Prescriptive Formality and Normative Rationality in Modern Legal Systems

Festschrift for Robert S. Summers

Robert S. Summers

Prescriptive Formality and Normative Rationality in Modern Legal Systems

Festschrift for Robert S. Summers

Edited by

Werner Krawietz
Neil MacCormick
Georg Henrik von Wright

Duncker & Humblot · Berlin

Die Deutsche Bibliothek – CIP-Einheitsaufnahme

Prescriptive formality and normative rationality in modern legal systems : Festschrift for Robert S. Summers / ed. by Werner Krawietz ... – Berlin : Duncker und Humblot, 1994
ISBN 3-428-07895-0
NE: Krawietz, Werner [Hrsg.]; Summers, Robert S.: Festschrift

Porträtfoto: Dagmar Ossig, Fotostudio Münster

Satz bzw. Fremddatenübernahme: Fotosatz Voigt, Berlin
Druck: Berliner Buchdruckerei Union GmbH, Berlin
Printed in Germany

ISBN 3-428-07895-0

Foreword

My Friend from Halfway, Oregon – A Most Unusual American Academic Career

I.

On September 19, 1933, Robert S. Summers was born in a farmhouse about five and a half miles from Halfway, Oregon, a remote village in a small valley called "Pine Valley" on the south side of the Wallowa mountain region in Eastern Oregon, a dozen miles from the Snake River which marks the border between Oregon and Idaho. His father, Orson W. Summers, now deceased, was born in the same general area (and was a distant relative of Abraham Lincoln). His mother, Estella Robertson Summers, of Scottish descent, still lives on the family farm.

1. As Robert Summers has elsewhere recorded, in the schools of Pine Valley Union High School he was recognized as one who should "go away to a university", and his parents and teachers saw that he went to the University of Oregon, in Eugene, where he enrolled in September of 1951, and from which he graduated with high honors in 1955. (There, too, he met his wife, Dorothy M. Kopp, mother of their five children.)* According to an article in the *Cornell Law Forum* for November, 1990, two of his teachers at the University of Oregon, Professors Egbert S. Wengert and H. Thomas Koplin, encouraged him to apply for what was then called a "junior" Fulbright Scholarship to study in England for a year after graduating from the University. He applied, and in the annual statewide competition received one of the two Fulbright awards allocated to seniors graduating from Oregon universities and colleges that year. Receipt of this award was an absolutely pivotal event in his life.

a) During the year 1955-56, Summers studied for one year as a Fulbright Scholar at the then new University of Southampton in England. While there, he formed what was to become a life-long attachment to England (and to Scotland, which he also visited then and from whence ancestors of his mother had emigrated in the nineteenth century). In that year he also met and became acquainted with the distinguished Oxford jurist, Professor H. L. A. Hart, who visited Southampton to give a guest lecture in April of 1956. This was the

* Brent Gordon, b. 1956; William Charles, b. 1959; Thomas Kopp, b. 1962; Elizabeth Anne, b. 1964; and Robert Orson, b. 1969.

beginning of a relationship that Summers had with Hart which lasted until Hart's death, on December 19, 1992.

b) Summers entered Harvard Law School in 1956, and received the LL.B degree in 1959. While there, he studied jurisprudence under Professor Lon L. Fuller, and the criminal law, and much else about law in general, under Professor Henry M. Hart. Roscoe Pound, though long since retired from the active faculty, was still a frequent presence at the Harvard Law School. Summers has recorded that he also became acquainted with Pound (in the fashion of a student), and read many of his writings. Most important, H. L. A. Hart was a visiting professor at Harvard during Summers' first year there. Summers saw him frequently, and Hart encouraged Summers' growing interest in legal theory.

c) In his second year at Harvard, Summers found Fuller's course in jurisprudence to be extraordinarily stimulating, especially since Fuller and Hart were then locked in their famous debate over the subject of Hart's Holmes Lecture, delivered at Harvard in April 1957, and called "Positivism and the Separation of Law and Morals". Summers, of course, heard this lecture, and discussed it at length with Hart after it was delivered. The written version of the debate between Hart and Fuller appeared in the pages of volume 71 of the *Harvard Law Review,* in February of 1958. With two teachers as stimulating and powerful as Hart and Fuller, it comes as no surprise that Summers ultimately chose to pursue an academic life in law, with legal theory a major interest.

2. Upon graduation from Harvard Law School in 1959, Robert Summers returned to his home state of Oregon where he practiced law in the Portland, Oregon law firm of King, Miller, Anderson, Nash and Yerke. After a little more than a year, he received an offer from Dean Orlando J. Hollis to become a member of the University of Oregon Law School faculty in Eugene, Oregon. In the fall of 1960, he started teaching contracts and commercial law, as these were the subjects then open. He soon introduced a course in legal theory.

a) At this time, Summers developed a strong interest in offering a broadly based and liberally oriented course about law not to professional law students but to university undergraduates as part of their general education. In 1961, he began teaching such a course, and prepared materials for use as a text in the course. The materials were eventually published in 1965 as his first book, with Charles G. Howard as a co-author. The title was *Law, Its Nature, Functions, and Limits.* The book is now in its third edition, and has been widely used in American universities as a text for general education courses on law.

b) As later recorded in the *Cornell Law Forum,* H. L. A. Hart, who was in the Fall of 1962 a visiting professor at the University of California at Los Angeles, traveled to the University of Oregon where he presented two lectures. At this time, Hart invited Summers to spend a year on research in residence in Oxford. Hart also discussed with Summers an early draft of Summers' first substantial essay in legal theory, a review article on Hart's then recently published book, *The Concept of Law* (1961). The essay was later published in the *Duke Law Journal* as "H. L. A. Hart's Concept of Law" (1964). The essay considers the central theses of this justly celebrated book, and develops a critique of it as somewhat reductionist in its analysis of legal phenomena, especially legal precepts and legal institutions, both of which Hart analyzed almost exclusively in terms of rules.

3. In 1963, the Uniform Commercial Code became law in many American states, including the State of Oregon. This Code had been drafted chiefly by the well-known American legal theorist and commercial law specialist, Karl N. Llewellyn. Since Robert Summers had been teaching in this field, he had had occasion, during the preceding year and a half, to compare the Code with the Oregon statute and case law which the Code was to supersede. These efforts marked the beginning of his life-long study of the Uniform Commercial Code and the case law growing out of it. In 1962, he published his first substantial article on a branch of this subject ("Secured Transactions Under the Uniform Commercial Code"). At that time, he also responded to many requests of the Oregon State Bar Association and of local county bar associations to lecture to practicing lawyers on the Code and on developments thereunder. His records of public lectures that he has given reveal that over the next thirty years, he would deliver more than a hundred such lectures to practicing lawyers and judges not only in Oregon but also in New York, California, Michigan, Tennessee, Ohio, Virginia, Washington, Florida and Minnesota. For such efforts, Summers has received various citations. For example, on June 19, 1987, the Minnesota Bar Association, by Special Resolution, awarded a Certificate of Merit to Summers (and one to his co-author, James J. White): "In recognition of, and in appreciation for, his high achievements in Legal Scholarship and Education, which constitute invaluable contributions to the Administration of Justice, the Facilitation of Commerce, and the Orderly Maintenance of Our Society."

4. During the academic year 1963-64, Robert Summers was a Visiting Associate Professor at Stanford Law School. Also visiting at Stanford that year were the British jurist, Graham Hughes, and the Australian jurist, Julius Stone. These other, more senior, personages offered the basic courses in legal theory while Summers taught contracts and commercial law. But in addition to many fruitful discussions, there were other notable events during the year. Thus, Summers has recorded that he and Professor Hughes went to Berkeley in March of 1964 where they spent an afternoon as guests of Professor Hans Kelsen. Kelsen at this time was probably the most influential living jurist in the world. He was then 83 years old, and Summers recalls that he was still most lively in discussion.

5. In the course of the year at Stanford, Summers applied, with the support of H. L. A. Hart, for a grant – a special fellowship in legal philosophy funded by the Rockefeller Foundation and administered by the Social Science Research Council. The grant was sufficient to enable him and his family to spend the year 1964-65 in Oxford, where he studied legal theory under Hart.

a) During the fall and winter terms at Oxford, Hart arranged for weekly discussions in his rooms in Kybald House, at University College. Summers' personal diary indicates that the procedure was usually for Summers to deliver a paper to Hart on Thursdays, which Hart would review in advance of their Saturday morning sessions. The topics varied greatly, ranging from differing models of justification in appellate judicial decision-making (e.g., for overruling a precedent, for creating an exception to a doctrine, for resolving a case of first impression, for upholding a finding of fact), to central issues in the Hart-Fuller debate (still going on at that time), and to general standards of criticism in legal philosophy. Summers has recorded that in discussion Hart had only one "speed", namely "high", and that he had a remarkable capacity for combining strong criticism with strong encouragement. Summers says that he often left these discussions feeling both "down" and "up" at the same time. The focus was on working out solutions to specific problems, and on method, technique, and approach. In two essays, Summers has summarized various aspects of the methodology current in Oxford legal theory at that time: "The New Analytical Jurists" in the *New York University Law Review* (1966), and "Notes on Criticism in Legal Philosophy" in *More Essays in Legal Philosophy* (1971).

b) The year 1964-65 was uniquely important for Summers in still another way. Largely self taught as a philosopher, it afforded him an opportunity to attend classes, lectures, and seminars offered by Oxford philosophers. In particular, he attended lectures or seminars by Peter Strawson, Gilbert Ryle, J. O. Urmson, Richard Hare, Isaiah Berlin, John Lucas, A. J. P. Kenny, and Phillipa Foot. This was in addition to lectures by Hart on Kelsen, and on rights and duties in the utilitarian tradition. During the year, Summers began what was to become his most important article in private law, an analysis of good faith in contract and commercial law. Summers has recounted many features of the Oxford scene during 1964-65 in a short essay: "Legal Philosophy at Oxford" (1966).

c) Summers' diary during this year in Oxford reveals that he became acquainted with, among others, Patrick Atiyah, Peter Carter, John Finnis, Peter Hacker, A. M. Honoré, A. J. P. Kenny, John Lucas, Geoffrey Marshall, Joseph Raz and Francis Reynolds, all Fellows of Oxford colleges and pursuing research in philosophy, law, or related subjects. Summers also became acquainted in this year with A. H. Campbell, a Fellow of All Souls College, and then Professor of Jurisprudence at the University of Edinburgh, who was later to introduce him to another theorist who would become his co-author, Neil MacCormick. Summers has maintained nearly all of these and still other relationships, intellectual and personal, in Britain, and he has renewed them more intensively at periodic intervals when spending sabbatical years in Oxford in 1974-75, 1981-82, and 1988-89. Indeed, Oxford has been, for him, a kind of second intellectual habitat, and he now resides there for three or four months each year.

6. Upon his return to the University of Oregon in 1965, Summers concerned himself with the research in legal theory and law he had begun in Oxford, with extensive lecturing to Oregon State Bar groups on the Uniform Commercial Code, with organizing and co-chairing a conference at the University of Colorado sponsored by the Association of American Law Schools for teachers of general education courses about law for undergraduates, and with editing the first of two collections of essays in legal philosophy published by Blackwells in England and the University of California Press in the U.S.

a) At this time, he also concentrated on finishing his article, "Good Faith in General Contract Law and the Sales Provision of the Uniform Commercial Code" which he completed in the summer of 1967, when he was thirty-three years old. The article, which he had begun in Oxford while working at what had been the desk of J. L. Austin, drew on Austin's "excluder" analysis of the meaning of certain types of words, and defended the thesis that good faith is not used in contract and commercial law as the name for a formally definable set of necessary and sufficient conditions for use of the words "good faith", but rather is generally used to "exclude" or proscribe on particular occasions a heterogeneous variety of forms of bad faith.

b) Once so conceptualized, American scholars could see clearly for the first time that the United States already had many judicial precedents on good faith extending far beyond the acknowledged doctrine of "good faith purchase". Indeed, Summers identified many such precedents in his article. This proved to be a significant revelation, given the wide-ranging potential of a general legal obligation of good faith. Summers' personal records include a letter about the article that he received from Professor Friedrich Kessler of Yale Law School in which Kessler concluded: "I think all of us working in the field of contracts owe you a real debt of gratitude for having written it." The seventy-two page article has been the most widely cited essay in the American legal literature on the subject of good faith in general contract law and the Uniform Commercial Code. Scholars and judges have referred to the essay as a "classic" and as "seminal". In 1970, when Section 205 on good faith in the proposed second Restatement of Contracts was before the American Law Institute for consideration, the director of the project, Professor Robert Braucher of Harvard, stated in the Institute's official proceedings that he was "indebted for its formulation to Professor Summers". Section 205 represented one of the three most important developments in the whole of American contract law between 1929, when the first Restatement of Contracts appeared, and 1979, when the second Restatement was completed.

c) Summers later published another article of similarly wide ranging applicability: "General Equitable Principles Under Section 1 - 103 of the Uniform Commercial Code" (1978). From the evidence of footnotes, it is apparent that scholars, judges, and practitioners have frequently relied upon this article as well. The good faith article and the article on general equitable principles deal with what might be called the morality of contract and commercial law.

7. For the fall semester of the 1968-69 academic year, Summers accepted an invitation to be a visiting professor at Cornell Law School and moved to Ithaca, New York. While there, he taught basic commercial law and the required first-year course in civil procedure. From the experience of teaching civil procedure, he developed a deep interest in what he came to call "process values", later the subject of another extended article. Also at this time, he entered into a contract with West Publishing Company to publish a casebook for commercial law courses with co-authors Richard E. Speidel and James J. White. Much of the visiting semester was spent on this project, and the first edition of this book was published in 1969. In 1993, it appeared in its 5th edition, and it has been widely used in American law schools for over twenty years. Before Summers returned to the University of Oregon in January of 1969, the Cornell Law School Faculty voted him a permanent offer of appointment, which he ultimately accepted. Summers' private papers include letters indicating that the Cornell offer was made largely on the basis of his writings on commercial law, including the subject of good faith (which had caught the eye of the distinguished Cornell comparativist, Rudolf Schlesinger), and on the basis of the quality of Summers' classroom teaching.

a) In subsequent years, Summers has often returned to the University of Oregon, and he taught the law school summer session there in 1980. In three short essays he has paid tribute to three former University of Oregon law faculty colleagues: Chapin Clark, Frank R. Lacy, and Hans A. Linde.

b) The Cornell appointment, which Summers took up in August of 1969, also marked the beginning of three years of extensive public service by Professor Summers as a consultant and co-founder of the "CLEO" Program co-sponsored by the Association of American Law Schools and the national bar associations. "CLEO" was the name for the Council on Legal Education Opportunity, founded to provide special opportunities for minority students to attend law school. CLEO contributed to a major increase in minority enrollments in law schools across the United States.

8. In the period 1969 to 1974, before his first sabbatical leave from Cornell, Summers published a number of articles and books. One of the articles, "The Technique Element in Law" appeared in 1971 in a *Festschrift* for Hans Kelsen.

It differentiated five basic ways in which law discharges its social functions: (1) the grievance-remedial technique, (2) the penal technique, (3) the administrative-regulatory technique, (4) the public-benefit conferral technique, and (5) the private-arranging technique. This framework also provided the structure for the second and third editions of his book: *Law, Its Nature, Functions, and Limits,* published in 1972, and again in 1986 respectively (with Cornell colleagues as co-authors). The framework has also figured as the conceptual foundation for books and articles by several other scholars.

a) Pursuant to a deep interest in providing liberal education about law for the lay citizen, Summers in 1973 also co-authored two books on law for grade school and high school students published by Ginn and Company of Boston. These books were used in American public schools for many years.

b) It was also in this period that Summers published his lengthy article on process values ("Evaluating and Improving Legal Processes – A Plea for Process Values", 1974.) This article defined "process values" as values realizable in the course of the workings of legal processes, values that are prizeable whether or not their implementation affects the quality of outcomes. In the article, various process values such as procedural fairness, orderly deliberation, institutional legitimacy, and appropriate impartiality are identified and subjected to analysis and evaluation. This article contributes to the analysis and improvement of procedural systems, and also criticizes utilitarian moral theory for its overemphasis on outcome values to the neglect of process values.

c) But perhaps Summers' most substantial contribution in this period was the appearance of the first edition of J. White and R. Summers, *The Uniform Commercial Code* (West Pub. Co. 1972), a book now about to go into its fourth edition and which today takes two forms, a single volume for students and a three volume treatise for practitioners, judges, and scholars. Today this is the most influential scholarly work in what is the largest field of private statutory law in the United States. The work has been cited in court opinions over 3000 times. As the *Cornell Law Forum* records, numerous judicial opinions in federal and state courts refer to "White and Summers" as the Code's "foremost" or "leading" commentators, and cite the book as the leading authority on commercial law. Chief Justice Ellen Peters of the Connecticut Supreme Court and former professor at Yale Law School once wrote of the book that it has been "enormously and deservedly influential".

9. In September of 1974, Summers returned to Great Britain for another sabbatical year in Oxford. In that year, he was affiliated with Balliol College (where Dr. A. J. P. Kenny, Dr. Joseph Raz, Donald Harris, and Paul Davies were Fellows). Summers' diary and the *Cornell Law Forum* reveal that in the course of that year, he delivered twenty-four guest lectures or seminars at universities in Britain, in Scandinavia, where his hosts were Professors Torstein Eckhoff, Folke Schmidt, Aleksander Peczenik and Stig Jørgensen, and in

Vienna and Salzburg, where his hosts were Herbert Hausmaninger, Theodor Tomandl, Günter Winkler and Ilmar Tammelo. His lecture and seminar topics included "process" values, the limited efficacy of law, and the technique element in law. While in Denmark, he had the privilege of spending an afternoon and evening with Professor Alf Ross, who reflected at length on developments in twentieth-century legal theory.

a) It was during this year that Professor Summers began a preliminary study of the elements of general theories of law that are essentially instrumentalist in nature. He did not confine himself to American theorists, but also studied the writings of Jeremy Bentham and Rudolf von Jhering. The first published essay to issue from this work was called "Naive Instrumentalism and the Law", a contribution to a *Festschrift* in honor of H. L. A. Hart on his seventieth birthday.

b) On returning to Cornell in the Fall of 1975, Summers continued his work on instrumentalist legal theory, concentrating on American thinkers such as Roscoe Pound and Karl Llewellyn. In the summer of 1976, he also prepared a first draft of a lengthy article on "goal" reasons and "rightness" reasons in judicial decision-making. In that same summer, with his colleague Roger Cramton, Summers also taught a basic course on "elements of law and legal process" to a group of 25 professors of economics for one week under the auspices of the Institute for Law and Economics, then at the University of Miami and directed by Henry Manne. Summers continued teaching such groups of university economists annually for twelve years. This assignment ultimately inspired a 42-page article in the *Oxford Journal of Legal Studies* on the nature of economic reasoning as applied to law, which Summers co-authored with his former student Leigh B. Kelly. The essay includes the first relatively comprehensive account in the legal literature of the basic criteria for judging the utility of substantive reasons of any type in making and justifying judicial decisions ("Economist's Reasons for Common Law Decisions", 1981).

c) It was also in this period that Summers had his second experience with field research, the first having been in 1967 as an interviewer of judges, lawyers, and others for the Brookings Institution study of the administration of the bankruptcy laws. (*Bankruptcy – Problem, Process, Reform* (1971)). His second experience at field research was as a participant-observer of the administration of New York State's "Taylor Act", a body of law designed to regulate the negotiation and implementation of collective bargaining contracts between state governmental employees and their employers. The Taylor Act was a model statute widely copied in other states. Professor Summers served as principal negotiator for several school districts and municipalities, and then prepared and published a monograph under the auspices of Cornell University's School of Industrial and Labor Relations: *Collective Bargaining and Public Benefit Conferral – A Jurisprudential Critique* (1976). The monograph is critical of the way in which the Taylor Act impinges upon representative democracy, especially at the local level. The monograph was discussed in academic journals, and in the New York Times and other newspapers.

d) In the Spring of 1976, Summers was invited to conduct seminars on topics in judicial decision-making for judges of the Washington State appellate courts. According to his records, this was the first of a dozen such seminars he presented over several years as part of continuing education programs for the judiciary in Oregon, Washington, Tennessee, New Hampshire, Massachusetts, Arizona, Wisconsin, Virginia, and Florida.

e) Effective July 1, 1976, Summers was appointed by the Board of Trustees of Cornell University the "William G. McRoberts Professor of Research in the Administration of the Law". This endowed chair provided him with special research support and teaching flexibility.

10. The summer of 1977 took Professor Summers to Australia where he was a visiting professor at the Australian National University in Canberra and at the University of Sydney. He also gave lectures at a number of other universities in Australia and New Zealand and attended the World Congress of the International Association of Social and Legal Philosophy, which was held at Sydney. In subsequent years, he attended such "IVR" congresses in Basel in 1979 (where he met Aulis Aarnio, Werner Krawietz, and Robert Alexy), at Helsinki in 1983, at Athens in 1985, at Edinburgh in 1989 and at Göttingen in 1991.

a) In 1978, Summers published in the *Cornell Law Review* one of his principal articles in legal theory, 82 pages in length: "Two Types of Substantive Reasons – The Core of a Theory of Common Law Justification." In this article he differentiated "goal" reasons from "rightness" reasons, and argued that rightness reasons, contrary to much modern moral and economic analysis, have justificatory force, too. They derive this force not from goal-serving effects but from the way in which rightness norms apply to past interactions of the parties involved. The article analyzed the structure and force of rightness reasons in judicial decision-making more systematically than had been done earlier, and sought to refute the utilitarian thesis that rightness reasons, because they are past-regarding, cannot have, as such, any force at all. "Thank you" does not really mean "more please"; it has force of its own.

b) Also in 1978, Summers published in the *Harvard Law Review* the first fruits of his intermittent studies of the legal theory of his former Harvard teacher, Lon L. Fuller: "Professor Fuller's Jurisprudence and America's Dominant Philosophy of Law."

c) In January of 1978, Summers gave a lecture at the University of Hamburg: "Current Trends in American Legal Theory." This was the first of more than fifteen lectures and seminars that he presented between 1978 and 1993 at various German universities, including, in addition to Hamburg, the Free University of Berlin, the University of Munich, the University of Göttingen, the University of the Saarland, the University of Münster, the University of Hannover, the University of Tübingen, the University of Heidelberg, and the University of Trier. Just as Summers' entry upon the English and Scottish legal world two decades earlier had proved to be a special source of growth for him, his introduction to the German legal world and the German tradition in legal theory was to prove, as he has put it elsewhere, "distinctively enriching". From the late 1970's, Summers took an increasing interest in German legal theory, including especially the writings of Jhering, Heck, Radbruch, and Weber. From the 1980's on, Summers was regularly a guest for brief periods at German universities, and in 1985 he was a visiting professor for an entire semester at the University of Vienna.

11. In the fall of 1981, Summers presented the first of about a dozen special lectureships he was invited to deliver at various universities between 1981 and 1993, mostly in the United States. These included the Sherman Lecture at Boston University Law School in 1981, the Harris Lecture at Indiana University Law School in 1983, the Patterson Lecture at Duke University Law School in 1984, the Halle Lecture at Case Western Law School in 1987, the Higgins Lecture at Lewis and Clark College of Law in 1988, the Seegers Lecture at Valparaiso University School of Law in 1989, the Hamlyn Lecture at the University of Edinburgh in 1989, the Altheimer Lecture at the University of Arkansas in 1991, the Goodhart Lecture at the University of Cambridge in 1991, and the MacDermott Lecture at the University of Belfast in 1992.

a) During 1981-82, Robert Summers was again in Oxford on sabbatical leave, having been elected a Visiting Research Fellow at Merton College. At this time, he was completing final work on two books, one to be published by Cornell University Press on American pragmatic instrumentalist legal theory, and one on Lon L. Fuller for the "Jurists – Profiles in Legal Theory" series edited by Professor William Twining and to be published by Stanford University Press. Summers' diary records that during this sabbatical year, he also presented twenty-three lectures and seminars at various universities in England, Scotland, Scandinavia, Germany and elsewhere in Europe. In the winter term of that year, he also hosted a small informal conference in Oxford attended by Professors Aulis Aarnio, Aleksander Peczenik, Robert Alexy, Neil MacCormick, Geoffrey Marshall, and John Lucas. Most participants read short papers, and this was followed by discussion.

b) Professor Summers and Professor Patrick S. Atiyah, University of Oxford, agreed in the summer of 1982 to enter upon a long-term project to write a book comparing levels of formality in the English and American legal systems. In that year, Summers had already published an article that was one of the fore-runners of this book: "Working Conceptions of the Law".

c) Also in the summer of 1982, and as the preface to *Interpreting Statutes – A Comparative Study* (1991) records, the idea of forming a group of legal theorists to do a comparative study of interpretive practices in nine Western countries was conceived by Professors Peczenik, Pattaro and Summers in the Italian Alps during a joint holiday. The agreed aim was to identify significant similarities and differences in such practices, and consider whether any similarities exist at the level of deep structure. The research group was actually formed in Helsinki during the IVR Congress in 1983, with Professor Aulis Aarnio as host. The group completed its work on interpretation through several workshops held at the Center for Interdisciplinary Studies at the University of Bielefeld. After publishing the book referred to above, the group has been at work comparing the role of legal precedent in the same nine countries. After a meeting on this topic at Cornell Law School in 1993, the group will finish its work during two further sessions in Italy and Finland. Summers has served as chair of the group since its founding, with Neil MacCormick as co-chair.

12. Summers' book, *Instrumentalism in American Legal Theory,* was largely completed in Oxford in 1981, and was published by Cornell University Press in 1982. This book provided an account and critique of the rise and reception of legal theory in the United States from the end of the nineteenth century up to the middle decades of the twentieth century, and was the first book to conceptualize and systematically draw together various tenets of American instrumentalist legal theory. An earlier version of the book had already been published in Dutch. An abridged German translation appeared in 1983: *Pragmatischer Instrumentalismus und amerikanische Rechtstheorie,* translated in final form by Dr. Thomas Laker of Göttingen and Professor Herbert Hausmaninger of the University of Vienna, and published by the Karl Alber Verlag of Freiburg. The English-language version of the book was reviewed in a dozen periodicals. One European reviewer remarked that it "includes profound insights about the nature of law and legal method, mostly indicated in the particular context of pragmatic instrumentalism and yet possessing universal importance".

a) This book, appearing in English, and in German and Dutch translations, and appearing in summary form in articles published in English, Italian, Japanese and Russian, demonstrated the coalescence of American philosophical pragmatism, sociological jurisprudence, and legal realism, and reconstructed the resulting general theory in terms of a set of basic pragmatic instrumentalist tenets. Among the leading tenets, stated in very general terms, were these: (1) the purpose of legal theorizing is to make law more useful for "social engineering", (2) the main purpose of law itself is the more or less utilitarian one of serving the "wants" or "interests" of the citizenry, (3) law is essentially a set of tools – instruments – to be deployed as a kind of technology in accord with the findings of social science, (4) the judges in the legal system are to play major roles in making and implementing policy through law, (5) the essential criterion for identifying valid law is predictive – that is, valid law consists of whatever officials in power, especially judges, may be predicted to do, and (6) the efficacy of law ultimately derives from the monopoly that officials of the system have over the use of state coercion, force and direct action. Summers subjected these and other tenets both to positive analysis and evaluative critique.

b) His reconstruction of main currents in early to mid-century American legal theory yielded novel results. His reconstruction exposed similarities of view that justified grouping together such otherwise disparate thinkers as Dewey and Gray, and Pound and Frank. At the same time, his reconstruction revealed that the American instrumentalist movement could be illuminatingly bifurcated into a "mainstream" in which certain views of Holmes, Pound, Gray, and Dewey were widely influential, and an "extremist wing" characterized by certain realist views most stridently expressed in the 1930's but which never became widely or continuously influential. At the same time, Summers argued that his work identified constructive general directions of thought in instrumentalist theorizing which provide an important corrective to the common view that many "realist" theorists were merely destructive trashers. In a debate with Professor Michael Moore, published in volume 69 of the *Cornell Law Review,* Summers defended the methodological principles that guided his reconstruction of twentieth-century American legal theory. The most concise account of Summers' views of the leading tenets and strengths and weaknesses of American pragmatic instrumentalism, "Pragmatic Instrumentalism and American Legal Theory", appeared in 1982 in *Rechtstheorie.*

13. In 1984, Robert Summers' book on the life and work of Lon L. Fuller was published by the Stanford University Press in the Great Jurists series edited by Professor William Twining. The book was entitled, simply, *Lon L. Fuller.* Summers dedicated it as follows: "For Lon L. Fuller of Harvard and H. L. A. Hart of Oxford, who jointly and severally rejuvenated the subject of legal theory in our time." Between 1926 and 1939, Fuller was successively a professor of law at the University of Oregon, the University of Illinois, and at Duke University. From 1939 until 1972, when he retired, he was a professor at Harvard Law School, having succeeded to Roscoe Pound's chair in 1948. Fuller, with Holmes, Pound, and Llewellyn, was one of the leading American legal theorists of the last 100 years. Fuller was also a major critic of American pragmatic instrumentalist legal theory. Himself an original thinker, he was highly conversant with European legal thought, and especially admired the writings of the great German jurist, Rudolf von Jhering.

a) As Summers demonstrated in his book, Fuller was a leading proponent of what might be called secular natural law theory. Fuller showed that notions of value – of what "ought to be" – figure in the very existence of rules and that law is inherently value laden. He argued that it is impossible to draw sharp lines between law and morals. More than any thinker before him, except perhaps for Rudolf von Jhering, Fuller stressed law's essential purposiveness and the necessary "direction-giving quality" of the purposes of law. Fuller had demonstrated at length in his *The Law in Quest of Itself* (1940) that there can be no universally applicable "master" criterion by which judges can determine whether any given rule is a valid law of the system. Fuller also wrote more illuminatingly than anyone before him on the complexities of law's means and ends and on the interactions between means and ends in legal ordering. In Summers' view, Fuller's sophisticated analyses of law's means and ends provided a major corrective to crude instrumentalist theories of law. In his book on Fuller, Summers also offered some critical commentary. The book was widely reviewed and well received.

b) Summers spent most of June and July of 1984 in Göttingen at a Goethe Institute studying German. He was already acquainted with some members of the Göttingen law faculty, and he found the intellectual atmosphere there most congenial. He had numerous professional discussions with Professors Ralf Dreier, Okko Behrends, Franz Wieacker, and Robert Alexy, all then at the University. That summer, he completed an influential article, "Toward a Better Theory of Legal Validity". After presenting the article in the form of a lecture to the Göttingen law faculty and as a seminar topic at Professor Arthur Kaufmann's Institute at the University of Munich, he published it in *Rechtstheorie*.

c) In the fall of 1984, Summers attended a conference on Reason and Law organized by Professor Enrico Pattaro at the University of Bologna. There he presented a paper on "Why Common Law Courts Seldom Need to Assess Closely the Comparative Force of Conflicting Substantive Reasons" (1987). This essay was a development of his work on the nature and role of substantive reasoning in judicial decision-making. In the article, Summers sought to show that when two substantive reasons conflict in a case, it is often not necessary to choose between them on the basis of their comparative weight. Rather, there will often be a preferable basis for choice *on other grounds,* e.g., the suitability of the reason for encapsulation in a well-defined rule.

14. Robert Summers was a Visiting Fulbright Professor at the University of Vienna Faculty of Law in the spring of 1985. During this period, he gave a course of lectures comparing developments in English and American legal theory from 1776 to 1976. The lectures later served as part of the basis for two chapters on legal theory in his book with Professor Atiyah. At this time, Summers also gave guest lectures at universities in Graz, Budapest, Tübingen, and Jerusalem.

a) On returning to the United States, Summers resumed work on the book he was writing with Professor Atiyah, and devoted much of the next two years to that project. In 1986, he was appointed by the President of the Association of American Law Schools (A. A. L. S.) to chair and organize a Conference for Teachers of Jurisprudence which was held in March of 1986. He devoted much time to this conference, which attracted many teachers of legal theory and also many teachers of first-year law subjects interested in incorporating more legal theory into their courses.

b) Summers was invited to the Soviet Union in December of 1986 under the auspices of the International Exchange of Scholars (IREX) program and the U. S. State Department. He presented one lecture at the Institute of State and Law in Moscow on "America's Dominant Legal Theory in the Twentieth Century", which was later translated into Russian, and one lecture on good faith in contract law at the University of Tashkent in Uzbeckistan.

c) In 1987, after more than twenty years of teaching in the field of contracts, Summers, with his Cornell colleague, Professor Robert Hillman, published a casebook for first-year law school courses in that subject: *Contract & Related Obligation: Theory, Doctrine, and Practice* (West Publishing Company). This is a somewhat distinctive teaching tool in its emphasis on the variety of lawyer roles in contractual matters, its focus on the special problems of law created by private parties, its stress on substantive as well as formal reasoning in judicial decisions, and its presentation of materials on contract theory.

15. At the end of 1987, Robert Summers and Patrick Atiyah of Oxford published their book *Form and Substance in Anglo-American Law*. This was the product of a five-year collaborative effort in which the book went through four complete drafts. In their preface the co-authors wrote: "This book has throughout been written jointly. Each of us has had a hand in writing and rewriting (often several times) every chapter." The book was published by Oxford University Press, and was immediately acclaimed in the United States, in Scandinavia, in Europe and in Britain. Professor John Fleming of the University of California, wrote in the *International and Comparative Law Quarterly* that the book is a "profound" work with an "original methodology". Professor Jerzy Wróblewski of Poland in his review in *Archiv für Rechts- und Sozialphilosophie* characterized the book as an "extremely rich and interesting comparative analysis". Professor Xavier Blanc-Jouvain of Paris, in the *Revue International de Droit Comparé*, commented that the book is "a brilliant treatment of fundamental questions about law". Dr. N. A. Andrews, in the *Cambridge Law Journal*, wrote: "Not since Holmes and Pollock exchanged their letters has there been such a sustained and absorbing communion of American and English legal minds."

a) This complex book cannot be briefly summarized, but a few remarks are in order. It offers, first, a new way of analyzing legal reasoning in terms of more "formal" or more "substantive" styles. This analysis, which is worked out in some detail, is offered as a contribution to legal theory in its own right.

Second, the book then develops the differences in legal reasoning and in legal systems in England and America, arguing that the English is a rather "formal" system and the American, more "substantive". Thirdly, the book explores a wide range of cultural, institutional, and historical factors influencing the formal style of the English system, and influencing the substantive style of the American. This exploration is of relevance not only for comparative studies, but also confirms the argument in the first part of the book that the English system is relatively more formal.

b) As he has indicated subsequently, Professor Summers' work on this book altered his perspective on general theories of law. He has come to believe that it is unlikely that there can be a single, general correct legal theory even for all western systems. Hart's general legal theory, for example, fits the more formal English system, whereas Fuller's theory fits the more substantive American system. Truth in legal theory is, to an extent, relative to the legal system in question.

16. In 1988-89, Professor Summers returned to the University of Oxford for a further sabbatical leave, and resumed his relationships there with colleagues working in philosophy, politics and law. This year marked the beginning of intensive work on what Summers now calls "the formal character of law", or "a general theory of formality in law". At the end of the sabbatical year, he presented the special Hamlyn lecture to close the Fourteenth IVR World Congress held at the University of Edinburgh. The lecture was entitled "Theory, Formality and Practical Legal Criticism", and was later published in the *Law Quarterly Review.* In the course of the sabbatical year, Summers also gave fourteen lectures at various universities, including presentations at a symposium on the Legitimacy of Law in Tampere, Finland, a *Festschrift* symposium at the University of Göttingen in honor of Professor Franz Wieacker, and a series of lectures while a Guest Professor at the University of Münster (to which he returned in 1993 for further lectures, hosted by Professor Werner Krawietz).

a) In 1989-90, several developments may be noted. Summers lectured on the topic "Peirce and America's Dominant Theory of Law" at the Charles Sanders Peirce Sesquicentennial held in September at Harvard University. Later that fall, he lectured at the Max Planck Institute on Comparative Law in Hamburg on "Form and Substance in Anglo-American Law", and on the "Comparative Statutory Interpretation Project". During 1989 and 1990, he served as President of the American Section of the International Association of Social and Legal Philosophy ("IVR").

b) On May 24, 1990, he was awarded the degree of Doctor of Laws, *honoris causa,* by the University of Helsinki, during the 350th anniversary celebration of the founding of that University. At the award ceremony, he was cited for his work in private law and in legal theory, and for the way he had attempted to bridge American and European legal thought.

c) Later that summer, he served as a member of the law faculty of the Salzburg Seminar in American Studies, where he lectured on form and substance in Anglo-American law, and on contract law in a market economy.

d) In the summer of 1991, the first fruit of the Comparative Statutory Interpretation Project, which had been formed in 1983 with members from nine countries, was published under the title *Interpreting Statutes – A Comparative Study,* co-edited by D. Neil MacCormick and Robert Summers. It included nine chapters reporting on basic issues of interpretive practice in each of the countries in the project. In addition, there is an introductory chapter, a chapter on methodology, a comparative chapter, and a chapter on "interpretation and justification". Professor Summers co-authored these four chapters, and contributed a chapter on statutory interpretation in the U.S. Supreme Court. Some of the more significant features of the book are these: a novel general framework for the systematic analysis of a wide range of types of interpretive argument; extensive analysis of particular types of argument; a finding that all nine countries in the project share a common core of eleven types of arguments; a discovery that conflicts between argument are resolved not only by weighing and balancing but also by resorting to other important techniques, including processes of cancellation; the identification of differences in interpretive practices and justificatory styles of opinion writing, and treatment of possible explanations for these (especially of an institutional kind). Among the early reviews of the book is one by Professor John Bell, who wrote in the *Oxford Journal of Legal Studies* that the book "will long be an essential and valuable resource for anyone seriously studying statutory interpretation". In another review Professor Theodor Tomandl of Vienna wrote that the book is a "pioneering" work that explores "major new dimensions" of the subject.

e) For the 1991-92 academic year, Summers was elected by the Cambridge Law faculty as the Arthur L. Goodhart Visiting Professor of Legal Science at Cambridge University. The Goodhart Visiting Professorship, tenable for one academic year, was founded in 1971 in honor of Arthur L. Goodhart who had been an academic lawyer in Cambridge and in Oxford, founder of the *Cambridge Law Journal,* Professor of Jurisprudence in Oxford prior to Hart, and Master of University College, Oxford. Visiting scholars appointed to the chair from Europe who preceded Summers include professors Andre Tunc of Paris, Folke Schmidt of Stockholm, Xavier Blanc-Jouvain of Paris and R. C. Van Caenegem of Ghent. From the United States, prior holders of the chair include professors John Fleming of Berkeley, Guido Calebresi of Yale, John Hazard of Columbia, Arthur von Mehren of Harvard, and Charles Alan Wright of Texas.

f) Summers has summarized the 1991-92 year in "An Academic Year in Cambridge" published in the *Cornell Law Forum* (1993). Much of his research that year was devoted to development of his theory that law is formal in character, and he presented the Goodhart Lecture before the Cambridge law faculty on this subject on December 4, 1992. This lecture was later published under that title in the *Cambridge Law Journal.* In the course of the academic year, Summers conducted a weekly seminar at Cambridge for graduate students on legal formality. The *Cornell Law Forum* indicates that he gave fourteen lectures and seminars elsewhere in Britain and on the Continent in that year, many on the subject of formality. In May 1992, Duncker & Humblot published his book entitled *Essays on the Nature of Law and Legal Reasoning,* a collection (as revised) of previously published articles, including several on formality in law.

17. In 1992-94, Summers completed, with his co-author, James J. White, two new volumes of the practitioner's edition of their treatise on the Uniform Commercial Code: a volume on Article 2A on leases, and a volume on Articles 3 and 4 and 4A on negotiable instruments and wire transfers. In May of 1993, Summers lectured at the celebration marking the 100th anniversary of Professor Karl N. Llewellyn's birth, held at the University of Chicago. In the fall of 1993, Summers and White began the process of assisting the Institute of Private Law in Moscow with the drafting of a new code of commercial law modeled in part on the Uniform Commercial Code. This project is also co-sponsored by American Aid for International Development (AID), an organization of the United States government.

a) At present, Professor Summers is working mainly on three long-term book projects: the fourth edition of J. White and R. Summers, *The Uniform Commercial Code,* a book on statutory interpretation, and a book on what he calls the formal character of law. As he conceives the law, all basic types of legal phenomena are formal. Thus, for example, source-oriented criteria of legal validity (e.g., due enactment by a legislature), statutory and common law rules, accepted methods of interpretation, the principle of *stare decisis,* and adjudicative processes, are all essentially formal, though in differing ways.

b) So, too, are features of the legal system viewed as a whole. It is formal in its structure, formal in the coherence of its norms, and formal in its basic modus operandi, for example. Moreover, the appropriate formality of law, of basic legal phenomena, and of legal systems is justified by various general rationales for formality such as predictability, citizen autonomy and self-direction, avoidance of disputes, and equality before the law. Appropriate formality itself also tends to beget law good in content, and inappropriate formality or lack of due formality tends to beget law bad in content. These and related themes are neglected in modern legal theory, especially in the United States, and to an extent in Britain and Europe as well. According to Professor Summers, a book of the right kind here would not only contribute to the rehabilitation of formality in those systems where it has been neglected, but would correct a major deficiency in traditional legal theory. In the course of his work on this book, Summers is drawing to some extent on ideas of formality articulated by the nineteenth-century German jurist Rudolf von Jhering.

c) In recognition of his work in contract law, commercial law, and legal theory, the University of Göttingen, on February 2, 1994, voted to award Robert Summers an honorary doctorate in law.

II.

Robert S. Summers is best known among his European colleagues as a legal theorist. He entered upon the post-war legal theory scene in the early 1960s. As he himself has written, at this time in the United States, tenets of philosophical pragmatism in the writings of John Dewey and William James, the sociological jurisprudence of Roscoe Pound, and the legal realism of Karl Llewellyn and others, had coalesced to form a relatively distinctive and dominant general theory of law which Professor Summers has called "pragmatic instrumentalism". Other major American developments in the general theory of law during the second half of this century have included what might be called the "legal process school" founded by the late Professors Henry Hart and Albert Sacks, the "rights thesis" of Ronald Dworkin and others, the "law and economics" movement associated with Richard Posner and Guido Calebresi, and, somewhat later, the "Critical Legal Studies" school, and its offshoots known as "feminist jurisprudence", and "critical race theory". Lon L. Fuller stood apart from such developments, practicing his own distinctive brand of secular natural law theory, including a reinterpretation of the ideal of the rule of law.

Elsewhere in the post-war Western legal world, legal theory evolved very differently. In Britain, Oxford analytic philosophy provided the leading models in legal theory, with Professor H. L. A. Hart the premier exemplar. On the Continent, Kelsenian positivism continued to be influential. There was a special revival of natural law theory led by, among others, Gustav Radbruch of Heidelberg. There were also developments in sociological jurisprudence in Germany and developments in realist jurisprudence, especially in Scandinavia. More recently, various theorists have refined legal thinking in terms of concepts of practical reason.

When Robert Summers became an Assistant Professor of Law at the University of Oregon in the early 1960's, he did not, either immediately or thereafter, subscribe to any of the various American movements in legal theory. He was specially influenced by Oxford analytic philosophy and by H. L. A. Hart in particular. At the same time, however, he was influenced by an adversary of Hart's, Lon L. Fuller, on whose life and work Summers has written extensively.

Although Professor Summers has done as much as any of his contemporaries to acquaint British, German, Scandinavian, Italian and other European thinkers with the distinctive American version of instrumentalist legal theory that he calls "pragmatic instrumentalism", he should not himself be classified as a subscriber to that type of theory. He has not even worked out very many of his own ideas and positions from the viewpoint of that type of theory. His writings on American instrumentalist theory have consisted largely of a scholarly effort to reconstruct, analyze and evaluate its leading tenets, and, where the theory was sketchy and incomplete, to suggest lines of further development. It may be that Professor Summers is best known in Europe for this work, which includes books in English, German and Dutch.

Rather than develop and refine an existing general theory of law, or attempt to work out a general theory of law of his own, Professor Summers has concentrated most of his creative theoretical efforts on more discrete problems of legal theory. His contributions here include a systematic account of the five basic techniques of legal implementation in any legal system (especially "The Technique Element in Law"); extended work on the nature of substantive reasons in law, itself a major branch of practical reasoning (especially "Two Types of Substantive Reasons"); elaborate treatment of what might be called the "morality" of commercial law ("Good Faith in General Contract Law and the Sales Provisions of the Uniform Commercial Code", "General Equitable Principles Under the Uniform Commercial Code"), a lengthy article on "process values", that is, values that may be realized in the course of the workings of a legal process but not necessarily also in its outcomes ("Evaluating and Improving Legal Processes"); a substantial treatment of the nature and limits of economic reasoning in judicial decision ("Economist's Reasons for Common Law Decisions"); and the systematic differentiation and analysis of basic modes of argumentation in the interpretation of statutes ("The Argument from Ordinary Meaning" with G. Marshall).

There is, however, one major exception to the generalization that Professor Summers has tended to concentrate his creative efforts on relatively discrete problems of legal theory. Over the last few years, he has been working out a more wide-ranging general theory of the nature, varieties, and importance of form and formality in modern legal systems. His interest in this fundamental topic did not originate in, but was certainly stimulated by, his collaboration with Professor Patrick S. Atiyah of Oxford on their well known book: *Form and Substance in Anglo-American Law* (1987). The current state of Professor Summers' work on legal formality is best seen in three articles: "The Formal Character of Law" (1992), "Der formale Charakter des Rechts II" in *Archiv für Rechts- und Sozialphilosophie* (1994), and "The Formal Character of Law III" forthcoming in *Rechtstheorie* (1994).

III.

Taking one's cues from the European practice, it is most unusual that a legal scholar would be honored with a *Festschrift* as early as his sixtieth birthday. It is still more unusual that the circle of friends and colleagues contributing to the *Festschrift* would stem from a dozen different countries, a truly international group. Legal scholars rarely enjoy much attention outside their own legal circles at home, and Robert Summers is the exception that establishes the rule. He is well known abroad, and his reputation there reflects a judgment on the part of the greater international scientific community about the high quality of his work.

The sketch of Robert Summers, whom we are celebrating with this *Festschrift,* would, however, be incomplete if one sought only to characterize the researcher and his work. All who know Robert Summers personally – and a good number of those who have contributed to this volume are close to him – value and appreciate his openness and enthusiasm, his boundless energy and vigor, indeed, his lust for life. His great warmth, his fairness in the give-and-take with those who challenge his views, and his ability to engage in self-criticism have won him many friends and admirers over the years. And last but by no means least: What would my friend Robert from Halfway, Oregon, be without Dorothy, their five children, and a growing brood of grandchildren?

IV.

I should like to add heartfelt thanks – in the name of the other editors, too – to all of those who have contributed to the *Festschrift.* Their collegiality and support have helped to minimize the burdens of the editorial work. Special thanks are due to Dean Russell K. Osgood, Cornell Law School, for support on a number of fronts. Special thanks, too, to Professor Herbert Hausmaninger, Vienna, and to Professor Stanley L. Paulson, presently in residence in Göttingen, for translating a number of papers into English and for refining the English of other papers.

What with fairly severe constraints on time, not everyone who was invited to contribute to the *Festschrift* was able to do so. Still more painful for the editors – not least of all with an eye to the range of themes and problems examined here – is the fact that they were by no means in a position to invite contributions from all of those with whom Robert Summers has worked and exchanged ideas over the years. This note of regret has particular application to Robert Summers' European colleagues, who are, I am afraid, not as well represented here as they ought to be.

I should like to thank the publisher Duncker & Humblot GmbH, in Berlin, above all, its director Professor Norbert Simon, who generously support this volume from its inception. The publisher, too, takes special pleasure in celebrating Robert Summers!

I thank, too, my assistants in Münster for their valuable help in the work on the *Festschrift,* especially Dr. Petra Werner and Andreas Schemann. My secretary, Andrea Freund, deserves warm thanks for her tireless efforts in seeing the manuscripts to the press. The painstaking work of reading the proofs was undertaken by Markus Ausetz and Matthias Neeb; they, too, have my special thanks.

Münster, March 1994

Werner Krawietz

Table of Contents

I. Definition and Theory in Jurisprudence Reconsidered

II. The Concept of Law Redefined

III. Form and Substance in Legal Argumentation: The Case of Roman, Greek, and Canon Law

IV. Legal Doctrine as Rational Reconstruction of Law

I. Definition and Theory
in Jurisprudence Reconsidered

Is Legal Science a Social Science?

By Aulis Aarnio, Tampere

I. Background

1. Sometimes one sees definitions according to which everything that studies *society* is a social science. This kind of definition rings hollow when the social scientific nature of legal science is considered. The definition says nothing about research or society. Nor does a standard definition which is based on the *research object* (the social, economic or political sphere) solve the question set in the title. According to this kind of definition, law is a field of "its own nature" which is not covered by social science.

Traditional characterizations of legal science do not make the issue less problematic. In particular, certain trends of legal positivism have wanted to "abolish" such elements in law which are of interest in the social sciences. This abolition has included morals as well, and thus the philosophy of values has been excluded from legal science. *Hans Kelsen,* among others, represented such a "pure" legal science. At the other extreme, there are theories which hold that legal science should be *restored* specifically to the empirical social sciences. Representatives of German "sociological" trends were among the many who followed this line of thought at the beginning of 1900s. In Finland, similar kinds of notions arose as late as the 1970s.

2. My strategy is not to *define* (stipulatively) either social or legal science so that the dilemma could be solved per definitionem. Reality does not follow a theorist's definitions. Thus, I neither accept the traditional definition of the object field of the social sciences nor commit myself to any specific endeavor to restore legal science to the social sciences. Although it may be paradoxical, my conception of the issue rather closely resembles Kelsen's way of thinking but on a different basis. Though my conclusions are somewhat similar to Kelsen's interpretations, one should not, however, generalize this to concern anything other than the relation of my theoretical approach to the "pure legal science".

Instead of rendering precise definitions, the aim here is to delineate the *rational reconstruction* of social science, on the one hand, and of legal science, on the other, in order to obtain that mutual "core" which the social sciences as social sciences and legal science as a social science share. In other words, to discover the linkage which combines research on different sectors and problems.

As mentioned above, a broad definition of the social sciences (that is, the notion that everything which studies society is a social science) is useless if nothing is said concerning the *concept of society* under consideration. When we try to specify this concept we will immediately be confronted by the statement: society *as such* does not exist. Society is a combination of various kinds of individuals, interest groups, etc., all of which have their own expectations, roles and function models. Society is nothing but interaction between people and society and – as *Kauko Pietilä* has expressed it – society is always "present" when there is interaction between people. This is also why the genuine research object for social science is interaction, it lies within those processes which create *consistency* in the eternally changing relations between people.

Thus, society *as such* is not an *ontologically* empirical object to which the propositions refer. One cannot observe society itself (an sich), only phenomena in which society is "present" can be objects of our observation. This is why, in the ontology represented by *Karl Popper,* society is a concept of a higher order than the world 1 consisting, for example, of physical objects and human beings. Society is a *theoretical object* manifested in the phenomena observed by empirical research.

If this is accepted as a point of departure, the following argument by Kauko Pietilä can be taken as a vantage point in further elaboration. He says that the research object of social science is, in the true sense of the word, the kind of sociation (Vergesellschaftung) that is present in certain behavior (interactional phenomena) of people. Thus, social science is studying people's activity as a specifically *sociating* activity, not as separate phenomena such as leisure behavior, health care, education, etc. Social science asks: what kind of society is born in this behavior, in the interaction between people?

People interact with each other as individuals, groups, institutions, etc., and it is essential to study those linkages and mediating mechanisms which make interaction social. In a way, society *exists* in those interaction relationships.

This is what Kauko Pietilä implies when he says that social science should not study phenomena as embedded in a society, but society as existing in the phenomena. The field of the social sciences (for example, sociology) should not be fragmented into the sociology of sports, health care, education, etc., but one should try to find the very element which unifies the fragmented object field of the social sciences. Hence, criminology is not a social science only because it studies a phenomenon thought to be social-scientific, namely crime. It is social science if and only if it analyzes – if ever – *society* which exists in this phenomenon. In this case, the social facts are studied as *social interactions which generate society.*

In the following the problem will be outlined against this conceptual-theoretical background. Let us ask: in what specific sense legal science is or can be social science if social science is reconstructed to be research on social interactions which generate society? In answering this, a short introduction to the reconstruction of legal science is necessary.

II. On Legal Science

1. For hundreds of years, the task of legal science in the *social division of labor* has been connected to (legal) *norms*. In a certain specific sense, legal science studies the valid system of legal norms in society.

From this point of view, it would be justified to discuss legal science in its plural form. The legal sciences include *legal dogmatics* (in German: Rechtsdogmatik), abbreviated here as *LD;* legal history, the sociology of law and comparative legal science. The oldest and most overwhelmingly essential of these is LD. It is based on Roman Law but its origin in the present sense can be rather reliably dated back to 1099. At that time, the first faculty of legal science was established in Bologna under guidance of *Irnerius*.

In the following, the analysis is condensed solely to the "social character" of LD. Thus, the question in the title can be defined more precisely as follows: is LD a social science? This dilemma is especially relevant because the main part of the research conducted in the world under the name of legal science is specifically LD. There is also an obvious reason for this.

The tasks of LD have been and still seem to be determined by society because LD obviously satisfies a constant social interest of knowledge, in other words, the need to know something about the *substance of the valid legal order*. This answers the question: what are the binding legal norms in society?

2. Thus, the social role of LD was already established at an early stage, and until today, this role has determined not only the social but also the *scientific function* of LD. To understand its scientific function one has to outline, on the one hand, its *task* and, on the other, its *object*. The tasks of LD are:

(i) to clarify the contents of the valid legal norms, i.e. the *interpretations* of statutes etc., and

(ii) the systematic (re)organization of legal norms, i.e. the *systematization*.

3. Through the tasks characteristic of LD, its object is determined, and additionally, the way in which it deviates from the other branches of the legal sciences. Although both LD and the comparative study of law analyze norms, the distinction is clear. The comparative study of law is interested in the substance of *foreign* norms and LD in valid law. Legal history focuses its studies on the norms (or institutions) which *have been valid* in the past.

Considering the subject of this paper, the relationship between LD and the sociology of law is the most interesting one. Usually, this relationship has been outlined as follows.

While LD is interested in *norms,* the sociology of law concentrates its attention on *regularities* (invariance), i. e. how individuals and groups actually function in society. If the task of legal sociology is interpreted in this way, we can say that it describes, explains and predicts the activities of individuals, groups or institutions. This kind of problem area does not interest LD because it has to answer to the question: what ought to be done in situation x?

Precisely in this sense, the sociology of law (as well as the history of law) has a double function. The sociology of law can be understood as an assistant producing material for LD when it, for its part, tries to find out the substance of norms. The sociology of law pays attention to such fields which the research interest of LD does not cover, for example, the macro-problems of society. Thus, the sociology of law helps to understand, for example, political/social linkages of legal institutions, their ideological background, etc.

LD is not *independent* from the results produced by its parallel research fields but compared to these fields LD is relatively autonomous, determined only by its basic tasks and its research object. In the following, the interpretative task of LD will be analyzed from this point of view.

III. On Interpreting Legal Norms

1. The interpretative task of LD includes the answer to *two* sub-elements of the problem: (1) which norms are legally valid (the question of validity), and (2) what is the content of valid norms (the question of interpretation).

Interpretation, for its part, can be understood in at least three different ways. To illustrate this I will use the terminology of *Jerzy Wróblewski,* a Polish philosopher of law. In the broadest sense of the word (sensu largissimo), interpretation is everything that concerns the understanding of some expression, event or process either animate or inanimate. This concept of interpretation is of no interest from the viewpoint of LD. Interpretation in a broad sense (sensu largo) means the clarification of the meaning of a certain expression. This kind of interpretation produces meaning statements describing the meaning section covered by the expression. Though this concept of interpretation has some relevance also in regard to LD, it is not the interpretation meant here.

Using Wróblewski's concepts, an interpretation relevant for our purposes is the *specification of the meaning,* i. e. interpretation in a restricted sense (sensu stricto). The meaning of an unclear term will be restricted to cover a certain meaning or certain meaning alternatives.

From this point of view, interpretation is always a "restrictive" act. The semantic meaning alternatives are reduced to cover the legally possible and those alternatives which do not suit the situation are cut off. Actually, the core of interpretation – if this line of thinking is followed – is to make a *choice* between different meaning candidates.

Considering the concept of interpretation, it is important to distinguish the *text* (expression) and its *meaning* from one another. This distinction makes it possible to understand the object of LD in such a way which justifies its research practices. It is only natural to think that LD studies *norms* when examining the substance of valid law. However, norms as objects of research are ontologically problematic.

Legal materials are the language in which something of the legal order is expressed. They are the tools of social communication. Thus, a statutory text gives *information* on binding legal norms and the text of a precedent gives information concerning the decision itself. In this sense, we can say, for example, that a *norm* is the meaning content of the statute and an analysis of the content of the statute gives (more specified) information on norms which we cannot otherwise grasp.

Thus, norms are issues "mediated by language", the ontology of which must be outlined bearing this special characteristic in mind. When talking about the "existence" of norms one necessarily has to refer to the meaning contents of text clarified by interpretation. Thus, a norm "exists" in the same specific sense as the meaning of an expression "exists" in language. This is why discussion on the interpretation of *norms* is not perfectly accurate. As a matter of fact, we "grasp norms" through language and this is why legal interpretation is always the interpretation of *texts,* it is a linguistic matter, and therefore, LD is an interpretation science. Primarily, texts – not norms – are its subject-matter. And this is the core in consideration of the research object of LD.

2. In regard to interpretation, it is possible to distinguish two different situations. If the meaning of the text is *clear* (obvious) and there are no application problems, one can talk about a *routine decision.* An example of this is a parking ticket. Thus, it is characteristic of a routine decision that no interpretative problems exist in it at all. I do not take any stand here as to whether this kind of unproblematic situation can be reasoned linguistically, and if so, on what conditions it is possible.

A so-called *hard case* is the opposite of a routine decision, and it always includes a choice made between alternative meanings as described above. In the following, legal interpretation will be analyzed solely from the viewpoint of a hard case because only in it are, for example, themes distinctive to LD exposed.

The basic structure of a hard case could be described as follows. There is an expression P to be interpreted, and let us suggest a cluster of semantically possible interpretation alternatives (T1 ... Tn) for P. In the next stage, one has to select some alternatives which are legally possible (T1 ... T5). Finally, the interpreter has to select *one* of the legally possible meanings (for example, T1) as the decision which can be "reasoned in the best possible way". Thus, it is not adequate only to suggest the interpretation T1, it must be reasoned, too.

3. Reasoning is carried out by using certain material (sources of law). Here, statutes, legislative drafts, precedents have been considered to be this material. Thus, the concept of statute covers all the official provisions, irregardless of the procedures of their enactment. Hence, a "statute" can be, for example, a decree or the decision of a city administrative court. In this respect, the view of this paper follows the notions of validity outlined by Hans Kelsen.

Legal data has often been called a *source of law* (rättskälla in Swedish; Rechtsquelle in German). This expression is figurative: law "wells forth" from some source. From the viewpoint of interpretation, the question is only *which kind of reasoning material makes the interpretation T1 justified.* If interpretation is understood as a choice between different meaning alternatives, the source material – for better or worse – legitimates (justifies) the choice in question.

The legal materials are language and if the text to be interpreted is inaccurate, vague, ambiguous or there are gaps or contradiction in it, the interpretation is always justified by referring to *other texts.* Precisely in this sense, interpretation can never hide "behind language" or in "reality" beyond language. The justification of legal interpretation merely means a formulation of a *consistent,* or in other words, coherent set of such statements that forms a convincing description of the meaning of the statement to be interpreted.

4. To cite *Ludwig Wittgenstein,* interpretation is like seeking "horizontal" confirmation for the interpretation to be suggested. It is a question of the internal dilemma of language which allows it to proceed to a "vertical" text, in other words to find out whether the suggested interpretation can be confirmed by "outside language" using some data (or a cluster of data) of an empirical nature. This is why legal interpretation is not *empirical* research in the traditional sense of the word. Thus, LD should conceptually be linked with the so-called human sciences rather than with those ulilizing the empirical approach to research.

This can be argued in another sense, too. Hard case situations often include *value-based choices.* This is the case already in the stage when the priority order of various source materials is decided upon. On the other hand, often the interpreter is also forced to use analogy (similarity) and an analogy relationship is always non-cognitive and based on values. Eventually, legal interpretation can also include moral conceptions or ethical choices, such as, a decision on the interpretation of the social basis of abortion.

Thus, in hard cases the reasoning of the chosen interpretation alternative cannot be totally *neutral in regard to value.* If or when this is the case, the easiest way to decide on the "fate" of LD would be to define it as a non-scientific activity. This would also solve the problem as to whether LD is a social science or not. A science would simply be defined to be value-neutral and all of that which is excluded by this definition is *per definitionem* not science. In Finland as late as in the 1970s, for example, this attitude towards the dilemma was fashionable. However, this stand does not solve the problem. LD does not cease to exist if it is defined as not being a science, nor does its social relevance diminish, and LD will not disappear from the universities of the world. What is even more important: a *positivist* definition of science skips the essential, i.e. the question as to whether it is possible or not to *control* the "unscientific" statements of LD in some rational way.

5. Due to this reason, it is justified to change the whole formulation of the problem and to precisely ask for those control mechanisms which produce – if they are properly utilized – the most reliable statements possible of LD. However, if the control cannot be empirical in a traditional way, what is it then?

To analyze this issue, we have to *accept* as granted that LD is an activity consisting partly of value choices, and at the same time, an activity which satisfies the societal interest of knowledge. If and when *this* point of departure is accepted one can ask *how* LD could fulfill its task in a most satisfactory way. Instead of butchering a cow, it is better to try to milk it rationally, or at least, to set rational conditions for milking. In this case, it is worthwhile to spend some time examining some fundamental problems. Let us illustrate them from a historical perspective.

IV. The Rational Acceptability of Interpretation

1. In a constitutional state, it is essential that an individual is entitled to a reasoned *expectation of legal protection.* It is one of the cornerstones of the rule-of-law principle. An individual must be entitled to legal protection against other individuals as well as against the state.

From the societal point of view, it is not an indifferent issue how this expectation is realized. In an authoritative community, where the status of the officials' machinery is powerful, often the *authority brought by the status* is sufficient. An interpretation is "right" simply because it is given by a legal court or another authorized interpreter. Until the late 1950s this was the case in Finland, where legitimacy attitudes, originating from the period of Russianization during Russian rule (1809 - 1917), strongly marked the machinery of legal proceeding and citizens' attitudes towards it.

Since those days, the attitudes towards the legal system have changed. Even if we do not speak about the lack or crisis of reliance, it is nonetheless obvious that the authority given by status is no longer sufficient. This holds true also as far as the legal machinery is concerned. It has to *earn* its authority by deeds, i.e. "beyond" mere status. The decision must be justified. Considering legal interpretation, the demand for justification can be simplified to mean *reasoning*. Actually, we can say that a judge's (and a scholar's) social responsibility is nowadays expressly a responsibility for reasoning. Citizens are no longer satisfied with information as to *how* the case was decided, they also ask *why* the decision was as it was. *This question* can be answered only by giving the reasons for the decision.

Due to this development, legal argumentation in several countries has especially become a focus of debate. In this, it is not a question of a fashionable theoretical whim but of a demand which has the nature of social origin and which has been brought about by the changes taken place in a democratic society. *Here* is also the crucial point in which the modern theory of legal argumentation adapts to the ideas presented by *Jürgen Habermas* on the modern constitutional state. In Finnland, *Kaarlo Tuori* has presented significant remarks on the issue expressly in the same line.

2. *Why* is it important in the modern democratic society to reason a decision? The answer is a simple one. It is essential to *avoid arbitrariness* in legal interpretations. It means, moreover, the *elimination of randomness* in legal interpretation or vice versa predictability. According to habits both in the everyday and theoretical use of language, it is natural to further modify the demand for predictability so that we presume the *thinking process to be rational.* Arbitrariness can be avoided if and only if discretion satisfies the minimum demands of rationality.

The demand to avoid arbitrariness draws our attention to the *discretion procedure,* to the way in which the interpretation proposal is achieved, i.e. to the procedural side of the issue. Rationality, which is assumed here, can be called communicative rationality. In various contexts, I have called it D-rationality because the discursive nature of discretion is emphasized in it.

However, it is not sufficient merely to satisfy the operations of rationality. It is also a question as to whether the *final result* produced by the procedure is acceptable or not. The law of Nazi Germany is often used as an example of how rationalty *as such* does not guarantee justice, unless some substantial demands are included in the concept of rationality. People can be blindly destroyed as a result of an extremely rational activity. And this does not concern only Hitler's Germany. Stalin's Soviet Union, Pol Pot's Cambodia, etc., are good examples of this. In a brutal dictatorship, not only the violations of human rights but also the weak points of legal machinery in general become visible.

Thus, in addition to *formal* rationality, we also set *criteria concerning the content* of law. The adjudication has to fulfill at least two extra preconditions:

(a) Every decision must be *based on a valid law* (the basic demand of legality), and additionally,

(b) Decisions must fulfill the *minimum moral demands* (the linkage between law and morality).

Specifically, the last-mentioned demand was the core of criticism against the law of Nazi Germany. Its moral base was not solid although the decisions in most cases fulfilled the demands of formal law. (Actually, Nazis maintained the validity of most of the norms established before Hitler's regime).

3. As mentioned above, the justification must be *internally* homogeneous, i.e. *a set of statements* which justifies the final decision must fulfill certain basic demands of coherency on which, for example, *Robert Alexy* and *Aleksander Peczenik* have written. The more homogeneous totality the reason forms – or the more elements it has – the more convinced we can be that this reason is *the best* of the possible reasons.

However, the formulation of a coherent set of statements presupposes weighing and balancing. It is not a logical operation. Thus, some extra demands have to be set for the justification procedure. They are demands which particularly concern the rationality of the process. From the societal point of view, the interpretation cannot accidentally end up to be a (very) coherent set of statements. It is essential also to control *how* this coherency was achieved. And here we find the most burning social question of legal interpretation, the question of opening the decision-making process so that it can be controlled.

4. Interpreted in this way, the theory of rational argumentation can also be characterized as a *critical* theory. It offers a measure or a model which make it possible to evaluate actual interpretation processes and their results. Rational argumentation and other demands referred to above together form an *ideal* which can be more or less approached by true processes. In this respect, legal interpretation is governed by a kind of *regulative principle:* try to produce such a decision which can be accepted by rationally thinking individuals (a rational audience). Actually, the regulative principle announces two basic demands of legal interpretation, that is rationality and acceptability (of content). Here is one of the meeting points between LD and social science. Before we look at the social scientific nature of LD from an interpretative point of view, the focus must, however, be placed on the other main task of LD, i.e. on the systematization of legal norms.

V. Systematization

1. Let us first make a distinction between legal *order* and legal *system*. Legal order is the sum of legal norms, a complex totality of numerous norms enacted in different times and contexts. It is, to a certain extent, an organized whole but because of its broadness it is very laborious to master it as such. As an example of this, the difference between the publication of the Statutes of Finland (a collection of all statutes) and the books of the Law of Finland I - II can be mentioned. The latter include a selected and systematically organized collection of statutes already published in the Statutes of Finland in their due time.

To master the statutes (norms) presumes that norms are *further* organized in comparison to the collection in the Law of Finland. This task of further organization has naturally become a part of LD. It is, as mentioned before, actually one of the two basic tasks of LD. Legal theorists describe this task remarking that LD reformulates the collection of norms so that the whole is:

- more abstract and general, and, thus
- more like a review and easier to master than pre-systemized law.

The (legal) systematization of norms is a kind of *a bearer of* legal *tradition*. Each "generation of norms" is based on certain basic concepts, on a model to analyze legal and social reality. If society accepts private ownership we cannot avoid the concept of ownership, neither can we escape from the distinction between personal and real estate, or from the concept of form, activities concerning trade, purchase, exchange, gift, renting or hiring out. We need concepts of contract, authorization, invalidity, compensation for damage and many other basic concepts. We also have to lean on numerous principles which support our legal conception, for example, such principles that no one is allowed to benefit from his/her wrongful act, that good faith must be protected, and that primarily the one who acts first must be protected (the principle of time priority). These concepts and principles constitute the *core of* legal *tradition*. They are, as *Robert S. Summers* emphazises, the *form* of it.

This tradition (form) for its part, is manifested in the legal system, for example, in the statutory order of succession or in the doctrine of contract. This system mediates the structures of thinking from one generation to another and maintains the consistence of legal order. The system of legal norms can be compared with the grammar of spoken and written language. We do not *choose* grammar when we learn to speak. Grammar precedes our individual language, we learn it, we adapt it, even though language and grammar are under rules of slow change. Grammar is not solid, unchanging or constraining everything. It is an *absolute* condition of the thinking process, a tool which can be modified on certain terms and which is changing along with the world. Grammar, just as systematization, is like the bank of a river, gradually it changes its location and form but always exists somewhere. The river *has* its bank. (Wittgenstein, *On Certainty*).

2. Without going into theoretical details, it is time to describe systematization with an example. To make it understandable, some basic concepts must be defined. Since the Middle Ages, lawyers have considered that law is realized *in relationships between individuals,* or briefly, in personal relationships. When one owns real estate, it is not a question of a relationship between the owner and the *object* but of the owner's relationship with *other people.* Rights and obligations are manifested *in* human relationships and *as* human relationships. From this point of view, debate on the rights of animals is not only *legally* problematic but also impossible.

A personal relationship, for its part, is constituted of human *behavior.* It is an outcome of communication, interaction and integration to a certain functional system. The behavior of type A produces personal relationships X while type B produces relationships Y, etc.

When a certain personal relationship is organized by a legal norm it becomes a *legal relationship.* A norm acts as a social "mediating material". A norm and only a norm gives *legal relevance* to the personal relationship and social behavior constituted in it. The same personal relationship can become sociated or be socially relevant in many other ways, too, but only the norm makes it interesting from a legal point of view.

Normally, a person simultaneously has *several* legal relationships in regard to society. Some complexes of relationships constitute (together) an individual's *legal status.* Therefore, a creditor's legal status means a complex of norms according to which a debtor has to pay the demanded debt under the threat of a sanction. A legal status can be logically organized by rights/obligations, liberties/claims, capacities/liabilities. A classic of this kind of an analysis is the American scholar *W. N. Hohfeld.*

Hence, the social character of law is "present" *in* those phenomena (behavior) which are made legally/socially relevant by legal norms.[1] They are built in the legal relationships between individuals, groups, etc. As a matter of fact, law *is* society manifested (partly) in those phenomena (relationships). And if we consider society, in this sense, to be organized expressly and specifically through law, we can also consider LD to be a *fundamental social science.* Here, I do not take any stand concerning this notion but even if the statement on the social character of law is formulated like this, it has something relevant to say in regard to the theme. I will return to this issue at the end of my presentation.

[1] For this notion I owe my gratitude to Kauko Pietilä who has directed my attention to this problem from the viewpoint of the social sciences.

3. As a typical example of this, the status of an owner has often been used. It is an apt example not only because of its social importance but also because of its complex structure. The especially problematic task is to describe the transfer of ownership or protection of ownership in atypical situations.

In the following, a reduced description of the owner's legal status will be given. From it a kind of a typical model of legal status will be generalized so that we can see what systematization means in legal context. At the end, based on the given model, we return to the *relationship* between systematization and interpretation because it enables us to make a needed conclusion of the theme.

The status of an owner as an *institution* consists of several different *components*. The right of ownership is not a "substance" which ontologically exists like physical objects. In this respect, ownership and other legal concepts belong to the same institutional category as, for example, the concept of power. Ownership is a *collective appellation* to a very complicated complex of norms which regulates what, on the one hand, an owner and non-owner are permitted to do or not to do, and, on the other, what they are obliged to do. The components of ownership are:

- owner's *right of possession* (possessio in Latin),
- the owner's *competence* to dispose of his/her property, for example, by renting it, etc., and
- the owner's *legal protection* in certain situations of transfer, for example, when a previous owner tries to vindicate the object due to some mistake which has taken place during a former stage of the process.

Each of the described components can be broken into subcomponents, and these to smaller components, etc. However, each one of the (sub)concepts *ultimately* refers to some *valid legal norm*. As a matter of fact, the concepts "lump together" an enormous collection of norms into such subaggregates that they can be mastered in a rational way in practice. A rough outline of the setting (from which subcomponents are excluded) could be the following:

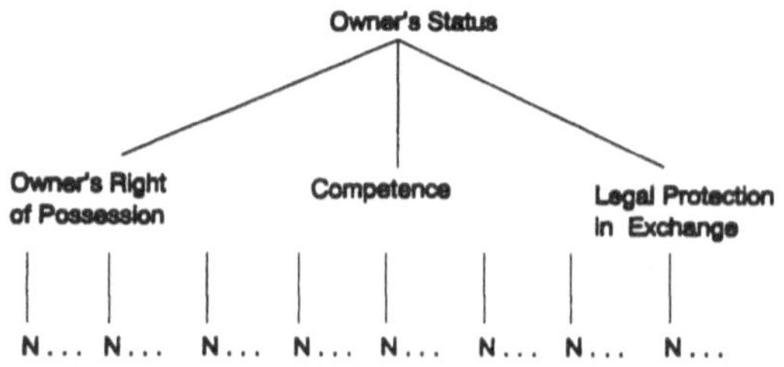

Figure 1

4. The same presentation can be detached from the owner's status and *generalized* to concern every description of legal status. In this case, the model takes the following shape:

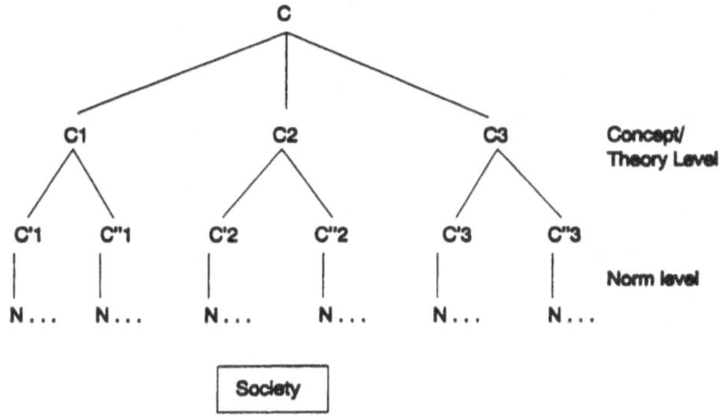

Figure 2

When (systematization) LD functions on the concept/theory level it can be called *theoretical* as to its nature. On the other hand, LD as an interpretive science is *pragmatic* because it has the function of solving practical legal (interpretative) problems.

Between these two exists an *interaction relationship:* systematization is reflected in interpretations and interpretations "test" the constancy of systematization. Only such ways of reorganizing legal norms can survive which produce "legal understanding" that satisfies the needs of the respective legal community. This is why norms cannot be systematized in just any possible way. Instead, all systematizations are based on something. As mentioned previously, systematizations are the bearers of legal tradition, and being such, they are bound to that "grammar" which maintains the legal order and offers grounds for legal self-understanding.

Yet, the *dynamics of law* is most clearly manifested in the changes of systematizations. One could illustrate the issue – being aware of the specifications needed in the illustration – by speaking about the *reinterpretations* of the paradigm of LD. The paradigm itself (LD as legal science) does not change but the way in which the "basic grammar" of law is interpreted is changing.

VI. Is Legal Science a Social Science?

1. Naturally, the answer to the question does not only depend on how LD is characterized. We also need a definition of social science. As far as the latter is concerned, we inevitably have to take a stand on the research object of

social science, that is *society*. Above, some clues have been given on the direction we could trace the answer from which.

2. *If* only such research is considered to be social scientific, the statements of which can be *confirmed empirically*, then LD does not belong to this family of sciences. LD, as pointed out before, is interpretative by its nature. The confirmation of interpretative statements is resolved basing on the *coherence* of the set of statements presented to support the interpretation.

In regard to LD – and from the internal viewpoint of LD – empirical social science can only be a device of interpretation. Empirical research produces, for example, data which can be utilized as a justification material or it helps to understand the functions of legal institutions and thus, indirectly opens new perspectives for interpretation.

3. If the demand of empirical confirmation *is not set* in this way, the relationship between LD and social science turns out to be of different nature. Assuming that social science can be thought to study – as Kauko Pietilä assumes – society (as existing) in phenomena, LD clearly seems to be one of the social sciences. LD expressly interprets linkages (norms) through which people's personal relationships become legalized and in this way sociated. From a certain point of view, law is society *in* those phenomena that LD is studying, and thus, LD is a study of these normative "reciprocating mechanisms". It is an interpretative research, that is a human (moral) science, but *in this* specific viewpoint it is inevitably also a social science, the truth of which is measured by coherence.

Nevertheless, in this respect LD has often lost (or forgotten) its sociated nature and social-scientific character. If LD is not clearly aware of the fact that its research object actually *is* society *in the above outlined sense,* it becomes a mere interpretation of symbols. In this case, LD turns from actual questions to a purely linguistic level, it becomes uncontaminated interpretation. This being case, LD only interprets for the sake of interpretation, it concerns only the level of mere language, it corrects and specifies language as language. To quote *Peter Winch,* LD only "clears trash from language".

If this is the case, the independence of LD in regard to its object becomes distorted, it would "abolish" itself from society and – from itself. And vice versa: LD can be a *sociating agent* only if it recognizes the social character of its object and thus, the fact that in interpreting legal data it is *inevitably* a social science. However, if LD only concentrates to choose "societally important objects" as its subject-matter or *participates* (politically) in society by interpretations, it is only superficially societal, it does not mean sociation. LD is not a field of legal *policy,* it represents legal *research.* And what is most important: LD is not interested in phenomena *as such* but in society as existing *in phenomena.*

In this respect, *theoretical* LD is in a key position. In it, the object of LD becomes obvious, that is legal relationships as a theoretical object. Theoretical LD analyzes on a conceptual level those linkages which constitute personal relationships to become legal relationships, and further, legal statutes (and institutions). Thus, legal relationships form the framework of pre-understanding (Vorverständnis) which guides interpretation and this framework inevitably (or at least, implicitly) always includes a picture of society. Therefore, the family resemblance of theoretical LD with (theoretical) social science is obvious.

The difference lies, more or less, in the fact that concepts of theoretical LD offer a *normative* framework to perceive society. It is a conceptual body of the world of "Ought" ("Sollen") which was so much emphasized by Hans Kelsen. However, normativity is not essential when the social-scientific nature of LD is evaluated. The normative concepts of LD have the same *function* as the descriptive concepts of other social sciences have in regard to the object of social science. Thus, in the field of law, theoretical LD fulfills exactly the *same function* of formulating theory as theory of any other field of research does, and in *this* point, one cannot prove any difference of principle between theoretical social science and (theoretical) LD.

References

Aarnio, Aulis: Laintulkinnan teoria (Theory of Legal Interpretation). Juva 1989.

– The Rational as Reasonable. Dordrecht 1987.

Alexy, Robert: Theory of Legal Argumentation. Oxford 1989.

Peczenik, Aleksander: On Law and Reason. Dordrecht 1989.

– Rätten och förnuftet (Law and Reason). 2 a uppl. Lund 1988.

Pietilä, Kauko/*Sondermann,* Klaus: Sanomalehden yhteiskunta. Sosiologinen tutkimus Helsingin Sanomista (Newspaper Society: A Sociological Study on a Finnish Daily). Forthcoming.

Summers, Robert S.: Essays on the Nature of Law and Legal Reasoning. 1992.

Summers, Robert S./*MacCormick,* Neil D.: Interpreting Statutes: A Comparative Study. 1991.

Tuori, Kaarlo: Oikeuden rationaalisuus. Max Weber ja Jürgen Habermas oikeuskehityksen tutlkitsijoina (Rationality of Law: Max Weber and Jürgen Habermas as Interpreters of Legal Development). Helsinki 1988.

Comparative Law and Legal Theory

By John Bell, Leeds

1. Introduction

A major contribution of the recent work of Robert Summers is to demonstrate the importance of comparative law for legal theory. In *Form and Substance in Anglo-American Law,* he and Patrick Atiyah argue that attention to the dimensions of formality and substativeness in a range of aspects of the legal system from procedure to rule-making and rule-application can illuminate the fundamental character of law. Indeed, this focus points to sharp differences in two members of what are commonly perceived as members of the same 'legal family' by comparative lawyers. This work encourages the jurisprudent to engage with the idea that law is not simply a set of norms or social facts, or even values, but a complex set of features defining and expressing a legal culture. In *Interpreting Statutes,* he and Neil MacCormick use the comparative method to analyse issues of jurisprudential interest in the area of statutory interpretation, and again relate these to specific legal cultures.

The position developed in these works is well summarised in the conclusion to *Form and Substance,* where Atiyah and Summers argue that:

> In our view, then, the primary subject matter of jurisprudence is not a single universal subject matter, abstracted from the variant phenomena of law in all societies. It should, rather, consist of the relevant features of the phenomena of law in one or more particular societies.[1]

To suggest that legal theory should use comparative law is nothing new. Much of nineteenth century jurisprudence drew first on Roman law and then on anthropology in order to explain general issues about law. For instance, John Austin's notion of 'general jurisprudence' was concerned with 'the exposition of principles, notions, and distinctions common to all systems of law'.[2] He was concerned to draw lessons from particular systems which would indicate something about the nature of law in general. Likewise, those who founded the modern comparative law method were concerned to find among the diverse rules and institutions of contemporary legal systems some general

1 *Form and Substance in Anglo-American Law* (Oxford 1988), p. 418.

2 *Lectures on Jurisprudence* (1834, 5th edn. by R. Campbell, London 1885), p. 1073.

principles which could constitute a *ius commune* around which legal unification could aspire.

The Summers approach is distinctive in that Summers and his collaborators are concerned to focus on specific problems and what can be concluded from them, rather than general issues about the nature of law.[3] Similarly, Basil Markesinis argues for a more specific focus to comparative law research, with attention paid to 'relatively narrow and manageable problems, avoiding those over-worked accounts of "les grands systèmes de droits contemporains"'.[4]

Despite these warnings, this paper seeks to draw from the methodology of comparative law some lessons for a general legal theory. It suggests that law is best viewed as a tradition within a legal community, rather than essentially as rules or norms of conduct. Within such a view of law, the central interplay between a community and its norms of conduct can be appreciated. I will suggest that this analysis of law is greatly helped by the work of Robert Summers, and it extrapolates from the unique contribution he has made both to comparative law and legal theory.

2. Jurisprudential Method

Comparative law and jurisprudence share a similar methodology. The method of jurisprudence has been to give definitions to law in a number of ways. The first, hermeneutical approach, adopted, for instance, by Hart, requires a jurisprudent to look at ordinary language: what do people call 'law'?[5] Hart does not set out hard-and-fast criteria for what is to count as law. David adopts much the same approach in his introduction to the *International Encyclopedia of Comparative Law*. He notes the diversity of views about the meaning of law and the function it plays, but with this warning, he leaves the various systems claiming to be legal systems side by side in the exposition of law.[6]

In one sense, this is valuable, in that it allows the phenomena to speak for themselves. It tries not to distort what is being done in a particular society. On the other hand, as any translator knows, the ability to communicate between countries depends on the existence of conceptual, and not simply terminological, equivalence. For example, a language like that of the Tswana may not have a word for 'law' on its own. 'Mekgwa le melao' is a compound concept covering 'law and customs'. One might wish, as Comaroff and Roberts did, to

---

[3] P. S. Atiyah and R. S. Summers, *Form and Substance*, p. 416.

[4] B. Markesinis, 'An Expanding Tort Law' (1987) 103 LQR at 396.

[5] *Definition and Theory in Jurisprudence* (Oxford 1953), *The Concept of Law* (Oxford 1961), pp. 3 - 4.

[6] *International Encyclopedia of Comparative Law*, vol. 1, ch. 1, paras. 1 - 4.

give an account of that concept in operation in a particular society.[7] But broader and valuable lessons can be gained by drawing comparisons with other societies, even though these latter do have a clearer distinction between 'laws' and 'customs'. It may be sufficient to adopt what Zweigert and Kötz describe as the negative aspect of functionality – to attempt to eradicate all preconceptions of one's own legal system when studying another.[8]

For this reason, a more stipulative definition of law is usually found helpful in a comparative exercise and in jurisprudence. Authors try to set out criteria for what is to count as law. Such a general definition of law focuses, as Finnis suggests, on the 'central case',[9] though it does not frequently exclude other phenomena coming within the idea of 'law'. Thus, while Austin talks of 'laws improperly so-called' and keeps the command of the sovereign at the centre of a definition of 'law', Kelsen is prepared to see more count as law, even though he maintains his central paradigm of law as coercive and part of a system of sanctions applied by officials.[10] Other features of law can be interpreted in the light of the pardigm feature or function. Thus Finnis accommodates unjust laws by saying that, although they may comply with formal criteria of validity, they are not central cases of the principal function of law, which is to give guidance about the requirements of practical reasonableness to the good citizen.[11] Like David, jurisprudents need to provide answers not merely to the question of definition, but also to the question of function.

A way round the difficulty of coming up with an adequate stipulative definition would be to focus specifically on the different tasks which law performs in different societies. Taken to an extreme example, Roberts has suggested that, at least in studying tribal and other less complex societies, we should compare functions without troubling ourselves whether they should count as 'law' at all. He argues that, given the lack of 'fit' between our own legal arrangements and the control mechanisms of those societies, our own legal theory is not really applicable and that we are best focusing on the way two main functions are performed: the maintenance of order and the resolution of disputes.[12] More typically, legal theorists have tried to develop a more sophisticated analysis of the functions which law plays in society. Thus, the work of Llewellyn on defining 'law jobs' is but one example of how a function-based analysis could be developed, not simply for so-called primitive systems, but also for modern systems. In an sense, this is the height of pragmatism: 'law' is simply a tool to perform certain jobs. Such function-centred thinking almost dispenses the theorist

---

7 J. L. Comaroff and S. Roberts, *Rules and Processes* (Chicago, 1981).

8 *An Introduction to Comparative Law* (2nd edn trans. Weir, Oxford 1987), p. 32.

9 J. Finnis, *Natural Law and Natural Rights* (Oxford 1980), pp. 9 - 11.

10 H. Kelsen, *Pure Theory of Law* (Berkley 1967), esp. pp. 34 - 9.

11 Ibid., p. 360.

12 S. Roberts, *Order and Dispute* (Harmondsworth, 1979), pp. 27 - 8.

from defining 'law' as a whole. How the individual jobs are best performed is a matter of what works in the circumstances of a particular society. A definition of 'law' in general is merely contingent and inessential.

In a sense, a functional approach already informs the paradigm which forms the core of the stipulative approach. Which functions are the ones which are central to law: providing coercive support to dispute resolution, setting standards to guide good citizens, adjudication of disputes, or whatever? A more specifically functionalist approach merely moves discussion of functions to centre stage. A theory of law takes these various analyses of functions and suggests that there is a priority between them which can be extended across a range of societies to form a basis for studying law in general. It is this functional approach which provides the link to the methodology of comparative law.

3. Comparative Law Approaches

Comparative law approaches have typically used a 'functional-equivalence' approach to comparison between legal systems. To quote Zweigert and Kötz,

> The basic methological principle of all comparative law is that of *functionality*... Incomparables cannot usefully be compared, and in law the only things which are comparable are those which fulfil the same function... The proposition rests on what every comparatist learns, namely that the legal system of every society faces essentially the same problems, and solves these problems by quite different means though very often with similar results.[13]

This approach shares much in common with the jurisprudents. There is a need to look at the law in terms of social function and then to see how problems are resolved, whether by law or otherwise.

But comparative lawyers also look beyond specific functions to the ways in which they actually operate in particular societies. Even where the same functions are performed in a society, there may well be differences in the end result because of the peculiarities of the legal context in which those functions are performed. Thus Kahn Freund argued

> given two or more countries with fairly similar political, economic, social and cultural structures, the questions which the law is asked to answer are likely to be similar, and so are the answers likely to be given; but the methods of arriving at the answers may be very different in the light of different structures of the legal sources and different traditions of legal argument. The questions and answers result from social necessity, the road to be travelled from the question to the answer is laid down by jurisitic doctrines and methods.[14]

[13] Op. cit., p. 31. Cf. the criticism of J. Hill, 'Comparative Law, Law Reform and Legal Theory' (1989) 9 OJLS 101, 104 - 5.

In more neo-Marxian terms, law stands in a quasi-autonomous relationship to the forces of social formation and social necessity.[15] Law has its own life which shapes the character of the performance of particular functions. In order to explain this particular idiosyncracy of law, comparative lawyers frequently rely on identifying legal families among legal systems. Such families represent specific legal traditions exemplified usually in several jurisdictions. David relied on two phenomena to identify such a 'family': an ideology and a set of legal techniques.[16] Thus western law and socialist law or muslim law are separated by ideology – there are different views about the individual and the community or about the relationship of law and morals which fundamentally characterise the systems. On the other hand, common law and Romanistic-German law are separated by legal technique and history, rather than by an ideological or political differences. Zweigert and Kötz offer a more sophisticated analysis of the features which serve to define a legal 'family'. They suggest that the crucial feature making one legal system distinct from another is its 'style' and they list five features as crucial for that style: its historical background and development, its predominant and characteristic mode of thought in legal matters, its distinctive institutions, the legal sources it acknowledges and handles, and its ideology.[17] There are thus a cluster of features which concur in defining a distinctive legal way of doing things, which may or may not coincide with the social or political features which make a country distinct.

Although the idea of legal families is problematic,[18] it does, however, have some value as in legal analysis. In the first place, it focuses on the specifically legal aspects of law, the way in which the character of law is not wholly determined by the social and political functions which it performs. That fundamentally similar societies in the West can belong to different legal cultures and operate in distinctive legal fashions demonstrates the importance of the purely legal tradition within which similar social functions have to be carried out. Summers has contributed to this analysis by the notion of the 'vision of law'. In *Form and Substance,* Atiyah and Summers identify within the single 'legal family' of the common law two distinct 'visions of law', a formal approach typical of England and a substantive approach typical of the United States. Such

---

[14] 'Common Law and Civil Law – Imaginary and Real Obstacle to Assimilation' in M. Cappelletti (ed.), *New Perspectives for a Common Law of Europe* (Brussels 1978), 137 at 148.

[15] I. D. Balbus, 'Commodity Form and Legal Form: an Essay on the Relative Autonomy of the Law', in C. E. Reasons and M. Rich, *The Sociology of Law* (Toronto 1978), ch. 3.

[16] R. David, Les grands systèmes du droit contemporain (10th edn by C. Jauffret-Spinozi, Paris 1993).

[17] Op. cit., p. 69.

[18] See M. Ancel, 'Le comparativiste devant les systèmes (ou "familles") de droit', in H. Bernstein, U. Drobnig and H. Kötz, Festschrift für Konrad Zweigert (Tübingen 1981), 355, 358. See also Zweigert and Kötz, op. cit., p. 74.

a vision is 'a set of inarticulate and perhaps even unconscious beliefs held by the general public at large and, to some extent, also by politicans, judges, and legal practitioners, as to the nature and function of law – how and by whom it should be made, interpreted and enforced'.[19] Such a view about the law may be held widely or merely narrowly within a legal community, though they consider that, even where a well-informed opionion is likely to be held only by legal professionals, public perceptions can be correlated quite well with the visions found in the two societies.[20] Their suggestion is that the legal tradition is not radically autonomous from the functions assigned to law by society, even if the form this takes may be adapted. Similarly, Van Caenegem suggests that differences between legal systems may not result so much from different cultures or 'national spirits' but from the way in which legal institutions interact with political circumstances. The weakness of politics in Germany might give rise to a 'professors' law' whereas a different political structure might permit the development of judges' law as in England.[21]

The emphasis on legal families takes us away from attention to law as a system of rules to the network of a tradition. The list of features given by David and Zweigert and Kötz focus on legal techniques, concepts, institutions and history, as well as the more general political or social ideology which informs legal practice. The central feature of the Atiyah and Summers analysis is more functionally dynamic. It suggests that there is a vision of law which renders coherent the practice of a particular legal community. But when we consider whence this vision comes, we find a strong role for the legal community in the form of courts, law schools, and lawmakers who mediate and articulate in structural form the expectatons of the wider community. Their analysis also suggests that such a vision is sustained as a tradition. Rules and functions operate as part of a tradition of legal ways of doing things which has various complex relationships to the kind of society in which it operates and the functions it accords to law.

4. Law as Tradition

The basic suggestion of this paper is that a tradition has three features: it is a process in which actors are engaged, it sets the context for decision-making, and it is a group of people engaged in the activity of the tradition and shaping it.

The concept of a 'legal family' encapsulates the idea that there is a tradition or way of dealing with legal rules which affects the way in which they will

[19] *Form and Substance,* p. 411.

[20] Ibid, pp. 411 - 2.

[21] R. C. van Caenegem, *Judges, Legislators and Professors* (Cambridge 1987), pp. 71 - 2.

apply. As Atiyah and Summers point out in relation to English and American law, broadly similar rules may apply in the two systems, but, within a different vision of law, this may lead to different consequences. Fidelity to rules is a feature of the formalist tradition which is not shared to the same extent by a substantivist tradition, where rigid application of rules may be avoided in order to achieve a substantively fairer result. The rules have to be understood within a process of interpretation specific to the legal system or legal family. But it is clear from their exposition that they envisage such a vision of law being first rooted in the practice and discourse of the profession, and 'when elements of a general theory of law become firmly embedded in the legal culture and in the content and workings of the law in a particular society, so that they become part of the general stock of ideas, much political and legal discourse will be cast in the language of that theory'.[22] The other features identified by Zweigert and Kötz such as history, predominant mode of thought on legal matters, distinctive legal institutions and concepts, techniques and methods go well beyond looking at law as rules or even functions. They shape the character of the rules to be applied and all these elements contribute to the nature of a tradition.

The concept of a tradition can appear negative. Tradition seems a break on development and invention. Thus David sees the inertia of routine and an attachment to accepted solutions as particular obstacles to legal progress in progress towards the unification of the rules of legal systems, a 'blind attachment to the past'.[23] But 'tradition' in the sense I wish to describe has a dynamic and life-giving possibility. Even routines among lawyers and accepted solutions, which David describes as 'obstacles' to the desirable unification of law, can be seen to serve positive social values. Such stable practices help create legal certainty, leaving scope for the development of a coherent and consistent legal regime. Such a legal system might more easily gain the confidence and respect of citizens. In addition, drawing on prior experiences saves time and avoids unnecessary errors in legal development. None of these virtues is conclusive against legal change or even unification. But they are not trivial values in a legal system.

A tradition may be defined as a complex of rules, concepts, institutions and practices which characterise the way the law works in a particular area. These features build together into a process. In short, a tradition is a way of doing things, which is handed down and shapes the way in which the law operates.

The notion of 'tradition as a process' suggests that law is fundamentally an activity which carries on a tradition. I will suggest that, in the first place, the central activity of a lawyer, interpretation, is a process of interacting with a

---

[22] Ibid, p. 412.

[23] See *International Encyclopedia of Comparative Law,* vol. 2, ch. 5, para. 63, also paras. 57 - 59.

tradition. Secondly, the tradition provides a framework for thought in resolving problems.

Martin Krygier suggests that the central feature of law as a tradition is the way in which law operates as a process mediating between past and present. Law is both an institutionalised form of the past, and has an authoritative present in which that past plays a normative role in relation to decisions, values and beliefs in the present.[24] Not only is it normative, it also provides anchorage for expectations of citizens about how they should behave towards one another.

The central feature of most modern legal systems is the text – of statute, case-law, or legal doctrine. The activity of reading and interpreting these texts is central to the activity of law, since they are the sources of applicable rules. It is a commonplace that the meaning of such texts is not simply accessible out of their legal context. Words are chosen by draftsmen for their meaning and resonance within a body of existing law, and those draftsmen are involved in making alive that body of law for a particular situation. The later interpreter has to connect the text with the current corpus of law, also drawn from the tradition, in order to distil its meaning. Law is thus engaged in a process of using and interpreting a received tradition of texts. As Betti put it,

> It is precisely by living in the tradition of the case law that jurists realise in themselves the continuity in the life of the law, blend in coherent harmony the data of the tradition with the new acquisitions, point out the links between the letter of the law and the thought handed down.[25]

Similarly, Gadamer argues that,

> In our continually manifested attitude to the past, the main feature is not, at any rate, a distancing and freeing of ourselves from what has been transmitted. Rather, we stand always within a tradition . . .[26]

Being within the tradition makes possible the activity of understanding the law – knowing what to look for and how to use legal materials. Of course, there is scope for freedom in interpretation, and even for a degree of innovation. As Gadamer goes on to say, the process of understanding and application of a text is part of the evolution of the tradition in relation to contemporary circumstances.[27] But even totally novel issues, such as how to deal with surrogacy contracts are not determined *ex nihilo*. Judges and legislators determine a solution negotiating within the legal tradition, typically by way of analogy with accepted solutions.[28] Law is thus a process which is inherently traditional.

---

[24] M. Krygier, 'Law as Tradition' (1986) 5 Law and Philosophy 237, esp. 240.

[25] E. Betti, *Interpretazione della Legge e degli Atti Giuridici* (Milan 1971), p. 66.

[26] H.-G. Gadamer, *Truth and Method* (London 1975), p. 250.

[27] Ibid, pp. 261 and 294.

[28] See J. Bell, in P. Cane and J. Stapleton (edd.), *Essays for Patrick Atiyah* (Oxford 1991), ch. 5.

Such reasoning within a tradition is not an isolated task. The interpreter is part of a legal community which is involved in making a set of legal texts and values operate in a given society. The decision made has not only to be situated within a tradition, it also has to be justified in terms compatible with the tradition. The correctness of the interpretation given is judged by reference to the legal audience, those knowledgeable and skilled in the law.[29] The legal text comes to the interpreter as part of a legal past to be fitted into the law as it now exists. The text is not purely an historical document; it has a normative content which reaches out to the present. The lawyer is thus not an antiquarian, seeking to understand a tradition in its past. Rather the lawyer seeks to maintain an appropriate continuity between past and present. This may involve significant development, but this must be a defensible development of the tradition. In Dworkin's terms, the solution must satisfy a threshhold of 'fit' with the rest of the law. Thus the process of interpretation is firmly connected with a legal community as the guardian, privileged exponent, and preserver of the tradition. The techniques that new law students learn are the perspective of that legal tradition as understood within the legal community. This tradition of ideas, language and concepts shapes the legal practice of a community. The legal audience to whom justifications for interpretations are addressed is to some extent ideal – the legal interpreter seeks to demonstrate that her conclusion is correct to anyone who cares to examine the argument. But the ideal audience is also instantiated in a concrete legal community. What is accepted by the particular community will count as strong evidence for what the ideal community would accept as a rational conclusion from the rules and principles of that system.

Although the very activity of law is traditional, there are specific features of the language, concepts, and techniques which constitute the tradition and which set the framework for legal thinking. At a simple level, the language of law has a precision because it expresses a set of concepts embedded in a structure of legal thought which has been handed down. That structure of concepts provides not only precision for dealing with established problems, it also provides a framework within which lawyers can talk about new problems. For example, the issue of public sector strikes is handled very differently in continental European and common law legal systems. In the former, such as in France, it is taken as obvious that public employees should not be governed by the same regime as private employees. Public employees perform a public service to fulfil the objectives of the general interest defined by the state. In some cases, they are able significantly to affect public order or security. In order that their public service function be fulfilled, public employees must accept limitations on the right to strike. Notably, the 'continuity of the public service' imposes on them a duty to maintain a minimum service and this over-

[29] See J. Bell, 'The Acceptability of Legal Arguments', in P. Birks and D. N. MacCormick, The Legal Mind (Oxford 1986), pp. 55 - 7.

rides the right to strike as a civil liberty.[30] In some cases, this will effectively defeat the right to strike altogether, as in the case of the army. Common lawyers start from different premises and concepts. Employment is a matter of contract, and thus of private law. Prohibitions must form part of the terms of the contract. In addition, the right to strike is a civil liberty which is not easily overriden in favour of the government (the preferred term, since 'the state' does not have the same sense in the common law as in other systems). While the public interest justifies specific prohibitions on strikes by the army or police in both systems, the idea of a minimum service is not accepted in the common law in part because of the conceptual structure within which lawyers have to reason. Such concepts and their relationships shape legal thinking, and give a specific character to legal systems.

Classifications, such as public law, private law, or the separation of legal and religious norms, are fundamental to ways of thinking. They set the framework for much legal discussion and generate a further chain of distinctions which makes any comparison between systems not sharing such basic classifications difficult. As Geoffrey Samuel has suggested, it may be possible to explain one system in terms of the classifications of another, and the use of such terms may be valuable.[31] All the same, this process is often difficult.

Law is not only a process of making present the rules and values contained in a tradition. Lawyers have to confront new problems and develop new solutions. On issues such as the validity of surrogacy contracts or dealing with the treatment of a person in a permanent vegetative state, then the tradition does not provide specific answers. All the same, continuity with the tradition is an important feature of the solutions reached. They must fit coherently into and build on the existing law. In this sense, there must be a threshhold of 'fit', as Dworkin suggests. In addition, the concepts and values around which the solution must be found come from the tradition, enriched by further thinking and development. Even legislative solutions introduce novel ideas within a context of established principles and procedures, if they are to work effectively. The idea of organic development is complemented by the necessity that any new decision to take full account of the existing state of the law and the expectations which it has generated. It may well be that many of the existing rules of law have been adopted through historical or geographical circumstance, or for other accidental reasons, and the solution adopted is only equally as good as

[30] See CE 7 July 1950, Dehaene, Leb. 426, and CC decision no. 79 - 105 DC of 25 July 1979, Strikes on Radio and Television, Rec. 33: see J. Bell, *French Constitutional Law* (Oxford 1992), pp. 160 - 2.

[31] G. Samuel, 'Civil and Commercial Law: A Distinction Worth Making' (1986) 102 LQR 569; ibid, 'Public Law and Private Law: A Private Lawyer's Response' (1983) 46 MLR 558; G. Samuel and J. Rincques, *The English Law of Obligations in Comparative Context* (Nijmegen 1991).

any other solution.[32] To follow David, different justifications may be acceptable in different systems. The reasons for differences are not just ideological. Different geography, historical accident, and just taking different turnings can account for different solutions. Ideas of justice in such a context can genuinely be different between legal systems without ideological difference. Once such legal differences are in place and generate equally acceptable conclusions, then it is difficult to move away from them. Indeed, the history, legal concepts, legal techniques, etc which define a particular legal system cannot be ignored without creating injustice in relation to the established expectations of citzens under the systems.

In other words, there may be no ideological objection to any alternative solution. But any legal change must take account of what has been entrenched, for it would be unjust to ignore the expectations which the current state of the tradition has generated. In addition, additions to the law must not be so inconsistent with the rest of the law as to cause problems for the future. Thus, for decisions which have to be taken based on novel policy considerations, the tradition forms an important part of the context.

The tradition is not just rules and processes, but is essentially the practice of people who operate and perpetuate the tradition. As a traditional activity, law is what specific institutions and professions do, and how they operate. For example, institutions and professions often generate and perpetuate distinctions. Thus, in France, the existence of two separate higher courts for public law and private law, each staffed by different personnel, tends to lead to an accentuation of the divisions between the branches of law, and to different ways of doing things which continues the public/private divide. In religious systems, the institutional competence of religious courts and the role of priests within them ensure a close link between religious and legal ideas of justice.

The existence of institutions brings us to the heart of a legal tradition. A tradition is a set of practices among a caste of lawyers. This point is made by Simpson who argues that

> the common law system is properly located as a customary system of law in this sense, that it consists of a body of practices observed and ideas received by a caste of lawyers, these ideas being used by them as providing guidance in what is conceived to be the rational determination of disputes litigated before them, or by them on behalf of clients, and in other contexts. These ideas and practices exist only in the sense that they are accepted and acted upon within the legal profession, just as customary practices may be said to exist within a group in the sense that they are observed, accepted as appropriate forms of behavior, and transmitted both by example and precept as membership of the group changes.[33]

[32] R. David, vol. 2 , ch. 5 no. 66.

[33] A.W.B. Simpson, 'The Common Law and Legal Theory', *Oxford Essays in Jurisprudence* (2nd series ed. A. W. B. Simpson, Oxford 1973), 79 at p. 94.

As a distinct caste, lawyers help to perpetate certain ways of doing things as part of their professional identity. In this sense, law is what lawyers do. The social phenomenon of law, the tasks or functions which it performs are linked intimately to the issue of where this caste of lawyers fits into society. What is a 'legal issue' may amount simply to where a lawyer, or a particular kind of lawyer, would be brought in. It is perfectly possible (indeed it happens frequently) that what is seen as a legal issue in one country is not so seen in another (for instance in the control of elections, commerce). Van Caenegem notes the way in which a legal tradition may be shaped by different actors. He identifies the categories of legislator's law, judge's law, and professor's law. Each has different content and each a different lead group. The character of the law, as well as its content, owes much to these groups shaping its development.

The importance of the legal community in this context is seen most centrally in the texts and decisions which are made, and then preserved by the legal community. They are written by lawyers for lawyers. Thus, in their commentary on the comparative method in studying statutory interpretation, Summers and Taruffo write that, in giving reasons for decisions 'the judge writes as a professional lawyer for those who share the legal culture. Since the legal culture is a culture of experts, we have here a dialogue among experts'.[34]

The actual legal community is the guardian of the tradition and is responsible for the induction of new members. This emphasis on the legal community does not mean that there is necessarily a single orthodoxy. As Terry Eagleton remarks, there might appear in the work of Gadamer and others a suggestion that there is a single mainstream 'tradition' which provides the correct reading of a text.[35] But he argues that the tradition typically is a locus of conflict and debate. In any legal tradition, there is usually something similar. There are competing interpretations and practices, for instance, about the values for which the English legal system stands and how these should be implemented. For example, the debates on civil liberties, prisoners' rights, the rights of immigrants and asylum seekers would be resolved by some by adopting a Bill of Rights or interpreting English law in accordance with it, while others would not see such an approach as in keeping with the common law. But such a debate goes on centrally among the community of lawyers, who, whatever their divergences, have much in common in their approach to what is a good legal solution and how to justify it. The existence of conflict does not deny the existence and importance of tradition, at least in the legal sphere.

It is this community, and not simply the rules and concepts which it uses, which have a history. Legal education in the English common law is different

[34] MacCormick and Summers, *Interpreting Statutes,* p. 495.
[35] T. Eagleton, *Literary Theory: An Introduction* (Oxford 1983), pp. 72 - 3.

from that in the United States and in continental Europe. This gives rise to different central reference groups within the legal community. Legal doctrine elaborated by academic lawyers still does not have the authority as in the other systems. Judicial sources, led by a very small group in the House of Lords, have a much greater priority, and their conception of what is legally correct prevails. Ways of presenting legal methods are also distinct. Thus in the MacCormick and Summers book, the rules of common law countries on admissible evidence for interpreting statutes are fuller than in continental Europe where it is the role of the judge, rather than the advocates, to discover the applicable rules of law. As a result, it is easier to see the approach to interpretation in the former systems than in the latter.

5. Conclusion

While jurisprudence focuses on a general definition of law in terms of a principal function. Comparative law, I have argued, draws attention not only to the cultural, social, religous, and economic setting of a legal system, but also to the specifically legal tradition, which has a significant effect on the way functions are performed. It is, of course, possible and valuable to analyse law in terms of the reasons for action it provides, or in terms of its paradigm role within society: providing social stability and state coercion, or guiding individual conduct in situations of problems of coordination. Various legal theorists have done so. This paper has been suggesting that, if we want to look at the phenomenon of law in its own right, then we are best focusing on it as a tradition situated among a legal community which both mediates its pastness to the present, and offers an authoritative standard for its interpretation and development.

It is this broader perspective on law which Robert Summers has so successfully demonstrated in his recent works of comparative law. Law is seen as the product of a particular society with all its specific social, economic and political concerns, as well as its distinctive legal community. Comparative law of this kind does provide the concrete basis for discussion of a general theory of law, and for a more illuminating theory to be developed. In that way, comparative law has lessons for legal theory.

Legal Principles

By Torstein Eckhoff, Oslo

I. Introductory Remarks

Robert Summers has contributed greatly to the analysis of legal reasoning.[1] He has, among other things, together with P. S. Atiyah developed a conceptual apparatus which I have found very useful.[2]

In this article I intend to give a survey of different kinds of propositions usually called "legal principles" and to say something about their bases and their functions in legal discourse. The distinction made by Atiyah and Summers between substantive and formal reasons, and their elucidation of different types and degrees of formality are highly relevant in this connection. To this I will return in the last section of the article.

II. Some Characteristics of Legal Principles

The term "principle", derived from the Latin "principium", is found in many languages (French "principe", German "Prinzip", Norwegian "prinsipp"). It is among other things used to denote normative propositions phrased in abstract general language (other names for such propositions are "maxim" and "topoi"). In different legal systems there exist a large number of such propositions which aim at giving answers to questions of law. An example taken from the case Riggs v. Palmer[3] is the principle that "no one shall be permitted to take advantage of his own wrong". This sounds convincing. In most cases it will certainly not be advisable to let a person profit from his own wrong. But the wording of the principle should not be taken literally. There are situations in which the law permits a person to take advantage of his wrongs, for instance in the case of adverse possession. It seems to be a common trait of most legal principles that they give an immediate impression of

[1] Robert Summers, *Essays on the Nature of Law and Legal Reasoning* (Schriften zur Rechtstheorie, Heft 151, Berlin 1992) is a collection of his articles previously published in different periodicals.

[2] P. S. Atiyah and Robert S. Summers, *Form and Substance in Anglo-American Law* (Oxford 1987).

[3] 115 N.Y. 506; 22 N.E. 188 (1989).

rightness, but that they are too general and too vague to give reliable answers to all questions covered by the wording.

Certain legal principles are not formulated in terms of normative propositions, but bear the names of states of affairs which are, or can be, based on rules of law. Examples are "the principle of freedom of speech", "the principle of cabinet responsibility" and "the polluter-pays-principle". A similarity between these principles and the above-mentioned is that principles of both kinds are generalizations which may embrace a number of particular rules.

III. How Principles Come into Being

Principles are usually not the products of deliberate decisions made by legislatures or courts, but are developed in the profession over time. It is often impossible to say when a principle first came into being. The reason to which it refers can have been taken into account several times by judges and other decision makers without even being mentioned in any court opinion. And it can have been mentioned several times and in several different ways before it was linked to a particular verbal formulation.

Different factors can have impact on the formation of legal principles. They may have their basis in substantive reasons of fairness or rightness, or in existing rules of law, or in both of these sources. Some principles serve as abstractions which in a broad, general way sum up a body of rules. An example is the principle of freedom of speech. But the sum of a body of rules is usually not called "a principle" unless it can be given a formulation which sounds finer or nobler than the particular rules, and which often has a broader field of application than the particular rules. Rules of law are often criticized, but one seldom hear any criticism of legal principles.

Propositions having the characteristic traits of principles may be adopted as statutory provisions by constitutional assemblies or legislators. The due process clause and the equal protection clause of the United States Constitution may serve as examples. Another example is article 1 of the German Constitution providing that "Die Würde des Menschen ist unantastbar. Sie zu achten und zu schützen ist Verpflichtung aller staatlichen Gewalt." The authoritativeness which a principle gets by being incorporated in a written constitution or statute may make it an argument of greater weight. But apart from this its use in legal reasoning, to which I will return, may be rather similar to the way other principles are used.

In European legal history there have been schools of thought with a marked preference for principles. The cultivation of principles is particularely prominent in the so-called *topic*-reasoning which is based on ideas originating from Aristotle and developed further by Cicero. Aristotle distinguished between "dialectical" and "apodeictic" reasoning. The latter proceeds from premisses that are "primary" and "true" so that the "apodeictic syllogism" would yield full certainty of truth. "Dialectical-reasoning" (or "rhetorics"), on the other hand, yields probabilities only. It is based on arguments which "all, or most men, or the wisest" regard as true. Arguments of this kind he called *"topoi"* (which literally means "places"; the Latin term "loci" is used by some writers). Topoi (or loci) then are "seats of argument". They are propositions, ideas, or grouping of ideas made worthy to serve as anchors for argument because of acceptance by men generally, or by those most wise and illustrious. Some of Aristotle's topoi serve as bases for the judging of questions of fact. Others are normative propositions carrying the distinctive mark of principles.

In the Middle Ages topic-reasoning played an important part in some European countries. A number of *topoi-catalogs* were compiled. They contained numerous principles which had been used, or were considered suitable for use as legal arguments. But gradually the topic-movement lost ground, and it was almost forgotten until it was revived in the 1950-ies; by the German scholar Theodor Viehweg,[4] the Belgian Chaim Perelman,[5] and the Australian Julius Stone.[6]

Viehweg's book aroused considerable interest in Germany, and it led to an extensive debate.[7] A central theme in the writings of the topic-sympathizers was their criticism of legal formalism, according to which rules of law decide cases, and deductive reasoning is assumed to give inevitable results. Opposing this rigid and narrow adherence to formal logic they maintained that there existed leeways for choice in judicial decision-making. But this did not mean that choice was arbitrary. Choices should be based on reason and guided by principles (topoi) of a non-stringent but still trustworthy quality.

The old tradition of compiling topoi-catalogs was resumed by Gerhard Struck. In his book Topische Jurisprudenz (Frankfurt a. M. 1971), Struck drew up an annotated list of 64 different principles which he had selected on the basis of occurrences in court opinions and legal literature. Some of them are old and well-known in Latin formulations in different legal systems, for instance

---

[4] Theodor Viehweg, *Topik und Jurisprudenz* (1953, 3 Aufl. München 1965).

[5] Chaim Perelman and L. Olbrecht-Tyteca, *The New Rhetoric. A Treatise on Argumentation* (French edition 1959, English translation Notre Dame and London 1969), Chaim Perelman, *The Idea of Justice and the Problems of Argument* (London 1963) and *The Realm of Rhetoric* (Notre Dame and London 1982).

[6] Julius Stone, "Reasons and Reasoning in Judicial and Juristic Argument" (in *Legal Essays, a Tribute to Frede Castberg,* Oslo 1963, pp. 170 - 197) and *Legal System and Lawyers Reasoning* (Stanford, Calif. 1964).

[7] See for instance Martin Kriele, *Theorie der Rechtsgewinnung* (Berlin 1967) pp. 114 - 53, Gerhard Otte, "Zwanzig Jahre Topic-Diskussion" (in RECHTSTHEORIE 1970, pp. 183 - 97), Gerhard Struck, *Topische Jurisprudenz* (Frankfurt a. M. 1971) and *Zur Theorie juristischer Argumentation* (Berlin 1977) and Lothar Bornscheuer, *Topik* (Frankfurt a. M. 1976).

"Et audiatur altera pars" (the other party should also be heard) and "In dubio pro reo" (the onus of proof of guilt is on the prosecution).

IV. Different Functions of Principles

Most principles have various uses.

Sometimes they are used as brief descriptions of certain aspects of a legal system. When informing a foreigner of Norwegian law I could for instance tell him or her that "in our constitutional law we have adopted the principle of cabinet responsibility", or that "the polluter-pays-principle is recognized as a goal to be achieved, but it is not yet completely implemented in our environmental legislation". The information given by referring to general principles is of course inaccurate. But still it is useful in many situations to be able to communicate in general terms instead of being led into a jungle of details. It may also give a better understanding of the particular rules to know that they together can be seen as manifestations of a certain principle.

Another function of principles is to serve as arguments in debates on questions of legal policy. A present debate in the Nordic countries can be mentioned as an example. It was started by the Finnish legal scholar Thomas Wilhelmsson who published a book where he argued that social considerations should be taken into account in contract law.[8] One of the problems discussed in the book is that of private households who because of unforeseen circumstances, for instance sickness or unemployment, had become unable to serve their debts. Wilhelmsson argued that these people should be helped, and he introduced a "principle of social force majeure" which in his opinion could justify exceptions from the rule that lack of money is no excuse for nonperformance. Wilhelmsson's book attracted much attention and his points of view were discussed in all Nordic countries. The main reason for this was certainly that his ideas were new and that they were related to questions of great practical importance. But it may also have played a part that he had summed up his arguments in a new principle which was bound up with the well known concept of "force majeure". His principle has not obtained general recognition, but it is well suited to attract attention, and it may also have helped to make Wilhelmsson's arguments more convincing for some of his readers.

Principles can also play a part in the making of new law by legislators or courts. They can serve as grounds for interpreting or changing laws and as patterns or models for rules. In other words, they may serve as a kind of "normative raw material" out of which new law is made.

---

[8] Thomas Wilhelmsson, *Social Sivilrätt* (Helsinki 1989), English edition *Critical Studies in Private Law* (Dordrecht/Boston/London 1992).

Some principles are, as mentioned, abstractions which in a general way cover a body of existing rules. Such principles are often conceived of as something more than a summing up of rules. They may for instance be characterized as the "underlying" principles of which the rules are "manifestations". And they will often serve as models for new rules. A case in point is the reforms of adminstrative proceedings which were carried through in Norway in the early post-war period. Principles governing court procedure, for instance the principles that there should be a fair hearing, an unbiased decision-maker, a right to legal advice and representation etc., served as models for the legislation. A central theme in the legislative debate was the extent to which these ideals could be put through in administrative law without too much prejudice to administrative efficiency. The reasoning was in other words based on analogies to court procedure, but not so much to the particular rules of civil or criminal procedure as to the underlying principles. These were conceived of as sufficiently abstract to cover both the existing rules of court procedure and the somewhat different rules of administrative procedure which were considered. A principle can in other words serve as a bridge between existing law and law that comes into being, thereby facilitating the use of analogies.

The use of principles as a way of justifying analogies is accessible for judges as well as for legislators. In Norway a body of rules, or even a single general rule which is suited for analogical application, is often said to be a "manifestation" of an "underlying" principle. Application of such a rule in a case which is not covered by its wording, may be justified by maintaining that the case falls under the principle of which the rule is a manifestation.[9]

Another way in which a principle may be used in judicial decision-making is to serve as a guiding standard determining that a certain substantive reason is a relevant argument which the law will take into account. This does not necessitate a particular decision because other reasons may argue in the opposite direction. In such cases the reasons must be weighed against each other.

Ronald Dworkin, who first called attention to this function of principles,[10] used as one of his examples the case of *Riggs v. Palmer.*[11] Here the court had to decide whether an heir named in the will of his grandfather could inherit under that will, even though he had murdered his grandfather in order to acquire the inheritance. The court began its reasoning with the admission and effect of wills, if literally construed, would give the property to the murderer. But the court continued to note that:

---

[9] I am indebted to Svein Eng for this and other examples.

[10] Ronald Dworkin, "The Model of Rules", 35 University of Chicago L. R. (1967), reprinted under the title "Is Law a System of Rules?" in Robert S. Sumers (ed.), *Essays in Legal Philosophy* (Berkeley and Los Angeles 1968) and in Ronald Dworkin, *Taking Rights Seriously* (London 1977) Ch. 2. The following references to Dworkin are to the book last mentioned.

[11] 115 N. Y. 506, 22 N. E. 188 (1989).

> "all laws as well as all contracts may be controlled in their operation and effect by general, fundamental maxims of the common law. No one shall be permitted to profit by his own fraud, or to take advantage of his own wrong, or to found any claim upon his own iniquity, or to acquire property by his own crime."

The court decided against the murderer on grounds of the quoted principle. But two judges dissented. They felt bound by the language of the statute. In addition they argued that the murderer, who served his term in prison, would get additional punishment if he were deprived of the inheritance. How much attention the majority paid to these counter arguments is not revealed in the court's opinion. They were in any case out-weighed in the court's opinion.

V. Alleged Differences Between Rules and Principles

Dworkin in the mentioned article (Taking Rights Seriously p. 24) argues that the difference between legal principles and legal rules is a logical distinction.

One of the arguments adduced in defence of this point of view is that "Rules are applicable in an all-or-nothing fashion. If the facts a rule stipulates are given, then either the rule is valid, in which case the answer it supplies must be accepted, or it is not, in which case it contributes nothing to the decision." Principles, by way of contrast, "do not set out legal consequences that follow automatically when the conditions provided are met". A principle rather "states a reason that argues in one direction, but does not necessitate a particular decision" (p. 26).

At first sight the quoted characterization of rules seems to be too categorical. A rule can be vague or ambiguous and there may be other rules to which it relates because they give definitions, make exceptions, or state additional requirements. But Dworkin's meaning is probably that *when* all questions of doubt concerning the validity and content of rules are solved, and *when* the relevant facts are found, then the legal consequences follow directly from the rules. To this I have no objections.

Dworkin has contributed greatly to our insight in the functions of legal principles by pointing to the fact that, even if a principle looks like a rule, it should, when used in legal reasoning, be interpreted as what I use to call a "guiding standard" (or "guideline", Norwegian "retningslinje", German "Richtlinie").[12] But this does not mean that the standard is without legal consequences. The legal consequence of a guiding standard is that the reason to which it refers should be considered a relevant argument. In other words, it

---

[12] In the article "Guiding Standards in Legal Reasoning" (29 Current Legal Problems, London 1976, pp. 205 - 219) and in Eckhoff / Sundby, *Rechtssysteme* (Schriften zur Rechtstheorie, Heft 129, Berlin 1988, chapter 6) I have discussed different kinds of guiding standards and their use in weighing-processes.

answers a question, but a different kind of question from that answered by a rule. I do not find it natural to characterize this difference as a "logical" distinction.

Another difference between principles and rules is, according to Dworkin (p. 26) that: "Principles have a dimension that rules do not – the dimension of weight or importance." I would rather say that it is not the principles, but the reasons to which they refer that have the dimension of weight. Most principles do not say anything about the weight of the reasons. And if anything is said it is, as a rule, only an approximate indication. The normal situation is, in other words, that the weight is not fixed beforehand but is determined by the decision-maker in light of the circumstances of the individual case. Also rules are sources of reasons with different weights. For instance, the statute invoked in *Riggs v. Palmer* gave a weighty formal reason in favour of the murderer, even if it was out-weighed by the substantive reason that he should not profit by his own wrong.

Also a third difference, mentioned by Dworkin (pp. 26 - 27), is in my opinion based on a mistake. He contends that conflicts between two principles are resolved by taking into account the relative weight of each of them, whereas the concept of weight is irrelevant if two rules conflict. In this case one of them cannot be a valid rule. – What makes this comparison misleading is that the term "conflict" does not mean the same thing in the two cases. When Dworkin talks about conflicts between rules he has in mind inconsistencies which must be eliminated. Such conflicts are conceivable also between principles. For instance, it follows from one principle (guideline) of sentencing that the age of the offender should be taken into account, whereas another principle says that age should not be taken into account. Also in this case it is necessary to eliminate the inconsistency, and it is done in a similar way as when rules are inconsistent, for instance by giving one of the principles priority and regarding the other as invalid, or by making them compatible by means of reinterpretation. This kind of conflict is different from the situation in which two reasons pull in different directions. In the latter case the task is not to eliminate an inconsistency, but to weigh the reasons against each other. No invalidation or reinterpretation of the reasons take place as a result of the weighing-process. This applies to reasons derived from rules as well as to reasons derived from principles. In *Riggs v. Palmer* the formal reason that the plain meaning of a statute ordinarily must be followed was out-weighed. This led to a modification of the law of succession, but the plain meaning-principle continued to exist as a weighty argument in new cases.

Thus we are left with only one of the alleged differences, namely that principles, when used in legal reasoning, (often) operate as guiding standards which state reasons that must be weighed against possible counter-reasons. This interpretation of principles is a natural consequence of their wide and vague wording. If they should be taken literally, they would say too much. This applies both to principles which have their basis in substantive reasons of fairness or rightness and to the principles which in a broad general way sum up a body of rules. The latter type is, as mentioned before in section IV, often conceived of as something more than merely a summing up of rules. These principles have in other words a "surplus-meaning" which may be taken as a reason for extending the scope of the rules.

However, it cannot be taken for granted that what is said here holds true of all principles. As pointed out by Robert Alexy, there are normative propositions, usually called "principles", which must be taken literally.[13] He mentions as an example the principle "nulla poena sine lege" (no punishment without a law making the act punishable) which in many legal systems is followed as a rule without any exception. Another possibility is that a normative proposition is saying too much, but that this is taken care of by regarding it as a rule to which certain exceptions must be made.

VI. Differences Between Principles and Rules Which Have Exceptions

What is the difference between a principle of the type invoked in *Riggs v. Palmer* and a rule which has exceptions? Why can't we regard the proposition "no one shall be permitted to take advantage of his own wrong" as a rule to which there are a number of exceptions? Dworkin's answer (p. 25) is that exceptions to a rule "in theory, at least" could all be listed, whereas cases where it is permitted to take advantage of one's own wrong

> "are not, even in theory, subject to enumeration, because we would have to include not only these cases (like adverse possession) in which some institution has provided that profit can be gained through a wrong, but also those numberless imaginary cases in which we know in advance that the principle would not hold".

This explanation is called in question by Alexy (pp. 68 - 71). His point is that also exceptions to rules may be impossible to enumerate, because we don't know in advance whether a court of law in the future will find it appropriate to make a new exception to the rule.

The crucial question is in my opinion not whether it is possible to enumerate exceptions, but if a restructuring of the principle into a framework of rules and exceptions would distort its meaning. This I think would be the case. The principle does not aim at answering the numerous questions which had to be answered if one should try to translate it into a body of rules and exceptions. And reasoning based on a general and vague principle is quite different from reasoning on the basis of rules and exceptions. In the latter case only two alter-

---

[13] Robert Alexy, "Zum Begriff des Rechtsprinzips", (RECHTSTHEORIE, Beiheft 1, Berlin 1979, pp. 59 - 87). The following references to Alexy are to this article.

natives are available: A case will either fall under the rule which leads to a decision in one direction, or it will fall under an exception which leads to a decision in the opposite direction. A principle, on the other hand, invites a more flexible kind of reasoning. One is not tied to the task of deciding whether a fact falls under a certain category or not, but one is free to take into account all circumstances of the individual case which one finds relevant and to weigh the pros and cons.

VII. Use of Principles as a Compromise Between Formal and Substantive Reasoning

A characteristic feature of legal principles is that they are shaped largely by reasons of substance. Some of them state norms that command ethical allegiance in the community. Others refer to states of affairs which are regarded as desirable, for instance the principle of freedom of speech. Their *content formality* – in the sense this expression is used by Atiyah and Summers[14] – is therefore low. One could imagine a legal system where reasoning in terms of principles never occured, but where, on the basis of substantive reasoning, the same results were reached as those based on principles in another system.

But this does not mean that legal principles are of no importance. They may have what Atiyah and Summers (p. 12) call *authoritative formality.* This may help to secure the recognition of the substantive reason incorporated in the principle as a relevant legal argument. It may also have the effect of giving the reason greater weight than it would have had without the authoritative backing.

The authoritativeness of a principle can be high or low – depending upon its source. The criteria determining the degree of authoritativeness may differ from one legal system to another. But usually principles embodied in written law will be regarded as having the highest formal authority. The embodiment of a principle will tend to increase the weight of the substantive reasons which can be derived from the principle. But when the content formality is low substantive counter-arguments will not be excluded from consideration.

Another source of authority are court decisions. If a principle is relied upon by a superior court, this may give it a certain degree of authority. Usually the principle will not be regarded as the *ratio decidendi* of the decision. Riggs v. Palmer, for instance, can be cited as a precedent for the rule that a murderer cannot inherit from his victim. But it is not regarded as precedent for the principle that nobody is permitted to take advantage of his own wrong. The fact

---

[14] P. S. Atiyah and Robert S. Summers, *Form and Substance in Anglo-American Law* (Oxford 1987) p. 13. The following references to Atiyah and Summers are to this book.

that a principle is used by a court as a decisive argument may, however, be sufficient to give the principle status as a recognized legal argument. But this formal recognition will not necessarily increase the weight of the substantive reasons incorporated in the principle.

Natural law ideology may also serve as a source of authority. Some legal principles have been conceived of as having their source in natural law. And even when this is not explicitly stated has there been a veneration for principles, and ways of arguing with principles, which bear traces of natural law thinking.

The fact that legal principles usually are shaped by reasons of substance, but that they still may bear a certain stamp of authoritativeness, places reasoning on the basis of principles in a border-field between substantive and formal reasoning. The use of principles in legal reasoning may indicate that a need is felt to take substantive reasons into account, but that one does not feel free to do that, or not free to give the substantive reasons sufficient weight, unless they are embodied in a recognized principle. In the development of legal systems frequent use of principle may serve as a stage in an evolution from more to less formality.

Dual Concept of the Legal System?

The Formal Character of Law from the Perspective of Institutional and Social Systems Theory

By Werner Krawietz, Münster

It is with great pleasure and enthusiasm that I join in this *Festschrift* to the American legal theorist and scholar, Robert S. Summers, the William G. McRoberts Professor of Research in the Administration of the Law, at Cornell University in Ithaca. It is especially fitting that I do so with a contribution on the topic of formality in law, for I have learned much from Professor Summers on this subject. I recall to mind with special pleasure our discussions on legal rationality and related matters when I was his guest in Cambridge, at Goodhart Lodge during a short weekend in May 1992, and then in September of the same year, in Ithaca, on the occasion of my visit at Cornell.

I.

1. What is my position on Professor Robert Summers' *overall thesis,* namely, that the law is formal in character? As a background remark that bears on my own contribution, it is important to see that I basically agree with Summers' approach to law and with what he has said about the formal character of law and legal systems in his *Goodhart Lecture* on 'The Formal Character of Law' held in Cambridge in 1991.[1]

I regard the distinction that Summers draws between *form* and *substance* of the law, the latter understood here as the "substantive content" of the law, as fruitful and as a promising point of departure for further investigation. I, too, am of the opinion that the definitive character of a legal rule is a formal feature of the configuration of a rule, and that it is in some way independent of the substantive content of the rule.

Moreover, I believe that legal formality can properly co-determine the content of a law. Legal formality gives the socio-normative structures rational support (but this can also be claimed in the other direction: social structures and institutionalized normative expectations give the legally formalized normative

[1] Published in: Cambridge Law Journal 51 (1992), pp. 242 - 262.

expectations rational support – and this, too, is a formal feature of law. Incidentally, this is the underlying thesis of my own contribution.).

My own contribution is with respect to the question: What does it really mean to say that "law is formal in character"? I try to answer this question from the standpoint of an institutional and systems theory of law.[2]

2. It is from this standpoint, too, that I view a number of general points made by Summers, which I will simply list here, for I do not propose to consider them further:

- that all major types of legal phenomena are formal in some significant way or ways;
- that such formality is pervasive and indispensable, and that one can identify rationales special to formality which even serve to justify high levels of legal formality;
- that concerning the formal features of rules and other legal precepts, one can identify particular formal attributes which pertain to the structure, or configuration, or shape, or the manner in which these rules have been established.

What I regard as of central importance, here, is that there be a relation of complementarity between formality and the substantive content of the rules, and that there be second-level rationales behind formality, which give the normative structures a rational underpinning.[3]

3. I also agree with what Summers says about the source-oriented criteria of legal validity, the formality of the binding force of the law, especially the formality of *stare decisis,* and the formalities of the restricted power of judges while interpreting or modifying the law.

What Summers says about the formality of the law and legal system taken as a whole (formality of governmental structure, coherence formality, formality of legal continuity and of the liberal state) strikes me as especially persuasive. Indeed, my only fear here is that I shall be driven to apologizing for having agreed with Summers over such a broad spectrum.

---

[2] For some details, see Werner Krawietz, "Paradigms, Positions and Prospects of Rationality – The Changing Foundation of Law in Institutional and Systems Theory", in: Anders Bratholm et al. (eds.), Samfunn – Rett – Rettferdighet. Festskrift til Torstein Eckhoffs 70-Årsdag, Oslo 1986, pp. 452 - 465, at 456ff.

[3] See H. L. A. Hart, The Concept of Law, Oxford [1]1961, p. v: "Many important distinctions, which are not immediately obvious, between types of social situation or relationships may best be brought to light by an examination of the standard uses of the relevant expressions and of the way in which these depend on a social context, itself often left unstated." For some details, see Werner Krawietz, "What Does it Mean 'To Follow an Institutionalized Legal Rule'? On Rereading Wittgenstein and Max Weber", in: Archiv für Rechts- und Sozialphilosophie, Beiheft 40 (1991), pp. 7 - 14.

In order to identify all these formal features of law and of legal systems, and in order to describe them in a way that is adequate to their social dimension, one needs an appropriate conceptual framework that is applicable to *all* legal systems, namely, in a global perspective. We lack, indeed, the concepts required for an adequate understanding of legal formality, and because of this, we cannot grasp all of its normative claims – and, I might add, for the same reason we cannot grasp its factual, institutional and systemic claims either.

4. I share, then, the result of Summers' "overall thesis that law is formal in character" in the "two-pronged" sense that this view reaches "to all basic types of legal phenomena *within* a legal system" *and* to the legal system viewed *as a whole,* in its structure and its mode of functioning *within* the societal context, that is, in the different social environments to which it refers.

I am of the opinion that Summers' "overall thesis" can be expanded to cover the *system of legal systems,* that is, the international order existing between and among legal systems, of which Summers does not speak. This phenomenon, too, can be characterized under the aspect of an *international legal formality.*

5. However, I should like now to turn to certain critical points, which I might put to Summers as queries. They are, for the most part, conceptual in character and speak to the following basic concepts in his framework of legal theory:

(1) the concept of legal rule

(2) the concept of legal structure

(3) the formality of legal continuity

(4) the priority or ranking of the sources of law (formal scheme of priorities, or "prioritisation")

(5) the formality of a normative jurisprudence that tries to identify and to describe the structure and functions of modern law, that is to say, of modern legal systems.

I see a certain difficulty in the notion that the conceptualization of *all* these *formal features* of law and legal system are dependent on theory, so that in some circumstances we may well be faced with competing theoretical approaches and, indeed, a pluralism of theories. This, to be sure, is something that Summers himself mentions, if only in passing.

II.

My own view of the law, which prompts the queries that I put to Summers, is to be differentiated from Summers' – perhaps not in fundamentals but quite possibly in the sense that in my own analyses of the formality of the law, I consider myself as perhaps more concerned with the societal underpinnings of the problem.

Today there are at least two contrasting approaches to the study of law which are not only current in the United Kingdom and in the United States, as William Twining[4] has pointed out, but – I would want to add – in more or less all countries and in all state law systems around the world. The first of these, which – following Twining – I shall refer to as the *black letter law approach,* is sometimes known as *legal formalism* or *legalism.* In this view, the study of law consists predominantly in the exposition, analyses and criticism of the rules of positive law in force in a given jurisdiction.

The alternative, which I shall refer to here as the *contextual approach* to law, holds that rules are important – indeed, a central feature of law – but for the purposes of understanding, criticizing or even expounding the law, the study of rules is not enough. Legal phenomena need to be set in some broader *political, cultural, economic* or other *social context* in order to understand legal formality in its dependence on, rather than simply in its independence from, the content of law.

Obviously, no analysis of the formal features of law, or of legal systems, can forego a *textual approach* altogether. In this sense, Summers' view and my own presumably lie somewhere between the two contrasting positions adumbrated above. Still, in my own case a contextual orientation is no doubt more evident, for I regard *every structural element of the law* as being, at the same time, *a part of the social structure.* It is precisely at this juncture, as I see it, that a formal feature of all law is given expression. Now I do not presume to know whether Summers is ready to go this far, namely, qualifiying the cognitive interests and the like that are bound up with the law.

In his *Goodhart Lecture,* Summers refers to the fact that some German theorists, for example, the late Karl Engisch, have contributed to the systematic study of legal formality. In this connection I might invite attention to the fact that there is in fact a whole string of German authors, from Max Weber to Schelsky, who have considered questions of the formal features of law and legal systems. Indeed, in precisely these features they have seen the expression of a *rationality par excellence.* In his theory and sociology of law Max Weber distinguishes expressly between the "formal" and the "material" (substantive) rationality of the law, and regards the further development of the law in a global perspective as determined and shaped through an ever growing formalization of the modern law. Helmut Schelsky, following Weber, addresses the formal rationality of the law, too, namely, in his well-known essay "Juridical

---

[4] William Twining, "Identification and Misidentification in Legal Processes: Redefining the Problem", in: Anders Bratholm et al. (eds.), Sammfunn – Rett – Rettferdighet. Festskrift til Torstein Eckhoffs 70-Årsdag, Oslo 1986, pp. 725 - 743, 726.

Rationality" (1980).[5] He sees the formal rationality of the law in the formality (= *rationality*) of, if you will, a "juridico-institutional practice of the law as legislation and adjudication", which is organized through a division of labour and is ordered according to rules. He interprets this notion in the light of an institutional and systems theory of his own.

Weber, who successfully integrated his legal theory and sociology of law, organized his work around the idea of legal formality and rationality, and pointed out that a particular legal institution or mode of thought is rationally independent of the substantive content of law. As far as his concept of legal rationality is concerned, he differentiated among at least four different meanings of the formal/material rationalization of law, the details of which I cannot go into here.[6] His "Sociology of Law" is centered on the *modern* legal system, on the ways and consequences of the "rationalization" of the law, that is, the development of those formal juristic qualities of legal institutions which are characteristic of it today. Legal argumentation seeks to establish the relation of meaning – as distinct from the causal relation – that links different rules, principles, practices and forms of thought. Social reality, including law and legal order, consists not of brute facts or data presented to scientific investigation, but of actions and practices that can be apprehended only be reference to some rationale, some meaning, that is attached to the relevant behaviour.

As far as the formal features of rules and other legal precepts are concerned – *prescriptive formality* in the sense of Robert Summers – the concept *rule,* if I consider it in the light of Max Weber's theory of norms, appears to me to be problematic. In particular, I do not think it appropriate to identify the concepts *norm* and *rule,* as is done here. I would like to distinguish between "norm" and "rule". The *legal rule* can be understood (i) as a norm-sentence, (ii) as a rule in the form in which it is actually complied with – which rule underlies, then, the corresponding behaviour. If one follows this conceptual distinction, the formal features of legal rules and legal systems can be characterized and described more precisely.

In other words, I would follow Weber in resisting the tendency to identify *norm* and *rule*. The "foundations" of Weber's theory of law are not found in "Economy and Society" and therefore, not in his "Sociology of Law" either. Rather, the "foundations" are found in his well-known critique of Stammler's legal theory, published in 1907.[7] There Weber establishes *in nuce* the basis

---

[5] See Helmut Schelsky, "Die juridische Rationalität", in: Schelsky, Die Soziologen und das Recht. Abhandlungen und Vorträge zur Soziologie von Recht, Institution und Planung, Opladen 1980, pp. 34 - 76, at 36ff., 48, 54.

[6] See Wolfgang Schluchter, Die Entwicklung des okzidentalen Rationalismus. Eine Analyse von Max Webers Gesellschaftsgeschichte, Tübingen 1979, at pp. 130ff., 135f., 141ff.

[7] See Max Weber, Critique of Stammler. Translated with an introductory essay by Guy Oakes, London 1977, pp. 57ff., 98ff.

of his sociological theory of norms. In this inquiry, Weber conceives of the linguistic "norm" and the lived "legal rule" – that is, the legal norm transformed in human behaviour – as structural elements of an institutionally regulated *form of social life.*

By comparing the rules of a game to legal rules, using the "paradigm of the game scat", he shows that the rules of a game, like the rules of the law, form a system that is established institutionally and for the long run – a system of orientational points of view, imposing structure on the players' sphere of activity. Thus, one can view compliance with the playing rules as a "presupposition" of a concrete game without thereby taking any position on the actual cause or result of the game.

In fact, all such playing rules, including those of the law, permit one to make better guesses about the moves of the other players than one could make without the rules, for the activities of the other players, too, are subject to these normative premises ("expectations").[8] The decisive function, then, of all socially established and institutionalized legal rules as human "artifacts" is exactly like the function of playing rules; it lies in the fact that everyone "can orient his own action to the clear *expectations* created (by these rules)". *Rule* and the *structure* of rules are, on this view, embedded and only observable *in the form in which they are complied with,* namely, through human behaviour, which for its part is dependent upon institutionalized behaviour patterns into which we have been, so to speak, trained.

A similar view is found in the *theory of norms* developed by *Theodor Geiger.* Geiger, with his realistic and normative formation of the concept of law, has always taken as his point of departure a distinction predominant in German socio-legal thought ever since Ihering and Max Weber, namely, the distinction between "linguistically formulated norms" (verbal norms, norms expressed in words) and "subsistent rules", embedded in and underlying human behaviour. The latter are, for Geiger, "rules in the actual sense". In every case, the linguistically formulated norm sustains a "demand expectation", specified for a certain situation and, by way of support from the respective system-bearing group, directed to the "conduct" of the respective norm addressees. Underlying, therefore, every social "system" (including the legal system as a "particular form of conduct coordination") are certain standardizing expectations of conduct.

It is not the potential for a collective organized reaction in the form of sanction or coercion that is of primary importance in understanding Geiger's

---

[8] On this point and on what follows, see Werner Krawietz, "Taking Legal Systems Seriously: Legal Norms and Principles as Expectations, in: Werner Krawietz, Leopold Pospišil, and Sabine Steinbrich (eds.), Sprache, Symbole und Symbolverwendungen in Ethnologie, Kulturanthropologie, Religion und Recht. Festschrift für Rüdiger Schott zum 65. Geburtstag, Berlin 1993, pp. 361 - 384, at 366ff., 370f., 376f.

theory of norms. Rather, what is of special relevance is the concept of normative expectation ("demand expectation", "expectation of conduct"), a concept of central importance in Geiger's theory of norms, in particular, his theory of legal norms.

Luhmann defends a similar view, which takes as its point of departure the separation of the concepts *norm* and *rule,* without expressly inviting attention to them. Norms are formalized or symbolized linguistically by norm-sentences, which should not be identified with norms as such – that is, with meanings – or with rules. The formation of normative structures is transposed to the formation of social expectations. Social expectations of a normative character are, so to speak, the *deep structure of all social institutions and systems.* For Luhmann, therefore, similarly as for Weber and Geiger, the law is "not primarily a coercive system at all but rather a facilitation of expectations", which with the help of the rules of the law ("selection of behavioural expectations") is established institutionally for the long run and functions as a more or less generalized "structure of social systems". Luhmann's well-known definition of law thereby acquires its plausibility; it is a definition in which neither coercion nor sanction nor the use of force by a state legal staff plays a role: "We can now define law", he says, "as the structure of a social system that is based on congruent generalizations about normative expectations respecting behaviour". At the same time, as one can easily recognize, Luhmann's theory of norms lies entirely within the intellectual tradition of German theory and sociology of law.

With an eye to the sociological concept of law – at any rate in German theory and sociology of law – ranging over Ihering, Max Weber, and Geiger to Schelsky and Luhmann, we might draw the following conclusion from the discussion, as it has proceeded thus far. The chief achievement of all legal institutions lies in the *formation of normative expectations.* Neither coercion nor sanction nor the existence of a legal staff is in the end the decisive structural element of the legal norm. The decisive element is, rather, the expectation selected by means of the legal norm and unfolding with expressive (prescriptive) effect.

According to the view defended here, however, all normative expectations that are given legal expression are specified and determined – namely, by institutions, organizations, and social systems – as fundamentally societal in structure, a theme I have developed elsewhere.[9] A means of access to the structure of the law understood now in terms of normative expectations arises only at the point at which one conceives of the whole of the law as embedded in the diverse forms of social life. A *formalization of these normative expectations,* which are formed in social institutions and organizations or – another

[9] See ibid., pp. 371ff., 377.

characterization – in social systems, can be seen in the fact that the state provides certain normative expectations, namely, those it has selected, with its "stamp of approval", that is to say, it gives expression to them as valid law.

III.

Let me turn briefly to the investigation, to which I have already alluded, that I published a short time ago together with several of my colleagues.[10]

Remaining open thus far is the question of where the achievement of German theory and sociology of law lies, a field in which – ever since Ihering, Max Weber, and Theodor Geiger – development has been unusually rapid, particularly following the Second World War. Insofar as theory construction vis-à-vis the law since the end of the 1960's is concerned, the question might be answered by pointing to the institutional and systems theory of Schelsky, Krawietz and Luhmann, which was developed very quickly and continues to have a lasting effect, right up to the present day.[11]

My own efforts have been directed to an integration of the two theoretical approaches with an eye to their use as a conceptual framework and foundation for a theory of norms.[12]

The theory of institutions and social systems takes as its point of departure the idea that law – considered genetically – is formed in social institutions, in organizations, and in social systems such as marriage, family (including, of course, communal living arrangements outside of marriage), and ownership, and that law is also formed in interactional social systems and organizations, highly bureaucratic in part, such as corporations, workers' unions, churches, and trade unions and associations. Against this background, a purely state concept of law, holding that all law is state law, must appear entirely ill-conceived. The institutional and systems theory replaces diffuse notions of "society" with a network of social relations that connects all individuals, social institutions, and organizations to the decision-making bureaucracies – be they state, inter-state, or supra-state units. This move puts the theory in a position to understand legal norms, like the legal order, as elements and components of the respective social structures of expectation, which are established through the medium of law and its procedures within the context of social life.

---

[10] Werner Krawietz and Michael Welker (eds.), Kritik der Theorie sozialer Systeme. Auseinandersetzungen mit Luhmanns Hauptwerk, Frankfurt a. M. 1992.

[11] Characteristically, Hart, too, sees his theory – quite apart from its concern with analysis – as "an essay in descriptive sociology". Hart, The Concept of Law (Fn. 3), p. iv.

[12] See Werner Krawietz, Recht als Regelsystem, Wiesbaden 1984.

My own version of systems theory, in particular, a systems theory of law, must be distinguished in a number of respects from that of Luhmann's – distinctions that I cannot go into here.[13] I would mention, however, that my own theory is distinguished above all through a distinct sequencing in theory construction, through greater consideration of the law and of various legal systems, as well as through the integration of essential insights of modern norm theories.[14] The central point of our critique is, however, the following: In his opus magnum "Soziale Systeme", a treatise on general social systems theory, which we have criticized in the book that I refer to above, Luhmann excludes organizations alltogether. Moreover, norms and normative systems are only mentioned in passing.[15] Legal systems organized by the state are not considered at all.[16] Our "Critique of Social Systems Theory" sticks to these points.

Here I would simply like to take up one point that is, I believe, important for an assessment of what Robert Summers considers under the label of *formality of governmental structure, formal legality,* and *formality of the liberal state.* I can endorse what he says here but would like to relativize a bit the status of the modern state vis-à-vis the question of legal formality, and moreover suggest, again vis-à-vis the question of legal formality, that a distinction ought to be drawn between (1) state law and (2) societal law.[17]

Under the conditions sketched here, the abandonment of a purely monistic (state) concept of law becomes well nigh inevitable, as an institutional and systems-theoretic conception of the theory of norms is in a position to show. In the theory and sociology of law, monism – that is, a monistic concept of law – is customarily understood as reflecting the view that law *ex definitio* is solely the law of the state and, accordingly, only law issued by the state or somehow derived therefrom is worthy of the name.

As an explanation drawn from institutional and systems theory is able to show, in the legal system of the modern society, a state legal system, there is neither an apex point nor a centre from which intra-systemic control could be brought about. Central control in earlier forms of state sovereignty may have

---

[13] Ibid.

[14] See Werner Krawietz, "Staatliches oder gesellschaftliches Recht? Systemabhängigkeiten normativer Strukturbildung im Funktionssystem Recht", in: Werner Krawietz and Michael Welker (eds.), Kritik der Theorie sozialer Systeme (Fn. 10), pp. 247 - 301, at 251ff., 261ff., 276ff.

[15] Ibid., pp. 251ff., 259ff.

[16] Ibid., pp. 262ff. See also Petra Werner, "Soziale Systeme als Interaktion und Organisation. Zum begrifflichen Verhältnis von Institution, Norm und Handlung", in: Werner Krawietz and Michael Welker (eds.), Kritik der Theorie sozialer Systeme (Fn. 10), pp. 200 - 214, at 200ff., 206f., and Andreas Schemann, "Strukturelle Kopplung. Zur Festlegung und normativen Bindung offener Möglichkeiten sozialen Handelns", in: ibid., pp. 215 - 229, at 222.

[17] See Werner Krawietz, "Staatliches oder gesellschaftliches Recht?" (Fn. 14), p. 262.

been administered from a single position – for example, from the monarch at the apex of a political community, from a kaiser, from a czar, or a U.S. president – although even this possibility will be met with skepticism in some circles. In the modern state legal system, organized as it is by means of a division of labour, and with diverse decision-making processes (legislation, administration, adjudication), the possibility of central control from a single position is precluded by the fact that the individual partial and subordinate formations of the system can be observed in relation to each other only to a very limited extent.

The concept of law cannot, then, be concentrated alone on the state and its law qua medium of political action. One must also keep in mind the possibility that there is, within the state legal system, also non-state law, that is, genuinely societal law, existing alongside state law. This is to say that in the future the theory and sociology of law will have to devote more attention to, and show more regard for, the forces of communal formation and social self-regulation, and this entirely apart from the state legal systems and their mechanisms of politico-legal decision-making.

This sheds new light both on the *ranking of the sources,* which Robert Summers correctly sees as emerging from within state law, and on the "formal prioritisation" that is tied to that ranking; both surely belong to the formal attributes of the modern liberal state.

From the standpoint of societal law, as that concept is explicated by institutional and systems-theoretic research, it must be noted that social systems, understood in the sense of regional societies that are nonetheless directed by legal systems, are essentially constructed not hierarchically but rather "heterarchically". This form of self-hierarchisation, as I have called it elsewhere, does not prevent us from distinguishing between formal and informal law – as I do, drawing on Weber. Here my own view converges with that of my friend Robert Summers on the formality of the law.

Four Quadrants of Jurisprudence

By Neil MacCormick, Edinburgh

This essay offers a view about the character of legal understanding by plotting four of its points of reference and deliberating on the tensions between them. Its thesis is that there are four key points of reference that can usefully be mapped out as four distinct quadrants of juristic thought. Most of the great debates about law can be re-appraised against this map. The four quadrants in question are tentatively dubbed 'raw law', 'doctrinal law', '"Society"' and 'Fundamental Values and Principles'. For graphic presentation, I portray them as four quadrants thus:

Law in Social Science	Fundamental Values and Principles
Raw Law	Doctrinal Law

The standpoint of the essay is at some meta-theoretical level, poised above the intersection.

I offer this essay in honour of a much admired colleague and friend, whose own contributions have contained much in the way of reflection on the character of jurisprudence and legal doctrine as intellectual disciplines, as well as some distinguished first-order contributions to both. It was in the 'Statutory Interpretation Group', later jocularly re-entitled 'The Bielefelder Kreis', led by Bob Summers that a group of us began to think out the idea of 'rational reconstruction' that in our view captures the essential method of good doctrinal work. In the second chapter of *Interpreting Statutes: a Comparative Study* (1991) edited by Bob and myself, there is an attempt to work out what it involves, and I try to carry the idea a little further forward here. The present text is somewhat experimental and preliminary, as is appropriate to its dedicatee's age of new beginnings, so I have dispensed with footnotes. There will be time enough for those in later more fully elaborated versions of the present thoughts. I have to acknowledge, though, that its first reading was to a colloquium in the University of Texas School of Law in July 1993, convened by Professor Michael Churgin, and that the text took its present form through engagement with some recent work by Professors Jack Balkin and Tom Seung of the University of Texas at Austin; to them and to other colleagues who gave helpful criticisms at that colloquium, I am most grateful. Even that gratitude does not equal my thanks to Bob Summers for companionship, colleagueship, friendship and encouragement over the twenty years of our acquaintance.

1. Raw Law

Perhaps the most uncomplicated way to think of law is to think of it as activity. Indeed, it seems to be a great deal of activities. It is what judges do in their courts, what advocates argue before the courts, what solicitors toil over in their offices, what corporate legal advisers advise on, what bureaucrats implement, what legislative draftsmen draft, what legislators legislate. It is perhaps even what ordinary citizens attend to as they fill in tax forms, subject their cars to annual testing, take out insurance on their lives or houses, pay the mortgage interest or the rent. Law in everyday life is activity on the grand scale – a bewildering plurality of activities. It is, of course, anyone's guess how all these disparate activities hang together, if at all. Notoriously the law-ways and practices of one court house are never quite like those of any other. What goes on in your office is never quite what goes on in your neighbour's. As legal practice, and legislation and case-law, grow everywhere more specialised, the problem of finding a vantage point to see the whole wood amid the forest of individual trees grows more, not less, problematic.

So far as I can see, law as activity always presents itself to new practitioners as mysterious, bewildering, intimidating – it comes as a shock to find what it's really like after the relatively ordered and systematised accounts of it that the law school gave them. As they grow more experienced, they grow more specialised, and perhaps their own specialism, and the tricks of their trade, and their routines, become more comfortable and familiar; but that cuts one off from even quite close colleagues in different lines of work with their own tricks, routines, craft. Laypeople, even laypeople who are legislators, usually seem to have even more fragmentary, even more episodic, even more bewildering, images of law. Most of the time, anyway, for most laypeople, and for most off-duty lawyers the law is an abstraction apart from ordinary concerns. *Law in Everyday Life,* by Rudolf von Ihering, is a witty if nightmarish reminder of this. Every event of every day can be re-cast as legally significant, starting with the contract of sale you thoughtlessly enter into as you exchange a few coins for your morning paper. Legal over-awareness would make a Midas of us all, turning to law all that our minds touch. But sane people, I suppose, don't live like that. Law as activity is spiky, episodic, transitory. Now you see it, now you don't. Its fragments and episodes perhaps belong within some coherent framework. But this is, at the level of everyday life, pious hope, not proven fact. The coherence of law is not, I think, an immediate part of lived experience.

Another way to put all this is perhaps as follows: Law as a phenomenon presenting itself to human beings in ordinary life seems at best fragmentary and chaotic. Indeed, it is a question whether law does present itself to us as 'a' phenomenon, or as a 'phenomenon' at all. What one thing or class of things phenomenally present to our ordinary consciousness is 'law'? Certainly, 'law', 'legal', 'lawful', 'unlawful' and other cognate terms crop up in daily talk, and so does talk about crimes, or murders, or thefts, contracts, damages for negligence, reports of famous trials (usually criminal) and the like. There are 'lawyers' known to us, going about what we and they take to be the business of the law; there are lawmakers, legislators in Parliaments or Congresses, judges and policemen and other 'arms of the law'. The world of everyday phenomena is a world rich in allusion to law, even if that very 'law' itself, as distinct from courthouses, law offices, jails, parliaments is somehow intangible, obscure, off-stage.

'Raw law' might be as good a term as any for alluding to this law-as-activity, law-as-lived, law-as-phenomenon apart from and prior to any particular explanatory scheme or theoretical understanding. Raw law is the unexamined substratum of brute fact (if any) that gives theorised, scholarly law-constructs whatever anchoring they have in the real world. There does seem to be some such substratum, of which we all (everyone in our kind of society) are to some extent aware, albeit taking very different degrees of interest in it. This is not to say that we have any pre-theoretical way of being sure that we all have the same or even similar awareness of it.

But nobody, or nobody likely to read this essay, actually does approach the matter purely pre-theoretically. And even when we try the thought-experiment of abstracting from theory as far as we can, it seems absurd to deny that raw law at least includes decisions which are or purport to be authoritative and which are taken by or in the name of state authorities or other institutional authorities. These can be decisions directed at individuals or decisions of a more general purport about general rules to be observed by people at large. These decisions, especially the ones directed to individuals do seem to have effects on individuals' lives and activities, sometimes drastic and far-reaching ones.

2. Doctrinal Law: Rational Reconstruction

Raw law occupies one of the four quadrants of my map of legal understanding – the bottom left. Opposite, in the bottom right, I place doctrinal law, law-as-science, legal dogmatics. This has a great deal to do with construction of an organised and organising view of decisions imputable to raw law. At least from the time of Gaius, and probably earlier, there have been legal scholars at work, capturing raw law and systematising it, but at the same time transforming it. Doctrinal law is no episodic and fragmentary mass of intermittent and scattered activity. On the contrary, it is systematised – parcelled off into law public and private; constitutional, administrative and criminal – tax law, too, now; persons, things, and actions; alternatively: family law; property; trusts; succession; contract; torts/delict; commercial law; company law; securities law; evidence and procedure, civil and criminal; and so forth. These can be displayed as structured bodies of norms, bearing in principle at least some systematic interaction with each other. We think of our law as coming in discrete but interrelated branches and subdivisions. These demarcations are in broadly similar terms observed across the whole range of contemporary legal systems, and our specialisations remain bearable and intelligible because legal scholarship is possessed of one (or a few) schemata indicating how all these disparate expertises fit together as parallel inquiries into different parts of the system. Even the most critical of contemporary Critical Legal Scholars seem in the main content to work critically and deconstructively within the schemata rather than to challenge them.

Certainly we see now an increasing 'globalisation of law'. This creates a growing sense of trans-systemic scholarly unity or at least collaboration – contracts lawyers, intellectual property scholars, family lawyers, constitutional lawyers get together to study and analyse their slice of the law across national systems. But this seems in fact to enhance rather than to weaken the paradigmatic force of the older systematisations of law. And indeed it remains part of the more or less unanalysed givens of contemporary legal thought that law comes in systems, and that there is normally one system per state, with due allowance for federations and anomalous cases like that of the English and Scottish legal systems, which contrive to share a single non-federal state. But in general the trends of the times are against the old self-sufficiency of states and state-law, and a new pluralism seems to be emerging.

'General Jurisprudence', *'Allgemeine Rechtslehre', 'Theorie Générale du Droit'* as one of the traditional branches of legal learning has served as a metascience to legal sciences of the first order. As Hans Kelsen and some of his followers have most clearly seen, the pretension of legal sholarship to scientific status, to being a real and autonomous branch of scholarship, has required the backing of a specific epistemology, giving an account of the presuppositions required to validate any claims doctrinal legal scholarship may make to count as a true department of knowledge and of learning, rather than to being simply a trade school. The conditions for viewing law as system, and the conceptual frameworks within which the elements of system are statable as interacting parts of a dynamic whole have to be worked out. Needless to say, legal theory of this sort gives rise to a great deal of highly contestable issues – but no more so than does first-order legal doctrine, which is also characterised by perennial debate and mutual criticism, as the law journals show.

How are we to characterise the nature of the work carried out in doctrinal legal scholarship? One answer current in contemporary jurisprudence presents legal doctrine as engaged essentially in the 'rational reconstruction of law'. This has been put forward in some work by Robert Summers, Zenon Bankowski, Jerzy Wróblewski and myself, following on hints dropped by Martin Golding in his reading of Kelsen; and Jack Balkin has advanced a similar idea in a different framework. The idea of 'reconstruction' here depends on what I said already about 'raw law'. Raw law is transformed by jurists into law-as-system. The idea of law as structured and analysable body of norms or rules and principles and the like is not something just given in our experience of phenomena. The system-quality of law depends essentially upon the existence of a scholarly practice of rationally systematising legal experience. Of course, that scholarly practice has had a feed-back effect into law-as-practice, which has in turn transformed the materials to be grasped, analysed, explained and systematised in juristic doctrine.

'Rational reconstruction' here, as also in the natural sciences, confronts data which in our consciousness are fragmentary, episodic, and incomplete; by postulating structural and transformational principles, we enable ourselves to re-interpret the phenomena as parts of a coherent and well-ordered whole. The rationality at stake is a matter of logical consistency and more-than-logical coherence. Factual statements and explanations of a relatively concrete and particularistic kind are represented as instantiations or 'determinationes' of broader explanatory principles. In natural science these are ultimately underpinned with extremely general descriptive principles of a cosmological character. In legal science the organising principles are normative in character. The ordering and re-ordering of phenomena in these terms, and the apprehending of them in terms of the postulated conceptual framework amounts to 'reconstructing' them, never just 'seeing them as they are' apart from any theory. All that we see apart from theory is a chaotic flux of activity and process.

But surely it makes a difference that in legal science we deal with law as the product of human decision and human will? Surely the difference between cosmological-descriptive scientific principles and constitutional-normative legal ones is too great to permit any facile analogising of doctrinal law with natural science? Surely the very idea of legal science begs the main question? Isn't it a breathtaking ideological *démarche* to mask the inevitably ideological activities of doctrinal law as some kind of (presumably neutral, value-free) 'science'? Here, we stand poised on the edge of deep waters to which we must later return. For the moment, a shallow answer may at least disarm objection to the point of suspended disbelief. Of course we must note the implicit place of values in the rational reconstruction that legal doctrine performs. There is no possibility at all of a value-free legal science, or of value-free doctrinal law. For most certainly the idea of a coherent legal order requires the construction of law as first a body of mutually consistent rules, just in the sense of logically noncontradictory rules, but then also secondly as a practically coherent set of rules.

For a set of rules to be presented as practically coherent, they must fulfil the test of normative coherence. That is, relatively concrete rules (or rule-formulations) have to be made intelligible as standards in view of some value or values their observance is supposed to realise, whether as intrinsic or as instrumental means to their realisation. The framing of such values in terms of normative generalisations is the formulation of legal principles. Principles can in turn be articulated more or less generally or abstractly and thus in at least a rough hierarchical order. Local and general value-priorities have to be postulated, to make possible a relative weighing of principles in situations where their application leads to conflicts of decision. In some way, the whole congeries of values and principles has to be thought of as delineating a defensible form of life for humans in political communities and societies, or else the reference of the postulated rules to those principles and values will fail the 'coherence' test.

This remains a shallow view so long as we leave open the question of the type of commitment that doctrinal legal scholars must make to the principles and values through and around which they make their accounts of law coherent ones. At the very least, and very obviously, these values have to be imputed to 'the law' as its values. This requires a not fantastic belief that there exist law-upholding and law-observant social and political agents (judges, legislators, for example) for whom the postulated values are seriously held commitments, animating individual activity at the level of raw law, and capable of transforming raw-law activity into reflective engagement with law as system. But need the doctrinal scholar have just that commitment herself or himself? How far is scholarly detachment possible here? Would it be a virtue if possible? How far would a relativistic view of legal values be seriously tenable as accounting for all that needs be taken here into account? These are the deep questions, but their answer belongs to review of the fourth quadrant.

Meantime, it is important to observe the potential interaction between doctrinal representations of law and raw law at the level of decisions exercising power over individuals or groups. Legal doctrine cannot be a description of how decision-makers actually behave. It is a statement of an ideal order of decision-making, stating norms that decisions could fulfil or not. The order is an order of system-dependent oughts. It is the order which the legal system as reconstructed by doctrine and theory stipulates as obligatory. Actual decisions that depart from the ideal order do not invalidate it, for it is in this sense ideal-normative, not descriptive. But as ideal, it is ideal relativised to system and by-and-large actual order, not ideal by direct reference to fundamental principles and values, that is, to our fourth quadrant.

3. Law in Social Science

For the moment, let us switch attention to the top left quadrant, the quadrant of 'Law in Social Science'. Here, we postulate some conception of society as an intelligible context of human activity, and we confront well-established academic disciplines dedicated to exhibiting its intelligibility. Economics constructs society around a market-place of rationally choosing individuals, and develops theorems and explanatory systems to model the real performance of real economies in real societies. Or, in Marxian mode, it depicts social order as riven with tension through the different orientation of different classes to the means of production, distribution and exchange. Sociology constructs ideal types of different forms of social order, *Gemeinschaft or Gesellschaft,* or different ideal types of authority, traditional, charismatic or legal rational, and explains legal order in terms of different ideal types of rationality or irrationality in social ordering; or it produces some structural-functionalist account of the characteristics of 'systems' and models social systems (including legal system) accordingly. History portrays the collective past as an intelligible narrative, and prepares for a future that carries on the human story in an intelligible but nondeterministic way. Political science constructs a view of politics out of theories about the power of persons or groups in social relationships, and conditions for the acknowledgement of power as legitimate authority (while political philosophy is concerned with the actual legitimacy of power, and the rights of persons and groups in relation to power and its exercise, hence finding its place in our fourth quadrant). Political science commonly shares its theoretical framework with one of the other social sciences, and has often a particular affinity with legal doctrine, at any rate in the sphere of public law.

If one thing is obvious, it is that 'raw law' is a part of the society that these social sciences postulate (in so far as 'society' is for them also a pre-theoretical phenomenon, we ought to speak of 'raw society' in this context). Society is what the social sciences seek to explain or describe or (as I would again say) rationally reconstruct in accordance with their own principles and schemata of explanation. It has often been claimed that they (or some one or other of them) necessarily give a better account of raw law than does legal doctrine, precisely because they seek to explain it in some kind of reductionist and usually also predictive way. Law is explained in terms of non-law, say in terms of market economics or Marxist economics, and the law's self-description through legal doctrine is sidelined as in some way merely epiphenomenal, a part of the explanandum, not of the explanans. To really understand what is going on, you must strip away the legal self-constructions and understand raw law at the level of economic rationality, or class struggle, or societal form, or autopoietic system, or as a moment in the grand march of events seen more broadly, or whatever.

Lawyers, especially academic lawyers, are by no means immune from doubt about the validity of legal dogmatics, certainly in its traditional form. Realism in America remains the classic example of constructive self-doubt in the legal academy. At the minimum, there can only be value in maintaining some scepticism about the 'law in books' as a guide to the 'law in action'. Raw law, law as activity and decision, is clearly dynamic and ever-changing. Doctrinal law is subject to the danger of stasis, as debate forms and rages around topics settled more by academic fashion than the contemporary reality of a dynamic social process. For practitioners who confront their law raw in tooth and claw, scepticism about neatly rational reconstructions in the legal texts and law journals is no doubt an essential strategy for professional survival. Doctrine may be, should be, of help in making sense of lumps of statute and precedent, and intractable problems of fact; but the real solution of the real case or the real drafting or advisory problem is never going to be something that can be read directly off the pages of the law review; and the internal dialectics of legal academia may draw doctrinal attention to points of scholarly dispute at the cost of attention to ongoing movements in the raw law. So Karl Llewellyn's exhortation to us to be critically aware of rule formulations as though they were predictions rather than normative formulae made a valuable point. Attempts to get out there and find out what is really going on can only be salutary – in the end it should lead to reconstructions of the law that are far more rational, as Llewellyn triumphantly showed in relation to commercial law and the development of the Uniform Commercial Code.

If there were not that feed-back into the doctrinal law from moments of fresh appraisal of the raw law, there would have to be some radically different recourse to understanding it. And here come in various versions of 'law and society' studies, the point of which is precisely to reconstruct the law rationally through the schema of one or another social science, on the ground that this is a better, a truer, a more objective understanding; not lawyers' ideology masquerading as legal science. This has always struck me as unconvincing, for the following reason. 'Law' is a conceptual category more than it is a raw reality. Even 'raw law' is already a theoretical idea; it identifies that un-theorised substratum which is the very object of a historically cohesive and powerful body of learning. For economics or sociology to try to access law-as-distinct-from-legal-doctrine-and-legal-theory would be illusory. In fact, as Kelsen said about Eugen Ehrlich's sociology of law, such an attempt could not yield anything that would be a sociology 'of law', it would just be sociology simpliciter. Anything recognisable as 'law' in the historic sense would slip through a net constructed so as to exclude normativistic legal theory or doctrinal law. Such an exclusion might certainly be both useful and interesting in its own way. It could tell us what it is like to think of society and social action and social interaction without making recourse to any of the familiar constructs of the law and legal institutions. Having studied this, one might return with a fresh eye to legal doctrine. At the very least, a reconsideration of doctrinal legal problems in terms of economic theory or sociology is likely to be illuminating in the development or re-appraisal of legal doctrine. For example, it may help in making better sense of the order of values and principles implicit in the task of making doctrinal law practically coherent. But that is a very different matter from supposing that the one could, without loss, be supplanted wholly by the other.

Although a social science might attempt to capture raw law directly as a feature of society, and account for it exclusively in terms of the preferred discipline, it would inevitably fall short in the attempt. Far more satisfactory would be an approach that acknowledged the practice of doctrinal law as itself a part of the totality of social action and interaction, one intimately involved with and interactive with raw law. A sociology of law or an economics of law or a history or anthropology of law would then aim to account for the systematisers and their systematisations as well as that which they systematise. A vivid and interesting example of this is provided in current sociology of law in the theory of law as autopoietic system proposed by Niklas Luhmann and Gunther Teubner. They deal with doctrinal law as a key part of what the sociology of law has to grasp and explain. Most illuminatingly, they treat legal dogmatics and legal theory as essential to the idea of law as a self-referential and self-producing system. For doctrinal law is precisely the system's self-observation, its consciousness of itself, without which it would lack the character of 'system'. Such a sociology does not offer to supplant doctrine, but to show its place in the whole ordering of law and of society.

4. Fundamental Values and Principles: Natural Law and Integrity

The fourth quadrant, the top right-hand corner, is reserved for fundamental values and principles. Here belong our apprehensions of justice and of the foundations of human well-being and well-doing. Whatever ethical principles are to be deemed fundamental, whether procedural principles of rational discourse or substantive principles of right conduct, belong here. So do theories of human rights as moral absolutes. Here, we are concerned with ideals as pure ideals; the 'ought' by which we finally criticise whatever is; the possible world which is our template for critique of the actual, of the world as we find it; the possible world that we try to make more actual in our own conduct.

Perennially controversial is the ontological status of such ideals, and hence the way in which this quadrant is related to the others is open to no less controversy. It will not be doubted that each human being has at any given time some ultimate value or values informing what s/he does and thinks. How far an individual's values are or have to be stable over time; how far they are learned and inculcated, how far chosen; how far a reflection of culture and milieu, how far a matter of individual choice and attitude, or of intuition and awareness; all these are perennial questions. Deep-held values are certainly an important constituent part of ideologies, but that does not tell us whether or not they are or can be also apprehensions of an underlying truth about the universe and our place as humans in it.

However that may be, it is not open to doubt that human activity is, as such, value-oriented. Whatever raw law is also, it is fundamentally a matter of activity. So there is certainly a link between the bottom left and the top right quadrant. Law-activity, like all activity, aims to realise value. But this need not be more than purely subjective value, and nothing in the bottom left quadrant guarantees any co-ordination or consensus of the multiplicity of different subjectivities that interact in the activities of raw law. Chaos and conflict quite as much as system and consensus will surely be marks of purely phenomenal raw law. How then can order be found or imposed?

One possibility would be by direct reference to the top right quadrant, to values considered as objective features of the universe. The true or sound element of phenomenal raw law would be that which matched up intelligibly with true or sound values. By expounding the coherent and true structure of the human good, one would articulate the very principles for constructing order out of the incipient chaos of raw law. A historic instance which seems to me to approximate to just such a direct systematisation against an account of fundamental values is that provided by Plato's *Republic,* and some early Christian writings, deriving human value from the will and goodness of a God whose integrity guarantees the coherence of the created world, seem to have a similar quality. St Augustine's *Civitas Dei* is perhaps a plausible example.

A second possibility would take a more tentative view either of the ontological underpinnings of the fourth quadrant, or of the human possibility of knowing for certain how exactly to order them. An agnosticism about the absolute reliability of any particular formulation of values and principles would seem to justify a more relativistic view of any such formulation applied to the task of systematising law. Whatever the ultimate truth about values in the realms of being and of knowledge, we could aim at a systematisation of law that made sense of it in terms of some chosen set or scheme of values imputed to the raw law and its operative principles, and used to reconstruct it as a defensible overall scheme of practical co-operation and social co-ordination.

The person engaged in the systematisation is, of course, engaged in a human activity, and thus necessarily orientated to some value or values. But this activity is an element of 'science' understood in its broad sense, as any production of systematic knowledge. So the value most fundamentally engaged in this activity is truth and understanding of a speculative kind rather than of a practical kind. The scientist wants to know what practical values make it possible to see the phenomena (the raw law) as some kind of coherent and rationally purposive totality. But that does not commit the scientist as practical human being to those same values, even though s/he must be fully capable of grasping and entering into them as though s/he were fully engaged. Indeed, some degree of detachment as well as of (at least heartily simulated) engagement is required by the attachment to the scientific project of explanation and understanding.

The true history of doctrinal law seems to me to have followed this trajectory. Especially in the beginnings of modernity, after the shock of reformation in Europa and the visible cancellation of a single institutional church's confident certification of (at least the possibility of) one grand scheme of indisputable values, and after similar events led to the development of distinct sovereign states each asserting an independent law of its own, there came the great age of Institutes of National Law, starting perhaps with Grotius' *Inleidinge* (Introduction to the Dutch Jurisprudence) and running through to the remarkably late systematisation of English law in Blackstone's *Commentaries* of 1765 (by contrast, Stair's *Institutions of the Law of Scotland* was already in print in its first edition in 1681). Later, in all jurisdictions came the great treatises on discrete branches of law, and then, after codification wherever that occurred, the commentaries on the Codes and their subdivisions.

Codification, and (even where no full codification was attempted or achieved) the growth in significance of statute law over custom and case-law, produced a further tendency to relativisation of values in legal exposition. For the legislator's will shapes the statute, and so the values that the legislator aimed to realise by enacting the statute are available as the rationalising framework for apprehending it systemically; the wider the sweep of the statute (none wider than that of a Code), the more comprehensively so. At the same time political or legal theories, or ideologies, that stress the sovereignty of the state and refer the existence of law to the will of the sovereign reinforce the asserted appropriateness of the willed values behind law as the proper source of its organising principles. The advent of democracy, and the aptness of deference to the now-sovereign people, has a reinforcing effect on this line of thought. The reception of legal positivism as command theory of law or *Gesetzespositivismus* is not so much either a cause or a consequence of all this as simply one element in it.

What is in any event clear is how it comes about that the bottom right quadrant, the quadrant of legal doctrine and legal theory, can and should be conceptualised as independent of the bottom left and the top right, though referring to both of them. A scholar can be in relation to her/his scholarly work politically disinterested and metaphysically agnostic while being fully committed to understanding, and can in that light construct or reconstruct a body of intelligible and systematised law out of the fragments and decisions and enactments of the raw law. An awareness of the relativity of value to law; a refusal to certify the present law's values as eternal truths; is a strength, not a weakness in such scholarly work, and remains so even if it is the case that fundamental values do exist as part of the furniture of the universe, a true grasp of which would illuminate the perfect account of an ideal human legal system. For it would be a travesty to claim that any legal order anywhere gets very close to being that, and it is comical to look back to the confidence of claims to absolutism made in earlier times, for example in the days when Herbert Spencer's *Social Statics* was taken to be a fundamental doctrine of the US Constitution because also a manifest truth of human nature; or when the common employment doctrine was confidently certified to be not only a sound proposition of English law, but a necessary doctrine of universal jurisprudence.

Nevertheless, it is important to acknowledge the continuing vitality of the claim that both of the lower quadrants make sense only on the assumption of ultimate objectivity in the top right. The powerful arguments of John Finnis in *Natural Law and Natural Rights,* or of Michael Moore or Ernest Weinrib in illuminating essays about the law, show the weight we must acknowledge in the thesis that human life is deeply unintelligible if not by reference to objects of endeavour which do not only belong to subjective impulse and desire, but which simply are goods for humans such that inherent or innate drives toward them are evidence for rather than constitutive of their goodness. In this perspective, the possibility of sound doctrinal scholarship in law depends not only on the good of knowledge (pursued through scholarship) but also on reference to the structural role of the other practical values that really do belong to human good, and also to derivative principles like those of justice, both commutative and distributive. Ronald Dworkin's theory of law as an interpretive concept, constructed around the idea of the integrity of a political community, does not seem to say anything very different in terms of the relations of my quadrants, except if his insistence on integrity amounts to relativisation of organising values to the actual values of the given legal system, interpreted with an eye to whatever are the objectively soundest values and principles, so as to make of them the best they can be, while still being genuinely anchored in the constructed system and behind that the 'raw law'.

The Finnisian view, if accepted, has far-reaching implications for the top left quadrant as well as the others. For it is his express claim that the basic values have the same foundational force in relation to the other social sciences as for legal science. Sociology, psychology, economics, anthropology, political science, in so far as they study human action and interaction under one or another specialised set of categories, must nevertheless orient the categories they construct towards what is of true value, or fail to shed light on the human predicament. This is a bold claim, many would say an impossibly audacious and errantly foundationalist claim, to make about the social sciences. But it must be conceded that Finnis's approach gives one perspective on the unity of the human and social sciences, and lets us see that while they have different orientations to topics of human interest, they do hang together. For human interests are portrayed as interests in the good as it really is, not in merely arbitrary and fleeting desires. The coherence of the other social and human sciences with legal science, and their potential for mutually valuable interchange as scholarly enterprises will obviously also be guaranteed by the common value-orientation that constitutes the unity of the human sciences.

This is all far from unchallenged or unchallengeable. A rival view would reverse the supposed hierarchical ordering between natural law theory and the social sciences. According to the rival view, it is the social sciences, or some, or one, of them that constitute objective knowledge, while natural law can express only a subjective orientation to values in a particular socio-historical conjuncture. Exposed to critique are then the very doctrines that natural law theories advance, and the philosophico-theological tenets on which they ground those doctrines. These tenets are not ultimate truths that found all modes of human knowledge, but are rather themselves to be re-explained as deliverances of ideology. Natural law ideas purport to legitimise a grand sweep of practices and ideas (and to delegitimise a grand aweep of rivals). Either they are sound and genuinely achieve that which they purport, or they are unsound, and must then necessarily be re-interpreted as mere ideology. For they have the characteristic ideological ambition to give a comprehensive foundation for an entire world view and set of practices, including a purported unification of the whole realm of social science. The claim to self-evidence of the basic propositions of natural law theory is a mark of their ideological status, not a certification of their true character.

One main strand in Critical Legal Studies is just such an attack on objectivism in legal doctrine and legal theory. Roberto Unger's presentation of a body of 'deviant doctrine', backed with argument aiming to show that this is at least as plausible as traditional legal doctrine challenges the proponents of the latter to bring forth the value-credentials of their view. Legal materials, Unger claims, are open to more than one rational reconstruction, and a radical reconsideration of fundamental values will lead to a radical reconstruction of law. Jack Balkin, if I read him rightly, would acknowledge that such a 'Critical' approach is no less ideological a project than that of regular or mainstream doctrine. For him the point is not whether legal studies can proceed without ideological underpinnings. On the contrary, the question for him is: 'What ideology?' together with the question whether scholars will be open and articulate about their ideological stances, or refuse to acknowledge them. Such a position, as noted, inverts the ranking of the top left and top right quadrants as against that favoured by natural lawyers or Dworkinians. For no values are conceived to stand above society in an ideal realm; instead, values are to be understood as immanent in cultures and individual life experiences, transformed by and transforming the individual in that very experience. So the confident departure from highest-order objective values and principles either into social science or into legal doctrine is unavailable. There must simply be a dialectic between legal doctrine, social science and philosophy, in which the different subjectivity of each participant in the effort of understanding is fully acknowledged, and in which values emerge as moments in that dialectic. Certainly, Balkin makes a persuasive case for the view that there has to be a dialectic between deconstruction and reconstruction if legal doctrine is to maintain a cutting edge of critical rationality.

A different possibility is represented by social scientific thought in its more imperialistic phases, when it, or some particular favoured strand in it, purports to have captured the whole high ground of worthwhile human understanding. This generates the claim that all else is explicable from this one privileged standpoint, including scientific theories and practical principles and values, not least those deployed in the construction of legal doctrine. There has always been a tendency toward this view in Marxist and Marxistic sociology. And certainly there have been moments in which claims made for the sociology of law as the mistress of the legal sciences have tended in the same direction in British academic legal debate; but those times are long past. The large claims of law and economics never seem to have gone quite so far in the way of the grandest imperialism, though the claim to provide a comprehensive restatement of legal doctrine is itself a bold one (and, to me, implausible).

5. Quadrants as Ideal Types

One could go on in this vein at considerable length, but surely more than enough has already been said to make clear how the present 'four quadrants' schema is supposed to provide a useful intellectual map against which to plot the nature and role of legal doctrine, legal theory the philosophy of law, and studies of law in society from the angle of one or another of the social sciences. It is in any event high time for an acknowledgement that contents of each of the quadrants are to be understood as ideal types. Especially of 'raw law' it has to be conceded that wholly untheorised, un-schematised, absolutely raw law is quite unlikely to be found in pure form in any contemporary society. Surely all or nearly all of legal activity in modern societies is strongly informed by systemic and doctrinal conceptions. Legislative assemblies and even more their committees and commissions are advised on the state of the existing law by doctrinal scholars, and law reform is sometimes at least carefully planned to fit into the pre-existing system according to a certain understanding of it. Judges write opinions in the manner of law review articles, and law review articles do the return compliment of playing back a judge-centred view of the law. Judges indeed are often distinguished legal scientists in their own right, and academics brought into judging can make distinguished contributions, nowhere more noticeably than in the European Community, whose law has been developed by a strongly academic Court of Justice from the very partial materials of the foundation Treaties. Journalists dealing with legal affairs tend to be specialists strongly influenced by the law of the schools. Raw law is everywhere contaminated with theory. And yet it is not itself theory or doctrine; there is always a gap, however small. Theory and doctrine are reconstructions aimed at and guided by an apprehension of fragments of raw law; there is much interaction between the two; but they are still not the same thing.

Certainly, at the higher appellate levels, and in constitutional courts in modern systems, there is an extraordinarily high doctrinal-theoretical content in judicial opinions. No doubt the need to determine a particular controversy, and to take some account of the justice of the particular case all-things-considered exposes judicial reasons to pressures not relevant to the issues of pure 'legal science' involved in doctrinal scholarship (though scholarly work sometimes falls short of its present ideal type when its authors take to crusades of their own). But the drawing of a line between highest-court constructions of law and scholarly reconstructions thereof is hazardous. Here, the line between raw law and doctrinal law is blurred to the point of vanishing. Perhaps that is just why sociologists of law and legal realists have been so insistent with warnings against appellate-court-itis in jurisprudence, and so intent on raising the inquiry how far the grand doctrinal constructs of appellate decision really do account well for the lived experience of law in the lower courts, and outside of courtrooms. The more the higher courts are assimilated in their opinion-production to doctrinal scholars of the law, the more the question arises how far they themselves are in touch with, or successful in shaping the more undifferentiated parts of raw law. To say that they have authority over the rest, and that the rest ought therefore to follow the law as declared at the highest levels is either simply to repeat doctrine as though it were description, or it is nothing to the issue. If there were need for an intermediate category to describe this almost-doctrinal law it should perhaps be 'operative doctrinal law'.

Conversely, it need not be supposed that there is much absolutely pure legal doctrine to be found. The school or schools of pure legal exegesis are things of the past, perhaps because they did their work pretty well. Very little of the more interesting contemporary work is absolutely pure in the Kelsenian sense. History, economics, sociology, political science are readily drawn into the process of constructing coherent accounts of legal values and their development. The doctrinal analysis of law is almost always improved by intellectual engagement with other disciplines. But it remains the case that there is a decisive difference between an adoption of economic or sociological or political-scientific or indeed historical ideas for the purposes of strengthening a doctrinal account of some branch of law and its past and possible future development, and work which is itself economics, or sociology, or political science, or history, even where these address themselves toward legal institutions as the primary focus of inquiry. Finally, so far as concerns fundamental values, there is no hard-and-fast line to be drawn between a person's own deepest judgements and those elements of evaluation that are intrinsic either to legal doctrine or to one or other of the social sciences. But that does not justify ignoring the role played in thought by values that actually are fundamental or at least are held as fundamental by a particular thinker, nor the fact that their being held as fundamental sets them apart from values that figure in the other quadrants.

6. Legal Positivism and Legal Science

Intellectual maps present a beguiling temptation, in that they become objects of intrinsic pleasure to their creators, who proceed to neglect the original purpose of explaining something else besides the map. There is a risk of that here, but it does remain the present objective to explain something other than the four quadrants themselves. What I have wanted to stress is the both-true-and-false aspects of the neo-Kantian idea that a science constitutes its own object. Legal science is an interesting case in point. It would be absurd to suppose or to say that the things here called 'raw law' are summoned into being by legal science or legal theory. The object in that sense is not at all the creature of the science. But the concept of 'law', especially where this is taken to be cognate with 'legal system', so that whatever is recognised as law is taken to be or belong to some form of systemic totality, surely belongs only to raw law as transformed by legal science. Law-as-system is the conceptual category devised and refined by dogmaticians and theoreticians from the Greek and Roman classical times forward to the present day. It gives us a way of seeing and differentiating the legal in social experience. The brute facts that constitute raw law are independent of any science; their being singled out and conceptually identified as 'law', even as 'raw law' does depend on the availability of the conceptual framework.

Was law not political then? Had the invention of legal systems nothing to do with the struggle by emergent states for independence, recognition, sovereignty, legitimacy? Of course it was political, too. In the perspective of the third quadrant, one can see that the second also is a praxis, has a history, was moulded and motivated in part by forces it did not create, though not less really also motivated by disinterested regard for truth and active commitment to pursuing it. This value-orientation no doubt has in turn also its social and economic history (but without the value of truth and its pursuit, what would we make of the offerings of social and economic history or any other social science?).

This, I believe, tells us something about the meaning and emergence (from the late eighteenth century forwards) of legal positivism. In the British tradition at least, we should recall that the basis of this was to do with a differentiation of sciences, namely the differentiation of the 'science of (positive) law' from the 'science of legislation'. The issue was whether one could scientifically describe a body of law as a project distinct from that of discussing programmes for rational utilitarian reform of that body of describable law. Kelsen's legal positivism a century or so later was also concerned about the possibility of science. In the context of a social democratic politics and of the rise of a scientific sociology which saw itself as aiming for predictive (causal or probabilistic) theses about society (including its law), it was a serious question whether there could be a normative legal science which was a true contribution to objective knowledge, not an essay in ideology. If so, what was the character of such a science, and on what presuppositions did it proceed? Kelsen's answer shows that it is possible for there to be a normative science, so long as its norms are presented only hypothetically, being dependent on a presupposed Grundnorm which is itself only an hypothesis, resulting from an act of thought, not of will, as Kelsen puts it. Such a legal science proceeds on the basis of a principle of imputation which is fundamental to a normative appreciation of the world in the same way as the principle of causality is to a physical or predictive science.

There is a case to be made out along these lines, but later work has made it clear, as was indicated above in discussion of the second and fourth quadrants, that values and principles enter into legal science in a crucial way. The process of rationally reconstructing law as coherent normative order requires the formulation of governing values and principles so as to make sense of the whole and create the possibility of practical coherence in presentation and apprehension of law. It seems to me quite clear that this does not of itself involve the jurist in direct reference to what are for her or him fundamental or absolute values, or the best version of the objective values that hold for us all as human beings. The usefulness of legal doctrine is as a picture of the actually-ideal order of a given law-community, not as a picture of an absolutely-ideal order. To construct that is a different task, and an important one. But it belongs to legal and political philosophy as the exploration of perfect ideal order. The guiding value of legal science as science is the pursuit of understanding and truth, not exploration of pure ideals. Its 'scientific' character in the sense intended here gives it a privileged quality as understanding, a point on which I appear respectfully to differ from Jack Balkin. The disengagement at this point from absolute values amounts to a differing also from Finnisian natural law.

The usefulness of doctrine as rational reconstruction is very great. It was acknowledged at the end of Section 1 above that actual decisions do not necessarily replicate doctrinal ideal order. But they can, and it is possible to demand that they do. The special gift of legal doctrine to politics is that it sustains the possibility of demands for the Rule of Law, for the governance of laws rather than of arbitrary discretions. This depends on the governing law being objectively statable, and stated. Although law-statements are not themselves to be confused with statements of fundamental ideals, their public availability is a part in one fundamental political value, that of the Rule of Law. Even when they are put forward with proper scholarly detachment, this is not a morally-neutral enterprise.

A corollary is that legal doctrine can become corrupt if made available in the potential legitimation of evil. Gustav Radbruch and others are right in urging legal scientists to withhold their services in respect of regimes that subvert fundamental values and principles, not within the range of reasonable dispute about fundamentals but beyond any reasonable reading of these. The question, it seems to me, is not whether the Nazis counted as having 'law' or not. If the issue is about raw law, no doubt they had many of the activities of decision-making that others have; that they were oriented to values of their own is not in much doubt either. But the practical challenge is whether anyone ought to have reconstructed as 'law' of a practically coherent kind the enterprises in which these people were engaged. Here no value of understanding can outweigh in my judgement the evils of ostensible endorsement and partial legitimation of what was done. There are other ways to secure understanding of these pathological cases. This might be thought an unsatisfactory answer to the question: 'But was it law or not?' I hope I have shown why in my view that is the wrong way to put the question.

Unity of the Legal System

By Aleksander Peczenik, Lund

1. Dissolution of the Law?

Legal reasoning is based on the assumption of unity of the law.

No doubt, this assumption has been put in question. *Hans Peter Graver* (1992, 132ff.), e.g., claims that different norms can be generated in different parts of the legal system (id. 140). The doctrine of the sources of the law varies, too, from one part of the legal order to another (id. 141). His conclusion is "that the classical concept of valid law and the conception of a uniform legal system attached to the state can no longer be upheld in a realist theory. It follows that one rather should speak about (various) normative systems in one society than about valid law. Different norms are valid in different systems" (id. 151).

2. The Assumption of Unity

No doubt, such theories are supported by empirical evidence. Yet, the empirical data do not imply the analytical consequence of the collapse of the legal system. Neither do they imply dissolution of the concept of legal validity. Validity and unity of legal system is a basic *assumption* of the lawyers, of a similar character as causality assumption in natural science. Such assumptions can be neither demonstrated nor falsified within the science in question. They are taken for granted and determine (define) what counts as this kind of science.

3. Validity-tests

In order to understand the role of the validity assumption, let me start with some remarks about legal validity-tests. *Robert S. Summers* (1985, 76ff.) has thus made the distinction between the following types of such tests: (a) source-oriented, (b) content-oriented, (c) process-oriented, (d) acceptance-oriented and (e) effectiveness-oriented.

a) The doctrine of the sources of the law determines the relation between legal validity of particular norms and their origin. A norm is thus legally valid, if it was created in the legally correct manner, stipulated by higher legal norms.

b) As regards the content-oriented test of validity, what matters is the relation of the law to morality. Some norms, mainly principles, are thus legally valid if constituting conclusions of a set of premises including both correctly created legal norms and moral norms, identifiable due to their content.

c) As regards the "process-oriented" test, one may claim that valid law must possess some qualities, necessary to make the process of its application morally justifiable. "Thus ... a statute may not be counted as law because not sufficiently intelligible to be administered in a law-like manner, or ... because improperly retroactive" (id., 76). Since insufficient intelligibility and retroactivity are properties of the content of the law, these examples of the "process-oriented" test of law seem to be a special case of the content-oriented test b.

d - e) One may also claim that legal validity in some cases requires that the putative law passes a test of actual acceptance and effectiveness.

4. The Validity-Tests as Juristic Assumptions

When a law-theorist states precisely what the validity-tests are, he may assume a descriptive or a normative point of view. He may thus describe the fact that the lawyers use these tests. He may also state that the tests are justifiable, and thus should be used. Such a normative theory must, however, give the reader some information about what "justifiable" means in this context. One important sense of the (essentially contestable) concept of "justifiable" is the following. In our legal culture, nobody can simultaneously ignore all or nearly all of these tests and still claim to have performed *legal* reasoning. "Justifiable" in this sense means the same as "necessary for legal reasoning". Legal practice is the basis of this kind of justifiability. But the justificatory force of the legal practice is not "given" in a hard-data empirical observation. It is *assumed* by a legal theorist. In this sense, the normative theory is based on the descriptive one. The fact that the lawyers and jurists actually use these validity-tests in their practice and scholarship is also a justification of the conclusion that the tests should be used.

5. The Grundnorm as a Validity-Basis

As regards the source-based validity-test, the lawyers thus *assume* the *Grundnorm* in Kelsen's sense. The laws inherit their validity from the legally valid Constitution. Then, the lawyers take for granted the *Grundnorm* that the Constitution is valid, that is, ought to be obeyed (cf. Kelsen 1960, 203f.).

The theory of the *Grundnorm* as the validity-basis is too complex to be discussed in the present paper. Let me merely make the following points.

a) The *Grundnorm* is merely an assumption which the lawyers take for granted. How can an assumption constitute a "ground" for legal validity? The "ground" *justifies* the law. How can a mere assumption do it? One possible answer to this question is this. The fact that the lawyers and jurists take the *Grundnorm* for granted in their every-day practice of legal argumentation is the same as existence of this *Grundnorm*. The *Grundnorm* thus exists in the practice of argumentation. This practice is the basis of legal validity.

b) In a normal society, all lawyers and jurists thus implicitly assume the *Grundnorm*. In a society exposed to extremely unjust exercise of power, the unconditional *Grundnorm* becomes contestable. In such a society, at least some lawyers rather tend to assume a conditional *Grundnorm* which needs a profound justification (cf., e.g., Alexy 1992, 154ff.). The following conditional *Grundnorm* seems to be coherent with Alexy's definition of the law (id., 201).

If a normative system has the following properties:

- it claims to be right;
- it includes a constitution and norms created in accordance with it;
- both the constitution and the norms created in accordance with it are efficacious *im grossen und Ganzen,* that is, actually followed in most relevant cases, and, at the same time, not extremely unjust; and, finally,
- the system also includes principles and other normative arguments, on which the practice of application of the law is actually based, or must be based in order to fulfil the claim to be right,

then the constitution of this normative system ought to be obeyed.

6. The Grundnorm and Unity of the Law

According to Kelsen, the *Grundnorm* is also the ground for the unity of the law. All norms whose validity can be derived from the same *Grundnorm* constitute one system of norms. The *Grundnorm* is their common validity basis. It also decides that a certain norm belongs to a certain legal order. This *Grundnorm* converts a variety of norms into unity, since it is the basis of validity of all norms that belong to this legal order (cf. Kelsen 1960, 197).

7. The Grundnorm and Identity of the Legal System

Certainly, a mere reference to the *Grundnorm* does *not* give the lawyers any information about *what* norms belong to the same legal order. In other words, the *Grundnorm* does not solve the "identity problem" of the law (cf. Raz 1970, 104).

In this context, the following must be stated.

a) The abstract formulation of the *Grundnorm* is incomplete. There are many legal systems, each one having its own *Grundnorm*. In the Swedish law, one thus assumes the *Grundnorm* "the Swedish constitution ought to be obeyed", in the German law the *Grundnorm* "the German constitution ought to be obeyed", etc.

b) To answer the question, What norms belong to the constitution?, one needs a complex information about, *inter alia,* the *content* of many legal norms, some perhaps belonging to the constitution, others not belonging to it (cf. Dworkin 1968, 205).

c) The *Grundnorm* helps to answer this question, since it implies that only one legal system is valid in one state and that this system is based on one constitution.

8. Continuity of a Legal System

Temporal continuity of a legal system gives raise to difficult problems, since it is *not* interrupted by the fact that a new constitution is enacted, perhaps in violation of the old one. So was the case, e.g., in Norway 1905. To answer the question, When is the continuity of a legal system interrupted?, one must evaluate the changes of the system as a whole, not merely of its constitution (cf. Eckhoff and Sundby 1991, 215). The constitution decides which other norms belong to the valid legal system. Legal changes of the system do not interrupt its continuity. Illegal changes do it, provided that they are sufficiently extensive and profound.

This evaluation of continuity has, however, the above-mentioned connection with the *Grundnorm*. The *Grundnorm* compels the lawyer to assume that there always is only one valid legal system in one state, and then to ask the question of continuity of this system.

9. Legal System and Its Entourage

Determination of the borderline between a legal system and its entourage depends, too, on many criteria. A norm belongs to the system if the system has produced or adopted it. Among the system-produced norms one must pay special attention to meta-norms, evolved in the legal argumentation practice, i.e., validity-norms and principles determining the sources of the law. These meta-norms decide what is to be counted as binding law. When various authorities interpret the same legal text in different manners, all the interpretations belong to the same legal system (cf. Eckhoff and Sundby 1991, 219). Adoption, on the other hand, consists in the fact that norms created or developed outside of the system are included into it by means of legislation, practice of the authorities or private practice (e.g., contracts). For instance, some foreign laws are thus adopted *via* implementation of domestic rules of international private law. But the domestic legal system is always a lawyer's and a jurist's starting point. He serves only one master, that is, the legal order of his own society. He presupposes a *Grundnorm* which enables him to always consider valid law as one legal system, regardless inconsistencies between various norms. If different authorities interpret a statute in different and mutually inconsistent manners, all the interpretations belong to the same legal system, since they are legally justifiable by means of an argumentation presupposing one and the same *Grundnorm*.

10. Some Conclusions

In their practice of argumentation, the lawyers show a disposition

- to regard the law of a state as one legal system;
- to regard inconsistency and insufficient coherence as defects of this system; and
- to eliminate the defects by legal interpretation.

The fact that the lawyers show this disposition in their argumentation practice means that the social norm "a state's law should be interpreted as one coherent system" *exists* in the lawyers' argumentation practice. This practice is the *unity basis* of valid law.

So is the case regardless what legal philosophy one adopts. It applies, e.g., both to Kelsen's legal positivism and Alexy's non-positivist theory of law.

The only successful way to criticise the assumption of unity of the legal system is evaluative, e.g., one can try to show that the assumption has some disadvantageous consequences. In fact, however, its consequences are mainly positive. The assumption strengthens the democratic state of law, since it helps to submit various kinds of norm-giving parliamentary control. If a sociologist shows that the parliament actually lost the control, the lawyers should not merely state that the legal system collapsed but the must try to save it, both by interpretation *de lege lata* and by criticism *de lege ferenda*.

11. Briefly about Coherence

The unity of the law is *one of many* juristic assumptions, expressing the idea of coherence.

The main idea or the *concept* of coherence can be expressed in the following way (cf. Alexy and Peczenik 1990, reprinted with some additions in Peczenik 1989, 158ff.).

The more the statements belonging to a given theory approximate a perfect supportive structure, the more coherent the theory.

- The word *"theory"* is used here in a broad sense, covering both descriptive, for example empirical theories, and normative or evaluative theories (norm systems or value systems).
- The statement p *supports* the statement q if, and only if, p belongs to a set of premises, S, from which q follows logically. (In an extreme case, q follows from p alone).

  (Concerning the relation between coherence and support, cf. Peczenik 1983, 88ff.; Aarnio 1987, 198ff.).

This definition of support assumes logical correctness. *Logical consistency* is thus a necessary but not sufficient condition of coherence.

Certainly, any p together with an arbitrarily added premise supports any conclusion whatever. However, this weak concept of support may be used as a starting point of discussion. Inappropriate additional premises are to be eliminated, *inter alia* by the criteria of coherence.

The degree of *perfection* of support depends on the degree to which the criteria of coherence are fulfilled. Criteria of coherence make the concept of coherence more precise.

12. Some Criteria of Coherence

One can distinguish between three kinds of criteria.

a) Criteria Concerning the Supportive Structure

A deeper and broader support makes a theory more coherent. *Ceteris paribus,* the degree of coherence of a theory depends on such circumstances as

- how great a number of supported statements belongs to it;
- how long chains of reasons belong to it;
- how great a number of connections exists between various supportive chains belonging to the theory, e.g., how many chains of reasons support one and the same conclusion; and
- how many statements belonging to the theory are relevant in the type of reasoning the theory uses.

b) Criteria Concerning Concepts

General concepts are a "cement" holding the pieces of a theory together. *Ceteris paribus,* the degree of coherence of a *single* theory depends on such circumstances as

- how great a number of universal statements belongs to it;
- how great a number of general concepts belongs to it; and
- how high the degree of generality of these concepts is.

Ceteris paribus, the degree of coherence *between* various theories depends on such circumstances as

- how great a number of resemblances exists between concepts they use;
- how great a number of conceptual cross-connections exists between them.

c) Criteria Concerning the Subject Matter of the Theory

Ceteris paribus, the degree of coherence of a theory depends on such circumstances as

- how great a number of cases it covers; and
- how great a number of fields of life it covers.

The degree of coherence is determined by weighing and balancing of these criteria.

13. The Unity Assumption and Coherence in Legal Dogmatics and in Legal Practice

Increased coherence is the purpose and the point of interpretation in legal dogmatics. In legal practice, however, the purpose is more limited. Only the norms applicable to the considered case are to be considered. Their coherent reworking can decrease their coherence with other legal norms. Moreover, the norms are made as coherent as the case requires, together with its possible role as a pattern-establishing precedent. The interpretation increasing mutual coherence of norms in the considered case may decrease their coherence in other cases. Consequently, unity of the law is assumed both in legal practice and in legal dogmatics, but in two different manners. In legal practice, it is assumed as much as the decided case and its possible precedent function requires. In legal dogmatics, it is assumed to the extent enabling the scholar to establish a total view of the legal system as a unity.

From another point of view, the unity assumption is, however, stronger in legal practice than in legal dogmatics. In practice, the decider *must* solve the case, and thus he must regard the law as unity to the extent demanded by this purpose. In legal dogmatics, a scholar must put the *question* whether the law can be regarded as a unity. He must even *try* to answer this question in the affirmative. But when all juristic attempts to interpret the law as a unity fail, he can peacefully give up. He did his best, and yet the chaos cannot be avoided.

14. Brief Remarks on Assumptions Underlying Legal Interpretation

The unity assumption, the coherence assumptions and the assumptions concerning validity-tests are completed with a number of assumptions underlying the interpretation of law. Let me briefly mention some of them.

a) Assumptions of Relevance

Lawyers and jurists utter *prima-facie* legal statements and definitive legal statements. General normative statements of the socially established law, such as statutes, have almost always *prima-facie* character, since they do not definitively determine legal conclusions and decisions in particular cases. However, they are legally relevant, since they must be taken into account in legal weighing and balancing of considerations jointly determining the conclusion.

A *prima-facie* norm- or value-statement is *relevant* (and thus *assumed*) in legal thinking if our culture compels us to take it into account when performing a legal weighing and balancing. So is the case, if all or almost all lawyers and jurists who belong to our legal culture often solve legal questions as if they have taken for granted that such prima-*facie* norm- and value-statements may not be ignored when one performs a legal weighing and balancing. Certainly, each of these statements can be confronted with counter-arguments. But in our culture, nobody can simultaneously ignore all or nearly all of them and still claim to have performed *legal* reasoning. Various sources of the law, such as binding statutes or precedents, are *particularly relevant,* that is, they have a privileged position in legal reasoning:

- Their *weight* in the law is so great that only particularly strong substantive reasons are sufficient to override them.
- They are apt to *explain* legal decisions. It is thus quite natural to say "A was sentenced to prison *because* the statute required it".
- They are also *necessary* from the legal point of view. Without sources of the law, a conclusion has no legal support.

b) All-Things-Considered Legal Statements

Such a weighing is supported by several argumentative steps but the ultimate step cannot be justified by further reasons. In this way, each act of weighing and balancing is based on the arbitrary *assumption* that the final argument is a sufficient foundation of the whole chain of reasons.

Yet, one can speak of a weighing being more or less *correct*. More precisely, the idea of correctness of legal reasoning implies, among other things, the following *assumptions*. *Ceteris paribus,* a definitive weighing and balancing is better, the greater number of relevant *prima-facie* reasons is considered. A definitive legal weighing and balancing is correct only if it is an all-things-considered weighing, taking into account all relevant *prima-facie* value- and norm-statements, applicable to the discussed (actual or hypothetical) case (cf. Peczenik 1989, 76f.).

15. Assumptions and Knowledge

a) The Problem

Both practical lawyers and jurists thus *assume* that legal reasoning should make the law as coherent as possible. Among other things, they *assume* that some tests indicate that the norm in question is valid law. They also *assume* that the correct interpretation of valid law consists of weighing and balancing of the socially established sources of the law and moral values. Finally, they *assume* that only one system of law is valid in a single state.

The assumptions rest on social *conventions*. Yet, one may speak about legal *knowledge*. Can knowledge be conventional? Is not all knowledge *true*? Can truth be conventional?

b) Truth of Practical Statements?

In *formal logic,* no reason exists to make a distinction between truth of theoretical and practical statements. Logicians thus construct calculi with two values, 1 and 0. If the calculus shows that a statement has the value 1, then the statement is true in the formal sense.

However, outside of formal logic, the distinction is important. "Truth" is an *ontological* concept, i.e., a concept presupposing something about the world.

Generally speaking, a statement is true if some knowable facts are precisely such as the statement tells us; and it is reasonable to assume that these knowable facts correspond to what is the case (i.e., to the real world "in itself"; cf. Peczenik 1989, 183f.). Can norm- and value-statements correspond to the world? In particular, Can a *juristic* statement about valid law be true, i.e., correspond to what is the case?

The following epistemological assumption is reasonable (cf. id. 186f. and 307ff.).

Definitive (not merely *prima-facie*) norm- and value-statements are neither true nor false, but they can be correct or incorrect. Correctness is to some extent determined by the world itself. However, it implies no ontological claim that a correct sentence corresponds to what is the case.

Cf. Popper 1966 vol. 2, 384f.:

> "First, both proposals and propositions are alike in that we can discuss them, criticise them and come to some decision about them. Secondly, there is some kind of regulative idea about both. In the realm of facts it is the idea of correspondence between a statement or a proposition and a fact; that is to say, the idea of truth. In the realm of standards, or of proposals, the regulative idea can be described in many ways, and called by many terms, for example by the terms 'right' or 'good'."

Coherence, consensus and pragmatic success are criteria of correctness, that is, they indicate that a norm- or value-system is correct in the discussed sense. More precisely, the following *assumptions* seem to be reasonable.

Ceteris paribus, the more coherent a norm- or value-system, the closer it approximates the ideal of correctness.

Ceteris paribus, the higher the probability that a norm- or value-system would be unanimously accepted in a discourse fulfilling the demands of sincerity, openness, impartiality and allocation of the burden of argument, the closer it approximates the ideal of correctness.

Ceteris paribus, the higher the probability that acceptance of a norm- or value-system would help an individual to achieve his goals, the closer the system approximates the ideal of correctness.

c) The Conclusion

In the light of these philosophical *assumptions,* a high degree of internal coherence is a good explication of the juristic concepts of correctness and legal knowledge. The concept of coherence rests on more *assumptions*. Unity of the law is *assumed* in a similar manner. If all these assumptions are accepted, one can justify the more specific juristic assumptions, implied by such practices as the implementation of legal validity-tests and the juristic weighing and balancing.

The unity assumption is one of many assumptions inherent in the legal thinking. In our culture, nobody can simultaneously ignore all or nearly all of these assumptions and still be regarded as a skilful lawyer or jurist.

Legal practice sets the standards determining who is to be regarded as a skilful lawyer. Legal practice is one of many practices, each setting its own standards of perfection, for instance determining who is a good father, a good citizen and so on. Indeed, our life consists in participation of such practices.

No doubt, all practices rest on social conventions. But these practices and conventions are a part of our *form of life* (cf. Peczenik 1989, 145 ff.). No justification can be stronger than this link with the form of life. In this sense, the assumption of the unity of law is justified.

Certainly, a scepticist may use empirical data to argue that the legal system has collapsed and the concept of legal validity has been dissolved. But these sceptical conclusions do not follow from the data alone but merely from their combination with his view that the juristic assumptions are to be refuted. This sceptical view, however, is itself an assumption. This negative assumption is by no means more certain than the positive ones.

The difference is only this. Juristic assumptions make our common social life easier, sceptical assumptions make it more difficult. It is up to you to make the choice.

References

Aarnio, Aulis (1987): The Rational as Reasonable. Dordrecht/Boston/Lancaster/Tokyo.

Alexy, Robert (1992): Begriff und Geltung des Rechts. Freiburg/München.

Alexy, Robert / *Peczenik,* Aleksander (1990): The Concept of Coherence and its Significance for Discursive Rationality. Ratio iuris. Vol. 3 No. 1bis.

Dworkin, Ronald (1968): Comments on the Unity of Law Doctrine (A Response). In: M. K. Munitz and H. E. Kiefer (edd.), Ethics and Social Justice. Albany, NY.

Eckhoff, Torstein /*Sundby,* Nils Kristian (1991): Rettssystemer. 2 ed. by Torstein Eckhoff. Oslo.

Graver, Hans Peter (1992): Normative systemer – skisse til en opplösning av rettsbegreppet, in: Ken Uggerud (ed.), Forvaltningsrett og rettskildelaere. Kritisk-juridiske artikler. Oslo.

Kelsen, Hans (1960): Reine Rechtslehre. 2 ed. Wien.

Peczenik, Aleksander (1983): The Basis of Legal Justification. Lund.

– (1989): On Law and Reason. Dordrecht/Boston/London.

Popper, Sir Karl R. (1966): The Open Society and Its Enemies. 5 ed. London.

Raz, Joseph (1970): The Concept of Legal System. Oxford.

Summers, Robert S. (1985): Toward a Better General Theory of Legal Validity. RECHTSTHEORIE 16.

Adequacy of Societal Norm-Systems

The Issues of Modern ius et non-ius

By Mihály Samu, Budapest

I. Introductory remarks

The question of *ius* and *non-ius,* more comprehensively the problem of the differentiation and interaction of different norms, and the analysis of the adequacy of these norms in the expression of societal requirements often has posed a problem.[1]

1. One frequently encounters the view in public thinking that many rules are not required and much regulation is not necessary. It is also assumed that life would be freer without regulation and norms. Apart from this view (perhaps even independently of it) one also encounters attitudes *denying* the necessity of particular legal measures and aspiring to reduce the authority of legal norms and the role of the law in general. It is especially noteworthy how many people in public life, politics, and certain academic and professional fields hold that legal regulation has a limiting effect on human relations. This raises difficulties in public affairs.

2. In these views one encounters an *aversion* to legal regulation and the law in general. However, a general aversion to legal regulation often does not go hand in hand with opposition to all kinds of regulation. One frequently experiences an ambivalent approach when people, taking a negative stand toward the law, nevertheless readily accept and obey other non-legal rules. Thus, for instance, teachers uphold and naturally follow the norms of teaching and education, public servants the norms of bureaucratic prescription, members of various occupations (e.g. accountants, doctors, electricians, etc.) their professional norms, merchants the rules of trading, producers or workers generally the rules of production, religious communities the religious (ecclesiastical) norms, voluntary organizations (political, scientific, artistic, sport, etc.) their charters or statutes. Yet many of these groups may take a negative stand toward the law and regulation.

---

[1] "A society has a very wide variety of social standards and norms, and people must be able to tell which are legal and which are nonlegal." R. S. Summers, Instrumentalism and American Legal Theory, Cornell University Press, 1982, p. 101.

3. It should be added, however, that in the public opinion of some countries one also encounters an attitude contrary to the above, in which the *omnipotence* of legal regulation is taken for granted. According to this, the various tasks of societal evolution can only be solved by legal regulation and the adoption of a definite legal measure is considered sufficient for solving social problems. This overestimation of the law and exaggerated confidence in legal measures has so penetrated public thinking that people believe social problems are to be solved primarily by new legal measures. (Perhaps this is the corollary of statism in common opinion and of positivism in legal thinking).

4. It may also be demonstrated by empirical facts that the essence of any regulation, i.e. its social necessity, is seldom clearly seen in public and scientific thinking. This stems primarily from the fact that neither the substance, content and size of social regulation, nor the differentiation and interaction of societal norms is yet theoretically worked out in the social sciences; this is a *scientific gap* – a terra incognita.

5. The question may be posed whether the content of a regulation is just or unjust, right or wrong, adequate or inadequate for regulatory needs and requirements. These questions can be answered precisely if we examine them in the framework of one set of norm-systems – legal, political, economic and cultural.

6. In earlier legal thinking the separation of law and morality attracted great attention for various reasons. Kant's opinion that law is an external rule directing human action (norm heteronomous) while morality being an inner one (norm autonomous), has been particularly popular in the human sciences. The content, comprehensive nature and the division of these regulations were, however, not clarified, with the exception of differentiation between their sanctions, as in legal positivism. In the course of analysis of the relation between law and other norms it has become a commonplace that there are a number of different norms in society (e.g. morality, etiquette, and religious rules). Recent literature also distinguishes between norms related to politics, state administration, army, trade, organizations, technical fields, economics and cultural life, etc. There are theoretical problems concerning the separation of this *ius* and *non-ius* in general, and in particular the place and role of different norms in a regulation-system. A special problem is the relation of law and citizens' rights, the rules of organizations, technical norms, and expert knowledge of management systems. We can state that some researchers seek to find in legal science the means of discovering the relationship of various types of norms in order to understand the role of law precisely.

II. The directive force of regulation and norms

1. When considering the existence of society, the questions necessarily arise: Why is regulation necessary in society? Why is it necessary to direct and control human behavior? Why are various aspects of social coexistence regulated by different norms?

It can be emphasized that regulation stems from the elementary needs of human coexistence, that history produces regulation and norms by necessity. In other words, the organization and regulation of certain aspects of production, exchange, property, distribution, division of labor, transport, communal life, administration of public affairs, sex relations, family life and private affairs is an elementary necessity of society. Such regulation facilitates the production and reproduction of the conditions of social existence in general.

It is a historic fact that in social coexistence different interests and controversies arose and generated a need to direct and regulate them. The activity of persons had to be socially regulated by norms; these were formulated by tradition, instinctively at the beginning and later by consciously shaped norms. These norms were destined to organize and regulate the behavior of individuals, their interactions and the reproduction of their social conditions. In other words, the reproduction of social existence cannot do without regulation; since the *cooperation* of individuals calls for social direction and the harmonization of human activities by norms. Under changing societal circumstances, meeting this need presupposes the regulation of human activities and the emergence of different norms; the behavior of people is directed by norms and maxims.[2]

2. In the course of determining human activities, the definition of aims, the incorporation of certain models of human behavior as norms (law or moral value), and the subjugation of individual wills to these aims, must be naturally conceived of as *power relations.* The setting of goals as well as their definition in norms is required so that these goals may be realized through activities of people within power relations. In social coexistence the regulation of human activities arises as part of power relations.[3]

Regulation, as an integral part of the power-system is intertwined with the governing of society. Here, power means the comprehensive direction of society, the ordering of the activities of communities and individuals. Furthermore, the paramount facet of social direction is the regulation, organization and administration of society, the operative solution of everyday problems, and the assurance of the permanent functioning of social coexistence requiring

---

[2] John Austin, Lectures on Jurisprudence, London 1872, Lp. 118.

[3] See Mihály Samu, Korrelation von Macht und Recht, RECHTSTHEORIE, 23. Band 1992, Heft 2, pp. 187 - 206.

stability. Regulation emerges as a necessity in order to deal with all these tasks and at the end to bring them about coercively if necessary.

We have to pay special attention to the fact that ensuring reproduction requires repeated activities and supporting attitudes from the members of society (community).[4] In the framework of regulation, individuals are obliged to repeat their actions; for this purpose, the social actions and relations are definitely and continually regulated by norms, requirements, expectations, and standards; and these apply to the future as well. By ensuring the continuous repetition of human activities, the norms perpetuate a certain behavioral model; they prescribe positive actions, and attitudes, and they set basic prohibitions defining anti-social or anti-community behavior. The norm on the one hand, defines in general form the behavior individuals should follow, and adds the threat of force to the obligation, on the other.

The essence of regulation may thus be summed up as an expression of the need for regulation, and as part of the system of power relations, regulations prescribe repeated activities of individuals in a general obligatory and lasting form, in order to secure the social life. Corbonnier's concise definition of the essence of the norm as the general and lasting prescription of power[5] is correct.

According to historic experience, communities (societies) fall apart without power-regulatory institutions. Societies cannot exist (cannot reproduce themselves) without norms.

3. The underlining of the "power character" of all regulation can give rise to certain misunderstandings. Since power relations are primarily regarded as macro-social relations, the fact that they – including regulation – can and do arise also at the meso- and micro-social levels is often disregarded. In fact power – at all different levels – integrates the whole society, and the individual "subjugates his own will to the law" not only in his/her work, but also in other relations of social coexistence. In the course of history, norms emerge as a consequence of differences between the reproduction of the life of individuals and that of the society between primary and secondary teleological suppositions, and between *macro-, meso- and micro-power* relations. This explains the great variety of regulations.

The fact that a majority generally obey the norms is another fundamental characteristic of regulation and of power practice. This characteristic is manifest in the level of legitimacy accepting the power-normative system as right and just (see Max Weber's argumentation). To a great extent, this acceptance is due to the socialization process of the society (by means of education, information, mass-communication and the judiciary in the modern societies). Not

---

[4] Agnes Heller, A mindennapi élet (Everyday Life), Budapest 1970, p. 204.

[5] J. Corbonnier, Sociologie juridique, Paris 1972, p. 132.

only is there conscious acceptance and the observance of the norms, but also an emotional identification with them.[6] In this regard, the state enforcement of rules plays a subordinate role. The question of force, i. e. the sanction of the societal rules, is often treated in a biased way in the literature. Force is underlined as a conceptual characteristic of some norms, while the lack of this is detected in the case of other norms. Of course, a certain manifestation of force is present in all forms of regulation (even in communal disapproval, censure, self-control and also in the form of a satiric sanction). Besides this, force is also relative; it is only for those who do not accept its authority or content, and not for the others, who do.

Acceptance and observation of norms, and the possibility of enforcement are interrelated and complement one another. This interrelation requires an appropriate proportional relation between the two aspects. When in a regulative system the proper proportion between coerced enforcement and voluntary observation of the norm is not present (mostly because of the preponderance of the coercive element) the regulation may eventually become distorted, and ineffective.

III. The historical bonds of regulation

1. One would arrive at too abstract an explanation of regulation, unless the historical bonds of regulation are given due emphasis. It is an obvious fact that regulation emerges according to historic conditions, and that historical development leads to changes of regulation and to adjustments to the actual situation; regulation emerges always and everywhere in concrete, changing practical connections.

The histories of human societies have, by necessity, produced power relations, including regulation connected to the development of social consciousness. The level of social consciousness and that of cultural development influences the standard of regulation to a significant extent; norms are mainly the result of generalized thinking. Consequently, in the process of norm-making, it is possible to work out general rules which shape human attitudes for longer periods, ensure a stable system of coexistence, and create human values.

It is almost a commonplace to say that there are qualitative differences in regulation in respect of primitive, precapitalist, and modern societies. The development of ancient societies did, of necessity, produce the consolidation of communal forms of living; power relations also emerged as connecting, integrating factors of social coexistence; direction, defense, organization and

---

[6] Lukács points out: every regulation postulates "that the general, practical manner of the activities of members of society should 'voluntarily' at least apparently voluntarily follow these regulations". György Lukács, A társadalmi léte ontologiájéról (On the Ontology of Social Existence), Vo. II, Budapest 1976, p. 18.

reproduction of social life were realized by self-government and self-regulation. The customs, taboos, and beliefs of those societies crystallized as specific forms of regulation.[7] These norms ordered the life of the community to the most minute details; the primitive forms of production, the natural division of labor, public life, everyday coexistence, sex relations, the life of the individual from the cradle to the grave.

The regulation of social relations and human activity is essential also for the civilization. The only difference is that this regulation is carried out by way of different systems or norms, with macrostructural regulation decisive; in most instances one finds a preponderance of *legal regulation.* After the emergence of civilization, the legal norms expressing and fixing social stratification became separate from the traditional communal rules. The traditional norms existed for a while parallel with legal provisions and other new norms. The law became separated from the uniform system of regulation in the form of customary law, and written law trying to replace the right of the strongest, the vendetta, the compensation, the communal "administration of justice" and the communal settling of disputes. This is not merely a conflict between traditional and new norms, but also a contradiction of the spontaneous and conscious kind of norm-making. Conscious law-making and new regulations (contrary to the norms of customary law) became dominant in the law.

In the course of modern history spontaneous regulation can no longer meet social needs. Conscious regulation is required. The necessity of institutional regulation produces the separation of the regulative activity within the power-system, and special institutions become established to work out the rules for the regulation of social relations (solution of conflicts, settling of disputes, remedying offenses).

2. Actual historical comparisons reveal major differences in the norm-systems of various societies. In some social systems, measures regulating certain social relations have a religious (church) character, while in others these relations are controlled by legal norms (e.g. one society regulates marriage and inheritance with religious norms, another society with legal provisions).

Considering the great variety of systems, it is also obvious that different societies and states develop different regulative solutions. On the basis of some common features as well as solutions of an identical nature in individual systems of regulation, specific groups can be identified, following specific models of regulation. The most typical differences between various norm-systems arise from their different role and place in the given society. Thus, in some societies the dominance of religious or legal norms may be observed. Elsewhere political or military norms, customs or traditions, economic or cultural norms are of a greater or lesser importance.

---

[7] William Sumner, Népszokások (folkways), Budapest 1978, p. 92.

The different importance of the various systems also determines the inner *hierarchy* of the normative model, having at the top of the hierarchy the dominant norm-system. Thus religious norms are the most important in the regulative system of theocratic states, the primacy of military norms is asserted in military dictatorships, party-political, or military norms are preponderant in totalitarian dictatorships, and law is dominant in constitutional democracies.

In respect to the various solutions, the question arises: what is the explanation for the dominance of the religious (or political) norm in one regulative system, and of the legal norm in the other? The answer is: the different importance attributed to the specific systems of norms, hierarchies of rules, and differing regulative solutions depends on the peculiarities of historical development of a power-system and, within that, on the different solutions in terms of social direction. Specific regulative models are defined primarily by the historical traditions. Apart from that, the specific regulative model of a nation, a society or a state is naturally determined by the achievements of the political struggles of the given era, the regulative concept and practice, and the inner hierarchy of the given normative system. Concisely, one may say that the regulative model depends on power-systems – on how a state or ruling factor meets the demand for regulation, taking into consideration given historical precedents and conditions.

IV. The place of law in a regulation-system

1. In the course of historical development, the law has particular importance in the sphere of many layered regulations according to social needs. The law differs from other norms in that it emerges at the macro-social level of power-system. In the inner hierarchy of the regulative system, the law fills a special function; regulates social practice in accordance with the intention of the ruling factors and decisive power-interests. The regulative system can be reinforced by the concentration of the regulative activity. One of the manifestations of this is the ousting of local, regional rules, customs, and their substitution with the law, and the creation of a uniform system of norms.

Thus the law is one instrument in the integration of the power system, and in the consolidation of centralized regulation. The lawyers here play a special and interesting role, as a special professional branch (or caste) of the society able to sum up the complicated labyrinth of the law, and to assert it in legal practice.[8]

2. Historical experience proves that the separation of legal norms in order to meet social needs arises as the result of conscious regulation-making activity. This conscious activity emerges as the rationality of legal regulation in

[8] Agnes Heller (note 4), p. 149.

more developed legal systems. It contains the direction, planning and foresight of human activities. Thus, it becomes a necessity to shape norms which aim not only at ensuring the stability of existing conditions, but also at regulating attitudes to be expected in the future. This led to the building up of legal order, the precise fixing of legal regulations, and the observation of norms. The requirement of making the legal regulations calculable emerged subsequently, and led to *putting the law in writing*. This of course does not result automatically in the observance of legal regulations, since this depends on the stability of society and the assertion of the norms. (It is a commonplace that the observing of legal norms is supported first of all by moral norms and maxims.)

But the law also contributes to guaranteeing social stability by way of building up its own order and stability. This means first of all securing the continuity of the content of law, its existence over a long period of time. In other words, the frequent changing of the content of law is a harmful practice. Aristotle recognized this: "reckless reformation of existing laws is in fact a weakening of the power of the law."[9]

V. The balance and hierarchy of norm-systems

1. In the framework of power systems, the totality of regulation, in other words the mutual relation of norms, and their mutually complementing role, the unity of regulation must not be overlooked. The differing qualitative character of the various kinds of norms does not dissolve within the totality of regulation: each system of norms exists independently and has its own rules. Their separation and independent role result in the realization and effectiveness of the comprehensive purposes of the normative order. The totality of social regulation spans the whole of society, the various relations and the attitudes of people.

The development of regulation proves that there are no sharp borders between the various systems of norms. They often overlap and take over roles from one another. Owing to this, it is not possible to establish in an exact manner which concrete attitude, or what kind of action can be regulated by one or some other kind of norm.

In spite of the various regulative solutions, a requirement may still be outlined, even if not exactly defined: the independent role of the existing kinds of norms must be guaranteed in the system of regulation, the balance and proportion of the rules must be upheld within the hierarchic order. Normative order and social coexistence are made possible by the harmony of the norms. Cs. *Varga* formulates this firmly: "In itself, the law is insufficient for con-

[9] Aristotle, Politika (Politics), Budapest 1969, p. 135.

cretely influencing social attitudes. Various forms of legitimation, institutions of religion and morals, and a whole series of ideological incentives are needed to maintain the effectiveness of the law."[10] Historical experience also proves the need for the harmony and the hierarchic proportion of the various kinds of norms. When the disproportionate role and the one-sided preponderance of some kind of norm are evident in the regulative system, the regulation becomes abnormal, distorted and ineffective.

The hierarchic relation and balance of the various norms adjusts also to the characteristics of concrete social conditions. In the various concrete relations of society, the hierarchy of norms follows peculiar and different solutions. The hierarchical interaction of the norms asserts itself in accordance with concrete social relations. The interaction of the norms arises differently under differing social (economic, political, family, community, religious, cultural) conditions; one or another norms may become preponderant or primary. Thus, for instance, in the regulation of family relations, religious norms, customs and law play roles along side the primacy of moral norms. Technical rules of production dominate in economic relations, and moral, legal, or political norms play secondary roles. On the other hand, the primacy of political norms or of the law is natural in the management of public affairs, where moral and religious norms, and customs and traditions play lesser roles.

The hierarchy, balance, and interaction of norms must be secured also in the regulation of various social relations, since the disintegration of the traditionally established regulative order causes social tensions and regulative crisis.[11] If, for instance, the primacy of political or governmental norms would be forced upon the regulation of family or economic relations, (since the families and the economic relations have their own norms, that is self-regulation as an independent norm-system) in place of primacy of moral and economic norms, the regulative balance of these relations would become upset. Regulation would likely be ineffective.

The inner hierarchy of this interaction mechanism asserts itself, with appropriate differences, both in the field of comprehensive regulation of social life, and in that of detailed concrete social relations. Comprehensive and detailed regulation is realized with regard to the inner coherence and order of regulative systems. The purpose of comprehensive regulation is to ensure order in the macro-, meso- and micro-social relations of social coexistence, that is the normative order.

2. In concrete relations, the normative order governs the everyday life of people. Under complicated conditions of social reproduction, regulation ful-

---

[10] Csaba Varga, A. jog helye Lukács György világképében (The Place of the Law in György Lukács: World View), Budapest 1981, p. 188.

[11] Hubert Rottleuthner, Legal Evolution and the Limits of Law, in: Law, Morality, and Discursive Rationality, Helsinki 1989.

fills its purpose, naturally, with many-faceted interactions of the various norms. The varieties and rules of social practice that developed in the course of history are merely *intermediary* forms, and developed originally also as such, in order to better regulate social life.

The various forms of norms extend over the whole lives of people; the most comprehensive of the various norms is the law. The fundamental question is whether the various norms are able to govern the conduct of individuals (citizen's) under concrete social conditions. The majority of individuals generally show conduct in agreement with the norms. And the parallel, concerted effect of the various norms significantly contributes to this.[12] Individuals are generally not conscious of the fact that they are complying with various norms. The general observation of the norms by the majority of people emerges in social coexistence under the material and formal effects of the normative order. Within this majority, however, the norm-obeying conduct of individuals evolves under the influence of different factors, and on the basis of different motives. In the sociology of law a distinction is made between two kinds of conduct; the acceptance of the norms emotionally and intellectually, on the one hand, and behavior adjusted to norms, on the other. In both cases people not only observe the rules, but also influence others to adjust to the normative regulations.

The observation of social norms is produced in society and in the various communities by a peculiar process of socialization. As a result of this, different values permeate the personality, and generate attitudes that appear in the concrete human relations.

3. The level and differentiation of the system of values in a given society has a considerable influence on comprehensive regulation. These *values* work their way into the normative order, and their acceptance and assertion become a necessity.

The entwinement of regulative and value systems produces specific kinds of responsibility related to the various norms. Thus a distinction can be made between moral, legal, economic and political *responsibility* according to the types of norms. And beyond these, there is also responsibility for professional conduct, organizational responsibility, etc.

There are no right boundaries between norms but the interaction of norms does not signify the interchangeability or the mixing of one form of *responsibility* with another. Thus, for instance, one cannot mix up political, moral, or organizational responsibility with legal, though their complete substitution for each other is a phenomenon observed very frequently. Actually, political or

---

[12] "When the moral and religious ideas of an individual run parallel to the legal order to which he is subject, his lawful behavior is often due to those moral and religious ideas." H. Kelsen, General Theory of Law and State, Cambridge 1945, p. 24.

economic responsibility can be deduced mostly from political or economic norms and legal or moral responsibility may be connected with these only in the complex overall system of regulation.[13]

As the consequence of the functioning of the normative order, the whole of communal coexistence is comprehensively regulated and within this the development and stabilization of individual responsibility are furthered. The various forms of responsibility work their way into the everyday relations of social coexistence, and in the process of socialization, individuals acquire fundamental values and normative orientations. This is the basis of responsible social actions or individual attitudes.

The observance of norms is primarily based on community attitudes and consciousness developed in the course of socialization. Besides this, the *sanctions* attached to the various norms have to be employed. The balance of various sanctions is a fundamental requirement of a normative order. The inappropriate sanctioning of various behavior, or over-emphasis on the sanctioning of a particular kind of norm (disregarding the others) may impair overall social regulation. For instance when legal sanctions are not in harmony with moral ones accepted in the community, the efficiency of legal sanctions is limited. Disproportion of sanctions, their exaggerated severity or lenience may impede the effectiveness of the normative order as a whole.

The law occupies a specific position among the various societal norms on the basis of its special character as a power-system. The legal system is an intermediary in dictatorship and in democracy; it is the first instance of regulation in a democratic constitutional state, though its primacy in the hierarchy of social norms can be substituted for by some other type of norm.

The special role of law can be explained by its characteristic features as a distinctive system.[14] Modern legal systems claim special consciousness (in legislation, in jurisdiction, and in observance). A legal system consists of a framework of consequential, mutually connected, contradiction-free rules built upon one another. The system ensures the remedying of wrongs, and the resolution of legal disputes by formal processes. The legal system provides an appropriate proportion of voluntariness and force. It makes calculability possible. It contributes to the stability of social order. It makes possible the introduction of legal values into everyday coexistence. It furthers the reinforcement of responsibility of citizens and the general acceptance of norm-observing attitudes. These basic features of the law contribute considerably to the realization of normative order.

---

[13] See Péter Szilágyi, A jogi felelősség alapja (The basis of legal responsibility), in: Felelősség és szankció a jogban (Responsibility and Sanction in Law), Budapest 1980, p. 108.

[14] Werner Krawietz, Recht als Regelsystem, Wiesbaden 1984.

An interesting consequence of the high differentiation of norms is manifest in the administration of justice in modern legal systems. When the differentiation of norms is rudimentary, knowledge of other (moral, political and religious) norms can be taken for granted. In more complicated systems, however, automatic knowledge of other norms no longer can be taken for granted. The use of expert knowledge in the administration of justice becomes an elementary requirement. This enables the court to consider whether a person (a clerk, an engineer, a doctor, a skilled worker, etc.) acted in accordance with professional and technical norms and this is the basis for the establishment of legal responsibility in the relevant instances. Beyond that, expert opinions based on scientific knowledge must also be considered when the subjective elements of human behavior are judged.

The existence of the system of experts, as a specific phenomenon, indicates that scientific and professional knowledge has become a necessity in establishing legal regulation and responsibility. This system enables one to get an insight into fundamental human actions and attitudes on the basis of scientific knowledge. In this a special part is played by the law. The law is capable of ordering the fundamental social relations in modern societies more soundly and more effectively on the basis of scientific knowledge.

VI. The adequate regulation and new needs

1. The assertion of normative order in modern societies brings in its train the conscious shaping of regulation, and this ensures first of all the independent role of the systems of norms, their hierarchy and interaction. It is of primary importance to use adequate regulatory solutions for the ordering of certain attitudes, behavior and personal activity. The regulatory needs which evolve in consequence of social changes must be precisely formulated and put in writing as new regulations (or as amendments of the existing ones).

The question always arises whether the existing regulatory system is capable of meeting new regulatory needs. Historical experience is ambivalent in this respect. In some instances legal norms can flexibly meet new needs. Some regulatory systems can even facilitate the emergence of new kinds of norms, and incorporate them into the system of interaction among different norms. In other instances, regulatory systems are unable to accommodate new types of norms because of the conservative character of the systems.

The conservative or progressive nature of the normative order affects the whole of society, and determines the character of the system of social direction. Owing to this, the solutions of the leadership are the primary factors (beside other spontaneous or non-significant social factors) in determining the suitability of societal regulation to new needs, the adaptability and efficiency of the normative order.

Historic experience shows a tendency for societies to exaggerate the special role of the law, i.e. through the voluntarism of the leadership, and statism. In these instances no attention is paid to the inner characteristics of the law and the peculiarities of other norm-systems. Non-legal content in legal norms is not enforceable yet may be set in legal frame.

The special nature of law – its formal nature and enforceability – give a particular prestige to the law in the system of societal regulation. The tendencies and practical solutions connected with power interests are often expressed not in adequate norms, but in the general framework of legal regulation. The fundamental reason for this is the possibility of using punitive sanctions in the regulation of certain attitudes. On the other hand, however, if the enforceability of the norm set in legal frame is doubtful, the legal regulation may be ineffective. For instance: political decisions or police measures may take legal form, with law regarded as a political instrument. In dictatorships, politics assume the role of the law, and law becomes a subordinate instrument of political propaganda. Democratic progress, however, brings with it the emergence of the real societal role of the law, and a parallel separation of the political and legal norms.

2. The establishment of regulation corresponding to given social requirements is, therefore, a fundamental necessity for the direction of society and for ordered social life. The separation of political demands and norms from the law arising in this relation is particularly significant.

The separation of political and legal norms refers not only to the political norms as such but also to the administrative ones as well. It is also necessary to separate the administrative orders issued by governmental leadership from legal rules. An administrative order is generally addressed to concretely defined persons who are to carry out some action or to demonstrate some definite attitude. In contrast, the legal provision is a general regulation expressing some typical attitude, and having universal validity for the whole society, i.e. the conduct of individuals must be in accordance with the legal rule.[15]

So we can state that in modern societies the political and administrative norms as special norm-systems appear in the framework of a regulation system which is influenced and supported by legal and moral norms. At the same time, self-regulatory systems exist in the economic and cultural sphere. The solutions of *self-regulation* of different spheres are significant in their own spheres, but they are regulated by morality and law as well.

A special problem can be posed by the norms of different professions and organizations in economic, political and cultural life. Different organs have their own norms of self-regulation which may interrelate with legal norms.

---

[15] Peschka, A Modern jogfilozófia alapproblémái (The Basic Problems of Modern Legal Philosophy), Budapest 1972, p. 268.

These facts are not expressed in scientific thinking. The political, economic, and cultural norms and rules of professions and organizations are qualified in legal content and character. It is accepted that modern legal progress brings in its train the development of professional or organizational law. On another view, the legal character of professional, technical and organizational norms is denied. This latter opinion has not yet been echoed enough in literature though the exclusion of regulations non-legal in character from the law. The corollary of this is the separate treatment of professional-technical and other norms. The dividing line between law in general and professional political, economic, and cultural norm-systems can be drawn by precise stipulation of their borders on the basis of their own content and peculiarities.

Legal thinking is inclined to include rules concerning organizations in the law. Yet it is impossible to agree with this view. It is true that the growth of legal material related to organizations comprises an exaggerated increase of legal provisions. This results in *over-regulation* rendering legal regulation confused. The legal regulation of the activity of organizations is aimed at the regulation of everyday practice which, by virtue of its very nature, requires frequent changes. In addition, regulations of an organizational character (administration, documentation, procedure, operation, accounting, inventory handling, security, labor protection, etc.) find their way into the law and contradict the traditional features of the law – rationality, formal character, integration into the process of socialization, etc. Furthermore, legal responsibility arising from these statutory provisions is not clearly defined, and even its assertion in the course of legal proceedings is doubtful. As a consequence, organizational statutory provisions are definitely different from legal regulation concerning individuals and the relations between individuals and organizations.

One is justified therefore in concluding that the rules directly ordering the attitudes, rights and obligations of individuals or the relations between individuals and legal entities unquestionably belong to the law, while the norms dealing with the inner activities of organizations recently put into legal form represent a separate variety of norms, because these norms are sui generis – a special system of norms of a non-legal character.

Organizational norms themselves are differentiated according to the structure and the institutional division of society. Separate types of rules can be ascertained in the framework of state: in the parliament, the executive, the organs of self-government, the armed forces, political parties and associations, and economic and cultural organizations. The division and inner character of the organizational norms naturally need clarification based on further research.

3. After we have become aware of some of the practical contradictions of societal regulation, we have to point out that – based on complex social cir-

cumstances – the system of regulation itself becomes more complex. In relation to this, we may ask whether the existing variety of norms is capable of expressing new regulatory requirements. As a characteristic feature of historical progress, it can be pointed out that one or another of the existing kinds of norms will be in tension with new regulatory requirements. The greatest problem is to find where the various types of existing norms must give way to the development of new varieties.

When this general question is analyzed in relation to the law, it is found that the law is flexible. It can expand and adjust to new circumstances. In preceding epochs the law was able to embrace also occupational-technical and organizational norms. It is a fact, however, supported by historic experience, that the law loses its legal character and efficiency if it continues to expand too far. It can be said that, based on quantitative growth, the modern regulatory system has reached a qualitative turning point. The economic-political-cultural-technical and the organizational varieties of norms have become separate and are calling for separation from the law. The division of norms is now making possible first of all the consolidation of the norms of the legal and the non-legal (the political, economic, cultural). Furthermore, true and exact expression of varieties of norms promotes harmony in systems of regulation, and efficiency and sound hierarchy in the normative order.

II. The Concept of Law Redefined

A Definition of Law

By Robert Alexy, Kiel

I. Three Elements

A person who wishes to define or describe the concept of law must deal with three elements: (1) due enactment, (2) social efficacy, and (3) substantial correctness. The vast number of definitions of law proposed in the history of legal philosophy can be explained by two reasons. The first is that the three elements just mentioned, the concepts of due enactment, social efficacy, and substantial correctness, are open to very different interpretations. The second consists in the fact that the three elements, however interpreted, can be weighed against each other in various ways. Only the second point will be discussed here.

The logical space of possible definitions of law can be conceived as a triangle. If we put social efficacy at corner *A*, substantial correctness at corner *B*, and due enactment at corner *C*, we have the following picture:

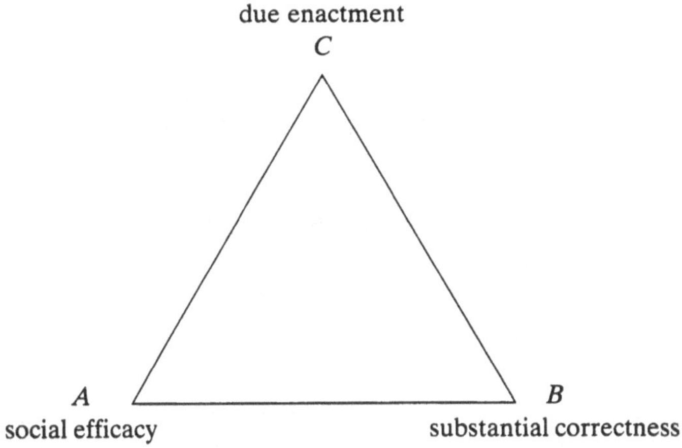

All positivist concepts of law are located on the line between *A* and *C*. The more realistic or sociological they are, the closer they are to *A*; the more juristic or authoritative they are, the closer they are to *C*. In any case, and that is the only point of interest here, as long as a concept of law remains on the line between *A* and *C*, meaning that law is exclusively defined with reference to due enactment and social efficacy, we have a positivist concept of law. If we interpret "substantial correctness" as "moral correctness" this corresponds exactly to the positivist thesis about the separation of law and morals.

The most radical non-positivist conception of law is located in point B. A definition of law that rests there disregards the facts concerning due and authoritative enactment and social efficacy. Point B represents a pure natural law theory which derives all content of law and all its validity from substantial moral, theological, or other justifications. That is not a theory generally of interest to lawyers and it generally is not a theory attractive to reasonable men or women asking what the law of their society is. There is a broad consensus today that the right placement of the definition of law lies somewhere between the line $\overline{AC}$ on the one hand and point B on the other. Regrettably nobody can tell exactly where the magic point is. As the definition of law is not a geometrical matter we cannot find that point by methods of geometry. We have to leave our triangle-picture. But before doing so, one additional insight can be gained. The whole space between A, B, and C belongs to non-positivism. As soon as the smallest step is taken from any point on the line $\overline{AC}$ towards B, elements of moral or substantial correctness are included in the concept of law and that concept turns from a positivist into a non-positivist one. The smallest infusion of morality suffices.

II. Three Levels

The correct "point" we are looking for cannot be determined by any simple formula. A complex theory is needed that takes into account all relevant arguments put forward in the longstanding discussion of the concept of law and results in a definition fixing our point as exactly as possible. I will start at the end of such an enterprise by stating a definition of law. The definition I propose contains three steps and proceeds as follows:

"Law is a norm-system which:

(1) implicates a claim to correctness; and

(2) consists both of the norms making up a by-and-large socially efficacious constitution, except for any norm that is extremely unjust; and consists also of the totality of the norms that are enacted pursuant to such a constitution, being norms that exhibit at least a minimum of social efficacy or the chance of being socially efficacious, and that are not extremely unjust; and to which

(3) there belong those principles and other normative arguments on which the procedure of applying law is founded and/or has to be founded in order to satisfy the claim to correctness."[1]

---

[1] R. Alexy, Begriff und Geltung des Rechts, Freiburg/München 1992, p. 201; cf. also R. Dreier, Some Remarks on the Concept of Law, in this volume.

The first step of this definition corresponds to what I propose to call the argument of correctness, the second to the argument of injustice, and the third to the argument of principle. To defend my definition means to reveal those arguments.

III. Five Distinctions

The argument about what law is has been going on for more than two thousand years and its success, measured by an achievement of consensus, has been limited. Perhaps, one can break the impasse by making distinctions which shed a new light on old arguments and permit new ones. My argument will rest on five related distinctions. They cannot be fully presented in this article but I will mention them.

The first distinction is between a concept of law that *includes the concept of validity* and one that does *not.* The inclusion of validity means the inclusion of the institutional and social context of law. The exclusion of validity leads to a concept of law comprising only norms as semantic entities. The latter considerably facilitates defending positivism.

The second distinction is between the legal system as a *system of norms* and the legal system as a *system of procedures.* It is easier to argue for non-positivism when the process of creation, interpretation, and application is included in the concept of law.

The third distinction is, perhaps, the most important one. It is the distinction between the *observer's* and the *participant's* perspective, which is close to Hart's distinction between an internal and an external point of view.[2] The participant's perspective is occupied by someone who, within a legal system, produces arguments about what the legal system commands, prohibits, or permits, and about what powers it confers. The observer's perspective, on the other hand, does not ask what the *correct* decision in a certain legal system is, but how a decision has been, is, and will be *actually* made in a certain legal system. The observer's perspective provides the best environment to support positivism, the participant's for non-positivism.

The fourth distinction is about two different kinds of connections between law and morality: *classifying* and *qualifying* ones. One talks about a classifying connection if one claims that norms or systems of norms, which do not fulfill a certain moral criterion, lack the quality of legal norms or of legal systems, that is they are not classified as law or valid law. A qualifying connection, on the other hand, is at issue if someone claims that a norm or a system of norms, which does not fulfill a certain moral criterion, may be regarded as a legal norm or a legal system, but is nevertheless a legally faulty legal norm or a leg-

[2] H. L. A. Hart, The Concept of Law, Oxford 1961, pp. 86f.

ally faulty legal system. It is decisive that the claimed fault is legal, not merely moral. This distinction facilitates the task of non-positivism considerably. It is much easier to fill the space of our triangle with a qualifying connection than with a classifying one. I will try to combine a complete qualifying connection with a rather limited classifying one.

The fifth distinction is between *analytical* and *normative* arguments. An analytical argument is one which explains the inclusion of moral elements in the concept of law as conceptually or linguistically necessary, impossible, or merely possible. On the other hand, the theses of connection or separation are based on normative arguments if one argues that the inclusion or exclusion of moral elements is necessary in order to fulfill a certain norm or to reach a certain aim. I will try to explain with analytical arguments that there is a qualifying connection. A classifying one can only be substantiated if normative arguments are added.

IV. The Argument of Correctness

The argument of correctness provides that individual legal norms and decisions as well as legal systems as a whole necessarily raise a claim to correctness (Anspruch auf Richtigkeit). This claim is not exclusively legal. It is rooted in all kinds of reasoning and as far as reasoning, that is asserting, arguing, and asking, are necessary components of the human form of life, it is founded in human nature.

The claim to correctness raised in law is, therefore, a special case of a much more general claim to correctness. The fact that it is always implicit in law can be shown by an analysis of legal propositions which explicitly deny it.[3] It would be close to a paradox if a constitutional convention approved the following sentence as first article of a constitution:

(1) *X* is a sovereign, federal, and unjust republic.

A similar fault would be commited by a judge announcing the following verdict:

(2) The defendant is – wrongly, because the valid law was interpreted incorrectly – sentenced to life imprisonment.

The bizarre character of both statements is a result of a contradiction between what is said and what is necessarily implied by acts like writing a constitution or making a legal decision. In both statements the claim to correctness is implicitly raised and explicitly denied.

---

[3] For a similar argument, cf. N. MacCormick, Law, Morality and Positivism, in: Neil MacCormick/Ota Weinberger, An Institutional Theory of Law, Dordrecht/Boston/Lancaster/Tokyo 1986, p. 141.

The claim to correctness has a classifying character only with respect to legal systems as a whole. Norm systems which do not explicitly or implicitly raise this claim are not legal systems.[4] Apart from this the claim to correctness plays only a qualifying role. Legal systems which make this claim but do not fulfill it do not lose their legal character or validity just for this reason. But they are legally faulty systems. The latter applies correspondingly for individual norms if they do not raise or fulfill the claim to correctness.

The argument of correctness considered so far has three important functions. First, in its classifying role, it delimits legal systems from systems of brute power. Second, in its qualifying role, it leads to an understanding of what it means to participate in a legal system. Third, both in its classifying and its qualifying role, it provides the basis for the arguments of injustice and of principle necessary to substantiate the second and the third part of my definition.

V. The Argument of Injustice

The argument of injustice says that duly enacted and socially efficacious individual norms lose their legal character and by this their validity once the threshold of extreme injustice is crossed; in short:

Extreme injustice is no law.

This can be traced back to the famous formula proposed in 1946 by Gustav Radbruch,[5] the Radbruch-formula, which has been applied by German courts after 1945 in decisions dealing with Nazi-law[6] and again after 1989 in decisions concerning DDR-law, especially in the decision of November 3, 1992 by the German Federal Court of Justice involving a wall-shooting.[7]

The Radbruch-formula does not totally conflate law and justice. According to it, a law can be even severely unjust and yet remains law as long as it is not extremely unjust. This formula demands much less than most declarations of human rights, for not every violation of a human right is extremely unjust. If we use our triangle-picture we can say that with Radbruch we proceed only a

---

[4] Cf. R. Alexy (fn. 1), pp. 57ff.

[5] Cf. G. Radbruch, Gesetzliches Unrecht und übergesetzliches Recht (1946), in: Gustav Radbruch. Gesamtausgabe, ed. by A. Kaufmann, vol. 3, Heidelberg 1990, p. 89.

[6] Cf. BVerfGE 3, 58 (119); 3, 225 (233); 6, 132 (198); 6, 309 (332); 6, 389 (414f.); 23, 98 (106); 54, 53 (67f.); BGHZ 3, 94 (107); 23, 175 (181); BGHSt 2, 173 (177); 2, 234 (238f.); 3, 357 (362f.).

[7] BGH, NJW 1993, 141 (144ff.); cf. R. Dreier, Gesetzliches Unrecht im SED-Staat? Am Beispiel des DDR-Grenzgesetzes, in: Strafgerechtigkeit, Festschrift for Arthur Kaufmann, ed. by F. Haft/W. Hassemer/U. Neumann/W. Schild/U. Schroth, Heidelberg 1993, pp. 57ff.; R. Alexy, Mauerschützen. Zum Verhältnis von Recht, Moral und Strafbarkeit, Hamburg 1993.

little bit from the line $\overline{AC}$ towards B. The rest of the space of ABC remains, as far as classification is concerned, strictly positivist in result. This is true only from a participant's point of view. If we take up the role of an observer even extreme injustice, if duly enacted and socially efficacious should be classified as law.[8]

The Radbruch-formula and by it the second part of my definition can only be justified by normative or practical arguments. The ambiguity and vagueness of the term "law" exclude settling the argument about legal positivism by means of conceptual analysis. Elsewhere I have tried to distinguish eight arguments for and against the Radbruch-formula: the arguments from language, clarity, efficiency, certainty, relativism, democracy, superfluousness, and candour.[9] I must confine myself here to four points: First, if radical relativism or scepticism were right, my argument would collapse. I assume that judgments concerning extreme injustice, like genocide or ethnic cleansing by murder of men and rape of women, can be rationally justified and are objective in character. Second, the Radbruch-formula involves only small losses of clarity, legal certainty, and democracy. These values are also infringed by any everyday constitutional adjudication. Naturally, there are borderline-cases. The wall-shooting case, mentioned above, is an example. But the existence of borderline-cases is, as such, not a refutation of the distinction. Third, many authors maintain that a non-positivist concept of law has no desirable effects. I think, the opposite is true. A predominant or general acceptance of a non-positivist concept of law increases the risk for people who, in a tyranny, commit legally sanctioned injustice or take part in it. This could lead to a situation in which people who do not have compunctions against taking part in injustice, or would even enjoy doing so, could be motivated to avoid taking part in injustice or at least to soften it. This is, perhaps, one of the strongest arguments for the Radbruch-formula. The strongest argument against it is now to be mentioned as point four. It is the argument from candour. Does the application of the Radbruch-formula entail hidden retroactivity and by this breach of *nulla poena sine lege?* I think that is not the case because our formula can only act in a negative way. It cannot sustain punishment like, for instance, that of murder. It can only overthrow specific provisions of a tyranny which led during its existence to non-punishment. If those provisions are declared void from the beginning there is a certain restriction of the *lex scripta*-rule, but it is, due to its negative character, a limited one. And because tyrannic provisions permitting extreme injustice can never become law there is no violation of the requirement of *ius praevium.*[10]

---

[8] Cf. R. Alexy (fn. 1), pp. 53ff.

[9] Id. (fn. 1), pp. 72ff.

[10] Id. (fn. 7), pp. 30ff.

VI. The Argument of Principle

The argument of injustice is concerned with an exceptional situation of the legal system: that of extremely unjust law. The argument of principle, justifying the third part of my definition, refers to the legal system in its everyday application. It begins with the open texture of law manifesting itself in vagueness, contradictions and collisions, gaps and, sometimes, even by decisions contrary to the wording of a statute. The argument of principle says that all those principles and other normative arguments involved in the decision of a hard case in order to satisfy the claim to correctness belong to law. This leads to a necessary incorporation of moral principles and moral argumentation in law.[11]

The argument of principle refers to the participant's perspective and the procedural aspect of law. The necessary connection between law and morality maintained by it is only of a qualifying character. If we call the classifying connection "hard" and the qualifying "soft" we can say that the whole space of our triangle is filled by the soft, but only a rather small area by the hard connection between law and morality. This cannot be different in a social world which is constituted by a tension between the real – in our case due enactment and social efficacy – and the ideal – in our case substantial correctness.

---

[11] Id. (fn. 1), pp. 117ff.

Some Remarks on the Concept of Law[1]

By Ralf Dreier, Göttingen

Virtually all the problems of the philosophy of law and of legal theory can be found in the debate on the concept of law. The following remarks consider some aspects of these problems. I begin with a short look at Kant's exposition and discussion of the concept of law. In the second section I analyse the main structural elements of (the) positivistic concept(s) of law. The third section covers the two main objections to (the) positivistic concept(s) of law raised in

[1] In 1984 Robert S. Summers kindly invited me to give some lectures at the Cornell Law School in Ithaca. One of the lectures dealt with the concept of law. Professor Summers proposed publishing this lecture in the American Journal of Jurisprudence. The editor, Professor Charles E. Rice, agreed but asked me to shorten the manuscript. For several reasons I hesitated to do so, and so the text remained unpublished. Eight years later, when Professor Krawietz (in November 1992) invited me to contribute to the present volume, I reread the manuscript and found that, in a revised and shortened version, it would still be worth publishing, for I had not substantially changed my view of the concept of law in the meantime. Moreover, I thought this volume would be a fine place to dedicate the article to Professor Summers, not least of all because it reflects rewarding discussions I had with him during several months in 1982 and 1984 when he was my guest in Göttingen. At any rate, through this publication I wish to express my deep gratitude to Robert S. Summers over the past ten years. – In German, the core ideas of this paper have been published in: R. Dreier, Der Begriff des Rechts, in: Neue Juristische Wochenschrift (NJW) 1986, p. 890 - 896 (reprinted in: R. Dreier, Recht – Staat – Vernunft, Frankfurt/M. 1991, chap. 4), and in a booklet: Rechtsbegriff und Rechtsidee. Kants Rechtsbegriff und seine Bedeutung für die gegenwärtige Diskussion, Frankfurt/M. 1986 (Würzburger Vorträge zur Rechtsphilosophie, Rechtstheorie und Rechtssoziologie, Heft 5). Both articles have prompted some remarkable critiques, e.g.: Norbert Hoerster, Zur Verteidigung des Rechtspositivismus, NJW 1986, p. 2480 - 2482, and W. Krawietz, Neues Naturrecht oder Rechtspositivismus? Eine kritische Auseinandersetzung mit dem Begriff des Rechts bei Ralf Dreier und Norbert Hoerster, in: RECHTSTHEORIE 18 (1987) p. 209 - 254. A reply to my critics may be found in R. Dreier: Neues Naturrecht oder Rechtspositivismus? In Erwiderung auf Werner Krawietz, in: RECHTSTHEORIE 18 (1987), p. 368 - 385; Zur gegenwärtigen Diskussion des Verhältnisses von Recht und Moral in der Bundesrepublik Deutschland, in: R. Alexy / R. Dreier / U. Neumann (ed.), Rechts- und Sozialphilosophie in Deutschland heute, Stuttgart 1991 (ARSP Beiheft 44), p. 55 - 67, and in additional remarks to chap. 4 of "Recht – Staat – Vernunft", pp. 117 et seq. The debate continued at a conference of the German section of the IVR 1988 in Göttingen, documented in: R. Dreier (ed.), Rechtspositivismus und Wertbezug des Rechts, Stuttgart 1990 (ARSP Beiheft 37). Robert Alexy elaborated the arguments against (the) positivistic concept(s) of law in his book: Begriff und Geltung des Rechts, Freiburg/München 1992, which originated in a common research project of both of us. – The following text is a shortened and revised version of my Ithaca Lecture 1984. I am grateful to Dr. Delf Buchwald for his assistance in revising the text. The footnotes are limited to a minimum. Occasionally I refer to the recent debate.

recent discussions. The concluding section summarizes the results of these reflections.

I.

"What is law?" This question, Kant writes,

> "might confuse the legal scholar, who does not want to lapse into tautology or, instead of offering a general solution, refer to what the statutes of a given place at any one time intend, just as the hallowed challenge 'What is truth?' might confuse the logician. The question 'what is law ?' *(quid sit iuris),* i.e. what the statutes of a given place at any one time say or said, is a question he might be able to answer, but whether that which the statutes intend is right, and the general criterion with which one might identify law as well as non-law *(iustum et iniustum)*, will remain hidden from him if he does not, for a time, abandon those empirical principles and search for the sources of these judgements in pure reason ... in order to establish the foundation for a possible positive legislation. A purely empirical theory of law (like the wooden head in Phaedrus's fable) is a head that may be handsome – if only it also had a brain!"[2]

It is worthwhile to take a closer look at this approach to the question. "The law", says Kant, is determined by the positive law statutes, i.e. according to the context, statutes founded on publicly known laws, especially state legislation. But the fact that a statute has been laid down in a legislative procedure is not in itself enough to determine whether it is "law" (in the sense of "right law"), i.e., just or reasonable. To determine its justness or reasonableness, one needs a general criterion "by which one can identify law as well as non-law *(iustum et iniustum)*". This criterion cannot be found empirically, i.e., by poring over statute books. It can only be found in "reason". Kant, without any hesitation, thereby equates "law" and "non-law" with "justice" and "injustice", respectively. Positive statutes are worthy of the name "law" only if they are just or, as we are impelled to add by way of interpretation, if they have a relation to justice founded on reason.

Does this mean that unjust statutes, because they are not "law", are not binding? This is far from being Kant's opinion. He denies any right of resistance (or, in modern terminology, of civil disobedience). He emphasizes that it is the citizen's duty to adhere to the statute even if it is unjust or unreasonable, and that it is the judge's duty to apply it. "The origins of sovereign power", says Kant, "are inscrutable, i.e. the subject should not actively pry into these origins ...".[3] And he continues:

---

[2] Kant, Metaphysik der Sitten, Rechtslehre, Einleitung § B, Werke, ed. Weischedel, Darmstadt 1956 sq., vol. IV, p. 336 = ed. Königlich Preußische Akademie der Wissenschaften, Berlin 1902 et seq. (AA), vol. VI, pp. 229/30. – All translations into English are by the present author.

[3] Kant, op.cit., § 49, Allgemeine Anmerkung A, Werke, vol. IV, p. 287 = AA vol. VI, p. 318.

"If the learned lawyer, as he ought to, proceeds as a government official does, he does not look for the laws guaranteeing 'Mine' and 'Thine' in his own reason, but in the book of statutes which has been sanctioned by the highest order and has been made publicly known. One cannot in fairness demand of him that he prove the truth and rightness of the statutes and defend them against the objections raised by reason. The statutes declare things to be right – to question the rightness of the statutes themselves must be bluntly rejected by the lawyer as absurd. It would be ridiculous to deny the duty to follow the highest order's publicly declared will, on the grounds that this is supposedly not in accord with reason. It is precisely here that the government's esteem lies – in that it does not allow its subjects the freedom to judge what is just and what unjust, but judges this itself by means of the statutes passed within its law making power".[4]

What, then, is the general criterion by which we can distinguish law from non-law? Must it be derived from reason or from the highest legislative power? And if there are, as Kant appears to assume, two kinds of law, on the one hand natural law, i.e. law based on reason, and on the other hand, the positive law, how do they relate to one another? And why does he call an empirical theory of law, i.e. an exclusively positivistic theory, "brainless", if, in his opinion, the lawyer is practically compelled to reject any question as to the rightness or the justice of the state's laws on grounds of unreasonableness?

Kant's answers to these questions are basically simple and clear, and they are still relevant today, despite some incongruities brought about by the passage of time. Kant's concept of law is, in general, not an empirical but a normative one, more precisely: a concept of law based on reason. It names the criteria which, though originally confused, form the basis of any cognition which is directed to identifying a norm as a legal norm – a legal norm being one which reason obligates us to adhere to. To become aware of these criteria and to explain them is the task of legal philosophy. The definition of law in this sense, according to Kant, reads as follows:

Law is "the totality of conditions under which the will of one individual is compatible with the will of others by a general law of freedom".[5]

This definition[6] comprises natural law as well as positive law. It is the expression of a general principle of law which is, in turn, derived from the

---

[4] Kant, Streit der Fakultäten, Werke, vol. IV, p. 287 = AA vol. VII, pp. 24/5.

[5] Kant, Rechtslehre, Einleitung § B, Werke, vol. IV, p. 337 = AA vol. VI., p. 230.

[6] It must be noted that Kant himself quite clearly saw the problems of adequately defining the concept of law (or, for that matter, of any "concept given a priori, e.g., substance, cause, law, equity, etc."). On Kant's discussion and on some general problems connected with defining fundamental concepts within and by means of a natural language, in contradistinction to definitions within the framework of a formal semantics, see D. Buchwald, Der Begriff der rationalen juristischen Begründung, Baden-Baden 1990, pp. 263 et seq. – Buchwald sees three main problems: (1) avoidance of circular definitions; (2) avoidance of mere nominal or stipulative definitions; and (3) development of definitions that contain necessary and sufficient conditions for the recognition of something as falling under the concept defined.

highest principle of practical reason in general, the categorical imperative. The categorical imperative says, in its basic formula:

> "Act so that the maxim of your will may always serve also as a principle of general legislation".[7]

The general principle of law says:

> "Act externally so that the free exercise of your own will is compatible with the freedom of everyone in accordance with a general law".[8]

With the help of a growing number of general anthropological and sociological premises, Kant deduces his system of natural law from this principle.[9] And this system of natural law includes a norm which, as the fundamental norm of positive law, demands that positive law statutes, under the condition of the existence of state-organized (constitutional) legislation, take priority over the natural law. Accordingly, it is imperative to comply with positive laws, even if they are unjust or unreasonable. The justification of this requirement is to be found in the rational principle of legal certainty and in the fact that positive laws, too, formulate conditions under which the will of one individual is compatible with the will of others by means of a general law of freedom.

Natural law, then, has a double function wherever there is state legislation. It provides a justification for the legal and moral validity of the positive laws, and it specifies the rational requirements that the legislature is obligated to follow in making positive law. Both tasks are integral parts of the *philosophical* theory of law. A *purely juridical* theory of law may limit itself to the study of positive law. This theory is "brainless" because and insofar as it does not consider the necessary relationship between law and reason. This is not a weakness, though, provided there is a philosophical theory of law to do its thinking for it.

Of course, one may ask whether Kant's theory of positive law can be classified as a positivistic one. That depends on the definition of legal positivism. The answer is "no" if we define it, as it is usual and useful, by means of the thesis that there is no necessary relationship between law and morals – "law" meaning positive law, and "morals" meaning that set of norms traditionally called "natural law", "law of reason" or "justice". For Kant's theory implies such a relationship. This relationship is even stronger if we interpret Kant's theory as one which justifies the priority of positive law over natural law only if the state, in its function as legislator of positive law, fulfils certain minimal requirements of the rule of law. There are, I think, good reasons for such an

---

[7] Kant, Kritik der praktischen Vernunft, I 1 § 7, Werke, vol. IV, p. 140 = AA vol. V, p. 30 in fine.

[8] Kant, Rechtslehre, Einleitung § C, Werke, vol. IV, p. 338 = AA vol. VI, p. 231.

[9] Compare R. Dreier, Recht – Moral – Ideologie, Frankfurt/M. 1981, chap. 10 (Zur Einheit der praktischen Philosophie Kants), esp. pp. 289 et seq.

interpretation because Kant was one of the founders of the theory of the *Rechtsstaat,* i.e. of a constitutional state. The natural law thesis according to which positive law takes priority over natural law has to be enriched, then, by ethical requirements derived from the rule of law.

II.

To put it figuratively the positivist thesis of the separation of law and morals cuts off the umbilical cord between reason and positive law. After this intervention, the positivist is left with two sets of elements with which to define the concept of law: elements of authoritativeness and elements of the effectiveness of a norm or a system of norms. In consequence, one can distinguish two main streams of positivistic definitions of law: those based on authoritativeness and thoses based on effectiveness. The classical example of an authoritativeness-oriented definition stems from John Austin, who regards law as the sum of the commands of a sovereign supported by sanctions.[10] Classical examples of effectiveness-oriented definitions are Holmes's ("The prophecies of what the courts will do in fact, and nothing more pretentious, are what I mean by the law")[11] and Max Weber's ("an order will be called *law* if it is externally guaranteed by the probability that coercion (physical or psychological) to bring about conformity or avenge violation, will be applied by a *staff* of people holding themselves specifically ready for that purpose").[12]

There is a great variety of positivistic definitions of law. This is so because their two main characteristics – authoritativeness and effectiveness – can be defined and combined in different ways.[13] The concept of authoritativeness requires the distinction between norms of general conduct, norms laid down by an authority and norms which regulate the procedure of creating norms. The concept of effectiveness can be defined in terms of regular compliance with a norm or by the fact that non-compliance is punished with sanctions. And both compliance with a norm and punishment in case of non-compliance can be characterized by an external and by an internal aspect of behaviour. The external aspect relates to observable behaviour, the internal aspect relates to the motivation which determines the behaviour. A combination of authoritativeness and effectiveness would, for example, be possible by defining law as the sum of all norms which have been laid down in accordance with the constitution of a legal system, and which are, on the whole, socially effec-

---

10 Cf. J. Austin, Lectures on Jurisprudence (1861), vol. I, 5th ed., London 1885, pp. 88 et seq.

11 O. W. Holmes, Collected Legal Papers, New York 1920, p. 167.

12 M. Weber, Wirtschaft und Gesellschaft, ed. J. Winckelmann, Köln/Berlin 1964, p. 24.

13 For the following I generally refer to H. Kelsen, Reine Rechtslehre, 2nd ed., Wien 1960, and H. L. A. Hart, The Concept of Law, Oxford 1961.

tive. Furthermore, the question "what is law?" can be asked from different perspectives, e.g., on the one hand, from an onlooker's perspective (or external point of view) and, on the other hand, from a participant's perspective (or internal point of view). Sociologists and ethnologists usually scrutinize legal systems from an onlooker's perspective, whereas citizens, officials and judges normally look at the law of their system from a participant's perspective.

These remarks may suffice to make clear why legal positivists have hitherto failed, even among themselves, to come up with a generally accepted definition of law. Nevertheless, the manifold positivistic analyses of the concept of law, whether from a sociological or from a legal point of view, have introduced many insights of lasting import into this field of study.

The difference between legal and sociological versions of positivist definitions of law can be said to be essentially based on the difference between the onlooker's and the participant's perspective. Of course, this is a simplification, for a specific kind of onlooker's perspective is also characteristic of certain legal occupations. This is especially so in the case of the attorney who, a reflection of his professional viewpoint, looks at the law by asking how the courts are likely to decide a case. Therefore, juristic definitions of law, which define the law by predicting what the courts will do in fact, are typical attorney-oriented definitions.

However, the "classical" or prototypical participant's perspective in the field of law is the perspective of the judge. The question "what is law?" is, for him, less a question of how he has decided in the past or how he will probably decide in the future, but one as to how he *ought to decide* the present case. This perspective forms, indeed, the basis for the great majority of legal analyses and definitions of the concept of law.

Judge-oriented versions of the concept of law are especially common in analytic theories. Kelsen's and Hart's theories are representative examples. Both combine the elements of authoritativeness and of effectiveness and both share similar basic tenets. Law is, according to Kelsen, a "normative order of human behaviour supported by sanctions", whose normativity is founded on a presupposed basic norm, which says:

> "One ought to obey a constitution which actually exists and is, on the whole, effective, and the norms which are laid down according to the constitution, and are, on the whole, effective".[14]

Hart, who avoids a definitional formula, characterizes developed legal systems as a

> "combination of primary rules of obligation with secondary rules of recognition, change and adjudication".[15]

---

[14] Kelsen, op. cit., pp. 45 et seq., 219.
[15] Hart, op. cit., p. 65.

Hart's rule of recognition is comparable in its function to Kelsen's basic norm. However, it is not, in contradistinction to Kelsen's basic norm, either a transcendental or fictional condition for the cognition or the legal validity of norms, but a socially effective rule for the identification of valid law by virtue of its acceptance.

In what follows I refer to that positivistic concept of law which has found its highest development in the studies of Kelsen and Hart.

III.

In the contemporary debate, two main objections against the positivistic concept of law are discussed: the argument from injustice (or from non-law) and the argument from principles.

1. The *argument from injustice* was provoked by the perversion of law in totalitarian dictatorships. It says that there are norms and systems of norms which are unjust to such a degree that their legal validity and/or legal character has to be denied. It is, however, neither always clear whether the argument refers to the concept or to the validity of law nor how both of these relate to one another. It is, I think, enough to interpret the argument as saying that legal validity is an element of the concept of positive law and that, therefore, propositions about validity imply propositions about the concept of law. Substantively, the argument from injustice appears in two versions. The first refers to single norms, the second to systems of norms.

a) The classical formulation of the first version stems from Gustav Radbruch.[16] The formula suggested by him reads as follows:

> "The conflict between justice and legal certainty should be resolved in such a way that the positive law, supported by legislation and sanctions, takes priority, even when it is substantively unjust or inexpedient, except when the discrepancy between positive law and justice is so unacceptable that the positive law, as 'unjust law', has to yield to justice".[17]

The criteria of justice on which the interpretation of the formula is based are, in Radbruch's theory, taken largely, from the tradition of human rights.

The German Federal Court of Justice and the German Federal Constitutional Court have adopted this formula in a number of leading cases.[18] Perhaps

---

16 See G. Radbruch, Gesetzliches Unrecht und übergesetzliches Recht (1946), reprinted in: G. Radbruch, Rechtsphilosophie, 8th ed., Stuttgart 1973, pp. 339 - 350.

17 Op. cit., p. 345.

18 See BGHZ 3, 94 (107); 23, 175 (181); BGHSt 2, 173 (177); 2, 234 (238); 3, 357 (362 et seq.); BVerfGE 3, 58 (119); 3, 225 (233); 6, 132 (198); 6, 389 (414 et seq.); 23, 98 (106); 54, 553 (67 et seq.). Compare B. Schumacher, Rezeption und Kritik der Radbruchschen Formel, Diss. Göttingen 1985. – Concerning statutory non-law in the German Democratic Republic see BGH NJW 1993, pp. 141 et seq.

the most important of these is a decision of the Federal Constitutional Court from February 14, 1968.[19] The question at issue in this decision was whether the German or the Dutch law of inheritance was applicable in the case of a German Jew who had emigrated to the Netherlands in 1938 and was later declared deceased. The answer to this question turned on the validity of the 11th decree of the German *Reichsbürgergesetz* from 1941, which deprived Jews who had emigrated of their German citizenship for racial reasons. The court's own headnotes 1 - 3 of the decision are:

> "1. The validity of National Socialist statutes can be denied if they so evidently contradict fundamental principles of justice that a judge who applied them or recognized their legal consequences, would create non-law instead of law.
>
> 2. In the Eleventh Decree of the *Reichsbürgergesetz* from November 25, 1941 (RGBl I S. 772), the conflict with justice reached such an unacceptable degree that it must be regarded as void from the beginning.
>
> 3. Non-law laid down by legislation, which obviously conflicts with constitutive basic principles of law, does not become law in that it is applied or followed."

In the international debate on legal theory the Radbruch formula has prompted a great deal of discussion. In particular, H. L. A. Hart has rejected it emphatically, arguing that it would confuse the distinction between moral duty and legal duty.[20] Unacceptable consequences of morally objectionable laws are, according to Hart, not to be removed by the judge's modifying the concept of law in an ethical sense, but by the legislator's making retroactive laws. This alternative, indeed, formulates a crucial problem, namely, who should correct the perversions of law in a totalitarian dictatorship after the collapse of such a system. Of course, this is primarily the duty of the legislator. But the question remains what a judge should do if the legislator, for whatever reasons, fails to carry out his duty. The decisions of German courts mentioned above show that it leads to unacceptable results if judges, in such cases, insist on the positivist separation thesis. The legal theorist should bear this point in mind, and he should take care to see that discussion on the concept of law does not lead to results which are at the expense of the citizens. In my view, the Radbruch formula, despite its vagueness, has proved to be a practicable as well as an adequate modification of a judge-oriented concept of law.

b) A second version of the argument from injustice has been presented by Martin Kriele.[21] It refers not to single norms, but to state-organized systems of

---

[19] BVerfGE 23, 98.

[20] See H. L. A. Hart, Positivism and the Separation of Law and Morals, 71 Harvard Law Review (1958), pp. 593 - 629. On the debate on this point between Hart and Fuller see R. S. Summers, Lon L. Fuller, Stanford/Cal. 1984, pp. 33ff., 44ff. Compare R. S. Summers, Professor Lon L. Fuller's Jurisprudence and America's Dominant Philosophy of Law, in: R. S. Summers, Essays on the Nature of Law and Legal Reasoning, Berlin 1992, pp. 77 et seq.

[21] M. Kriele, Recht und praktische Vernunft, Göttingen, 1979, chap. 5.

norms. Kriele's thesis is that there is a necessary relationship between legal duty and moral duty, i.e. there is a duty to obey the law of a legal system, "provided that the system 'on the whole' is ethically justified".[22] This condition is, according to Kriele, fulfilled if the law is part of a system which is based on the principles of the democratic and constitutional state. The main practical consequence of his formula is the possibility of justifying acts of resistance in a totalitarian system, after its collapse not only morally but also legally, i.e., judicially.

In this respect, the Kriele formula serves essentially the same functions as the Radbruch formula, especially as it is a further tenet of Kriele's theory that not all norms in totalitarian dictatorships are invalid, but that there is, in those systems, a "direct legal legitimization" for laws and institutions which are not specific to any such system and which are, taken by themselves, ethically justified or justifiable. Furthermore, the Kriele formula may have practical consequences for the problem of recognition of states or governments in international law, i.e., the question under which conditions a state or government should be recognized by other states as being a legal subject in international law. The prevailing opinion on this question considers the principle of effectiveness to be decisive. However, it is contested whether and in what sense the principle of effectiveness has to be modified by elements of the principle of legitimacy. The Kriele formula, in terms of a theory of the concept of law, opts for such a modification. I will set the point aside in this article.

2. The *argument from principles* says that all developed legal systems include legal principles which, by virtue of their structure or the nature of their validity, go beyond the positivistic concept of law. The form in which it is currently most often discussed was first worked out by Ronald Dworkin.[23] In Germany, Robert Alexy has taken up Dworkin's theory, partially, I think, improving and partially modifying it.[24] The foundation for the principles argument is the distinction between rules and principles. This distinction is expressible in terms of a theory of structure as well as in terms of a theory of legal validity. Consequently, there are two versions of the principles argument: a structure-oriented one and a validity-oriented one.

a) With respect to the *structural* difference between rules and principles, I refer mainly to Alexy's theory. Alexy defines principles as optimizing precepts, which can be fulfilled to varying degrees, and rules as stipulations, which are either fulfilled or not. In other words: Principles are norms which

---

[22] Op. cit., p. 117.

[23] R. Dworkin, Taking Rights Seriously, 2nd ed., London 1978.

[24] R. Alexy, Theorie der Grundrechte, Baden-Baden 1985, chap. 3 and 'Zum Begriff des Rechtsprinzips', in: RECHTSTHEORIE, Beiheft 1, Berlin 1979, pp. 59 - 87. See also J.-R. Sieckmann, Regelmodelle und Prinzipienmodelle des Rechtssystems, Baden-Baden 1990.

state the duty to pursue certain aims or goals; rules are norms which state operative facts and legal consequences, the latter of which being applicable whenever their operative facts exist. In this sense all norms are either rules or principles.

But the same norm-sentence can be interpreted as a rule and as a principle. An example is Art. 5 par. 3 sentence 1 of the German Constitution (*Grundgesetz,* Basic Law), which reads:

"Art and science, research and teaching are free".

The normative content of this sentence can, with respect to science, be expressed in the formula:

"Science ought to be free".

If one interprets this formula as expressing a principle, one takes the norm to state:

"The state is obligated to facilitate the greatest possible freedom of the sciences."

If one interprets the formula as expressing a rule, one arrives at the norm that, e.g.:

"The state is forbidden to interfere in certain activities which qualify as scientific activities."

The structural difference between rules and principles is especially manifest in solving conflicts of norms. These are either conflicts between rules or collisions of principles. Whereas conflicts between rules can only be resolved if one of the rules is invalidated or altered by adding an exception-clause, a collision of different principles has to be resolved by weighing them and by then determining which of them takes priority in an individual case or in special types of cases. The conditions under which one principle, for example, that of the greatest possible protection of privacy, takes priority over another, for example, that of the greatest possible freedom of the press, suffice to form a rule which expresses the legal consequences of the more weighty principle, for example, the prohibition of certain breaches of privacy by the press. Thus, colliding principles are transformed into rules, and in this respect principles include a methodological dimension.

Up to now I have mentioned sentences conferring basic rights as examples of normative sentences which can be interpreted as principles. Further examples are the *Staatszielbestimmungen,* e.g., in German constitutional law, the principles of the rule of law, of democracy and of the welfare state. They are principles insofar as they obligate the state to optimize constitutionality, democracy and the general welfare of the state. If one takes these principles together with the principles of human rights, especially those of human dignity, of freedom and of equality, one can say that the main principles of modern ethics and political morality are incorporated in the German Constitution as principles of positive law.

It is obvious that these principles exhibit an opening of law towards morals. According to Kelsen and Hart, this opening is to be interpreted as giving the judge the power to fill in the positive law with moral and political principles which, however, do not form a part of the positive law. The corresponding positivist thesis had already been formulated by John Austin: "So far as the judge's arbitrium extends, there is no law at all".[25] The argument from principles, to the contrary, says that even where the positive law is open-textured and vague a judge is not free to excercise his discretion but is legally bound by legally valid principles, directing the evaluation and weighing of individual and collective goods or interests.

An instructive example for the conceptual implications of the principles-theory (or "value-theory", as it is often called with respect to the adjudication of the German Federal Constitutional Court) is the decision of the Federal Constitutional Court from February 14, 1973, in which the question was discussed whether the judge has power to decide *contra legem*. The central passage of the opinion reads:

> "The law is not identical with the whole of the written laws. Over and above the positive-law enactments of the state there can be '*ein Mehr an Recht*' (a surplus of law) which has its source in the constitutional legal order as a holistic unity of meaning and which can operate as a corrective to the written law; to find it and to deliver it in decisions is the task of adjudication. Under the Basic Law, the judge is not constrained to apply legislative directives to a case within the bounds of possible literal meaning. Such a conception would assume that the positive legal order of the state does not, in principle, contain any gaps, a state of affairs that is acceptable as a general postulate of legal certainty but unattainable in practice. Judicial activity does not consist merely in recognizing and pronouncing on the legislator's decisions. The task of adjudication can demand, in particular, that evaluative assumptions which in the constitutional legal order are immanent, but are not or are only incompletely expressed in the texts of the written laws, be elucidated and realized in decisions by an act of evaluative cognition which, admittedly, is not lacking in volitional elements. The judge must thereby avoid arbitrariness; his decision must be based on rational argumentation. It must be understood that the written law does not by itself serve the function of solving a legal problem in a just way. The judicial decision then fills this gap according to the standards of practical reason and the 'community's well-based general ideas of justice'".[26]

The passage raises a number of questions which are of great interest for the theorist of law. Here I refer only to its implications for the concept of law. They lie in the thesis that the legally valid law has an "overriding capacity" which is based on the constitutional legal order as a whole and which consists

[25] J. Austin, op.cit., vol.II, p.664.

[26] BVerfGE 34, 269 (287).

in the positive law's directedness towards justice and reason. When interpreting and applying the positive law the judge has to take this directedness into consideration. Therefore, the office of the judge, as the court says in another decision, "is, in a certain way, based on the idea of law itself".[27]

Robert Alexy has elaborated the principles argument in three steps, as follows:

(1) the *incorporation-thesis,* stating that every legal system which is at least minimally developed, necessarily contains principles in the defined sense;

(2) the *morality-thesis,* stating that the necessary existence of principles in legal systems leads to a necessary connection between law and a given morality;

(3) the *coherence-thesis,* stating that it is legally obligatory in legal systems to develop a system which contains all principles which must be taken into account, and which allows that they be weighed appropriately.

Together with other elements of his theory of law – the claim-thesis which says that single legal norms and single legal decisions as well as legal systems raise a claim of rightness; the special case-thesis, according to which legal discourse is a special case of general practical discourse, and the discourse-theory, which formulates the requirements of rationality of legal as well as of general practical discourse – Alexy develops the direct antithesis to the positivist's separation-thesis: the concept of law should be defined in such a way that it includes moral elements.[28]

b) Whereas Alexy analyzes only the structural difference between rules and principles, Dworkin goes beyond this and stresses the difference between these norm-categories in terms of the theory of *legal validity*. The guiding idea is that the legal validity of rules can be subjected to a "test of pedigree" whereas that of principles cannot. "Test of pedigree ", in this context, means the positivist criterion for the identification of law as law – a criterion as defined, for example, by Kelsen's basic norm or by Hart's rule of recognition, i.e., a criterion by means of which one can recognize whether a norm is a legal norm valid in a given legal system. Therefore, the validity-oriented version of the principles argument states that principles, by virtue of the nature of their validity, go beyond the limits of the positivistic concept of law.

It is characteristic of Kelsen's basic norm and of Hart's rule of recognition that the criteria they mention refer exclusively to the authoritativeness and the effectiveness of a norm or a system of norms and do not require that the contents of norms be examined. Dworkin believes that principles cannot be identified in this way; rather, they elude all criteria of identification which can be formulated in a basic norm. On the contrary, they are characterized by a

---

[27] BVerfGE 3, 225 (235).

[28] See R. Alexy, Begriff und Geltung des Rechts, pp. 39 et seq.

flowing transition between legal and purely moral principles, even though the latter, if part of the "political" or "community morality", may have the power to overrule precedents. Examined more closely, there are, as I understand it, at least four kinds of principles in Dworkin's theory: firstly, principles which are expressly stated in the constitution or in the written laws of a legal system; secondly, principles which are not expressly stated but which can be considered legal by virtue of the "institutional support" afforded them by laws, precedents, doctrinal theories and legal customs; thirdly, purely moral principles, i.e. those without clearly definable "institutional support", which can, however, be used as legitimate reasons for a judge's decision, because they are part of the "community morality"; and, fourthly, moral principles which must be excluded from the list of legitimate grounds for a court's decision due to the system's constitution or its basic moral-political principles.[29]

Flowing transitions can be found especially between the second and the third category. Hitherto, Dworkin has rejected suggestions that the concept of institutional support be employed as a criterion for the identification of principles as valid law.[30] In his view, the test of institutional support cannot be decisive because it is not possible to specify in general how much and what kind of institutional support a principle must have to qualify as valid law. Dworkin's conception, therefore, does, in fact, go beyond the positivistic concept of law. His own concept of law, of which he does not offer an explicit definition, is accordingly and, I think, unnecessarily underdetermined.

This underdetermination may be remedied in either of two ways. The first has already been described: to use what Dworkin rejects, namely the test of institutional support as a criterion capable of identifying principles as valid law. This criterion is, on the one hand, vague enough to preserve Dworkin's intentions, and, on the other hand, not more elusive than, for example, the criterion of effectiveness in Kelsen's basic norm theory. There is, however, a second possibility, which I find preferable. It would have to be elaborated in two steps. The first step would be to show that every developed legal system

---

[29] On the general discussion of the nature, status and functions of legal principles in Dworkin's theory of law see, e.g., M. Cohen (ed.), Ronald Dworkin and Contemporary Jurisprudence, London 1983 (including, among others, J. Raz, Legal Principles and the Limits of Law, op.cit., pp. 73 - 87, and N. MacCormick, Dworkin as Pre-Benthamite, op.cit., pp. 182 - 201); M. Bayles, Principles of Law, Dordrecht 1987; S. Utz, Rules, Principles, Algorithms and the Description of Legal Systems, Ratio Juris 5/1992, pp. 23 - 45; A. Peczenik, Weighing Rights, in: D. N. MacCormick / Z. Bankowski (eds.), Enlightenment, Rights and Revolution, Aberdeen 1989, pp. 175 - 196; A. Aarnio, Taking Rules Seriously, in: ARSP Beiheft 42, Wiesbaden 1990, 180 - 192. – Along with Alexy, the German debate has been influenced by J. Esser, Grundsatz und Norm in der richterlichen Fortbildung des Privatrechts, Tübingen 1956; F. Bydlinski, Fundamentale Rechtsgrundsätze, Wien/New York 1988; U. Penski, Rechtsgrundsätze und Rechtsregeln, JZ 1989, pp. 105 - 114.

[30] See R. Dworkin, op.cit., pp. 338 et seq.

contains a set of basic principles, and that the remaining principles stand in a derivative and/or an associative relation to those basic principles. The six main principles of the German Constitution mentioned above – dignity, freedom, equality, constitutionality, democracy and the welfare state – could perhaps be considered as defining that set of basic principles in legal systems, at least in those with democratic constitutions. The second step would be to prove that this set of principles enjoys constitutional status in the legal system under consideration, i.e., that they either directly or indirectly belong to the written or unwritten constitution of the system. A basic norm could then be formulated as a criterion for identifying principles as valid law which, like Kelsen's, would point to the constitution.

However, the principles theory remains, when modified in this way, within the limits of the positivistic concept of law at least with respect to the theory of validity. In terms of this theory, those limits would first be trespassed if one regarded the difference between the principles in categories three and four (i.e. between those that are inside and those that are outside of the "community morality") as being not only a question of the constitution of a given legal system but as a question of the concept of law – in other words, if certain principles, for example, the principle of racial segregation, were to be excluded from the concept of law for reasons drawn from a point of view of law in general, rather than seen from the point of view of a given legal system. The principles argument changes, at this point, into the argument from injustice.

IV.

In this last section I would like to summarize the above considerations and supplement them with a handful of additional remarks.

1. Law is a complex and manifold phenomenon which can be an object of scientific research and conceptualization from different perspectives. In particular, a distinction has to be made between the sociological, the ethical and the legal perspectives. The legal perspective, at its core, is characterized by the judge's perspective, and the judge's perspective is defined by the task which the judge, by virtue of his office, has to perform. In all developed legal systems this task is to decide cases in a methodologically correct way according to the valid law. The question "what is law?" is, therefore, from the standpoint of the judge, essentially the question "what is valid law?".

2. There are at least three concepts of validity: a sociological, an ethical and a juristic one.[31] The sociological concept refers to social validity, the ethical

[31] For the following see R. Dreier, Recht – Moral – Ideologie, chap. 6 (Recht und Moral), esp. pp. 194 - 198.

concept to moral validity, and the juristic concept to the legal validity of a norm or a system of norms.

a) A norm is *socially* valid if it is socially effective, and it is a socially valid *legal* norm if it is socially effective in a specific way, namely – following the external aspect – if the behaviour of the members of a given social system either conforms with the norm or, in the case of non-conformity, is sanctioned by courts. Social validity in this sense is a statistically measurable phenomenon.

b) A norm is *morally* valid if it is ethically justified, and it is a morally valid *legal* norm if it is – in its substance – directed at external and potentially coercible behaviour. Problems of the operative provisions of a norm referring to internal behaviour (intention, conscience, etc.) may be left aside here.

c) It is more difficult to define the *juristic* concept of validity. The current positivistic definition reads:

> A norm is *legally* valid if it is created in a formally correct way and if it does not collide with superior norms of positive law.

If one accepts the objections to the positivistic concept of law, one has to complete this definition not only by introducing elements of the social effectiveness of norms and systems of norms but also with elements of substantial rightness.

3. As has already been said, the argument from injustice, especially the Radbruch formula, has proved in the adjudication of German courts to be a practicable and adequate modification of merely positivistic concepts of law. The same holds for the argument from principles, especially in its structure-oriented version, if one looks at the value-based adjudication of the German Federal Constitutional Court. Both arguments have thereby received noteworthy confirmation through judicial practice. The consequences for the concept of law can be summarized in the thesis that the concept of positive law, in the sense of legally valid law, is not an empirical but a normative one. A constitutive element of this concept is the directedness of positive law to justice and reason. That means: Norms and systems of norms which claim to be law can fall so far short of this claim that they must be denied the character of law. And norms and norm-systems are, in cases of vaguenesses and norm-conflicts, to be interpreted according to their claim. The task of legal theory and of the philosophy of law is, not least of all, to explicate the directedness of positive law towards justice and reason which is manifest in its claim to be legally valid law.

4. A definitional formula can only be the last step in a set of elaborate conceptual reflections. I proposed such a formula in one of my earlier studies.[32] Robert Alexy has improved this formula substantially. His definition reads:

[32] NJW 1986, p. 896 = Recht – Staat – Vernunft, p. 116. The definition reads: "Law consists of those norms which belong to the constitution of a system of norms organized

"The law is a system of norms, which

(1) raises a claim of rightness,

(2) consists of the sum of norms which belong to the constitution of the system, the norms being, on the whole, socially effective and not extremely unjust, as well as of the norms which are laid down according to this constitution, are at least minimally socially effective or applicable and are not extremely unjust, and which system

(3) comprises those principles and other normative arguments on which the procedure of applying the law is or must be based in order to fulfil the claim of rightness".[33]

I think that this definition is a very interesting development of the concept of law, well worth further discussion.[34]

5. I should not wish to close without saying that the foregoing remarks on the concept of law proposed here stand squarely in the tradition of Kant's philosophy. The dated elements of Kant's theory of law lie in the fact that Kant, on the one hand (in the tradition of Montesquieu), understands interpretation in applying law as a mere execution of statutes and that he, on the other hand (in the tradition of Hobbes), gives a one-sided priority to the peace-oriented function over the justice-oriented function of the positive law. Fundamental to his concept of law, however, are not those somewhat anachronistic elements, but rather the directedness of law towards reason. Kant works out this direction within the framework of his theory of practical reason. The principles of this theory are, as the contemporary debate in ethics as well as in the philosophy of law shows, as topical today as ever. Kant's natural law-based thesis that the positive law takes priority over natural law (or more precisely: over the law of reason) serves to remind us of the weight which, in all constitutional and democratic legal systems, ought to be given to the principles of legal certainty, democracy and the separation of powers.

---

in a state or on the international level, if this system is on the whole socially effective and, in a minimal sense, ethically justifiable, and of those norms which are laid down according to this constitution, if these, taken by themselves, are socially effective or have at least the chance to become socially effective and which are, in a minimal sense, ethically justifiable."

[33] Begriff und Geltung des Rechts, p. 201.

[34] It should be noted that it is also worth discussing whether it is expedient to define the concept of law regardless of its validity. I have proposed such a definition in: Göttliches und menschliches Recht, in: Zeitschrift für evangelisches Kirchenrecht, vol. 32, 1987, pp. 289 - 316, at pp. 292 - 294 (law = the totality of norms for external human behaviour applicable by courts). This definition has been elaborated by Delf Buchwald (op. cit., at pp. 263 et seq., 275 et seq.). On the possibility of establishing necessary relations between law and morality on the level of the concept of law itself (together with the idea of rational justification of court-decisions) see D. Buchwald, op. cit, at pp. 276 et seq., esp. 293 et seq.

Legal Reasoning and Personal Convictions

By Kent Greenawalt, New York

I. Introduction

Robert Summers, by his intellect, energy, and friendship, has done as much as any legal scholar in the United States to create a genuine international academic community. He has also made notable contributions to the subject of reasons in law.[1] Since I have been intrigued by the limits of reason in judicial decision and have been puzzled by the diametrically opposed conclusions the highest courts in Germany and the United States reached about abortion roughly two decades ago, I decided to use this occasion to focus on those conclusions and to suggest how they look from a broader perspective of reasons in law. One of my themes is the place of religious convictions in judicial decision; that theme seems particularly appropriate, because I know that Professor Summers has religious convictions that matter in his life.

II. The General Problem

The general problem I am considering is that for some cases no combination of legal materials (such as statutes and cases) and ordinary legal reasons yields a decisive conclusion.[2] I shall not try to defend this proposition against possible alternatives, but I do need to explain carefully what it is that I believe.

I am not endorsing a deeply skeptical position about the law and its content. There is in the United States a group of "critical legal scholars" who suggest

---

1 See especially Robert S. Summers, Two Types of Substantive Reasons: The Core of a Theory of Common Law Justification, 63 Cornell Law Review 707 (1978); On Why Courts in Cases Not Governed By Binding Law Seldom Need to Assess Closely the Relative Justificatory Force of Conflicting Substantive Reasons, Carla Faralli and Enrico Pattaro (eds.), Reason in Law, pp. 207 - 33 (1987); Robert S. Summers and Leigh B. Kelley, 'Economists'. Reasons for Common Law Decision – A Preliminary Inquiry/ Oxford Journal of Legal Studies 213 (1981).

2 As with many of the general points in this essay, I have discussed this question elsewhere, most fully in Law and Objectivity (Oxford and New York 1992). In Religious Convictions and Political Choice (Oxford and New York 1988), I consider the special place of religious understanding in political judgment and, to a lesser extent, legal judgment. I am working on another book on "public reasons" and self-restraint in politics, tentatively titled Political Self-Restraint.

that the language of legal norms is rarely conclusive and that "legal reasons" are typically contradictory (and thus rhetorical ploys) rather than genuine aids in resolving legal issues. I believe, on the contrary, that the language of directly relevant legal norms, understood with attention to purpose and context, is often conclusive and that, even when it is not, background legal reasons frequently point strongly in one direction rather than the other. All I claim is that *sometimes* the legal materials and legal reasons, together, are not decisive.

When I say that these are not decisive, I mean more than that the resolution of a case is hard to determine and will be debated. I mean that even a perfect judge could not resolve the case on those bases alone, without injecting of something else. For example, in common law systems, the legal status of behavior often depends on whether the behavior is "reasonable." Although usually such determinations are made by juries (or other finders of fact), sometimes they are made by judges and amount to determinations of law. This occurs in the United States under the constitutional bans on "unreasonable" searches and seizures and "cruel and unusual punishments." Judges must decide in some cases whether particular searches are unreasonable or particular punishments are cruel. In these instances, it is obvious that the *directly relevant* legal language, "reasonable" or "cruel," does not by itself settle whether a practice is all right. Judges must look elsewhere. I believe that the same is sometimes true when judges must make more complicated interpretations of law, but I shall use these simpler examples as illustrations.

There are at least three places judges could look to resolve such questions. One is the entire corpus of legal materials, which may indicate important reasons for decision and orderings of value. Conceivably, the perfect judge could make a determination on this basis alone. A second possible source of decision is social morality, the community's sense of what is right and wrong. A third avenue for a judge is to ask what is *really* right, what has come to be called in the American literature an independent judgment of moral and political philosophy. To take the punishment example, judges would ask what is genuinely cruel, under the best moral views, not simply what would count as cruel if one surveyed all the legal materials or community perspectives.

From limited contact,[3] my sense is that German and other continental theorists are generally more confident about the power of the corpus of legal materials to resolve things than are most American scholars. This difference in view is surely related to differences between code and common law traditions and to differences between continental legal cultures, which aim strongly for

[3] My main source of understanding was an intense three-week conference on criminal law justifications and excuses at the Max Planck Institute for Foreign and International Criminal Law in Freiburg, Germany, in 1984, organized by Albin Eser and George Fletcher. I also learned a great deal at a conference on comparative constitutional law in Belgrade two years later.

unanimity, anonymity, and summary statements of reasons in judicial opinions, and common law cultures, which often have non-unanimous, named, and expansive opinions. Also, the ideas that codes are comprehensive and that more specific legal norms are closely tied to pervasive general principles that govern the system help explain why continental law is more often considered complete.

Few American scholars believe that the corpus of legal materials, somehow interpreted without the introduction of outside values, can resolve all cases. Some, like the legal realists and critical legal scholars, are pervasively skeptical about what law settles; others agree with Benjamin Cardozo[4] and H. L. A. Hart[5] that the law resolves much but leaves gaps that must be filled in by "legislative discretion;" a few follow Ronald Dworkin in claiming that a right answer does exist for every case but that "right answer" may depend on an independent judgment of moral and political philosophy with which the legal corpus is interpreted.[6] Even Americans who grasp the differences between continental and common law contexts are usually dubious that codes can yield decisive answers for all cases.

If the legal materials, including reasons drawn from them, cannot resolve all cases, can a combination of legal materials and community morality do so? One prominent American scholar does believe this is possible for the common law (he does not discuss statutory and constitutional cases),[7] but I believe the suggestion founders on the reality that community morality is often inconclusive and that some moral and political judgment is needed to determine *what counts* as community morality. Community morality and the entire set of legal norms and legal reasons are often crucial for decision, but sometimes judges have to make independent judgments of moral and political philosophy to resolve cases. That premise leads to the second aspect of our general problem: how are judges to make such judgments?

The difficulty about independent moral and political judgments concerns the bases on which they might be made. Judicial opinions are written as if decision is based on objectively valid reasons whose force does not depend on the personality of the judge. Is this a reasonable expectation for independent moral and political judgments? Were there an objective, recognized way to make such judgments, the expectation would certainly be reasonable. What we find, however, are areas of agreement and areas of disagreement about the substance of such judgments and the methodology by which they are made,

---

4 See Benjamin Nathan Cardozo, The Nature of the Judicial Process (New Haven, Conn. 1921).

5 See H. L. A. Hart, The Concept of Law (Oxford 1961).

6 See, e.g., Ronald Dworkin, Law's Empire (Cambridge, Mass. 1986).

7 Melvin Eisenberg, The Nature of the Common Law (Cambridge, Mass. 1988).

not any generally accepted way to make these judgments. Whether there is *any* objective way that does not depend on the perspectives of particular judges is disputed. Skeptics claim that all we can ultimately say about many moral judgments is that they are the ones made by particular persons or groups at particular times and places. Others believe in objective grounds, establishable by reasoned analysis, despite the failure of many (or all) people yet to recognize the correct manner of doing things. Still others believe in objectively correct answers, and a (more or less) reliable way of arriving at them, but they acknowledge that something beyond reason is necessary to establish that. The question that mainly concerns me is whether and how judges should make these independent judgments, and particularly whether they appropriately rely on what I call intuitive moral convictions and religious convictions. It is just this question that I believe the abortion cases raise in such stark fashion. I address the two cases before returning to my more general themes.

III. Roe v. Wade: Searching for a Ground of Decision

Roe v. *Wade,*[8] decided in 1973, is the central American constitutional decision on abortion. It has set the groundwork for subsequent constitutional cases, and for a ferocious, highly divisive, national public debate that continues unabated. In *Roe* v. *Wade* the Supreme Court held that upon the medical judgment of a doctor, a woman has a federal constitutional right to terminate a pregnancy before the fetus is viable. During the first trimester, the state must leave the decisions about having an abortion and about medical procedures to a woman and her doctor. During the second trimester, a state can regulate medical procedures for abortion in order to protect the pregnant woman's health. Only after viability can a state proscribe abortion; even then a woman has a right to have an abortion if a medical judgment has been made that one is necessary to preserve her life or health.

Roe v. *Wade* is one of the most important constitutional decisions of the century, and it is controversial on many counts. I shall concentrate on one crucial element: how does the Court determine that up until viability a state's interest in protecting prenatal life is not sufficiently strong to justify prohibiting most abortions? The Court's reasoning to support this determination proves elusive. Before I address that reasoning, I will indicate how the determination fits in constitutional context.

During this century, one of the most important of general constitutional questions has been whether the federal constitution protects "substantive" rights that are not, like liberty of speech and religion, specifically enumerated.

---

[8] 410 U.S. 113.

At one time, the Court held various state welfare measures, such as minimum wage and maximum hours legislation, to be unconstitutional infringements of a liberty of contract that is not to be found explicitly protected in the Constitution.[9] The Court relied on the post-Civil-War fourteenth amendment, which provides that states cannot "abridge the privileges or immunities of citizens" or "deprive any person of life, liberty, or property, without due process of law..." Although the "privileges or immunities" language seems more apposite, an early decision had sharply restricted its coverage, so the Court used the "due process clause." During 1930's "substantive due process" was largely abandoned. All that appeared to be left was the idea that a state regulation must be rationally related to an appropriate objective.

The origin of modern substantive due process was the 1965 case of *Griswold* v. *Connecticut.*[10] The Court decided that a state cannot prohibit a married couple from using contraceptive devices. The main opinion relied on various specific guarantees to establish a "right of privacy" that extended beyond the reach of any specific provision. Another opinion found support in the vague ninth amendment, which says that the enumeration of some rights shall not be construed to deny others retained by the people. Two other concurring opinions rested more exclusively on due process under the fourteenth amendment.

In *Roe* v. *Wade,* the Court considered a Texas law that forbade most abortions. In the United States, unlike most European countries, basic criminal law is a matter for individual states, not the national government. Absent some federal constitutional right, states may regulate as they choose, and they may adopt radically different approaches to subjects. That, indeed, was how abortion was treated in 1973; some states had enacted laws permitting wide choice about abortion, but most states retained highly restrictive rules.

Two threshold questions in *Roe* v. *Wade* were whether a fetus is a person under the fourteenth amendment and whether a woman's interest in terminating her pregnancy falls within the "right of privacy" established in *Griswold.* The Court dealt with the first question rather summarily. Assuming that a restrictive law would be appropriate if a fetus were a person whose life was protected by the amendment, it noted that other constitutional references to "persons" seemed to mean postnatal life and it pointed to freer abortion practices during most of the 19th century as helping to establish that direct constitutional coverage of fetal life was not intended. Although *Griswold* had emphasized the privacy of sexual relations, in the sense of privacy as a shielding from public view, the Court found little difficulty in treating the constitutional "right of privacy" as covering the pregnant woman's claim to control her body, a claim that involves fundamental autonomy more than privacy in a

[9] The best known case was Lochner v. New York, 198 U.S. 45 (1905).
[10] 381 U.S. 479.

narrow sense. The Court then invoked what had become the standard approach for regulation of fundamental rights: restriction of the right is acceptable only if the state presents a compelling interest that cannot be achieved without restricting the right.

Some of the next steps in the analysis were fairly simple. First, the state could not restrict abortions for everyone as a means to discourage premarital sex. Second, given medical advances, the pregnant woman's own safety could not be invoked as a reason to prevent her from having an abortion. This left the state's asserted interest in protecting fetal life. Since a highly restrictive law was obviously an appropriate *way* to protect fetal life, the crucial issue became whether the state's interest in protecting that life was compelling. That is the question on which I focus.

Justice Blackmun's opinion for the Court in *Roe* v. *Wade* has been severely criticized, largely because the opinion gives no satisfactory answer to the critical question of valuation. The opinion starts out with a remarkably honest statement of pitfalls:

> We forthwith acknowledge our awareness of the sensitive and emotional nature of the abortion controversy, of the vigorous opposing views, even among physicians, and of the deep and seemingly absolute convictions that the subject inspires. One's philosophy, one's experiences, one's exposure to the raw edges of human existence, one's religious training, one's attitudes toward life and family and their values, and the moral standards one establishes and seeks to observe, are all likely to influence and to color one's thinking and conclusions about abortion.[11]

Justice Blackmun goes on to say that "Our task, of course, is to resolve the issue by constitutional measurement, free of emotion and of predilection." But some fifty pages later, the reader is still wondering whether that has been accomplished and how it could be accomplished.

Much of the opinion's effort is directed toward showing that for most of the history of England and the United States, criminalization of abortion has been more limited than it is under the Texas statute, but Justice Blackmun acknowledges that the Texas approach is typical of the preceding century. The Court also relies to some extent on the fact that for many kinds of civil legal rights, an early fetus is not protected as a person.

The Court undertakes an analysis of the relevance of the Hippocratic Oath that would be amusing if the subject were not so serious. The opinion relies on the work of L. Edelstein who concluded that the Oath's strong rejection of abortion represented a Pythagorean doctrine that was not generally accepted in ancient Greece. A decided change took place at the end of antiquity, when resistance against abortion, supported by the emerging teachings of Christianity, became common. Dr. Edelstein suggests that the Oath is a "'Pythagorean

[11] 410 U.S., at 116.

manifesto and not the expression of an absolute standard of medical conduct.'"[12] The Court concludes that this "is a satisfactory and acceptable explanation of the Hippocratic Oath's apparent rigidity." Given the Court's own summary, the Oath was not apparently rigid in its origin; it *was* rigid, in accord with the controversial views of the Pythagoreans. Justice Blackmun provides no basis for us to suppose that the Oath has shifted from being rigid to being apparently rigid (although that could happen to a document as interpreted over time). If the Oath's rejection of abortion was *originally controversial,* how much difference should that make if a consensus about the position emerged with the end of antiquity? 1500 years of consensus is a rather long time. Justice Blackmun writes as if Dr. Edelstein's analysis undercuts any force of the Oath as a support to restrictive abortion laws, but he is mistaken.

Eventually, the opinion reaches the central question whether the claim of Texas to protect fetal life is a compelling interest sufficient to justify the restriction on abortion. The Court again recognizes the difficulty of its problem:

> Texas urges that, apart from the Fourteenth Amendment, life begins at conception and is present throughout pregnancy, and that, therefore, the State has a compelling interest in protecting that life from and after conception. We need not resolve the difficult question of when life begins. When those trained in the respective disciplines of medicine, philosophy, and theology are unable to arrive at any consensus, the judiciary, at this point in the development of man's knowledge, is not in a position to speculate as to the answer.[13]

After a brief survey of competing views, the Court concludes that "by adopting one theory of life, Texas may [not] override the rights of the pregnant woman that are at stake." It then proceeds:

> With respect to the State's important and legitimate interest in potential life the "compelling" point is at viability. This is so because the fetus then presumably has the capability of meaningful life outside the mother's womb. State regulation protective of fetal life after viability thus has both logical and biological justifications.[14]

For the Court to find that the interest in preserving fetal life *is not compelling prior to viability* is surely to take a stance on the value of the fetus. Finding that viability makes a critical difference for the value of fetal life is to adopt one among a number of controversial positions. The Court had earlier acknowledged that if the fetus was a person under the Fourteenth Amendment, a restrictive law would be justified. One way of understanding the claim of Texas was that the state chose to consider the fetus as having the same value as a person under the Fourteenth Amendment. In different terminology, it had decided that even an early fetus is a human being, as entitled to protection

---

[12] Id. at 132.
[13] Id. at 159.
[14] Id. at 163.

as a new born baby. That determination lies very close to an answer to the question of "when life begins." The Court says it will not resolve the latter question, but its rejection of the Texas claim seems to be a resolution in favor of the view that (full, fully counting) human life does not begin before viability.[15]

If the Court's actual reasoning was inadequate, what might it have done instead? It could have decided that, in light of disagreement and uncertainty, a state can value fetal life as it believes best. A decision accompanying that rationale would have permitted rather than invalidated restrictive state laws. The Court could have undertaken a systematic attempt to resolve the problem of valuing fetal life. Had it done that, it would have needed to give some indication what role personal and religious judgments could play. Since I believe the problem of valuing the fetus does not yield fully to systematic reasoned evaluation, and any systematic approach would have generated intense disagreement, I think the Court wisely eschewed that effort. The Court could explicitly have given great weight to the view of doctors about what should be done about abortion. (I say "explicitly," because Justice Blackmun had a longstanding relationship to the Mayo Clinic, and one of the implicit subtexts of the opinion is respect for doctors.) It could have tried to gauge prevailing community sentiments on a national basis, perhaps allowing restrictive laws if those were supported by dominant or substantial sentiment. The Court might have said that the pregnant woman's control over her body and over the decision whether to have a baby are so important they can be limited only if there is a strong consensus that doing so is appropriate. That approach would have yielded a decision in favor of the right to abortion, because no consensus either way existed at the time.

Any of these courses would have been subject to strong objection, but any of them might have represented a coherent resolution of the central problem. Instead, the Court refreshingly admitted the problem's difficulty, but then retreated into a realm of legal statement and came up with a legal conclusion that rested more or less on thin air. The Court effectively resolved the question it denied it could resolve, and failed to present any convincing basis for doing so.

IV. The Ruling of the West German Federal Constitutional Court: The Apparent Supremacy of Legal Values

Two years after the United States had rendered its landmark decision, the West German Constitutional Court reviewed an act of the federal parliament

[15] Indeed, its decision that a state cannot forbid abortion of a viable fetus when that is needed for the "health" of the mother seems to reject the view that even a viable fetus counts as much as a new born baby.

dealing with abortion.[16] In the Federal Republic of Germany, the Constitutional Court has explicit responsibility to deal with constitutional issues. It is not in the hierarchy of ordinary courts, as is the United States Supreme Court, and it need not wait for a typical legal case to arise, as must federal courts in the United States. In this instance, the "first division" of the Constitutional Court reviewed the Abortion Reform Act of 1974 upon the request of federal deputies who had opposed it (Christian Democrats) and the governments of some of the provinces. The Court declared that the act inappropriately eliminated criminal penalties for early voluntary abortions, reasoning that the Constitution required greater protection for unborn life.

As with the American case, I shall focus on one aspect of the Court's decision: its conclusion that because the value of the early fetus is so great, Parliament may not choose to eliminate criminal penalties for abortions performed during the first trimester of pregnancy. Initially, I place this resolution in context.

The new act represented a significant change in the law of abortion. From the middle of the nineteenth century, German statutory law had strictly banned abortion, although the law's effect had been moderated by a 1927 decision of the Supreme Court that held that an abortion necessary to preserve the life or health of the pregnant woman was not punishable. In 1972, there was extensive debate over abortion legislation, and more particularly over the desirability of allowing a woman and her physician to have complete discretion to abort during the first three months – a "term" approach – or, instead, requiring some special reason, such as the woman's life or health, avoidance of a seriously defective child, or extremely harmful social consequences of birth for the woman, to justify an abortion – an "indications" approach. Premature dissolution of Parliament ended the debate without legislation.

The 1974 act adopted the term approach for the first twelve weeks of pregnancy; any woman could have an abortion if it was performed by a licensed physician and had been preceded by counseling. Criminal penalties continued to apply after that period unless there were medical, eugenic (avoidance of a defective child), or ethical indications to justify abortion. The primary rationale in parliamentary debate for making the law more permissive was not that a woman had an absolute right to control her body, but rather that illegal abortions had sharply increased and that the regime of counseling would better protect unborn life than criminal sanctions. The Constitutional Court held that the act was invalid in eliminating punishment in the absence of indications recognized by previous decisions.

[16] The Abortion Decision of February 25, 1975 of the Federal Constitutional Court, Federal Republic of Germany, Translated and Introduced by Edmund C. Jann (Washington, D.C. 1975).

A crucial premise of the Court's decision was its conclusion that prenatal life is protected by the Basic Law (Constitution), which states, Article 2, paragraph 2, sentence 1, that "Everyone shall have the right to life. ..." The Court considered this fundamental right to life as a reaction to the disregard for life of the Nazi era. The Court's opinion quickly concludes that:

> Life in the sense of the developmental existence of a human individual in any event begins, according to established biological-physiological findings, on the 14th day after conception (implantation, individuation). ... The development process thus begun is a continuous one which manifests no sharp caesuras and does not permit any precise delimitation of the various developmental stages of the human life. ... The right to life is guaranteed to everyone who "lives"; no distinction can be made between individual stages of the developing life before birth or between prenatal and postnatal life.[17]

Against the argument that "everyone" in common parlance means completed human beings, the Court says that the sense and purpose of the provision extends to developing life; otherwise human existence would not be adequately safeguarded against intrusions by the state. Further, broad coverage was intended by the Parliamentary Council considering the constitutional language.

According to the Court, the Basic Law not only forbids the state from encroaching on life; it commands the state to play a protective and supporting role for life.[18] Although a woman has a right to free development of her personality, the protection of the life of the fetus, inevitably destroyed in an abortion, "must be given priority." Disapproval of the termination of pregnancy must be clearly expressed in the legal order. Although it is incumbent on legislators to decide how to fulfill the state's obligations, the criminal law has traditionally protected the elementary values of community life. The time-phase rule of the new law does not do justice to the state's obligation to protect life, since the counseling system that is substituted for criminal penalties during the first twelve weeks does not adequately express disapproval of abortion and will fail to prevent abortions that lack adequate justifying reasons.

Two judges dissented, not a common practice for the Constitutional Court. They object to the Court's finding of a constitutional duty to issue penal norms, noting that nothing in the legislative materials dealing with the right to life indicated an obligation to protect prenatal life by penal sanctions.[19] They urge that the Court "overlooks the *singularity of the termination of pregnancy,*" and that the Court's acknowledgement that the legislature may permit abortion on ethical, eugenic, and social indications shows that the Court leaves room for the historical legal distinction between prenatal and postnatal life.

---

[17] Id. at 51.

[18] Id. at 57.

[19] Id. at 100.

The dissenters agree with the majority that as far as *government encroachments* are concerned, no distinction should be made between prenatal and postnatal development, but contend that such a distinction is warranted when the woman's right to abort is at stake. The single female judge (Rupp-v. Brunneck) says that "the refusal of the pregnant woman to permit the fetus to develop into a human being within her body is, not only according to the natural feelings of the woman but also according to the law, something entirely different from the destruction of independently existing life."[20] She regards as entirely appropriate a time-phase approach that corresponds with a process of development.

In sharp contrast with the majority opinion in *Roe* v. *Wade,* the Court does not mention the bewildering multiplicity of views about abortion. Relying only on legal materials, it constructs a justification that is coherent and systematic, leaving no gaps in its reasoning to confuse the reader. But is what it says convincing?

Someone who has only my degree of familiarity with the German materials cannot confidently answer this question, but various steps in the process of reasoning seem dubious. Although "everyone" in the sentence of the Basic Law that guarantees a right to life might mean only human beings already born, I think the Court offers a persuasive argument, from the purpose of the provision, that *government encroachment on prenatal life* would be a violation. This point was accepted by both the dissenters and the federal government defending the law. It does not follow, however, either that the protection extends to voluntary actions by pregnant women or, if it does, that the interest in life at early stages outweighs the woman's claim to control her body.

What the Court says about stages of development is elusive. Even if one grants that "life" in a sense that falls within constitutional protection exists after 14 days, the right to life at this stage need not already be as powerful as that of a new born baby. One can believe that the intrinsic value of the life increases with its develoment. Indeed, as the dissenters urge, the Court, in its acceptance of abortions justified by indications, implicitly seems to acknowledge that prenatal life need not be counted *as worth as much* as postnatal life. The Court says correctly that there are no subsequent sharp stages (except birth?), and that precise delimitation of stages is impossible. That, however, does not settle the validity of a law that makes periods of time crucial. A legislature might say: "We agree that there are no precise stages at which the value of life raises sharply, but there is an incremental development and increase in value over time. A time-phase law is not meant to map exactly sharp breaks in ethical evaluation; but its somewhat crude representation of a gradual development is the best the law can do." The Court does not really explain

[20] Id. at 105.

why the beginning of individual life at 14 days already brings *a very high valuation* or why the absence of sharp stages of development should preclude the only kind of recognition of increasing value of which a legislature is capable. (Indeed, courts themselves must sometimes make decisions that draw a line at a particular point, when *exactly* where to draw the line along a continuum seems arbitrary.) Even given the Court's conclusions that the Basic Law reaches "life" 14 days after conception and that the Basic Law can set obligations for the government to protect against the taking of life by private individuals, it is hard to find from within the law a clear basis for saying that acceding to the choice of the pregnant woman is not one appropriate stance for the state to take during the early weeks of pregnancy.

The move to liberalize abortion laws, which occurred simultaneously in most liberal democracies, was closely connected to increasing concern for the rights of women. That the highest constitutional courts of two countries should reach different outcomes is not itself surprising; one might have expected judges to defer to legislative determinations about this troubling problem, for which so much depends on how greatly one values the developing fetus. What is genuinely startling is that the West German and American courts were willing to reach contrary results in the teeth of legislature determinations they rejected. The German Court invalidated federal legislation. The law the United States Supreme Court held unconstitutional was not some isolated, outdated relic of an earlier era; it remained the dominant approach among the fifty states despite pressure to liberalize. Moreover, in a companion case, *Doe* v. *Bolton,* the Court held unconstitutional a substantially more liberal Georgia statute.

One perceptive observation about the two decisions is that the German Basic Law and the Constitutional Court take a more communitarian approach to rights than do the Supreme Court and the legal culture in the United States.[21] In Germany constitutional provisions recognize limits on rights for common welfare, and individuals are not conceived as autonomous units exercising their freedom. *Roe* v. *Wade* gives overriding effect to the liberty of a pregnant woman; the German Court is not hesitant to impose a duty on her to complete a pregnancy in order to preserve the life of the fetus. Still, it remains remarkable that the Constitutional Court takes a provision that undeniably was mainly adopted to prevent state *encroachment* on individual freedom to compel state prohibition of behavior that many regard as properly within the sphere of a woman's essential freedom.

---

[21] See Donald P. Kommers, Abortion and the Constitution: The Cases of the United States and West Germany, in Edward Manier, William Liu, David Solomon (eds.), Abortion 83, 106 - 08 (Notre Dame 1977); Donald P. Kommers, Liberty and Community in Constitutional Law: The Abortion Cases in Comparative Perspective, 1985 Brigham Young University Law Review 371.

V. The General Problem and Possible Resolutions

The abortion decisions illustrate how judges may deal with problems when the purely legal sources seem to leave alternatives open, and a crucial valuation may need to be made on other bases. One feature of the cases does not arise in ordinary code, or statutory, or common law interpretation: the courts had to determine whether to override legislative decisions on constitutional grounds. This aspect of constitutional review creates the possibility that courts can simply defer to clear legislative choices. In what follows, I disregard this special feature in favor of more general comments about situations when legal sources seem to leave open some important valuation, such as the valuation of an early fetus and a comparison of the importance of preserving its life against the claim of freedom of a pregnant woman whose body will be severely burdened for the months of pregnancy and whose life will be unalterably affected if she gives birth and keeps the child.[22]

For circumstances like these, the following questions about judicial choice are important: Will judges be influenced by "extralegal" evaluations? If so, will these evaluations include sources that are personal in some sense? Is there a correct result that does not depend on such evaluations? Should judges self-consciously take "extralegal" evaluations into account? If so, should these include sources that are personal in some sense? Should "extralegal" evaluations, possibly including those based on personal sources, be included in legal opinions? These are immense questions, and I shall deal with them summarily.

1. Actual Influence of "Extralegal" Evaluations, Including Personal Sources

I believe the answers to the first two questions are easy. Despite any legal mythology to the contrary, judges are influenced by extralegal evaluations, and these include what I call personal sources. Nominees for federal judgeships routinely assure Senators in the United States during the confirmation process that they can decide without regard to their own personal moral convictions; but they are wrong. On something like the abortion issue, judges will be influenced *to some degree* by what they believe as nonjudicial human beings about abortion, and this influence will extend to personal intuitions and religious convictions.

It is time now to explain what I mean by a "personal" source of judgment. Some bases for evaluation may reach beyond the law, but have interpersonal force in reason. Dominant social morality is one such basis; interpersonal reason can assess its stance on many subjects. Judges may suppose that domi-

[22] The possibility of adoption is not a full answer to the concern about a baby's effect on the woman's life, since many women are loathe to give away a child to whom they have given birth.

nant morality should help determine the content of law whether or not they agree with that morality. Of course, social morality may be unclear or divided on a subject and often one may need to make controversial moral and political judgments to decide just how to construct social morality; but *sometimes* any plausible construction of dominant social morality will yield the same conclusion about a problem. For example, dominant social morality in all (or nearly all) western democracies now strongly supports the moral right of a married couple to decide whether to use contraceptives – the central issue in *Griswold* v. *Connecticut.*[23]

Apart from social morality, there may be ways of reasoning about moral and political problems that have interpersonal validity, and that are accessible to the common reason of human beings or of virtually all members of a relevant culture. The German Court so presents the conclusion that after 14 days, the fetus is a life with an independent interest in protection. For this determination, the Court does not depend mainly on legal materials. Rather, it assumes that the conclusion is self-evident once one reads off the scientific data that by 14 days a final individuation of the embryo has taken place. A much more complex interpersonal basis for judgment might be provided by a dialogical theory of moral truth. According to this theory, what is morally right is what people would agree to in ideal conditions of undominated dialogue. A judge might suppose that he or she could make an evaluation from that perspective. Another interpersonal ground for evaluations may be fundamental choices that a society has made. For example, one conclusion may fit better with basic premises of liberal democracy than another.

What I mean by "personal" sources are bases for evaluation that to some important degree lack such an appeal to interpersonal reason. A judge might simply have a strong feeling that a practice, such as early abortion, is bad or good without belief that the feeling has interpersonal validity at all. Or, the judge may think that the valuation does have interpersonal validity but is not subject to interpersonal reason. Suppose that the judge has religious convictions that indicate that early abortion is a grave wrong. The judge's understanding is that religious truth is known by faith through the special grace of God, and is not accessible to reason alone or even to a combination of reason and a will to believe. Unless the judge's religious convictions are shared by an overwhelming proportion of the citizenry, the judge has what he regards as a source of truth that is not accessible to the reason of many fellow citizens. Even if the judge happens to believe that this religious truth *is accessible to reason,* nonetheless many fellow citizens will think its claims lie in a domain in which fundamental truths are not establishable by reason. By "personal

[23] What I mean by a moral right here is a right to freedom from coercion by others. Some people who believe that married couples have this moral right also believe that the use of contraceptives by those couples is morally wrong.

sources," I mean roughly bases for evaluation not subject to interpersonal reason.[24]

My claim here is that *all* these "extralegal" sources do sometimes affect the conclusions of judges, because judges are incapable of blotting out fully bases of evaluation they employ in ordinary nonjudicial capacities. No doubt, in some circumstances, scrupulous judges will lean over backwards *not to be affected* by "extralegal" sources of evaluation, adopting a result contrary to what they believe is true according to those sources. What judges are not capable of doing is acting in total disregard of extralegal sources of evaluation.

I am not asserting that the amount of influence is a constant. Forms of legal culture and judicial decision make a difference. For example, a legal culture that emphasizes the primacy of legal sources, that trains a professional judiciary (rather than selecting judges from a general body of trained lawyers), and that strongly discourages individual opinions, may reduce the influence of extralegal evaluations. Thus, I do not assume these evaluations have the same influence in Germany and the United States, only that they have *some influence* in any legal regime.

2. The Possibility of Correct Results That Do Not Depend on Extralegal Evaluations

The question about correct results is more complicated, and I shall barely scratch its surface. Is there a correct result to all legal cases that does not depend on extralegal evaluations? It is fairly clear that in the United States the best answer to some legal problems is not to be found exclusively in the legal materials, but depends on some judgment about community morality, or what is really right from a moral and political point of view, or both. It may be said that these judgments are not outside law, because the legal system somehow directs judges to decide in this manner; but, even in that event, judges must make evaluations that do not come only from legal materials and ordinary legal reasons. Given the greater coherence of comprehensive codes and the assumption that broad values are to be drawn from the codes themselves, the *need* for extralegal evaluation may be substantially less in most code systems. Perhaps some theorists think that rarely, if ever, does a need for such evaluation arise, believing that the legal materials, understood with the broad values of the legal culture, provide a correct answer for someone who is capable of discerning the implications of the materials without any outside judgment of his own. My sense at a conference on justification and excuse in criminal law[25] was that some German theorists did think the code and its basic principles provided such answers to every conceivable problem. Although my own skepticism *may* flow from an insufficient grasp of code systems, I doubt that;

[24] Obviously, there are subtle matters of degree I am disregarding here.

[25] See note 3 supra.

and I think the German Court's abortion case may illustrate the need for extralegal value judgments, when different value judgments leading to contrary results would fit as well with the existing legal framework.

3. Self-Conscious Use in Individual Judgment and Opinions

The difficulty of the remaining questions depends on one's answer to the last one. If one thinks that a correct answer can be drawn from the legal materials themselves and appropriate legal reasons (however difficult the task may be for human judges), one will probably conclude that judges should attempt to decide exclusively on the basis of legal sources and should rely on those exclusively in opinions. (Perhaps one could make an argument for some limited use of "extralegal" evaluations to support debatable legal evaluations, but I do not discuss that possibility.) The troublesome questions arise if one concedes that the legal sources alone are not adequate to yield correct results in some cases. In what remains, I proceed in accord with my own belief that legal sources cannot resolve all issues. (Although my discussion rests on distinguishing reasons that derive from legal sources from extralegal evaluations, I do not suppose the distinction is neat and easy. A full effort to address this topic would require careful attention to this problem, and the writings of Robert Summers would provide an important source of illumination.[26])

Should judges self-consciously rely on "extralegal" evaluations? Initially, one might suppose that *if* some cases cannot be resolved without extralegal evaluations, it follows that judges should self-consciously rely on such evaluations; but that conclusion is far from obvious. Suppose, first, that in the great majority of cases, exclusive reliance on legal sources will yield correct answers to legal questions, second, that judges cannot confidently identify when extralegal evaluations are required, and third, that people have little confidence in the ability of judges to make good extralegal evaluations. On these assumptions, the system might well work best if judges consciously limited themselves to legal sources. One's answer to what judges should self-consciously do will depend partly on one's estimate of the frequency and ease of identification of cases when legal sources are inconclusive, and on one's sense of the ability of judges to make extralegal evaluations. The argument for self-conscious reliance on extralegal evaluations is strongest when the need for reliance is evidently apparent and some reasonable interpersonal standard, such as community morality, presents itself as a basis for making the evaluation.

Should judges self-consciously rely on personal sources? Insofar as possible, legal cases should be decided on the basis of grounds that are subject to

[26] See the articles cited in note 1, supra.

reasoned interpersonal evaluation. Thus, the arguments that judges should not rely on personal sources are stronger than the arguments that they should not rely on sources of extralegal evaluation that are fully subject to interpersonal reason.[27] Someone might wish to limit any self-conscious extralegal evaluation to bases judges think can be defended by interpersonal reasons that are very widely accepted within the culture, ones of the sort Professor Summers has explored in depth.[28] Nevertheless, for some instances in which legal sources need supplementation, evaluations that rely on bases subject to interpersonal reason may be evidently inconclusive (perhaps this is true about the critical evaluations in the abortion cases); one *might conclude* that it is better for judges then frankly to rely on their own personal sources of judgment than to delude themselves into supposing that legal sources or other interpersonal criteria yield a result.

Should "extralegal" evaluations appear in opinions? Although the United States Supreme Court discusses extralegal evaluations in *Roe* v. *Wade,* it does not rest its decision on them. The connection between its conclusion and reasoned use of legal sources is much less clear than the similar connection in the West German case; but both opinions purport to base decision on legal sources,[29] not on some other kind of evaluation of the comparative status of an early fetus and a pregnant woman. Explicit reliance on legal sources helps give the appearance that legal judgment does not depend on the individual perspectives of particular judges.

From the standpoint of the appearance of impartial decision, *explicit* use of personal sources is much more threatening than explicit use of extralegal evaluations that claim to be rooted in grounds with reasoned interpersonal validity. It, of course, follows that explicit use of personal sources would help particularly well to strip away illusions of objectivity and impartiality. For appellate courts with unanimous or majority opinions, explicit reliance on personal sources would require a great change in how opinions are written, since the reasons offered are presented as ones with force for all the judges who join them.

VI. The Connection to Wider Political Debate

The abortion decisions may illustrate something else important that I have not yet discussed: the effect of legal reasoning on public debate. Abortion

---

27 If one thought that virtually all "extralegal" evaluation comes down to personal sources, that *might* strengthen one's resistance to any self-conscious use of extralegal evaluations.

28 See note 1, supra.

29 In the German decision, the conclusion that a life exists after 14 days is not based on legal sources, but it is treated as a self-evident application of undisputed scientific facts.

reemerged in Germany as a crucial issue after reunification joined the highly permissive legal regime of the East with the moderately restrictive regime in the West. (I say moderately restrictive, because early abortion remained widespread under the legal guide of "indications".) Whatever people's actual convictions may be, public political discussion has taken place largely within the terms set by the Court. Those terms assume a high value of the life of the fetus from the earliest stages, and are cast largely in the language of means and ends of how to accomplish objectives the Court has specified.[30] Of course, this may have been partly for the Court's consumption, in what has proved to be an unsuccessful attempt to persuade it to accept a law substantially more permissive than what has existed in the Federal Republic.[31] But whatever people's motivations may have been, the debate so far seems to have been much more civilized than that in the United States, in which "sexist" and "murderer" are among the milder terms employed by competing forces. When courts purport to resolve problems exclusively on the basis of some systematic code of legal values, the consequence may sometimes be a less shrill tone for public discussion, though perhaps at the expense of spontaneity, candor, and originality.

VII. Conclusion

I have suggested many possibilities. Finally, I state my own conclusions about judicial action, although without defending them here. These conclusions are based heavily on American experience, but I do not yet see why my views are wrong for civil law countries if they are right for the United States. I am against explicit reliance on personal sources in opinions; I believe opinions should represent a process of public reason, even if that representation is not fully accurate. Opinions should explicitly include other extralegal evaluations only when the need for reliance on them is appropriate and fairly clear and the sources for judgment are very widely conceived to be subject to interpersonal assessment and to be appropriate within the society. I accept a somewhat wider range for self-conscious reliance on extralegal evaluations than will be evident from opinions and, in very rare cases when other sources are evidently inconclusive, I think it is all right for judges to rely self-consciously on personal sources.

---

[30] I owe a great deal to a seminar paper by Oda Friedheim, entitled The Abortion Debate in Germany – A Viable Compromise or an Illiberal Outcome. The paper summarizes the relevant history and the 1992 legislative debate.

[31] The new legislation, again, allowed women to have abortions during the first three months of pregnancy. The law was held invalid by the Constitutional Court, but the opinion was somewhat more accommodating than the 1975 opinion. See German Court Restricts Abortion, Angering Feminists and the East, N. Y. Times, May 29, 1993, p. 1, col. 1.

Conceptually Necessary Links between Law and Morality

By Sterling Harwood, San José

1. Introduction

I will try to reconcile some of the major views on the question of the separation of law and morals. I will argue that there are some conceptually necessary connections between law and morals. I will argue against leading separatists, including legal positivists and legal realists. There are two basic ambiguities in the separatists' claim that there is no necessary connection between law and morals. First, the word 'necessary' is ambiguous. The central claim is not that there are no particular legal systems where law and morals are necessarily connected. Rather, the claim is that law, as such, need not be connected in any way with morals. So a particular legal system where law and morals are necessarily connected would not be a counterexample to the claim. Second, the word 'morals' is ambiguous. It may mean positive or critical morality. I will deemphasize positive morals and argue for a necessary connection between law and critical morals. In section 3 I clarify the distinction between positive and critical morals.

So I will deny that law, as such, need not be connected in any way with morals. While I avow that law is morally fallible, and an unjust "law" can be a law, I will argue that there are moral constraints on what can count as law, which is inherently prima facie good. In section 4 I argue against John Austin's separatism, showing that his three main tenets form an inconsistent triad: (1) utilitarianism; (2) the separation of law and morals; and (3) the imperative theory of law as commands. In section 5 I cover Hart's view that law's general rules are procedurally just in treating like cases alike. I also ask if the three social defects Hart thinks law cures are also moral defects. In section 6 I support and apply Fuller's view that law must be a purposive achievement of moral significance. Section 7 concludes my paper. To begin well, we need at least a rudimentary idea of the two things claimed to be separate. The next two sections, 2 and 3, try to supply this.

2. The Separatists' View of Law

The separatists are generally legal positivists (including legal realists), and thus endorse a source-based view of law. Law, on this view, is determined by the actions of officials (judges, on the view of legal realists such as Oliver Wendell Holmes, Jr.) who create and lay down the law, and thus are the sources of the law. For example, Austin says all law can be reduced to commands.[1] Others, Hart for example, disagree and require legal systems to involve acceptance of certain social rules by the people or key officials.[2] Fuller resisted the idea that law can be defined in terms of necessary and sufficient conditions. Fuller thought acceptance was a necessary condition for law, and he even toyed with a definition using necessary and sufficient conditions, but he refused to adopt it.[3] Instead, he enumerated eight elements of legality: that rules be (1) general, (2) promulgated, (3) prospective, (4) understandably clear, (5) internally consistent, (6) possible to obey, (7) stable, and (8) congruent with official acts.[4] Since the elements implied eight ways to fail to make law, they imply necessary but not sufficient conditions for law. Since the separatists thought law was created only by a certain social *context,* the law created could have any *content,* and, therefore, need not be moral. And since the separatists argued that the source of law was human, they thought law must be, as humans are, morally fallible, that is, not necessarily moral. As we shall see, I will argue that the necessary moral value of law is not a matter of any necessary *content* of the law, nor a matter of morally infallible humans, but a matter of some minimal but necessary moral value inherent in the human social *context* that creates law.

I cannot describe a necessary link between law and morals unless I say something is necessarily true of law. In sections 4 and 5 I will simply use certain separatists' claims about what is necessarily true of law. In sections 6 and 7, however, I will support and apply Fuller's view that law necessarily is purposive activity, which some key separatists also accept. Note that family resemblances, some of which can be necessary conditions for law, perhaps serve to

[1] John Austin, The Province of Jurisprudence Determined (1832). For a good introduction to some key issues, see, Edmund L. Pincoffs, Philosophy Of Law, Ch. 8 (1991). For challenging views seeing law as patriarchal commands, see generally, Patricia Smith (ed.), Feminist Jurisprudence (1993).

[2] H. L. A. Hart, "Positivism and the Separation of Law and Morals," 71 Harv. L. Rev. 593, 606 (1958).

[3] Lon L Fuller, "Positivism and Fidelity to Law – A Reply to Professor Hart," 71 Harv. L. Rev. 630, 638 - 43 (1958), and Robert S. Summers, "Professor Fuller on Morality and Law," in More Essays In Legal Philosophy (ed.), Robert S. Summers 114 (1971).

[4] Lon L. Fuller, The Morality of Law (rev. ed. 1969). For insightful analyses of Fuller's view here, see Alan R. Mabe, "Fuller and the Internal Morality of Law," 13 Southern Journal of Philosophy 515 (1975), Robert S. Summers, Lon L. Fuller 36ff. (1984), and Michael Martin, The Legal Philosophy of H. L. A. Hart 219ff. (1987).

identify law better (at least for my purposes here) than do definitions using necessary and sufficient conditions. I am not committed to using family resemblances, rather than necessary and sufficient conditions, to define law. I am merely suggesting that perhaps we can conceive of law using family resemblances in order to be as noncommittal as possible so as to avoid begging questions. To get a rough idea of what law is claimed to be, consider the following family resemblances of law: Fuller's eight elements of law (which imply that law must be clear and followable), a human source of coercive commands or socially accepted rules, and the monopoly of force. More can and will be added. One can largely reconcile the various views defining law in terms of necessary and sufficient conditions by taking, with a grain of salt, the grains of truth contained in each of these views and putting them into a *set* of family resemblances which gives us a working definition of law. So, if one's intuitions are not satisfied that any one of the foregoing resemblances would, by itself, suffice to form a legal system, one should be comforted by knowing that each resemblance, considered alone is admittedly extreme and certainly would at best be a black sheep in the family of legal systems.

3. What is a Critical Morality?

Frequently, the separatists are fundamentally wrong about morality. They fail to distinguish adequately between positive morality and more enlightened critical morality. Due to this failure, they see many problems with morality that simply do not exist. Gewirth exposes this type of error, which he calls the fallacy of disparateness. He says people commit this fallacy when they, for example, compare *normative* science with *positive* morality and then decry the shortcomings of morality when it does not measure up to science.[5] Such people do *not* count astrology, Christian Science, scientology, assorted medical quackery, phrenology and creation science (among others) as science. Yet they count Nazism, cannibalism, loyalty, charity, apartheid, Christianity, and humanism (among others) as morals. The error is that the word 'science' is used *normatively* to exclude dubious or notorious sciences, whereas 'morals' is used *descriptively* and so lumps all sorts of monstrosities together with moral views worthy of the name. Such people consider all that is done in the name of morality as the practice of morals, but they do not classify as the practice of science all things done in the name of science. So, because the deck is stacked, morality does not stack up to science.

The separatists respect science largely because science progresses. But, at least arguably, morality also progresses. And there are normative moralities which form critical morality. For example, utilitarianism, which the separatists

[5] Alan Gewirth, "Positive 'Ethics' and Normative 'Science'," 69 Philosophical Review 311, 311 - 15 (1960).

endorse as their theory of value, is a critical morality.[6] Further, Hart, a separatist, admits that morality progresses.[7] And Gewirth notes that moral progress occurred, for example, in the "development of the ideals of modern liberal democracy."[8] Slavery was abolished. Suffrage was extended. Moral progress, however modest and limited, was made in large part through moral argument establishing a morally correct consensus on major moral issues such as racial and sexual equality.

Fuller claims his eight elements constitute a morality because they form a view that considers humans as responsible agents.[9] Summers rightly criticizes Fuller's view as overinclusive.[10] For etiquette and other pseudo-moral systems see humans as responsible agents.[11] Touchstone tests to identify critical morality (e.g., Fuller's test of responsible agency) are, like the essentialist definitions used to identify law, wrongheaded. Like law, critical morality is too complex to define in that way. Critical morality, which is what I seek to link necessarily with law, is, like law, best defined by family resemblances. Dworkin supplies some resemblances (e.g., treating like cases alike, and treating immutable characteristics as morally irrelevant).[12] More exist, including one which I will use in section 4, below. So, we should not follow the separatists by decrying in advance the complexity of morality. For, as with the task of defining law, we do not want procrustean precision or pigeonholes which oversimplify complexities of morality. Morality may just be inexact. Even quite a few sciences, in the separatists' normative sense of 'science', are not exact sciences.

4. A Necessary Link in the Imperative Theory of Law

John Austin was a utilitarian.[13] And Austin was a separatist; his famous slogan was "The existence of law is one thing; its merit or demerit another." In this section I will argue that the following three tenets form an inconsistent

---

[6] Robert S. Summers, Instrumentalism And American Legal Theory Ch. 1 (1982).

[7] Hart, supra note 2, at 619 - 20.

[8] Gewirth, supra note 5, at 330.

[9] Fuller, supra note 4, at 162.

[10] Summers, supra note 3, at 128 - 30.

[11] For an instructive table summarizing how several norms treat humans as responsible agents, see, Louis P. Pojman, Ethics: Discovering Right And Wrong 5 (1990).

[12] Ronald M. Dworkin, Taking Rights Seriously 248 - 53 (rev. ed. 1971).

[13] Hart agrees with this classification of Austin's view. See, Hart, supra note 2, at 597. Bentham was another utilitarian separatist who believed in the imperative theory of law. Thomas Aquinas said "law is imposed on others as a rule and measure." Summa Theologica, The Basic Writings of Saint Thomas Aquinas, ed. Anton C. Pegis, Vol. II. (1945), "Whether Promulgation is Essential to Law?," answer to Obj. 3. Thus, Aquinas believed the imperative theory, and implied it was compatible with a necessary link to morality, a link he thought forged from rule by divine right of kings. See the text accompanying note 50 below.

triad: (1) utilitarianism; (2) the separation of law and morals; and (3) the imperative theory of law.

Austin, in his imperative theory of law, says "A command, then, is a signification of desire."[14] His imperative theory says that the sovereign's commands are habitually obeyed by the bulk of those commanded. Thus, a legal system, by definition, *necessarily* involves the habitual satisfaction of the desires motivating the commands that are laws. According to utilitarianism, the satisfaction of any desire has some moral value. So, a utilitarian who believes the imperative theory of law is constrained to believe that there is a necessary link between law and morals. Bentham also believed in the imperative theory, and so this analysis applies to his view, too.

One may object that the habitual satisfaction of the sovereign's desires need not involve the maximization of happiness, and thus need not meet the moral requirements of utilitarianism. True, habitual satisfaction does not imply the greatest good for the greatest number. The sovereign could be a tyrant whose habitual satisfaction comes only at the cost of much greater suffering experienced by millions. But habitual satisfaction does imply some significant degree of satisfaction of desire. And that suffices to show that Austin, as a utilitarian, must admit that any legal system, by definition, is a minimal moral achievement, even if this achievement is overridden by greater suffering. The necessary, habitual satisfaction inherent in a legal system necessarily creates a presumption in favor of the morality of the legal system. The presumption may be overridden (e.g., by the suffering of millions), but, according to utilitarianism, even if the presumption is overridden the legal system is nonetheless prima facie good. The prima facie moral goodness of the legal system is not eliminated by being overridden, for the habitual satisfaction exists even when it also involves a greater amount of suffering. And utilitarianism says the existence of satisfaction is always good. I will deal below with the question of whether one must, to rebut the separatists, claim that a connection greater than the one above is necessary between law and morals (e.g., whether one must claim that an unjust or immoral law is no law at all).

5. Necessary Links in Hart's Theory of Law

It seems "Hart is the best-known advocate in contemporary philosophy of law of the separation of law and morality."[15] Still, Hart admits that there is, in a sense, a natural necessity between law and moral principles against murder, violence and theft, since no legal system can survive without constraining mur-

[14] Austin, supra note 1, at Lecture I, fourteenth paragraph.

[15] Martin, supra note 4, at 210. See also, Timothy C. Shiell, "Making Sense Out Of A Necessary Connection Between Law And Morality," 1 Public Affairs Quarterly 77, 84 (1987).

der, violence and theft. But this connection between law and morality is not necessary but contingent on five facts that Hart notes about human nature and the human condition.[16] So I do not count this as the necessary connection with morality that I want to find in the definition or concept of law itself.

But three of Hart's other views suggest such necessary links. First, Hart claims that in unclear, penumbral cases "judges must [i.e., necessarily] legislate and so exercise a creative choice between alternatives..."[17] Hart suggests that penumbral cases will necessarily arise in any legal system, since law necessarily involves language, which will necessarily involve penumbral cases concerning various words in the language. Further, Hart says that law, by definition, has rules of adjudication. Thus, judges are necessarily included in any legal system. Now, when one chooses, one expresses a preference. Since the judge is legislating, he makes the law he chooses, and thus satisfies his preference. Hart, however, is not committed to utiltiarianism or any morality implying that the satisfaction of any preference is morally good. But Hart's view does imply a necessary link between law and the critical morality of utilitarianism (or any other morality implying that the satisfaction of preferences is a prima facie good). I explore this sort of argument in detail in section 6.

Second, Hart suggests a very different necessary link by saying:

> If we attach to a legal system the minimum meaning that it must consist of general rules – general both in the sense that they refer to courses of action, not single actions, and to multiplicities of men, not single individuals – this meaning connotes the principle of treating like cases alike ... [*O*]*ne* essential element of the concept of justice is the principle of treating like cases alike. This is justice in the administration of the law, not justice of the law. So there is, in the very notion of law consisting of general rules, something which prevents us from treating it as if morally it is utterly neutral, without any necessary contact with moral principles. Natural procedural justice consists therefore of those prinicples of objectivity and impartiality ... which are designed to ... minimize the risks of inequalities in this sense.[18]

Hart seems committed to the notion of law consisting of general rules, since he thinks law consists of primary and secondary *rules* (including rules of change and rules of adjudication) unified under a *rule* of recognition. Such social rules are necessarily general. Hart seems committed to implying that law necessarily has some pure procedural justice, since Hart says a legal system must, by its very meaning, consist of rules which are general in the sense that they apply to courses of action and to multiplicities of persons.[19] (Note that Austin claimed that all laws were general, distinguishing them from occasional or particular

---

[16] H. L. A. Hart, The Concept of Law 190 - 93 (1961).
[17] Hart, supra note 2, at Section III.
[18] Id. at Section IV.
[19] Id. at 623.

commands.[20] Thus, this necessary link might also apply to Austin's concept of law, though we would have to convince Austin, a utilitarian, that justice is a moral value.)

But is Hart right to infer from the fact that the justice of treating like alike is procedural that law is "without any necessary contact with moral principles"? I think not, since 'any' and 'contact' are extremely broad, and since justice is itself a moral principle. And the procedural justice of law's generality closely resembles Fuller's inner morality of eight ideals for law to be followable, which we saw in section 2 and which I will examine further in section 6. Hart is right to say that treating like cases alike can involve merely the procedurally just administration of a substantively unjust law, for example, "All blacks shall be enslaved for ten years." But treating like cases alike will achieve some minimal fairness not only in that no blacks will receive any favoritism (each black will be impartially treated as the equal of every other black) but also in that no blacks will be enslaved for more than ten years, and in that no non-blacks will be enslaved. This is a minimal moral achievement even if the legal system is, on balance and all things considered, unjust and immoral.

Finally, there is in Hart's theory one more area with some promise of supplying a necessary link between law and morality. Hart advances three elements, secondary rules, in his definition of law.[21] Each element, by definition, is designed to cure a social defect in a pre-legal society which has only primary rules, rules which only impose obligations. My aim is to show that some of these social defects are also moral defects. If some of them are moral defects, then there would seem to be a necessary connection between (Hart's concept of) law and (critical) morality. Hart says

> It is plain that only a small community closely knit by ties of kinship, common sentiment, and belief, and placed in a stable environment, *could* live successfully by ... a regime of unofficial rules. In any other conditions such a simple form of social control *must* prove defective and will *require* supplementation ...[22]

Since ethics concerns living well, Hart's requirements to "live successfully" seem to concern morality. Defects hindering successful living are moral defects.

One might object that we cannot get a *necessary* link to morality from curing these defects, since Hart excepts certain small communities. But Hart says only that such communities *could* live successfully, not that they must or will. And his claim is also fully compatible with saying that the communities will live successfully *despite* the defects. A community may overcome the defect

---

20 Austin, supra note 1, at Lecture I.

21 Hart, supra note 16, at Ch. 3.

22 Id. at 90 (emphasis added).

without using secondary rules, but the moral defect was still there to be overcome – and secondary rules necessarily would have overcome the moral defect. The cautious Hart's extreme language suggests that the defects would be less severe but still present even in the communities he might seem to except. He says of one particular defect that without secondary rules "in any but the *smallest* societies" it will "continue *interminably* . . ."[23] Further, we know that, as a contingent fact, there are communities that are not so small etc. So, if Hart is right, we know that in those larger communities there is a necessary connection between law and morality. Law *would* necessarily diminish defects in such societies – and as a matter of (contingent) fact it does.

The first defect is uncertainty. In the pre-legal society "doubts arise as to what the rules are or as to the precise scope of some given rule, [and] there will be no procedure for settling this doubt."[24] Now, is this social defect of uncertainty also a moral defect of the society? It clearly is. Uncertainty in the applicability or application of the law is bound to involve unfairness, since uncertain people will lack due notice and fair warning of what is to be punished, and how severely they are to be punished. Since there are no secondary rules at all, the level of uncertainty is bound to exceed any acceptable minimum of uncertainty. The application of uncertain law necessarily involves some degree of unfairness. If law, by definition, helps reduce this degree of unfairness, as Hart suggests, then law and morality are necessarily connected.

The second defect is "the *static* nature of the rules."[25] A society with only primary rules has no rules providing for changing the rules. Such rules would be secondary rules or power-conferring rules, rather than rules merely imposing obligations. Is such a static society morally defective? Almost always, yes, since it is so often the case that society must adapt to changing circumstances or changing individuals. But this is a contingent fact of human nature and the human condition, a fact like the five facts Hart notes involving the minimum content of natural law. So the second defect seems not to be necessarily a moral defect. Thus, even if law necessarily cures the defect, it does not follow that law and morality are necessarily connected.

The third defect is "the *inefficiency* of the diffuse social pressure by which the rules are maintained. Disputes as to whether an admitted rule has . . . been violated will always occur . . ."[26] First, must disputes be morally disadvantageous? No, they need not be. On the contrary, disputes over what the law is *can* be scholarly, instructive and invigorating. The history of scholarship is the history of disagreement. Second, is such inefficiency necessarily a moral defect?

---

[23] Id. at p. 91 (emphasis added).
[24] Id. at 90.
[25] Id. at 91 - 92.
[26] Id. at 90 - 91 (emphasis in original).

Arguably not, since the social pressure's ends or means *can* be entirely evil. Still, efficiency per se would seem necessarily to have *some* moral value, even if it were outweighed by the evil of the social pressure's ends or means. Inefficiency seems necessarily at odds with "successful living." We will explore this further in section 6.

So some of Hart's three elements of law have a necessary connection with morality. Hart makes it quite clear that law necessarily, by definition, is effective in diminishing the three social defects. He says:

> There are ... two minimum conditions necessary and sufficient for the existence of a legal system. On the one hand those rules of behaviour which are valid according to the system's ultimate criteria of validity must be generally obeyed, and, on the other hand, its rules of recognition specifying the criteria of legal validity and its rules of change and adjudication must be effectively accepted as common public standards of official behaviour by its officials.[27]

So Hart's theory can hardly rule out a necessary connection between law and morality, and even has some promise of providing such a connection.

6. Fuller's Necessary Connection

Law is necessarily a purposive activity. The purposes are those of the persons who create and use the law. But even Fuller, who thinks there is a necessary connection between law and morals, admits that such purposes can be immoral.[28] So what is the necessary link with critical morality? If we, like the separatists, adopt utilitarianism – a critical morality, we can properly say that the satisfaction of a law's purpose is necessarily and intrinsically a *prima facie* moral good. Fuller was no utilitarian. But, as we shall see, while a utilitarian must accept a necessary connection, my argument will also show that the necessary connection does not depend on the correctness or acceptance of utilitarianism. Utilitarianism favors the satisfaction of all desires and purposes, even legal purposes. The law's purposes are the desires of the lawmaker or a complex of desires or values embodied or embedded in the law. But the satisfaction of these desires is only a *prima facie* moral good. For the law's purpose may be, for example, sadistic, and so fail to maximize the satisfaction of all desires.

Some object that Fuller's alleged morality is not a morality but only a technology of efficiency. But utilitarianism, which the separatists accept, says efficiency in the satisfaction of human purposes is a moral value – indeed, the only moral value. And we will see how, according to Fuller, law involves human

---

[27] Id. at 113. Dworkin, supra note 11, at 20 - 21, interprets Hart to imply that the rule of recognition is a necessary and sufficient condition for law.

[28] Summers, supra note 4, at Ch. 3, especially p. 73.

purposes. One might also object that Fuller's alleged morality of law cannot be a morality providing a necessary connection between law and morality. For Fuller's alleged morality does not necessarily yield moral results. But this objection is too demanding. Utilitarianism is a counterexample to the objection. Utilitarianism is a morality, yet it does not guarantee moral results. For (the most common version of) utilitarianism requires the maximization of *expected* utility, which is probabilistic rather than necessary. Murphy's law (i. e., what can go wrong will go wrong) can counter any morality. No plausible morality can make moral results necessary.

One may object that my use above of *'prima facie'* is just another way to say that something is not necessarily what it appears to be on the face of it (or at first glance). Perhaps *'prima facie'* can be so used, but I do not so use it here. *'Prima facie'* means the moral good of satisfying the law's purpose can be overridden. For example, the frustration caused by a law that frustrates other purposes can override the importance of satisfying the law's purpose. But that it can be overridden does not imply that when it is overridden it is *eliminated.* The satisfaction of the legal purpose is a permanent but surmountable moral good (good, for short). It need not be good on balance, but the satisfaction of a legal purpose *conceptually* cannot be *all* bad.

One may object that the foregoing arguments show an improper disregard for the morality of means. First, the legal purpose or its means might be intrinsically evil and thus perhaps entirely evil; for we need not fully accept utilitarianism as the relevant critical morality. Second, nothing above says the deontological values of the means of satisfying the legal purpose can override the alleged moral good of satisfying that purpose.

Both objections fail. First, the costs of means should be morally considered. My point is merely that some *minimal* good is necessary, not that goodness on balance is necessary. The minimal good necessary need not prevail when balanced against other good and evils, including the goods and evils of the means to the law's end. This is why I claim merely a *prima facie* good.

Further, I do not exclude all deontological theories from critical morality. I use utilitarianism above to achieve reconciliation and persuade the separatists, who have utilitarianism as their theory of value. But not all deontological views (nor all teleological views) are sufficiently enlightened to be critical moralities. Moreover, I reject any deontology that says satisfying human purposes embodied in laws is intrinsically – regardless of the consequences – not even a *prima facie* good. For I support, as an element of critical morality, the tenet that, *ceteris paribus,* the satisfaction of any purpose is good. Note that I am not thereby assuming that utilitarianism is true; for it stands for much more than my tenet. Yet because utilitarianism implies my tenet, the separatists will accept my tenet *and* utilitarianism will still be a critical morality. The tenet is a part of critical morality and a *family resemblance* helping to identify critical moralities.

One may object that my tenet implies that satisfying sadistic purposes is, *ceteris paribus,* good. I admit this implication is problematic, but I accept it since it is so heavily qualified. The tenet implies merely that, all other things being equal, sadistic satisfaction is to some unspecified degree a minimal good. *Moreover,* it is not good *qua* sadism; it is good *qua satisfaction.* The satisfaction of the collective desires embodied in law, which results from the satisfaction of the law's purpose, is necessarily *prima facie* good. Second, I can readily allow deontological values to override the good of satisfying a legal purpose. Perhaps even the sadism of a purpose can override the good of its own satisfaction. Still, the good of its satisfaction (and conversely the evil of its frustration) is not eliminated but only overcome (overridden). I must insist on its continued existence even when it is counterbalanced (overridden) because a *necessary* connection cannot admit of even one counterexample. Finally, I probably do not even need to claim such a minimal *prima facie* good, since I can claim merely that frustrating such purposes is *prima facie* and minimally *bad.* This move lets me avoid saying, for example, that sadistic or racist satisfaction is somewhat *good.* And this move seems soundly based on the principle that gratuitous, needless, pointless or purposeless suffering or frustration is morally bad. Any morality that denies this principle seems implausible, and thus is not a critical morality.

Ryle gives an independent argument which supports my idea that law necessarily involves a minimal good. Ryle uses the idea of "achievement verbs" to infer conceptual truths about ordinary activities. Ryle did not explicitly have law in mind, but consider his examples. He says: "Just as a person cannot win a race unsuccessfully, or solve an anagram incorrectly, since 'win' means 'race victoriously' and 'solve' means 'rearrange correctly', so a person cannot detect mistakenly..."[29] Ryle's idea is precisely the same point Max Black makes with a medical example.[30] A doctor who regularly killed his patients by giving them poison instead of medicine is not practicing medicine in those cases. He is not even practicing medicine poorly; for he is failing to practice medicine at all. The verb 'treat' (in the medical sense) is another of Ryle's "achievement verbs." Some *minimal* success or good is required for treatment. Summers uses Black's example to illustrate a point made by Fuller. Fuller's point is that a system satisfying all the principles of legality still could not be a legal system if it *completely failed* to serve human *interests.*[31] Utter failure is below the minimal success required for the "achievement sense" concept of law. And human

---

[29] Gilbert Ryle, The Concept of Mind 238 (1949).

[30] Fuller, supra note 4, at 155 - 57 and Summers, supra note 3, at 39.

[31] Summers, supra note 4, p. 39.

interests are directly and intimately related to the purposes of humans.[32] Fuller makes several more points which seem to form a position both supported by Ryle's views and consistent with my arguments for a necessary connection.

Fuller says his eight elements constitute an internal or inner morality of law.[33] We saw in section 5 how Hart says that law's generality, which closely concerns Fuller's eight ideals for law to be followable, involves pure procedural justice (i.e., treat like cases alike, which, as we saw above, is one of Dworkin's family resemblances of critical morality). But in this section I emphasize a different necessary connection between law and morality, a link between law and – not procedural justice – but substantive ends of humans. Fuller says the eight are "means toward a single end."[34] This end is the achievement of a minimal legal order. He says "law is the enterprise of subjecting human conduct to the governance of rules," "an activity and ... the product of a sustained purposive effort."[35] He states: "Law, as something deserving loyalty, must represent a human *achievement*..."[36] He says law "must be worked for" and that law is a "collaborative human *achievement*."[37] Similarly, Fuller says one cannot interpret without minimal success, and that one cannot do the enterprise or activity called law without minimal success.[38] Notice that Fuller calls law an achievement and an *activity*. This fits well with Ryle's "achievement *verbs*." Indeed, Fuller says his eight elements are standards of minimal success that, when conversely stated, describe eight ways to *fail* to make law.[39] Likewise, ignoring purposes when interpreting particular laws leads not to a bad interpretation or even a misinterpretation, but to *no* interpretation *of* that particular law at all. For 'interpret' is an achievement-sense verb, implying that some minimally successful link is established between the putative interpretation and the thing allegedly interpreted. Summers makes the same basic point when he says Fuller thinks an interpretation must itself at least be sufficiently 'congruent' with the form of law which it purports to interpret to count as an interpretation *of* that law.[40] This necessary, minimal success allows Fuller to say rightly that "even bad laws ... have a claim to our respect."[41] He says "[t]his morality of order must be respected if we are to create anything that can be called law, even bad law."[42] Both this

---

[32] On this point, see, e.g., Kurt Baier, The Moral Point Of View 99, 106, 117 - 18, 202 - 03, and 209 (1958).

[33] Fuller, supra note 4, at 168.

[34] Id. at 104.

[35] Id. at 106.

[36] Fuller, supra note 3, at 632.

[37] Id. at 646 and 648.

[38] Summers, supra note 4, at 39 - 40 and Fuller, supra note 4, at 155 - 57.

[39] Fuller, supra note 4, at 39, 110, 129 and 148.

[40] Summers, supra note 4, at 110ff.

[41] Fuller, supra note 3, at 632.

order and the minimal success necessary for interpretation intimately involve the satisfaction or effectuation of purposes. Fuller says we should interpret *particular laws* in light of their purposes and to effectuate the human purposes embodied in them.[43] As for *legal systems*, he says:

> If laws, even bad laws, have a claim [based on critical morality] to our respect, then law must represent some general direction of human effort that we can understand and describe, and that we can *approve in principle even at the moment when it seems to us to miss the mark.*[44]

Fuller's idea is very similar to my surmountable but ineliminable good of satisfying legal purposes. Laws *necessarily* deserve respect as laws, for as laws they always represent at least some minimal human achievement of purposes that is worthy of some respect. As we have seen, the achievement of an enforced law is the satisfaction of the collective human desires embodied or embedded in the law, and we have seen that it is a tenet of critical morality that the satisfaction of human desires is a *prima facie* good.

One may object that law does not necessarily embody purposes of moral value. For the collective desires embodied in a law may *merely* be the desires of legislators long dead. Utilitarianism, for example, does not value the satisfaction of what we take to be the desires of the dead. I agree; such satisfactions are not the psychological satisfactions utilitarians value. But the objection is inconclusive for three reasons. First, Hart admits that even in hard cases judges are "implementing a 'purpose' which it seems natural to attribute (in some sense) to the rule itself rather than to any particular person dead or alive."[45] Second, philosophers from Aristotle to Joel Feinberg have defended the claim that we have *some* duties to give *some* respect to the wishes or purposes of the dead.[46] Third, I challenge the idea that a particular putative law serving *absolutely no* one's purposes is a law. True, it may be on the books and comply with all source-based tests of law and law's pedigree. But no one *wants* to enforce it, and so it goes unenforced. If an official wanted to enforce it, the law would have some purpose. So the law's *prima facie* good purpose need not be the purposes of the original lawgiver(s). For the satisfaction of any living

---

42 Id. at 645.

43 See Fuller, supra note 4, pp. 106 and 118, and Summers, supra note 4, Ch. 2.

44 Fuller, supra note 3, pp. 632.

45 Hart, supra note 2, at 627.

46 See, Aristotle, Nichomachean Ethics, Book I, Ch. 10, Joel Feinberg, Rights, Justice, And The Bounds Of Liberty 173 - 76 (1980) and Joel Feinberg, Harm To Others: The Moral Limits Of The Criminal Law 79 - 91 (1984). See also, Joan C. Callahan, "On Harming The Dead," 97 Ethics 341 (1987), Don Marquis, "Harming the Dead," 96 Ethics 159 (1985), Barbara Baum Levenbook, "Harming the Dead, Once Again," 96 Ethics 162 (1985) and "Harming Someone After His Death," 94 Ethics 407 (1984), and George Pitcher, "The Misfortunes Of The Dead," 21 American Philosophical Quarterly 183 (1984). All of the above, except Callahan and Marquis, argue that the dead can be harmed or wronged.

person's purpose is a *prima facie* good. A "law" which goes unenforced due to complete apathy, and which serves no one's purposes or interests, is no law; for the requirement of an "achievement-sense" concept of law, which I defended above, is not met. Moreover, the separatists (e.g., Holmes) who saw law as predictions of what courts *will enforce* would agree that such dead "law" is not law.[47] Such a pointless "law" might technically be a law on the books, but it would not be a law in action, a genuine law.

Further, the "achievement sense" concept of law is very much like a functional definition of law. Summers says Fuller endorsed a functional definition of law. An engine, for example, is defined or identified by how well it *satisfies* the purpose or function for which it is created or used. Summers summarizes the view, saying: "[T]he question 'Is this assemblage a steam engine?' overlaps mightily with the question, 'Is this a good steam engine?'"[48] Foot endorses this precise point about the definition of artifices. (Law is a human creation, and hence an artifice.) Foot states:

> [L]et us suppose that never in the history of this community were knife-shaped objects used as we use knives. These people have objects which look just like knives, are made of the same material and so on, but they only use them for some quite different purpose, such as marking plots of land. If asked whether they had knives we should not say, 'Yes, but they use them for quite different purposes from us', but rather 'No', explaining that they did as a matter of fact have things just like our knives, but that these were actually markers... [S]ince 'knife' is a functional word in the strong sense 'good knives cut well' must be held to be some kind of analytic proposition.[49]

Foot's view of markers resembles my view of an unenforced "law" which serves no one's interests. Such a "law" is just like a law in that it takes the same legal form on the books, but it is not used as a law must be used, and so it is not a law. It does not have the definitive purposes of law. Again, the separatists defining law in terms of the purposive patterns of officials' behavior would agree with me here.

Suppose *each* enforcer enforces the laws of a legal system not because he accepts any law (or even the legal system generally) but solely because he fears being punished by the other enforcers for refusing to enforce. Fuller says acceptance is a necessary condition for law.[50] So, he would say the example is not a legal system. Similarly, Hart's requirement that certain people accept the law (i.e., the internal aspect of the law) implies that the example is not a legal system.[51] But even if we reject this reasoning, the example is not a counterexample to my necessary connection. For, while the enforcers do not *ideally*

---

[47] See, Summers, supra note 6, at Ch. 5.
[48] Summers, supra note 4, at 25.
[49] Philippa Foot, Virtues And Vices 134 - 35 (1978).
[50] Fuller, supra note 3, at 638 - 43.

want to enforce, they want *on balance* to enforce the law. The satisfaction of the latter want is still a *prima facie* good.

7. Conclusion

Finally, one may object that the law's necessary good I describe is too slight to fulfil the spirit of the usual claims that laws and morals are necessarily connected. The good is slight, but recall this is the *necessary* moral force law has just in virtue of being law. So, law *always* has moral force. Moreover, my view can consistently agree that the moral force is dramatically greater as we move from discussing the black sheep of the family of law to more typical laws. But the objection may assume that the only opponent of the separatists is the one who claims that an unjust law is no law at all. But this is only the most extreme version of natural law's necessary connection between law and morals. Fuller's version, which claims only a prima facie necessary good, is a less extreme version. Indeed, not even Aquinas seems to have believed the extreme version. He cites Augustine's view that "a law that is not just *seems* to be no law at all."[52] But Aquinas need not say that all is as it seems. Elsewhere Aquinas implies that genuine laws can be to some extent unjust.

> Human law has the nature of law *in so far* as it partakes of right reason ... But *in so far* as it deviates from reason, it is called an unjust law, and has the nature, not of law ... Nevertheless, even an unjust law, *in so far* as it retains some appearance of law, through being framed by one who is in power, is derived from the eternal law; for all power is from the Lord God ...[53]

Aquinas believes that monarchs have the power to rule by divine right. And he sensibly believes that justice is a matter of degree (i.e., something can be more unjust or less unjust than something else). He concludes that even unjust laws can be genuine laws so long as a monarch ruling by divine right has issued that law. So not even Aquinas, the classic opponent of the separatists, goes to the extreme of insisting that an unjust law is no law at all.

David Lyons notes that separatists such as Holmes, Austin and Bentham were unified and motivated in their separatism "because they held that law could not be criticized intelligently unless its fundamental features were first identified and understood" and "because they wished us to see the law for what it is and [then] to direct it in morally more justifiable ways."[54] Does my analysis reconcile the separtists' critical and reforming motivation with a necessary link between law and morality? I think so. Lyons distinguishes two mar-

[51] Hart, supra note 15, at Ch. V, Section 2. See, Ronald M. Dworkin, Law's Empire 35 (1986).

[52] Aquinas, supra note 12, at Question XCVI.

[53] Id. at Question XCIII (emphasis added).

[54] David Lyons, Ethics and the Rule of Law 69 (1984).

kedly different formulations of separatism. The first claims, meekly, that law is morally fallible and that "any sound legal theory must leave room for moral criticism of law."[55] As we just saw, Aquinas avows that law can have less than the full degree of justice, and thus is morally fallible and criticizable. But Lyons concludes from the truth of this meek separatism that "Any theory implying that law is inherently good, right, and just will bear a heavy burden of implausibility."[56] Lyons' use of 'Any' seems to make his claim somewhat overstated, since there are many versions of a necessary connection, including my version of law as prima facie moral, that leave much room for moral criticism of law and yet claim that law is, prima facie, inherently good, right, and just. Aquinas' emphasis on the *degrees* of justice helps us to see this point. In short, 'inherently' does not mean *'fully.'* So I can claim that all law is inherently moral yet leave ample room for moral criticism of law by denying that all law is fully moral and affirming that law is only prima facie moral.

Lyons' second, bolder formulation of separatism claims "there are no [necessary] moral constraints on what can count as law."[57] I deny this bolder formulation, since I have argued that nothing which causes completely pointless, purposeless, gratuitous suffering or frustration can be law. Fortunately for my project of reconciling the separatists with their foes, Lyons admits that he finds the dispute too unclear to tell if the separatists and their foes would disagree about the second formulation. Lyons says merely that "[d]isagreement about this [second formulation] might be the basis for the conflict between natural law and legal positivism."[58]

Further, especially considering Fuller's quite different approach, Fuller's views are remarkably more reconcilable with the separatists' ideas than most believe.[59] Indeed, Hart says that if Fuller's inner morality of law "is what the necessary connexion of law and morality means, we may accept it. It is unfortunately compatible with very great iniquity."[60] (As I have argued, a necessary connection between law and morality can be merely a prima facie moral good, and thus compatible with very great iniquity.) Fuller's eight ideals are procedural, and he even criticizes Hart's tentative and substantive necessities of law. Moreover, the purposes of the law, which are so crucial for Fuller, need not have any particular moral *content.* Nor need they have, all things considered, moral content. Nor need they be, on balance, moral laws or purposes. All of this is consistent with the separatists' source-based view of law (though

[55] Id. at 67.

[56] Id.

[57] Id.

[58] Id. at 68.

[59] But I am not alone in reaching this conclusion. Michael Martin would agree that the views of Hart and Fuller are "much closer than is usually supposed." See, Martin, supra note 4, at 209.

[60] Hart, supra note 16, at 202.

Fuller's legal philosophy is elsewhere clearly inconsistent with their view). And Fuller is even a vigorous anti-formalist, as were the separatists.

In conclusion, several of the major views on the separation of law and morals are closer together than they are usually thought to be. Ambiguities often cloak their close proximity to one another. One might be tempted to conclude that the necessary connection between law and morals is not much to brag about. For it is merely a *prima facie* moral good which can, depending on the injustice of specific legal purposes and the circumstances, be easily overridden, or perhaps it involves only the *prima facie* evil of gratuitous, needless, pointless and purposeless suffering or frustration. But the necessary connection is of much theoretical significance, since neither the critical, reforming spirit motivating the separatists nor the motivations of natural lawyers such as Aquinas and Fuller requires that the necessary connection be much more to brag about than the connection I advocate. Further, the necessary connection is significant enough to include both prima facie considerations of procedural justice and prima facie considerations of utility. Furthermore, both sides can agree that a much stronger connection could be typical (though not necessary) of the family of legal systems.[61] The necessary connection may misleadingly seem less significant to some because it is so *theoretical.* But the issue concerns a *conceptually* necessary connection, not a *practically* necessary one, which separatists such as Hart admit exist and even advocate.[62] The *modest,* conceptually necessary connection I show solicits the critical attitude toward law that the separatists so admire. A more robust yet necessary connection between law and morals would perturb the separatists, imperil much of the reconciliation attempted above, and prove difficult to show.[63]

---

[61] See Fuller, "A Reply to Professors Cohen and Dworkin," 10 Villanova L. Rev. 655, 665 (1965), and Fuller, supra note 4, at 223 - 224.

[62] Hart, supra note 16, at Ch. 9 Section 2. On a practical link between law and morals, see, Wolfgang Waldstein, "Is There A Natural Law?," 10 Vera Lex 1 (1990).

[63] I thank Robert Summers and Philip E. Davis for their comments on earlier versions of this paper. I also thank the American Society for Value Inquiry for accepting this paper for presentation at its meeting with the American Philosophical Association's Central Division in April of 1990, and thank William Aiken for serving as commentator on that occasion.

Pragmatic Instrumentalism and the Future of American Legal Education

By Erik M. Jensen, Cleveland*

Law, after all, is not religion, not physics, and not just an applied social science. Law is law.

Robert S. Summers[1]

In an influential series of writings in the 1970s and 1980s, Robert S. Summers described, criticized, and sometimes praised America's dominant philosophy of law, pragmatic instrumentalism.[2] It was among Summers's major contributions to see the common core in several intellectual movements that had generally been studied separately – philosophical pragmatism, sociological jurisprudence, and the moderate wing of legal realism[3] – and to see the continuing influence of the common tenets on American legal philosophy. In Summers's view, pragmatic instrumentalism is a "fourth great tradition in Western legal theory, alongside analytical positivism, natural law philosophy, and historical jurisprudence".[4]

Pragmatic instrumentalism reached its ascendancy in the mid-twentieth century – the period from the 1940s to the 1960s – but it is still with us to a great extent. Dominant philosophies do not disappear overnight. While the practice of law in the United States may be undergoing structural changes that could have far-reaching consequences, it has not changed fundamentally in the last few decades.[5] And a lawyer today could dip into the work of many of

---

* Professor of Law, Case Western Reserve University, Cleveland, Ohio.

1 Robert Samuel Summers, Instrumentalism and American Legal Theory 271 (1982).

2 Id.; Robert S. Summers, Professor Fuller's Jurisprudence and America's Dominant Philosophy of Law, 92 Harv. L. Rev. 433 (1978) [hereinafter Summers II]; Robert S. Summers, Pragmatic Instrumentalism in Twentieth Century American Legal Thought – A Synthesis and Critique of Our Dominant Theory About Law and Its Use, 66 Cornell L. Rev. 861 (1981); see also Robert S. Summers, Lon L. Fuller (1984); R. S. Summers, Naive Instrumentalism and the Law, in Law, Morality and Society – Essays in Honor of H. L. A. Hart 119 (P. M. S. Hacker & J. Raz eds., 1977).

3 That is, not including those realists who reduced law to little more than what judges eat for breakfast – the practitioners of "gastronomic jurisprudence." See Summers, supra note 1, at 37.

4 Id. at 19.

5 I concede that the American legal profession is at a "crossroads of change." Robert L. Nelson and David M. Trubek, New Problems and New Paradigms in Studies of the

the most prominent "theoreticians"[6] of pragmatic instrumentalism – men like Felix S. Cohen, Jerome N. Frank, John Chipman Gray, Oliver Wendell Holmes, Jr., Karl N. Llewellyn, and Roscoe Pound – and read with profit.[7] For the most part, these men used language that came from the same planet on which legal practice was taking place. Many practiced law themselves.

But the intellectual footprints of those giants are disappearing. There is much wrong with pragmatic instrumentalism and, if it were being superseded by something demonstrably better, one might not mourn its passing. Unfortunately that is not the case. With the appearance of such new movements as law and economics, critical legal studies, and feminist legal theory,[8] fragmentation in the academy is so great that jurisprudential scholars can no longer agree on much of anything, including the issues for discussion. Practitioners of traditional jurisprudence – and from the perspective of the 1990s the pragmatic instrumentalists are traditional – have been called a "dying breed".[9]

The new movement scholars generally make no attempt to speak to the bar. Even if the new movements have as yet had little impact on American legal practice,[10] however, the effects are strong among law faculties. American legal academics have always overestimated their influence on young lawyers-to-be,

---

Legal Profession, in Lawyers' Ideals / Lawyers' Practices: Transformation in the American Legal Profession 1, 1 (Robert L. Nelson et al. eds., 1992). And the "sense of stability [of big law firms] has been shaken." Marc Galanter and Thomas Palay, The Transformation of the Big Law Firm, in Lawyers' Ideals, supra, at 31, 61. But despite the pervasive rhetoric about declining professionalism, most American lawyers operate today as most American lawyers did thirty years ago. If legal practice has changed, it is not because of philosophical changes, but because of such factors as clients' becoming more cost conscious.

[6] The term is in quotation marks because the pragmatic instrumentalists were skeptical of grand theories.

[7] With the exception of John Dewey, the other prominent pragmatic instrumentalists identified by Summers are relatively unknown today: Joseph W. Bingham, Walter Wheeler Cook, W. Underhill Moore, and Herman Oliphant. Summers, supra note 1, at 23, 284 - 88. Dewey, while renowned, was often not accessible to a general audience.

[8] Law and literature and critical race theory perhaps belong here as well. I use the term "movement" to mean only that writers in these areas have some sense of common goals.

[9] See Gary Minda, Jurisprudence at Century's End, 43 J. Legal Educ. --- (1993) (forthcoming). At many law schools, the issues of traditional jurisprudence – like What is law? and How is judicial discretion to be constrained? – continue to be taught in courses denominated "Jurisprudence." But the courses that most law schools now have in law and economics, feminist jurisprudence, critical legal studies, and other alternative perspectives have trumped traditional jurisprudence. I suspect that more American law students now read Toni Morrison for a law school class than read H. L. A. Hart or Karl Llewellyn (not counting Llewellyn's Uniform Commercial Code).

[10] Law and economics has had its successes in this regard, with the appointments of Richard Posner and Frank Easterbrook to the federal bench. But in the battles between the Chicago jurists and the real world, the real world has often won. See generally Richard A. Posner, The Problems of Jurisprudence (1990) (evidencing a softening of Posner's original law and economics principles).

but it is hard to imagine that at least a few tenets of these movements are not filtering into receptive and often unreflective student minds. If nothing else, the disarray in legal theory must be apparent to students at the major law schools. The process of lawyering may ultimately be affected and, as I shall argue, that is cause for more than a little concern.

It is the thesis of this essay that some of the modern jurisprudential movements share several core tenets with pragmatic instrumentalism, and those tenets are generally the least admirable ones. In retaining and at times extending the worst aspects of pragmatic instrumentalism, the American legal academy is becoming "de-lawed":[11] the idea that law has independent significance (apart from, say, politics, economics, race, or gender) is in decline.

As is suggested by the quotation with which this essay begins, Bob Summers does not accept the de-lawing of law schools. He is a student of legal philosophy with his feet firmly planted in substantive law – contract and commercial law.[12] He combats de-lawing for many reasons, I am sure, but one is fundamental: rejection of law as an independent concept and therefore as an independent discipline is a rejection of the rule of law.

Part I of this essay briefly describes pragmatic instrumentalism. In Part II I outline and criticize some of the traits common to pragmatic instrumentalism and the more prominent of the new movements. That discussion leads to Part III, which recounts the "canon debate" that seems to have developed in American legal academia. Finally, I provide some thoughts on Bob Summers and the direction of American legal education.

I. Pragmatic Instrumentalism

In his first work using the term, Summers justified his choice of "pragmatic instrumentalism":

> This philosophy is "instrumentalist" in that it conceives of law not as means-goal complexes but merely as means to external goals. It is "pragmatic" in several ways. It focuses on law in action and on the practical differences that law makes. It stresses the roles of legal actors and their technological "know-how." It is experimentalist. It is pragmatic, too, in its professed contextualism – its reliance on time, place, circumstance, interests, wants, and the assumed malleability of reality rather than on theories, general principles, and the "nature of things" as sources of ends and means.[13]

No one, it is fair to say, ever identified himself as a pragmatic instrumentalist. In that sense, pragmatic instrumentalism is a creation of Robert Sum-

[11] The term is borrowed from my colleague Arthur Austin.

[12] I was once described as having followed the Summers model in this regard. I can imagine no higher praise.

[13] Summers II, supra note 2, at 435.

mers: it was he who saw the commonalities – something approaching a general theory – that tied the different thinkers together intellectually. But America's dominant legal philosophy was no less real for its after-the-fact explication.

Summers did not claim that the most prominent pragmatic instrumentalists were in agreement on all significant issues. For example, legal realists would have found little to agree with in the work of a legal positivist like John Chipman Gray, who was nonetheless a pragmatic instrumentalist.[14] Regardless of such tension, which is inevitable in any intellectual movement, the leading pragmatic instrumentalists adhered to more than enough common tenets to justify viewing their core beliefs as a distinct, and often sophisticated, direction of thought.[15]

II. Pragmatic Instrumentalism and the New Movements

The new jurisprudential movements – such as law and economics, critical legal studies, and feminist legal theory – are products of the 1970s and 1980s, which is to say that they are partly celebrations of (or reactions to) the 1960s. Although some have suggested that critical legal studies is legal realism in different guise, the new movements are not simply revivals of the intellectual groups that comprised pragmatic instrumentalism.[16]

While not revivals, critical legal studies and law and economics do have some relationship to pragmatic instrumentalism.[17] In particular, they share value-skepticism; a conception of law, and of society as well, as malleable; and interpretational principles that reflect value-skepticism and the belief in law's malleability. "Formalism" in law is disparaged, and "law" is deemed to be so driven by underlying forces – be they economic, political, racial, or gender-based – that it has little significance apart from those forces.

As Summers was always careful to emphasize, pragmatic instrumentalism has given American legal theory much that is praiseworthy. Among other things, it was a needed corrective to the sometimes mindless formalism that antedated it, particularly among judges.[18]

Pragmatic instrumentalism has also had costs for the American polity, however. Because of value-skepticism and the related discounting of notions of a common good, pragmatic instrumentalism understated the importance of prin-

---

[14] See John Chipman Gray, The Nature and Sources of the Law (2d ed., 1921).

[15] See Summers, supra note 1, at 23.

[16] The purported relationship between critical legal studies and legal realism has been challenged by some CLS scholars. See, e.g., Mark Kelman, A Guide to Critical Legal Studies 12 - 13 (1987).

[17] Feminist legal theory fits less well here for a number of reasons, including the obvious lack of women among the prominent pragmatic instrumentalists.

[18] See Summers, supra note 1, at 279.

ciples of social order.[19] It underestimated the extent to which the very idea of "law" places limits on law's use in effecting significant change. And its principles of interpretation, grounded in that moral skepticism, reduced analysis of the written word to a secondary place in understanding law. These faults continue today and are exacerbated in the modern movements.

1. Value-Skepticism

The pragmatic instrumentalists had a theory of value, but it was one that looked primarily to the wants of individuals.[20] The merit of those wants was not subjected to intellectual scrutiny; they were accepted as givens, to be satisfied if possible.[21]

That theory of value (which, in a sense, denigrates theories of value) is familiar to practitioners of law and economics, who also give primacy to individual wants and desires: the market facilitates the maximization of those unexamined cravings. But value-skepticism is not confined to law and economics. Judge Richard Posner recently wrote that "the foundations [of traditional jurisprudence] have been kicked away. Today we are all skeptics."[22] Posner is right about the skepticism of modern legal academics generally (although he is wrong if he means that the traditional foundations were reasonably discarded).

The skepticism is tied, as both cause and effect, to the cultural and ethical relativism that began with the pragmatic instrumentalists and that pervades American law schools today. The skepticism is directed at the values that underlie law but, directly or indirectly, it also calls into question the idea of law itself. Witness the omnipresent student belief that nearly any position can be reasonably advanced in a legal matter: law is viewed by many as just a "game",[23] with no inviolable core. Taken to its extremes – and the early practitioners of critical legal studies were superb at reaching extremes – this view can lead to the conclusion that the law is radically indeterminate.[24] And radically indeterminate law is not law at all.

Extreme skepticism destroys our ability to evaluate particular laws and legal systems. Consider this example of cultural relativism, taken from a generally

---

19 See generally The Principles of Social Order: Selected Essays of Lon L. Fuller (Kenneth I. Winston ed., 1981).

20 Although the term "interests" was sometimes used, it referred to desires or wants of individuals. It carried no evaluative connotation.

21 See Summers, supra note 1, at 41 - 59.

22 Posner, supra note 10, at 453.

23 See Robert Granfield, Making Elite Lawyers: Visions of Law at Harvard and Beyond 61 - 65 (1992).

24 For a balanced discussion of the "fundamental contradiction" thesis that gave rise to radical indeterminacy, see Kelman, supra note 16, at 258 - 62.

fine work written by the current president-elect of the Association of American Law Schools, Rennard Strickland: "[W]e cannot judge the laws of a people by the standards of the people of another time and another place. To do so does violence to the very concept of law as a living institution."[25]

Preserving the concept of "law as a living institution" is precisely what should keep us from abdicating our evaluative responsibilities.[26] Of course we should not ignore historical context, but we should also not limit evaluative standards to those prevailing in a particular society at a particular time, without regard to the intrinsic merit of those standards.[27] One hopes that the laws of Nazi Germany – to take an easy case – should be evaluated using principles other than those of Nazism itself.[28]

Few would deny that a level of skepticism about purportedly eternal truths is desirable. But a radical skepticism that denies the possibility of eternal truths, even midlevel truths, can lead to something approaching nihilism.[29]

In a widely noted 1984 essay, Paul Carrington made a related point (and was subjected to heavy criticism for doing so) in questioning the foundations of the critical legal studies movement: "One cannot believe in one's professional skill and judgment as a lawyer unless one also has some minimal belief in the idea of law and the institutions that enforce it."[30]

Much the same criticism can be levelled at proponents of law and economics. Such scholars do not deny a human nature, of course, but most

---

[25] Rennard Strickland, Fire and the Spirits: Cherokee Law from Clan to Court xiv (1975).

[26] Cf. Walter Berns, Taking the Constitution Seriously 236 (1987) ("The Framers ... charged [the Supreme Court] with the task, not of keeping the Constitution in tune with the times but, to the extent possible, of keeping the times in tune with the Constitution.").

[27] Cf. Harry V. Jaffa, Crisis of the House Divided 371 (Washington paperbacks, 1973) (the "task of statesmanship" is "to know what is good and right, to know how much of that good is attainable, and to act to secure that much good but not to abandon the attainable good by grasping for more").

[28] One might even question, as Fuller did, whether Nazi laws were "law" as we should understand the term. Does not the concept of law, that is, have its own immutable characteristics? See Lon L. Fuller, The Morality of Consent 40 - 41, 54 - 55, 107, 123, 155, 158 (rev. ed. 1974). That is a question many modern students would not consider worth asking.

[29] See James Q. Wilson, The Moral Sense, 87 Am. Pol. Sci. Rev. 1, 9 (1993) (citations omitted):

> [T]he unwary philosopher [can be led] to suppose that if a sentiment does not settle everything, it cannot settle anything or to infer that if people make different choices, they must do so on the basis of different sentiments. The first error leads to logical positivism; the second, to cultural relativism; and the two together, to modern nihilism or, at best, to "liberal irony."

[30] Paul D. Carrington, Of Law and the River, 34 J. Legal Educ. 222, 226 (1984); see also id. at 227 ("More than a few lawyers lack competence because they have lost, or never acquired, the needed confidence that law matters.").

legal economists would be skeptical that nature has anything to tell us about the qualities of goodness or fairness.

Modern commentators forget that widespread questioning of the existence of eternal values is a recent phenomenon. The founding generation in the United States, after all, held certain truths to be "self evident" – that "all men are created equal" and "endowed by their Creator with certain inalienable rights".[31]

This is not to suggest consensus on what the enduring values are. Nevertheless, there was once substantial agreement that eternal values exist and that we, as reasoning beings, should be trying to discern and understand them. As James Q. Wilson puts it, "We may disagree about what is natural; but we cannot escape the fact that we have a nature, that is, a set of traits and predispositions that limits what we may do and suggests guides to what we must do."[32] We cannot escape it, but most of us don't believe it.

In a wonderful new work, Wilson writes of man's "moral sense," finding empirical support for the proposition that man – *by nature* – has at least rudimentary senses of fairness, of sympathy, of morality generally. He concludes that "all of the predictions that follow from a purely relativist view of human nature are, so far as one can tell, false".[33]

Certainly the existence of different cultures – historically and today – does not prove the rightness of relativism. As Leo Strauss explained, "[B]y proving that there is no principle of justice that has not been denied somewhere or at some time, one has not proved that any given denial was justified or reasonable."[34]

By disregarding conceptions of a higher good, as it largely has, modernity undercuts principles of social order and the rule of law. It may not be politically correct to quote him, but Allan Bloom got it right when he asked rhetorically: "[W]hen there are no shared goals or vision of the public good, is the social contract any longer possible?"[35]

My description of modernity will strike many as overblown, and a slippery slope from skepticism to nihilism is not inevitable. I am sure no modern legal scholars are willing to identify themselves as nihilists. But ask modern scholars for principles that might be used to explain why the philosophical bases of their movements are superior to anything else, and most would be hard-

---

[31] It should go without saying, although I guess it doesn't these days, that the term "men" in this context is not gender-specific.

[32] Wilson, supra note 29, at 8.

[33] Id. at 3.

[34] Leo Strauss, Natural Right and History 9 - 10 (1953).

[35] Allan Bloom, The Closing of the American Mind 27 (1987).

pressed to reply. Is the very idea of "law" merely a passing fancy in man's history, with no underlying *natural* theoretical justification?[36]

2. Malleability of Legal Principle; Interpretation

"Recent Russian history should have put to rest the view that everything is learned and man is infinitely malleable," writes James Q. Wilson,[37] but it has done no such thing. The new movements follow pragmatic instrumentalism in seeing few constraints on what can be accomplished in reordering society through legal engineering, with law as a "tool".[38] Law is susceptible to nearly limitless manipulation to achieve desired ends – or so it is believed.

Good lawyers are trained to look for, and make use of, ambiguity and uncertainty in legal language. But the perceived fuzziness of legal doctrine today goes far beyond that (as it did historically with many pragmatic instrumentalists). For example, the radical indeterminacy thesis of early critical legal studies clearly pointed to (in fact, it invited) the manipulation of "law" for almost any end.[39] The law and economics world is somewhat less malleable in that economic principles impose constraints on behavior and on what the law can reasonably hope to accomplish. Nevertheless, the language of law is thought to be so flexible that it can encompass economic principles whether or not there is any specific reference to those principles.

The malleability of doctrine can be seen in the techniques used in many American law school classrooms and legal writings to interpret judicial opinions. The goal is not to understand (and criticize) the published reasoning of the judicial author. Instead, the intention is to figure out what was "really going on" in the court's deliberations, and that may bear little relationship to the written opinion. The search is for unarticulated exercises of power or unexplicated economic trends that were driving the judges. Many of the interpretational excesses of legal realism are commonplace in today's academy.

The subordination of the analysis of reasoning in judicial opinions manifests itself in two different, but related, situations: interpreting individual opinions and deriving principles from lines of cases.

---

[36] Modern scholars might seek to defend law's importance in terms of fairness, but they would be reluctant to take the next step to see any grounding of "fairness" in nature.

[37] Wilson, supra note 29, at 9.

[38] Cf. Granfield, supra note 23 (present-day student perceptions of "law as a tool," suitable for nearly any goal).

[39] This is not to say that critical legal scholars would have approved any end. In its infancy CLS was a decidedly political movement, with strong Marxist overtones. But the purported indeterminacy made law an instrument of power that could be used for evil as well as for good. Indeed, law as a disguise for power was one of the crits' major criticisms.

If we are studying the works of a great mind and we have some reason to think that he was constrained in what he could write, we might very well want to figure out what he was really trying to say: to go beneath the surface, to read between the lines.[40] And we might want to do that in interpreting a single judicial opinion, when we know that all sorts of forces were pressing on the judges – forces of which they must have been aware, but which they might not have wanted to acknowledge for one reason or another.[41] For example, I agree that, in a limited way, the Supreme Court follows the election returns, and it would be silly to read any important Court opinion with no sense of extrajudicial factors.

But we would follow that informed process to read and understand *the opinion,* which is, after all, the law. It is a truism, but worth repeating, that the law in a published case is not only the result; it is also the reasoning.[42] If the language and reasoning of opinions are disregarded, in what sense is a Supreme Court opinion law? For that matter, in what sense is anything law that has been reduced to writing – a statute, a regulation, or an opinion – if the scope of interpretation is not constrained by the written word? Yes, judicial opinions may contain rationalizations, but rationalizations are reasons and can be evaluated on the merits.

The distressing neglect of the written word has also become common in analyzing historical bodies of law. When commentators analyze lines of cases (which may number in the hundreds), they often purport to look for consistent principles that (they say) must have been driving courts over the years. For examples, I direct you to any law and economics analysis that sees economic rationality behind the common law even though the judges involved made no mention of efficiency.[43]

---

[40] See Leo Strauss, Persecution and the Art of Writing 22 - 37 (University of Chicago ed., 1988).

[41] Planned Parenthood v. Casey, 112 S. Ct. 2791 (1992), presented the extraordinary spectacle of three Justices (O'Connor, Kennedy, and Souter) openly justifying continued deference to Roe v. Wade, 410 U.S. 113 (1973), the landmark abortion decision, not because the decision was right, but because overruling *Roe* could seriously weaken the Court's capacity to exercise its judicial power. It is no surprise that judges think about institutional stability in resolving cases, but it is unusual for judges to be so open about concerns that do not go to the merits of the matter.

[42] That distinction is often disregarded in discussions of the famous desegregation case, Brown v. Board of Education, 349 U.S. 294 (1954). Acceptance of Brown as constitutional analysis has become a prerequisite for judicial appointment in the United States. See Ronald Dworkin, The Bork Nomination, 34 N.Y. Rev. Books, Aug. 13, 1987, at 3, 3. But the required acceptance of *Brown* is symbolic rather than substantive. The actual opinion in *Brown,* which emphasizes that education in common values is necessary for good citizenship, is no longer taken seriously in a society moving toward multiculturalism.

[43] E.g., Richard A. Posner, Economic Analysis of Law 251 - 55 (4th ed., 1992) (describing the "implicit economic logic of the common law").

Now, my complaint is not with the use of modern doctrine to suggest a more appropriate way that cases could have been analyzed historically. It is perfectly proper to argue that, if the judges had had the benefits of our modern learning, they could have done a better job of analysis while coming to the same results. And I see no objection to the proposition that newly discovered, superior principles ought to be taken into account in future analysis.

It is something else altogether, however, to assert that principles which were not expressed (and could not have been expressed given the level of economic learning at the time) must have been motivating jurists. What is gained intellectually by pretending that the implicit reasoning was something it could not have been?

Legal scholars often say they have found rationalizing principles that create consistency in lines of cases otherwise apparently in disarray: something like "The results in two centuries of railroad cases are consistent with the application of my principle *x*." But as a description of historical fact, such consistency is phony, and manufactured history adds nothing to the value of a principle.

If the rationalizing principle has justificatory power, it should survive on its merits; the principle becomes no more powerful as reason simply because decades of cases could have been decided, but were not, on the basis of the principle. And a weak principle also derives no authority from the fact that it could have been used to decide cases in the past. The authoritative power of precedent, which may protect weak as well as strong principles, should not attach to principles that in fact were not used by decision-makers.

Perhaps it is time in the United States for a reconsideration of the value of formalism – of reading statutes narrowly and reading judicial opinions with a sense of the opinions *as written*.[44] One sometimes wonders whether the term "formalism," when used disparagingly (as it usually is), is a synonym for "law," as that term was traditionally understood. To be sure, we need to reject mindless formalism, as the pragmatic instrumentalists did, but we should not forget the benefits of a principled formalism.[45]

---

[44] Reluctance to pay attention to the written word can be found in many legal contexts. See, e.g., Berns, supra note 26, at 233 - 36 (discussing refusal of Supreme Court Justice Brennan to give weight to clear constitutional language permitting capital punishment).

[45] The values of formalism are better understood by our British colleagues, as John Tiley demonstrated in his look at, and rejection of, American tax jurisprudence's "substance over form" doctrine. See John Tiley, Judicial Anti-Avoidance Doctrines: The US Alternatives, 1987 Brit. Tax Rev. 180 (1987); Judicial Anti-Avoidance Doctrines: Some Problem Areas, 1988 Brit. Tax Rev. 63 (1988); Judicial Anti-Avoidance Doctrines: Corporations and Conclusions, 1988 Brit. Tax Rev. 110 (1988). Bob Summers has spent a great deal of intellectual effort in considering British-American differences in the importance of form and substance. See P. S. Atiyah & R. S. Summers, Form and Substance in Anglo-American Law (1987). In fact, his first publication – as a young assistant professor at the University of Oregon – was an examination of form versus

3. Influence of Other Disciplines; The Law as Law

Is law just politics? Or economics? Gender? Race? Something else? It is now common to criticize the idea that there is a "distinctive space for law".[46]

The issue is not whether other disciplines should be used to inform legal analysis. Of course they should. It would be folly to make law without taking into account economic factors, for example.

Furthermore, we can all concede that law is in some sense politics; it is not and cannot be a closed system of purely neutral logic. We know that American legal bodies could not have been immune to the demands of industrialization, which meant that decisions on the whole supported that development. And the law in the United States has unquestionably been dominated by males, and white males to boot. The well-to-do by definition have done better than the less successful.

But it does not follow that because politics (or economics or whatever) affects the law that law is nothing but politics. It is demonstrably not the case that white males always act in ways intended to further the interests only of white males. Nor do courts and legislatures act only to further the interest of the rich and powerful. And so on. The flaw in the arguments used to denigrate the idea of law today is the same one that justly condemned the extreme wing of legal realism: the conceded existence of what might be called extra-legal factors does not mean that law is nothing but such factors.

The debate about whether law is in some sense distinctive is at the center (I believe) of the so-called "canon debate" in the American legal academy. I discuss that debate in the next section of this essay.

III. The "Canon Debate" in American Legal Education

1. The Mysterious Legal Canon

The theme of the 1993 Annual Meeting of the Association of American Law Schools, held in San Francisco in January, was "Multiple Cultures and the Law: Do We Have a Legal Canon?" The answer – a largely orchestrated answer – was a resounding No.

---

substance in the tax area. A Critique of the Business Purpose Doctrine, 41 Or. L. Rev. 38 (1961). Cf. Robert S. Summers, Lon L. Fuller 3 (1984) (noting the many influential legal academics who began their careers at Oregon – modestly omitting the name of Summers).

[46] See, e.g., Andrew Goldsmith, 'Positively Postmodern Stanley' and Other Law Stories, 56 Mod. L. Rev. 248, 253 (1993) (seeing nothing in law apart from politics and the pain and violence of daily life) (reviewing The Fate of Law (Austin Sarat & Thomas R. Kearns eds., 1991)).

Those responsible for planning the sessions seem to have concluded that the question was not even one for serious academic discussion. Of the five speakers at the Meeting's plenary session, only one was arguably a defender of traditional legal values and scholarship.[47] One speaker's address was followed by a standing ovation from, I estimated, one-third of the audience. Was this an academic meeting or a political rally?

A follow-up session, "Learning from the Canon Debate: Law, Culture, Perspective," presented under the auspices of the AALS Executive Committee, included six speakers, none of whom spoke in defense of anything like tradition or academic rigor. Two of the speakers described themselves as one-time "canonettes," participants in traditional academic discourse, who had since come to see the errors of their ways.[48]

Even if defenders of the canon (whatever that might be) were to be excluded from the discussions – a decision impossible to justify in an academic setting – one might have expected some clear exposition of what was being attacked. But no speaker defined the legal canon.

In English departments, for example, there is some sense of a real canon debate, at two levels. On one level, the debate focuses on additions to and deletions from a generally accepted body of knowledge: given limited time both inside and outside class, should, say, Toni Morrison displace a dead white eurocentric male on a reading list?[49] Canon debates of this sort always go on, in all branches of the university, as our subject matters change incrementally. At another level, however, the debate in English departments considers whether there is *any* body of knowledge that an educated person in the field should be familiar with.[50]

The legal-academic analog to such disputes is not obvious. No one means (I hope, although I'm not sure) that a student who is a future commercial lawyer need not study the Uniform Commercial Code. Would the most extreme critic

---

[47] The speakers were historian Patricia Limerick, literary theorist Stanley Fish, and law professors Derrick Bell, Patricia Williams, and Cass Sunstein. I characterize Sunstein as the defender of tradition within that group (although, to be fair, I should note that Limerick's rollicking address contained some defense of traditional values). Most of these papers are to be published (somewhat revised) in the Journal of Legal Education, volume 43, number 1.

[48] "Canonette" comes from the names of backup groups to popular singers (like Ray Charles and his Rayettes). Those groups mouth sounds, often nonsense words, without thinking.

[49] Cf. T. Walter Herbert, Breaking the Deadlock at the Heart of Literary Studies, Chron. Higher Educ., Mar. 3, 1993, at A52 (noting how "the party of revision" regards Hawthorne as "the ultimate dead white guy").

[50] Similarly, historians have had their disputes about what historical subjects should be studied. At the plenary session, Patricia Limerick, a historian of the American West, noted the difficulty that her sub-discipline had in becoming recognized in the academic reward structure.

of legal tradition seek the services of a lawyer who has no grounding in the appropriate area of substantive law?

The canon under attack at the AALS Meeting seems to be a more diffuse, but higher order, set of ideas. It apparently includes rationality, rigor, and the Socratic method. It may include moderate or conservative political views. And I am afraid it includes the idea of law itself.[51]

2. The Legal Academy Today (with a Reference or Two to Bob Summers)

If the canon under attack is what I think it is, I have no doubt that Bob Summers is an unrepentant canonette. He is a superb scholar and the best example I know of the traditionally rigorous Socratic teacher. Bob has spent his academic life training young lawyers-to-be in legal doctrine that matters – contracts and commercial law – while trying to convince those often doubting students that being a good lawyer (and a good person) also requires a firm grounding in jurisprudence, history, the arts. Had Sir Walter Scott not already said it, Bob Summers might have done so: "A lawyer without history or literature is a mechanic, a mere working mason; if he possesses some knowledge of these, he may venture to call himself an architect."[52]

In a very real, but very peculiar, sense, Bob has prevailed in one of his great battles: American law schools are now filled with "perspectives" courses. In many respects, that is a very good thing. Who can complain if students are exposed to the broadest range of ideas?

Unfortunately the one perspective that is being driven into a secondary position at many of America's law schools is that of *law* itself – law as distinct from politics, economics, race, or gender. It is precisely that perspective which is new for so many students and in which they should therefore be immersed. If they wish to do so, however, students can graduate from most schools having had minimal contact with substantive law outside the required first-year courses.[53] The students' legal training might touch the law in only its most abstract forms.

---

[51] Sometimes those characteristics are – very, very sadly – condemned as white male values. How did we get (or return?) to the point where self-proclaimed defenders of women and minorities can suggest that women and minorities are inherently less rational than white males? Or that the American political regime, with its emphasis on individual rights, is in some fundamental sense male? Cf. Catharine MacKinnon, Toward a Feminist Theory of the State 229 (1989) ("To be a person, an abstract individual with abstract rights, may be a bourgeois concept, but its content is male."); id. at 163 ("The state is male jurisprudentially, meaning that it adopts the standpoint of male power on the relation between law and society.").

[52] Guy Mannering 259 (reprint 1964) (1815), quoted in Bryan A. Garner, The Elements of Legal Style 211 (1991).

[53] Even those requirements are in decline, explicitly or implicitly, at many schools.

As the value of law has come increasingly into question in the academy, the tone of scholarly debate has declined. The de-lawing of law schools has coincided with the increasing politicization of American academia[54] and the stultifying effects of "political correctness." Some have ridiculed the idea that there is anything like an "atmosphere of scholarly paralysis, censorship, and intimidation" in the American academy today,[55] but it is true.

The legal academy rewards the new, which often means the silly,[56] and that inevitably affects the tone of scholarly debate. Loud, obnoxious, ridiculous positions – the "new" – are increasingly common in the literature. Does the serious scholar ignore the ridiculousness, hoping it will sink from its own weight, or engage it politely, thereby giving it greater intellectual credence than it deserves?[57]

The classroom, too, is under stress. Rigor of the sort that Bob Summers has always insisted on now meets serious student resistance; we have seen the creation of a literature that presents law students as members of an oppressed group.[58] Students "more interested in policy than law"[59] – as if the two were entirely discrete bodies of learning – urge that emotionally and politically charged statements should be given at least as much weight in class as cool, rational analysis, and they are getting support for that position from a steadily increasing number of professors.

As if all of this weren't bad enough, the academy faces another challenge to its independence. The organized bar is understandably bewildered by goings-on in law schools,[60] and it is reacting to jurisprudential fragmentation by push-

---

[54] See Granfield, supra note 23, at 8 - 9; see generally Roger Kimball, Tenured Radicals: How Politics Has Corrupted Our Higher Education (1990).

[55] E.g., Toni Morrison, Introduction: Friday on the Potomac, in Race-ing Justice, En-gendering Power xi (Toni Morrison ed., 1992).

[56] See Daniel A. Farber, The Case Against Brilliance, 70 Minn. L. Rev. 917, 917 (1986) ("The ... traits of novelty, surprise, and unconventionality that are considered marks of distinction in other fields should be considered suspect in economics and law, in which thoughtfulness may be a more important virtue.").

[57] As an example of an attempt to engage overblown and often patently ridiculous authors on their own ground (and using similarly polemical language), see Kenneth Lasson, Feminism Awry: Excesses in the Pursuit of Rights and Trifles, 42 J. Legal Educ. 1 (1992) (less than restrained criticism of radical feminist writings). But see John A. Siliciano, Fighting with Angry Women: A Response to Lasson, 42 J. Legal Educ. 461 (1992) (criticizing Lasson for not engaging radical feminists on high intellectual ground); Kenneth Lasson, Comments in Reply, 42 J. Legal Educ. 467 (1992) (finding no such ground).

[58] One of the most recent examples of whining is Richard D. Kahlenberg, Broken Contract: A Memoir of Harvard Law School (1992).

[59] Id. at 180.

[60] See, e.g., United States v. Six Hundred Thirty-Nine Thousand Five Hundred and Fifty-Eight Dollars in United States Currency, 955 F.2d 712, 722 (D.C. Cir. 1992) (Silberman, J., concurring) ("many of our law reviews are dominated by rather exotic offerings of increasingly out-of-touch faculty members").

ing for increased emphasis on skills training.[61] Excessively clinical law schools should be no more palatable in an academic setting than law schools without law, but the pressures from outside university walls to lessen the separation between law schools and legal practice will be hard to resist.

*

Can the rule of law survive if law is seen as derivative, malleable, and excessively rational?[62] Do we want a world in which "law" is determined by emotion rather than reason? Is the only alternative in legal education the clinical law school?

It is more than a little sad that an essay written as a tribute to Bob Summers has so negative a tone. What Bob has stood for his entire life – rigor, discipline, *legal* reasoning – is under attack in the American academy, and, in some institutions, the good guys have surrendered and withdrawn from the field.

I am pessimistic about the direction of the American legal academy, and I suspect that Bob is too. Nevertheless, my unhappiness does not mean that I think Bob's work has had no influence. Quite the contrary. He has been one of the most important figures in American legal education in his generation.

And there are some hopeful signs in the academy. Most law and economics scholars no longer insist on using an efficiency thesis to explain everything, and critical legal studies has few believers left in radical indeterminacy. Furthermore, there remains the core of American legal educators who, for varying reasons, have been largely immune from the strident jurisprudential battles.

Perhaps the greatest reason for hope is that Bob Summers is only sixty, and I see no signs that he is willing to give up the fight for superior legal education and scholarship. We can anticipate another thirty or forty years of exciting and interesting intellectual work from him.

---

[61] The "MacCrate Report" is the most prominent example. American Bar Association Section of Legal Education and Admissions to the Bar, Legal Education and Professional Development – An Educational Continuum: Report of the Task Force on Law Schools and the Profession: Narrowing the Gap (1992).

[62] Granfield, supra note 23, at 76 - 77.

Ethical Aspects of the Concept of Legal Standard

By Enrico Pattaro, Bologna

1. Presentation

This paper consists of two parts. The first (sections 1 - 5) is a general attempt to place the notion of legal standard within a context, or more properly a tradition, of ethical discourse. The second (sections 6 - 11) develops the distinction between legal standard and legal rule and deals more specifically with the ethical issues involved in the notion of legal standard.

2. A Tradition of Ethical Thought Behind the Concept of Legal Standard

The history of Western thought has displayed a remarkable degree of thematic and conceptual continuity from its ancient Greek beginnings. In the natural sciences this continuity remained unbroken until the seventeenth century, when the scientific revolution led to the abandonment of the Aristotelian model: in the humanities and social sciences it was maintained until the nineteenth century and the birth of philosophical positivism.

In the natural sciences the break with the old model was complete and definitive, for the discovery of entirely new objects of research, along with theoretical and conceptual tools which were far more powerful and no less comprehensive than the old, rendered it genuinely obsolete. In the humanities, on the contrary, and in the social sciences, the old themes, theories and conceptual models for a time maintained their place alongside the new, or sometimes reappeared after a long absence. This was because, in the humanities and the social sciences, the new models did not always produce better results, or new objects of enquiry, or more powerful and more comprehensive theories and concepts than the old.

The notion of legal standard is a good example of just such a renaissance, for it revives, under the relatively modern label "legal standard", ancient themes and conceptual models which contain elements not only of Aristotelian but also of Roman, medieval, and, most importantly, baroque thought.

The themes thus revived by the notion of legal standard are those of prudence or practical wisdom, of judgement and of wit (or common sense): all of them conceived since the ancient Greek philosophy as typical of moral, political and aesthetic domains. Prudence (or practical wisdom), judgement and wit (or common sense) are intuitive faculties *par excellence,* and as such suited to deal with the specific circumstance and the individual case, as required by moral and political life as well as by aesthetics.

In the works of baroque thinkers, and particularly in their moral, political, aesthetic and literary treatises, great emphasis was placed on the need to reduce wit to an art, according to Matteo Pellegrino. This is evident in works on the reason of state; and in the poetical treatises of, for example, Baltasar Gracian, Emmanuel Tesauro and John Lyly. Their aim was to establish and make explicit the rules of prudence, to expose the art of politics (understood as a way of acquiring and preserving power), and to lay down the canons of literary good taste. The writings of the Marquis Bouhours, Mme. Dacier and Lodovico Antonio Muratori further exemplify this trend.

Law is a mixture of prudence, judgement and common sense. From Aristotle's *epieikeia* (fairness) to Roman law and the *jurisprudentes* of medieval law, until the European codifications, and the French Civil Code in particular, legal minds continued to develop such great themes running through Western thought. Legal thinkers, especially in the seventeenth century, the baroque period, insisted that *jus* should be *in artem redactum* as other matters of judgement and prudence. They thought, in other words, that rules (or "standards", to use the modern term) of prudence, judgement, fairness and common sense should be laid down to define limits and provide a set of criteria to act as guidelines, the domain of prudence, judgement etc. being so fluid and open to subjectivism.

3. The Current Revival

In modern times these themes have made their reappearance in the new rhetoric of Perelman (1958), which attempts to preserve the notion of the reasonable in any discourse on values. Previously, in 1953, Theodor Viehweg had published a booklet, *Topik und Jurisprudenz,* in which he reclaimed topical, dialectical and "prudential" discourse for legal reasoning.

Even Jürgen Habermas, in the radical restructuring of the relation between theory and practice which constitutes the central idea of his work, did much to rehabilitate the rhetorical and humanist approach to those disciplines which deal with social conduct, in opposing, for example, the *prudentia* of Giambattista Vico to the voluntarism of Hobbes.

As recently as 1987 Aulis Aarnio, from an analytical point of view, published a book in which he speaks of what is reasonable and acceptable in ethical and legal discourse in terms which (apart from his expressed intentions) hark back through Perelman and Habermas to Aristotelian themes and methods of analysis. In this same trend of legal-philosophical thought I put, in a way, the works by Robert Alexy and Aleksander Peczenik.

4. Roscoe Pound on Legal Standard

When we consider Roscoe Pound's classic definition of legal standard, we see that the idea of prudence and of "prudential" reasoning plays an important role: it is, indeed, one of the central moral aspects of the idea of legal standard. This is why I have gone so far back, to the Greeks and to the division between the sciences and the humanities, in tracing its origins.

Roscoe Pound writes:

> Roman lawyers worked out certain standards or measures of conduct, such as what an upright and diligent head of a family would do, or the way in which prudent and diligent husbandman would use his land. In similar fashion English equity worked out a standard of "fair conduct" on the part of a fiduciary. Later the Anglo-American law of torts worked out, as a measure for those who are pursuing some affirmative course of conduct, the standard of what a reasonable, prudent man would do under the circumstances. Also the law of public utilities worked out standards of "reasonable service", "reasonable facilities", "reasonable incidents" of the service, and the like. In all these cases the rule is that the conduct of one who acts must come up to the requirements of a standard. The significant thing is not the fixed rule but the margin of discretion involved in the standard and its regard for the circumstances of the individual case.

According to Pound, there are three characteristics of legal standard:

(1) It involves "a certain moral judgement upon conduct", which should be "fair", or "conscientious", or "reasonable", or "prudent", or "diligent".

(2) Legal standard, moreover, does not involve "exact legal knowledge exactly applied". On the contrary, it requires "common sense" about "common things", or "trained intuition about things outside of everyone's experience".

(3) Finally, legal standard is not "formulated absolutely and given an exact content": it is "relative to times and places and circumstances"; it must take account of the facts of the particular case; and to some degree it implies that "each case is to a certain extent unique".
(Roscoe Pound, *An Introduction to the Philosophy of Law,* revised edition, New Haven, Yale University Press, 1955, pp. 57 - 58.)

5. A First Conclusion

One could easily quote passages from Aristotle, Aquinas, Vico relevant to the Pound's characterisation; or from Pascal, for example, where he opposes the *esprit de finesse,* to the *esprit de géométrie* and identifies in the *esprit de justesse* the moment at which the *esprit de finesse* is applied. He says further that it is applied "naturally and without artifice", not by reasoning but by intuition.

In these passages we would find the same ideas which Roscoe Pound synthesized into the three characteristics of legal standard: the idea of a moral judgement upon conduct that should be reasonable, prudent, diligent, and so on; the idea of common sense and trained intuition; and the idea of the uniqueness of every case.

Whatever else these ideas suggest, they contain the essential strands of that tradition of ethical thought which, from Aristotle's *Nichomachean Ethics* has as its central theme the idea of prudence as a practical virtue which enables us to find, by a mixture of intuition and rationality, or rather reasonableness, the "only right answer" to a particular case.

This is perhaps the most important ethical aspect of legal standard. It shows that legal standard is concerned not only with morality but also, and particularly, with critical morality: in other words, morality that derives not only from conduct and custom (which constitute positive morality) but also from reflection, analysis and ethical theory. The tradition of thought to which I have appealed in order to show how it has shaped the idea of legal standard is, in all the different guises in which it has appeared and reappeared throughout history, one of the two great traditions of Western ethical thought: the other is represented by the rationalist doctrine of natural law.

Both the ethics of what constitutes reasonable conduct in a particular case and the abstract ethics of the rationalist doctrine of natural law are attempts to provide a critical basis and "objective" criteria for the moral choices that we make.

6. Many Distinctions in the Distinction between Legal Rule and Legal Standard

I shall now turn to other and more specific ethical aspects of legal standard in the context of the distinction between legal standards and legal rules.

I have noticed that contemporary writers, when discussing the distinction between legal standard and legal rules, never make it clear whether the distinction in question is between a legal rule and the prescription of a standard or between a legal rule and an actual standard. An actual standard is a standard which already exists in social practice and may be taken as a model of conduct: it is the object of a prescription.

I believe that we must distinguish between a prescribed standard and the prescription of a standard.

We must also distinguish between the prescription of a legal standard and other types of prescription, where what is prescribed is something other than a standard.

And we must, finally, distinguish legal standard from other models of conduct which exist in social practice and differ from the legal standard.

7. Legal Standard vs Legal Rule

Clearly, the prescription to comply with a given standard is in itself a legal rule, a linguistic formulation by a legislator or judge, whereas a standard is a model of conduct practised in social life. In other words, the prescription of a standard does not itself derive from the sphere of custom.

What *does* derive from the sphere of custom is the standard itself, the object of the prescription. The first and the most interesting and striking difference between legal standard and legal rule is then a difference in kind: the same difference existing between statutory law and custom. A legal rule is a prescription and it belongs to the domain of statutory law. Legal standard, on the contrary, is a model of conduct which exists in social reality and thus belongs to the domain of custom. Indeed, this is a particularly important aspect of legal standard, for it is also because it is grounded in custom that it has a moral dimension.

8. Legal Rule vs Prescription of a Legal Standard

The difference between a legal rule and the prescription of a standard is of another sort. A standard is itself the object of a legal rule which prescribes its application. The distinction, then, is here between different species of legal rules. While the difference between legal rule and legal standard is one of kind, the difference between a legal rule which prescribes the application of a legal standard and a legal rule which prescribes something else is a difference of species.

I shall now consider some of the differences between a legal rule which prescribes a standard and a legal rule which prescribes something other than a standard.

First of all, the prescription of a standard is not a rule that prescribes a certain well-defined conduct, as is the case, for example, of rules of conduct which forbid theft or murder.

Nor is it even a rule of competence, that is to say a rule which grants to a body or to an individual the power to make law: the rules which grant regulatory power to an administrative organ, or invest judges with the power (and impose on them the duty) to act as if they were legislators (this is for instance the case of art. 1 of the 1907 Swiss Code), or grant the power to settle a question according to fairness or according to the nature of things, are classic examples of such rules.

Nor, finally, can it even be said that the prescription of a standard is simply a rule of vague or indeterminate content, like rules which establish certain legal consequences in case "one causes grave bodily harm", or when "failure to abide by a contract is of little importance": in such cases determining what constitues grave bodily harm or when the failure to abide by a contract is of little importance is left up to the courts.

9. The Prescription of a Legal Standard Defined

The prescription of a standard is, in my view, to be counted among the rules referring or appealing to other rules for the discipline to be applied. Such are, for instance, the rules which appeal to Roman or canon law, or to international treaties, or to other laws applicable either directly or by analogy, or to general principles of law, to customs and to local traditions. And the rule which prescribes an appeal to a standard is another rule of the same kind.

Furthermore, the prescription of a standard, particularly by this sort of appeal, defines a way of conduct rather than a specific conduct; the rule does not prescribe *what* we should do but rather *how* we should act in doing what we are called upon to do. It might, for example, prescribe that when we are responsible for the administration of other people's assets we should act as a diligent husbandman does when using his land; or that we should act fairly when preparing, concluding or performing a contract; or that we should be diligent, prudent and reasonable in the exercise of a function or a duty.

One might say, then, that a rule which prescribes a standard prescribes certain virtues. Some of these, like prudence, or diligence, or good faith, are civil virtues, and are prescribed by an appeal to relative models as they are practised in society. Clearly, this further aspect of the (prescription of a) legal standard – the prescription of virtues – is a moral aspect.

The standard appealed to, then, is a model of conduct to be found in existing social practice. Like custom, it belongs to the factual, social and psychological realm, and as such it is of a different kind from prescriptions which define, by linguistic formulations, abstract models of conduct. One might say that the legal standard is "law in action" rather than "law in books"; or, better still, that it is "morality in action" to which appeal is made by laws in books.

10. Legal Standard as Distinguished from Habit and Custom

We must now define a more specific aspect of legal standard, by distinguishing it from other kinds of models of conduct which exist in social practice: habit and custom.

Habit is not, in the strict sense, something obligatory. It is a uniformity of conduct and not a measure of correct conduct; it does not constitute a parameter of conduct.

Nor is habit necessarily the expression of conscious and critical aptitude with regard to conduct. On the contrary, one could even say that it is never, or only very seldom, such an expression. Legal standard, on the other hand, is a model of conduct which entails the idea of the right action, and moreover this right action is arrived at by the exercise of critical judgement. Habit entails no such idea.

The idea of the right action with regard to a standard is touched on by Roscoe Pound when he writes that a standard is an average measure of correct social conduct (R. Pound, *Administrative Application of Legal Standard,* p. 12). And the idea of the correct action – of the rightness of an action – is, in turn, a characteristically moral idea.

The idea of the right action is in fact common to both custom and legal standard. But there are other characteristics of legal standard which distinguish it from custom: first, the legal standard entails the exercise of a critical moral sense, whereas custom entails only positive morality; and second, legal standard is flexible and elastic, while custom is rigid and fixed.

If we were to establish a hierarchy it might look something like this: Habit belongs to the domain of non-critical and non-obligatory social practice. It does not touch on the realm of morality: neither on that of positive morality, because it lacks the idea of the right action, nor on that of critical morality, because it lacks the idea of critical judgement. Moreover, habit is rigid.

Custom belongs to the domain of positive morality. Unlike habit, it involves the idea of the right action, but not the exercise of the critical faculty. Moreover, it, too, is neither flexible nor elastic, but rigid.

Standard, on the other hand, belongs to the domain of critical morality. Because it involves morality, it entails the idea of duty and rightness; and because it involves the critical faculty, and is the fruit of reflection, it is sophisticated. Finally, it is not rigid, but flexible and elastic.

11. Summary of the Ethical Aspects of Legal Standard

To recapitulate: it seems to me that we can distinguish at least the following ethical aspects of legal standard, taking them to be perspectives or viewpoints from which legal standard may be considered to belong to the domain of ethics in certain senses of the term:

(a) Legal standard *is addressed to the domain of practice*: it is a model of conduct. As such, it belongs to the domain of ethics in the traditionally accepted broad sense of that term, which includes morality (or ethics in the strict sense), law, politics and economy, and which excludes, for example, art, religion and science.

Note that on this view the legal rule which prescribes the standard, as well as other legal rules, also belongs to the domain of ethics, as well as the standard prescribed.

(b) Legal standard is also a model of conduct which *belongs to the domain of practice*. It exists in social practice; it is not a written, formulated, promulgated rule; like habit and custom, it exists as a psychological attitude and a model of conduct present on an intersubjective level within a group, a class, or a social milieu.

On this view, legal standard belongs to the domain of ethics in another sense of the term, a sense derived from the opposition of *ethos* and *eidos,* practice and theory, action and thought. Legal standard not only addresses itself to conduct (which written laws typically also do); it *is* a certain kind of conduct.

If we want to claim that ethics does not exist outside social practice, we should not include the legal rule in the domain of ethics; but we *should* include legal standard. On this view, a legal rule does not belong to the realm of ethics even if it prescribes a standard, while the standard prescribed does. What we have here, in other words, is an appeal by the domain of law (or of legal rule) to the domain of morality (or of legal standard).

(c) Furthermore, legal standard is a model of conduct which *belongs to the domain of qualified practice*. This is to say that legal standard, like custom but unlike habit, is a real model of conduct involving the idea of duty: the idea of right action, and correct conduct, independently of the end (for example, independently of the wish to obtain something useful) or the motive (for example, independently of the fear of sanctions) of the action or conduct.

If we want to claim (as I do) that the idea of duty and of correct conduct is essential to morality, we will want to include legal standard in the domain of ethics.

(d) Legal standard is also *a model of the exercise of certain virtues*. The legal rule which prescribes a legal standard (for example, the diligence of a head of family) prescribes a civil virtue by appealing to the standard recognised as appropriate to the correct exercise of the prescribed virtue.

An accepted sense of the term "ethics" involves reference to virtue. Ethics in this sense concerns legal rules (which prescribe virtue and, by appeal or reference, prescribe the relative standard) as well as the prescribed standard, which is no more than the correct way of exercising the virtue in question.

(e) Legal standard *aims to arrive at the just solution of each specific case*. Indeed, Aristotle defines *epieikeia* (fairness) precisely as justice in the specific case. He compares fairness to the measuring rule used by the masons of Lesbos, which could be adapted to the curves and rough surfaces of the terrain because it was made of supple and elastic materials. Aristotle sometimes also used the term *gnome* (judgement) to mean the capacity to judge of what is equitable.

The domain of ethics is often defined in opposition to the domain of law. This is not only, or not principally, because, unlike law, which is abstract, ethics is grounded in practice, but also, and most importantly, because it deals with the concrete and the specific where law does not: it concerns itself with concrete cases and specific situations. "Situational ethics", for example, concerns itself with specific situations, and it is one accepted sense in which the term "ethics" can be understood. I do not mean by this to imply that legal standard can be reduced to a version of situational ethics. Rather, and more simply, I mean to point out that some kinds of ethics, situational ethics among them, presuppose adherence to the particularities, and sometimes the unique nature, of the specific case; and that legal standard involves (this is mentioned in the third characterisation of it which Pound supplies) an ethical dimension even on a "situational" view of ethics.

(f) Finally, legal standard *belongs to one of the two most important traditions of Western moral thought.* This is the point I tried to elaborate in the first part of this article (sections 1 - 5). Among the principal streams of Western moral thought there are two which stand out by their richness and their antiquity: the rationalist tradition of natural law, which produced ethics that were *more geometrico demonstratae,* and the tradition of the reasonable, which centred on the ideas of prudence and practical wisdom (*phronesis*) and judgement (*sunesis, eusunesia, gnome*) and produced methods and procedures apt to judging concrete (as well as "hard") cases. Legal standard belongs to this latter tradition.

Was it a Legal Order?

By Hubert Rottleuthner, Berlin

One of the favorite occupations of legal theorists is constructing definitions of law. It is by no means always clear what questions they aim to answer by doing so. It may be that the goal is to employ the definition to assist in distinguishing legal norms from other sorts of norms (for example, and most often, from those of morality). Or it may be to formulate normative criteria that will enable one to distinguish between valid and invalid norms (say, because they are unjust), in which case the ability to recognize which norms are legal norms is presupposed. Many of these definitions appear to contain abbreviated versions of legal theories buried somewhere within, for example, theories about the origins, development and functions of law (avoiding close scrutiny of their assumptions).

Not only is it important that it be made clear to what questions a proposed definition is addressed, but also it ought to be specified what relevance the definition may have to the solution of concrete legal problems in particular societies. A "realistic" legal theory should be concerned with real problems and not just with joining in a debate with historical or contemporary authors or having an impact on purely internal controversies in the realm of theory. And finally, a proposed definition should be so formulated that it can be applied to the realities of social life; so that it would be possible with its assistance, for example, to decide whether a particular norm under examination is one of law or of morality, or whether it should be considered to be valid within a particular legal system, or whether one may properly call that normative system a legal order at all, etc.

In what follows my effort will be to discuss several of such definitions in order to determine whether they are capable of shedding light on the question whether the legal order of the German Democratic Republic (GDR) was a legal order in the sense of (Western) definitions – as it was held to be according to the internal Marxist-Leninist understanding of the GDR. I will undertake to determine if using these definitions can contribute to a more precise understanding of that legal order by attempting to see to what extent it fulfilled their criteria.

An effort of this kind is not merely of theoretical interest but may have practical consequences. Events that took place in the GDR are now under juridical examination through legislation, judicial decisions and administrative determinations in the Federal Republic of Germany. It may also contribute more generally to an understanding of the way law functioned in the so-called former socialist countries, as part of the background to the establishment of new legal systems in places where, according to many political figures and legal theorists, new legal orders are being erected on the ashes of previous systems, after a long period in which lawfulness was lacking.

I. Some Recent Definitions of Law

My starting point is three definitions that have been put forward in recent years:

> "Law is the totality of norms that belong to a state-organized or international system of norms, insofar as these are by and large socially efficacious and exhibit a minimum of ethical justification or capacity for ethical justification, as well as those norms adopted under this constitution, insofar as they exhibit a minimum of social efficaciousness or the potential to be socially efficacious and a minimum of ethical justification or capacity for ethical justification."[1]

> "Law is a system of norms that (1) raises a claim of justness and (2) is part of a totality of norms that belong to a by and large socially efficacious constitution, insofar as they exhibit a minimum of social efficaciousness or potential social efficaciousness and are not extremely unjust, and to which (3) the principles and other normative arguments belong, on which the procedures of application of law depend or must depend in order to fulfill the claim of justness."[2]

> "Law is a totality of social norms (1) whose efficacy is by and large guaranteed by organized coercion, (2) whose application and establishment requires an appropriate authorization and (3) whose claim to be binding presupposes a belief in their legitimacy."[3]

These definitions have the following in common:

- Law is understood as a quantity of *norms,* more specifically the norms of a constitution and those norms which issue from it (Alexy adds: principles, arguments, procedures).
- Issuance (and application) of norms *according* to a constitution or some type of higher authority is what makes these norms elements of a legal order, within which they have validity.
- *Justness:* this characteristic is treated differentially. In one a minimum of ethical justification or capacity for ethical justification is required of the constitution and the other norms; in another, law should raise a claim of just-

[1] R. Dreier, Der Begriff des Rechts, Neue Juristische Wochenschrift 1986, pp. 890 - 96 (896).

[2] R. Alexy, Begriff und Geltung des Rechts, Freiburg/München 1992, p. 201.

[3] P. Koller, Theorie des Rechts. Eine Einführung, Wien/Köln/ Weimar 1992, p. 44.

ness; in yet another the claim of legal norms to be binding presupposes "belief in their legitimacy."

- Social *efficacy* of the norms of the constitution and the norms issuing from it: This characteristic is usually qualified in some way. They should be "by and large" efficacious, or a "minimum" of efficacy or "capacity for efficacy" is called for. (Koller, in the tradition of M. Weber, Geiger and others, adds that efficacy must be guaranteed through organized coercion.)

I want to touch briefly upon a few problems that I see in these definitions: The question can be raised whether norms are the only "element" of law, that is, whether law can be defined solely in terms of norms. If Alexy accepts certain actions, namely "procedures" (and does not seem to mean only the *norms* of procedures), then the door is open to include a wide range of elements. Max Weber, for example, understood law as a "social order", meaning a conglomeration of norms, actions, institutions (e.g., the legal profession, the personnel of courts). For sociology of law, in any case, it is appropriate to have a concept of law that works with a multiplicity of elements – actions, persons (groups), organizations, etc. – all of which have a *reference to legal norms*.[4]

With respect to the problematic notion of a "totality of norms" I will go into greater detail later, in discussing the questions of justness and efficacy. The notion seems to make sense insofar as the validity of a particular norm needs to be defined in relation to an "entire" legal order. But that raises the question of what defines the entirety or unity of a legal order. According to Dreier and Alexy that should be the constitution, yet that is also itself an element of the "totality of norms".

The definitions make it possible to explicate an important aspect of the relationship between law and morality, namely the question to what extent a definition of law can succeed without recourse to moral elements.[5] The neutrality of a proposed definition is not marred by the use of moral arguments to support a definition that does not itself include moral elements. A necessary relation between law and morality is said to exist – by definition, so to speak – if elements in the definition appear which cannot be determined without resort to moral values. This is definitely the case for the elements "a minimum of ethical justification or capacity for ethical justification" (Dreier) and "not extremely unjust" (Alexy). It is possible, however, that a definition may contain moral elements that can be descriptively "reduced", that is, are susceptible to being operationalized for empirical investigation. This may be true for the element "belief in their legitimacy" (Koller). Similarly, the existence of the

---

[4] See H. Rottleuthner, On the Sociological Concept of Law, in: Prawo w zmieniajacym sie spoleczenstwie, Kraków 1992, pp. 43 - 55 (German version in: ARSP Beiheft 44 (R. Alexy, R. Dreier, U. Neumann, eds.), Stuttgart 1991, pp. 300 - 11).

[5] I am thankful to a yet unpublished manuscript by Klaus Füßer for important clarifying suggestions.

characteristic "claim of justness" in Alexy's definition could be established by an investigation of the statements made by the legislator with respect to the norm in question (with the predictable result being that, of course, something good was desired, if not the very best.)

II. On the Justice and Legitimacy of Law in the GDR

Article 17, sec. 2 of the German Unification Treaty denominates the GDR as a "SED[6]-regime of injustice" (but simultaneously recognizes the validity of the legal system of the GDR to a degree that it rarely enjoyed when the GDR still existed.) There also have been references to the "system of injustice" of the GDR.[7] And there has been widespread use of the term "rule of injustice *(Unrechtsstaat)*" as a forceful attempt to create a counter-concept to "rule of law *(Rechtsstaat)*".[8] Labels of this kind have the entire state system as their target. Does that mean that in the GDR there was not a particle of law? No legal order at all? What can the definitions considered above contribute to the effort to answer this question?

What is it that is being evaluated in employing the criterion "not extremely unjust" or "a minimum of ethical justification or capacity for ethical justification"? Is it the totality of all of the norms that have been adopted under the constitution as well as the constitution itself? That would presuppose that one already had employed some concept of law to distinguish between the law and other phenomena (non-law), that is, if one defines law as a set of norms, between legal rules and non-legal rules (e.g., moral or customary). The further distinction between what is (legally) just and (legally) unjust could be made only after this neutral, basic distinction was made (for which the above definitions would yield little).[9] Once the potentially legal norms are identified, the above-named moral criteria must be applied – and, note, it must be to their "totality". Needless to say, no one has made the effort to grasp and evaluate all of these norms. Rather, isolated examples are offerred to draw a conclusion – what conclusion? – about the character of the totality of the norms.

---

[6] *Sozialistische Einheitspartei Deutschlands* = Socialist Unity Party.

[7] E.g., Landgericht Berlin, Urteil 20.1.1992, Neue Juristische Wochenschrift 1992, pp. 691 - 96 (695).

[8] H. Sendler makes the statement that the GDR "at its core" was an *Unrechtsstaat* (illegal/unjust state), Neue Justiz 1991, pp. 379 - 82; later, he said it was so "only" at the core, Zeitschrift für Rechtspolitik 1993, p. 3. – H. Roggemann (Neue Justiz 1992, pp. 377, 382) employs a compromise formulation: "pre-rule of law state" *(vorrechtsstaatlicher Staat)*. It is important to emphasize, in any case, that the criteria for "just" law are not congruent with those for "rule of law" *(Rechtsstaatlichkeit)*.

[9] Perhaps Koller is attempting to introduce this approach by using the formulation "norms, which by and large are effective through the guarantee of organized coercion".

The following examples, at least, many of which are standard examples,[10] should permit one to determine just what it is that is being evaluated. On the one hand, it appears that it is legal norms "as such" which are held to be "extremely unjust" or "not capable of justification". On the other hand – and this is definitely more frequently the case – it is particular actions or activities which are said to be incompatible with legality.

Among those norms of which it is said that one can see their unjust character "as such" are included, e.g.,

- the offense of *Boykotthetze* (political agitation) set out in Art. 6 of the constitution of 1949 (in force until 1968).[11] In this instance highly indefinite sanctions, up to and including the death penalty, were attached to an offense whose elements were stated in extremely vague terms.
- For the commission of economic crimes, the threatened punishments were horrendous, and, at least by western sensibilities, completely excessive (especially in the 1950s).
- The case of the law for the protection of the GDR border of 1982 is more difficult.[12] It is not immediately apparent that it restricts one from leaving the limits of the national border (sec. 9). The provision for employing weapons does not on its face sound "extremely unjust". But during the so-called *Mauerschützenprozesse* (trials of GDR border guards – after unification – for having shot or attempted to shoot people who had tried to escape over the border) there came to light an entangled skein of directions to the border guards consisting of normative orders from lower levels of the hierarchy plus guidelines, instructions, and commendations which were partly unofficial. This mish-mash makes it extremely difficult to determine which of these formal and informal norms were unjust *ab initio* or what aspects of the actual practice of the use of weapons on the border, if any, could be seen as inherently contrary to law, that is, according to GDR "criteria" – or were so according to universal criteria, that is, western principles of respect for humanity. One would have to make the assumption that the addressees had been empowered to shoot through the deliberate construction of ambiguity, leaving them receptive to orders or even hints from their superiors.
- Was Para. 213 StGB-DDR, which made it illegal "to cross the border illegally" a law that was "extremely unjust" *ab initio*? Could judges, therefore,

[10] E.g., Sendler, Zeitschrift für Rechtspolitik 1993, p. 4; see also K. Lüderssen, Regierungskriminalität, Frankfurt a.M. 1992.

[11] "Agitation against democratic bodies and organizations, incitement to violence (assassination) against democratic political leaders, public manifestation of religious, radical, or ethnic hatred, militaristic propaganda as well as agitation for war and all other actions directed against equality are offenses under the penal law," that is, subject to sanctions ranging from one year in prison to the death penalty.

[12] Gesetz über die Staatsgrenze der DDR, 25. 3. 1982, GBl. I, p. 197.

who sentenced people on the basis of Para. 213 be charged with "perversion of law" *(Rechtsbeugung)*?[13]

- After October 3, 1990 (the date of official unification) the GDR rule that judges could give legal advice in matters in which they might later be called upon to make decisions was seen as blatantly incompatible with having an independent judiciary. However, one must take into consideration, at least, that the constitutional clause that was the basis for the independence of judicial decision-making (Art. 96 of the Constitution of 1974) had a completely different interpretation in the GDR.[14] Legal counseling by judges was thought to be completely consistent with it; the prevailing view was that it was beneficial to those seeking legal redress, and many of them made use of it. It is at this point that the general problem of a moral evaluation becomes clear: to what extent one accepts the "internal" evaluation and interpretation of a legal system; how far one applies "external" values and interpretations (in which case the internal perspective is seen only as a naked lie, as propaganda or illusionary).

With respect to actions which themselves were violations of GDR law, the following kinds of examples are given:

- Various types of crimes of office: corruption through high party functionaries and government officials; intervention in judicial proceedings[15] or other government decisions by party functionaries; violations of the election laws through fraud, as in the last communal elections in the spring of 1989.
- Obtaining privileges through government officials or party functionaries, or through certain lawyers (e.g., in connection with requests for emigration).
- Violations of telephone privacy and other forms of eavesdropping by the secret police *(Stasi)*.[16]
- Expropriation of goods that could be traded for hard currency, e.g., using repressive taxes or other forms of extortion to obtain valuable antiques.

Another category of interest are those cases in which judges and other legal personnel *(der Rechtsstab)* disregarded the norms then in force:

- Perversion of law *(Rechtsbeugung)* by judges and prosecutors; the primary instance of this are the so-called Waldheim cases, in which just about every

---

[13] This would have to be rejected under the criteria that were employed in the trials by West Germany of the former Nazi judges for perversion of law (in which, between 1948 and 1950, only two professional judges were convicted).

[14] As was also, for example, the category "statutory judge".

[15] Compare this with the extreme examples from the 1950s: F. Werkentin, Walter Ulbricht als oberster Gerichtsherr, in: Vorgänge 1991, pp. 1 - 15.

[16] It is appropriate in this connection to call for an international comparative study of legal regulation of the activities of secret police.

procedural rule was knowingly violated, monstrous penalties were imposed, and not the least effort was made to require proof of individual guilt.[17]

- Decisions under Para. 213 in cases arising out of failed attempts at "illegally crossing the border".
- Dismissals of employees who had filed papers for emigration; in these cases the required judicial procedure for dismissals was ignored – on the basis of an (unpublished) internal directive.

The list could be continued.[18] But it still would not answer our question: *When does a list of examples of illegallity and injustice permit one to draw the conclusion that the "totality of norms" had an unjust character?*

There were ample grounds to conclude that the Nazi regime had a total lack of a legal order, because in that instance not a single fundamental principle was bound to be respected (e.g., that of equality before the law). The mere utterance of the Führer's will could have the quality of law (though, presumably, not his commands to his sheep dog), and wide areas of government activity lay entirely outside legal control. Nevertheless, after 1945 the Allies – primarily on practical grounds – declined to declare invalid all of the statutes and official decisions of the Nazi regime (including the judgements of the *Volksgerichtshof,* the so-called People's Court, and the *Sondergerichte,* the special tribunals), and then be faced with making only particular exceptions. Instead, the Allied Control Commission enumerated those particular laws it had decided to declare invalid.[19] – Therefore, once again, the question may be posed, how does one arrive at an evaluation of the "totality of norms"?

Alongside this question, I already have put forth a further one: just what, exactly, is to be evaluated? Only the norms? Or must other phenomena, especially those actions closely linked to legal norms, be brought into view? The examples mentioned above which are claimed to demonstrate GDR-injustice *("DDR-Unrecht")* clearly have shown that it is not so much "norms as such" which are scrutinized as it is particular activities, of which in some of the cases it is completely unclear whether they were in pursuance of the norms then in force or in violation of them.

In this connection a third problem surfaced: from what perspective should the evaluation actually be made, and to what extent should the understandings

---

17 With respect to this complex, see W. Eisert, Die Waldheimer Prozesse. Der stalinistische Terror 1950. Ein dunkles Kapitel der DDR-Justiz, Esslingen/München 1993.

18 Not usually mentioned is the use of the death penalty in the GDR (with the exception of the twenty-four executions in the Waldheim cases and the Smolka case); cf. K. Schmude, Fallbeil-Erziehung. Der Stasi/SED Mord an Manfred Smolka, Böblingen 1992. The death penalty was abolished in the GDR in 1987; the last execution took place in 1981 (after about 180).

19 The Law on Rehabilitation *(Rehabilitationsgesetz)* of 1992 also speaks of damage from particular "decisions in violation of the rule of law".

of the "participants" be taken into account? This point can be clarified by considering the other criteria cited in the definitions – "a claim of justness" or "belief in their legitimacy". So far as it is the constitution of the GDR that is called into question, one would have to say that it had "a claim to justness". For instance, after a substantial period of public debate, which led to alterations of the original draft, a referendum was held on the constitution of 1968.[20] The real difficulty in analyzing the legal orders of the countries of "actually existing socialism" lies precisely in the fact that they articulated the highest values – Justice, Humanity, Peace, Friendship among Peoples, Equality, Fraternity, the Common Good, not to mention Humanism, Democracy and every other universal value imaginable. Yet these good intentions ("Come what may, I love you!"[21]) were bound up with a monopoly of coercive benevolence and – at least during the Stalinist phase – with a readiness to destroy anything that was labelled as belonging to the "enemy" or its ways. It was this bombastic-moralistic feeling of self-worth that had the effect of removing almost all scruples in the manipulation of legal norms. At the same time that it was an *expression* of this absolute "claim to justness" it stood as an *instrumentarium* at the disposition of the socialization-dictators. One cannot smooth over the distinction between what was believed and what was done by declaring the official values to have been a mere façade; the problem still remains how can one describe the "real" actions without taking into account the declared beliefs. What concepts can be employed, in which the actors could still recognize themselves?

This phenomenon, the instrumental proviso in a thoroughly moralistic law, makes it nearly impossible today to say anything meaningful about the "belief in their legitimacy". The official moral rhetoric that then existed does not in itself raise doubts about the existence of such a belief. The results of opinion studies made in 1989 in the GDR, which include questions that go to the issue of acceptance of legitimacy, are difficult to interpret. One cannot regard the degree of acceptance as merely a consequence of an effort to satisfy the wishes of the interviewer. Even less convincing are assertions by the west that the GDR populace always had held certain legal rules to be invalid. Now, after a

---

[20] One cannot write that off as pure propaganda noise. Ulbricht himself was sceptical whether a referendum could be won (Cf. Protokoll der 5. ZK-Tagung, 21. 3. 1968, pp. 126ff. – Institut für die Geschichte der Arbeiterbewegung – Zentrales Parteiarchiv (IfGA ZPA) IV 2/1/373). Cf. also the analysis of the particular proposals: Bericht vom 18. 3. 1968 über die Ergebnisse der Volksaussprache für die ZK-Tagung (IfGA ZPA IV 2/1/372); and see the "highly confidential" appendix containing a detailed statistical assessment of the proposals.

[21] Security Minister Mielke spoke this way in his last speech before the *Volkskammer* (the GDR Parliament) in Fall 1989. The claim that the Marxist-Leninist *ideology* is "inhumane" per se is the expression of the kind of stupidity that reflects nothing more than one's belief in one's beliefs.

period of transvaluation of values, it would be completly impossible to test that.[22]

A fourth problem, finally, must be discussed: What would the application of the definitions considered above consist of – even if the three problems just mentioned were solved? Would the result be that a yes/no determination could be made? That it would be established that there was a legal order or there was none? Or is there a way to avoid such a dichotomy?

A strategy often adopted to characterize the legal order of the GDR is to recur to the terminology of Ernst Fraenkel's book, *The Dual State,* that is, his distinction between a normative state and a prerogative state.[23] He employed it to characterize the system of rule under the Nazis in the period up until about 1938. This distinction has the advantage, at least, that unlike that between *Rechtsstaat* (rule of law) and *Unrechtsstaat* (rule of unjustice), it is not so loaded down with value judgments, but it still is a dichotomy.

The application of Fraenkel's categories to the legal situation in the GDR does not produce the conclusion that it was on the same level as the Nazi state. On the dimension of terror, of racist and military horror, they are far too wide apart.

> "The entire legal system has become an instrument of the political authorities. But insofar as the political authorities do not exercise their power, private and public life are regulated either by the traditionally prevailing or the newly enacted law ... Normal life is ruled by legal norms. But since martial law has become permanent in Germany, exceptions to the normal law are continually made."[24]

The problem of applying Fraenkel's distinction to phenomena other than the Nazis is grounded in the fact that the differentiation between normative state and prerogative state directs us to diverse facets of the situation which I wish to pursue briefly in what follows.

(1) One is the matter of what *criteria* were employed by the courts and other government agencies. Did they apply the statutes (normative state) or were they guided by expediency and discretion (prerogative state)?

---

[22] Therefore, the courts also should avoid making projections out of the blue as did, for example, the Landgericht Berlin in its explanation of the judgement of 20. 1. 1992 on the "Legal community of the former GDR citizens", Neue Juristische Wochenschrift 1992, pp. 691 - 96 (695). – In the light of the free floating projections made in the west the decision of the Volkswagen Foundation not to finance a proposed investigation of the change in the legal consciousness in the new German states is a scandal.

[23] E. Fraenkel, The Dual State, New York: Oxford University Press, 1941 – In this connection it is important from a methodological point of view to note that Fraenkel does not depend on the laws, edicts, etc., but rather on (published) court decisions and particular passages in legal treatises.

[24] Ibid., p. 57.

(2) Another is that the two regimes had different kinds of *actors* (whether they were in the courts or, for example, in the Gestapo). The prerogative state, in Fraenkel's usage, refers to the *Volksgerichtshof* and the special tribunals.

(3) A further distinction is in the respective *jurisdictions*. That is, whether courts, government agencies, etc. were responsible for dealing with political or apolitical matters. When, e.g., state or Party offices were exempt from judicial review, from prosecution or from civil liability – even if that was done itself by judicial decision – then it falls in the category of the prerogative state.

(4) One can also recognize a *functional* distinction. The normative state provides a framework for the rational calculation needed in a capitalist economy. The prerogative state serves the purpose of coercive production of community and the destruction of worker's organizations (labor unions).

(5) The *means* selected for application also can be a ground of distinction – whether judicial judgments were employed (whatever the kind of courts) or whether the state employed extra-judicial "preventive detention".

(6) Finally, it appears that the two types of state have different *addressees* as their target. One is reserved for the "Aryan" Volk; the other is aimed at "dealing with" the Jews and others who were outside the privileged group.

Thus, it is not so easy to apply the two categories without first working through some of their dimensions. The differentiation only makes sense insofar as it can be developed out of the underlying dichotomy. What encroaches most on its utility is that it is mainly usable to place a value on something: in the normative state acceptable decisions are made; in the prerogative state we find that such decisions have been replaced by injustice and illegality, etc.

The greatest disadvantage of Fraenkel's distinction is that even after attempting to list an internal differentiation of its categories it still rests on a blunt dichotomy. Methodologically speaking, the measuring device is too crude. To characterize a legal order one must do more than merely employ a classificatory scale, and especially not one that has only two points on it, regardless of whether they are rule of law/rule of illegality or normative state/prerogative state[25]. It is true that it is common in the usual way of doing things in the world of legal doctrine to operate with such dichotomies, which conclude in a yes/no, valid/invalid, legal/illegal decision and do not recognize any spectrum between these extremes.[26] But terms such as "minimum" and "not extremely" that appear in the definitions we have considered are not so

[25] Sendler's attempt to clarify matters by calling the GDR a state that was "only at the core a state of injustice/ illegality" is the failed effort to achieve a wider differentiation while remaining within a dichotomy (without reaching, e.g., for a trichotomy). That effort succeeds (or rather fails) by employing the metaphor "core".

[26] Even if that part of the argument that deals with "principles" in contrast to the part that deals with "rules" is conducted on an ordinal basis (cf. R. Alexy, Theorie der Grundrechte, Baden-Baden 1988), a determination must be made categorically (e.g., constitutional or unconstitutional).

far from an approach that considers the matter to lie on a spectrum. The authors, however, did not work through these problems.

III. On the Efficacy of Law in the GDR

No doubt it is well known that the efficacy of legal norms always was "measured" more exactly than their justness. It is a further truism that in the analysis of efficacy one must go beyond the legal norms "as such" to include consideration of actions and their consequences. For this purpose the fundamental distinctions customarily drawn in effectiveness research in sociology of law are at hand:

- law in the books/law in action
- legal norms/legal reality
- imposed order/living order
- formal (official)/informal

etc.

Even if effectiveness research encompasses a wide range of objects in addition to legal norms and only takes them as a starting point, the predicate "effective" is reserved for the norms (in contrast to predicates such as "just" or "capable of being justified" which may be applied not only to norms but also to other phenomena, e.g., actions). To this extent we can exempt here the kinds of problems discussed above in II. Likewise, the question of the relationship between the external and the internal value perspectives is not so serious in the case of effectiveness research, since it already is incorporated in the fundamental distinctions employed in sociology of law, mentioned above.

Two questions, however, nonetheless are raised if one applies the previously considered definitions to the law of the GDR:

(1) *How can one determine the efficacy of the entire legal order (and not simply a particular legal norm)?*

Should one continue the process of working with examples and juxtapose examples of effective and ineffective norms? Does "by and large" effective mean that a large quantity of particular norms are followed, applied, and made use of to a great extent? Certainly, a large number of norms in the GDR can be pointed out which achieved a high degree of recognition – not only by being invoked in propaganda but also in the institutionalization of an actually working system for registration and analysis.

However, is that what is meant in the statement of the requirement that the totality of norms displays a minimum of social effectiveness or potential effectiveness? If so, then here too – as in the evaluation of justness – a large percentage of the norms would have to be tested. But in practice no one actually argues this way. The arguments, to the extent that any are made, focus on the effectiveness of secondary norms according to which the state officials were to do their work (concerning the alteration of law, its application, etc.).

It is time to recall the general theoretical structure underlying any test of effectiveness.[27] A legal norm is effective if, after it has been issued, this or that goal is achieved which was the purpose of the legislator(s). In most cases in order to determine the effectiveness of a legal norm two theoretical steps are required: first, a theory must be employed to explain why a norm that has been adopted is more or less followed, applied, or made use of. Second, a theory must be employed to explain the effects of these activities in relation to the legislatively desired end-state. Only when the norm-following, -applying, or -using activities actually are that which brings about the conditions that correspond to the goals of the legislator(s) can one speak of effectiveness.[28] Only in the classical criminal law do both aspects coincide – e.g., when by compliance with the prohibition of murder the good sought by the legislator already is accomplished.

But what would that mean for an entire legal order or even for the entire constitution? What are their goals or purposes? An answer must be provided before the definitions mentioned above can be usable. Thus, in the case of the GDR, one would have to investigate the degree of observance or use of all of the possible legal norms (if that were imaginable) – and still one would be faced with the task of determining what the goal of the legal order in the GDR was.[29]

The definitions, in their focus on law, lead one to neglect the non-legal and the extra-legal (that does not mean the illegal). A glance at the society of the GDR and its law, however, makes the trans-legal step easy:

(2) *What role does law play, after all, in a society – in comparison to other ordering mechanisms? From a societal perspective is it only marginal?*

The question here is not the well worn topic of "legalization" – the quantity of legal regulations, the number of fields of legal regulation, the depth of pen-

---

[27] See H. Rottleuthner, Rechtssoziologie und Rechtstheorie, Freiburg/München 1982.

[28] One cannot speak of the goal of the legislator as being that people do not cross the street against the red light; it must be viewed as the reduction of the risk of accident. One can then inquire how a higher degree of compliance effects the rate of accidents.

[29] If one takes, e.g., Art. 2 of the GDR Constitution of 1974 into consideration: "The decisive task of the developed socialist society is the further increase of the material and cultural standard of living on the basis of a high tempo of development of socialist production, increasing scientific and technical progress and the growth of the productivity of labor," one would have to conclude that the pursuit of this goal failed miserably, even violated the constitution.

etration of legal regulation – but rather the effectiveness of legal mechanisms of regulation in comparison to other mechanisms of regulation. With respect to the GDR this topic touches on the issue of the relationship between the Party and the State.[30]

The role of the party was not regulated by law. Only in Art. I of the Constitution of 1968 was there mention of the leading role of the Party[31] – and nothing else. However, the Party structure was regulated in statutes of the SED. One might ask in this connection whether the norms of the Party, i.e., especially the statutes, didn't fulfill all of the criteria of law (since they include substantive definitions, sanctions, procedures, jurisdictional rules, etc.). But these rules applied only to the Party members and thus did not raise any general obligation of conformity such as that which was required by legal norms.[32]

What put in question the role of law as a general mode of regulation and orientation was the fact that nowhere was there a definition of the influence the Party organization was supposed to have over state officials. On the one hand the separation of the Party from the State was given emphasis; on the other it was official policy that the Party had a continuous responsibility for political and ideological oversight over its members – and where that responsibility ended never was established clearly.

Of course, in countries of the west it also is possible for political parties to exercise great influence outside of the parliamentary halls. And one cannot necessarily discover this influence by examining the norms of the constitution. It may well be that the existence of several political parties, with a relatively equal measure of power among them, guarantees a certain degree of political pluralism. Nevertheless, the larger parties may become a kind of clique, may make their "arrangements", and through deals, there may be a kind of nepotism that transcends party lines. The example of Italy demonstrates an extreme form of such entanglements.

In western "parliamentary democracies" the influence of political parties over the state bureaucracy is accomplished primarily via membership in a party, i.e., through the existence of the role of party member. By contrast, in the GDR and other countries that styled themselves socialist, a party

---

30 The dualism of which Fraenkel writes was located within the Nazi *state,* which in his view was only on the margin touched by the unregulated relationship of the Party (NSDAP) and the state under the Nazis.

31 "The German Democratic Republic is a socialist state of the German nation. It is the political organization of the working people in the cities and on the land who together under the leadership of the working class and its Marxist-Leninist Party are realizing socialism."

32 In the classical discussion of the problem of distinguishing a state from a band of robbers it often is pointed out that robber bands also have a normative structure. But the norms that are valid within the robber band are not the legal norms that are valid for the entire social system. See Alexy, op. cit. (fn. 2), p. 60.

apparatus existed as a full scale institution alongside the institutions of the state. In the GDR it consisted of the Politbüro, the Central Committee with its various departments, the Party Control Commission, local and district offices, the party cadre groups in workplaces.[33] Fundamental loyalties could be secured by communicative interventions that relied on the fact that officials also had their roles as party members (one sees this in workplace meetings and party gatherings) – and almost all of the judges and state's attorneys were members of the SED. Even that was not sufficient. Parallel to whatever legal systems of regulation existed, decisions in particular cases and on personnel matters were prepared and made in Party bodies (at the highest level, in the Central Committee's "Department for State and Law"), which decisions were expected to be implemented by state officials. There were also informal bodies, e.g., leadership councils, in which representatives from both state and party worked cooperatively. Unpublished normative acts also imposed duties on employees of state offices, requiring them to follow the Party line.[34] The rules were so arranged that it always was possible to direct a particular proceeding to the "right" person (determining the venue of the case within the prosecutorial system, removing it to the Attorney General, granting the chief judge the power to take any matter into his own hands, etc.). Of course, insofar as the administration of justice was a mass production bureaucracy it was not normal to review and intervene in every proceeding; but through a dense system of reporting it was possible to inform higher authorities about "politically sensitive" cases. When it was needed, the mechanism of legal regulation by the Party was standing by.

In the GDR the notion of a "unity of state power" rather than a separation of powers was propagated (on the basis of the supposed classlessness, since the class system had been overcome), but this unity was undercut by the existence of a system of paralegal power of the Party over the state. The status of the state was undercut by the para-legality of the Party.

The interweaving of the state apparatus and the Party machine relativized the legal order into an instrument at the Party's disposal. Law did not provide the framework for the society as a whole; one could more accurately say that

---

[33] One must imagine, e.g., what it would be like if there were a party organization of the Social Democrats within a court, so that a party secretary would sit in sessions of the presidency of that court. See, with respect to the direction of the GDR judiciary by the Party, H. Rottleuthner, Steuerung der Justiz in der DDR, Kritische Vierteljahresschrift für Gesetzgebung und Rechtswissenschaft 1992, pp. 237 - 264 and my contribution for the 16th IVR World Congress "The Conformity of the Legal Staff", in: Rechtstheorie – Beiheft 15, Berlin 1993, pp. 441 - 50.

[34] An internal provision of the Ministry of Justice of 25. 6. 1956 specified, for example: "Sec. 1 Personal Responsibility: (1) Every employee is personally responsible for carrying out the political line of the working class and for fulfilling the assignments made to him" (Bundesarchiv – Abteilungen Potsdam, P-1/1603/309).

of the Party-hydra. I do not know how the definitions considered above can deal with this phenomenon.

IV. A Plea for an Ordinal Concept of Law

The central characteristics of justness and efficacy employed in the definitions are not formulated categorically: a legal order should demonstrate a "minimum" of justification or capacity for justification; it should not be "extremely" unjust. And certainly one could measure the degree to which there is "belief in its legitimacy". It should be "by and large" efficacious; it should possess a "minimum" of efficacy. All of these are expressions that point towards a gradual (if not quantitative) concept of law, that means, towards an ordinal (or even interval) scale against which a legal order could be measured as more or less, greater or smaller, etc.[35] What is required is a gradated concept of law, a gradated or gradual concept of legal order. It is already entirely customary in sociology of law to employ a gradated concept of law, and it has proved itself in both synchronous and historical comparisons.[36] In any case the dimensions and entities[37] that are considered are quite various – and thus one should correctly speak of gradated concepts of law.

Elsewhere in legal theory this notion is not very widespread, sorry to say. A pathbreaking suggestion was made by Lon Fuller:

> "When we realize that order itself is something that must be worked for it becomes apparent that the existence of a legal system ... is always a matter of degree."[38]

And it is well known that Bob Summers, who we honor here, has worked on the problem of how the dimensions of the formality of law (of a legal order) can be measured on a sophisticated scale.

For the questions we have been discussing about the justness and efficacy of law Fuller's approach remains of great interest – simply because he managed to connect both aspects in an interesting way. If law represents a social order whose goal is to make possible fundamental social orientation beyond the everyday coordination of behavior that is taken for granted and beyond the unusual instances of agreement through consensus achieved by persuasion, then it is the task of legal theory to develop the premises of a theory of action

---

35 Sendler also speaks of the possibility of a gradation between a state under the rule of law *(Rechtsstaat)* and a state that lacks it *(Unrechtstaat)*, but he does not develop the notion.

36 See, e.g., E. Blankenburg, Recht als gradualisiertes Konzept, Jahrbuch für Rechtssoziologie und Rechtstheorie vol. 6, Opladen 1980, pp. 83 - 98.

37 That is, whether one is speaking of norms, actions, persons (groups), or organizations.

38 L. Fuller, Positivism and Fidelity to Law: A Reply to Professor Hart, Harvard Law Review 71 (1958), p. 646.

for the success of such a project of social orientation. That is the task Fuller undertook in specifying his well known eight criteria of an "internal morality of law":[39]

- the norms should be general (no ad hoc decisions);
- they should be available to everyone – be published;
- nor retrospective directions;
- and as precise, clear and understandable as possible;
- a legal order should not contain contradictory directions;
- they cannot demand the impossible;
- they should not be altered too often;
- and finally the officials working under them must be bound by the law; they must apply the law.

These criteria encompass determinants of the content of "legitimate" law and do not grant a blank check to the moral judgement of the user of a definition (minimum of justification, not extremely unjust). The criteria relate to the quality of the work of the lawgiver primarily, but also include the activity of applying the law. According to Fuller's approach they must be susceptible to application on an ordinal scale and/or it must be possible to construct an index out of them, that means, a standard against which the magnitude in each of the eight dimensions could be weighed, with which a measure for the "morality" of a legal order could be established. Likewise, it should be possible to use this to determine to what extent the orientation function of the legal order has been achieved or could be achieved. In the first instance this is only hypothetically possible, since it must still be investigated empirically – following the two-step method for effectiveness research – in what way the norms so qualified are actually followed, applied, or used and with what consequences for the action orientation of society.

To elaborate this using one example from the law of the GDR: the Supreme Court of the GDR issued "guidelines" for interpretations of the lower courts. Many of these guidelines were not published, but instead were distributed internally to the courts and only selectively to the practicing lawyers.[40] How did this practice effect the orientation of the populace?

In particular, Fuller's final criterion is of great significance for an analysis of the functioning of the GDR legal order. It reveals that contradictions in general principles rained down on the heads of the legal personnel in the form of orientation-paradoxes. Thus, the judges were charged with the realization of

[39] L. Fuller, The Morality of Law, New Haven 1969, p. 39.

[40] See F.-Ch. Schroeder / D. Gräf, Geheime Rechtsprechungsanweisungen in der DDR, in: Recht in Ost und West 1987, pp. 291 - 94.

the principle of Party loyality and at the same time the principle of socialist legality;[41] the independence of the judiciary (in making interpretations of the law) passed badly with the measures for the securing of "unified interpretation of the law in every court".[42] Judges and prosecutors were left in the dark on when they should be more repressive and when they should apply more lenient, educational sanctions in a criminal justice system that was subject to political intervention. They were pulled in one direction or the other by the forces of political opportunism.

There is much work still to be done on Fuller's proposal. There are a whole row of problems to be solved (problems of measurement, scale niveau of the particular dimensions, construction of indices, etc.) And of course, the question of additional dimensions can be raised,[43] e.g., the matter of the existence of a differentiated discourse or the extent to which a hermeneutic extends throughout the legal order (which note already is sounded in Alexy's definition). For these can contribute to greater precision and thus to better orientation. Reflecting on the experience of GDR law, one might also think about the issue of structural unclarity. Thus, for many years the tasks of the Ministry of Justice and of the Supreme Court in the guidance of interpretation remained unclear even at the normative level (without this necessarily constituting a case of contradictory rules).

In any case this further work should concentrate on the legal orders that lie at hand (including those examples that are historically available). The analysis of the formerly socialist legal orders offers a wide field in which to labor, especially because we are no longer limited to the official documents but also have access to information about what was going on "backstage", that is, we can see how they really functioned. Similarly, as we study legal orders that are still operating we should take this kind of realistic view – no matter how strong the pressure may be to direct our vision only to the just and effective sides of the law.

---

41 "If my decision is legally correct, it will be politically wrong. If it is politically correct, it will be wrong in legal terms." (Bericht über die Arbeit der Justizorgane im Bezirk Leipzig vom 14. 7. 1956, p. 3 – IfGA ZPA IV 2/13/103).

42 Art. 93, sec. 2 GDR-Constitution of 1968 (sec. 3 in the version of 1974).

43 See R. Summers, Professor Fuller on Morality and Law, in: Journal of Legal Education 1966, pp. 1ff. 19ff.

III. Form and Substance in Legal Argumentation: The Case of Roman, Greek, and Canon Law

Formality and Substance in Classical Roman Law*

By Okko Behrends, Göttingen

I.

(1) Roman legal science, reflecting at least four hundred years of continuous literary debate, of ever increasing complexity, coped over a long period of time with the problem of formality and the place it occupies in the law. From the beginning there was no doubt that rules and concepts that are structured in such a way as to be socially effective without the aid of substantive (and, as such, necessarily casuistic) arguments, are essential to law. The problem that persisted, however, was how to define – by a basic conceptual argument justifying formality itself – the limits of formality and the point at which immediately effective substantive arguments had to be taken into account. The scientific debate ended with an interesting and to a certain extent open compromise.

This final compromise was the result of a deep antagonism in Roman legal thinking, fought out between the two imperial Schools – the Sabinians and the Proculians – and informed by a dual heritage handed down from Republican times, where in the age of Cicero the classical legal system in the strict sense, uniquely founded on formal rules and concepts, replaced a preclassical system based on a dualistic natural law theory that had tried to harmonize good faith solidarity of social life with the principle of private will submitted to compliance with strict forms.[1] This antagonism between classical and preclassical law and its persistance in the confrontation between the Sabinians, renewing preclassical jurisprudence, and the Proculians, standing for the leading classical traditions, is an early example of a phenomenon that constitutes an ever-recurring experience in legal history and comparative law and seems best understood on the model of a pendulum. A major shift from a substantive to a more formal system took place in the last century, not only in European legal history but in American as well.[2] After the pendulum had then swung back

* I am greatly indebted to Prof. Stanley L. Paulson for a thorough correction of my first draft and for many valuable suggestions.

[1] For the most recent illustration of this paradigm-shift see O. Behrends, Die *bona fides* im *mandatum.* Die vorklassischen Grundlagen des klassischen Konsensualvertrags Auftrags in: Festschrift Wolfgang Waldstein (1993), in print.

[2] Wieacker, Privatrechtsgeschichte der Neuzeit (1967), 249ff., 430ff.; Gilmore, The Ages of American Law (1974), 19ff., 41ff.

very forcefully at the end of the last century, it appears, at the end of the present century, there will once again be a reassertion of formalism, especially in such countries as the United States and the Federal Republic of Germany, where substantive reasoning in law with its immediate effectiveness has in the interim again taken a more or less unchecked lead.[3]

(2) The answer that the classical Roman system initially gave to the problem of formality was very clear. The classical lawyers declared that nothing is law unless it is laid down in hard and fast rules or in clearly demarcated concepts. Nothing was admitted into their *ratio* or *ars iuris,* as defined by this jurisprudence, which did not meet these conditions.

The result was, of course, an extremely rigid legal system. The system was made workable, however, by a very clever device. Substantive arguments demanding an extension or correction of the formal law were not excluded; rather, they were admitted, but with a clear distinction – they were brought in only at a level beneath the formal law. Thus, within the formal system the classical law could deny all open texture[4] to legal rules and nevertheless fulfill all demands for casuistic justice, this by permitting the use of equity principles, relegated to a lower level. So it was that the body of law *(ius)* situated at the level of legal science remained intact, while in real life the needs of substantive justice were met. Whatever was done at the factual level, did no harm to the formal law.

The handling and development of these secondary rules, not law in the sense of *ius* but socially effective, were entrusted to the judiciary (in the Roman case to magistrates and judges, both laymen, the latter often a one-man jury, sometimes a bank). In this way the Roman courts could create rules of great importance, notwithstanding their inability to alter the letter of the law. The guiding principle was: When substantive reasons required it, the magistrates and judges could create rules of their own, based on the authority of the magistrate and on the duty *(officium)* of the judge, but could not create or alter law itself (ius).

To give examples: The magistrate could not make an heir in law; if equity demanded it, however, he could grant the factual possession of the inheritance to another person. In this case the legal heir retained his status as heir, although all the benefits went to the possessor of the inheritance. If the judge

[3] See Robert S. Summers, The Formal Character of Law, in: 51 Cambridge Law Journal 238ff. 1992.; P. S. Atiyah and R. S. Summers, Form and Substance in Anglo-American Law. A Comparative Study in Legal Reasoning, Legal Theory and Legal Institutions. For Germany, see O. Behrends, Struktur und Wert. Zum institutionellen und prinzipiellen Denken im geltenden Recht, in: O. Behrends, M. Dießelhorst, R. Dreier (eds.), Rechtsdogmatik und praktische Vernunft (1989), p. 138 - 174.

[4] Used here in the sense made popular by H. L. A. Hart, The Concept of Law (1961).

required a buyer who had delayed payment of the price to pay interest, the duty he created was not part of the formal law, that is to say, the interest was not *in obligatione,* not part of the formal debit, but depended uniquely on the command of the judge *(officio iudicis),* who for his part was entitled to such discretion in all procedures with particular equity clauses.

This classical division between formal rules and concepts constituting the body of the law *(ius)* and the extensions and corrections given to it by the courts (magistrates and judges) was omnipresent in classical law and formed a coherent whole, because both parts of the effective law were strictly supervised by the leading lawyers of Rome. In fact, in legal questions, the magistrates and judges, being as a rule laymen, were normally nothing more then mouth-pieces of the *iurisconsulti.* In sharp contrast to modern courts, which sometimes tend to develop a legal philosophy of their own, the Roman courts were, intellectually speaking, totally at the mercy of the leading lawyers and their authoritative teaching and counsel in the concrete cases.[5]

Later on, this initial system was modified more and more by moderating the idea of the immutable formality of the *ratio iuris* and admitting, too, adjustments in the concepts and rules themselves. This represented, of course, a deep and essential encroachment on the classical idea of formality which might have destroyed it totally. The classical foundations of formalism, however, were so strong that the pattern persisted beneath this compromise: If it was true that formalism suffered a great deal, it was also true that formalism remained in the lead, with the result that substantive argument, now admitted at the level of the law, operated for the most part casuistically in the manner of exceptions to formalism stemming from equity. And this fact was present not only in the consciousness of classical lawyers in Roman times, but was felt later as well, wherever Roman law exerted its influence.

(3) Before considering some details, it will be useful to look more closely into the notion of formality as I use it in this paper. I use it here not only in the sense that formal concepts and rules can be applied, without the aid of substantive arguments, in a hard and fast way. This content-oriented sense of formality is, to be sure, always implied as an essential feature of the classical legal system; in fact, it was also present to a certain extent in the formality of its pre-classical predecessor, limited there to strict law.

But formality in the classical law has had (as its predecessor) primarily a functional aspect, seldom referred to in modern discussions. Classical formal-

---

[5] Lawyers' counsel, often asked for by the parties, was binding. There was a possibility of choice for the judge only when counsel for the plaintiff and that for the defendant differed. The figure transmitting the information from the sophisticated legal literature to the magistrates was the *assessor,* who when the magistrate pronounced something wrong was in fact held responsible. See for details Behrends, Der Assessor zur Zeit der klassischen Rechtswissenschaft, in: Savigny Zeitschrift, Rom. Abt. 86 (1969), 192 - 226.

ity was focussed not on decision making, but on the organization of the legal system in all its aspects – for example, to name a few simple instances, on personal status and property rights and obligations (debits). The merits and limits of formality are thus illustrated in the classical law by questions as to who is a free person and as to what rules govern the acquisition of property and obligations (debits). The formal rules were not principally conceived of with an eye to application by the courts. Not even the law of torts was conceived of from the point of view of the courts. It was not asked under what circumstance the court would award damages. Rather, the classical question was: What are the legal conditions that must be satisfied for the injured person to acquire an obligation against the person who wrongfully caused the damage. The courts were, first of all, regarded as subservient to the legal system seen as a structured and preexistent matrix. The magistrates and judges had to apply the formal law, the *ars iuris* qua body of legal institutes, organizing social life.

Questions about this general rule were not raised by the fact that the magistrates and the judges often had to adjust the formal rules and concepts to the concrete cases by appealing to their secondary rules. These adjustments did not abolish the primary perspective of the Roman legal system, conceived of as a means of organizing social life. The secondary rules themselves moved only within a certain sphere inside or outside of the formal rules held to be over- or underinclusive. In this way, the adjustments also became part of the court's duty to engender respect by all participants for the legal organziation of social life. And when, finally, equitable adjustments were admitted on the primary level as well, this did not mean any change in the primary function of classical law.

Classical law, accordingly, was regarded as a set of structures and rules, serving human life and present in human life,[6] a bit like the field and rules of a play that one associates with a game, say, baseball. The umpire, of course, plays an enormous role in winning respect for them. But the structures and rules of the game are present even when he is not looking or is not called upon to interfere.

The idea that law exists only for resolving conflicts, for decison making and for the determination of single cases is totally alien to classical thinking. Of course, the magistrate and the judges had to work to bring litigation to an end and they favoured compromise of every imaginable sort. But the reductive notion that law is what the judge does, that it is nothing but "the prophecies of what the courts will do in fact, and nothing more pretentious" is far removed.[7]

---

[6] Hermogenian, Epitome of Law, book 1, D 1,5,2: "All law is established for the sake of man" (Hermogenianus libro primo iuris epitomarum *Hominum causa omne ius constitutum*). This view was extended to legal entities in so far as they were acknowledged fictiously as taking part in law of property and obligations.

[7] Holmes, The Path of the Law, 10, Harvard Law Review, 460 - 461, 1896 - 97. In the second half of his article, however, Holmes demonstrates that he had not studied the

On the other hand, the obvious fact that "The judge has the last word"[8] was by no means neglected. On the contrary, it was handled with great clarity in the way I have already mentioned. The secondary rules that the magistrate or the judge (supervised by the *iurisconsulti*) created by their own authority ranked in dignity as being beneath the law *(ius)*, being unable to alter its letter, but as far as their effectiveness in real life was concerned, they had the last word.

He who with the help of the magistrate received possession of what was left by the *de cuius* enjoyed all the benefits of an heir except the name. The interest that a buyer in delay was made to pay was real money, even if it was not formally *in obligatione,* but only created *officio iudicis.* And the creditor against whom the magistrate by request of the sued debtor granted an exception based on fraud *(exceptio doli),* retained his *obligatio* but as a pure form: the *exceptio,* founded on substantive reasoning of the secondary rules, took away the economic substance of the legal form by destroying the possibility of getting a favourable judgment.

In all these cases the last word was with the courts. And it was also admitted in classical theory that these secondary rules acquired validity and relevance only when the decision of the magistrate or the judge was rendered. Their validity rested on the power to command and to demand obedience, powers with which the magistrate is vested by the constitution and the judge, named by the magistrate, by the law of procedure. In the case of the magistrate this power is called *imperium,* in the case of the judge *officium.* Neither creates law *(ius),* but both have with their commands power over real life and in this sense what they say is final.

(4) Judge-made rules were thus very important indeed in the classical system, but being secondary rules they did not contribute to the overall picture of the law. The leading model was constructed from the primary rules and concepts regarded as *ius.* And because this primary model was oriented to the organisation of social life, namely by attributing status to natural persons and to legal entities, by formulating relations of status-holders to things (property rights) and to other persons (obligations), and by treating the right to go to the

Roman law, and read what he calls (p. 475) "Sohm's admirable Institutes" in vain by saying: "Theory is the most important part of the dogma of the law, as the architect is the most important man who takes part in the building of a house." Cf. note 9.

[8] Thus, the still influential John Chipman Gray, The Nature and Sources of the Law (1924), 171 - 172 citing Jhering, Geist, 4th edn., § 44 pp. 445 - 446 with a passage, expounding the problem of communication between law and judge (a problem formality strives to overcome) and citing also Bülow, Gesetz und Richteramt (1885), 6,7 (very influential as a precursor of the Free Law Movement) who defended the last-word theory very powerfully: Examples of Bülow's words in Gray's translation: "A judgment of a Court has the force of Law; it carries the whole force of the Law with it" and: "Not by its legislative, but by its judicial determinations, the law regulating power of the State speakes its last word."

law (the *actio*) as an offspring of the legal position defined by the *ratio iuris* – because of these factors, there was a strong tendency to mould the main products of the judge-made law in the same way.

A modern lawyer, who is used to a legal model centered around the state, which creates law by means of statutes and judicial decisions, will tend to enquire at this point into the nature of the structures out of which the legal system in the classical sense is constructed. The answer is: they exist, of course, only in law, and in a more superficial way in the mind of those who are concerned with them in their daily life and in the minds of the lawyers, too, replete with professional detail. For this reason we find them called, in technical language: incorporeal objects of thought *(res incorporales)*. Oliver Wendell Holmes, studying the Roman heritage in the common law, correctly perceived that it would be reductive to translate this term with "incoporeal right"; in fact it is a much more general term comprising all legal entities which lend structure to a scheme of organization. And Holmes correctly stressed the fictious, man-made character, the merely ideated character of these structures.[9] They are created and accepted because they are useful for the purpose of organizing a legal system for laymen and lawyers. The classical law, formulated in reaction to natural law theory, is in itself based on anthropological and humanistic foundations. Its legal system is decidedly conceived of as a man-made body of formal rules and concepts giving to social life the legal structures it needs. The long-term success of the civil law in history has shown that this approach was basically sound.

---

[9] Cf. O. W. Holmes, The Arrangement of the Law – Privity, in: Early Writings of W. O. Holmes Jr., (1930 - 31) 44 Harvard Law Review, 747 note 9 [republished from 7 American Law Review, 46 1872]. Holmes calls attention to an interesting mistranslation, which he traced back a hundred and fifty years and which he thinks very likely could be traced back much further: "The distinction between corporeal and incorporeal things is stated in Inst. 2, 2, §§ 1, 2, to be that the former are those *quae tangi possunt,* the latter *quae tangi non possunt, quae sunt ea* quae in jure consistunt. This is constantly translated, "which consist in a right", and being so interpreted, has led to the hopeless confusion of modern "incorporeal hereditaments" and to Austin's attack on the decison as senseless (Lect. 33). If we translate the phrase "which exist only in contemplation of law" or "which depend on the law for existence" and notice that the first instance is the *hereditas,* which is a *universitas* distinct from its components parts (D.50.16.208) and as much a fictitious thing as a corporation is a fictitious person, we shall be nearer to what the Roman lawyers had in mind, although we may not be able to justify all their examples." Holmes is right and his translation in fact explains all the examples given in classical times for *res incorporales,* including those of the first source in which the distinction is quoted (Cicero, Topica 5,26). Holmes would be astonished that the erroneous translation he castigated still persists (cf. Kaser, Kaser Röm. Privatrechts I^2 § 92 I 1, p. 376) and has prevented up to the present a full appraisal of the fundamental theoretical importance that the (sceptical but at the same time powerful) notion of objects existing only in legal thought has had for the formation of the classical and civil law.

II.

(5) Moving now to a concrete illustration of the final compromise, it seems appropriate to begin with a statement in which the ideal of formality was still expressed and defended with great vigour by a leading representative of the Proculian Law School. This sentence was uttered in a period when formalism had already yielded to a considerable extent to the new compromise.

Neratius, the leader of the Proculians in the time of Trajan and Hardian, formulated the classical point of view in his writings :

"The law can and should be definite".[10]

This means – the English rendition is due to the recent translation of the Digest organized by Alan Watson[11] – formality in the sense of clear definition as an inherent and necessary characteristic of law. It can and must be achieved everywhere.

The context of this observation underscores its principal importance and it is useful to examine it for a moment. Neratius develops the following argument: A law which can and must be regarded as definite is easy to know. Therefore the classical law is justified in formulating as a general rule that a mistake of law prejudices, while a mistake of fact does not. Law is a scientifically developed and limited set of concepts and rules,[12] and can therefore be known, at least where a lawyer is at hand;[13] the factual world is infinite and even a careful man can easily be mistaken in it.[14]

---

[10] Neratius 5 membranarum D 22,6,2 ... *cum ius finitum et possit esse et debeat.*

[11] The Digest of Justinian I – IV Philadelphia, 1985. English Translation edited by Alan Watson. The translators to whom I am thus indebted are Prof. Neil MacCormick, book 1; Prof. Geoffrey MacCormack, book 4; Prof. Peter Birks, book 12; the late Prof. J. A. C. Thomas, book 18, 35, 41 and 47; Prof. A. M. Honoré, book 22; the late Prof. Ben Beinart, book 44; Dr. Susan Hart, Mr. Andrew Lewis and Prof. Ben Beinart, book 45; and Professor Michael Crawford, book 50.

[12] The rule pertains of course essentially and primarily to the results of the classical jurisprudence. The doubts expressed by Kaser, Röm. Privatrecht I^2 § 59 note 60 p. 242 are not founded.

[13] This highly consequential limitation seems to be due to Labeo, who in fact knew that he had complicated the classical system a good bit. His idea was nevertheless not well received in the mainstream: cf. Paul, Mistake of Law and Fact, sole book (Paulus *libro singulari de iuris et facti ignorantia* D 22,6,9,3.), who, commenting on Labeos opinion, says: "This view is seldom appropriate *(quod raro accipiendum est)*".

[14] Paul, Mistake of Law and Fact, sole book: "It is a rule of law that mistake of law prejudices, mistake of fact does not." (Paulus *libro singulari de iuris et facti ignorantia* D 22,6,9,pr *Regula est iuris quidem ignorantiam cuique nocere, facti vero ignorantiam non nocere.*) The full text of Neratius *libro quinto membranarum* D 22,6,2 runs (Neratius, Parchments, book 5): "Mistake of law should not in any branch of the law be treated like mistake of fact, since the law can and should be definite, while the interpretation of facts often baffles even very careful people." *(In omni parte error in iure non eodem loco quo facti ignorantia haberi debebit, cum ius finitum et possit esse et debeat, facti interpetatio plerumque etiam prudentissimos fallat.)*

The sharp contrast between *ius* and *factum,* law and reality, in this rule, goes back to the founding of the classical jurisprudence. Its co-founder, Aquilius Gallius, used to say, whenever a question regarding the factual state of affair was put to him, that this is not up to me, this is the business of Cicero, the rhetor, thereby strictly limiting his competence to the formal law.[15] The technical distinction between formal law *(ius)* and reality *(factum),* as it is used in the classical law, was conceived of in the founding period of the classical legal system as contemporary theoretical sources prove.[16]

The preclassical tradition treated the problem of the mistake in law in an altogether different way, distinguishing between two parts of the law: These lawyers demanded that everyone know its strictly defined rights, but excused an individual who was mistaken as to the legal situation of the party with whom he happened to be dealing.[17] This rule is shaped in accordance with the preclassical distinction between individual rights, formulated by the *ius strictum* and the realm of social life governed by substantive natural law principles of the *ius aequum,* especially that of good faith. This rule also makes good sense, perhaps even better sense, than the classical rule. It is not unfair to ask that everyone know his proper circle of strictly defined rights and to let him bear to that extent the consequences of any mistake he has had to cope with. On the other hand, it is reasonable to assume that no one can know all the details of the legal situation with which he is faced in a relationship to others, and he can therefore be excused, provided that he has acted in good faith. Therefore, the casuistic recurrence of the preclassical distinction in the classical law is understandable. In the case of usucapion the iron-rule of the formalist, namely "an error of law never benefits", was limited with the help of the principle "good faith helps" in a case where the purchaser had good grounds (in the view of the lawyer deciding) for his mistaken belief that the legal situation allowed usucapion.[18]

---

[15] Cicero, Topica 12,51: "This does not refer to the law, but to Cicero, our Gallus Aquilis used to say whenever something was brought before him that needed discussion of facts." *(Nihil hoc ad ius; ad Ciceronem,' inquiebat Gallus noster, si quis ad eum quid tale retulerat, ut de facto quaereretur.)*

[16] Cicero, partitiones oratoriae 37, 129; Cicero, topica 23,90. The contrast between *lex* and *natura* or *institutio* and *natura,* made in the texts of Cicero, recurrs in the legal texts as the contrast of natural and civil equity (cf. e.g. Ulpian, Edict, book 31 (D 47,4,1,1): "This action, as Labeo wrote, rests on natural equity rather than on the civil equity" *(Ulpianus libro trigesimo primo ad edictum: haec autem actio, ut Labeo scripsit naturalem potius in se quam civilem habet aequitatem).*

[17] Pomponius, Sabinus, book 3 (D 22,6,3): "Not to know another's legal and factual position is very different from not knowing one's own rights. 1. But Cassius reports that Sabinus held that 'not knowing' does not cover the mistake of a slipshod and careless man." Pomponius libro tertio ad Sabinum *Plurimum interest, utrum quis de alterius causa et facto non sciret an de iure suo ignorat.* 1. *Sed Cassius ignorantiam Sabinum ita accipiendam existimasse refert non deperditi et nimium securi hominis.)*

[18] Cf. for the rule: Paulus, Sabinus book 32 (D 41,3,31,pr): "An error of law never benefits the possessor in the matter of usucapion. Accordingly Proculus says ... (i.e. no

The comparison between the different preclassical and classical treatments of the perennial question of mistake in law also offers a clear view on what happened when the paradigm shift took place. The idea of strictness, limited in the elder system to rules governing individual rights, was, in the new system, generalized into scientific formality and extended to the whole body of structured law. And whereas in the elder system strict law was complemented by the infinite social world ruled by natural law, in the new system structured law was complemented by the infinite factual world to which the magistrate, by means of his secondary rules, conceived as purely factual *(in factum concepta)*, lent some order.[19]

Ius finitum et debet esse et potest (the law can and should be definite) was the proud manifesto of the classical school. And this exhortation to formalism in the law, executed so visibly in the Institutes of Roman Law, was often pursued with renewed vigour in the different periods of the European history of the Roman Law.

(6) But the Roman Law also tells us a lot about the difficulties that such a scientific ideal will encounter. Living in approximately the same period as Neratius, the leader of the opposing school, Javolen, held quite a different view as to the ideal of definite law. He warned lawyers against putting forward definite rules or concepts and stressed the risk inherent in doing so. Such definitions could easily meet with a pertinent case, which would prove that they are over- or underinclusive.

Javolenus, Letters, book 11

Every definition in civil law is dangerous; for it is rare for the possibility not to exist of its being overthrown.[20]

---

help in the case that the formal consent of the tutor given to the contracting pupil was void)" [Paulus 32 ad Sabinum *Numquam in usucapionibus iuris error possessor prodest: et ideo Proculus ait...*]; for the correcting principle Pomponius, Quintus Mucius, book 24 (D 44,2,24,pr) "good faith (sometimes) benefits" (Pomponius 24 ad Quintum Mucium *Bona fides prodest*); for the casuistic concession African, Questions, book 21 (D 41,4,11): "The common opinion that one, who thinks himself to have bought something when in fact he has not, cannot usucapt, is, says [Julian] true insofar as the purchaser has no good ground for his mistaken belief; for if the slave or procurator whom he charged to buy the thing should persuade him that he had bought it and, on that ground, deliver it, the better view is that usucapion will follow." The decision is not entirely convincing; it privileges those buying with the help of servants and does not take into account that the knowledge of a servant should be imputed to the master.

[19] In the end, the rule that mistake in law prejudices was extended to the secondary rules of the magistrates. Cf. Paulus 44 ad edictum D 22,6,1,pr. The extension was not all that important because the praetor granted his protection based on fact *(in factum concepta)* very often only after very short delays, normally a year, and knowledge of this had always been at the risk of the interested party.

[20] Javolenus 11 epistularum D 50,17,202 *Omnis definitio in iure civili periculosa est: parum* (Haloander reads: *rarum,* which is adopted by the translation) *est enim ut non subverti potest.*

This attitude contends that definitions are dangerous, for he who puts forward a definition or a rule can easily be compelled to confess that the rule must be modified. And as we will see, this became in the end the common conviction of classical lawyers. Since, finally, they were all prepared to admit modifications of the legal concept for the sake of justice, no one could trust that a definition he advanced would endure.

I will illustrate this state of affairs with an example taken from the classical law of sale. A rule says that no contract of sale is conceivable without a thing sold.

Pomponius, Sabinus, book 9 D 18,1,8

There can be no sale without a thing to be sold.[21]

Like the complementary rule, which says that no sale is possible without a price in money agreed upon,[22] it is a rule and at the same time a definition of the concept "consensual contract of sale", which in order to be perfect as a mutually binding covenant in classical Roman law required nothing more than a meeting of the minds of seller and purchaser on the thing sold and on the price to be paid.

And this classical, formally defined concept of the contract of sale was acknowledged in both Law Schools from the time of Julian onward, because with Julian the Sabinians renounced their old adherence to the natural law idea that the basic idea of sale is not the formal bargain requiring money but a barter concluded and performed in good faith. With Julian too, the Sabinians opted for the classical bargain-model of sale with its considerable allowance for mutual profit-seeking and overreaching.[23] This option was part of an overall supplanting of natural law principles by formal concepts and rules of classical origin in the Sabinian School, leaving to the natural law tradition of this school only the role of a guide for interpretative adjustments of classical law formalism.

Our rule, which if a contract for sale is to come into legal existence requires with rigour, alongside a price in money, a thing sold, was initially meant to be

---

[21] Pomponius libro nono ad Sabinum D 18,1,8 *Nec emptio nec venditio sine quae veneat potest intellegi.*

[22] Ulpian, Sabinus, book 1 D 18,1,2,1: "There is no sale without a price" [Ulpian *libro primo ad Sabinus Sine pretio nulla venditio est.*); applied to a particular case Papinian, Questions, book 10 (D 18,1,72): "... the price was of the essence of the sale". (Papinianus libro decimo quaestionum ... *emptionis substantia constitit ex pretio.*)

[23] That is why the Sabinian Pomponius can in the Digest be made to state as his opinion that (Ulpian, Edict, book 11 [D 4,4,16,4]: Pomponius says that) "as regards the price in purchase and sale, the contracting parties are in the course of nature allowed to overreach each other." (Ulpianus 11 ad edictum *Pomponius ait in pretio emptionis et venditionis naturaliter licere contrahentibus se circumvenire.*) The good faith principle demanding a certain measure of partnership also in the finding of the price is here expelled. For further discussion see Zimmermann, The Law of Obligations. Roman Foundations of the Civilian Tradition (1990), 246 - 248.

an inexorable rule of the *ars iuris*. And this rigour was possible: as we know, in hard cases where this rule might produce injustice, the magistrate could help with his secondary rules of natural equity, which left the formal system intact.

This changed in the peak period of classical development, marked by the names of two outstanding figures, the Proculian Celsus, the promotor of natural law equity in his formal school, and the Sabinian Julian, the promotor of formalism in his.

Celsus gave a formal advice that falsified, as far as it went, the rule that a sale necessitates a thing sold. He decided that where liability is not expressedly excluded, the vendor of a debit is generally answerable for the existence of the debit.

Ulpian, Edict, book 32

When a debit is sold, Celsus says in the ninth book of his Digest that subject to contrary agreement, the vendor is not answerable for the debtor's solvency but only for the fact that he is a debtor.[24]

Where there is no debtor, there is no debit. If liability is defended where in reality there is no debit, this means of course an acknowledgement of sale without a thing sold. In this case the contract of sale makes the vendor liable to the buyer even if there was never a debit which could be transferred.

The equity of the decision on the other hand is obvious. A debit is a *res incorporalis*, an object which, as Holmes saw so well, exists only in the legal system and therefore cannot be perceived. The buyer who can thus easily be misled needs protection. And it is good policy to protect him without regard to the good or bad faith of the seller; the German Code, following Celus in its § 437 BGB, does just that.

Celsus had also some good technical reasons for his decisions. The secondary rules of the judiciary were in this case not easily accessible. The magistrate would have had difficulties in helping here. For according to his public edict on the casuistic treatment of fraud *(de dolo)* – in reality an invention of the lawyers who founded the classical systems – he granted his remedies normally only in the event that the other party had acted intentionally with knowledge of the non-existence of the thing sold.

On the other hand, costs for this promotion of equity are obvious, too. They concerned the purity of the system. The rule that a sale is not conceivable without a thing sold was no longer valid. The admission of a sale without a thing sold – in Roman terms "*sine re (incorporali)* – falsified it.

The civil system makes this encroachment on formality perfectly clear. The classical law made answerable with a civil action only a party already bound by

---

[24] Ulpianus libro trigensimo secundo ad edictum D 18,4,4 *Si nomen sit distractum, Celsus libro nono digestorum scribit, locupletem esse debitorem non debere praestare, debitorem autem esse praestare, nisi aliud convenit.*

a civil obligation. In the case of sale, the written civil formula with which the magistrate invests a judge with power to decide an action intended by the buyer, requires at the beginning that there be a valid sale. The pertinent text runs in English: What concerns the case that Titius bought from Seius a debit (*Quod Aulus Agerius* [John Doe] *de Numerio Negidio* [John Roe] *nomen emit*). This demonstration of the legal situtation brought before the case (in fact it was technically called *demonstratio*), had to be true.

With his decision of Celsus, the judge was compelled to call a sale also a contract even though there had never been a primary obligation to deliver a good sold – nobody can really be thought to be bound to deliver something which does not exist. Sale was now also a contract where there was only responsibility, in this case warranty for the existence of the thing sold. This must have been felt intensely, for the classical sale had insisted with such force on having for the individual sale a concrete object existing either in reality or as an individual legal structure in thought, that it never thought of admitting the important sale of generic goods.[25] With the decision of Celsus, sale became in a casuistic way also a mere warranty for the buyer, protecting his interest. The intrusion is still felt today, for § 440 BGB which perpetuates the decision of Celsus, is treated systematically as an exception to the rule, namely that § 306 BGB that initial impossibility nullifies the contract.

(7) So the Proculians learned – not for the first time but, with Celsus, with new intensity – the truth of the saying that the traditionally "natural law minded" Sabinians had known for so long: Every definition in civil law is dangerous, for it can be easily overthrown – or at least modified by an exception to the rule – whenever equity demands it.

[25] See for a recent discussion of this striking characteristic of classical Roman law Zimmerman (note 23), 236 - 238. The refusal to admit the generic sale cannot be explained in as highly sophisticated a system as classical Roman law by the influence of the primitive cash sale, which differs from primitive barter only by the use of money. If lawyers conceive of the idea that the simple consensual meeting of minds creates a mutual obligation of sale, i.e. a fully executory contract, how can they look at the same time on something so entirely different and simple as a cash sale or barter and feel moved by it? There must be a reason in theory. And this reason is not simply the tendency of the classical law, felt everywhere, to radicate its structures as fast as possible in concrete reality. It is in this case, I think, in the first line the common sense *(sensus communis)* approach of classical jurisprudence. A sale, even when promoted to an executory contract based on a meeting of the minds, is to common sense primarily an instrument promoting the circulation of concrete goods. The unilateral obligations always accepted generic goods (money, oat, wine etc.) and they could therefore serve to replace the generic sale by using two of them: but since these obligations were created initially for the refunding of loans, for them a generic content was normal. It can be added that in the unilateral obligation, performance was traditionally regarded as the way the debtor could liberate himself from the bond at his own cost and risk *(solutio)*, whereas the obligation typical for modern generic sale to procure goods from the promised genus (oat, wine etc.) for delivery would in classical terms have exceeded the boundaries of sale and belonged already to a species of work contract *(locatio conductio operis)*.

That this was – for the Sabinians – not a new insight at all, we learn from a famous sentence at the beginning of the last title of the Digest "Various rules of the (good!) old law",[26] in which Paul cites Sabinus approvingly:

Paul, Plautius, book 16 D 50,17,1

The law may not be derived from a rule, but a rule must arise from the law as it is.[27]

This means: You must not apply a rule blindly, simply as you find it in a law book; rather, you must always take into account that a rule is the expression of the whole law and therefore admits of modification whenever some legal principle demands it. If you do not, the rule, as the cited Sabinus proceeds, loses its forces *(perdit officium suum)* for not being a real rule of law.

To be sure, this sounds a bit like a truism. Thus, it is not surprising that the experience formulated in the exhortation: *non ex regula ius sumatur, sed ex iure quod est regula fiat* can, to a certain extent, be transferred to modern statute law. Modern codes generally bind one not to the letter but to the spirit of the law and hold the judge bound – as the German Grundgesetz (Art. 20 (3) GG expresses it directly – to the "statute and (!) the law". And since the German BGB regards every valid rule as a "Gesetz"[28] and therefore calls every norm accepted for legal decisions regardless of its origin a "Gesetz", we can adapt the exhortation to the situation of the BGB only by maintaing the equivocation of the term "Gesetz", meaning both in the BGB, statute and the norm established by extralegal interpetation. The sentence then runs: *non ex lege ius sumatur sed ex iure quod est lex fiat* (the law must not be derived simply from the statutory rule; rather, the norm to be applied must arise from the law as a whole, as it is).[29]

Within a statute this rule takes the form, forcefully enunciated by Celsus, that a lawyer should never rely on a single provision of a given statute but should endeavour to study all of them;[30] otherwise he will end up in the predi-

---

[26] *DE DIVERSIS REGULIS IURIS ANTIQUI.* The Pensylvania translations reads: "Various rules of early [!] law", which is misleading, because it suggests that the rules and the principles in this title were regarded by Justinian as no longer valid.

[27] Paulus libro sexto decimo ad Plautium D 50,17,1 *non ex regula ius sumatur, sed ex iure quod est regula fiat.* For a more detailed discussion of this famous fragment, see O. Behrends, Die Causae coniectio der Zwölftafeln und die Tatbestandsdisposition der Gerichtsrhetorik, in: Savigny Zeitschrift, Rom. Abt. 92 (1975), 162 - 185. The sentence later on became – in an anacronistic interpretation – a slogan of the Free Law Movement. See O. Behrends, Von der Freirechtsbewegung zu konkreten Ordnungs- und Gestaltungdenken, in: Dreier, Sellert (eds.), Recht und Justiz im "Dritten Reich" (1989), 48 - 49.

[28] Art. 2 EGBGB [Einführungsgesetz zum BGB): "Gesetz im Sinne dieses Gesetzes ist jede Rechtsnorm (A legal provision in the sense meant by this code is every legal norm)".

[29] In German: "Die anzuwendende Rechtsnorm folgt nicht einfach aus dem Gesetz, sondern aus dem gesamten geltenden Recht."

[30] Celsus, Digest, book 35 (D 1,3,24): "It is not lawyer-like practice to give judgment

cament of the modern university student who, confronted (in the case of a fictitious debit sold) with a sale with no object, will stumble on to § 306, nullifying such a sale, and will not find the Celsinian exception in § 440 BGB.

(8) The result achieved thus far requires further qualifications concerning the difference between overturning a rule and modifying it. Evaluating the sayings of Sabinus and the pre-Julian Sabinian Javolen, it seems that both lawyers really thought that a rule which proved to be underinclusive is completely overturned. The underinclusive rule seemed to them totally abrogated; in its place, a rule was formulated with the help of the notion of "the law as it is".

This makes sense in a legal system in which one proceeds in terms of natural truths that have to be uncovered and are uncovered more and more correctly. And so it is understandable to see this attitude formulated in the pre-Julian law school of the Sabinians, when it was still dominated by natural law.

This attitude makes no sense, however, in the classical systems based on institutes created by the sceptical belief that law is a value-guided system that introduces a legal structure in a world created by man and serves his needs qua social and cultural being. In such a system, where a rule serves to build a legal structure it is reasonable to differentiate between rule and exception: generally we demand for the emerging legal structure the fulfillment of the preconditions of the rule, but exceptionally – under circumstances casuistically described – the rule can be admitted in a deficient form.

In fact, the classical system did not have the lawyer thinking in terms of simply overturning a rule. The classical system, even in its latest development, left the lead to formalism, as I said at the outset. The experience with the secondary rule of the courts, having in fact the last word but leaving intact the civil law system, has obviously taught a lasting lesson and it provided what was, ultimately, the final answer of the classical system.

The classical lawyers were, in the end, highly conscious of the fact that with the new approach, the principles of justice and equity could modifiy the rules and concepts of the formal *ratio iuris*. The conflict that this compromise created was felt intensely. But the ideal of the *ius finitum*, the *ius* established in rules and concepts, was nevertheless maintained to the end.

In the following lines, perhaps the most famous words ever spoken by a Roman lawyer, the tension created by this new compromise cannot be missed. Celsus speaks as the head of the Proculian law school who held this office at the same time as Neratius and was as his colleague imbibed with the ideal of *ius finitum*.

---

or to state an opinion on the basis of one particular part of a statute without regard to the whole."

Ulpian, Institutes, book 1 D 1,1,1,pr

A law student at the outset of his studies ought first to know the derivation of the word *jus*. Its derivation is from *justitia*.[31] For, in terms of Celsus' elegant definiton, the law is the art of goodness and fairness.[32]

The splendid formulation stresses with new vigour the goal of the *ars iuris* – it has to serve substantive justice – but the means to that end are afforded primarily by the *ius finitum*.

Of course – in the new compromise – only primarily. Natural equity can now interfere immediately on the level of the classical law, as Celsus himself did in famous instances. The risk that a bad lawyers could do harm to the well defined body of the law is therefore lurking everywhere. Celsus was aware of this.

So he warned his colleagues passionately as to the dangers inherent in using equity indiscriminately, and did so, indeed, in a great outburst, all out of proportion to the simple case he had to decide: In formal law a debtor cannot purge his delay in delivering goods by offering them on a later term, but equity can allow the purge of delay *(purgatio morae)* if the circumstances are favorable. Celsus decided in this way, but with remorses which made him say:

Paul, Plautius, book 17, D 45,1,91,3

This is a matter of what is right and equitable in which type of case, he (Celsus the Younger) says,[33] lawyers often commit pernicious mistakes under the authority of the law.[34]

The fear of Celsus is quite clear. Because equity has now become part of the legal system, enforced with the full authority of legal science and no longer entrusted to the courts and their secondary rules alone, the possibly fatal consequences of error have become far greater.

(9) In the end this compromise of Roman Private Law was a combination of hard and fast rules of the classical types and leading principles, which cast a penumbra around the outer circle of the rules and concepts, a penumbra, in which in a casuistic fashion the rules and concepts could be extended and restricted. The original classical contrast between a uniquely formal law and the judiciary, which could not alter the letter of the law but did create rules of

[31] The translator of the Pensylvanian Digest (Geoffrey MacCormack; cf. note 11) notes rightly: "Jus cannot be exactly translated from Latin into English."

[32] Ulpianus libro primo institutionum D 1,1,1,pr *Iuri operam daturum prius nosse oportet, unde nomen iuris descendat. est autem a iustitia appellatum: nam, ut eleganter Celsus definit, ius est ars boni et aequi.*

[33] The Pensylvania Digest (note 11) here misses the point by translating: "one is often sadly misled by the influence of a (?) knowledge of the law".

[34] Paulus libro septimo decimo ad Plautium D 45,1,91,3 *esse enim hanc quaestionem de bono et aequo; in quo genere plerumque sub auctoritate iuris scientiae perniciose, inquit, erratur.*

their own, had been maintained in the final system only as a more or less fossilized relic.

This older, highly technical dualism between scientific formalism and secondary rules of the judiciary thus had no impact on the European legal systems. In exchange, the basic idea of the new compromise, namely that law should consist in the first place of clear cut concepts and hard and fast rules and should allow for substantive control only in the second line, in the form of a value guided casuistic, has been extremely powerful in the legal history up to the present day.[35] It would be easy to multiply examples. Fritz Schulz' admirable textbook "Classical Roman Law" cites while describing the narrow rules governing the claims for the recovery of an "unjustified enrichment" the natural law maxim, found also in the Digest, which seems to disregard all technical definitions[36] and comments correctly[37]: "To the classical lawyers this was a general idea or principle, not a legal rule". This explains why the narrow rules remained discernible, although, especially from Celsus onward, actions of restitution in law were overtly founded only on natural equity.[38]

The final result was a civilized balance between classical formality and guiding substantive principles of justice. It was a practical answer, one given by lawyers who have undergone all the experiences and endured all the tensions that formalism creates in a world where the individual case and the individual parties incessantly bring forward substantive arguments that in effect pose a challenge to formality.

The theoretical bases of the compromise could have been more stable and explicit. As it turned out, the final result was to a certain extent made up of heterogeneous parts, of classical legal rules organizing the main structures of law on the one hand, and natural law principles guiding concrete life on the other. The concept of natural equity, initially formulated to express the generally accepted values behind the formal system of classical law, had become more and more infused by elements of the preclassical natural law. A clear and reliable maxim as to the question of when either the one or the other side should prevail was not enunciated and was left to the practical work of the lawyers who showed in that work that they had learned from the long debate – namely, that formality serving freedom and individual rights is essential to law but needs as its complement principles of substantive justice preserving a

---

[35] See my Struktur und Wert, note 3.

[36] Pomponius, Various Readings, book 9 (D 50,16,206): "By the law of nature it is fair that no one become richer by the loss and injury of another". (Pomponius 9 ex variis lectionibus *Iure naturae aequum est neminem cum alterius detrimento et iniuria fieri locupletiorem.)*

[37] Fritz Schulz, Classical Roman Law (Oxford 1950), 610ff.

[38] See e.g. Ulpian, Edict, book 26 (D 12,4,3,7): "Can he recover? Celsus reports his father as holding that he cannot, but Celsus himself, influenced by consideration of natural equity [*naturali aequitate motus*], thinks that he can."

fair society. The quest for a modern explicit theory combining formality with substantive justice is open and might well be an eternal quest. Still, it is, in any case, a rewarding one. And so it is with special pleasure that I dedicate this paper to my friend Robert Summers, who – in trying to give formality in law its due – has embarked on this great task of legal theory.

Aristotle's Theory of Equity

By Jim Evans, Auckland

The last time I saw Bob Summers our meeting was dominated by discussion of statutory interpretation, a topic on which we were both working. The last part of the meeting was an animated discussion in the back of a car on the way to Syracuse airport about the difference between the meaning of a law and the practical judgment to which it was intended to give effect. We were discussing this difference as the cause of one type of problem of statutory interpretation. I had argued earlier that in modern legal theory problems that arise from this cause are often wrongly diagnosed as arising from imprecision in the meaning of a rule.[1] To understand this type of problem correctly, I had suggested, we need to go back to Aristotle's theory of equity, and the view of practical deliberation (deliberation about how to act) out of which it arises. We were exploring this topic on the way to the airport; but there was no time to finish the discussion. The flights of major airlines do not wait for the flights of legal philosophers. This essay, then, provides a chance to continue the dialogue. I hope that in doing so it may provoke a memory of at least one of many happy discussions. Long may the dialogue continue!

1. Introduction

Very broadly, Aristotle's argument is that because of our inability to foresee all the cases that come within a general law such laws are always prone to include instances for which the judgment that gave rise to the law is inappropriate. The special function of equity ("epieikia") is to remedy this defect by allowing the law to be departed from or modified in exceptional cases.

---

[1] E. g. by Roberto Unger 92. (Details of references are at the end of this essay.) Unger relies on a case quoted by Puffendorf. In Puffendorf's version a law is made imposing severe penalties on anyone who draws blood in the streets, and a barber who, in a street, opens a vein for medical reasons is charged under the law. This case, which is hypothetical, seems to have been designed to sharpen one of the points involved in the actual case, in which a barber cut a client by accident while shaving him in the street (see Thorne (1) 456). Both appear to have been much discussed. If the issue in the hypothetical case is did the makers of the law mean by "draw blood" "draw blood in an attack or fracas" the case is relatively trivial, and was not worth the discussion. It is interesting only if we assume the makers of the law meant draw blood in any way, at least intentionally, but did not think of blood-letting for medical purposes. On this understanding it is a case of conflict between meaning and judgment.

Aristotle gives only one example of the application of equity. I shall discuss it later, but it is not a very convincing example, so I shall take an example from St Thomas Aquinas, who, it is worth mentioning, understood the theory well, understood its basis in Aristotle's views about practical deliberation, and used it in a number of contexts.[2] In Aquinas' example a rule has been made by a city under siege that the gates of the city are to be kept closed at all times. On an occasion some defenders of the city, coming to the relief of the city are approaching the gates pursued at a distance by attackers of the city. The guards on the gates, St Thomas argues, may legitimately open them, contrary to the letter of the law. As a general rule observance of this law would serve the public welfare, but this is a case, not contemplated by those who made the law, in which complying with it would damage that welfare. That the law should be allowed to damage the common good in this unintended way is not to be tolerated.

The Aristotelian theory of equity has had a major impact on Western political and legal thought. I have tried to trace some aspects of this and found it a mammoth task. For the present two broad illustrations may be enough to give some sense of the influence of the theory. The first is that in the common law system the Aristotelian doctrine (as it became) formed an important part of the justification for the separate jurisdiction of the equity courts.[3] The other is that the doctrine was a received part of the learning on statutory interpretation in the English legal system from, at the latest, the publication of St German's Doctor and Student in 1524[4] until the early part of the nineteenth century. At that time it, or, more strictly, a broader doctrine of equitable interpretation of which it had then become a part[5] came under attack by strict constructionists.[6]

---

[2] The example is in Summa Theologica 1a2ae, Q96, A6 (Blackfriars vol 28, 137 - 141), where St Thomas discusses whether one who is subject to a law may ever act against the letter of the law. The example was almost certainly adapted from earlier writings for a case something like this featured in the Roman rhetoric tradition as early as 100 BC: see Bonner 30. "Epieikeia" (equity) is specifically discussed by St Thomas at 2a2ae, Q120 (Blackfriars vol 41, 277). St Thomas also relies on the theory in describing the character of derivative precepts drawn from the general values that ground the natural law. These precepts, though they generally apply, are not proof against all exceptions. Thus, it belongs to the natural law to return a thing loaned, but not if the object is to be used to attack one's country: 1a2ae, Q94, A4 (Blackfriars Vol 28, 87 - 91). That he understood the theory of equity as based on Aristotle's view of practical deliberation is made clear by (inter alia) his discussion of Aristotle's text in his Commentary on the Nichomachean Ethics, Lecture 16 (464 - 469).

[3] See e.g. St German 101 - 107; King James speech in the conflict between the common lawyers and the chancery in 1616, in Bacon Vol 5, 382 - 383; Nottingham 11ff.

[4] At the latest, because the doctrine was known by fifteenth century English jurists and writers even if it had not been made part of a developed theory of interpretation see Pecock (1443) 22 - 26; Fortescue (circa 1463) Vol 1, 214 (Ch 24). I am indebted to Doe 222 - 243 for leading me to these references.

[5] The other part of "equitable interpretation" came from interpretation "on the equity" of a statute: a process of extending statutes by analogy (see Thorne (2)). This pre-dated any extensive influence of the Aristotelian theory in the common law

Thereafter, when exceptions were made to statutes it was not under the ambit of the older learning, but on other grounds, such as that the meaning of the relevant words when they were read in context did not include the exceptional case.[7]

The older learning seems to have lasted longer in the USA, for I was surprised to discover recently that the first ground for the decision in the New York case Riggs v Palmer,[8] decided in 1889, a case made famous by Ronald Dworkin,[9] was the old common law learning on statutory interpretation that incorporated the Aristotelian theory.

In this essay I shall try to clarify Aristotle's argument by paying close attention to his text and by placing the argument within the broader context of his views about practical deliberation. This is undertaken in the next two sections. In the final section I shall make some further points about the theory that will help relate it more effectively to modern concerns.

2. Aristotle's Text

The principal statement of Aristotle's argument is in Book 5, Chapter 10, of the *Nichomachean Ethics.* I have sighted well over a dozen translations of this passage in English, and no two are exactly alike on details of the meaning. The difficulty is that the text is terse and elliptical, so that much depends on the way the translator construes the sense. My method of expounding the passage will be to set out in full the Ross translation[10] with occasional additions, and then follow this by a set of numbered notes that are related to bracketed numbers I have placed within the text.

"Our next subject is equity and the equitable (to epieikes), and their respective relations to justice and the just. For on examination they appear to be neither absolutely the same nor generically different; and while we sometimes praise what is equitable and the

approach to statutory interpretation. The two doctrines were first linked under one title by Plowden, although he recognised the difference between them: see his note to Eyston v Studd (1574) 2 Plowden 465, 75 ER 695; but later writers simply blended them into one doctrine: see eg Coke's Institute (1624) Bk 1, Ch 2, S 21, and the definition of equity in Cowel (1607). By the early nineteenth century the lawyer's learning on this topic had become confused and moribund. That it did not last long under attack is not surprising.

6 See, for example, Bacon's Abridgment (7th ed 1832) Vol 7, 259, where the traditional doctrine is carried forward from the text of older editions (along with a quotation in the Greek from Nichomachean Ethics 5, 10), but some doubts expressed in more recent cases are added in this edition.

7 E.g. Cox v Hakes [1890] AC 506; and see the discussion of In re Bidie [1949] Ch 121 in the last section of this article.

8 115 NY 506 (1889), esp. 509 - 511.

9 See Dworkin.

10 Aristotle, Nichomachean Ethics (1).

equitable man (so that we apply the name by way of praise even to instances of the other virtues, instead of 'good', meaning by epieikesteron that a thing is better), at other times, when we reason it out, it seems strange if the equitable being something different from the just, is yet praiseworthy; for either the just or the equitable is not good, if they are different; or, if both are good, they are the same. (1)

These then are pretty much the considerations that give rise to the problem about the equitable; they are all in a sense correct and not opposed to one another; for the equitable, though it is better than one kind of justice, yet is just, and it is not as being a different class of thing that it is better than the just. The same thing, then, is just and equitable, and while both are good the equitable is superior. (2) What creates the problem is that the equitable is just, but not the legally just but a correction of legal justice. (3) The reason [such a correction is needed] is that all law is universal but about some things it is not possible to make a universal statement which shall be correct. (4) In those cases, then, in which it is necessary to speak [pronounce] universally, but not possible to do so correctly, the law takes the usual case, though it is not ignorant of the possibility of error. (5) And it [the law when it proceeds in this way] is none the less correct; for the error is not in the law nor in the legislator but in the nature of the thing, since the matter of practical affairs is of this kind from the start. (6) When the law speaks universally, then, and a case arises on it which is not [adequately] covered by the universal statement, then it is right, where the legislator fails us and has erred by over-simplicity, to correct the omission – to say what the legislator would have said had he been present, and would have put into his law if he had known. (7) Hence the equitable is just, and better than one kind of justice – not better than absolute justice but better than the error that arises from the absoluteness of the statement [of justice]. And this is the nature of the equitable, a correction of law where it is defective owing to its universality. In fact this [the deficiency of universal laws] is the reason why all things are not determined by law, viz. that about some things it is impossible to lay down a law, so that a decree is needed. For when the thing is indefinite the rule also is indefinite, like the leaden rule used in making the Lesbian moulding; the rule adapts itself to the shape of the stone and is not rigid, and so too the decree is adapted to the facts. (8)

It is plain, then, what the equitable is, and that it is just and better than one kind of justice. It is evident also from this who the equitable man is; the man who chooses and does such acts, and is no stickler for his rights in a bad sense but tends to take less than his share though he has the law on his side, is equitable, and this state of character is equity, which is a sort of justice and not a different state of character. (9)"

Notes

(1) Aristotle takes it for granted that equity gives advice on matters to which justice also applies. He also takes it for granted that justice is good: the passage comes in the course of a discussion of justice (or the state of character of one disposed to act justly) as one of the virtues. However, he suggests we also think of equity ("epieikeia") as good, as is evidenced by the fact the word is sometimes used as a general term of praise in a sense wide enough to embrace other virtues than justice. ("Epieikesteron" is the comparative of the adjective from "epieikeia") But these facts create a problem: for if equity and

justice differ then when they conflict one must be good and the other not; in contrast, if both are good they do not differ, but this seems to make one redundant, and is contrary to the sense they are not exactly the same.

(2) More literally: "Justice and equity, then, are the same, and both excellent, although equity is the more excellent."[11]

(3) The root of the Greek words translated here as "legally" and "legal" is "nomos", the etymology of which is something positively assigned – hence a positive enactment. According to Douglas MacDowell, in *The Law in Classical Athens,* "by the fourth century *nomos* was the normal word for a statute, a law published in writing and validated by a political process".[12] In context the sense is, "equity is not the justice of the expressed law, but a correction of this justice".

(4) There is no word for "things" in the text: Aristotle just says about "some" it is not possible to speak (or pronounce) generally in a way that is correct. The reference of the word "some" is assumed. I suggest this is because Aristotle is repeating a point with which he expects his students to be familiar, and that the correct completion is "subject-matters". What he has in mind, I think, is the division between matters of theoretical reason, where certainty in the reasoning from universal to particular is possible – as in the employment of a correct syllogism – and matters of practical reasoning or deliberation where this is not possible.[13]

"Correct" should, of course, be understood here as meaning "adequate" or "right".

The word translated as "to speak" ("eipein") has also the sense of "to propose", as in moving a measure in the assembly. The broad scope of the word suits Aristotle's purpose, for he wants to contrast, in terms of their possible accuracy, declaring what is the case with declaring what is to be done. Hence he needs a term that covers both.

(5) This sentence as translated suggests the problem identified only occurs on some occasions on which the law pronounces universally (ie frames a general rule). I think this is misleading. The words translated as "but not possible to do so correctly" actually read "but (or 'and') not possible rightly". I suggest this phrase is not intended to help delineate the circumstances in which the law takes the usual case, but is rather an interpolation reminding the reader of what is true when the law does pronounce universally. The commas around the phrase (which are shown in reprints of the Greek text) might be better

---

[11] Cf Nichomachean Ethics (2) (Rackham translation).

[12] 44.

[13] Aristotle has already mentioned twice that there are no invariable laws to be resorted to in practical deliberation: see Bk 1, Ch 3, 1094b19 - 27; Bk 2, Ch 2, 1103b34-1104a10-.

understood as brackets. The sense would then be: "In those instances, then, in which it is necessary to pronounce universally (but not possible rightly) the law takes the usual case."

This interpretation takes Aristotle as saying that the problem is potentially present whenever the law pronounces universally. That fits with my interpretation of the previous sentence as stating that the source of the problem is a general difficulty with practical matters, and, as we shall see, that fits with what comes later in the paragraph. But a puzzle remains why Aristotle considers it is only sometimes necessary for the law to pronounce universally. The solution, I suggest, is that he had in mind the process of Greek law-making, which sometimes proceeded by general laws and sometimes by particular decrees. Certainly in Athens both forms of law-making were common, and quite a bit of learning existed about the relation between decrees and general laws. Decrees, for instance, could not over-ride a general law.[14]

(6) The root of the Greek word translated as "matter" (hēlē) is "material" – the raw stuff on which an artisan works. A more literal translation is: "the error is not in the law, nor in the law-maker, for naturally of this kind is the material of practical affairs".

(7) More literally: "Whenever, therefore, the law speaks generally, and there happens something outside of the general, then it is right where the law-maker has omitted something, and missed the mark, through speaking absolutely, to make right the thing omitted, by making law as the law-maker himself would make if he were present there, and if he knew."

(8) A leaden rule was used to get the profile of an irregular surface.

(9) The states of character are not strictly "equity" and "justice" but having a disposition to perform acts that are equitable or just.

3. The Wider Context: Aristotle's Views on Practical Deliberation

Whether or not one accepts my suggestions in notes 4 and 5 above, there is plainly a link between this passage and Aristotle's views on the nature of practical deliberation; indeed, he says as much – "naturally of this kind is the material of practical affairs". I believe one can not understand Aristotle's theory of equity fully unless one sees it as an aspect of his views about practical deliberation. I want, therefore, to say a little about these views and to link the theory of equity to them. Before starting I should record that Aristotle's views about practical deliberation have been the subject of some important recent writing to which I am much indebted.[15]

[14] See MacDowell, Douglas M 43 - 52.

[15] In particular, Wiggins; Ackrill; Nussbaum (1978), (1986) Chs 8 - 10; John McDowell; Burnyeat.

We may start by noticing the significance Aristotle gives to particular judgments made in a concrete set of circumstances. That these judgments have a special importance is a theme repeated often in the *Nichomachean Ethics*. Two examples will sufficiently illustrate the tenor of Aristotle's remarks.

The first is from Book 2, Chapter 2, in a passage in which Aristotle warns we should look for only as much precision in the study of practical matters as the subject allows[16]:

> "But let it be understood, before we go on, that all reasoning on matters of practice must be in outline merely, and not scientifically exact: for as we said at starting, the kind of reasoning to be demanded varies with the subject in hand; and in practical matters and questions of expediency there are no invariable laws, any more than in questions of health.
>
> And if our general conclusions are thus inexact, still more inexact is all reasoning about particular cases; for these fall under no system of scientifically established rules or traditional maxims, but the agent must always consider for himself what the special occasion requires, just as in medicine or navigation."

The word translated here as "scientifically established rules" is "techne", a skill, or regular method of making or doing something. There is no techne, or any set of instructions ("paraggelian"), for deciding what is appropriate in the particular case, the agent must just come to see what is appropriate.

The second illustration is from Book 6, Chapter 8, in which Aristotle contrasts the starting points in theoretical reason with those in practical deliberation. Here I use a translation – cum – paraphrase, as he calls it, given by David Wiggins[17]:

> "That practical reason is not deductive theoretical knowledge is plain. For practical wisdom is, as I have said, of the ultimate and particular – as is the subject matter of action. In this practical reason is the counterpart or dual of theoretical intuition. *Theoretical* intellect or intuition is of the ultimate, but in this sense – it is of ultimate universal concepts and axioms that are too primitive or fundamental to admit of further analysis or of justification from without. [At the opposite extreme] practical wisdom [as a counterpart of theoretical reason] also treats of matters that defy justification from without. Practical wisdom is of what is ultimate and particular in the distinct sense of needing to be quite simply perceived. By perception here I do not mean sense perception but the kind of perception or insight one needs to see that a triangle, say, is one of the basic or ultimate components [of a figure which one has to construct

---

16 1104a1, Peters translation 36. In The Fragility of Goodness, at 302 - 4, Martha Craven Nussbaum uses this passage to make similar, but different, points to those made here. I do not wholly agree with the analysis she gives on these pages. It seems to me her "mutability" and "indeterminacy" (an unhappy word for what she means) boil down to the enormous variety of situations human beings confront in life, the complexity of many of them from a practical point of view, and the impossibility of anticipating all these situations ahead of time. I shall comment in the text on what she calls "particularity".

17 1142a23. Wiggins 235.

with ruler and compass]. [For there is no *routine procedure* for analysing a problem figure into the components by which one may construct it with rule and compasses.] The analysis calls for insight, and there is a limit to what one can say about it. But even this sort of insight is more akin to sense perception than practical reason is really akin to sense perception."

One might reasonably ask what is it that is just perceived in such judgments. As I understand Aristotle, it is that which can make up part of a life that can be considered well-lived. Now, of course, such judgments can be both challenged and justified. We can consider all the predictable consequences of the act, in what character it should be understood, and how it can fit into an overall life. But the point is that when all these things have been considered we must just find the act acceptable or not. There can be no further justification of a different sort.

Although this ultimate character of particular judgments is important, it does not distinguish such judgments from general judgments (those applying to a class of cases[18]). General judgments may always be tentative, the best we can say being that, other things being equal, a certain type of act is desirable or appropriate in a certain type of circumstance. Nevertheless, the force of such judgments so far as they go must be just understood and does not admit of justification from without. This is most easily seen with regard to judgments that a type of act is desirable. The agent who makes this judgment must see the type of act as having one or more desirable features: and if we ask of any such feature why it makes the act desirable, and keep pursuing the enquiry long enough, we will trace the agent's perception to something she considers desirable for its own sake. That this thing is desirable for its own sake must just strike the agent: there can be no further justification.[19] Similar considerations apply to a judgment that a type of act is worthwhile, or can constitute part of a life that is well-lived. Such judgments must depend on the recognition of one or more things as worthwhile for their own sake, and that these things are worthwhile must be just seen. Worth comment here is that what is of worth in action, as that may feature in practical reasoning, could not be just written in the structure of the universe. For what was written would not move an agent to act unless the agent found it of worth, or found other reasons for performing it. But in the first case the agent would just have to find the content of what was written of worth, the fact that it was written being incidental; and in the second case the agent would, at most, be treating something else as worthwhile for its own sake. So in lacking ultimate justification outside of the agent's responses universal and particular practical judgments are alike.

[18] I use "general" in what follows rather than "universal" in order to cover both open and closed classes: that is classes picked out by terms that do not imply any limit to the number of possible members, and those picked out by terms that do.

[19] Which is not to say that such things may not also be seen as instances of, or as conducing towards, other things that are desired for their own sake.

True, to claim that the evaluations that ground particular practical judgments are ultimate, in the sense of lacking justification from outside, is a useful way of making an important point. For characteristic of particular practical judgments, especially those requiring any serious deliberation, is that they involve choosing between options that satisfy different packages of our conflicting concerns. To assert that the right balance between conflicting concerns must be just seen, is to assert that there is no single measure for settling such conflicts. That point is salutary, for, as Wiggins points out, there are many who would like to deal with the difficulties of choice by finding such a measure.[20] If there is no single measure to settle conflicts between the things we care about then we must just struggle to find choices that we can respect. But salutary as this is it does not distinguish particular practical judgments from general ones, for many general judgments involve a choice between conflicting concerns.

We need to consider further why the difference between particular and general practical judgments is important. That there is a puzzle about this is shown by the following consideration. Suppose one is asked to justify the judgment that a certain action is the right thing to do, or even an appropriate thing to do, in a certain particular circumstance. Obviously one will have to point to features of the circumstance and of the act proposed that show the act to be right or appropriate. Now, so long as one is concerned with justification in terms of standards that are assumed to apply to numbers of people it will be an assumption of the dialogue that if features of the same type were present in another case to which the same mode of justification applies, and were the only significant features present, the same judgment would be required. More than that, only features that are instances of general qualities other instances of which would, *certeris paribus,* justify the same judgment on other occasions (if present in a case to which the same mode of justification applies) can be used in such justification. For only such features can bring the case within a general standard. All of this applies to ethical justification – for in ethical discourse it seems that the relevant standards are expected to apply to all sane, mature, human beings. Thus, ethical dialogue, which is after all Aristotle's subject matter, depends on general judgments, what is said of particular cases holding only insofar as they are instances of open classes of case[21] to which such judgments apply. But then it becomes unclear how within this type of discourse general and particular judgments can differ.

Of course, the features that justify an ethical judgment in a particular case may be so complex that it is inconceivable that anyone should ever stand in the same position again: for often we are not just concerned with combinations of features, but features that may be present in different degrees. This is not to

---

[20] Wiggins 237.

[21] See n 18 for a definition of open classes.

the point. We are considering the logical character of such judgments and the practical likelihood of the features that justify a judgment recurring is not relevant. Also, if the right balance in a particular case must be just seen, then different people may see it differently. But, again, that does not affect the claim made. Our ethical judgments may be just our own, and we may only hope that we can come to some shared understandings with others, but if *we* hold that a particular action is right because of certain features of it, then *we* are committed to holding the same would be true in any like case.

I have been careful to limit my claims to justification, because it seems similar points do not hold of the motivation of action. A person may act in a certain way because of certain features of a situation without seeing themselves as acting on a general principle, and without any commitment to acting in the same way in a like case. Someone gets up in the night to tend a sick child: they might do so because they see this as a parent's role, or because they have assumed a responsibility, but no such general conception need apply – they might just respond spontaneously to the child's plight. Asked, they might explain, "I couldn't bear her unhappiness, I had to try to do something."

We need to be careful here. To perceive the case as being that of a child suffering the person acting must, of course, have recognised it as belonging to a type. All categorisation is like this. And, of course, he must have acted because he understood the situation as being of this type. But he need not have acted because he believed it was right to respond to this type of situation in this way (even if he believed this); nor need he have any commitment to acting in the same way in other cases of this type. Obviously, it would be a strange person who having responded to a particular situation in a certain way did not feel at least an inclination to respond in the same way in a like case – unless, of course, some general contemplation about the desirability of that type of behaviour had intervened in the meantime. We might worry about the fragmented character of someone, who without apparent reason, responded quite differently to apparently similar situations. But, again, that is a different point.

These comments can, I think, help us understand the force of an interesting remark made by Martha Craven Nussbaum in seeking to explain Aristotle's view about the significance of particular judgments in ethical assessment. She writes[22]:

> "Aristotle also thinks, in speaking of correct choice, of the ethical relevance of particular non-repeatable components of the situation. [–] The good friend will [–] attend to the particular needs and concerns of his friend, benefiting him or her for the sake of what he or she is in and of him or herself, not for the sake of some general good. Much of this 'in and of himself' will, as we shall see, consist of repeatable char-

[22] Nussbaum (1986) 304.

acter traits; but in love and friendship features of shared history and family relatedness that are not even in principle repeatable are permitted to bear serious ethical weight."

So far as ethical assessment is concerned, the important word here seems to me to be "permitted". Sometimes an assumption is made that morality forbids one to prefer one's family or friends unless one acts on a general moral principle that requires this: a principle of the form, "Everyone should treat their X in such and such a way in such and such circumstances". Now ethical contemplation can provide principles of this form: for instance, "a true friend ought to act in this way in this type of situation". Such principles can, of course, motivate: indeed it is important that they do. But to assume that it is wrong to prefer one's family or friends unless one acts on such a principle is a mistake. Nussbaum's use of the word "permitted" seems to me right. Much of the role of our ethical concern with such relationships is not to provide a motive, but in some cases to permit, in others to restrict, and in still others to applaud, acting on natural motives. However, this still means that ethical assessment deals in general standards that apply to all those subject to such assessment.

In any event, even if I am wrong that ethical assessment always deals with general standards, the judgments made in applying equity (in Aristotle's sense) ought almost always to be general judgments. In the first place the judgments equity modifies plainly are judgments about what should occur in a class of case, since equity modifies general laws. But in almost all cases the judgment that an exception ought to be allowed in a particular case should depend on a general judgment that an exception ought to be allowed in a class of case of which this case is an instance. To make an exception on the ground of features of one person that are not in principle repeatable would normally be a blatant breach of impartiality between citizens. There may be exceptions to this. An exception in favour of the sovereign might sometimes be justifiable (assuming there was no general doctrine covering this). Such an exception would normally apply to any sovereign, but conceivably a case might occur in which it was justifiable to allow an exception for just one sovereign. Any such case allowing an exception for just one person would need to be extraordinary. For almost all cases, then, equitable exceptions will need to be justified by general judgments.

But if that is so why are such general judgments superior to the general judgments that ground a rule? We are back to the question why are practical judgments in the particular case superior to general practical judgments when both are based on general features? The answer, I think, is that the *general* judgments made in particular cases are superior only in being based on additional relevant experience. They are not free from the inherent problems of general practical judgments – for an exception may need to be made to the general terms of the exception. But as judgments that can be adequately applied to the particular case they are superior in that they stand a chance of responding to all the general concerns that ought to be taken into account in that case. In the particular case we can hope to add to the general concerns that we weigh in a general judgment, not only recognition that these concerns are in fact present, but also the assessment that they are not outweighed by other concerns present in that case. Whereas, if Aristotle is right, when we make a judgment about a class of case not present to us, particularly an open class of case, we can not be certain that there will not be instances within the class in which the considerations we have taken into account are outweighed by others.

Applied to general ethical judgments this account yields just one way in which such judgments may, through oversight, prove inadequate in a particular case: the considerations which favour the judgment may, in a particular case, be outweighed by others. But applied to expressed general laws it yields two different ways in which application of the law in a particular case may not adequately reflect the judgment of those who made it. Firstly, a case may be within the meaning of the law, but, through oversight, the judgment that lay behind the law may not apply to it at all. The case may simply not fall within the considerations on which that judgment was based. (I shall say more about this in the next section.) Secondly, the considerations on which the judgment was based may be present, but outweighed. There is no sign that Aristotle recognised the difference between these two types of case. In the *Rhetoric* he gives an example of a case requiring application of equity that comes into the first category. His account of equity in the *Nichomachean Ethics* applies more plainly to the second type of case than the first, so if he had recognised the difference when he wrote that account he might have confined the concept of equity just to this. Alternatively, he might have modified his account. As there is no way of knowing about this I have elected to treat both types of case as within equity in a broadly Aristotelian sense, simply because I think that is the most convenient choice, and because cases of both types have been treated as within Aristotle's doctrine down through the years.

This, then, is my explanation of why equity is needed to correct general laws, but is it Aristotle's? Subject to any quibble about my ruling in the last paragraph, I think it clearly is, for this is pretty much what he says. The role of equity is to put *into the law* what the lawmaker himself would have put if he had known. Equity thus makes a general modification of a general law. Less clear is the relation between my account of the limitations of general practical judgments and Aristotle's remarks on the inexactness of discourse about the practical and the importance of particular judgments. I do not think what I have said here about general practical judgments fully explains these comments of Aristotle. Another source is that often in ethical appraisal, and even more often in living – with its mix of ethical and other concerns – we must make judgments that require such a sensitive reading of the situation, and such a complex balancing of concerns, that no rule could possibly prepare us ahead of time to make such judgments.[23] However, I do think that what I have said here about general practical judgments is part of the reason for Aristotle's comments. He does say that there are no invariable laws governing practical matters[24] and also stress that accuracy is only to be found in particular judgments; and although he does not say precisely why these things are so it seems reasonable to conclude he saw the first as at least part of the cause of the second. As to why there are no invariable laws for practical matters, that this is because we are always likely to overlook relevant concerns when making general judgments is sufficiently indicated in the passage on equity itself.

There is one more level at which the ground for the theory of equity can be stated. Behind the belief that we are always likely to omit relevant concerns from general practical judgments lies, ultimately, a view about human life and the human situation. I shall finish this section by setting out the beliefs of this kind that I think are the ultimate props for Aristotles's theory:

(1) There are many things human beings care about.

(2) Life confronts us with an enormous variety of situations in which such things compete, often in very complex ways;

(3) No measure exists for resolving such conflicts so that in cases of conflict we have just to choose between different things we care about, or between different compromises between them; and

(4) We do not have the ability to anticipate all of these situations.

The last point does not necessarily depend just on our inadequate powers of foresight. If there are an infinite variety of ways in which the things we care about can compete, as conceivably there are, then no matter how extensive our powers of foresight we would not be able to anticipate them all.

4. Some Comments on the Theory

This section is in the nature of a postscript intended to help relate what has been said to modern concerns, particularly about statutory interpretation. I shall make a number of discrete points.

(1) The need for equitable exceptions is not *the* cause of problems in interpreting laws, any more than, pace H. L. A. Hart,[25] vagueness is *the* cause of such problems. Like vagueness, it is one cause among a variety.[26]

---

[23] Cf Nussbaum (1986) 303 - 304.

[24] See n 12 above.

[25] See Hart Ch 7.

[26] I have attempted to give a broader survey of these causes in Evans Ch's 4 - 11.

(2) Aristotle assumes that equity both brings the law closer to justice and puts into the law what the law-maker himself would have put if he had thought of this case. These are two different things, and they need not coincide. Aristotle seems to assume that the law-maker aims to state what justice requires on some matter, and that he gets it broadly right. Perhaps stating what justice requires was the major task of law-makers in his time, although it is hard to believe it could have been the whole of it. In any event modern citizens are familiar with laws that do not state some aspect of justice, but aim at a public good instrumentally. They are also familiar with laws that do not get it broadly right: instrumental laws that are inept, and harsh and oppressive laws. If we think of equity just as an aspect of interpretation there can be equitable exceptions to any of these laws even if they do not bring the result closer to justice. Indeed, there could be equitable exceptions made by the members of a gang of bandits to the general commands of the bandit leader. Equity, St German said, is not "agaynst the cruelnes of the lawe".[27] He meant that applying it is consistent with believing the law involved is generally good. But the point can be taken another way. Equity, as a device of interpretation, is not concerned with the quality of the judgment behind the law at all, it simply allows the interpreter to meet oversight by putting into the law what the interpreter believes the law-maker would have put if he (or it) had thought of this case.

None of this suggests, of course, that in dealing with modern legal problems we should not assume that the laws we deal with were made for some good purpose. Nor does it suggest that public goods that may or may not have swayed the law-makers (in fact) had they recognised their relevance, should not be part of a standardised way of dealing with the problem Aristotle identifies. (See comment 6 below).

(3) I indicated earlier that there are two ways in which a gap may arise in a particular case between the meaning of a law and the judgment of those who framed it: (i) the meaning may include cases to which the judgment does not apply at all, and (ii) the meaning may include cases to which the judgment applies but in which the considerations it depended on are outweighed.

Interestingly, the only example that Aristotle gives of the application of equity is of the first type. It occurs in the *Rhetoric*,[28] which gives a broader account of equity than that in the *Nichomachean Ethics* – not merely in covering this type of case. The text is not very clear, but the case seems to be roughly this. A law is made against striking another with an instrument; one who strikes another with his hand is wearing a finger ring and is charged under the law. According to Aristotle, "he is guilty of a criminal act according to the written words of the law; but he is innocent really, and it is equity that declares

---

[27] St German 97.

[28] Rhetorica 1374a 35.

him to be so". Here the evil the law is directed against – the serious character of attacks with an instrument – is not present at all. The grounds for the law are not outweighed by something more important, as they would be, say, if a person were to attack another with an instrument in order to prevent a treason against the state: they simply do not apply.

It is not a very good example. Modern case-records enable us to do better. Consider, for example, the English case *In re Bidie.*[29] A family protection statute gave members of a testator's family who believed they were inadequately provided for in the testator's will an opportunity to seek from the court an order varying the disposition of the testator's estate. A time limit was imposed on the bringing of such proceedings in a section that read:

> "An order under this act shall not be made save on an application made within six months from the date on which representation in regard to the testator's estate [–] is first taken out."

"Representation" is a grant of authority to executors or administrators to administer an estate. In this case the deceased was believed to have died intestate and representation was granted on this assumption. Under an intestacy the estate would have gone to his widow. Some sixteen months later, and before the estate was distributed, a will was found which disinherited the widow. The earlier grant of representation was then revoked and a new grant made. Within six months from this grant the widow sought to pursue an application under the act and was met by the claim that representation had first been granted more than six months earlier.

The court held in favour of the widow on the ground that "representation" as used in the section did not mean representation generally, but only representation in respect of a will. The idea was that "representation" was used elliptically to mean "representation in respect of a will". This argument fails to convince when we consider that to have meant representations in respect of a will, as distinct from representations generally, the draftsperson would have had to realize that some representations granted in cases where an application under the act might be appropriate would not relate to a will. To have done that he would need to have thought of the possibility of lost wills found after a representation had been granted on an assumed intestacy, and if he had done that he would surely have recognised that the type of problem that occurred in this case could also occur when the first grant of representation was to administer a will later found to have been superseded by another will.[30] But, if he had recognised these possibilities and intended the act should not apply to them it is implausible that he would not have dealt with the point explicitly.

---

[29] [1949] Ch 121.

[30] The court equivocates about this problem, saying that is a case for another time (at 133).

The truth appears to be that the draftsperson overlooked the unusual case in which a will is discovered after a representation has been granted. The case is one in which the judgment behind a rule does not apply to a case within its meaning. We may reconstruct the relevant practical judgment as follows. A balance needs to be struck between (i) giving claimants a reasonable time to lodge their applications, and (ii) not delaying the distribution of estates unduly while administrators wait for potential claims. If potential claimants, or those responsible for them, have had six months to lodge their claims this is a reasonable time. So precluding claims after that time has elapsed strikes the required balance. However, in the case that had occurred the applicant had not had any time at all to lodge her claim. So the feature assumed to be present in each case to which the rule applies, the presence of which it was judged would make the application of the rule in such cases fair, was not present at all in this case. Hence the need for an equitable exception.

One may wonder how cases of this type can occur, since it seems strange that those who frame a law should ever identify as the cases to which it applies a different class of case from that to which their judgment applies. The explanation is that we may wrongly assume that all cases falling under a certain description will possess a feature, or set of features, that brings them under another description, and judge of them under the one description but refer to them under the other. We need not make this assumption generally, but may do so only in regard to a particular context. Presumably, the drafter of the statute considered in *In re Bidie* did not assume that all representations to administer estates relate to wills, he simply assumed that when people named in the act as potential claimants wanted to lodge a claim any representation granted would relate to the will the applicant wished to challenge. If we could be more careful in framing laws to identify the features we consider justify the application of the law, problems of this sort could be eliminated. So it is worth noting that there is not for these problems any cause that is in principle not eliminable, as perhaps there is for the outweighing type of case.

Of the outweighing type of case little more needs to be said. As modern examples we might take *Riggs v Palmer,*[31] in which a grandson who murdered his grandfather to inherit under his will was held not entitled to inherit although the statutes providing for the implementation of wills made no exception for this type of case; and *In re Sigsworth,*[32] in which a son who murdered his mother was held not entitled to inherit on her intestacy under an intestacy statute that on its terms would have given the estate to the son.

(4) In judging whether the point of a law applies in a particular case we should take account of a quite common strategy in law-making. Often legis-

---

[31] 115 NY 506 (1889).

[32] [1935] 1 Ch 89.

lators deliberately frame laws that apply to a wider class than they are concerned with as a means of being sure of capturing the narrower class, or as a means of doing so in a workable way.

Consider the following representative problem. A market is held most days Monday to Friday from 6am to around 11am. Sometimes it finishes a little earlier. Vehicles parked near the market clutter the area and prevent delivery vehicles making deliveries. The local authority could make a by-law saying, "No parking near the market while the market is in process, except for delivery vehicles". But this would invite endless argument. When, precisely, does the market stop being in process? What is *near* the market? What counts as a delivery vehicle? Instead it adopts a common expedient. It paints a yellow line alongside certain sections of road, and posts a notice backed by a by-law alongside these sections saying, "No Parking Monday to Friday 6am to 11am, without a delivery sticker.". Then it issues stickers to regular delivery vehicles. Now when someone parks in this area at 10.30am when the market has finished early, or on a public holiday, these are not cases for an equitable exception. For these cases possess the feature that was thought to justify the law – since this is being among the cases that it was judged necessary to prohibit in order to have a workable means of stopping parked vehicles interfering with the market.

(5) As the discussion of *In re Bidie* illustrated, recognising an ellipsis *is* not making an exception to a law. Often we use a general term intending it to be understood from the context as applying to some sub-class of the cases covered by its literal meaning. So, a bankruptcy statute may refer to "all creditors", meaning, in context, "all creditors who have proved their debt in this bankruptcy". To recognise such an ellipsis *is* to recognise the meaning of the rule, it is not to make an exception to it.

(6) Aristotle's discussion of equity identifies a problem that every legal system has to deal with. But the right way to deal with it is not necessarily to make an exception whenever it seems probable that those who framed or approved the law would have made an exception if they had thought of the case. Acting consistently with the judgment of the law-makers (which may involve going beyond their judgment) and avoiding the harsh results that would follow from an unqualified application of laws are important concerns; but they need to be balanced against another. This is protecting the ability of citizens and their advisers to rely on an understanding of the law that can be worked out from the content of statutes with reasonable confidence. Legal systems need to develop strategies for dealing with the problem that are sensitive to both these concerns.

In part, all legal systems deal with it by developing doctrines providing for exceptions. For example, the criminal defences of self-defence and duress are instances of doctrines dealing with the outweighing type of case. Sometimes such doctrines apply unless this would be inconsistent with the aims of the law. Some relating of the case to the judgment of the law-makers can then occur in deciding whether the doctrine applies. Consider for example the doctrine that strict compliance with procedural rules can normally be waived by the party for whose protection they were made. This can be seen as a doctrine for dealing with certain cases of the "judgment not applicable" type. But it applies only if it is not inconsistent with the purpose of the rule, as it would be, for instance, if the purpose were paternalistic – the aim being to protect persons from harming their own interests.[33] So a careful relating of a case to the judgment behind the law can occur in deciding whether the doctrine applies in a particular instance. In other doctrines scope for the weighing of conflicting concerns is allowed within the content of the doctrine itself (as for example, in the defence of necessity which allows a defence when compliance with the law would have damaged a value outweighing those promoted by the law).

Outside of these established doctrines a common, and sensible, strategy for the outweighing type of case is to allow exceptions when preference for the concern that argues for the exception over that which was intended to be promoted by the law is consistent with established policy followed elsewhere in the law. This may not absorb all the remaining cases of this type in which exceptions are justifiable, but in cases outside this range the ground for the exception should presumably be an evaluation that is a matter of notorious public understanding. In the "judgment not applicable" type of case perhaps the right standard is that the oversight of the legislature should be obvious.

References

Ackrill, J. L.: "Aristotle on Eudaimonia", in Amelié Rorty, Essays on Aristotle's Ethics, Berkley 1980.

Aquinas, St. Thomas Summa Theologica (1265 - 1274), Blackfriars, London and New York (1964 - 1966).

– Commentary on the Nichomachean Ethics, trans C. I. Litzinger, Chicago 1964.

Aristotle: Nichomachean Ethics (1), trans Sir David Ross, London 1925, 1963 reprint.

– Nichomachean Ethics (2), trans H. Rackham, 2nd ed, London 1934, 1962 reprint.

– Nichomachean Ethics (3), trans F. H. Peters, 12th ed, London 1916.

– Rhetorica, trans W. Rhys Roberts, in The Works of Aristotle, vol XI, ed W. D. Ross, Oxford 1924.

Bacon, Sir Francis: Lord Bacon's Letters and Life, ed J. Spedding, London 1869.

Bacon's Abridgment of the Law of England, 8 Vols, 7th ed, London 1832.

---

[33] See e.g. Ramia v African Woods Ltd [1960] 1; All ER 627.

Bonner, S. F.: Roman Declamation in the Late Republic and Early Empire, Liverpool 1949.

Burnyeat, M. F.: "Aristotle on Learning to be Good" in Amelié Rorty, Essays on Aristotle's Ethics, Berkley 1980.

Coke, Sir Edward: First Institute of the Laws of England, London 1628.

Cowel, Dr.: The Interpretation of Words and Terms Used either in the Common or Statute Laws of this Realm, London, intermittently from 1607 to 1701.

Doe, C. Norman: Central Concepts in Fifteenth Century English Legal Thought, PhD thesis, Cambridge 1987.

Dworkin, Ronald: "The Model of Rules" (1967) 35 University of Chicago Law Review 14; republished as "Is Law a System of Rules?" in Robert S. Summers, Essays in Legal Philosophy, Oxford 1968, 25.

Evans, Jim: Statutory Interpretation: Problems of Communication, Auckland 1988.

Fortescue, Sir John: De Natura Legis Naturae (circa 1463), in Works of Sir John Fortescue, ed Thomas Lord Clermond, trans Chichester Fortescue, London 1869.

Hart, H. L. A.: The Concept of Law, Oxford 1961.

MacDowell, Douglas M.: The Law in Classical Athens, London 1978.

McDowell, J.: "The Role of Eudaimonia in Aristotle's Ethics", in Amelié Rorty, Essays on Aristotle's Ethics, Berkley 1980.

Nottingham, Lord Chancellor: Prolegomena of Equity, manuscript copy by Francis Hargreave, circa 1675, Cambridge University Library (Manuscripts).

Nussbaum, Martha Craven: "Practical Syllogisms and Practical Science" in Nussbaum, Aristotle's De Motu Animalium, Princeton 1978.

– The Fragility of Goodness, Cambridge 1986.

Pecock, Reginald: Rule of Crysten Religioun (1443), ed W. C. Greet, Early English Text Society, London 1927.

St. German, Christopher: Doctor and Student (1524 in Latin, circa 1531 in English), Seldon Society (Volume 91), London 1974.

Thorne, S. E.: (1) "Statuti in the Post-Glossators" (1936) 11 Speculum 452.

– (2) "The Equity of a Statute and Heydon's Case" (1936) Illinois Law Review 202.

Unger, Roberto: Knowledge and Politics, New York 1976.

Wiggins, David: "Deliberation and Practical Reason" in Amelié Rorty, Essays on Aristotle's Ethics, Berkley 1980.

Publius Iuventius Celsus – The Profile of a Classical Roman Jurist*

By Herbert Hausmaninger, Vienna**

1. Introduction: Roman Jurists' Law

The 'classical' Roman law of the first two centuries AD was essentially 'jurists' law'.[1] The classical jurists were legal scholars who belonged to the Roman aristocracy. Their public service careers culminated in the highest administrative offices in Rome and in the provinces. They also functioned as legal advisers to the Emperor and as members of his state council. Until well into the Empire, the study and practice of law were considered a noble pastime with no immediate financial reward, but potentially considerable political benefits.

There were very few statutes that dealt with Roman private law. The key figure in the Roman legal process was the Praetor, a high state official who annually promulgated the Edict, a catalog of actions (similar to the former English common law writs) and other legal remedies that he would be prepared to grant. Although the Praetor considered himself bound by his own Edict, he would, in exceptional circumstances, also be willing to formulate a new remedy *(actio utilis, actio in factum)*. In this respect, he assumed a role similar to that of the English Chancellor when exercising equity jurisdiction.

All Roman litigation was initiated before the Praetor. Once he had selected a specific *actio* as the proper program for a civil suit, he would send the parties to a *iudex* (judge) who was to take evidence, hear oral argument and decide the case. Both the Praetor and the *iudex* were laymen, with little or no background or training in the law. They relied, therefore, on the opinions of the jurists, who were political friends, social peers and, above all, legal experts.

---

* This essay is dedicated in gratitude and with most cordial wishes to Bob Summers, eminent scholar of exceptional perspective and interests, generously supportive colleague, and enthusiastic friend of many years.

** Professor of Law, University of Vienna (Austria); Visiting Professor of Law, University of Virginia Law School and Cornell Law School.

1 See A. A. Schiller, Jurists' Law, in: An American Experience in Roman Law (1971) 148; The Nature and Significance of Jurists' Law, id. 199. M. Kaser, Römische Rechtsquellen und angewandte Juristenmethode (1986) 33.

The fundamental function of the Roman jurist, in the Empire as well as in the preceding Republic, was the formulation of a *responsum,* an expert legal opinion, in answer to a *quaestio,* a legal problem put to him by a Praetor or *iudex* or private parties involved in the initiation or decision of a law suit. The combined social and professional authority of the learned jurists gave their advisory opinions already in the Republic (at least de facto) the force of law. In truth, the jurists were the ones who decided the cases and determined the course of Roman legal development: the mainstream of Roman private law was constituted by a 'professors' law' as opposed to legislative or judicial law-making.

The Emperor Augustus and his successors granted the most outstanding jurists the right to deliver legal advice to the judge and the parties on behalf of the Emperor *(ius respondendi ex auctoritate principis).*[2] Thus the second century jurist Gaius was able to list the opinions of these jurists in his catalog of the sources of law in the technical sense, together with statutes, edicts, etc.[3] The judges' decisions were not considered binding precedents and thus were not reported. The legal writings of the jurists, however, functioned as authoritative works, recording leading and dissenting opinions of colleagues and predecessors, and providing persuasive arguments that could be used in future legal disputes.

The classical Roman jurists had at their disposal a broad range of formal and substantive reasons to support and justify their opinions. Among their more formal reasonings we find deductions from logic and grammar, references to the legislator's or the parties' intent, ordinary usage of language, analogy and so forth. Among the substantive arguments there is strong emphasis on values such as *bona fides* (good faith), *aequitas* (equity, fairness), *boni mores* (good morals, public policy), *utilitas* (practicability), etc.[4]

It has often been noted that classical Roman law as written by the jurists exhibits a remarkable conformity as to substance and even more so as to style. Although we do encounter differences of opinion, scholarly controversies, and even rival schools of thought, there appears to be a particularly strong concern for the professional authority of the law which would express itself in terse, matter of fact, technical language devoid of any oratory embellishment, emotion or personal idiosyncrasy.[5] The individual jurists seem to restrain their per-

---

[2] See F. Wieacker, Respondere ex auctoritate principis, in: Satura R. Feenstra oblata (1985) 71; T. Honoré, Emperors and Lawyers (1981) 4; R. A. Bauman, Lawyers and Politics in the Early Roman Empire (1989) passim.

[3] Gaius Inst. 1,7 ... *quibus permissum est, iura condere.*

[4] F. Horak, Rationes decidendi I (1969); F. Wieacker, Offene Wertungen in der römischen Jurisprudenz, in: Ausgewählte Schriften I (1983) 174.

[5] See the characterization of Roman legal language by F. Schulz, Prinzipien des römischen Rechts (1934) 55; W. Kalb, Roms Juristen, nach ihrer Sprache dargestellt

sonalities in favor of a common legal style, so much so that F. C. von Savigny, one of the leading 19th century authorities on the subject, would call them 'fungible persons'.[6]

This notion has, of course, become subject to scholarly challenge. But we shall probably never be able to write intellectual profiles of Roman jurists in the way we can individualize German scholars or American judges.[7] We may, however, attempt to sketch personal thought patterns, preferred arguments and approaches of one or the other Roman jurist, thus eventually gaining an additional dimension to Roman law, the substance of which has been so much more familiar to us over the centuries than its methodology, and the methodology of which has been subject to far more generalizing harmonization than attempts at discriminating individualization.

The following essay will focus on the legal reasoning of the classical jurist Publius Iuventius Celsus. It is a report on work in progress and will in part draw on research published (and more fully argued) elsewhere.[8]

2. Celsus: a Biographical Note

Although Publius Iuventius Celsus was one of the leading and highly influential jurists of his time, literary sources transmit only scant biographical data on his life and career.[9] We know that he served as Praetor in 106 or 107 AD, and at some time between 107 and 117 as provincial governor *(legatus pro praetore)* in Thracia. He then held his first consulship in the reign of either Trajan (98 - 117) or Hadrian (117 - 138), was a member of Hadrian's *consilium* (state council) and headed, together with Neratius Priscus, the so-called Proculian law school.[10] Celsus was Consul for the second time in 129 and at some later date governed the province of Asia as *proconsul.*

(1890) passim; M. Kaser, Zur Methodologie der römischen Rechtsquellenforschung (1972) 47.

[6] Vom Beruf unserer Zeit für Gesetzgebung und Rechtswissenschaft (2nd ed. 1828) 157; see also id. 29 "Selbst wenn wir ihre Schriften vollständig vor uns hätten, würden wir darin weit weniger Individualität finden, als in irgend einer anderen Literatur . . .".

[7] Let alone distinguish styles like in painting or music, cf. the exaggerated hopes of E. Seidl, Tryphoninus und Callistratus, Eranion in honorem G.S. Maridakis (1963) 231 "Was würde man von einem Kunsthistoriker sagen, der einen Rubens und einen Rembrandt nicht nach ihrer Malweise zu unterscheiden verstünde? . . ."

[8] See H. Hausmaninger, Publius Iuventius Celsus: Persönlichkeit und juristische Argumentation, Aufstieg und Niedergang der römischen Welt (= ANRW) II/15 (ed. H. Temporini, 1976) 382; Zur Gesetzesinterpretation des Celsus, Studi in onore di G. Grosso V (1972) 243; Zur Legatsinterpretation des Celsus, IVRA 35 (1984, publ. 1987) 16; 'Id quod actum est' als Argumentationsfigur bei Celsus, Festschrift für G. Wesener (1992) 159; Celsus gegen Proculus, 3. Festschrift für U. v. Lübtow (1991) 53.

[9] W. Kunkel, Herkunft und soziale Stellung der römischen Juristen (2nd ed. 1967) 146; R. A. Bauman (supra note 2) 221.

[10] Pomp. D 1,2,2,53. On the Proculian school see infra at note 25.

The young Celsus was introduced to legal science by his own father, who preceded him as head of the Proculian school. It was probably the elder Celsus who according to the historian Cassius Dio prominently figured in a conspiracy against the Emperor Domitian but managed to escape the penalty.[11] The younger Pliny's account of a heated senate debate in which the younger Celsus played a leading role sheds little light on the jurist's general personal traits or legal style.[12]

3. Legal Writings: the 'digesta'

Fortunately, the surviving excerpts from Celsus' legal writings speak a clearer language than the scarce references to the jurist in other Roman sources, and they promise to support a number of conclusions concerning the jurist's personality and reasoning.[13]

Celsus published *digesta* in 39 *libri* or volumes. The standard size of a *liber* (papyrus scroll) was between 1500 and 2500 lines of 34 letters each.[14] In Justinian's Digest we possess 141 excerpts from the Celsus *digesta,* ranging in size from one to 90 of such standard lines and amounting to a total of approximately 1500 lines or roughly 2% of the original work. In addition, Celsus opinions are referred to in 139 excerpts from the works of other jurists, most notably Ulpian's, who frequently quotes Celsus at length and even verbatim, thus offering valuable additional material facilitating an appraisal of the jurist's legal argument and style.[15]

As far as the system of the Celsus *digesta* may be reconstructed, it follows the order of subject matter in the praetorian Edict (*libri* 1 to 27) and a – later to become stereotype – list of *leges* and *senatus consulta* that are usually commented on in works of this type.[16] While the *digesta* are the only work of Cel-

---

[11] Cass. Dio 67,13; R.A. Bauman (supra note 2) 182 and 222.

[12] Epist. 6,5; for political background and highly speculative deductions see R. A. Bauman (supra note 2) 222 - 228.

[13] The older literature on Celsus may be found in F. Casavola, Giuristi adrianei (1980) 280. See also his substantive remarks id. 33 and 107. Recent studies include V. Scarano Ussani, Valori e storia nella cultura giuridica fra Nerva e Adriano: Studi su Nerazio e Celso (1979) and P. Cerami, La concezione celsina del 'ius' – Presupposti culturali e implicazioni metodologiche I: L'interpretazione degli atti autoritativi (1985). A forthcoming study by B. Kauffmann promises to focus on the influence of Celsus on *senatus consulta* and *constitutiones* under Hadrian, see M. Memmer, W. Selb (eds.) Romanistik 1991 (1991) 83.

[14] See L. Wenger, Die Quellen des römischen Rechts (1953) 91.

[15] Of these citations Ulpian provides 118, Pomponius 9, Paul 6, Marcian 4, Julian and Maecian 1 each. The Emperor Justinian refers to Celsus once in his Institutes and twice in his Code.

[16] Cf. the *digesta* written by Julian and Marcellus: P. Krüger, Geschichte der Quellen und Litteratur des Römischen Rechts (2nd ed. 1912) 143.

sus from which at least a number of extracts survive, several double citations by later jurists make it plausible that Celsus in composing his *digesta* exploited earlier writings of his own that were originally published as *commentarii* (lecture notes or a student hornbook), *epistulae* (letters) and *quaestiones* (problems, i.e. real or hypothetical cases discussed with students).[17] His *digesta* do not present themselves as exhaustive or systematic treatment of topics, but rather exhibit a colorful mixture of tracts, letters and opinions, often maintaining the original question-and-answer form in which legal advice and legal instruction were most commonly given. This lack of editing appears to be a fortunate circumstance in that it provides us with the immediate and unadulterated impact of a spirited and at times polemical, perhaps even sarcastic, temperament that has often been taken to be the single most characteristic feature distinguishing Celsus from the traditional, bland style of his more genteel colleagues.[18]

4. Personality and Style: Polemical and Elegant?

It seems indeed to be a specialty of Celsus to criticize other jurists' views as ridiculous, silly or inept (*ridiculum, stultum, ineptum et vitiosum,* etc).[19] In the Middle Ages a *responsum Celsinum* generally designated a scathing reply to a stupid question.[20] One should, however, refrain from attaching excessive weight to this observation. *Ridiculum* sporadically occurs in the writings of other jurists as well,[21] and Celsus himself uses the word with some restraint, i.e. only in an impersonal sense, without naming names. He shows the same restraint in using *absurdum,* a term rather frequently employed in a similar fashion by his colleagues.[22] He does, however, once call a specific jurist's opinion *stolida* or stupid.[23] But for the most part he uses simply *falsum* (wrong) when disapproving of a particular jurist's view. *Falsum* is rather common in classical usage. It is, for instance, frequently employed by Iavolenus or Paul when commenting on the works of Labeo.

---

[17] Five of these citations survive in Ulpian's works, demonstrating that Celsus wrote at least 11 *libri epistularum,* 12 *libri quaestionum* and 7 *libri commentariorum.*

[18] Cf. F. Wieacker, Amoenitates Iuventianae, IVRA 13 (1962) 1.

[19] H. Hausmaninger, Publius Iuventius Celsus: Persönlichkeit und juristische Argumentation, ANRW II/15 (1976) 386. See also the critical review of this study by M. Talamanca, Bull. dell'Ist. di dir. rom. (= BIDR) 80 (1977) 254.

[20] D 28,1,27 ... *non intellego quid sit, de quo me consulueris, aut valide stulta est consultatio tua: plus enim quam ridiculum est* ... Cf. P. Kretschmar, Quaestio Domitiana – Responsio Celsina, Zeitschr. der Savigny-Stiftung f. Rechtsgeschichte, rom. Abt. (= ZSS) 57 (1937) 52.

[21] H. Hausmaninger (supra note 19) 386 note 27.

[22] Id. 386.

[23] Vat. 75,5 ... *Sabinus responderit, ut et Celsus ... refert ... quam sententiam ipse ut stolidam reprehendit* ...

Furthermore, Celsus seems perfectly capable of phrasing his criticism in friendly and obliging terms. He thus sounds like a politely deferential Supreme Court Justice when writing in D 33,10,7,2 "although I am strongly moved by the reasoning and authority of Tubero I shall not dissent from Servius".[24] Still, comparing the occurrence of pointedly hostile remarks to more moderate criticism or even praise for the opinions of others, it must be admitted that Celsus does not resist the temptation when an opportunity for a quick stab presents itself. But we may take some comfort from the observation that he does not quote a colleague only when he can make a fool of him.

Celsus was reared in the traditions of and ultimately succeeded his own father as head of the Proculian law school. It would thus seem natural that he quote Proculian authors more frequently than legal writers from the rival Sabinian school.[25] What comes as a surprise is that he rejects approximately one-third of the Proculian opinions he cites in his *digesta,* and Proculus, the venerable founder of the school, receives the harshest treatment of all.[26] Must we then assume that Celsus breaks with school traditions or that he wants to demonstrate how much smarter he is than his famous predecessor?

The school conflict itself is based primarily, as Peter Stein[27] and Detlef Liebs[28] explain, on different perceptions of legal method. The Sabinians seem to be more pragmatic, relying on custom, and deciding new cases on an ad hoc basis with more concern for reasonableness than for consistency. The Proculian approach appears to be more rational, giving more attention to matters of principle and logic, and at the same time more innovative, prepared to create new legal forms. We possess hardly any material that would link Celsus explicitly to some of the known school controversies.[29] With one exception, we see him neither endorse nor reject typical Proculian positions.[30] What does this tell us about his pointed attacks on Proculus?

Judging from the six specific cases in which the confrontation takes place, Proculus is criticized by Celsus with good reason. Celsus invariably exhibits a

---

24 See infra at note 53.

25 A. M. Honoré, Gaius (1962) 22.

26 H. Hausmaninger, Celsus gegen Proculus, 3. Festschrift für U. v. Lübtow (1991) 53.

27 Two Schools of Jurists in the Early Roman Principate, Cambridge Law Journal 31 (1972) 8.

28 Rechtsschulen und Rechtsunterricht im Prinzipat, ANRW II/15 (1976) 197; see also G. L. Falchi, Le controversie tra Sabiniani e Proculiani (1981); R. A. Bauman (supra note 2) passim; T. Giaro, Von der Genealogie der Begriffe zur Genealogie der Juristen: De Sabinianis et Proculianis fabulae, Rechtshistorisches Journal 11 (1992) 508.

29 I have argued in Celsus und die regula Catoniana, Tijdschrift voor rechtsgeschiedenis (= TR) 36 (1968) 469 that Celsus attempts to resolve a school conflict concerning the scope of this particular rule.

30 The exception is D 12,4,16. See H. Hausmaninger (supra note 26) 61.

greater facility to distinguish and to generalize, a broader theoretical perspective and more consistency as well as better common sense. He clearly emerges as the stronger and more interesting jurist.[31]

The common element of all negative criticism of Proculus by Celsus is irony. It may be argued that youthful passion and an uncompromising sense of scholarly 'rightness' and mission provide at least partial explanations of his disrespectful style. One may also speculate that especially the young Celsus could have felt himself 'boxed in' by the authority of his father on one side and the professional weight of Neratius, the prominent statesman and his elder colleague in the leadership of the Proculian school on the other side. He could hardly accomplish emancipation by openly distancing himself from the one or the other (although cautious dissent from both is occasionally visible in his work).[32] Thus Proculus may have served as the vicarious object of aggressive polemic aimed at 'parental' authority by an equally intelligent and impatient jurist.

Two further observations on context may add to this perspective. First: Insofar as Proculians reject tradition per se as a valid legal argument, Celsus criticizing Proculus may not be considered improper. It should be noted that Proculus himself strongly criticizes Labeo,[33] his own predecessor and one of overwhelming legal authority. Celsus thus stands in a teaching tradition that does not believe in swearing on the master's words. And most likely it was in the context of law teaching, striving to hold the attention of his students, that Celsus adopted a more colorful style than his colleagues, or at any rate chose not to edit it out of his manuscripts before publication. His pose of arrogant irony may thus be as much an attempt to win personal profile as an effective teaching tool. We might not be surprised to encounter this type of personality in one or the other leading law school even of today.

Second: Celsus is the jurist to whom Ulpian refers most often as 'elegant'. What does this attribute denote in the hierarchy of praise among jurists? Is it equivalent to an Oxford don's faint praise of a Cambridge colleague's work as "a stimulating book" (adding, tongue in cheek, "I lost no time reading it"), or to a judge's reference to the "fine opinion" from which he is about to dissent? Our modern suspicions are not borne out by the classical texts. Ulpian generally cites other jurists in an extremely dry, matter of fact style, without embellishment or flattery.[34] Against this background, five commendations of Celsus

[31] Id. 62.

[32] Cf. Ulp. D 12,4,3,7 ... *et refert patrem suum Celsum existimasse repetere eum non posse: sed ipse Celsus naturali aequitate motus putat repeti posse.* The Celsus attack on unnamed jurists (*quidam*) in D 41,3,27 almost certainly includes Neratius in view of the latter's opposing view in D 41,10,5,1. See H. Hausmaninger (supra note 19) 403.

[33] 14 (or two-thirds) of the Proculus references to Labeo are negative.

[34] H. Hausmaninger (supra note 19) 391.

opinions as "elegant" and one even as "not inelegant" (as a form of reluctant recognition all the more illuminating) do indeed stand out as exceptional tributes to this jurist.

'Elegance' in these references implies more than a special choice of words. It characterizes acuteness of thought, demonstrated in a striking or subtle illustration of principle, or to an attractive idea which transcends traditional legal categories.[35] In D 3,5,9,1 Ulpian reports with obvious enjoyment how Celsus elegantly ridiculed an opinion held by Proculus.[36] In that particular case, Celsus skilfully pointed out the abstract principle that the unhappy Proculus had missed in his shortsighted case-by-case approach. At least in Ulpian's eyes, derision of one jurist by another could be justified by elegance in execution.

5. 'Bonum et aequum': Substance over Form?

Traditional approaches to Celsus have either focused on one conspicuous element of his style, thus misconstruing his personality as that of a somewhat rowdy polemicist,[37] or on an aspect of substance, namely his famous definition *"ius est ars boni et aequi"* (law is the art of accomplishing what is reasonable and fair), making the latter appear a singleminded and overriding concern[38] on the part of Celsus to achieve a 'social balance of interests'[39] in each and every case. It should be realized, however, that Celsus' reference to *bonum et aequum* is specific and limited in scope.[40]

The first illustrative case is D 12,1,32, where A asks B and C each for a money loan. B orders his debtor X to give the requested amount to A. In accepting the money, A believes that X is the debtor of C (not B). Thus there is no contract between A and B. Yet Celsus considers it reasonable and fair *(bonum et aequum)* that B should get his money back. The Roman law of unjust enrichment was a tightly compartmentalized sphere of *ius strictum* at that time. There were actions available only for specific fact situations. Celsus, however, moved toward a bold generalization, granting an abstract *condictio* based on what he considered the underlying principle of the existing specific remedies: no one should be enriched at the expense of another.[41]

---

35 Id. 389; see also P. Stein, Elegance in Law, Law Quarterly Review 77 (1961) 242.

36 ... *sed istam sententiam Celsus eleganter deridet* ... See H. Hausmaninger (supra note 26) 55.

37 F. Wieacker (supra note 18) 1.

38 M. Bretone, Note minime su Celsus filius, Labeo 9 (1963) 331, reprinted without change in Tecniche e ideologie dei giuristi romani (1971) 91 and 2nd ed. (1982) 193.

39 P. Cerami (supra note 13) passim, critical discussion by H. Hausmaninger, IVRA 36 (1985) 162.

40 H. Hausmaninger (supra note 19) 399.

41 Id. 402.

That Celsus should use *bonum et aequum* as an argument for granting a remedy of the strict law must have come as a shock to his contemporaries. But Celsus obviously loved to stun his colleagues. His very definition of the law in D 1,1,1 pr. as *ars boni et aequi* was an audacious attempt to combine two spheres that were traditionally strictly separated by the jurists. Rhetoricians and philosophers might have tried to integrate *bonum et aequum* into their concepts of law. Jurists knew better. They occasionally incorporated *bonum et aequum* or other values like *bona fides* (good faith) as standards of behavior or liability in specific remedies, but refrained from considering them as general sources or overriding principles of law. Celsus was the first and, until the late classical jurisprudence, the only jurist using *bonum et aequum* in his reasoning. Ulpian, citing the Celsus definition of law almost one century later as 'elegant', must have still felt some surprise and a sense of paradox in this formula at his time.[42]

The most valuable citation to demonstrate the innovative character of Celsus in this respect is found in the works of the late classical jurist Paul (D 45,1,91,3): If a debtor through his own fault fails to fulfill his duty at the proper time, may the creditor as a matter of law simply refuse a belated delivery? Celsus says he may not. For the jurist this is a matter of *bonum et aequum,* so that his decision depends on the circumstances of the case. And he lashes out against those who would not differentiate: "in matters of *bonum et aequum",* he says, "pernicious mistakes are frequently committed under the guise of legal science", thereby attacking with fervor the perceived formalism of other jurists, who arrogantly brush aside what they consider to be extraneous and irrelevant to the law.[43]

Bonum et aequum is no doubt a most important and highly interesting argument in the work of Celsus, but it is only one among others. There are similar value judgments based on *aequitas, benignitas, bona fides* and so forth that are not simply embraced by *bonum et aequum.* And the substantive values that inspire Celsus on the one hand are checked and counterbalanced by more formal decisions upholding strict legal rules on the other hand.[44] Only a fuller explanation of his whole range of legal reasoning would ultimately permit us to assess the level of each element in the jurist's pyramid of legal valuations and arguments. Until such a comprehensive analysis has been accomplished, our profile of Celsus will remain tentative, and there is good reason to warn against premature and overly speculative generalizations concerning a 'Celsus methodology'.[45]

[42] Id. 401.

[43] Id. 400.

[44] Id. 403. See also O. Behrends, Gnomon 55 (1983) 237.

[45] See generally F. Wieacker, Zur Ideologie der römischen Juristen – Vom Gebrauch aktueller Erklärungsmodelle in der heutigen Romanistik, Festschrift für W. Flume I (1978) 233.

6. Statutory Interpretation: 'voluntas legis'

The compilers of Justinian's Digest included 141 Celsus excerpts in their anthology of 9142 selections from the writings of 39 jurists, spreading them over 430 'titles' or subject areas. When they composed Digest title 1,3 *de legibus senatusque consultis et longa consuetudine,* they included no fewer than 7 Celsus statements on sources of law and methods of interpretation in the total number of 41 fragments, thereby exceeding the average share of Celsus in Justinian's Digest by more than ten times.[46] One may assume that Celsus attracted the attention of Justinian's compilers by the special quality of his ideas and formulations in this area of the law. Four of the seven Celsus texts concern statutory interpretation. They come from different parts of the jurist's *digesta,* and have no doubt been lifted by the compilers from specific contexts that are not readily discernible today. Nevertheless, they appear as consistent parts of a whole, permitting us to reconstruct a theory of interpretation which, although not coherently stated, pervades the work of this particular Roman jurist.

Celsus is the first jurist who coins such timeless principles of interpretation as D 1,3,17 *Scire leges non hoc est verba earum tenere, sed vim ac potestatem* ("To know the statutes is not to memorize their words, but to understand their meaning and intent") – the canon of autonomy or immanence of hermeneutical criteria;[47] or D 1,3,24 *Incivile est nisi tota lege perspecta una aliqua particula eius proposita iudicare vel respondere* ("It is uncivil [unlawyerlike] to render a judgment or opinion on the basis of a mere section instead of examining the statute in its entirety") – the hermeneutical canon of totality.[48] His most interesting observation may well be the one in D 1,3,18 *Benignius leges interpretandae sunt, quo voluntas earum conservetur* ("Statutes are to be interpreted more benevolently, in order to preserve their intent"), where Celsus makes legislative intent the basis of a correction of the faulty wording of the statute, thus demonstrating how far he is prepared to go in emphasizing *voluntas* over *verba legis*.[49] That Celsus in using *voluntas legis* (legislative intent) refers to the 'historical' legislator and not to an actualized, contemporary 'teleological' standard becomes evident from D 1,3,19 *In ambigua voce legis ea potius accipienda est significatio, quae vitio caret...* ("concerning an ambiguous statutory expression one must choose that meaning which is free from fault...."): By not referring to legislative intent in this context Celsus signals that the latter

---

[46] Of the 41 excepts in this Digest title 9 each come from Ulpian and Paul, who contribute approximately one third and one sixth of the total text of the Digest, respectively. Celsus contributes only 1,5%. See H. Hausmaninger, Zur Gesetzesauslegung des Celsus, Studi in onore di G. Grosso V (1972) 246.

[47] Id. 247.

[48] Id. 250.

[49] Id. 256.

was unknown, and thus a subsidiary criterion of interpretation had to be introduced, the 'absence of fault'. This formula would have been superfluous had Celsus construed the concept of *voluntas legis* as permitting a jurist to read a statute as it appeared to be most useful in a contemporary situtation, in effect allowing him to substitute his own intent for that of the legislator.[50]

Celsus may have had only limited means for ascertaining legislative intent with respect to the historical purpose of a particular statute. The specific examples in our sources, where Celsus interprets one of the few statutory regulations in Roman private law, most notably the *lex Aquilia,* a comparatively well-documented tort statute of 286 BC, provide some positive proof of the jurist's concern for legislative intent and much deference to interpretive traditions. Moreover, there is also negative evidence, namely that he never contradicts his theories in the practice of interpretation.[51]

It has been noted that the principles of interpretation formulated by Celsus bear the mark of Roman rhetoric. This is not to be taken as a sign of intellectual dependence, but rather as one of courage and originality. Whereas rhetoricians used 'intent' and 'wording' as interchangeable, topical arguments, Celsus molded them into a stable legal doctrine. Whereas other jurists spurned the concepts and generalizations of Roman rhetoric, Celsus took the innovative step of critically selecting and modifying elements from the rich arsenal of arguments offered by the rhetoricians, using them creatively to shape abstract principles of a general theory of statutory interpretation.

7. Interpretation of Wills: 'voluntas testatoris'

Like other Roman jurists before and after him, Celsus devoted extraordinary attention to the law of succession, in particular to the interpretation of bequests. No fewer than four of the 39 *libri* of Celsus' *digesta* treat the topic of bequests,[52] and there is a sizeable number of texts shedding light on the approach chosen by Celsus to matters of interpretation. Surprisingly, however, only one of them projects a statement of principle. It is contained in D 33,10,7,2, a famous tract on *suppellex legatum* (bequest of household goods).[53]

---

[50] Id. 252. See also D. Medicus, Der historische Normzweck bei den römischen Klassikern, in: D. Medicus, H.-H. Seiler (eds.), Studien im römischen Recht (1973) 57, who demonstrates that among Roman jurists only Celsus and Gaius seem to have paid attention to the 'historical' legislator. The sources give no support to Cerami's theory (supra note 13 at 116) that Celsus considered statutes not as binding norms (to be interpreted as such) but rather as flexible 'models' for the disposition of cases in the light of *bonum et aequum*.

[51] Id. 263.

[52] *Libri* 15 and 16 treat the topic *de testamentis,* 17 to 20 *de legatis*.

[53] H. Hausmaninger, Zur Legatsinterpretation des Celsus, IVRA 35 (1984) 19. See also the critical remarks by M. Talamanca, BIDR 91 (1988) 847.

As reported by Celsus in this passage of his work, the republican jurist Servius had written that if someone had simply bequeathed 'the household goods' *(suppellex)* to his wife, it was necessary to ascertain the intent of the de cuius. This could be achieved by first determining under which heading of his household inventory he had originally entered the articles under dispute. But this should only apply to cases of doubt. If, for instance, the testator had recorded silver plate for table use, cloaks and togas under 'household goods', although these articles clearly belonged in different categories, namely *argentum factum* (silverware) or *vestis* (clothes), they were not to be considered part of a *suppellex legatum*: The standard of interpretation in these cases was to be the ordinary usage of language, not the personal linguistic idiosyncrasies of the testator *("non enim ex opinionibus singulorum, sed ex communi usu nomina exaudiri debere")*.

Tubero, a later jurist discussed by Celsus, had objected to this position taken by Servius. "What is the value of words," he said, "unless they are to demonstrate the intent of the person using them?" Tubero would thus respect the individual intent of the testator even if the latter's language clearly deviated from ordinary usage.

Celsus then came down on the side of Servius: *"non videri quemquam dixisse, cuius non suo nomine usus sit"*, the testator's intent cannot be considered if he did not express it in his will in terms of common usage. This position taken by Celsus is part of a long interpretive tradition to which Celsus adds nothing new as far as substance is concerned. His statement is, however, remarkable for its abstract, systematizing form.

In a great number of specific interpretation decisions Celsus uses the conceptual framework of *verba – voluntas*. In some of them he emphasizes that his decision is founded on both elements, but in most cases he bases his opinion expressly on *mens* or *voluntas* of the testator. In so doing he sometimes refers to an actual, sometimes to a hypothetical (presumably personal or typical) intent of the de cuius. In most of these cases the jurist seems to argue from presumed (typical) intent, the actual intent of the individual testator not being ascertainable. In comparing Celsus with other jurists one gains the impression that he made a greater effort to establish actual individual intent and was prepared to give this process more of a chance than most others. One is reminded of the jurist's similarly unique pursuit of legislative intent in the context of statutory interpretation.[54]

[54] Supra at note 49. This aspect has been overemphasized by V. Scarano Ussani (supra note 13) 136, 172, 199 and passim, who reads into it a philosophical doctrine of 'skepticism' and 'empiricism' as providing the basic 'methodology' of the jurist's work. See the critical reviews by F. Horak, Labeo 29 (1983) 186 and Ch. Krampe, ZSS 102 (1985) 593. For a more sympathetic appraisal see O. Behrends, Gnomon 55 (1983) 229. On Scarano Ussani's restatement of these ideas in Empiria e dogmi – la scuola proculiana fra Nerva e Adriano (1989) see R. Willvonseder, ZSS 108 (1991) 447.

Celsus occasionally attempts to facilitate upholding the presumed intent of the testator by means of assigning burdens of proof. Yet he never seems satisfied with convenient presumptions of intent as unassailable solutions to questions of interpretation. He always admits evidence to the contrary that might serve as specific proof of an individual intent of the de cuius. The most notable example of this attitude is offered in D 34,2,3, where Celsus successfully attacks an interpretive tradition which considered a husband's divorcing his wife to be an implied revocation of a previous bequest to her in his will.[55] To Celsus this is a question of fact to be explored by the judge, in which the actual individual intent of the testator has to be established. He reached a similar decision when the de cuius bequeathed an object and subsequently sold it. Justinian expressly endorsed this enlightened opinion in his Institutes.[56]

We may look with special interest at one text in which Celsus ostensibly contradicts his general thrust of favoring the testator's intent over the wording of the will. A woman had bequeathed her *ornatrices* (hairdressers) to a friend.[57] Celsus decided that slave girls who had been in training for only two months did not qualify under this term and would not be owed to the legatee, thus restricting the more generous decisions of other jurists. In taking this position Celsus seems to confirm his general principle of interpretation in D 33,10,7,2 whereby the question of intent may only be pursued within the framework of ordinary language.

There are cases concerning the interpretation of bequests concerning various special types of goods, e.g. *fundus instructus* (a farm with all necessary appurtenances) or *suppellex* (household goods), in which Celsus does not refer to his usual framework of *verba* and *voluntas*.[58] In these cases he obviously felt a stronger compulsion to abide by established tradition than to pursue the goal of systematic consistency. Furthermore, Celsus differs from many other jurists by not specifically favoring certain persons (e.g. the widow) in certain types of bequests, and he also makes no specific references to standards like *bonum et aequum* or *benignitas*. This is not to deny that some of these standards may have had a motivating influence, but only to point out the absence of express reference.[59] One's overall impression of Celsus' approach to the interpretation

---

[55] *Uxori legavit quae eius causa parata sunt et ante mortem divortit. non deberi, quia adempta videantur, Proculus ait. nimirum facti quaestio est: nam potest nec repudiatae adimere voluisse.* See H. Hausmaninger (supra note 53) 34.

[56] Inst. Iust. 2,20,12 *Si rem suam legaverit testator posteaque eam alienaverit, Celsus existimat, si non adimendi animo vendidit, nihilo minus deberi...*, rejecting the majority view expressed in Gaius Inst. 2, 198.

[57] Marcianus D 32,65,3 *Ornatricibus legatis Celsus scripsit eas, quae duos tantum menses apud magistrum fuerunt, legato non cedere, alii et has cedere, ne necesse sit nullam cedere, cum onmes adhuc discere possint et omne artificium incrementum recipit.* See H. Hausmaninger (supra note 53) 27; M. Talamanca (supra note 53) 849.

[58] H. Hausmaninger (supra note 53) 35.

[59] Id. 45.

of bequests is that of a fairly general and consistent emphasis on the testator's intent within a framework of ordinary language.

8. Interpretation of Contracts: 'id quod actum est'

A similar balance regarding personal intent and a sensible, practice-oriented allocation of the burden of proof may also be observed in Celsus opinions concerning the interpretation of contracts. A key notion in this field used by Celsus as well as by other jurists is *id quod actum est,* literally "what is meant by the transaction". For some jurists this is a typical, objective meaning of a contractual agreement, whereas others explore the individual intentions of the specific parties.[60]

The following case (D 19,1,38,2) best illustrates the views of Celsus.[61] A house has been sold, and the question arises whether water pipes that have not been expressly mentioned in the agreement are to be considered sold with the house. Proculus says that the case turns on *id quod actum est.* For Celsus this is not a satisfactory answer. To him the problem begins at the point where *'id quod actum est'* cannot be determined because the parties never thought of the water pipes. And he indicates with some irony that this seems to be the most usual situation. His subsidiary solution for this case is that the pipes should be considered to have been sold with the house, a solution that appears to make practical sense, treating objects inserted or included in the house as if they were fixtures of the house.

For Celsus, *id quod actum est* is invariably the individual, actual intent of the parties.[62] If this cannot be determined, Celsus does not replace it with a typical intent, saying that the parties seem to have intended such and such, but finds a solution outside any formula that would refer to intent. Since Celsus realizes that he must quite frequently provide a decision without being able to determine the parties' intent, he occasionally moves his initially subsidiary solutions into the foreground, suggesting burdens of proof that take account of the normal case, but always allowing for the possibility of actual proof of a different individual intent.[63] For the judge, the Celsus formula reduces the need for careful investigation of specific aspects of the case and of potential evidence outside the contract proper. Whereas other jurists like Julian would explore alternative versions of what the parties might have intended,[64] leaving to the judge to choose the most likely individual intent, Celsus prepares a decision

[60] See generally F. Pringsheim, Id quod actum est, ZSS 78 (1961) 1 - 91.

[61] H. Hausmaninger, 'Id quod actum est' als Argumentationsfigur bei Celsus, Festschrift für G. Wesener (1992) 160.

[62] Id. 174.

[63] Id. 175.

[64] Cf. D 17,2,52 pr. or D 18,1,41 pr.

based on the presumed impossibility of ascertaining individual intent, but leaving the door open to the parties to produce evidence rebutting the jurist's preconceived interpretation of their minds and conduct.

The interest Celsus exhibits in questions of evidence is unique among the jurists of his time. Classical jurists before Celsus traditionally restricted their attention to questions of law.[65] Celsus is even the first jurist to use the term *quaestio facti,*[66] and such questions of fact quickly gained importance after he had introduced the concept. His innovative approach was duly honored by Justian's compilers, who, like in their composition of Digest title 1,3 on sources of the law,[67] included an extraordinary amount of Celsus material in Digest title 22,3 *de probationibus et praesumtionibus* ('on evidence and presumtions').[68]

9. Celsus and Hadrian: the Jurist and his Emperor

Celsus is the first jurist to cite verbatim an imperial rescript, and it is hardly a coincidence that it dealt with a question of proof. The rescript concerns an interpretation of a statute forbidding the manumission of slaves before they have reached a certain age. Celsus reports the Emperor Hadrian in D 22,3,13 as saying "It is both hard and unjust, when a question arises with reference to someone's age and different statements are made, to accept preferably the one that is damaging . . .". This quote raises the question: Can we establish a link between the legal policy of the Emperor Hadrian[69] and the legal science of Celsus? Have innovative aspects of the work of Celsus been prompted by Hadrians philosophical persuasions or his practical political intentions? Conversely, might the eminent jurist have inspired some of the well-known legal reforms of the Emperor?[70]

Hadrian drew the most prominent jurists of his time, such as Neratius, Celsus, Julian, into his *consilium*[71] and assigned to this state council of expert advisers an important role in the further development of law. The honor of a

[65] Cf. Cic. top. 12,51 *Nihil hoc ad ius, ad Ciceronem.*

[66] D 34,2,3; D 24,1,47.

[67] Supra at note 46.

[68] In this Digest title Celsus takes second place among 12 jurists, contributing 5 of a total of 29 fragments and ranking between Paul (6 texts) and Ulpian (4).

[69] On Hadrian's reforms see B. d'Orgeval, L'Empereur Hadrien – Oeuvre législative et administrative (1950); F. Pringsheim, The legal policy and reforms of Hadrian, Gesammelte Abhandlungen I (1961) 91; H. Hübner, Zur Rechtspolitik Kaiser Hadrians, Festschrift für E. Seidl (1975) 61; M. K. Thornton, Hadrian and his Reign, ANRW II/2 (1975) 432.

[70] On this aspect see the useful tentative studies but premature generalizations in V. Scarano Ussani (supra note 13) 207 - 222 (id. 222 "il 'giurista della corona' negli anni decisivi della 'svolta adrianea'").

[71] SHA Hadr. 18,1. See J. Crook, Consilium principis (1955) 56.

second consulate in 129 seems to attest to Hadrian's special trust in and appreciation for Celsus. The interest Celsus shows for questions of evidence, thereby clearly transcending the traditional role of the classical jurist who would relegate questions of fact to the province of the court orator, is in all probability a product of his activity in Hadrian's council. Problems of proof occupy a conspicuous position in Hadrian's rescripts, especially those addressed to provincial governors.[72] To what extent those rescripts reflect the personal thought and language of Hadrian is difficult to judge. It seems less likely that he would care for technicalities, and one would expect a comparatively stronger interest on his part in either questions of general policy or equitable solutions. But Hadrian is not easy to fathom.[73] His Roman biographer informs us that the Emperor delighted in embarrassing professors of all disciplines.[74] We must not exclude the possibility that he could even compete with lawyers and would demonstrate this on occasion in a less than likely area of the law.

In a number of imperial rescripts concerning criminal cases, Hadrian places special emphasis on 'mens rea'.[75] Celsus pursues a similar line in increasing or diminishing contractual liability according to degrees of fault. There is one particularly significant case, in which Celsus seems to reflect a way of thinking and evaluation as we find it expressed in Hadrian's decisions. This is Celsus' discussion of the standard of liability of the depositary (a bailee for the sole benefit of the bailor) which the jurist wishes to extend to include negligence, saying (D 16,3,32):" For even if someone generally fails to be as diligent as human nature demands, he is not free from fraud unless he exhibits at least his own standard of care towards the deposited goods: for he violates good faith if he applies less care than in his own affairs."[76] There are several Ulpian texts that show Celsus making far ranging attempts to introduce liability for negligence into other areas of Roman contract law as well.[77]

It was Hadrian's ambition to eliminate harsh and inequitable aspects of the law. His rescript as reported by Celsus begins with the very words *"Et durum et iniquum est..."*, and in his epistle to Ramnius Martialis, Prefect of Egypt,

---

[72] Cf. F. Pringsheim (supra note 69) 93 note 14.

[73] Cf. SHA Hadr. 14,11 *Idem severus comis, gravis lascivus, cunctator festinans, tenax liberalis, simulator simplex, saevus clemens, et semper in omnibus varius.* Aurelius Victor, Epit. de Caes. 14, 6 calls Hadrian *varius, multiplex, multiformis.*

[74] SHA Hadr. 15,10 *professores omnium artium semper ut doctior risit contempsit obtrivit.*

[75] See R.A. Bauman (supra note 2) 264.

[76] See H. Hausmaninger, Diligentia Quam In Suis: A Standard of Liability from Ancient Roman to Modern Soviet Law, Cornell International Law Journal 18 (1985) 179 at 183. See also infra note 77 and, most recently, F. Mercogliano, 'Diligentia quam in suis' per i giuristi romani classici, Index 19 (1991) 379.

[77] H. Hausmaninger, Diligentia quam in suis, Festschrift für M. Kaser (1976) 269.

he elaborates "it is with great pleasure that I seize upon opportunities to grant a more humane interpretation of harsher decisions rendered by preceding emperors."[78] The jurists initially refrained from adopting this terminology of imperial legal criticism. The words *durum* (harsh or hard) and *humanum* (humane) are not found in the vocabulary of Neratius or Celsus.[79] Arguably, the jurists were bound more strongly by existing legal rules in their private law practice than the Emperor in the exercise of his *cognitio*. The participation of the jurists in this imperial *cognitio* did, however, influence them in their general practice. The 'humane' interpretation of the emperors encouraged and legitimized a 'benign' interpretation *(benigna interpretatio)* of the jurists.[80]

One generation after Celsus the jurist Marcellus gives a detailed account (D 28,4,3 pr.) of a discussion that took place in 166 in the council of Marcus Aurelius, the Emperor who also made his mark as a stoic philosopher. The Emperor, after listening to adversarial pleading, had his chambers cleared of all attendants, pondered the problem and declared "the present case seems to admit a more humane interpretation", thereby taking up the suggestion of the jurist Marcellus "to adopt, in a case of doubt, the more benign interpretation".[81] Celsus himself resorted twice to benevolence as an argument. Aside from his dictum concerning statutory interpretation in D 1,3,19 *(benignius leges interpretandae sunt...)*[82], we see him correct in D 8,3,11 a *subtilis ratio,* the strict and rigid application of the *ius civile*, with a more benevolent solution.[83] There are parallels to this mollification of *subtilitas* with *benignitas* in the writings of contemporary jurists like Iavolenus and Julian. And when Julian in D 28,2,13 pr. contrasts *subtilitas* with *humanitas,* his language sounds very much as if it were reporting a deliberation and decision of a case in Hadrian's *consilium*.[84]

The record shows that a *benigna interpretatio* by the jurist Marcellus moved the Emperor Marcus to adopt a humane decision. As regarding Celsus, one can only speculate whether his *benignitas* influenced Hadrian's *humanitas* or, conversely, the humanity of the Emperor encouraged benevolent opinions of the jurist in the realm of the *ius civile*. There is, however, one sphere of legal innovation on the part of Celsus, in which the priority of his thought is clearly demonstrable: His use of *bonum et aequum* as a critical tool of legal analysis

[78] BGU I, 140 in: Fontes iuris romani anteiustiniani I (rev. ed. S. Riccobono, 1941) nr. 78. See H. Hausmaninger, 'Benevolent' and 'Humane' Opinions of Classical Roman Jurists, Boston University Law Review 61 (1981) 1139 at 1149.

[79] Id. 1151.

[80] Id. 1155.

[81] Id. 1147.

[82] See supra at note 49.

[83] H. Hausmaninger (supra note 78) 1144; see also H. Hausmaninger, Subtilitas iuris, Festgabe für M. Kaser (1986) 64.

[84] Id.

and transformation is not a mere reflex of Hadrian's equity. As discussed above[85], Celsus refers to *bonum et aequum* in three significant contexts. In one of them the jurist Paul cites Celsus in a very unusual manner, introducing his opinion with the words *"Celsus adulescens scribit..."* ("the adolescent Celsus writes..."). This sounds rather condescending, keeping in mind that Paul (differing markedly from Ulpian in this respect) quotes Celsus very rarely in his work. But he approves his opinion in substance. The patronizing attribute *adulescens* probably aims at putting the overflowing pathos, the youthfully emotional attack, in its place. It may well be that Paul is quoting from the Commentaries, the lecture notes of the young law teacher Celsus, who is concerned with asserting himself forcefully vis-à-vis a petrified legal establishment. After all Neratius, his co-director of the Proculian law school and elder statesman with overpowering authority, seems to have insisted on a very conservative, traditional approach to the law[86] that may have irritated Celsus more than once.

Hadrian must have been impressed with the determination of Celsus to force the idea of *bonum et aequum* upon a law that had become too strict and rigid. Celsus was of Hadrian's age and came to the praetorship shortly after the Emperor himself had acted in that capacity. His spirited and lively temperament and his obvious interest in rhetoric and philosophy may have had additional appeal to an Emperor who felt bored in the comparatively unintellectual company of Roman senators.

10. Conclusion: Tradition and Innovation in Celsus and Classical Roman Law

Our perspective of classical Roman law and its development has been to a large extent determined by Justinian's compilers, by their assessment of the writings of earlier jurists that were at their disposal, by their decisions to excerpt from some jurists more than from others, and to strike or to preserve reports on scholarly controversies. Their work followed two at times contradictory orientations: the Digest was to serve both as a collection of authoritative law to be applied in contemporary judicial procedure, and as a documentation of classical legal thought to be used in law school instruction.[87] Thus, on the one hand, they drew heavily on the most recent and comprehensive commentaries of the late classical jurists Ulpian and Paul[88], and on the other hand, they reached back as far as possible to demonstrate early and broad legal sophistication on the part of more than 30 other classical jurists.

---

[85] Supra at note 43.

[86] See, despite some unconvincing generalizations, V. Scarano Ussani (supra note 13) 73 and R. A. Bauman (supra note 2) 203.

[87] See F. Wieacker, Vom römischen Recht (2nd ed. 1961) 242.

[88] Of the 9142 excerpts in the Digest 2464 are from Ulpian, 2081 from Paul.

Celsus does not figure prominently in the general pattern of Justinian's Digest. In the number of excerpts from his writings he ranks only twelfth among 39 jurists. The compilers excerpted an average of 3 to 4 fragments from each of his 39 *libri*. When, as in D 1,3 (on sources of law)[89] or D 22,3 (on evidence and presumptions)[90] they considerably exceeded this average, they surely had compelling reasons of substance and/or style. In other words, we may assume an element of originality on the part of Celsus that persuaded the compilers to go out of their way to select from his work instead of that of others.

Surprisingly, we find very little reference to Celsus in contemporary and immediately following Roman legal literature. The voluminous work of Pomponius, which abounds with citations to other jurists, rarely refers to him[91], Julian and Maecian each cite him once, most others do not quote him at all. Three observations may help explain this absence of Celsus citations in the high classical period. First, the 39 volume *digesta* of Celsus soon found themselves overshadowed by the 90 volume work and the towering professional prestige of his younger colleague Julian.[92] Second, perhaps due to his abrasive temperament, Celsus unlike Julian did not find himself surrounded with a circle of admiring students[93] who would subsequently promote their master's work. Third, the general usage of the time preferred the citation of older jurists to that of near contemporaries. Such a preference for older jurists – yet in combination with respect for contemporary standard works – seems to have been characteristic also of the late classical jurist Paul. To him, Celsus and most of the contemporaries of this jurist fell into an intermediary period worthy of neglect.[94] It is to Ulpian's special credit that he revived and paid due attention to Celsus, citing frequently and admiringly from his work, and probably inducing Tribonian, the chairman of Justinian's compilers, to follow his lead.

It is perhaps in this perspective that we can explain what made Celsus particularly attractive to such diverse minds as those of Hadrian, Ulpian and Tribonian, who each pursued a mission of both maintaining and improving law: It was no doubt his mastery of theory and practice, his acute perception

---

89 See supra at note 46.

90 See supra at note 68.

91 Pomponius has 52 citations to Labeo, 27 to Aristo, 26 to Quintus Mucius, 20 to Julian, but only 9 to Celsus. See A. M. Honoré (supra note 25) tab. laud. XI (at p. 171).

92 Justinian's compilers included 456 excerpts from Julian's work in their Digest.

93 See A. M. Honoré, Julian's Circle, TR 32 (1964) 1.

94 Paul's edictal commentary devotes more attention to the early classical writers Sabinus, Proculus and Cassius, citing them 31, 25 and 23 times, respectively, and even to republican jurists like Servius (12 citations) and Trebatius (11) than to Celsus (3 citations), Neratius (7), Aristo (3) and Marcellus (5). Paul does, however, cite Celsus' younger contemporaries Julian 59 times and Pomponius 39 times.

of reality and his capacity for generalization and abstraction; his originality of thought and formulation, at times aggressive yet not inelegant, frequently provocative and forward moving, formulating and applying principle, implementing substantive values, yet not sacrificing valuable tradition for the sake of logical consistency. His work seems to reflect and reinforce Hadrian's philosophy of social peace under strong autocratic leadership, tempered with humanity and moral demands upon men and laws. Ulpian's comprehensive restatement of classical law in his voluminous commentaries pays tribute to the creative originality of a colleague to which he himself could not aspire[95], whereas many a classical jurist between Celsus and Ulpian may have been jealous of his unusual intellectual range or at least uncomfortable with his personal style.

The function of Roman jurists in the Roman legal process transcended the mere scholarly exposition of existing law. This function may be analyzed in terms of a framework of tradition and innovation[96]: Despite their strong tendency to preserve legal traditions, Roman jurists also realized (some more, some less acutely) that the law must not be static and immutable, but must respond to new social circumstances and changing practical needs. They consciously accepted the challenge and responsibility to create new law. We may well agree with the way the second century jurist Pomponius expressed this idea in D 1,2,2,13, and we can hardly find a better protagonist to illustrate it than Iuventius Celsus: *"constare non potest ius, nisi sit aliquis iuris peritus, per quem possit cottidie in melius produci"* – "law could not exist, were it not for the jurist who shapes it for the better, day by day."

[95] Cf. T. Honoré, Ulpian (1982) 242.

[96] On this topic see generally D. Nörr, Pomponius oder "Zum Geschichtsverständnis der römischen Juristen", ANRW II/15 (1976) 497; Zum Traditionalismus der römischen Juristen, Festschrift für W. Flume I (1978) 153. Cf. also V. Giuffrè, Papiniano: fra tradizione e innovazione, ANRW II/15 (1976) 632.

Legal Formalism, Substantive Policy, and the Creation of a Canon Law of Prescription

By R. H. Helmholz, Chicago*

"A teacher can never tell where his influence stops." So runs a much quoted aphorism.[1] Behind it lies the thought that a teacher's ideas and words may be remembered and used by his students in contexts far different from those he had in mind when he stated them. I hope the aphorism is true. At least I can say that its veracity is supported by my experience (as the student) in reading and reacting to Robert Summers' work on the place of formalism in law.[2] My experience occurred in an admittedly unlikely corner of legal research: a study of the law of prescription in the classical canon law. His work caused me to think about the subject in a different way than I otherwise would have. It allowed me to see something that undoubtedly existed, but which I had not quite seen by myself: an interplay between formal enactment and substantive policy in the creation of a canon law of prescription. I doubt that Professor Summers would have predicted this.

I. The Problem

To what extent should the law admit the validity of claims which are contrary to established property rights or legal rules, when the claims are based on nothing more than long usage? This is an old and a continuing problem. For the medieval Church during the period of the formulation of the classical canon law (c. 1140 - 1300), it was also a most urgent problem. Such usages, many of them quite contrary to the stated rules, the material interests, and the settled assumptions of the clerical order, were common in early medieval Europe. Usurpation of ecclesiastical property was an undeniable fact of life. Government itself was weak. Even had it been stronger, ascertainment of what rights the Church held would not always have been possible, since so many of the transactions upon which society depends were purely oral.[3] Keep-

* Ruth Wyatt Rosenson Professor of Law, University of Chicago.

[1] It appears in Henry Adams, The Education of Henry Adams, chap. 20 (New York, 1931) 300, and is usually ascribed to the author; see, e.g., Bartlett's Familiar Quotations (14th ed. Emily Morison Beck ed. 1968) 777a.

[2] E.g., "The Formal Character of Law," Cambridge L.J. 51 (1992) 242 - 62.

[3] M. T. Clanchy, From Memory to Written Record: England 1066 - 1307 (Cambridge, Mass. 1979) 3 - 4.

ing reliable records was the exception, not the norm. It seems, therefore, that if the nascent law of the Church were to be brought effectively to bear upon the situation, as did indeed happen through the efforts of the canonists of the twelfth and thirteenth centuries,[4] the law of prescription would inevitably come into play. And that is what happened. The real problem would lie in formulating that law.

It would have been quite possible for the jurists who undertook the task of formulation to have put the problem in terms we would recognize as instrumental legal policy.[5] Had they taken that approach, they might have begun with the assumption that the canon law should have set its face firmly against the acquisition of right by prescription. Prescription grows out of a wrong. To admit its legitimacy within a religious legal system is thus to give law's sanction to a wrong. As the medieval writers sometimes expressed the point, the long continuation of a sin does not make the act less sinful. It only augments its sinfulness.[6] Moreover, in economic terms, the medieval Church would certainly have gained overall by the severe restriction of claims based upon prescriptive right. Medieval chroniclers perceived the usurpation of the Church's possessions by laymen to be a great endemic problem of their society. They were loud in condemning it. Even if one makes proper allowance for the pious exaggeration common among medieval monastic writers, one cannot think them wholly misguided.

On the other hand, in policy terms it would have seemed equally impossible to enact a legal rule that sanctioned no prescriptive rights whatsoever. To have done so would have upset too many of the assumptions upon which society rested, and it would have been entirely impossible to enforce. A more realistic jurisprudence all but required the admission of some sort of prescriptive right. The argument would have been all the stronger because many of the Church's rights themselves grew out of prescription. This was particularly so within the Church's organizational structure; many rights had become settled simply through long usage. Even as against the laity, to have embraced an abolitionist view of the subject would have threatened long established rights, rights which everyone assumed to be legitimate. Perhaps the Church would have gained overall thereby. But it is unlikely that the balance would actually have stood this way at the end, had the Church abandoned all approval of claims to prescriptive right. In fact, the Church would have given

[4] Harold Berman, Law and Revolution (Cambridge, Mass. 1984) 199 - 224.

[5] See generally P. S. Atiyah and R. S. Summers, Form and Substance in Anglo-American Law (Oxford 1987), the book which set me thinking about the problem in the terms found herein.

[6] Glossa ordinaria ad X 2.26.5 (Vigilanti): "Nota quod diuturnitas temporis peccatum non minuit sed auget." [This and all following references to the *Decretales Gregorii IX* are taken from an edition published in Lyons in 1556. References to canonical texts are given in the accepted modern form, described in 15 Traditio 452 (1959)].

away all *its* rights, and received only theoretical, unenforceable claims in return. From an instrumental point of view, it must have seemed that a more compromising policy was called for.

This instrumental way of thinking is not, however, how the canonists normally approached their task. Something like it did occasionally make its way into their discussion of problems involving the law of prescription. However, their normal approach was a more formal one. From Gratian, the "father" of the medieval canon law, right up through the writings of the later medieval commentators, the law was developed through reliance upon, and usage of, authoritative texts. These were the decrees of early Church councils, the decretal letters of popes, the Bible, and the texts of the classical Roman law that made up the *Corpus iuris canonici.*[7] Out of these sources the canon lawyers forged a law of prescription, principally by the process of what looks very like statutory interpretation. In their hands, the law of prescription turned out to be slightly different from that found in any one of the sources. It was a system not without faults and absurdities. But it was a sophisticated and remarkably durable system nonetheless.

II. Gratian's *Decretum*

The initial question was the legitimacy of any kind of prescription. Unlike customary rights,[8] which arose out of the tacit consent of those governed by the custom, prescriptive right was initiated in circumstances where usage violated an established right. Therefore, it was normally contrary to the desires of the person who held the right.[9] It was far from obvious that prescription should be sanctioned at all. Gratian raised the question in Causa 16 of his *Decretum* (c. 1140). Here is the case he put. A certain abbot was in possession of a Church; he had held it without interruption or objection for forty years, and he had nominated a monk to celebrate the Church's offices within it. However, the clergy of a nearby baptismal church now objected, claiming that the church in dispute was in fact a chapel within the precincts owned by their baptismal church. The right of nomination therefore belonged to them. Such dependent chapels were not at all unusual in the medieval Church, and the Causa assumed that it was so in this case. In the fashion characteristic of Gra-

---

[7] See generally Eltjo J. H. Schrage, Utrumque Ius: eine Einführung in das Studium der Quellen des mittelalterlichen gelehrten Rechts (Berlin 1992) 90 - 110.

[8] On this subject, there is now a very large collection of scholarship; see the recent treatments with bibliography: John Gilissen, La coutume, in Typologie des sources du moyen age occidental, A-III, I* (Brepols 1982); John P. McIntyre, Customary Law in the Corpus iuris canonici (San Francisco 1991).

[9] The *ius commune* developed six different distinctions between custom and prescription, holding however that they were not so fundamentally distinct that both could not be included in the same petition. See generally Johannes Franciscus Balbus (fl. 16 C.), Tractatus de praescriptionibus (Cologne 1573) Pt. 1 § Decimo et ultimo, nos. 3 - 12.

tian, the Causa of the *Decretum* asked several questions based upon it. The third, treated in Quaestio III, was: "Whether the rights of churches are to be taken away by prescription?"[10] Gratian's treatment thus placed the question of prescription's legitimacy into the context of a dispute within the Church, or (better said) between two competing churches, rather than in the context of a dispute involving lay usurpation of ecclesiastical possessions.

Gratian began his analysis with four texts from the earliest centuries of Christianity, each standing in favor of prescription: a canon from the Council of Chalcedon (451), a letter of Pope Gelasius (c. 494), and two canons from the Fourth Council of Toledo (633). All of them dealt with settling disputes over diocesan or parochial boundaries. They held that where these boundaries had remained unchanged *(immobiles)* and unchallenged for thirty years or more, they should not be challenged thereafter. These ancient canons were almost certainly following the outlines of the established Roman law of prescription, perhaps self-consciously that of the Christian emperors contained in the *Codex*.[11] However, for a modern student the prevalence of canons from Spanish councils is also worth noting. Indeed it is one of the most notable features of this Causa. The unsettled conditions in the Spanish Church in consequence of Moslem invasions and the Reconquest rendered the problem of fixing boundaries particularly urgent, requiring immediate consideration of the relation between the Roman law of prescription and the dictates and aspirations of the Christian religion.

None of the texts employed by Gratian explicitly considered the basic question of the justification for permitting prescription in the canon law. They did not address the question of what we would term "policy", and it must appear that this was not Gratian's primary interest. However, in the fashion very characteristic of the classical canon law, a reason for the rule allowing prescription was taken up in the *glossa ordinaria,* the medieval companion to the texts compiled by Johannes Teutonicus (d. 1245), which was copied into the margins of medieval copies of the *Decretum* and also of most early printed versions. The gloss explained that prescription had not been introduced into the canon law as part of the natural law. Indeed it was said to be contrary to natural right for one person to be made richer at the expense of another's right. Instead, the gloss suggested that prescription had been introduced "lest dominion of things be left forever uncertain," citing texts from the Roman law as support and in further explanation.[12] This understanding of the place of pre-

---

[10] "Tertio, an iura ecclesiarum prescriptione tollantur?" found in C. 16, rubr., in Corpus iuris canonici (ed. A. Friedberg, Leipzig 1879) I: 761.

[11] Cod. 7.39.7.

[12] Glossa ordinaria to Decretum Gratiani ad C. 16 q. 3 c. 4 s.v. legis: "nam de iure naturali non sunt praescriptiones inductae; nam de iure naturali iniquum est aliquem ditari cum aliena iactura, ..., sed ideo inventa est praescriptio, ne dominia rerum

scription turned out to have important consequences in the canon law of prescription, but characteristically, Gratian did not go into the possible consequences in this part of his Causa 16. Instead, he continued along the same path, compiling and distinguishing similar authorities. They had the effect of limiting the reach of the law of prescription, and along the lines suggested in the *glossa ordinaria*.

However, they were here introduced by Gratian's *dictum*, to the effect that they appeared to be contrary to the rule of the first four canons. The first of these authorities was a letter of the same Pope Gelasius dealing with the intrusion by one bishop into the spiritual rights of the other, specifically the assertion of rights by the bishop of Ancona over a church within a neighboring bishopric. Gelasius reproved the "temerity". Gratian, however, distinguished this case from the preceding four, by limiting its holding to dioceses whose boundaries were "certain and distinct". The *glossa ordinaria* also suggested that the prohibition applied only to acts of outright intrusion, thereby bringing it within the Roman law rule that kept prescription, at least in ordinary circumstances, from being asserted by those who had taken property by force.[13] One might therefore describe the papal letter as "being limited to its facts" by Gratian's treatment. One might note further that cases where the property rights were objectively "certain and distinct" were exactly those in which a third party was least likely to be able to intervene without acting as a *mala fide* intruder. Moreover, where the boundaries were known and fixed, the reason for permitting canonical prescription in the first place – to bring an end to uncertainty – would have been entirely lacking. Gratian himself, however, did not draw these reasons from his text; it was enough for him to distinguish this letter of Pope Gelasius from the preceding four and to draw a conclusion of law from that distinction.

The next contrary authority was again a letter of Pope Gelasius dealing with the subject of diocesan boundaries. This letter disallowed prescription, and it might be regarded simply as a restatement of the previous principle. However, in the *dictum* after the canon Gratian suggested that the decretal "might also be distinguished in another way."[14] That is, Gelasius' letter might be read as a statement that prescription was impossible where a possessor held property he was legally incapable of owning. One bishop cannot own rights that are essential to the episcopate of another. Neither may a cleric obtain the powers of a bishop by force of prescription.[15] Because they are legally distinct rights, not within the power of the possessor's office to hold, illegal possession of them

semper sint in incerto." [The Venice 1615 edition of the Decretum Gratiani is used throughout for quotations to the medieval gloss.]

[13] Glossa ordinaria ad id s. v. invasi.

[14] Dictum post C. 16 q. 3 c. 7: "Potest etiam aliter distingui."

[15] Glossa ordinaria ad C. 16 q. 3 c. 11 s. v. in ius proprium.

must be treated as a pure act of usurpation. It could not be the source of legitimate title.

This is the law today.[16] It should nonetheless not be regarded as a simple truism. In fact, the principle had enormous consequences for the Church. It meant, for example, that possession of tithes by laymen, even very long possession of tithes, would never ripen into legitimate ownership, since under the canon law, laymen could not legally own the right to collect tithes.[17] A quarrel over boundaries between two bishops may seem an unlikely circumstance in which to find an enormously consequential rule to be stated. So we do find it, however. Not a word of the canon treated the desirable consequences as a reason for adopting the rule. It seems not to have been thought necessary that "social policies" should be considered directly, though they might appropriately be used as illustration. It is entirely consistent with Gratian's normal approach to find the principle so drawn from one of the texts he selected.

Canons 13 and 14 follow, the one from a seventh century Church Council, the other from a ninth century papal letter. They limited the availability of prescription by disqualifying possession where the "furor of hostility" or even the "fear of hostility" had prevailed. Under them, the years when hostility had been present would not count towards the establishment of prescriptive right. Both came from lands where such hostility had been a fact of life: Spain and Germany. The principle they stated seemed self-evident to Gratian. God himself would be subject to rebuke, asserted the second of these canons, if possession maintained by force were to count towards establishing prescriptive right. Had not the Children of Israel been subject to the Pharaoh's yoke during four hundred and thirty years?[18] Yet God had led them out of slavery. It was not, therefore, to be supposed that Pharaoh's kind of bondage, or anything like it, should be the source of legitimate prescriptive right. That could not grow from pure force without contradicting this Biblical authority.

From this principle, it would be argued that lands that had once been in Christian hands, but had subsequently come under Moslem rule, should be restored, no matter how long they had been withheld from their original Christian owners. If not restored voluntarily, they might lawfully be taken back by force. The result was the Crusades, or at least an argument justifying the Crusades. Gratian, himself writing at the height of the Crusading movement, says nothing about this possibility inherent in his text. Nor does the *glossa ordinaria*. Whether the canonists had the lands in the Middle East in their

[16] In American law, the rule's primary importance lies in barring possessory claims to government property, but it also applies, for example, to title to wild animals or rights to marital status.

[17] See X 2.26.7 (Causam quae). Tithes were very frequently in lay hands during the Middle Ages, particularly in France and Spain, so that this was both theoretically and practically a very contentious point.

[18] The reference is to Exodus 12: 40 - 1.

minds when they worked out this doctrine, we cannot know. So far as their writing itself goes, they appear to have conceived their duty as concentrating upon collection of texts stating under what ordinary circumstances the several conditions existed that would prevent the running of the prescriptive period. Some of these continue to exist in modern law as "disabilities," like the minority of the true holder of the property right.[19] Others, like excommunication of the true holder, seem distinctly more medieval, although the reason for them was basically the same as in modern law. An excommunicate had no standing to sue.[20] The gloss lists nine such disabilities, and more would be adduced by later commentators.

The final canon of Causa 16 dealt with a claim of prescription against the Roman Church. The facts that gave rise to the canon are largely suppressed, but it came from a papal letter of the end of the ninth century that dealt with a royal claim of prescription against the rights of the Roman Church. The Pope's letter asserted that only prescription of more than 100 years should prevail against the Roman Church. The authority cited was Roman law, specifically an imperial decree allowing that long prescriptive periods to religious institutions as a matter of pious humanity. This papal response was an obviously effective way of dealing with an act by a king who himself claimed some of the power that the Roman law accorded to the ruler. The letter itself made no claim of special papal rights; it did no more than assert a privilege generally available to churches under the Roman law. However, as used by Gratian and as developed by the canonists, the rule was read as applying to the Roman Church alone. The civil law had here been, as the canonists themselves put it, "corrected" by the canon law.

Two aspects of this canon are notable by implication. First, albeit in limited circumstances, it did subject the Church's interests to prescriptive claims on behalf of the laity. Second, it staked out the canon law's independence from the Roman law of prescription. Both are important. As to the first, it might have seemed tempting, at least as a matter of policy, for Churchmen to claim all the privileges of the Roman fisc, against which prescriptive claims did not run. As Maitland once said, the medieval Church was a State, and claims to sovereignty were made routinely on the Church's behalf. Why not claim this normal attribute of sovereignty? This would have protected the rights of the Church against all contrary claims. Such an immunity to possessory claims might have been hard to vindicate in fact, but it might have seemed tempting to seek and valuable to assert. However, this final canon shows that such an immunity would not be asserted. That the 100 year period was limited to the

---

19 Gl. ord. ad C. 16 q. 3 c. 13 s.v. post liminio: "Alius est in pupillari aetate," citing a text from the Codex.

20 Id. "Item et tempore excommunicationis non currit praescriptio."

Roman Church alone in Gratian's treatment of it would have made this ecclesiastical self-denial all the more emphatic.

As to the second, the break with Roman law, it should be stressed that many of the canons, like this one, were based upon knowledge of the Roman law of prescription. Citing it explicitly or implicitly, the popes and Church councils had understood the temporal law to authorize prescriptive right within the Church itself. Here, in limiting the reach of this imperial decree to the papacy alone, the canonists were in effect asserting the independence of their law from that of the emperors, even while denying to the Church the full benefits of this imperial decree. By eschewing a privilege, they claimed a greater right. Accomplished without explicit discussion, the consequences were nonetheless of the greatest importance in the later formulation of the canon law of prescription, as we shall see. These consequences are manifest in the Decretals, the second principal part of the *Corpus iuris canonici,* that compiled by Gregory of Peñaforte and promulgated by Pope Gregory IX in 1234.

III. The Gregorian Decretals

The Decretals devoted a title of twenty chapters in its Second Book to the subject of prescriptive rights. These chapters accomplished several things. They restated and amplified rules found in the *Decretum,* drawing from them specific conclusions that the *Decretum* had contained only in embryo. They dealt with some of the detailed problems of procedure and evidence that inevitably arose in canonical practice and that Gratian had left largely untouched. And they enacted a requirement of good faith for all prescription under the canon law, a requirement that turned out to have large implications for the European *ius commune*. Except in correcting some of the inconsistencies in the earlier treatment, there was no break with the *Decretum* in this new compilation. It did, however, bring the law of prescription into the context of a working legal system to a much greater extent than the earlier work had. Gratian had been concerned with the basic question of whether prescription could be lawful at all. That principle established, it was necessary to care for some of the details.

The Decretals repeated virtually all the principles found in the *Decretum*: that the prescriptive period did not run in time of war, that only property the possessor could legitimately own could be acquired by prescription, and that force could not be the source of prescriptive title. The *Decretum* had been more textbook than statute book or case book, and it may have seemed useful or even necessary to state these in authoritative form. Certainly it must have seemed desirable to elaborate upon them in the many varied circumstances that arose in common practice. For example, the problem of interruption of the prescriptive period was dealt with in several decretals. Thus, it was established that while an episcopal see was vacant, possession by a cleric of tithes belonging to the bishopric did not count towards the forty-year prescriptive period.[21] In the case of the papal see, periods of schism were similarly not to form part of the 100 year prescriptive period.[22]

Likewise building upon the canons holding that in some situations prescription was not permitted at all, the Decretals specifically disallowed prescription for tithes,[23] procurations owed to apostolic legates and nuncios,[24] professions of obedience owed to prelates by their subjects,[25] and the rights of episcopal visitation.[26] The underlying principle throughout was that essentially spiritual rights should not be subject to prescription. They should never be determined by mere usage. There were enough such instances that, together with the cases in which a disability interrupted prescription, they came to be encapsulated in a handy mnemonic device for use by students of the canon law.[27] Such devices are measures of the importance this subject had in the medieval teaching of the Church's laws.

Necessarily raised in the Decretals were also several interpretive questions: for instance, the question of whether, prescription once begun, interruptions caused a new prescriptive period to begin, or were simply to be subtracted from the total in determining whether enough years had passed? A decretal of Pope Innocent III (1198 - 1216), the architect of a great deal of the law in this title, made the assumption that subtraction was to be used.[28] Although there was some authority on both sides of this question among the commentators, Innocent's turned out to have been the view taken by most commentators. A later writer, for example, spoke of prescription "sleeping" while the condition that prevented suit being brought continued to exist.[29]

Of the substantive details clarifying the scope of the law of prescription, perhaps the most important was that which fixed the applicable periods. Whereas most of the canons in the *Decretum* had either said nothing on the subject or had assumed a thirty year prescriptive period, a decretal of Pope Alexander III (1159 - 81) enacted that with respect to claims being made against the Church, a forty year period should henceforth prevail.[30] Otherwise, he made no change. It could be, and in fact was, therefore assumed that

---

21 X 2.26.4 (De quarta decime).
22 X 2.26.14 (Quum vobis).
23 X 2.26.7 (Causam quae).
24 X 2.26.11 (Accedentes).
25 X 2.26.12 (Quum non liceat).
26 X 2.26.16 (Quum ex officii).
27 It is given in the glossa ordinaria ad X 2.26.12 s. v. non obstante, towards the end.
28 X 2.26.15 (Auditis et intellectis); the word used is "subducere".
29 Innocent IV, Apparatus in libros decretalium (Frankfurt 1570) ad X 2.26.10, no. 1.
30 X 2.26.4 (De quarta decime).

the law of the Church had "canonized" the thirty year prescriptive period of the civil law in all suits against and among laymen.

This was not quite the end of the matter. There were other prescriptive periods for different sorts of claims, and things became complicated enough in the provisions found elsewhere in the canonical texts that the canonist Hostiensis (d. 1271) was able to list the stupefying number of fifty-five separate prescriptive periods allowed under the canon law.[31] However, most of these were straight-forward statutes of limitation for bringing suit, and some of them (as often happened in the literature of the canon law) were mere feats of juristic imagination.[32] It was Alexander III's decretal that contained the basic rule governing possession of most kinds of real and personal property. That decretal provided the workable base for computing the prescriptive period in most cases that arose under the Church's legal system.

Pope Alexander's decretal undoubtedly was legislative in character, although the forty year prescriptive period was not unknown in Roman law,[33] and although the decretal was formulated in response to a question that had been put to him. The only reason for the ten year extension given in the decretal was that, "the Roman Church does not admit a thirty-year prescription against the Church." Separation of the clerical order from the laity and a privileged status for the former was of course one of the cardinal tenets of the Gregorian Reform tradition,[34] and like much of the canon law that grew from that tradition, this decretal announced a rule discriminating in the interests of the Church. Asked to give a substantive reason for it, commentators were content with saying that ecclesiastical institutions were "favored" by the law.[35] Most, seeing no need for explanation at all, stated simply that Alexander III had corrected the canons found in Gratian's *Decretum*.[36] Papal legislation was a motive source of the canon law, a normal way in which formal enactments were made. Here is a textbook example.

It is also clearly correct to describe as a legislative act, one meant to correct the inherited civil law, a second feature of the Gregorian Decretals: the estab-

---

[31] Henricus de Segusio, Summa aurea, II, tit. de praesumptionibus, nos. 2 - 3 (Venice 1574 ed. col. 721).

[32] Id., for example, he lists the fact that under a text in the Decretum one became immundus for seven days after touching a cadaver. This seems a considerable stretch of the concept of prescription.

[33] Cod. 7.39.2 (praescriptio longissimi temporis), on which see Dieter Nörr, Die Entstehung der longi temporis praescriptio (Cologne 1969).

[34] See Colin Morris, The Papal Monarchy: the Western Church from 1050 to 1250 (Oxford 1989) 316 - 20.

[35] E.g., Rufinus von Bologna, Summa decretorum ad C. 16 q. 3 (Heinrich Singer ed. 1902) 360 (speaking specifically about monasteries).

[36] Glossa ordinaria ad C. 16 q. 3 c. 1 s.v. triginta: "Hodie non statur huic numero, extra de praescrip. de quarta."

lishment of good faith as a requirement for valid prescription. The requirement of good faith in the canon law meant essentially what it does today: that the possessor must have acted without knowledge of the true state of the title. He must have thought that he was possessing what was rightfully his to quality as a *bona fide* possessor.[37] Although one might think that the requirement was implicit in parts of the *Decretum,* it appeared as an unstated assumption more than as a rule, and that only in limited circumstances. In fact, Gratian had assumed that good faith would *not* be present in some of the cases in which prescription was successfully established.[38] Two chapters in the Decretals changed this. They made *bona fides* an explicit requirement for all claims. The first was a papal letter of Alexander III,[39] the second the decree *Quoniam omnes* of Innocent III's Fourth Lateran Council (1215).[40]

Roman law had admitted the possibility that a *mala fide* possessor could acquire title.[41] The canon law was consciously rejecting this part of its legal heritage. Echoing a phrase from St. Paul's Letter to the Romans – that "whatsoever is not from faith, is sin" – the Lateran Council decreed, "that no prescription, whether civil or canonical, shall be valid without good faith."[42] The moral underpinnings of the medieval canon law are readily apparent in this decree. A related requirement that the possessor have a *iustus titulus* to acquire prescriptive right, added to the Decretal law by Pope Boniface VIII in the Liber Sextus (1298), sprang evidently from the same source.[43] Although there were differences between the views taken by the medieval theologians and the canonists, here is a reminder that the canon law had spiritual ends in view. To acquire property through a knowing wrong could not be done without sin.[44] For the canon law to have embraced a rule that threatened "to divide man from God,"[45] seemed quite wrong to the canonists. At least it would have

---

37 See Balbus, De praescriptionibus, Pt. 3:2, no. 1.

38 Dictum post C. 16 q. 3 q. 15 § 1. Gratian does not mention bona fides as a requirement in all cases, and where required he also limited it to the start of the prescriptive period.

39 X 2.26.5 (Vigilanti).

40 X 2.26.20 (Quoniam omne).

41 On the concept in Roman law, see Herbert Hausmaninger, Die bona fides des Ersitzungsbesitzers im klassichen römischen Recht (Vienna 1964).

42 Rom. 14: 23: "Omne quod non est ex fide peccatum est."

43 Sext 2.13.1, generally defined as possession iusta causa, so that the requirement tended in practice to run together with the requirement of good faith. See Balbus, De praescriptionibus, Pt. 3:1. The background is the subject of Jules Fauré, Justa causa et bonne foi: essai d'explication des singularités de l'usucaption pro emptore en droit romain classique (Lausanne 1936).

44 Glossa ordinaria ad X 2.26.20: "Quicunque facit contra conscientiam aedificat ad gehennam. Et ideo statuit concilium quod nulla valeat praescriptio absque bona fide."

45 So put by Joannes Andreae, Commentaria in libros decretalium (Venice 1581) ad Sext 5.12.2, no. 20.

required elaborate explaining. It was here, through avowedly legislative enactment, that this "policy goal" of the canon law took effect.

IV. The Fundamental Problems

Explanation, together with determination of many difficult problems which still plague the law of prescription, was the task of the canonists in commenting upon the texts so far discussed. There were many such problems, large and small, and a sixteenth century commentator described the resulting law as "subtle and profound" as a consequence.[46] Among them was one to which Professor Summers has himself contributed in a modern setting,[47] arriving at a workable definition of what constitutes good faith in specific circumstances. Others included questions that have continued to vex the law of prescription, such as fixing the nature of the possession that must underlie prescriptive rights, determining the rights of co-tenants among themselves, and dealing with the changes caused by successive ownership.[48]

How the canonists attacked these problems is well worth studying. However, it is true that most of them could be, and were in fact, worked out within the framework of existing Roman and decretal law. In conceptual interest, they were dwarfed by two more basic questions, which amounted to real dilemmas for the commentators.[49] First, what should the law hold about the common case where knowledge of the true state of the title was acquired *after* the prescriptive period had run? And second, how should it formulate the proper relationship between the long-established civilian rules and the canonical requirements? Both were new problems. Neither was fully answered either by Alexander III's decretal or by the formal enactment of the Fourth Lateran Council. And both raised questions that caused the canonists to confront assumptions that were basic to their jurisprudence.

The first dilemma is easy to appreciate. If conscience provides the operative rule for determining prescriptive right, and if a person who has knowledge of the true state of the title of the thing he has possessed, what does it matter how many years have gone by? Why is it important exactly when his *mala fides* began? He may not have known at the time his possession started. He may not have known while it continued. But *now* he does know. The property really

---

[46] See Balbus, De praescriptionibus, Pt. 1, Proem. "subtilis et profunda, ac in variis multifariis et prope infinitis iuris partibus diffusa."

[47] Robert S. Summers, "'Good Faith' in General Contract Law and the Sales Provisions of the Uniform Commercial Code," Virginia Law Rev. 54 (1968) 195 - 267.

[48] See Balbus, De praescriptionibus, Pt. 1, for fuller treatment of these, and other issues.

[49] For some of the ramifications of the rule requiring good faith, see Thomas O. Martin, Adverse Possession, Prescription and Limitation of Actions: the canonical 'Praescriptio' (Catholic University of America, Canon Law Studies, No. 202, 1944)

belongs to someone else. Can he retain it without sin simply because the formal law appears to allow him to do so? It is far from obvious that he can, and there was respectable authority, particularly among contemporary theologians, holding that he could not.[50]

To have embraced the theologians' opinion would have required the canonists to ignore quite clear provisions of the Decretals, not to speak of the principal point made by Gratian's *Decretum:* that prescription was possible and ultimately consistent with the assumptions of the canon law. To have taken the negative position would also have reduced the place of successful prescription to a largely theoretical possibility, since actual disputes over prescriptive right normally arise only when the truth about the title becomes known. If *mala fides* at a late point in time always defeated the prescriptive claim, there would have been very little room for successful prescription under the law. It was therefore necessary for the canonists to attempt to reconcile the formal element of the law, the canonical enactments, with the claims of conscience.

The canonists did this in two different, but not mutually inconsistent, ways. One was to distinguish. Joannes Andreae (d. 1348), for example, suggested making use of the quite reasonable distinction between taking and retaining.[51] It might reasonably be thought that where the possessor had not himself taken the item, he should be treated more leniently than the possessor who had actually "usurped" it, allowing the former but not the latter to prevail when the truth became known after the prescriptive period. Hostiensis mentioned the possibility of treating the question of *bona fides* as a question of fact, allowing the choice to be made by the possessor himself according to the actual dictates of his conscience.[52] Alanus Anglicus (fl. c. 1210) suggested that a distinction be drawn according to whether possession had been *ex causa lucrativa* or not.[53]

The advantage of these distinctions – no small advantage in the eyes of the medieval jurists – was that they allowed the texts to be reconciled. Those texts which disallowed prescriptive title where knowledge had been acquired after the passage of forty years could be described as dealing with the situation where one side of the distinction applied. Those which allowed it could be described as dealing with the other. The disadvantage of the distinctions was that they seemed arbitrary, not being based upon any formal source of law. They also must have seemed intellectually unsatisfying. It could not be made wholly clear just why they were being suggested. Sometimes the law has to make do with such distinctions. The question of acquiring legal rights in prop-

---

50 This is usefully discussed by Hostiensis, Summa Aurea II, tit. de praescriptionibus, no. 3.

51 See at Sext 5.12.2, nos. 33 - 38.

52 Summa aurea, no. 3.

53 Glossa ordinaria ad X 2.26.5 s.v. noverit.

erty that belongs to someone else is inherently difficult. But most jurists seek a more elegant solution than that offered by these artificial distinctions. Certainly the medieval canonists did.

The solution they hit upon depended ultimately upon the power of the law and of the lawmaker. The canonists came to hold that the law itself created a wholly new title to the property. It was the law itself, not any action by the possessor, that extinguished the old title and created a new one. This is the same solution that modern American writers on the subject of adverse possession have reached, apparently without consciousness of this aspect of its history.[54] These writers would probably be surprised to discover their own solution being worked out by the medieval canonists because of a conflict between the claims of conscience and the necessity of establishing prescriptive right. Some of the steps taken along the way to the solution would surely surprise them. In any event, the ending place turns out to be pretty much identical in both contexts.

The canonists thus stated that the possessor, after completion of the prescriptive period, no longer held the property under the same title that had once belonged to the original owner. As the *glossa ordinaria* put it, "the laws make this mine and that yours".[55] Thus, as if by definition, the possessor could not be holding in bad faith once the prescriptive period had passed, because the original owner no longer had any interest in the property upon which claims of conscience could be founded. "The canons," it was concluded, "can give me a thing belonging to another, and I will be secure."[56] What no individual could do on his own, the law could.

It should not be concluded from this account that the canonists regarded their solution as resting simply upon legislative fiat. There were good reasons for it. Ownership should not be left forever uncertain,[57] and to upset a right established by prescription whenever its holder began to have *mala fides* would threaten to do just that. As we say today, so said the canonists: at some point the law must put an end to the upset of lives and minds caused by uncertainty and litigation. It was entirely rational to accomplish this goal by sanctioning prescriptive right and embracing the notion that the law created a new title.[58] The law was also justified in penalizing an owner who slept on his rights. If the opposite rule were to obtain, wrote Joannes Andreae, "the sin of

[54] See, e.g., Roger A. Cunningham et al., The Law of Property (St. Paul, Minnesota, 1984) § 11.7. The subject does, however, also have old roots in the English common law. See James Barr Ames, "The Nature of Ownership," in Lectures on Legal History (Cambridge, Mass. 1913) 191 - 209.

[55] Glossa ordinaria ad X 2.26.5 s.v. noverit.

[56] Id.

[57] Glossa ordinaria ad C. 16 q. 3 c. 4 s.v. legis.

[58] Joannes Andreae, Novella Commentaria ad Sext 5.12.2, no. 15.

negligence, which is contrary to the public good, would go unpunished."[59] Prescription was therefore not contrary to the *ius naturae,* as it might seem to be at first sight, because fully considered no person was actually being enriched at the expense of another. The original possessor deserved the loss that occurred to him; it was *damnum absque injuria.*[60]

The second fundamental problem for the canonists lay in determining the relationship of the requirement of good faith to established Roman law, which, although requiring good faith for some purposes,[61] contained no blanket requirement of continued good faith on the part of all possessors. The problem existed because the Fourth Lateran Council's constitution stated in so many words that it applied to "prescription both canonical and civil."[62] Had it, in effect, therefore nullified the civil law? And if so, by what right? What justification did the canon law have for intervening in what would otherwise be a purely secular matter? As the great jurist, Baldus de Ubaldis (d. 1400), phrased the commonly stated objection, "The pope cannot intrude himself into the affairs of laymen, since he is not a competent judge in their causes."[63]

Three different positions on this potentially divisive question were taken by the early canonists. One held that, rightly interpreted, the Lateran Council's decree did not reach prescription under the civil law at all. If so, the conflict was only apparent. Another held that to a "hierocratic" view: that the conflict was real, that canon law had overruled the civil law, and that it was entirely right to do so. A third, best articulated by Joannes Andreae, held that there was a possible conflict between the two rules, but that both positions were lawful and appropriate, given the disparate purposes of each legal system. The first and second of these are the easiest to describe. The third is harder to understand, but it is revealing about the inner nature of the canon law.

The argument that the decretals requiring good faith did not cover prescription under the Roman law depended on a careful, perhaps creative, reading of *Quoniam omnes.*[64] The words *tam canonica quam civilia* might be read as referring simply to different kinds of causes coming before the courts of the Church. Under the canon law, some matters were regarded as *spiritualia* (e.g. tithes); some as *temporalia* (e.g. ordinary rights in land). Either might become the subject of litigation in the ecclesiastical forum. The Lateran Council's

---

59 Id. at Sext 5.12.2, no. 12

60 Id.

61 For instance, *usucaptio* in Roman law required good faith at the start of the period (Inst. 2.6).

62 "ut nulla valeat absque bona fide praescriptio tam canonica quam civilis."

63 Commentaria ad tres priores libros decretalium Commentaria (Lyons 1585) ad X 2.26.20, no. 2: "Opp. quod papa non possit se intromittere de rebus laicorum cum sit iudex incompetens in causis eorum."

64 These arguments can be found in the glossa ordinaria ad X 2.26.20 s.v. tam canonica.

decree might be read, therefore, as stating simply that both of these would be judged by the good faith standard in that forum. If so, it would not prejudice the rules of the Roman law within its own forum. An alternate possibility was to say that the decree had been meant to apply to both civil and ecclesiastical pleas, but only in those geographical areas (of which there were many) where the Church held both spiritual and temporal jurisdiction. If this had been the meaning of the Council fathers, again no conflict existed, since the Church had an undoubted right to legislate in such areas and since the Roman law could continue to apply in all other circumstances.

To modern tastes, these readings of the language of *Quoniam omnes* may seem purely formal, if not actually perverse. They were, however, quite normal within the *ius commune*. Indeed, it was possible to go further, asserting for example that the canonical decree had been meant only to penalize *mala fide* possessors, and consequently that it had no application where the law's principal purpose was to penalize a record owner who had been negligent. The argument was that if the purpose of a statute in awarding land to the prescriptive possessor was to encourage record owners to be vigilant in protecting their rights, then the question of good or bad faith of the prescriptive possessor would be entirely irrelevant. The possessor's gain would be only an indirect and incidental result of a positive achievement, taking the property from the slothful (former) owner.[65] Thus the Roman law of prescription might continue to exist without coming into direct conflict with the canonical decree.

The second possibility of answering the question about the relationship of *Quoniam omnes* to Roman law was equally formal, although it reached the opposite result. It took the decree at face value, holding that the canon law had justifiably intervened *ratione peccati* in order to correct the Roman law of prescription. The canon law held itself bound to respect the independence of the temporal law in ordinary circumstances,[66] but not where the temporal law would lead men into sin. The basic idea was to avert danger to the souls of the people involved. This might be the situation here. If a *mala fide* possessor risked eternal damnation by retaining property to which he had no right, then the canon law was correct in stepping in to overrule the temporal law's rule. Salvation was undeniably more important than temporal advantage, and the Roman law, some said, had lost sight of this. Medieval canonists habitually

65 This argument is made by Bartolus de Saxoferrato (d. 1357), Commentaria (Venice 1615) ad Dig. 41.3.4.26, no. 2: "Sed ego prescribo per tuam negligentiam, vel potius tu perdis quam ego praescribam."

66 See, e.g., A. M. Stickler, "Sacerdozio e regno nelle nuove ricerche attorno di secoli XII e XIII nei decretisti e decretalisti," in Miscellanea Historiae Pontificiae 18 (1954) 479 - 505. Some wilder hierocratic claims were of course also made by some canonists in favor of the rights of the Papacy and the Church: as that all jurisdiction had been placed into the papal hands and that princes exercised it only as his agents. See generally Michael Wilks, The Problem of Sovereignty in the later Middle Ages (Cambridge 1963).

treated this sort of intervention as only "indirect". They regarded it as no denial of the independence of the temporal law, so that in this case it could be said that the canon law was simply correcting an inherited part of the law of prescription in the exercise of this salutary principle.[67]

The obvious difficulty of this interpretation was that it proved too much. Since most litigation involves wrongdoing of some sort, if the principle were applied rigorously, it would risk putting all jurisdiction immediately into the hands of the Church. Some of the canonists did not shrink before that possibility. Antonius de Butrio (d. 1408), for example, wrote that "it belongs to the Pope to annul all laws, constitutions, statutes and customs which foster sin."[68] In some parts of medieval Europe, the Church courts in fact attempted to put the rule into practice, even allowing it to be invoked in individual cases.[69] But the truth is that application of jurisdiction *ratione peccati* went contrary to normal ways of thinking during the Middle Ages. Most men, canonists among them, assumed a "Two Swords" approach, under which Church and State were bound to respect the legitimate exercise of the jurisdiction belonging to the other. Ecclesiastical jurisdiction *ratione peccati* therefore proved unacceptable to most civil lawyers and temporal officials. It subverted that principle. The canonists were themselves aware of the dangers in pushing the hierocratic view too far. Some among them saw the need for a different approach to the dilemma.

The most sophisticated such attempt to harmonize the Roman and canon laws of prescription was written by Joannes Andreae, commenting on the *Regulae iuris* inserted at the end of the *Liber Sextus*. This formed the third part of the *Corpus iuris canonici,* and was promulgated in 1298 by Pope Boniface VIII.[70] Joannes did not approach the problem simply by asking which law should prevail. He instead raised the possibility that on some level both might be equally valid. This may seem unlikely, but in fact it followed from his way of putting the problem. Joannes began with the uncontroversial assertion that the law of prescription should stand in conformity with the law of nature and that such conformity furnished a test of its legitimacy. Was it possible, therefore, that both might be "in harmony with the equity of the law of nature," even while taking opposite positions on the requirement of good faith in prescription?[71]

[67] E.g., Innocent IV, Apparatus (Frankfurt 1570) ad X 2.26.20: "Sed quid ad Papam de praescriptione inter laicos? Respondeo ratione peccati hoc statuit."

[68] Commentaria in libros decretalium (Venice 1578) ad id, no. 3: "Nota ad Papam spectare ut casset omnes leges constitutiones statuta et consuetudines peccatum nutrientes."

[69] See Eduard Eichmann, Der recursus ab abusu nach deutschem Recht (Breslau 1903) 14 - 15; Jorg Müller-Volbert, Die geistlichen Gerichte in den Braunschweig-Wolfenbüttelschen Landen (1973) 86.

[70] Novella Commentaria ad Sext 2.12.2.

[71] Id., no. 19: "et concordat aequitati iuris naturae."

It was. For the sake a greater good, Joannes noted, the law often permits consequences that it would not promote directly. It could, for example, legitimately require candidates for clerical office to answer questions about their past life that would be unlawful if asked of someone who was not a candidate. The ultimate good of protecting the clerical office from unworthy occupants rendered an intrusion, which would otherwise be unlawful, legitimate. Now the ultimate good of the Roman law was the preservation and enhancement of civil society. The civil law might therefore be acting in entire harmony with natural law if it adopted the rule of prescription best calculated to promote that good, even if the rule had incidental consequences that might be spiritually undesirable. Discouraging negligence by property owners and limiting the length of time during which quarrels and litigation could arise were proper ways of preserving right order within human society. "The public good," Joannes wrote, "is most seriously impeded by disputes that cannot readily be ended."[72] A rule of prescription framed to fit these ends was entirely justified. It would not become improper, still less would it be invalid, if the civil law left issues of conscience aside. In the eyes of Joannes, the relation between an adverse possessor and God neither were nor should have been of paramount importance to the civil law.

With the canon law, the situation was quite otherwise. The canon law's goal was to serve God's purposes in the world. Its rules must therefore comport with God's will and with the law of the Gospel; its rules were to be fashioned "so that men may attain to glory."[73] At least it seemed clear that the canon law must not endorse a rule that divided man from God, for that would violate its greatest good. Its rule of prescription, if it were to be in harmony with natural law, should therefore promote justice, whereas the rule of Roman law might simply promote peace. This difference required that the canon law concern itself with the inner man, and adjust its rule according to the adverse possessor's interior *bona fides*. Had not Jesus, in teaching that the man who lusts after a woman has sinned in his heart, also said that he had come not to abolish the law but to fulfill it?[74] He must have meant that the law of the church should look to a person's subjective intentions. Because the goals of the two laws were different, it followed for Joannes that they were not incompatible, even though they adopted different standards for the acquisition of prescriptive title. Indeed one could almost say that each had adopted the rule best suited for its inner nature.

---

[72] Id., no. 15: "quia bonum publicum maxime impeditur per lites quae non facile terminantur, et ideo illud legale ius quod imponit finem litibus talibus maxime congruit bono publico ac per consequens maxime concordat iuri naturali."

[73] Id., no. 20: "Nam suus finis principalis est ordinare in Deum et in legem Evangelicam ut homo gloriam assequatur."

[74] The reference is to Matt: 5:33 and 5:28.

V. Conclusion

The harmonization of Roman and canon law from the pen of Joannes Andreae was elegant and sophisticated, perhaps too sophisticated for the realities of everyday litigation. The stubborn question of law remained: Which law of prescription would actually be applied in actual cases? He wrote during the first half of the fourteenth century, and for a time, it seems, his answer described the realities of court practice. The civil courts applied their rule; the ecclesiastical courts applied theirs.[75] Gradually, however, the canonical principle came to prevail. By the fifteenth century, it appears to have become the rule applied no matter which forum the plaintiff had chosen. This change was not announced as the adoption of a new substantive policy, but as one in which the Roman law rule had been corrected by the newer regime of the canon law.

This change was accomplished, as it seems to me, by an interplay between instrumental policy and formal enactment. As in the creation of a canonical system of prescription as a whole, the canonists relied first of all upon formal rules, interpreting them in directions one might legitimately say were sometimes expansive and sometimes strict. They read these authorities, according to their understanding of the inner nature of the canon law, as well as of its evident purposes in the human society. In this respect, examination of the creation and development of the canon law of prescription may not implausibly be regarded as a fit subject for a volume honoring Professor Summers.

---

[75] See Baldus de Ubaldis (d. 1400), Commentaria (Venice 1595) ad X 2.26.20, no. 6: "Quaero numquid haec decretalis servetur in foro seculari? Dicit Bernardus quod non et verum est quod de facto non servatur." See also Bartolus de Saxoferrato, Commentaria ad Cod. 7.31.1, no. 2: "Item nota quod mala fides superveniens non interrumpit praescriptionem; secus de iure canonico."

The Lay-out of Arguments

By J. R. Lucas, Oxford

Arguments have been much misunderstood. Not only has it been assumed that they must be deductive, but it has been assumed also that, although often expressed in loose and elliptical form, they must be capable, if they are valid at all, of being expressed with absolute precision, as a set of necessary and sufficient conditions for the action in question to be appropriate. Mathematical arguments are capable of being stated precisely, and it has long been a reproach to workers in other disciplines that they do not manage to achieve equal precision in their work. The assumption is made that absolute precision is in principle available, and it is only a lack of rigour by practitioners in the non-mathematical disciplines that prevents them casting their arguments in satisfactory form, and the philosopher should, therefore, reconstruct arguments to conform with these requirements, evaluating those that do, and rejecting any that do not.

This assumption is false. Most arguments, not only about morals, but in the humanities generally, are of a different, dialectical, form. A case is made out *prima facie* and objections to it are made. These objections may be rebutted, and counter-arguments countered. Sometimes the argument may be conclusive, so that there is no more to be said, and often some consideration is decisive so that we have little doubt in making up our minds. But often we do so leaving open the possibility that further considerations could emerge which would justify a change of mind, and often we reach a conclusion only tentatively, saying that the facts support it *ceteris paribus*, other things being equal.[1]

It is clear that there are very many variations on this pattern of argument. We may object at the outset to the *prima facie* case so that it never gets off the ground, or we may shoot it down in full flight, or we may allow that it strikes home but still claim to escape its full force. These different counters may be met by different rebuttals, and the argument may be ramified in different ways. The possibilities are extremely complex. Searle criticizes Ross for not

---

[1] W. D. Ross, The Right and the Good, Oxford 1930, pp. 19ff.; H. L. A. Hart, "The Ascription of Responsibility and Rights," P.A.S. 1948, pp. 171-94; reprinted in A. G. N. Flew, Logic and Language, vol. I, Oxford 1951, pp. 145 - 65; J. R. Lucas, "The Philosophy of the Reasonable Man," Philosophical Quarterly, 1963, pp. 97 - 106; J. R. Lucas "Not 'Therefore' but 'But'" Philosophical Quarterly, 1966, pp. 289 - 307; S. E. Toulmin, The Uses of Argument, Cambridge 1958, pp. 57ff.

distinguishing them sufficiently,[2] and, indeed, there is a difference between the case where I argue "You ought to go to Sheila's party because I heard you say to her 'I hereby promise to go to your party" which you counter by saying "You should not pick up fag-ends: I only uttered those words as a philosophical example", and the case where my argument is countered "But I have had a telephone call saying my mother is ill, and I must go at once". In the former case there never was an obligation. Although your having uttered the words is *prima facie* evidence of your being under an obligation, the circumstance of their being uttered as a philosophical example entirely alters the case. So, too, if you were play-acting or sleepwalking. Other things being equal, to say 'I hereby promise to go to your party' creates an obligation: but other things are not equal, and the *prima facie* case is defeated by the special context of utterance. In the latter case, however, there was an obligation, only it was overridden by another more fundamental, more pressing, more important or more urgent obligation. An overridden obligation is not the same as no obligation or an extinguished obligation. If you had never promised to go to Sheila's party, or if you had promised but had subsequently been released from your promise, there would be no call on you to explain your non-appearance or present your apologies or make amends. If, however, you had promised, but the obligation had been overridden by another, then you would need to make it up with Sheila. Although you had done the right thing in going to your mother, you had failed to do what you had promised to do, and you owed Sheila an explanation. Once given, it should, of course, be accepted; she should lose no time in acknowledging your greater obligation to your mother, and expressing sympathy for you at a worrying time. But the fact that you owed her an explanation shows that the obligation was not extinguished by being overridden – as it would have been if she had cancelled the party –, and often the obligation remains in attenuated form – the next time she asks you to come you ought to make a special effort to be able to, even at the cost of considerable inconvenience.

Thus far Searle is right to warn against the dangers of oversimplification. But this scarcely diminishes the importance of the concept of the *prima facie* that Ross introduced. At each stage an argument is adduced which is not conclusive but is adequate. In normal circumstances, it is enough that I heard you say 'I hereby promise to go to your party' for you to have put yourself under an obligation: but there can be circumstances which render such an inference incorrect. I do not need to ascertain in advance that no such circumstances obtain. I am entitled on the evidence in my possession to draw that inference. But it is defeasible, and can be defeated should some exceptional circumstances obtain. If, however, on enquiry no such circumstances can be discovered, then

---

[2] J. R. Searle, "Prima Facie Obligations", in Joseph Raz, ed. Practical Reasoning, Oxford 1978, pp. 81 -90.

I may reckon that, having considered all the circumstances of the case, you really did put yourself under an obligation. Similarly, if once it is admitted that yourself are under an obligation, the inference can, other things being equal, be drawn that the obligation still holds. Such a presumption needs no further evidence to support it. But it can be defeated – if Sheila subsequently released you from the obligation, or said or showed that she did not reckon it to be a firm promise, or did not expect you to come or did not really want you to come; or if war breaks out, or she gets ill, or the university is closed down by the Minister of Education. In the absence of such special circumstances, the inference is valid, and you are under an obligation. From this it normally follows that you ought, indeed, to go to the party when the time comes, and that only by doing that will you have acquitted yourself well as man of your word. But other duties can arise, and in view of them you may conclude that in the event you ought to do something else. It seems quite reasonable to call the obligation to go to the party a *prima facie* obligation to distinguish it from what, after due consideration, you conclude you actually ought to do. Such a *prima facie* obligation may be overridden by a more important or more pressing one, and in that case you should carry out the latter with a good conscience and without repine, although, as we have seen, with due explanation and apology. There is a difference, which Searle is right to insist on, between this latter case and the others, because *prima facie* obligations on our part give rise to legitimate expectations on the part of others, and if we have to disappoint them, even for good reason, we still need to make amends. But in spite of this difference, there is an important similarity between the pattern of inference at the last and at earlier stages of the argument, and Ross was right to see that moral arguments, as well as many others, needed to be characterized in a quite different way from what had hitherto been assumed.

The dialectical nature of practical reason has important consequences. Even when there is no moral conflict, there are often reasons *for* an action and reasons *against*. Some of these reasons may meet others and defeat them, but often we shall be left still with reasons on both sides, and will have to decide between them. We deliberate and try and assess how weighty the reasons are on either side, and finally strike a balance. As the metaphor suggests, the decision is not an arbitrary one; but nor is it governed by some impersonal decision-procedure. We can criticize someone's decision, but we cannot replace it by the result of a standard application of an impersonal decision-procedure. It is a decision which has to be taken by somebody or other, using his judgement as best as he can. We may disagree with his judgement, and reckon that had the decision been ours, we should have decided differently. But then it is our judgement against his. We may be right, but we are not, save in exceptional circumstances, indisputably right. From this it follows that we cannot brush aside the reasoning of a decision-maker, even when we dissent from his decision, in the way we can ignore the calculations of a faulty arithmetician, the fallacious proofs of a would-be geometer, or the chemical analyses of an incompetent experimentalist. With moral argument – and many other forms of argument in the humanities – we have to enter into the reasoning of the man who strikes the balance, and not merely replace it by what we take to be the correct reasons. We have to consider not merely *the* reasons, but *his* reasons, and take not merely a third-personal, or rather omni-personal, standpoint but also a first-personal standpoint as well.

The interplay between first- and third-personal reasons is of great importance in moral philosophy. While we are deliberating we consider third-personal reasons for and against a particular course of action. When we have decided, we support our decision by reference to the reasons for *or* the reasons against, whichever are the reasons inclining towards the way we have decided. When asked to justify the decision we give our reasons, namely those reasons which in our judgement weighed most heavily with us. In deliberating we weigh the reasons on either side against each other, and in striking a balance we adopt the weightier as our reasons, which we cite thereafter in justifying our decision. We do not cite the reasons on the other side, but only our objections to them, if they are pressed on us. Although while we were deliberating we weighed them, they did not weigh with us in the event, and drop out of sight in our subsequent report of our reasoning. In discussing what is to be done, you and I may well agree on what are the relevant considerations on either side, but strike the balance differently, so that I decide one way giving as my reasons some of the considerations inclining one way and you decide the other way giving as your reasons some of the quite different considerations inclining the other way. In debate we largely agree on what the relevant considerations are, but in conclusion we cite entirely disparate selections from those considerations in support of diametrically opposed decisions. It is easy, then, in retrospect to concentrate on the difference of judgement while overlooking the similarity of consideration. And this makes our first-personal reasons seem more subjective and less inter-personal than they really are. Real differences of opinion mask considerable agreement in argument.

Suppose we are arguing about capital punishment. We agree that life is sacred, and that it is wrong to kill. One takes this as an absolute, and concludes that judicial execution is therefore wrong. The other contends that those who have killed have forfeited their right to life, and may be condemned to death to prevent their ever killing again and to deter any others who are tempted to kill. The debate widens. The advocate of the death penalty points out that even the abolitionist does not regard the prohibition of killing as being absolutely absolute, and will allow that a man may kill another in self-defence. The abolitionist points out that imprisonment is as effective a preventitive as execution, and claims that it is also equally effective as a deterrent; and he emphasizes the possibility of error in the judicial process. In the debate each takes the points made by the other. Both agree on the sanctity of life – the murderer's, his victim's, and other potential victims'. Both agree that wrongdoing merits punishment, and that crimes should be prevented and discouraged. Both agree that miscarriages of justice are very terrible, and not to be tolerated or made light of. But in giving their reasons for holding opposing opinions each will cite only those considerations which he finally takes as decisive, and will ignore the large measure of common ground. The advocate of the death penalty will instance the rights of victims and potential victims as paramount, the abolitionist the importance of the state's not compromising by its actions its stance on the absolute sanctity of human life. Their reasons – the reasons each adopts as his own in coming down on one side or the other – differ: but the reasons they recognise as relevant in debate are largely the same.

The dialectical structure of practical reason has the further consequence of making it informal. Few formal rules are applicable where everything depends on the response the other party makes. If I adduce an argument you may counter by denying the facts I allege, or by glossing them further – "although I did indeed utter the words 'I promise to pay you five dollars' I did so only as a philosophical example and not in order to make a genuine promise" –, or by denying the principle of morality I invoke, or by claiming that it does not apply in the particular case in question, or by acknowledging the force of my contention but claiming countervailing considerations which override it. My next move will depend on which move you make, and your counter on mine. There will thus be a rapidly widening variety of moves and countermoves, and no simple pattern that comprises them all. At each stage it will be necessary to consider the substantial point that has been made, and to address one's mind to that. No formula will fit all the twists and turns of dialectical argument, and we have simply to argue as best we can on the substantial merits of the case.

There are many different counters that can be made to an argument, but not all of them will be made. Although it is logically appropriate to respond to an argument based on the fact that I uttered the words 'I promise to pay you five dollars' by explaining that although I did, indeed, utter the words, I did so only as a philosophical example, it would often be untrue to make such a response, and often I concede that I not only uttered the words but did so with the intention of their being taken in the normal way. I concede, as in all honesty I must, many points, and concentrate on the crucial ones where my counter-argument can be substantiated, and if substantiated will carry the day. There is thus an important gap in the many points I do not contest between the degree of proof actually required and the degree that might on some occasion conceivably be required. Often it is enough that you heard me say 'I promise to pay you five dollars', but on some occasions we can conceive of we should have to consider the possibility of the words being uttered not in order to make a promise but to serve as a philosophical example, and then we should need to consider the whole context of the utterance. This possibility, however, does not lead to our always requiring evidence of context before we are justified in taking the words 'I promise to pay you five dollars' in the standard way. Once we are reliably informed that the words were uttered we are entitled to *assume* that they were intended to be taken in the standard way *unless* reasons are adduced for believing the contrary. Moral arguments do not proceed *more geometrico*. A geometrical argument is no argument at all unless it is absolutely watertight: a moral argument, together with most arguments in the humanities, is full of possible holes, but nevertheless holds water unless someone succeeds in picking an actual hole. A typical "proof" in morals, history or literary criticism is one which gives *adequate* reason for the conclusion in *the absence of* a convincing counter-argument, whereas a proof in geometry or mathematics generally is one which gives *conclusive* reason, a logically *sufficient* condition, for the theorem, with there being *no* logical possibility of any counter-argument whatsoever. Much therefore depends in moral argument on a possible hole not being an actual hole, on the other party's conceding the point rather than contesting it, on his letting it pass in silence rather than interposing a further 'but'. The argument from silence is of great importance in morals, as it is, in a different way, in history.

It might seem that the most effective strategy in argument was to contest each and every point made by the other side, so as to require them all to be proved up to the hilt: in this way one would maximise the chance of finding some weak points which would unhinge the whole argument. Many children and some inexperienced advocates adopt such a strategy, but it is less effective than they suppose. For often it is a matter of judgment whether an objection is cogent, and if someone shows bad judgement in putting forward objections which are not sustainable, it weakens the authority of his judgment over all, and in particular about those objections which might be sustainable. If I make out that when I uttered the words 'I promise to pay you five dollars' I was using them only as a philosophical example, I put you to the trouble of proving that I used them in the standard way: but if you succeed in doing this, I am seriously discredited, and my other arguments are correspondingly weakened. I am much more likely to be believed if I say simply that I had in fact discharged the debt, or that you had subsequently released me from my obligations, and do not also make out something that turns out to be demonstrably false. If I am wrong about that, as I evidently am, I may well be wrong on the other point too. So it is that in morals many reasons are often weaker than one: whereas nobody thinks Pythagoras' theorem less true because it can be proved in forty-seven different ways.

The dialectical structure of moral arguments reflects the fact they are practical arguments – arguments about what ought to be done – addressed to human beings, who are rational agents acting under conditions of imperfect information. Because we are human, we are fallible; because we are having to decide what to do under conditions of imperfect information, we have to live with our fallibility, and decide as best we can none the less. We cannot not decide. In the practical world of affairs, *tertium non datur:* either one does something or one does not; if one does not accept the invitation by the time the party comes, one has declined it. It is a rare luxury, mostly confined to academic life, to be able to suspend judgment. Usually we have to decide on the evidence available at the time, even though the evidence is inadequate and our judgement faulty. We have to make our minds up what to do, and shall be lost if we hesitate too long. I cannot dither, but must decide either to stand and fight, or to turn and flee while there is yet time. My decision may be wrong, and so there is always room for a further 'but' between the arguments and the final conclusion, allowing that the arguments were not bad but pointing out that in the event, in the light of some further factor or some further consideration, the conclusion was in fact the wrong one. Practical arguments are full of possible holes. But although it is inherent in taking decisions that we can be wrong, it does not follow that we cannot be right. We are rational agents, acting as best we can in the circumstances in which we find ourselves, and although we may not succeed in selecting the right response to the situation, some responses are more appropriate than others, and we may, and indeed often do, succeed in responding appropriately. So, although we can be wrong, there is a presumption of rightness. If a man judges something to be the appropriate response to a certain situation, the fact of his so judging is an indication in its favour. He may be wrong, but does not have to prove he is right. If we doubt the wisdom of his action, we may ask him his reasons, and may then fault them or point out reasons bearing the other way: but it is for us to make the counter-argument; he does not have to give his reasons and then go on to prove that they are good ones. Although it is theoretically possible, and may occasionally happen, that someone adduces a completely bizarre reason for an action or a moral obligation – "You ought to pay me five dollars", "Why?" "The number of the Beast in the Apocalypse is equal to the height of the great Pyramid measured in cubits" – to which the only response is a request for further explanation why such an alleged fact should constitute a justification for the obligation's obtaining, these cases are extremely rare. In nearly all cases the relevance of the reason is not in question. The once popular *riposte* "So what?" is nearly always inappropriate. Nearly always it is evident that the reason adduced is indeed a reason, as we should expect of a rational agent. It is very seldom that we do not recognise it as being a reason at all: rather, we question whether it is a good enough reason, or whether it is, although a good reason, overridden by other weightier ones, or whether, although in general a good reason, it is not inapplicable to this particular case.

Arguments between fallible rational agents are characterized by a good measure of disagreement but a greater one of mutual understanding. Because we are fallible, each is liable to error, and even if you are in fact right, I may be wrong, and so you will have to disagree with me. So we often disagree. But I can nearly always understand your reasons and enter into them, even though they are not for me the ones I adopted as the decisive ones. Hence on any particular issue we well may disagree, although we do not have to, but in articulating our reasons and adducing our arguments we operate against a background of mutual understanding and potential agreement. This is why argument is worthwhile. At the very least it engenders understanding. And by pinpointing the issues on which we disagree it reduces the area of disagreement and may lead to a complete resolution.

The dialectical structure of argument is not peculiar to moral argument. It is characteristic of all practical argument, and of all the humane disciplines, such as history and literary criticism, which are about human actions and reactions. In each case the fundamental concern is with the response of a human being to a set of circumstances. We make some deep metaphysical assumptions of shared humanity, believing that other people are in some deep respects like-minded with ourselves, but do not identify with them completely. Rather, we submit them together with ourselves to the impersonal ideal of rationality. We do not seek simply to understand, but also to judge or evaluate. Reasons are not simply first-personal reasons why the agent did or does or will do a particular deed, but also why he should have done it or should do it. We can identify with the agent to the extent of understanding why he did what he did or will do what he plans to do, and yet dissociate ourselves from him in reckoning his decision wrong, and in believing that in his shoes we should do differently. But by the same token we have to sit loose to our own opinions, and recognise that we too could be wrong, and submit our own views to criticism and possible correction. It is always difficult, notably in history, to combine the sympathetic with the critical role, and the critical with the self-critical. Historians have learned to be wary of the judgemental role in which the Kings of Judah are judged simply on the score of whether they did good or evil in the sight of the Lord. Tiberius, Caligula and Nero may have been bad men, but the historian hesitates now to anticipate the Day of Judgement, and is concerned to explain, rather than to evaluate, their actions. He seeks to understand why each acted as he did, to get inside him, and understand the action from inside. But that is impossible except on some assumption of common humanity. I cannot get inside Caligula's action in making his soldiers pick up sea shells unless I can see myself so circumstanced that I might be inclined to act similarly. It remains utterly opaque, the unintelligible actions of a madman, unless some circumstances are sketched in and some *rationale* suggested,[3] which makes sense of the action. Then, and only then, I can see why Caligula acted as he did, because I can see that perhaps I should have acted similarly if similarly

[3] As by J. P. V. Balsdon, The Emperor Gaius (Caligula), Oxford 1934, pp. 88 - 95.

situated. *Should:* I see as something which perhaps I should have done, something which perhaps was the reasonable thing to do; it is only by projecting myself into his situation, and considering my rational responses, that I can see things from his point of view; his first-personal reasons are accessible to me only because they are reasons, which can guide not just his actions alone but those of any rational agent, myself included. But *perhaps:* I do not have to adopt his reasons as my own whole-heartedly; it is enought that I can envisage that perhaps I should have done as he did, even though in his actual situation I should not have done so in view of some of the circumstances or some further considerations which he evidently did not take into account; perhaps, if those circumstances did not obtain or those considerations did not apply, I should and would have done as he did, and so I can appreciate what was behind his action even though in his actual circumstances and in view of all the considerations that applied, I should not and would not have done as he did.

Many modern historians, in their anxiety not to be judgemental, have failed to see the extent to which we must evaluate in order to explain. They suppose that all evaluation must be whole-hearted, and must lead us simply to praise well-doers and blame evil-doers, and in order to avoid that, they make out that history must be value-free. But it is, as we now can see, a false alternative. The Whig ideal of history is not the only one that allows evaluations. Granted the dialectical structure of practical argument, I can see why an agent acted as he did, and enter into his reasoning and understand the action from the inside, without whole-heartedly endorsing it. I can see that he had his reasons for acting, and recognise that that they were indeed reasons why he, or anyone, should do as he did, and yet interpose a mental 'but', citing other reasons bearing the other way, which would lead me to refrain from acting as he did. I can evaluate without endorsing, and can therefore explain and understand without needing either to condone or condemn. But, of course, I may be led to justify or condemn. In understanding the actions of Caligula, I may see why he acted in a certain fashion, and reckon that it was indeed a reasonable thing to do, and that he was, in this instance at least, unfairly traduced by Tacitus. In understanding his action, I may endorse it; although I may dissociate myself, interposing a further 'but', I may not, and may be led not only to appreciate his reasons but to appropriate them as what would have been my own; equally, I may dissociate myself, and reckon that although Caligula may have had some reasons, which in some circumstances might have led me to act similarly, in the actual circumstances of his case there were overwhelming reasons the other way, and his act was an act of folly or of great wickedness. Although to sympathize is not the same as to criticize, it carries with it the possibility of criticism. I cannot see things from someone else's point of view without entering into his position; but it is I who am entering in, and in evaluating his action from his point of view, I cannot help being in a position to evaluate it from mine. If I were to forswear all possibility of judging and criticizing, I should have to forgo all evaluation and explanation. The one carries with it the possibility of the other. But although I have to be able to justify and condemn, I do not have to be doing so all the time, or to make it the main task of the historian. The Whig interpretation of history sees it as a progress towards the Whig's present situation. But history need not be interpreted as a progress, and the present need not be seen as the end to which all things should move. The historian can be slow, rather than quick, to criticize or judge historical characters from his own standpoint. Although necessarily occupying his own standpoint, he may remember how different past ages were from his own both in their circumstances and in the moral principles inculcated into those living then and in the moral standards expected of them. If I were running the Trojan war, I should not act as Agamemnon did, or so I hope: but if I had been brought up as Agamemnon was, and had not read the dialogues of Plato or the prophets of Israel, and knew nothing of the civilities of Cicero or the teaching and self-sacrifice of Christ, can I be sure that I would not have been as aggressive and self-assertive as he? A certain degree of charity is appropriate in view of my inadequate appreciation of the whole situation in which he found himself. I may be able to put myself into his shoes, but can never put myself entirely into his skin, and so should be cautious in criticizing. Quite apart from this, the historian may hesitate to judge knowing that he, too, is subject to judgement, and that his own opinions and the moral principles of the present age are not necessarily correct. There is a certain self-righteousness about the Whig interpreter of history that we do well to eschew. Although in explaining we are in a position to criticize and on occasion must, we do not want to obtrude our judgements unnecessarily, any more than we do in the day-to-day business of our present age. I must on occasion pass judgement: it would be inhuman to recount all the actions of Caligula or Nero or Hitler or Stalin in an entirely neutral, value-free way. But our purpose in writing history is often to explain rather than to condemn, and so we are not cager to mark what has been done amiss.

Literature holds a mirror to life in a different way from history. It dispenses with the condition of actuality with all its consequential clutter. The poet, the playwright and the novelist portray possible people in possible situations responding in characteristic ways where adventitious circumstances do not obscure the plot or obstruct the course of poetic justice. Even more than in history we understand by entering in, seeing the situation from the agent's point of view, and being moved and responding in the same way as he. Literary criticism is one remove from literature, and is concerned with other things – the magic of words – besides the portrayal of character and the development of action. Nevertheless, much argument in literary criticism has the same dialectical structure as historical argument. An interpretation is put forward, and a *prima facie* case made for it by reference to various passages. Objections may be made on the basis of other passages, and these may be countered. Alternative interpretations may be suggested, which may or may not commend themselves in preference to the one originally proposed. What considerations are relevant will be largely agreed between the critics, but they may well differ in the assessment of where the weight of argument lies. In one respect there is an important difference between discussing a work of art and deliberating on a course of action. At the end of deliberation we have to decide, choosing one course of action and rejecting others: interpretations are not similarly exclusive, and although we may reject an interpretation on the ground that it seems inadequate, we do not have to on account of our seeing merits in another. Both interpretations may be illuminating, and if we find them so, we may accept them both.

Not all humane, not all practical arguments are moral arguments. We may confine our attention simply to understanding a man's action or a work of art, deliberately suspending judgement on it: or we may in our deliberations confine our questions to what is expedient, what is prudent, what is profitable, or what is socially or legally obligatory. In asking what I should do, I may exclude certain considerations – I may exclude consideration of the interests of others, or consideration of my own; I may be concerned solely with my duties as a citizen, or as a tutor, or as a don; I may look only to future consequences, or to past commitments. These exclusions and emphases colour the arguments, and the conclusions obtained. The tenor of some is moral – altruistic, utilitarian, or deontological: others we contrast with morality, and call them counsels of prudence, or reasons of state, or considerations of self-interest. But although the course of these arguments all differ, they all have the same general lay-out, and exhibit the same underlying dialectical structure.

Historical Models for the Unification of European Law

By Franz Wieacker, Göttingen

I.

The 'models' to be discussed here are not meant to be offered as guidelines for the concrete solution of contemporary problems: as we know, history cannot teach us anything in this respect, primarily because of the unrepeatability of the original conditions. Yet historical solutions may suggest common patterns in comparable constellations, and may thus indicate a framework for contemporary action.

1. The choice of our models must above all be determined by the comparability of the constellations. The foremost condition is the coexistence of a number of particular legal systems within *one* comprehensive legal culture, in which the aspiration to construct a higher common order can begin to develop in the first place. This condition seems to have been satisfied in the context of the three models that will be presented here:

(a) the Greco-Roman world of classical antiquity, which in its late phase coincides with the *Imperium Romanum;*

(b) the *Corpus Christianum* of high and late medieval Europe; and finally

(c) in a smaller measure, but closer to our times, the unification of law in the 19th century central European state formations: in the German Confederation (Deutscher Bund) and the early Bismarck Reich as well as in the Swiss Confederation (Schweizerische Eidgenossenschaft).

2. For these models we shall also require some type of code-key, which will enable us to connect historical findings with contemporary questions.

(a) There is in the first place the concept of the *'supranational'*. Actually, the modern binomial national/supranational attains an exact match only in the third model: in the relations existing between the particular state and the confederacy or federation in the 19th century. In the other models, supranationality signifies only a looser relationship of the particular to the higher unit.

(b) One must also take note of modes of *implementation* of the unification of law. Today we observe processes of legislation or codification by supranational organizations, on the level of a confederation or even a European super-state. Again this criterion is met only in the evolution from the general codes of a confederation to those of a federal state.

(c) As stated earlier, we cannot expect our models to provide guidance as to *contents*. The main reason for this is that at least the first two models represent very different modes of life. These were pre-technical civilizations, which employed only human and animal energy. In such a world, liability for extra-hazardous activities (risks created) and environmental problems would arise only on a small scale, and unification of law could not become an issue. But it may be interesting for the modern observer to note that in antiquity and in the Middle Ages the creation of supra-national law was promoted specifically in relation to trade with distant countries via sea or land, especially regarding risks to ships, freight and money transports, and the distribution or transfer of risk, including liability insurance.

II.

1. As to the first model we shall restrict ourselves, based on source availability, to Greek-Hellenistic-Roman antiquity. Of course, there had been trade on land (at first on a relay basis) and on sea in this geographic area since pre-historic times. Also, we have surprisingly extensive knowledge of ancient oriental law and business records. But secularized processes of lawmaking transcending the old pre-legal protection of this trade through simple barter or religious assurance and practices of hospitality have become apparent only in Greek, Hellenistic, and Roman legal texts. The partners in this supra-regional trade in the Mediterranean were generally city states, namely those of the Greek motherland and, most importantly, the Greek and Hellenistic colonies; later the economically and commercially hellenized Phoenician and Punic trade cities from Tyros and Sidon to Carthage; and finally, in the third century, the forcefully entering city of Rome. Its basis was the export of grain, oil, and foodstuffs by the prospering colonies in Sicily and lower Italy, in the Black Sea area, as well as in Punic Africa, in exchange for the large manufacturing production of ceramics, textiles, tools, weapons, and, last but not least, the works of the fine and applied arts.

2. With regard to the development of supra-national law under these conditions one must keep in mind that the partners were generally citizens of *city states,* in other words of communities whose identity was based on autonomous city statutes. Although the adoption of foreign city charters, e.g. the Athenian by Alexandria, may have eased legal transactions in antiquity as later in the Middle Ages, the settlement of disputes between citizens of different city states was principally a matter concerning the national court of the respective forum. Because the resolution of such conflicts lies in the interest of both cities affected, the legal protection of the foreign trade partners is assured to

the same extent as that of their own citizens in a foreign location. This protection is accomplished mostly in bilateral arbitration agreements, while multilateral compacts (as later in the Hansa) seem to be rarer.

Because of the wide scattering of Greek sources we will focus on the *Roman* law texts, which will, however, provide us with an impression of the total Mediterranean context. Already the Twelve Tables demonstrate equal access to legal transactions and civil procedure for the non-citizen, the *peregrinus* or *hostis* (the 'guest'). They refer to the foreigner characteristically in personal property trade relations, and tend to favor him instead of discriminating against him. The next pieces of evidence are Rome's very old treaties with Carthage, of which at least the second (of 348 B. C.) is well documented as a state and trade treaty between two powerful oligarchically ruled republics. What interests us most in this context is that they contain agreements with respect to their citizens concerning contract forms, contract documentation, and jurisdiction. The last of the early data indicates that Rome introduced a second official vested with jurisdiction over non-citizens, the 'peregrine praetor' *(praetor qui ius dicit inter peregrinos)* at the end of the first Punic war (242 B. C.), which firmly established the city in Mediterranean politics and trade. In taking this step, Rome obviously followed the Greek example of a *xénios kósmos* ('official for foreigners') for litigation between foreigners and for disputes between Romans and foreigners.

3. (a) When we ask how a common supra-regional law could grow from these sources, we must first address a preliminary question, namely, what type of law was it that such courts applied to foreigners? In so doing, we must attempt to separate ourselves completely from our habitual frames of reference. First, there was no private international law, i. e. rules for the application of foreign law by national courts, as were first created by medieval jurists in response to similar needs. Further: even the peregrine praetor does not apply a particular foreign law, not only because he cannot be expected to know it, but also because in Rome he is to exercise *Roman* jurisdiction. There was also no *principle of personality of law,* under which one was subject to the law of one's own tribe or city statutes wherever one went to court, as was the case in the Germanic successor states after the fall of the Roman Empire. Finally: the peregrine praetor could, of course, apply particular Roman *ius civile;* but this was limited to Roman citizens, cf. institutions like *manus*-marriage, emancipation, *sponsio* as an originally sacred promise under oath, or the ancient act of fraternization, which served to establish the agricultural or commercial communal property and partnership between brothers.

(b) In this situation the peregrine praetor, based on his unlimited jurisdiction over foreigners, uses his free discretionary judgement. Understandably, he will often by analogy apply particular Roman law (that is as such reserved for Roman citizens), or create similar business models specifically for foreigners, or insert the fiction *'si civis esset'* ('if he were a Roman citizen') in a form of action that had originally been reserved for citizens. But often he may feel compelled to rely on unwritten but generally acknowledged and practiced custom, legal institutions, and rules of international trade. And in so doing he is clearly on the way to supra-national law. For he finds these customs and rules in the principles of law known to and observed by all civilized peoples. The Romans call these principles *ius gentium* (a term which in contrast to its contemporary European usage does not confine itself to the 'recognized principles of public international law', but also includes universal private law).

This *ius gentium* is not the ideal natural law of the world citizens' state, the *kosmopolis* or the *consociatio humana* of stoic philosophy and Cicero, the powerful legal metaphysics of antiquity that was to become so influential in the occident. It is rather an empirical world exploration, the *historia,* as experienced by the Greek trader and colonist and his companion, the explorer. World-wide experience taught him, for example, that among most peoples bilateral business contracts as well as unilateral promises to pay a debt will be honored on the basis of good faith, and that ownership in personal property may be acquired through simple delivery. In their introductory works the Roman jurists, following the example of Greek ethnographers and comparativists, express this fact in a simple formula: all peoples live partly according to their own particular laws, partly according to universally accepted principles (Gaius Institutes I, 1). Thus the Roman *civitas* also lives partly according to *ius proprium Romanorum* (e.g. *patria potestas, sponsio,* and the ancient fraternization), partly according to *ius gentium* (e.g. property acquisition through simple delivery, formless consensual contracts that encompass the six most important types of exchange of goods and services as well as partnership).

(c) In the course of these developments, this supra-national common law was not recorded, let alone codified, in either Rome or in other parts of the Mediterranean world. This was at least in part due to the fact that for a long time there existed no supra-national legislative power, not even in Rome. But, as is the case today, firm and generally observed usages were created in the areas of maritime and supra-national trade.

It is possible that the most powerful non-Roman trade center, the Hellenistic Rhodes, had recorded such usages, and had even formulated them as city statutes, which as *lex Rhodia* ranged through legal texts for many centuries. But more likely these are general usages that, like the statutes of Ile d'Oléron or the Antwerp-York rule of our time, have become associated with the names of leading trade centers. In any case, they are recognized by trade partners as well as by local courts for foreigners, – even by the supreme jurisdiction of Rome which at the very time of its ascendancy to total, exploitative rule of the Mediterranean adopted from this common law the most important institutions of international maritime law, such as jettison at sea, the maritime loan, as well as the formless trade partnerships and currency-free transfer of payments. Rome's distinctive feature is the unparalleled skill of the Roman legal specialists in integrating these forms with sovereign ease into the grammar of the Roman *ius:* thus charter, piece transport of goods, and passage became part of Roman *locatio conductio,* the maritime loan became *faenus nauticum (pecunia traiecticia)* which had the function of maritime insurance, the transfer payments were accommodated by the ancient Roman *mutuum,* and the supranational trade company by the old tradition of fraternal partnership.

4. So far we have dealt with the supra-national commercial law of the Hellenistic-Roman Mediterranean. Yet regarding unification of law in antiquity, the trained jurist will probably first and foremost think of another process of historical dimension, namely, the expansion of *Roman law proper* within a supra-national Roman Empire. In our view, this process appears to demonstrate the victory of lawmaking by a supra-national super-state over the profusion of mostly ethnically determined laws of particular peoples. Even if this perception is not entirely incorrect, we must part from this established view. In the first place, the advance to the unity of Roman law does not occur directly through legislation, let alone codification, but through a process of personal integration of non-Romans through individual or collective grants of citizenship rights. At the same time, this is not a unification of law through the free consolidation of member states into a higher union, but the evolution of the occupation regime imposed by an expanding city state into a universal empire.

(a) Only in Italy, the core area, may we observe a process similar to the forming of a federal union. There the integration took place partly through the establishment of Roman or Latin colonies, and partly through grants of citizenship to individual municipalities, and it came to a conclusion with the grant of Roman citizenship to all Italics (89 B.C. in the course of the Social War). As a result, Italy virtually became a decentralized Roman unitary state with limited communal autonomy.

In contrast to this development in Italy, the 'occupation regime' of the Roman rulers controlled the provinces until the early Empire period. This implied absolute authority of the Roman *ius publicum* in areas such as public administration, levies and tax laws, public land law, discretionary criminal justice for non-citizens, and, beyond that, principally the supremacy of Rome's jurisdiction. However, Roman private law was in principle *not* applied to non-citizens. Its expansion could only take place through grants of citizenship to privileged groups or to individuals. In the west, these grants led to the acculturation and urbanization of non-Roman (in Roman eyes barbarian) Celtic, Iberian, Germanic, and Numidian tribes and settlements. In the east, they were primarily designed to win the allegiance of the Greek and Hellenistic upper classes to the Roman Empire. The *pax Romana* of the Flavian dynasty, and above all of the adopted emperors of the 'Golden Age of the Antonines', pursued these integration politics with great wisdom and historical success. Their side effect, which was similarly perceived as a privilege, was the enjoyment of Roman private law.

(b) But soon after, the wisely directed integration process ran out of control and 'tipped over' like an over-fertilized lake. In A.D. 212 the Emperor Caracalla granted Roman citizenship to virtually all residents of the *orbis Romanus,* apparently for reasons of fiscal, administrative, and military policy: they were now all citizens, and as such all of them, Romans and non-Romans alike, could be equally exploited as subjects of an expanding coercive state. In this context, only the unification of law is of interest to us. In fact the actions of the Roman authorities and courts did extend Roman private law to the masses of new citizens, and they often mastered this troublesome consequence with passable governmental skill.

The situation became more complicated, for at the end of that same century fundamental changes occurred in the Roman legal system itself, which accompanied the revolutionary reforms of Diocletian and Constantine. They were designed to cope with the great crisis of the third century, and actually accomplished that goal. These changes levelled ancient Roman legal traditions as well as the old local legal institutions and customs of other peoples living in the Roman Empire. At the same time, the local legal substrata ('Volksrecht') began to react to imperial law ('Reichsrecht'): in part because imperial legislation had to take the reality of non-Roman institutions (e.g. family and inheritance laws) into account; in part because local land law and forms of documentation were favorable to the aims of the new coercive state; and finally in part because under the influence of the church, Hellenistic and oriental legal conceptions also began to affect legislation. The result was a true advancement toward unification of law, but one brought about by legislative reaction to the daily troubles of a centralized super-state that found itself in permanent crisis, and one that can definitely not serve as a model for the growing together of a new common legal system on the basis of a voluntary association of components forming a union on a higher level.

(c) At this point, the cultured jurist will certainly raise his eyebrows: was not Justinian's famous codification the final crowning of legal unity in a universal imperial state? The fame is legitimate, the objection is not. Justinian's Digest and his Code are wonderful achievements of an academic and judicial culture in its final stage. But they are clearly not creative legislative accomplishments like the Code Napoléon or even the Austrian General Civil Code (ABGB) and the Prussian Code (Allgemeines Landrecht). They preserve the remains of a long expired legal science and disparate imperial laws of the last three centuries. Justinian's lateborn lawbooks had a far reaching effect on the later revival of the Byzantine Empire and on the southern Slavs and Russians, who had been won over by the Eastern church, and they were to have an immense impact – like that of a time bomb – on Western legal science. But their immediate area of influence soon became limited to the south of the Balkan peninsula, Anatolia, and the Byzantine redoubts in Italy. And even there their actual leverage remained marginal for centuries. Of all historical models for the unification of law on a supra-national level, this one seems furthest removed from being a useful paradigm for the solution of contemporary problems.

III.

We shall now look at the European Middle Ages.

1. For the historically interested jurist of today, the reception of Roman law in *Europe* as a result of the spiritual rediscovery of Justinian's Digests represents a model of progressive unification of a profusion of individual tribal, territorial and city laws. Modern legal historians, however, see this process very differently: as an ideological and intellectual 'revolution of the clerks', which scripturalized, scholarized and rationalized administration, diplomacy, and jurisdiction, thus giving trained professional legal specialists a one-sided as well as effective functional monopoly. Of course, the contents of Justinianic law penetrated all areas in which learned jurists functioned. But this did not necessarily imply unification of law. On the contrary, it remained a firm maxim that the Roman *ius commune* was *subsidiary* to all the narrower legal systems, even if it is true that the learned jurist, according to his understanding of the law, can only perceive documented law (such as statutes and city charters, Sachsenspiegel, Siete Partidas, Bracton's Leges Angliae). The 'revolution of the clerks' laid only a *legal foundation* for later unification: it did not provide a legal metaphysics like natural law or law of reason, but a general consensus-building pragmatic ideology, which rested as much on the group identity, the solidarity, and the mentality of the jurists as on a common grammar of concepts and methods. A substantive unification of law was accomplished only where political forces on the regional, occasionally also on the national level pushed for setting down the law in written form: so in the new legally oriented church of the high Middle Ages, in the ascending nation states of western Europe, especially in England, Castile, and Naples, as well as in the statutes of politically fragmented Italy, and in the city charters and the city charter families of the disintegrating Empire.

2. But there was another sphere in which supra-national law was formed pragmatically and almost uninfluenced by the *ius commune* of the academics. By somewhat broadening an established usage of language we may refer to this sphere as *ius mercatorum* or *lex mercatoria.* These are the international trade and maritime laws that have become supra-nationally acknowledged and

applied by arbitrators and local courts in the trade centers. (The parallels to the supra-national trade in goods and payments in classical antiquity [supra II a] and to the party-created law of today's major contract partners will be obvious.) The sources of this legal sphere were recorded business documents, usages and legal rules, similar to the formulas and usages of modern world trade since 'cif', and 'fob', and the Antwerp-York Rule. The regional centers were the Mediterranean (as apparent in the Catalonian Consolat del Mar and in the statutes and trade agreements of Venice and Genoa with Byzantium); north of the Alps the great arteries of the exchange of goods from the Eurasian landmass to western Europe; in maritime trade from Visby to the bureaus of the Hansa; in the overland trade from Cracow and Prague via Magdeburg and Nuremberg westward as well as southward over the Alps to Venice and finally to the seam-line between maritime trade in the south and north Atlantic, to the river estuaries of the Garonne, the Loire, the Seine, the Schelde, and the Thames (with the laws of Ile d'Oléron and the *lex mercatoria* of the English ports). Similar rules evolved for the transfer of payments in the trade centers of Flanders, northern France, upper Italy, and southern Germany.

3. This *lex mercatoria* constitutes, as is often noted today, the closest paradigm for that type of unification of law which today is realized not through the official lawmaking of delegated bodies of the European Community, but instead through self-regulation by international trade partners. Here as there we find the preponderance of pragmatic trade requirements and the objective conditions of international markets, a free alliance in the absence of organized supranational lawmaking authorities, and the flexibility, rationality, and economy of conflict resolution.

IV.

The historical paradigm for the counterpart, namely unification of law by legislative governmental power, may be found in the last of our three models, that is, that of *German and Swiss legal unification in the nineteenth century.* (The important parallel development in Italy will not be discussed here, for in that case national unity did not develop through federation but through a centralized unitary state.) Since this process is both spatially and temporally much closer to us, my remarks can be briefer.

A distinctive feature of this process is the interweaving of ideological, namely, democratic and national impulses with the substantive needs of a rapidly expanding bourgeois industrial and economic community. In this development, the national-democratic ideology typically *preceded* effective unification of law: for instance in France en route from the projects of the early revolution to the Napoleonic Codes; or in Germany in the course from the codification dispute between Thibaut and Savigny to the precipitous dreams of the Germanists' conventions prior to the March 1848 revolution and of the Paulskirche Assembly, up to the sober and successful work of codification between 1861 and 1896 (1861 Allgemeines Deutsches Handelsgesetzbuch [General German Commercial Code], 1865 Dresdner Entwurf des Obligationenrechts [Dresden Draft of the Law of Obligations], 1873 lex Lasker). A similar process may be observed with respect to Swiss and Italian unification of law. In most cases, drafts and legislation of member states performed a pilot function as, for instance, Bluntschli's Zürcher Privatrechtliches Gesetzbuch (Zurich Civil Code) of 1855/6 or the Sächsische BGB (Saxon Civil Code) of 1863.

V.

In conclusion we shall attempt to deduce from the examined models a *conceptual framework* for delineating the paths that lead to a supra-regional unification of particular legal systems.

1. The first condition was an overarching common legal culture, which was founded not so much on religious, denominational or philosophical legal metaphysics as on a pragmatic minimal consensus concerning the common features of the world one lived in and the advantages of a rapprochement or amalgamation of the regional laws. This requirement was satisfied in antiquity through the empirical *ius gentium* of all civilized societies, in the Middle Ages through the supra-regional trade and economic network, and in the nineteenth century through recognizing the necessity of freedom of movement and trade in an industrial society.

Yet ideological motives, too, fostered unification of law. Thus the Greek cultural ideals and the striving of the Stoa beyond the constrictions of the city states to attain the universality of the *kosmopolis* or the *consociatio humana;* thus in the Middle Ages the idea of the *Corpus Christianum* and the related idea of a Holy Roman Empire; thus in the nineteenth century the idea of 'nation une et indivisible' and the closely related concept of the unmediated relationship of the citizen to his state; thus today the ideas of a united Europe as well as a new community of peoples in the United Nations, both born out of the horrors of the Second World War and the fears of the cold war.

2. Further: Lasting unification of law will evidently succeed only through the free association of the members of a higher alliance: unity can in the long run not be *decreed.* Thus the Napoleonic lawbooks were indeed admirable achievements, in which profound legal erudition was paired with a great vision arising from the beginning of the revolution and with the political acumen of an extraordinary regent – more specifically, as the master-plan of a universal European monarchy, in which the will of the ruler, civil liberties, and human rights would be joined. But they won their well earned role as the core of the most important 'family' of legal systems on the continent only after the fall of Napoleon. In Germany the governments of Prussia, Bavaria, and Baden were

wise enough to maintain this legal heritage; in Italy, Spain, and the Netherlands it was finally secured only by the victory of the constitutional state. (It may be noted in passing that lasting unity of law likewise cannot be decreed tacitly through the exclusive solidarity of an international team of experts, answerable only to themselves.)

3. In relation to the *subject matter* of unification of law, the path has almost always led from the law of the specific supra-regional trade in goods, payments, and credit to the general law of obligations, and only at a later point to land, family property, and inheritance law, all of which are more deeply rooted in the historical, societal, and intellectual traditions and beliefs than are the more flexible and more mobile contract relationships.

This *gradus ad Parnassum* reflects the nature of things and has, therefore, repeated itself in the course of history: in the resistance of local law ('Volksrechte') against the Roman imperial law ('Reichsrecht') in antiquity; in the regional European land, inheritance, and family property laws' opposition to Justinianic law; and as late as in the reservations of member state legislation to contemporary codification. These matters will also offer prolonged resistance to the unification of contemporary European law, to say nothing of global unification, unless they are overcome by ideological and universal revolutions – may they occur with blaring violence or as quietly as in the liberal democracies of the West.

4. Let us take a final look at the *organization* in which the construction of supranational legal systems tends to take place. Naturally, it develops according to the manner and method in which lawmaking generally occurs in the respective legal cultures. If lawmaking is basically entrusted to legal specialists, it will occur principally through academic teaching, university study, opinions, and learned courts, as in the German reception of Roman law and as late as in the Pandectist legal science of the last century. If lawmaking originates with courts enjoying supra-national authority (as in the Oberhöfen [courts of appeal], Schöffenstühle [assessors' courts], admiralty courts, or national and international supreme courts) it will above all be effected through *judicial opinions.* As is well known, lawmaking of this kind can be found extensively in current European Community law. A *lex mercatoria,* in particular, will frequently spread through the adoption of statutes, city charters, usages, model formulas, and clauses from leading centers of trade. If, as today, the member states of a developing supranational unit are pledged to the lawmaking and codification monopoly of the nation state, the temptation will be especially great to hope for unification of law via legislation or codification by a supranational body, in the best case scenario by a confederation. The resulting difficulty that the codification ideal will be unfamiliar to some members of the new community belongs, as is well known, to the most acute problems of European unification of law.

IV. Legal Doctrine as Rational Reconstruction of Law

Countervailing against Environmental Subsidies

By John J. Barceló III*, Ithaca

I. Introduction

This paper deals with a proposal, put forward particularly by staunch environmentalists, to apply national countervailing duty law against countries that "subsidize" their producers through lax environmental standards. Legislation to this effect has been introduced in the United States Congress[1] and advocated in Senate hearings.[2] Professional journals also have carried articles advocating this approach.[3] I believe the proposal is misguided and likely to play into the hands of protectionists without advancing environmental goals significantly. After analyzing how the environmental subsidy concept would fare under existing GATT and United States countervailing duty law, I will describe these new proposals and discuss the problematic nature of using them as a weapon against so-called "environmental dumping". This paper does not oppose all forms of trade sanctions for environmental ends; it opposes only the

---

* A. R. Noll Professor of Law and Director, Berger International Legal Studies Program, Cornell University Law School. I am extremely pleased to be able to contribute to this Festschrift honoring Bob Summers, my good friend and colleague. I owe both a personal and professional debt of gratitude to Bob. He and I joined the Cornell law faculty together in the summer of 1969, but I was a beginning law teacher and he was already an outstanding teacher and scholar. He took an interest in me and my fledgling career (as I have seen him do for many others) and offered invaluable assistance and advice on all things important to a law professor's career – especially scholarship and teaching – and on many aspects of life beyond that. I am grateful that his friendship, advice, and wise counsel have continued uninterrupted since those early years. Bob has been an extraordinary scholar and teacher. Through his unparalleled productivity, creativity, energy, analytical rigor, and breadth of knowledge and interest, Bob has set standards for his colleagues and friends that have made us expect more of ourselves.

1 S. 984, 102d Cong., 1st Sess. (1991), hereafter Boren Bill, reprinted in: Trade and the Environment: Hearings on S. 984 Before the Subcomm. on International Trade of the Senate Comm. on Finance, 102nd Cong. , 1st Sess. pp. 53 - 55 (1991), hereafter Trade and the Environment Hearings.

2 Trade and the Environment Hearings, ibid., at pp. 1 - 5 (opening statement of Max Baucus, Chairman), hereafter Baucus Proposal.

3 T. Plofchan, "Recognizing and Countervailing Environmental Subsidies" (1992), 26 Int'l L. 763; D. Chapman, "Environmental Standards and International Trade in Automobiles and Copper: The Case for a Social Tariff" (1991), 31 Nat. Resources J. 449; K. Komoroski, "The Failure of Governments to Regulate Industry: A Subsidy Under the GATT?" (1988), 10 Hous. J. Int'l L. 189.

concept of treating so-called "lax environmental standards" as an actionable subsidy under national countervailing duty law.

The environmental dumping issue is part of a larger controversy concerning the relationship between environmental and trade policy. Though the linkage between these policies has been clear for years, environmentalists have only recently begun to speak out on trade issues. They were highly vocal on trade policy for the first time during the 1991 United States Congressional debate over whether to grant President Bush "fast-track" authority to negotiate a free trade agreement with Mexico and Canada. Environmentalists opposed the negotiations unless the President promised special attention for environmental issues. In that debate and thereafter, environmentalists and protectionists appeared to join in a classic "Baptist and bootlegger" coalition[4] that threatened President Bush's negotiating authority and that may yet decide whether the final agreement – the North American Free Trade Area (NAFTA) agreement[5] – is approved. To encourage approval, the Clinton administration has negotiated several supplemental agreements to NAFTA, including one on the environment.[6]

In September 1991, not long after the fast-track legislation passed, a GATT panel ruled in favor of Mexico in the famous Tuna-Dolphin dispute.[7] That decision particularly antagonized environmentalists, some of whom castigated the GATT as antiquated, out-of-step, and insensitive to environmental concerns. In the wake of this belligerent environmentalist reaction, GATT has issued an important report on environment and trade[8] and reactivated its task force on the subject. Scholars have also begun to devote increased attention to the trade-environment conflict.[9]

---

[4] The reference is to the supposed coalition in certain southern counties in the United States between teetotalling Baptists and bootleggers to support laws banning the sale of alcohol. See D. Vogel, Discussant's Comments, in World Bank, Discussion Paper No. 159, International Trade and the Environment 245 (1992).

[5] North American Free Trade Agreement, done in triplicate at Washington on Dec. 8, 17, 1992, at Ottawa on Dec. 11, 17, 1992, at Mexico City, Dec. 14, 17, 1992 (1993), 32 I. L. M. 289 (parts 1 - 3 of agreement), (1993), 32 I. L. M. 605 (parts 4 - 8 of agreement), hereafter NAFTA.

[6] Clyde H. Farnsworth, "3 Nations Disagree on Trade", N. Y. Times, May 22, 1993, § 1, at p. 33.

[7] United States-Restrictions on Imports of Tuna: Report of the Panel, GATT Doc. DS 211 R (Sept. 3, 1991), reprinted in (1991), 30 I. L. M. 1598, and 8 Int'l Trade Rep. (BNA) No. 38, at p. 1288 (Aug. 28, 1991), hereafter Tuna Panel Decision.

[8] GATT, Trade and the Environment, in (1992), 1 International Trade 1990 - 91, p. 19.

[9] See, e.g., T. Schoenbaum, "Free International Trade and Protection of the Environment: Irreconcilable Conflict" (1992), 86 A.J. Int'l L. 700; E. Weiss, "Environment and Trade as Partners in Sustainable Development: A Commentary" (1992), 86 A.J. Int'l L. 728; F. Kirgis, "Environment and Trade Measures After the Tuna/Dolphin Decision" (1992), 49 Wash. & Lee L. Rev. 1221; J. Jackson, "World Trade Rules and

For activists concerned about lax environmental standards in foreign countries, countervailing duty law is especially attractive. It is an accepted part of GATT,[10] and its concepts can be made to fit the problem – whether well or wisely is the topic of this article. It is "hard" rather than "soft" law. Procedures are in place, private parties have a right to bring a claim seeking a remedy and the remedy is mandatory (not subject to discretion other than that involved in applying law to facts).[11] The successful claimant wins more than a moral victory; the claimant wins new duties on offending country imports.

By contrast, the recently negotiated NAFTA agreement has no provision for "hard" trade remedies if one of the parties becomes a pollution haven. NAFTA, in Article 1114, contains a hortatory provision saying it would be "inappropriate" for a party to relax environmental standards to attract investment and that a party "should not" waive or derogate from existing standards to attract or retain investment.[12] Breach of this provision, however, brings only bilateral negotiations to correct the situation – or soft law. A countervailing duty regime, on the other hand, would allow a domestic enterprise to complain to national authorities who could impose an offsetting duty against offending imports. While in my judgment the negotiation strategy is a more promising means of actually raising environmental standards – at least as a first step – because it focuses on the real end desired, one can understand why some activists, and certainly protectionists, would prefer a unilateral regime with hard law results.[13]

A countervailing duty remedy may be attractive to activists for another reason – the regime's potential legality under GATT. The controversial Tuna-Dolphin dispute explains why this could be important. The dispute arose when

Environmental Policies: Congruence or Conflict" (1992), 49 Wash. & Lee L. Rev. 1227; "Symposium: Environmental Quality and Free Trade: Interdependent Goals or Irreconcilable Conflict?" (1992), 49 Wash. & Lee L. Rev. 1221.

[10] General Agreement on Tariffs and Trade, opened for signature Oct. 30, 1947, 61 Stat. A3, T.I.A.S. No. 1700. 55 U.N.T.S. 187, hereafter GATT, art. VI; Agreement on Interpretation and Application of Articles VI, XVI and XXIII, Apr. 12, 1979, GATT, 26th Supp. B.I.S.D. 56 (1980) (1979), 18 I.L.M. 579, hereafter Subsidies Code.

[11] See, e.g., 19 U.S.C. §§ 1671 - 1677g (1988) (U.S. countervailing duty law applicable to countries party to the Subsidies Code).

[12] See NAFTA, art. 1114, 32 I.L.M. at p. 642.

[13] Indeed, the Clinton administration sought hard-law trade sactions to enforce the supplemental agreements to NAFTA it championed, including the environment agreement, despite significant opposition from Canada and Mexico. See "Senator Baucus Blasts Canada, Mexico for Opposing NAFTA Trade Sanctions", 10 Int'l Trade Rep. (BNA) 902 (June 2, 1993). The environment agreement finally negotiated allows trade sanctions as an ultimate sanction, but only on United States-Mexican trade, not on Canadian trade, and only on the basis of a trilateral dispute settlement process. See North American Agreement on Environmental Cooperation, Arts. 22 - 36 & Annex 36A, 32 I.L.M. 1482 (1993).

the United States applied its Marine Mammals Protection Act[14] to ban imports of tuna from Mexico. Under the Act the United States may ban the import of tuna caught by methods that simultaneously kill or seriously injure a greater number of dolphins than allowed under United States standards. When the United States banned imports of Mexican tuna because Mexican tuna fishermen killed too many dolphins, Mexico complained to the GATT.

The GATT panel decided that the United States measure violated GATT Article XI, which prohibits quantitative restrictions on imports.[15] The United States had sought to justify the tuna ban under GATT Article III, which allows a country to impose a regulatory restraint on an imported "product" as long as the same restraint is imposed on domestic products. The panel concluded that Article III did not apply because the United States import ban sought to regulate not the product itself – the tuna – but the process used to produce the tuna.

The panel also decided that the United States measure could not be saved by the exceptions in GATT Article XX, paras. (b) and (g). These paragraphs allow a country to use trade barriers "necessary to protect human, animal or plant life or health"; or "relating to the conservation of exhaustible natural resources". The panel reasoned that these provisions were inapplicable because the tuna ban sought to protect dolphins that were outside the territory of the United States. The panel report has never been presented to the GATT Council for approval and thus is not technically authoritative, but it is certain to be influential.

The Tuna-Dolphin panel reasoning would seem to prevent the United States or any GATT country from *banning* imports solely because they were produced in a pollution haven country. But if the United States were to levy a countervailing duty instead, the reasoning of the Tuna-Dolphin case would not be directly applicable. The issue would then be whether such action was authorized under the GATT provisions concerning countervailing duties and subsidies. As we will see, some of the panel's reasoning may be indirectly relevant to that issue, but the decision would not be directly applicable.

Finally, it is important to put the Tuna-Dolphin dispute and the countervailing duty issue into context. There are two fundamentally different pollution problems that bring environmental policy into potential conflict with trade policy: *consumption pollution* and *production pollution*. Consumption pollution refers to pollution generated by the use or consumption of a particular product – for example, automobiles without catalytic converters, piping insu-

---

[14] Marine Mammal Protection Act of 1972, Pub. L. No. 95 - 552, 86 Stat. 1027 (codified with amendments at 16 U.S.C. §§ 1361 - 1362, 1371 - 1384, 1401 - 1407 (1988)).

[15] Tuna Panel Decision, supra, footnote 7.

lated with asbestos, or coal laden with sulfur. The pollution is released where the product is used or consumed. Production pollution refers to pollution generated by a production process – for example, manufacturing plants discharging excessive effluents into the air, or atomic power plants emitting harmful radiation into surrounding communities, or farmers releasing dangerous pesticides into ground and drinking water.

Of course the distinction is not airtight. Much of the pollution generated by a producer's plant comes from "consuming" input products, such as fuel and raw materials. A consumer driving a car to work pollutes the atmosphere as a part of his or her employer's production process. So producers consume and consumers produce. Nevertheless the consumption-production distinction usefully focuses attention on the source of the pollution. A manufacturing plant that produces automobiles creates pollution in a different location and of a different kind from the pollution that will arise when the automobiles themselves are used.

In the case of consumption pollution most trade regimes follow the destination principle, under which the standards of the country of destination would apply. This is the general rule for GATT[16] and the European Community,[17] although the EC is actively pursuing harmonization policies for product standards. In the case of production pollution the regimes are less clear, but decisions like the Tuna-Dolphin case and general principles of territorial sovereignty argue for an origin principle – generally the standards of the country of origin should apply.[18]

The issues discussed in this paper concern production pollution, not consumption pollution. Neither the Tuna-Dolphin case nor countervailing duty law constrains an importing country's freedom to adopt its own environmental protection, health and safety standards for products, whether domestic or imported. If the pollution potential or the safety or health risk is carried in the product itself, the product must meet the importing country's standards. Of course, the existence of diverse and inconsistent standards for internationally traded goods can be a barrier to trade and raises many difficult issues – all beyond the scope of this paper. Here I am addressing the conflicts that arise from inconsistent approaches to production pollution and, in particular, whether countervailing duty laws should be used to combat so-called "environmental subsidies".

---

16 GATT, Article III.

17 Treaty Establishing the European Economic Community, Mar. 25, 1957, 298 U.N.T.S. 11 (entered into force Jan. 1, 1958), art. 36.

18 For a general discussion of the destination and origin principles applied in the context of consumption and production pollution, see J. Barceló, "Subsidies and Countervailing Duties – Analysis and a Proposal" (1977), 9 L. & Pol'y Int'l Bus. 779, at pp. 818 - 21.

II. Environmental Subsidies and GATT

The GATT regulates countervailing duties and subsidies in two places, in the 1947 GATT agreement[19] and in the 1979 Tokyo Round Subsidies Code.[20] GATT Article VI authorizes member states to impose a countervailing duty against imports that have been subsidized – either in the production process (domestic subsidy) or upon export (export subsidy). The duty is limited to the net subsidy benefit the imported product received and can only be levied if subsidized imports cause (or threaten) "material injury" to a domestic industry in the importing country. GATT Article XVI contains provisions directly controlling member state use of subsidies, including obligations to report on their use and to consult with other countries concerning their effects. These are weak obligations; nothing in Article XVI binds parties not to use subsidies. In fact, GATT Article III treats domestic subsidies as entirely legitimate and provides that a party may pay such subsidies only to domestic producers.

These GATT provisions do not actually define the subsidy concept, except in the most general terms. Clearly, under Article VI, member states may countervail against subsidies paid on production as well as on export. They may also countervail against a foreign subsidy even if no GATT provision makes the subsidy illegal. The GATT thus decouples the right to countervail from the rather weak provisions in Article XVI aimed directly at regulating subsidies.

The 1979 Subsidies Code deals both with countervailing duties – sometimes called Track I – and the legality of using subsidies – sometimes called Track II. Track I seeks to prevent abuse of countervailing duties by detailing various procedural safeguards and requirements for finding material injury. Nowhere, however, do the Track I provisions define the term subsidy. Track II, for the first time, expressly prohibits some subsidies, namely export subsidies on non-primary products (non-agricultural products) as defined in an annex list.[21] The common feature of all items on the list is that the subsidy is conditioned on export of the product or export performance.

Track II expressly notes that domestic subsidies ("subsidies other than export subsidies"[22]) are legitimate policy instruments regularly used for various social and economic ends. Parties are only encouraged in hortatory terms to "seek to avoid causing" injury to a domestic industry in another country through the use of such subsidies.[23] Again, nowhere is the concept of a domestic subsidy defined. Also the decoupling of the provisions of Article VI (coun-

---

[19] GATT, supra, footnote 10.

[20] Subsidies Code, supra, footnote 10.

[21] Ibid.

[22] Ibid., art. 11 (1).

[23] Ibid.

tervailing duties) and Article XVI (direct regulation of subsidies) in the original GATT has been retained in the Subsidies Code. At least there is nothing expressly conditioning the Track I right to countervail against a subsidy on a Track II prohibition of that subsidy. Since the Subsidies Code is intended as a further elaboration of the GATT countervailing and subsidies provisions,[24] one must presume that the prior decoupling of GATT Articles VI and XVI is paralleled in the Code through a decoupling of Track I and Track II.

What then of the question whether countervailing against an environmental subsidy would be legal under the GATT and the Code? The answer turns on the meaning given to the concept "subsidy or bounty" in GATT Article VI and Track I of the Subsidies Code. A conservative definition would confine the concept to out-of-pocket government expenditures. This is the approach taken by the European Community in defining the analogous concept of "state aids" in the Rome Treaty. The European Court of Justice has ruled, for example, that a Dutch law fixing minimum prices for certain alcoholic drinks is not a state aid because it does not involve a charge on government funds.[25] Under such an out-of-pocket theory lax environmental standards would clearly not qualify as a subsidy.

States have used broader concepts of subsidy, however. The United States, for example, has long considered special tax breaks for a particular industry to be a subsidy and has countervailed against such practices.[26] To the author's knowledge this practice has never been challenged in GATT. A reduced tax burden is of course not necessarily beyond the reach of the EC "out-of-pocket" theory because it can be characterized as an "indirect" charge on public resources, a forgone collection of tax. Nevertheless, a special tax break for a given industry could also be analogized to a reduced regulatory burden on that industry. Taxes, after all, are often a form of government regulation. To apply this concept to an environmental subsidy, however, one would have to compare the environmental standards for the favoured industry with those applicable to other similarly situated industries in the same country. If environmental subsidies were so defined, I believe countervailing duties to offset them would have a reasonable chance of surviving a GATT challenge.

Most of the proposals in the United States to countervail against environmental subsidies, however, take a different approach. They propose as a benchmark some external standard, such as the environmental requirements

[24] The Subsidies Code is entitled: "Agreement on Interpretation and Application of Articles VI, XVI and XXIII"; see supra, footnote 10.

[25] Case 82/77, Openbaar Ministerie v. van Tiggele, 1978 E.C.R. 25.

[26] See, X-Radial Steel Belted Tires from Canada, 38 Fed. Reg. 1018 (Jan. 8, 1973); Rivers and Greenwald, "The Negotiation of a Code on Subsidies and Countervailing Measures: Bridging Fundamental Policy Differences" (1979), 11 L. & Pol'y Int'l Bus. 1447 at p. 1473.

of the importing country or of a multilateral agreement. While nothing in the GATT expressly forbids such a definition, two features suggest a GATT panel might have difficulty with it. First, it is similar to imposing environmental standards on a country extraterritorially – the very concept the Tuna-Dolphin panel rejected (although in a different context). Second, such a definition would sweep within it such a large range of state regulatory activity that countervailing duties would threaten serious restriction of world trade. That potential in the Tuna-Dolphin case also seemed to exert strong influence on the panel decision.[27] At one point the panel stated: "a contracting party may not restrict imports of a product merely because it originates in a country with environmental policies different from its own."[28] If that principle were transferred to the countervailing duty context, it would bar the countervailing duty proposals under discussion.

III. Environmental Subsidies and United States Countervailing Duty Law

Under existing United States countervailing duty law the same issue of how to define a subsidy would arise. The United States law generally complies with GATT and Subsidies Code requirements, although it contains some unique provisions. The United States statute includes in its definition of countervailable subsidies both export and domestic subsidies. Export subsidies are defined as those listed in the Subsidies Code annex.[29] For domestic subsidies, however, the United States law adds a new concept. It requires that a domestic subsidy must benefit a "specific industry".[30] This specificity test excludes all government programs with a generalized effect throughout the economy, such as public education and public highway programs; police and fire-fighting services; military and diplomatic protection; support for basic research; and so on.

Would the United States' specificity requirement prevent a finding of subsidy in the case of the "external standard" theory applied to pollution haven countries? If the test were whether a statute or regulation appeared on its face to provide benefits "generally available" to all industries, the answer might be yes. But the United States statute was amended in 1988 to define the specificity test as being met if in practice the subsidy is utilized or benefits only a specific enterprise or industry or group of enterprises or industries.[31] Thus, if in practice lax environmental standards benefit only certain pollution-prone industries, the specificity test would probably be met.

---

27 Cf. Tuna Panel Decision, supra, footnote 7, 30 I.L.M. at p. 1620, ¶ 5.27.

28 Ibid., at p. 1622.

29 19 U.S.C. § 1677 (5) (A) (i) (1988).

30 19 U.S.C. § 1677 (5) (A) (ii) (1988).

31 19 U.S.C. § 1677 (5) (B) (1988).

The definition of a subsidy would still remain a hurdle, however, under United States law. The statute speaks of a subsidy "provided or required by government action".[32] It says nothing about *inaction*. Also, nothing in the illustrative list of domestic subsidies in the statute even faintly resembles a concept of subsidy deriving from failure to regulate. The list includes:[33]

(1) provision of capital, loans, or loan guarantees on terms inconsistent with commercial considerations;

(2) provision of goods or services at preferential rates;

(3) grant of funds or forgiveness of debt to cover operating losses ...;

(4) assumption of any costs or expenses of manufacture, production, or distribution.

On the other hand the statute expressly states that the definition of subsidy is not limited either to the language "provided or required by government action" or the illustrative list.[34] Yet no decided case or agency decision has ever extended the subsidy definition to a government's failure to regulate its own industry to the level of some international or other nation's standard. Presumably, doubt that existing United States law could be extended to cover environmental subsidies has led to the proposals for amendments to achieve that end.

IV. Efficiency and Fairness Arguments for Countervailing against Environmental Subsidies

This final section discusses whether GATT and related national laws *should* be amended to permit countries to contervail against environmental subsidies. First I will describe the recent proposals in the United States for such an extension of countervailing duty law. Then I will evaluate the efficiency and fairness arguments that have been advanced to support these proposals.

The proposals fall into two categories depending on how they would fix the benchmark for measuring the existence and the amount of an environmental subsidy. The "unilateralist" proposals would take as the touchstone the environmental standards imposed in the United States on American producers in the same or equivalent industry.[35] The catchphrase here is to "level the playing field". Proposal advocates assert that if American producers must meet

---

32 19 U.S.C. § 1677 (5) (A) (ii) (1988).

33 Ibid.

34 19 U.S.C. § 1677 (5) (A) (1988).

35 See, e.g., Boren Bill, supra, footnote 1, §§ 3 (a), 3 (b) ("The amount ... shall consist of the cost which would have to be incurred by the manufacturer or producer of the foreign articles or merchandise to comply with environmental standards imposed on U.S. producers of the same class or kind of merchandise.").

burdensome and costly environmental standards, it would be unfair to force them to compete with foreign producers operating under non-existent or more lax standards.

The "multilateralist" proposals call for a negotiated Environment Code, patterned on the Tokyo Round Subsidies Code, that would set multilaterally approved environmental standards.[36] The proposals have not been clear as to whether such a code should expressly authorize the use of unilaterally administered countervailing duties against breaches of the negotiated standards, or whether – once such multilaterally approved standards were established – existing countervailing duty laws would apply of their own force to breaches of those standards. Putting this issue slightly differently, the question would arise whether countervailing duties could be imposed against countries not party to the proposed Environment Code. Proposal advocates appear to believe that such duties would be appropriate even against non-parties.

1. The Efficiency Argument

Although "level playing field" fairness arguments dominate the debate over these proposals, efficiency arguments also have surfaced. While I believe the fairness argument is considerably more important, something should be said about the efficiency claim. Advocates have asserted, for example, that failure to impose adequate environmental standards leads to a distortion of production in the country of origin that should be corrected by countervailing duties.[37] This argument is problematic at several levels. Perhaps it arises because "market efficiency" is the holy grail of trade policy and environmental advocates want to meet trade advocates on the latter's own turf. But the efficiency argument is unpersuasive.

Efficiency effects of trade policy can be analyzed from the perspective of either the importing country or the world trading system as a whole.[38] Viewed from the perspective of the importing country, the issue of whether countervailing against foreign subsidies raises or lowers the importing country's welfare has been thoroughly and effectively analyzed by Alan Sykes.[39] Sykes has

[36] See, e.g., Baucus Proposal, supra, footnote 2, at p. 3 ("I believe a GATT environmental code, largely modeled on the current subsidies code, should be negotiated."); Komoroski, supra, footnote 3, also takes a multilateralist approach.

[37] Plofchan, supra, footnote 3, at p. 778 ("[M]ost economic industrial decisions treat environmental costs as externalities not subsequently incorporated into production cost assessments. The countervailing of environmental subsidies should produce the beginning of worldwide internalization of environmental costs into calculations of production costs.").

[38] J. Bhagwati, Fair Trade, Reciprocity and Harmonization: The New Challenge to the Theory and Policy of Free Trade (Col. U. Dept. of Economics Discussion Paper Series No. 604, rev. ed., 1992), pp. 3 - 5.

[39] "Countervailing Duty Law: An Economic Perspective", (1989), 89 Col. L. Rev. 199.

shown that the most probable effect of countervailing duties would be to reduce importing country aggregate welfare; that the special cases in which welfare would be enhanced would not be detectable by reasonable administrative means; and that in any event the cases of welfare enhancement do not depend on the existence of foreign subsidies. These cases would depend instead on the existence of importing country monopsony power in the relevant industry. Thus Sykes rejects efficiency – from the importing country's perspective – as a justification for countervailing against subsidized imports. The basic point here is that cheap imports are generally a boon to an importing country no matter what causes them to be cheap.

Different issues arise, however, if one views the efficiency question from a global point of view. This appears to be the perspective of countervailing duty advocates. They reason from the premise that failure to internalize pollution costs in the production process leads to a distortion or market failure in the country of origin. They argue, in effect, that failure to internalize to the country-of-origin producer the external costs of pollution causes excess production and excess pollution damage in that country (and hence globally).[40] Thus, if we could eliminate this distortion or counterbalance it, global welfare would improve. But this is a problematic argument.

Even if we could establish that lax environmental standards distorted the market in the country of origin, countervailing duties would not be a sensible way to correct the problem. Economists have shown that the "first best" approach to correcting market distortion requires correction as close as possible to the distortion.[41] Thus a first best solution would call for a tax on the country-of-origin producer tied to its pollution output or a regulatory measure requiring the producer to decrease its pollution level. A duty imposed by an importing country misses all the production consumed in the country of origin and that part exported to countries that do not impose countervailing duties. It also opens another distortion (between world price and internal price) in the importing country, which reduces welfare in that country. Moreover, the requirement of material injury in the importing country – which is an element of countervailing duty law – is entirely unrelated to the efficiency goal of forcing producers to internalize pollution costs. Those costs should be internalized whether or not the failure to do so injures producers in the importing country.

Of course, if producer countries responded to imposed or threatened countervailing duties with higher standards or more effective pollution control, this would improve global welfare (on the assumptions made). But if that is the

---

[40] See, Plofchan, supra, footnote 3.

[41] See G. Denton and S. O'Cleireacain, Subsidy Issues in International Commerce (1992), p. 8; H. Johnson, "Optimal Trade Intervention in the Presence of Domestic Distortions", in Trade, Growth and the Balance of Payments, Baldwin et al. (eds.) (1965).

goal, direct negotiations seeking such environmental standards would seem more promising. Moreover, producer countries are likely to see countervailing duties, especially if tied to industry injury, as only thinly disguised protectionism. That could provoke retaliation rather than capitulation on environmental standards. Alternatively, producer countries will simply re-route their exports to countries that do not countervail for environmental purposes.

But even more problematic for the efficiency argument is the pollution-related external cost concept in the first place. The concept presupposes the existence of an objective or universal standard of allowable and disallowable pollution. But no such standard exists. There is no absolute or inherent level of impurities in surrounding air and water from a production process that can be labelled *a priori* an "external cost" imposed on those resources. The issue is always one of alternative uses of the same resources, either by competing producers, or individual residents in urban or rural communities, or nature-loving campers. To require a reduction in effluents emanating from a plant near a natural preserve imposes a cost on that producer and on all those who use the producer's product. Reciprocally, to allow the plant to spew out effluents unchecked imposes a cost on those who prefer an unpolluted natural preserve.

This is an issue that requires a society or nation to make trade offs in uses and to establish values for its own desired level of environmental purity. Not all countries, especially not those in different stages of development, will make the same trade offs. The air over Mexico City may be dirtier than the air over New York City, but that could be the way the Mexicans want it (given the alternatives), and hence talk of a market imperfection or distortion in Mexico would not be meaningful.[42]

Of course, I am not asserting that whatever level of pollution Mexico or any other country experiences at any given time is optimal for that country. A country may be so focused on employment or development goals that it underestimates the costs of pollution until levels become intolerable. Or producers may dominate the political process and skew outcomes to their own advantage and away from the social optimum. Yet even if one believes that producer-biased outcomes are likely in many countries, still there is no objective way of knowing how much pollution is the "right" amount for each country. Social welfare is not necessarily always advanced by shifting more pollution costs to producers under all circumstances. Currently Mexico appears almost desperate to improve Mexico City's air quality; but again, who other than Mexicans themselves can say at what cost, at what speed, and to what level?

---

[42] In fact, however, it seems that Mexico is strongly interested in reducing air pollution in Mexico City. See, e.g., "Mexico; Under A Cloud", Economist, April 4, 1992, p. 51.

The discussion thus far concerns cases in which the pollution is entirely localized within the country of origin. If instead the pollution spills over into a neighboring country, the neighbor has every right to object and seek some accommodation of its interests. If it is unsuccessful in direct negotiations, it may perhaps be justified in retaliating or pressuring the offending country in other ways. But a countervailing duty regime would be a poor form of retaliation or pressure. The cost to be countered through possible retaliation is the direct cost of pollution damage in the retaliating country, not the putative cost savings of producers in the country of origin stemming from lax regulations. Also, retaliation should be premised on the existence of injury to the retaliating country's environment, not on competitive injury to its local producers.

This is not to say, of course, that only environmental injury counts in the neighboring country. Competitive injury also counts and may well require response either internally through adjustment policies or in some cases through trade intervention. But existing safeguard (or escape clause) laws – authorizing trade intervention consistent with GATT Article XIX – are appropriate for such cases.[43] There is no convincing *efficiency*-based reason for a special countervailing duty regime to counteract environmental subsidies where products from foreign "dirty" producers cause competitive injury in another country.

The spillover case could of course involve spillover effects upon the global commons, not just effects upon a single neighboring country. An example would be excessive release of greenhouse gases or anti-ozone chemicals and gases. Here multilateral decision-making – as one finds in the Montreal Protocol[44] – would seem essential to bring the problem under control. In this con-

[43] See the United States escape clause law, 19 U.S.C. §§ 2251 to 2254 (1988).

[44] The Vienna Convention for the Protection of the Ozone Layer was signed in 1985 to respond to concerns about depletion of the ozone layer. The Parties added the Montreal Protocol in 1987 to establish specific targets for the elimination of ozone-depleting substances. Only three years later, in 1990, the Parties convened again to make adjustments and amend the Protocol to take account of newly discovered ozone-depleting substances and new evidence that ozone depletion was progressing faster than originally thought.

The Protocol, as amended, also seeks to influence the environmental policies of States not party to the agreement. Article 4 of the amended Protocol provides for the total ban of exports and imports not only of the controlled substances themselves, but also of products containing controlled substances, to and from States not party to the Protocol. If feasible, Article 4 also contemplates the total ban of imports from States not party to the Protocol of substances produced with, but not containing, the controlled substances.

See generally Vienna Convention for the Protection of the Ozone Layer, Mar. 22, 1985, S. Treaty Doc. NO. 9, 99th Cong., 1st Sess. 22 (1985), (1987), 26 I.L.M. 1529 (entered into force Sept. 22, 1988); Montreal Protocol on Substances that Deplete the Ozone Layer, Sept. 16, 1987, S. Treaty Soc. No. 10, 100th Cong., 1st Sess. 2 (1987) (1987), 26 I.L.M. 1550 (entered into force Jan. 1, 1989); London Adjustments and Amendments to the Montreal Protocol on Substances that Deplete the Ozone Layer, June 29, 1990 (1991), 30 I.L.M. 537, at pp. 539 - 41.

text I would not rule out use of sanctions or other forms of pressure against offending countries if authorized by a multilateral decision to enforce multilateral standards of widespread acceptance. Such a regime would have little in common with countervailing duties unilaterally imposed at the instance of domestic producers claiming competitive injury.

2. The Fairness Argument

The strongest support for countervailing against environmental subsidies comes from those who rely on general fairness norms to urge a "level playing field". They argue that United States producers who must charge higher prices to cover strict United States pollution standards should not lose sales to foreign producers who have lower costs because of lower or non-existent pollution standards.[45]

Perhaps the major objection to this argument is the Pandora's box problem: the inability to constrain the argument within reasonable bounds. If failure to regulate were to be considered a subsidy and each country were free to use its own regulatory standards and requirements (or some supposed multilateral standard[46]) as the benchmark for deciding the existence of such a subsidy, the world would soon be flooded by playing field leveling charges on imports that could bring trade to a halt or seriously impede it.

Burdens or costs are imposed on producers through a wide range of regulatory programs. In worker-related areas there are minimum wage laws, child-labor laws, maximum hour rules, worker safety standards – in the United States stemming from Occupational Safety and Health Administration ("OSHA") regulations – worker compensation schemes and accompanying insurance costs, social security taxes and pension regulations, and even worker rights in labor law. In consumer-related areas there are products liability laws and accompanying insurance costs, and health and safety regulations. In the business, financial and competition fields, there are antitrust laws, securities regulations, corporate minimum capitalization rules, even anti-foreign bribery rules. In the civil rights area there are anti-discrimination laws and regulations. The list is formidable and the cost burdens associated with these regulations surely vary from country to country, perhaps in some cases significantly. Under the level playing field argument presumably extra "fairness" duties

---

[45] See, e.g., Trade and the Environment Hearings, supra, footnote 1, at pp. 50 - 1 (prepared statement of Senator David Boren: "Environmental ... legislation can be costly and may place an American company at an extreme disadvantage in the world marketplace ... [The Boren Bill] allows U.S. companies to level the playing field by removing the cost advantage derived from freedom to pollute"). See also Komoroski, supra, footnote 3, at p. 190.

[46] I say "supposed" because I believe it is unreasonable to assume many such standards could be negotiated anytime soon in a global trade setting.

should be levied at the border to compensate for such cost burdens in all of these areas and any others of a similar nature. Surely this would be a happy day for protectionists and a sad day for consumers.

The GATT and national countervailing duty laws could be amended to include only lax environment standards as a "regulatory failure subsidy". The line could be drawn, but it would be arbitrary. There seems no obvious way to explain why producer burdens from one regulatory scheme are not just as unfair or do not require just as much equalization at the border as those stemming from other regulatory schemes. Indeed, compelled perhaps by the logic of their own argument, some commentators favoring environmental countervailing duties have not blinked at proposing the same solution for worker safety and wage levels.[47]

The fairness argument is often coupled with the claim that disparity in environmental standards will drive producers to relocate from the United States (or other strict standard countries) to lax standard countries. Environmentalists and others have particularly made that claim in United States debates over the proposed free trade agreement with Mexico. Empirical studies so far seem to show that only a limited number of industries would be affected by such pressures.[48] Indeed one would assume that industry relocation, if it occurred or were threatened, would be driven by more than one cost factor.

Suppose, for example, that an enterprise is trying to decide whether and where to relocate an existing plant or where to build a new one. Factors that are bound to influence the decision would include labor costs, availability of skilled labor, the strength of labor laws, the burden of taxes, the general regulatory burden in the country, the ease of travel and communication, the political and economic stability of the country, the availability of capital, the supply of raw materials and so on. Suppose in country "X" some of these factors cut against investment and some cut in favor of it, so that the ledger is evenly balanced. Suppose further that the existence of lower environmental protection costs tips the balance in favor of locating the new (or relocated) plant in country X. Is it meaningful or fair to focus exclusively on the environmental cost savings as the decisive factor in the investment calculus?

---

47 Chapman, supra, footnote 3, at p. 460.

48 See 9 [Current Reports] Int'l Trade Rep. (BNA) 2182 - 83 (Dec. 23, 1992) for a report of a study by Glenn Harrison, Professor of Economics at the University of South Carolina, which identifies four industries (chemicals, paper, petroleum and coal, and primary metals) as incurring at least 60% of the pollution-abatement costs in the United States and hence as likely to find lower pollution-abatement standards attractive. This is not, of course, the same thing as saying that pollution abatement costs are such a large part of total operating costs in these industries that they would actually choose to relocate to lower-standard countries.

All the factors mentioned, and others not listed, would surely have influenced the decision. Suppose some of the factors in X, such as the tax burden and political and economic stability, compare unfavorably to those factors in the United States. How should that be accounted for in analyzing whether country X has given an environmental subsidy to attract investment? Should the lower environmental protection costs be offset by the higher taxes and unstable economic and political climate? Why does fairness call only for a comparison of environmental protection costs?

It is true that in a few industries lax environmental standards may be so important as to play a dominant role in pressures to relocate enterprises, and in those industries there may be strong pressures in the United States to resist higher environmental standards or actually to lower existing standards.[49] This seems at least a theoretical possibility, even if recent studies tend to conclude that relocation for environmental reasons is likely to be an insignificant phenomenon.[50]

Even if such conditions existed in a few industries, that would not justify an across-the-board countervailing duty regime applicable in all cases of disparate environmental protection costs. Instead, it might argue for a special effort on the part of governments in high-standard countries to influence the government in, say, country X to raise its environmental standards for the industries in question, especially where X's standards are unreasonably low. If X's standards are truly unreasonable, there should be political gains to the government of X in raising them. Higher standards in X, rather than blocked imports from X, would be in everyone's interest.

If all else fails, if the industries in question are of sufficient importance (taking into account, among other things, the dislocation costs industry migration would cause), and if there is convincing evidence of likely migration, high-standard countries might be justified in seeking a remedy. For one thing, migration to pollution-haven countries could be seen as wasteful if one assumes that unreasonably low-standard countries will eventually succumb to steadily growing global and local political pressures to upgrade standards. I believe the preferred remedy would be for high-standard countries to subsidize their own enterprises to keep them in place.

Domestic subsidies have been shown by economists to be more efficient than trade interventions as instruments for retaining domestic production.[51] Trade intervention would only seem supportable as a last resort if domestic subsidies were politically unachievable. The difficulty of making the required

[49] Ibid.

[50] See BNA report, ibid., citing Harrison as claiming that in the context of NAFTA, "the plausible size of the migration [for environmental reasons] is of the second order of smalls".

[51] See Barceló, supra, footnote 18, at pp. 790 - 1 and sources cited therein.

decisions sketched above, the current evidence that the migration risk is low, and the danger of protectionist capture of the process would argue against any form of subsidy or trade intervention remedy, or at least would justify a heavy burden of persuasion before such actions were taken. In any event the anti-migration regime just contemplated is quite distinct from a countervailing-duty scheme.

It is true that the problem of regulatory-burden influence on competitiveness will increase as countries enter regional integration pacts that tear down other barriers to commerce and investment; it will become more pronounced globally if integration under GATT proceeds far enough. Increasingly, attention will turn to the influence of the regulatory milieu on new investment decisions, plant relocations and the pattern of trade. If the example and experience of the European Community is any guide, increasingly there will be demand to harmonize disparate regulatory practices – including environmental regulation. Dispute resolution procedures will be required and presumably some form of enforcement mechanism. But again the emphasis should be on achieving harmonized standards – as it is in EC law – and not on trade remedies for perceived abuses and certainly not on countervailing duties.[52]

V. Conclusion

This paper has argued that existing provisions of the GATT, the Subsidies Code and national legislation – at least in the United States – would probably not authorize countervailing against environmental subsidies. Thus, amendment of the GATT and national legislation would be necessary to put such a regime in place. At the same time, the paper has argued that neither efficiency nor fairness arguments make a persuasive case for such a regime.

The paper does not rule out the possibility that some form of retaliation or pressure – even involving trade intervention – might be needed and appropriate in dealing with environmental pollution that crosses national boundaries to injure either neighboring countries directly or the global commons. But this would be much more *ad hoc* and limited than an across-the-board countervailing duty regime, and the focus should be upon avoiding environmental harm, not competitive injury. Moreover trade intervention even in this context should be a last resort. The emphasis should be on multilateral standards and decision-making – at least in the global commons case – and the overriding goal should be adoption of appropriate and effective environmental standards in the offending countries. A countervailing duty law, by contrast, is likely to serve protectionism more than environmentalism.

[52] Countervailing duties are not permitted on intra-EC trade.

Good Faith Performance of Contracts in Late Twentieth-Century American Law

By Robert A. Hillman, Ithaca*

In the early and mid-twentieth century, courts imposed an obligation of good faith performance and enforcement of contracts in many American cases and in various contexts.[1] Robert S. Summers gathered and analyzed relevant cases in his seminal 1968 article, *"Good Faith" in General Contract Law and the Sales Provisions of the Uniform Commercial Code.*[2] Summers found that the decisions ruled out various types of bad faith performance, including "evasion of the spirit of the deal; lack of diligence and slacking off; ... and interference with, or failure to cooperate in, the other party's performance."[3] Courts also excluded inappropriate conduct involving "the assertion, settlement, and litigation of contract claims and defenses."[4] Such conduct included "asserting an overreaching or 'weaseling' interpretation or construction of contract language; taking advantage of another's necessitous circumstances to secure a favorable modification; ... and abusing a power to determine compliance or to terminate a contract."[5]

In light of the breadth of contexts in which courts employed good faith and the variety of conduct it ruled out, Professor Summers concluded that the principle has no general meaning of its own. Instead, the principle excludes various forms of inappropriate conduct depending on the context.[6] As such, good faith is a "safety valve" employed directly by judges to ensure a minimal level of fairness in the contracting process.[7]

Professor Summers saw that the "excluder" approach to good faith conferred on judges considerable (although not unbounded[8]), discretion to determine the conduct to be ruled out in a case and therefore might not appeal to

---

* Associate Dean for Academic Affairs and Professor of Law, Cornell Law School.

[1] Robert S. Summers, The General Duty of Good Faith – Its Recognition and Conceptualization, 67 Cornell L. Rev. 810, 812 (1982) [hereinafter General Duty].

[2] 54 Va. L. Rev. 195 (1968) [hereinafter Good Faith].

[3] Summers, General Duty, supra note 1, at 813.

[4] Id.

[5] Id.

[6] See Summers, Good Faith, supra note 2, at 199 - 207.

[7] Summers, General Duty, supra note 1, at 811 - 812.

[8] See generally id.

those preferring certainty in contract law. Yet, Summers correctly observed that no positive definition of good faith was possible because the concept did not lend itself to that kind of conceptualization:[9] The good faith obligation is "an unusually 'circumstance-bound' requirement, and excludes highly varied forms of bad faith, many of which become identifiable only in the context of circumstantial detail of a kind that defies comprehensive formulation in a single rule."[10] The task for judges, then, is to generate criteria for determining bad faith in particularized contexts and to formulate rules barring specific kinds of bad faith.[11]

In 1979, the American Law Institute promulgated section 205 of the *Restatement (Second) of Contracts,* which set forth an obligation of good faith performance in every contract.[12] Largely influenced by Professor Summers' analysis, Professor Braucher, the section's principal drafter,[13] did not attempt to define good faith. Instead Braucher acknowledged that

> "[t]he phrase 'good faith' is used in a variety of contexts, and its meaning varies somewhat with the context. ... Good faith performance or enforcement of a contract ... excludes a variety of types of conduct characterized as involving 'bad faith' because they violate community standards of decency, fairness or reasonableness.[14]

Not only has Professor Summers' analysis influenced the *Restatement (Second)* approach to good faith, courts expressly follow it as well.[15] In case after

---

[9] Id. at 817 - 821.

[10] Id. at 821.

[11] Id. at 822.

[12]. Restatement (Second) of Contracts § 205 (1979) provides: "Every contract imposes upon each party a duty of good faith and fair dealing in its performance and its enforcement."

[13] Summers, General Duty, supra note 1, at 810.

[14] Restatement (Second) of Contracts, § 205 Comment a.

[15] A sample of recent cases bears out this observation. See, e.g., Tymshare, Inc. v. Covell, 727 F.2d 1145 (D.C. Cir. 1984) (then Judge Scalia agreeing with the "excluder" analysis); Carma Developers, Inc. v. Marathon Dev. Cal., 2 Cal. 4th. 342, 372, 6 Cal. Rptr. 2d 467, 484 (1992) ("Instead of defining what is consistent with good faith and fair dealing, it is more meaningful to concentrate on what is prohibited"); Price v. Wells Fargo Bank, 213 Cal. App. 3d 465, 479, 261 Cal. Rptr. 735, 741 (1989) ("The term 'good faith' has been described as an 'excluder' phrase which is 'without general meaning (or meanings) of its own ...'"); Centronics Corp. v. Genicom Corp., 562 A.2d 187, 191 (N.H. 1989) (Souter, J.) ("The differences between the obligations of good faith ... are enough to explain why the commentators despair of articulating any single concept of contractual good faith, even after the more than fifty years of litigation following in the wake of the American common law's first explicit recognition of an implied good faith contractual obligation ..."); Nolan v. Control Data Corp., 243 N.J. Super. 420, 579 A.2d 1252 (1990) (quoting favorably from Tymshare, Inc. v. Covell's discussion of Summers); Best v. U.S. Nat'l Bank, 303 Or. 557, 562, 739 P.2d 554, 557 (1987) ("Because [good faith] must be applied to the entire range of contracts, definitions of good faith tend to be either too abstract or applicable only to specific contexts."); Garrett v. Bankwest, Inc., 459 N.W.2d 833, 841 (S.D. 1990) (good faith's meaning "varies with the context").

case, courts characterize good faith as an excluder with no general meaning of its own, cite Summers in support, and isolate criteria for determining bad faith in the context before them.[16] In light of the validity and acceptance of the conceptualization, analysts should seek to aid the effort by helping to formulate the criteria and, ultimately, the rules for defining bad faith in particular circumstances.

In just such an effort, I analyze in this essay some important recent good faith cases arising in a few of the contexts isolated by Professor Summers. I will consider the kinds of conduct that should be excluded as bad faith when a party allegedly asserts an overreaching interpretation of a contract clause or fails to cooperate in another's performance. These categories require distinguishing the laudable exercise of one's contract rights on the one hand and engaging in "sharp" practices on the other. They also raise the larger question of whether good faith reinforces freedom of contract or supports principles legitimizing judicial intervention in agreements. The topics therefore bring into focus fundamental issues of late twentieth-century American contract law.

I. Asserting an Overreaching Interpretation of a Contract Term

Several recent good-faith cases involve claims of bad faith arising when a contracting party exercised what appeared to be an express contract right. In two cases, involving remarkably similar facts (somewhat simplified here for discussion), a written employment contract entitled an employee-sales representative to commissions on sales in excess of certain quotas. Nevertheless, the contract also expressly permitted the employer to raise the sales quotas retroactively without notice and reason and thereby to slash the employee's compensation. Not surprisingly, in both cases, the employee claimed the employer exercised the power in bad faith to deprive the employee of earned compensation.[17] In another case, depositors' account agreements permitted their banks to set fees for checks written on insufficient funds. The depositors brought a class action against the banks alleging the banks acted in bad faith by setting the fees too high.[18]

Can the doctrine of good faith apply when a party exercises what appears to be an unfettered contract right? Under the excluder analysis, the question is whether such conduct can ever be ruled out as bad faith. Professor Summers

[16] See cases cited supra note 15.

[17] See Tymshare, Inc. v. Covell, 727 F.2d 1145 (D.C. Cir. 1984) (employer had unlimited discretion to modify or terminate employee's compensation plan in its "sole discretion"); Nolan v. Control Data Corp., 243 N.J. Super. 420, 579 A.2d 1252 (1990) (employer reserved the right to "make any retroactive, current and/or prospective adjustments or revisions to salaries, bonuses, [or] incentive compensation levels").

[18] Best v. U.S. National Bank, 303 Or. 557, 739 P.2d 554 (1987).

observed that asserting an "overreaching" interpretation of a contract term could be bad faith. But how could an employer's or bank's interpretation "overreach" if the contract expressly authorized the party's actions?[19]

Because of the elasticity of language, courts have largely abandoned the "plain meaning" rule of contract interpretation, which bars extrinsic evidence in determining a contract's meaning.[20] Mainly to support reasonable reliance on contracts, courts also interpret contract language according to a reasonable person's understanding – a party's actual intentions do not control.[21] Applying these principles to the sales-quota cases, for example, the question becomes whether an employer's retroactive alteration of its employee's sales quotas and compensation contradicted the employee's reasonable expectations, as determined in light of all admissible extrinsic evidence.[22] If so, the employer would assert an "overreaching" interpretation by claiming the contract authorized its actions.

Courts confronting such questions have recognized that even a clause purporting to grant sole power to a party does not necessarily permit the party to exercise the power "for any reason whatsoever, no matter how arbitrary or unreasonable."[23] Such an interpretation would likely contradict the other party's reasonable expectations because it would deprive that party of the fruits of the contract. In the case of a provision affording an employer "sole discretion" to alter sales quotas, for example, then Judge Scalia,[24] speaking for the court in *Tymshare, Inc. v. Covell,*[25] stated:

> [A]greeing to such a provision would require a degree of folly on the part of these sales representatives we are not inclined to posit where another plausible interpretation of the language is available. It seems to us that the 'sole discretion' intended was discretion to determine the existence or nonexistence of the various factors that

[19] "We are aware of no reported case in which a court has held the covenant of good faith may be read to prohibit a party from doing that which is expressly permitted by an agreement." Carma Developers, Inc. v. Marathon Dev. Cal., 2 Cal. 4th. 342, 374, 6 Cal. Rptr. 2d. 467, 485 (1992).

[20] See, e.g., Edwin W. Patterson, The Interpretation and Construction of Contracts, 64 Colum. L. Rev. 833, 838 - 842 (1964); Restatement (Second) of Contracts § 212 (1) and comment b (1979).

[21] See, e.g., Hotchkiss v. Nat'l City Bank, 200 F. 287, 293 (S.D.N.Y. 1913) (Learned Hand, J.). "We ask judges or juries to discover that 'objective viewpoint' – through their own subjective processes." Zell v. American Seating Co., 138 F.2d 641, 647 (2d Cir. 1943) (Frank, J.), rev'd, 322 U.S. 709 (1944) (per curiam). See also Charles Fried, Contract as Promise: A Theory of Contractual Obligation 82 (1981).

[22] "[T]he mere recitation of an express power is not always the test" of whether the parties left the decision to alter quotas to the absolute and "uncontrolled discretion" of the employer. Tymshare, Inc. v. Covell, 727 F.2d 1145, 1153 (D.C. Cir. 1984).

[23] Id. at 1154; Nolan v. Control Data Corp., 243 N.J. Super. 420, 433 - 434, 579 A.2d 1252, 1259 (N.J. Super. 1990).

[24] Judge Scalia is now Justice Scalia of the United State Supreme Court.

[25] 727 F.2d 1145 (D.C. Cir. 1984).

> would reasonably justify alteration of the sales quota. Those factors would include ... an unanticipated volume of business from a particular customer unconnected with the extra sales efforts of the employee assigned to that account; and ... a poor overall sales year for the company, leaving less gross income to be expended on commissions. ... But the language need not (and therefore can not reasonably) be read to confer discretion to [increase] the quota for any reason whatever – including ... a simple desire to deprive an employee of the fairly agreed benefit of his labors.[26]

Not surprisingly, many courts appear to agree with the above reasoning.[27] The approach appeals to a sense of justice, and by invoking the parties' intentions, it also theoretically preserves contractual freedom. But some also believe that determining the parties' expectations objectively "expand[s] the scope of 'consent' far beyond anything remotely close to what the parties had in mind."[28] Instead, the reasonable expectations test licenses courts to import interventionist principles such as fairness and justice. Did Judge Scalia decide what good faith ruled out, not on the basis of the parties' view of the meaning of the sales-quota adjustment clause, but according to the dictates of fairness and the like? More generally, does good faith rule out conduct based on the parties' intentions or according to societal values?

One response is that the issue is relatively unimportant – generally courts reach the same result under either approach.[29] Basically Judge Scalia reasoned that the parties probably did not intend to permit the employer to reduce the employee's compensation retroactively and arbitrarily because a reasonable employee would not agree to such an onerous provision.[30] Reasonable parties, in other words, intend to incorporate the meaning of terms society would find fair and just.

Although contracting parties may often tend to agree on relatively fair terms, the characterization of good faith matters. For example, whether an employer can *ever* in good faith exercise a clause expressly authorizing it to

---

[26] Id. at 1154. The reasoning is similar when the issue is a bank's right to set NSF fees: "[D]iscretion had to be exercised within the confines of the reasonable expectations of the depositors." Best v. U.S. Nat'l Bank of Oregon, 303 Or. 557, 564, 739 P.2d 554, 558 (1987).

[27] See, e.g., Best, 303 Or. 557, 739 P.2d 554 (1987). But see Corenswet, Inc. v. Amana Refrigeration, Inc., 594 F.2d 129 (5th Cir. 1979), cert. denied, 444 U.S. 938 (1979) ("for any reason" termination clause means any reason a franchisor deemed sufficient).

[28] Ian R. Macneil, Contracts: Adjustment of Long-term Economic Relations Under Classical, Neoclassical, and Relational Contract Law, 72 Nw. U.L. Rev. 854, 883 (1978).

[29] See, e.g., Mkt. Street Assocs. v. Frey, 941 F.2d 588, 596 (7th. Cir. 1991) ("[W]hether we say that a contract shall be deemed to contain such implied conditions as are necessary to make sense of the contract, or that a contract obligates the parties to cooperate in its performance in 'good faith' to the extent necessary to carry out the purposes of the contract, comes to much the same thing.").

[30] Tymshare, Inc. v. Covell, 727 F.2d 1145, 1154 (D.C. Cir. 1984).

eliminate an employee's gains arbitrarily depends on the source of good faith law. Suppose the contract in *Tymshare* expressly permitted management to change the sales quotas at any time "for the sole purpose of reducing or eliminating the employee's earned commissions." Suppose further that the employer points out and explains the legal effect of the clause before an employee signs the contract. Later the employer seeks to exercise the clause for the purpose expressed. Although we may be repulsed by such conduct, good faith should not apply if good faith excludes only conduct outside of the employee's reasonable expectations, because the employee should have reasonably expected the employer's actions. Of course, such a clause may be unenforceable on other grounds, such as unconscionability.[31] But that doctrine may not always apply, for example, because the parties may enjoy equal bargaining power. Good faith may be determinative.

My guess is that many courts faced with such harsh facts would find bad faith. If I am correct, good faith is not always tied to the parties' intentions. Instead, it can rule out conduct based on considerations of fairness and justice. Some courts may directly import these interventionist principles.[32] Other courts may engage in impressive judicial acrobatics to fit good faith within an assent framework, and then find bad faith.[33] In fact, some might claim that Judge Scalia's reasoning in *Tymshare* is itself an example of the latter.[34] After all, the contract appeared to authorize the employer's nasty behavior (recall that it permitted the employer to alter the quota plan "within [its] sole discretion"). Nevertheless, the judge reasoned that the employer could not in good faith reduce the sales quota arbitrarily because the parties did not intend to give the employer that power. By stretching assent beyond its natural limits in hard cases, courts may do more harm to the rule of law than by acknowledging the interventionist nature of good faith.[35]

This is not to say that good faith invariably utilizes outside principles. Freedom of contract remains an important goal of contract law, and courts do not lose sight of it even in good faith cases. Nevertheless, fairness in the contracting process is another important contract aim. Good faith reflects this dichotomy. It sometimes rules out conduct based on the parties' expectations, either express or implied. It also excludes conduct abhorrent to society.

---

[31] Id. at 1152 n. 5. See generally, Robert A. Hillman, An Analysis of the Cessation of Contractual Relations, 68 Cornell L. Rev. 617, 648 - 650 (1983).

[32] See, e.g., Best v. U.S. Nat'l Bank, 303 Or. 557, 565, 739 P.2d 554, 559 (1987) ("When a party has the contractual right to specify a price term, the term specified may be so high or low that the party will be deemed to have acted in bad faith regardless of the reasonable expectations of the other party.").

[33] Mkt. St. Assocs. v. Frey, 941 F.2d 588 (7th. Cir. 1991).

[34] Compare the court's reasoning in Corenswet, Inc. v. Amana Refrigeration, Inc., 594 F.2d 129 (5th Cir. 1979), cert. denied, 444 U.S. 938 (1979) ("for any reason" termination clause means any reason a franchisor deemed sufficient).

[35] See Summers, Good Faith, supra note 2, at 226 n.288.

From what has been said, we can now begin to formulate criteria for defining the behavior to be ruled out when a party allegedly asserts an overreaching interpretation of an express contract clause. Does the conduct deprive a party of the fruits of the contract? Is the motive of the party engaging in the conduct to deprive the other party of those fruits? Does contract language, interpreted objectively and in light of all the circumstances, bar such conduct? Is the conduct fair? If the answer to the first two questions and either the third or fourth question is "yes," good faith rules out the conduct.

II. Failing to Cooperate

Much modern contracting involves multiple interactions between familiar parties over an extended time period.[36] In light of the likelihood of changed circumstances, the parties to such agreements rarely draft complete agreements and, instead, rely on norms such as cooperation, flexibility, and trust to govern their relation.[37] The doctrine of good faith supports such arrangements by ruling out behavior that conflicts with these norms even when the contract does not expressly forbid the behavior and even when the conduct would not constitute fraud.[38] At the same time, parties to long term contracts generally do not owe each other a fiduciary duty – a duty to put the other's interests first.[39] The challenge for courts is to determine when a party's conduct, although between the extremes of fraud on the one hand and the violation of a fiduciary duty on the other, sufficiently offends to be characterized as bad faith.

Consider the following problem based on a major recent case.[40] Seeking to develop its property, a landowner enters a sale and leaseback arrangement with a large finance company. The agreement entitles the lessee (the former landowner) to request the lessor (the finance company) to finance improvements on the land and calls for good faith negotiations toward that end. If the negotiations fail, the lessee can repurchase the property from the lessor at a price based on a computation set forth in the agreement. Later, the lessee decides to seek financing, but not from the lessor. The lessee is unable to secure financing, however, because it does not own the land. The lessee therefore seeks to repurchase the property from the lessor, but the latter's price is too high. The lessee then realizes the formula for establishing the repurchase

---

36 Robert A. Hillman, Court Adjustment of Long-Term Contracts: An Analysis Under Modern Contract Law, 1987 Duke L.J. 1, 4 - 6.

37 Ian R. Macneil, Values in Contract: Internal and External, 78 Nw U.L. Rev. 340 (1983).

38 Mkt. St. Assocs. v. Frey, 941 F.2d 588 (7th. Cir. 1991).

39 Id. at 593.

40 Id.

price under the sale-leaseback agreement is very favorable, about one-third of the lessor's current asking price and below market value. The lessee also understands that it must request financing from the lessor before the repurchase option matures. The lessee also realizes that the lessor does not recall the agreement's repurchase option. The lessee therefore requests financing "pursuant to the lease," but never calls to the lessor's attention the repurchase provision.[41] In fact, the lessee hopes the lessor will reject the request. Does good faith rule out the lessee's conduct?

The lessee has no fiduciary duty to call the repurchase option to the lessor's attention.[42] Nor does anything in the parties' contract require the lessee to remind the lessor of this key term. Nevertheless, the question is whether a court should read such a requirement into the agreement on the basis of the good faith principle. Judge Posner responded affirmatively in *Market Street Associates v. Frey.*[43] Far from demonstrating the expansiveness of good faith, however, the judge strenuously flexed his muscles to convince that the parties' "constructive" intentions controlled.

Acknowledging the realities of long-term contracting, Judge Posner theorized that contracting parties impliedly condition their performance on cooperation from their counterpart because express provisions become "progressively less apt" as time passes.[44] The duty to cooperate thus "give[s] the parties what they would have stipulated for expressly if at the time of making the contract they had had complete knowledge of the future" and encountered no transaction costs.[45] Judge Posner concluded that tricking the lessor into selling the land to the lessee runs afoul of the duty to cooperate because it "would be the type of opportunistic behavior in an ongoing contractual relationship" that the parties would never have authorized.[46]

Judge Posner located the good faith obligation to cooperate as "halfway between a fiduciary duty ... and the duty merely to refrain from active fraud."[47] He knew this, not because good faith interjects moral and ethical principles into the law, but because the concept "is a stab at approximating the terms the

---

41 Id. at 591. The lessee wrote to the lessor-finance company "to ask again that you advise us immediately if you are willing to provide the financing pursuant to the lease." Id.

42 Id.

43 941 F.2d 588 (7th. Cir. 1991). In the actual case, the court reversed a summary judgment in favor of the lessor. Judge Posner, for the court, remanded for a determination of the facts. In dicta, he suggested that if the facts were as set forth in this essay, he would find bad faith.

44 Id. at 595 - 596.

45 Id. at 596.

46 Id.

47 Id. at 595.

parties would have negotiated had they foreseen the circumstances that have given rise to their dispute."[48]

The parties very likely never considered whether their lease included a duty to cooperate by reminding the lessor of its rights. Nevertheless, by tying the duty to the parties' presumed preferences, Judge Posner's conceptualization attracts admirers of contractual freedom. The problem with the analysis is that one suspects the parties likely would *not* have included a duty to remind if they had considered the matter. After all, the lessor was a large, experienced finance company, exceedingly familiar with sale-leaseback arrangements. The lessor, "an immensely sophisticated enterprise,"[49] surely would have assumed the responsibility for understanding its rights and obligations under the lease.

Despite his protestations, Judge Posner's real agenda may have been to advance his economic analysis.[50] He notes that good faith does not require "altruistic" behavior when the other party "gets into trouble in performing."[51] Otherwise, a party would be excused whenever a difficulty arose. On the other hand, a contracting party cannot "take deliberate advantage of an oversight by [a] contract partner concerning his rights under the contract. Such taking advantage [is] sharp dealing."[52] The latter should not be condoned because "it has no social product, and also like theft it induces costly defensive expenditures, in the form of overelaborate disclaimers or investigations into the trustworthiness of a prospective contracting partner."[53] In a nutshell, condoning the lessee's conduct would increase unnecessary "defensive expenditures."[54]

In reality, then, we must add to reasonable expectations and fairness an additional source of good faith as it is applied by courts: instrumental policy such as economic efficiency.[55] As with cases involving an "overreaching" interpretation of a contract term, good faith here reflects contract law's complexity and richness.

Again, let us conclude by suggesting criteria for defining the behavior to be ruled out in failure-to-cooperate cases such as *Market Street Associates*. Several factors control. Was the lessee aware of the repurchase provision and its effect? Was the lessee aware that the lessor had overlooked the term and would have acted differently had it been cognizant of the provision? Is the

---

48 Id.

49 Id. at 597.

50 See Richard Posner, Economic Analysis of the Law (3d ed. 1986).

51 Mkt. St. Assocs v. Frey, 941 F.2d at 594.

52 Id.

53 Id.

54 Id.

55 I leave for another day whether this is an appropriate factor and whether Judge Posner applied it correctly.

effect of the lessor's oversight a material windfall for the lessee? Does the lessee's conduct therefore conflict with the lessor's reasonable expectations? Is it unfair? Is it inefficient?[56] If the answer to each of the first three questions and any of the last three questions is "yes," good faith excludes the lessee's strategy.

Conclusion

Professor Summers' excluder analysis has withstood the test of time. Courts continue to utilize his analysis almost twenty-five years after he published it. His conceptualization underscores the expansiveness of the good faith principle. Recent cases reinforce this truth. Courts invoke fairness and social policy, even as they insist that the doctrine reflects the parties' expectations.

[56] Again, I leave for another day whether economic efficiency is an appropriate factor in good faith cases.

On the History of Justification and Excuse in Cases of Necessity*

By Joachim Hruschka, Erlangen

Current discussions among criminal law theorists of the difference between justification and excuse[1] were preceded by similar discussions among eighteenth century practical philosophers. The latter drew exceptionally lucid distinctions, which are still most valuable as they reduce the question at issue to its logical core. They also reveal that more is at stake than merely the justification-excuse distinction. Indeed, eighteenth century philosophers grasped the fundamental distinction between what today is referred to as "decision rules" and "conduct rules".[2] They recognized that justifications, as opposed to excuses, are part of the rules of conduct and furthermore that decision rules must be divided into two groups, each relating to a different level of imputation.

The purpose of this article is to provide an historical account of the development and import of these distinctions during the eighteenth century. It begins with an analysis of the Plank of Carneades case that Friedrich Gentz, a student of Immanuel Kant's, provided in 1793. At that time, the plank case had been

* This paper is based on an article of mine on the same subject, published in Goltdammer's Archiv für Strafrecht 138, 1 (1991). I would like to thank Sheila O'Laughlin for the translation of an earlier draft of the paper and Sharon Byrd for her most helpful comments.

1 George P. Fletcher, Rethinking Criminal Law 759 - 875 (1978); Paul Robinson, Criminal Law Defenses 1, 83 - 101 (1984); Glanville Williams, Textbook of Criminal Law (2d ed. 1983). – B. Sharon Byrd, 'Wrongdoing and Attribution: Implications beyond the Justification-Excuse Distinction', Wayne L. Rev. 33, 1289 (1987); Joshua Dressler, 'New Thoughts About the Concept of Justification in the Criminal Law: A Critique of Fletcher's Thinking and Rethinking', UCLA L. Rev. 32, 61 (1984); George P. Fletcher, 'The Right and the Reasonable', Harv. L. Rev. 98, 949 (1985); Kent Greenawalt, 'The Perplexing Borders of Justification and Excuse', Colum. L. Rev. 84, 1897 (1984); Miriam Gur-Arye, 'Should the Criminal Law Distinguish Between Necessity as a Justification and Necessity as an Excuse?', Law Q. Rev. 102, 71 (1986); Donald L. Horowitz, 'Justification and Excuse in the Program of the Criminal Law', Law & Contemp. Probs. 49, 109 (1986).

2 Meir Dan-Cohen, 'Decision Rules and Conduct Rules: On Accoustic Separation in Criminal Law', Harv. L. Rev. 97, 625 (1984); see also George Fletcher, Rethinking Criminal Law 491 - 92, who uses the terms "question of wrongdoing" and "question of attribution" to express this distinction; and with slightly different expressions, Paul Robinson, 'Rules of Conduct and Principles of Adjudication', U. Chi. L. Rev. 57, 729 (1990).

the paradigmatic example of necessity for centuries. Gentz's analysis reveals a clear recognition of the difference between justification and excuse (Part I). The sources of the justification-excuse distinction lie in the natural law doctrine of the seventeenth and eighteenth centuries (Part II). As early as 1754, Joachim Georg Daries, a philosopher and authority on natural law, distinguished three different cases of necessity, thereby connecting each of these cases to a separate type of defense to a criminal charge. One of them is the typical case of justification, which Daries clearly saw as being a rule of conduct. Two of these defenses regard what are now called "decision rules", or "rules of imputation" (Part III). Kant's own analysis of the Plank of Carneades case in 1797 is based on these distinctions. It indicates that, from a logical point of view, justifications and excuses cannot belong to the same class of rules within a legal system (Part IV).

I. Gentz's Analysis of the Plank of Carneades Case

In his 1793 article 'Commentary on Professor Kant's Raisonnement on the Relationship between Theory and Practice'[3] Friedrich Gentz criticizes his former professor's essay 'On the Common Saying: That May be True in Theory, But is of No Practical Use'[4], published only a few months earlier. In this article Gentz comments on revolutions:

> Whenever and amid whatever manifold of conditions . . . we encounter examples in history of small or large, specific or general, popular rebellions we can always assume, without danger of error, that as a consequence the *Law* has been violated. The diversity of circumstances in which a rebelling nation found itself results merely in a diversity of excuses for the unlawful action. The decision to push an enemy with whom one occupies a narrow plank after shipwreck into the sea rather than to surely drown, is indeed never *justified,* but probably will be *excused* (since in extreme danger one would have to be heroic to respond to the call of duty). Similarly, although it always remains *unlawful,* it can still be considered very *pardonable,* when a nation provoked to the extreme by tyranny casts off its yoke in rebellion. However, that which mankind *forgives* can never be a rule in a system of *Law,* and nothing within the theory of state may contradict the concept of Law. Consequently, it must be maintained absolutely: that a rebellion against the lawful sovereign, even if induced by inhumane oppression and bloody tyranny, is an impermissible action.[5]

[3] Friedrich Gentz, 'Nachtrag zu dem Räsonnement des Hrn Professor Kant über das Verhältniß zwischen Theorie und Praxis', Berlinische Monatsschrift 22, 518 (J. E. Biester ed., 1793); also published in: Kant / Gentz / Rehberg: Über Theorie und Praxis, 89 (Dieter Henrich ed., Frankfurt am Main 1967).

[4] Immanuel Kant, 'Ueber den Gemeinspruch: Das mag in der Theorie richtig sein, taugt aber nicht für die Praxis', Berlinische Monatsschrift, 22, 201 (1793) (hereinafter cited as ‚Theory and Practice'); also published in Kant's gesammelte Schriften, 8, 273 (Preußische Akademie der Wissenschaften, and other Academies, ed.; hereinafter cited as A. A.).

[5] "So oft und unter so mannigfaltigen Umständen uns in der Geschichte die Beispiele von kleineren oder größeren, spezielleren oder allgemeineren Volksempörungen

Interesting here is not Gentz's position on the right to rebel, but rather the distinction between justification and excuse. It is this distinction which makes his position possible, and he employs it as a matter of course. "Justification", according to Gentz, implies that a prima facie unlawful act, when reconsidered, proves not to be unlawful afterall. Consequently, the absence of a justification means that the deed which at first seems unlawful, remains unlawful under closer examination. In contrast an "excuse" presupposes the unlawfulness of a deed, including the absence of a justification. An excuse is granted when one pardons the perpetrator for the act, when one forgives him. The act excused is not "permitted" or "allowed", for every permission or allowance is the basis of a justification. According to Gentz, a permission, and therefore a justification, would be a rule that belongs to the "system of Law". A rule that is the basis for forgiveness, however, necessarily lies outside of this system.

The example Gentz uses to demonstrate the difference between justification and excuse is a classic one, which, according to the depiction of Lactanz, was raised for discussion by Carneades.[6] At least since its treatment in Samuel Pufendorf's *De Jure Naturae et Gentium* of 1672,[7] the example has been standard in European legal literature. And at least since that time, it has been common to speak of cases like the Plank of Carneades case as "casus necessitatis".[8] The works of Pufendorf served as the decisive incentive for discourse on cases of necessity during the following centuries.[9] In particular, Pufendorf raised the question of whether a "jus" or a "favor necessitatis" should be recognized.[10] The solution offered by Gentz in the plank case implies that the

---

begegnen mögen, können wir, ohne alle Gefahr zu irren, immer sicher annehmen, daß das Recht dabei verletzt worden sei. Die Verschiedenheit der Lagen, in welchen rebellierende Völker sich befanden, wirkt bloß eine Verschiedenheit in den Entschuldigungsgründen für die widerrechtliche Handlung. Denn so, wie der Entschluß, einen Feind, mit dem man sich im Schiffbruch auf einem schmalen Brette befände, lieber in die See zu stoßen, als unvermeidlich selbst unterzugehen, zwar nie *gerechtfertigt* werden, wohl aber (weil in der äußersten Not schon Heldenmut dazu gehört, sich bloß von Pflichtbegriffen leiten zu lassen) *Entschuldigung* finden wird, ebenso bleibt es zwar immer *unrechtmäßig*, kann aber für sehr *verzeihlich* gelten, wenn eine durch Tyrannei aufs äußerste gebrachte Nation ihr Joch durch einen Aufstand abschüttelt. Da jedoch das, was man der Menschheit *nachsieht,* nie zur Regel in einem System der *Rechte* werden kann, dem Begriff des Rechts aber in der ganzen Staatstheorie nichts widersprechen darf, so muß es schlechterdings dabei bleiben: daß eine Rebellion gegen das rechtmäßige Oberhaupt, wäre sie gleich durch die unmenschlichste Bedrückung und durch die blutigste Tyrannei veranlaßt, eine unerlaubte Handlung ist." Berlinische Monatsschrift, 545 - 46; Kant / Gentz / Rehberg, 106 - 7 (emphases in the original).

6 L. Caelius Firmianus Lactantius, Divinae Institutiones, Lib. V Cap. 16, Opera Omnia, Pars I, 451 (Samuel Brandt & Georg Laubmann eds., Pragae, Vindobonae, Lipsiae MDCCCLXXXX).

7 Samuel Pufendorf, De Jure Naturae et Gentium libri octo, Lib. II Cap. III § 11 (here cited in the editio secunda, Francofurti ad Moenum MDCLXXXIV).

8 The expression "casus necessitatis" e.g. in Samuel Pufendorf, De Officio Hominis et Civis libri duo, Lib. I Cap. V § XVIII (Londini Scanorum MDCLXXIII).

9 See e.g. Hans Welzel, Die Naturrechtslehre Samuel Pufendorfs, 89 et seq. (1958).

actor does not have the right to push the other from the plank, or in the language of Pufendorf, a jus necessitatis does not exist. Yet there remains a favor necessitatis with which the act, which remains unlawful for lack of a right of necessity, can be forgiven. In the terminology used by Gentz himself: necessity provides the actor not a justification, but rather an excuse.

II. Natural Law Authorities on Justification and Excuse

Gentz's analysis of the plank case presupposes the availability of the pertinent concepts. The clear distinction he draws between the notions of justification and excuse and its consequences for solving cases such as the plank case demand an understanding of the distinction's exact nature within given sets of legal or moral rules. Although the words "justification" and "excuse" or their counterparts in other European languages had been in use for some time, the interrelationship of the corresponding concepts was initially unclear. Interesting is the development preceding Gentz's own work that led to the use of the words "justification" and "excuse" in a way that corresponds to modern terminology.[11]

Excuse, the older of the two concepts, traces back to ancient moral philosophy and Roman law. The concept of justification had also been commonly understood at the time Gentz wrote. Hugo Grotius used it in 1625 quite prominently at the beginning of the second book of *De Iure Belli ac Pacis*. Grotius discusses in great length the question of how a war can be justified. One must understand that the latter concept includes private wars, which we today no longer refer to as "wars", but rather as cases of "self-defense". In this context Grotius introduces the term "causa justifica",[12] which, in his famous French rendition of 1724, Jean Barbeyrac translates as "la Raison justificative".[13] Grotius' authority, and that of his translator, brought about a rapid recognition of this concept during the eighteenth century. Consequently, Gottfried

---

[10] See e.g. the titel of Lib. II Cap. VI in Samuel Pufendorf, De Jure Naturae et Gentium: "De Jure et Favore Necessitatis".

[11] The fact that the words "justification" and "excuse" can be employed without the distinction between the pertinent concepts being clearly understood is illustrated quite well in the discussion of necessity in Regina v. Dudley and Stephens, 14 Q.B.D. 273 (1884): "Now it is admitted that the deliberate killing of this unoffending and unresisting boy was clearly murder, unless the killing can be *justified* by some well-recognised *excuse* admitted by the law. It is further admitted that there was in this case no such *excuse* unless the killing was *justified* by what has been called 'necessity'." (emphases added).

[12] Hugo Grotius, De Iure Belli ac Pacis libri tres, Lib. II Cap. I § I, 167 (B. J. A. de Kanter-van Hettinga Tromp ed., Lugduni Batavorum MCMXXXIX).

[13] Le Droit de la Guerre et de la Paix. Par Hugues Grotius, Nouvelle Traduction, par Jean Barbeyrac ... Avec ... de nouvelles Notes du Traducteur. Tome Premier, 203 (Amsterdam MDCCXXIV).

Achenwall had no difficulty speaking of "caussa iustifica" or "ratio iustifica" in his *Ius Naturae* published during the 1750's and 1760's. Achenwall even uses the term "ratio justifica" to describe the permission to intrude upon the legally protected interests of an innocent third party in a situation of necessity,[14] thereby severing it from its initial connection with the notion of self-defense.

De Jure Belli ac Pacis is also relevant for the actual differentiation between justification and excuse. Grotius writes "necessitas si non defendit tamen excusat", "if necessity does not defend, it nevertheless excuses".[15] The relationship between "defensio" and "excusatio" in this passage is admittedly rather opaque. Furthermore, the relationship between "defensio" here and "causa justifica" at the beginning of the second book of Grotius' work is left to one's imagination. Pufendorf does not provide any better clarification. In reference to the plank case he says what is more excused than approved ("adprobatur") because of necessity, should certainly not be understood as a general rule of action.[16] Thus Pufendorf merely replaces Grotius' "defensio" with "adprobatio", and fails to comment on the relationship between what is approved and excused. Nor do Pufendorf's other discussions of the concept of necessity shed light upon this relationship. Barbeyrac, however, translates the Grotius' text with the words "la Nécessité, qui fournit toujours, sinon dequoi se justifier entiérement, du moins dequoi s'excuser",[17] thereby equating "defensio" with "bringing a causa justifica to bear" and using the expressions "justifier" and "excuser" contrastively. Indeed it is most probable that this translation is the source of the common eighteenth century practice of making a joint reference to "justification" and "excuse". In 1780, Ludwig Julius Friedrich Höpfner, for example, explains that he intends "neither to justify nor to excuse" the publication of his writings on natural law.[18] Additional examples of this usage can also be found in the writings of other German lawyers,[19] although the practice is not limited to Germany. Francis Hutcheson's remarks

---

[14] On Achenwall's "Sola laesio [est] caussa iustifica coactionis" see Gottfried Achenwall, Ius Naturae, § 260 und 265 (editio sexta emendatior, Gottingae MDCCLXVII); cf. also § 260 in each of editio quarta emendatior, Gottingae MDCCLVIII, and editio quinta emendatior, Gottingae MDCCLXIII. On "ratio iustifica" for ius eminens, see Gottfried Achenwall, Iuris Naturalis pars posterior § 146 (editio quarta emendatior. Gottingae MDCCLVIIII; editio quinta emendatior. Gottingae MDCCLXIII; editio sexta emendatior, Gottingae MDCCLXVIII).

[15] Grotius, De Iure Belli ac Pacis, Lib. III Cap. XI § IV Nr. 7, 744.

[16] Pufendorf, De Jure Naturae et Gentium, Lib. II Cap. III § 11: "quod per necessitatem ... magis excusatur, quam adprobatur, hautquidquam in communem agendi regulam esse trahendum."

[17] Barbeyrac, supra note 13, at 864, No. 4.

[18] Ludwig Julius Friedrich Höpfner, Naturrecht des einzelnen Menschen, der Gesellschaften und der Völker, preface to the first ed. 1780, 1 (Gießen 5th ed. 1790).

[19] See e.g. the letter by Ernst Ferdinand Klein to Kant dated December 22, 1789, A.A. 11, 117 - 8; Paul Johann Anselm Feuerbach, Revision der Grundsätze und Grundbegriffe des positiven peinlichen Rechts, VI, 103 (Erster Theil Erfurt 1799).

on the good, though not sufficiently good, consequences of an action: "they may extenuate the guilt, but do not justify the action",[20] remind us again of Barbeyrac's translation of Grotius, which was famous not only in Germany, but in Scotland as well.[21]

A passage in Alexander Baumgarten's *Initia Philosophiae Practicae Primae*[22] of 1760 is also interesting in this context. Baumgarten offers the distinction between "imputatio facti" and "imputatio legis", "imputation of the deed" and "imputation of law." He understands imputatio legis explicitly as "applicatio legis ad factum, s[ive] facti sub lege subsumptio" or "application of the law to the deed or subsumtion of the deed under the law".[23] When a court, a "forum externum", undertakes an imputatio legis, reasons could indicate that the law, either entirely or partially, should not be applied to the deed in question. In particular, these reasons could be given even though the elements of the deed satisfy the definition of an offense. When arguments are presented, according to which the law cannot be attributed at all, Baumgarten speaks of an "exculpatio", while he uses "excusatio" when arguments are presented according to which the degree of attribution of the law is reduced.[24] Grotius' juxtaposition of "defensio" and "excusatio" is easy to recognize in this text. In light of Barabeyrac's translation and common usage in the second half of the 18th century, it also makes sense to translate Baumgarten's "exculpatio" and "excusatio" with "justification" and "excuse".

Achenwall's *Ius Naturae* and Baumgarten's *Initia Philosophiae Practicae Primae* are the sources of Gentz's concepts, for Kant used these works as the basis of his lectures on natural law, practical philosophy, and moral philosophy, and Gentz attended Kant's lectures in Königsberg.[25] Kant's own copy of

[20] Francis Hutcheson, A System of Moral Philosophy, I (published from the original Manuscript, by his son Francis Hutcheson London MDCCLV); here cited from Collected Works of Francis Hutcheson, Facsimile Editions V, 231 (Bernhard Fabian ed., Hildesheim 1969; hereinafter cited as Collected Works). Cf. also Francis Hutcheson, An Inquiry into the Original of our Ideas of Beauty and Virtue (London MDCCXXV) (Collected Works, I, 156 (1971)).

[21] Barbeyrac, however, may be not the only source of Hutcheson's remark since William Hawkins, followed by Adam Smith half a century later, made the distinction between "justifiable" and "excusable homicide" as early as 1716. – See William Hawkins, A Treatise of the Pleas of the Crown, Book I, 69 et seq. (In the Savoy 1716); correspondingly in 3rd ed., 69 et seq. (MDCCXXXIX), and Adam Smith, Lectures on Jurisprudence, The Glasgow Edition of the Works and Correspondence of Adam Smith, V, 111 (report dated 1762 - 1763) and 477 (report dated 1766) (R. L. Meek, D. D. Raphael & P. G. Stein eds., Oxford 1978).

[22] Alexander Gottlieb Baumgarten, Initia Philosophiae Practicae Primae (Halae Magdeburgicae 1760); also published in A. A. 19, 7 et seq.

[23] Id. at § 125.

[24] Id. at § 195 - 98.

[25] On Kant's relation to Gentz, cf. the editor's introduction in Immanuel Kant, Kleinere Schriften zur Geschichtsphilosophie, Ethik und Politik (Karl Vorländer ed. 1913) (unaltered reprint, Hamburg 1964 XXXI - II).

the *Initia* shows that he translated Baumgarten's "exculpatio" with "justification".[26] Gentz seems to have taken even the plank case from Kant, as Kant often discusses the example, for instance in his essay 'Theory and Practice' in 1793,[27] to which Gentz then responded in his article.

III. Daries' Differentiation Between Three Types of Necessity

Although the explanation of Gentz's terminology seems to be satisfying at first sight, problems remain with his thesis "that which mankind forgives can never be a rule in a system of Law." If one takes the thesis seriously, the rules of excuse form a system of their own, which is not to be confused with the system of Law concerning rights, duties and justifications. Even though this consequence is possibly indicated by Pufendorf in the passage quoted above,[28] it is expressed by neither Achenwall nor Baumgarten. On the contrary, Baumgarten's juxtaposition of "exculpatio" and "excusatio" suggests that both defenses belong to one and the same set, the difference lying exclusively in that an "exculpatio" totally excludes imputation, whereas an "excusatio" merely limits it. According to Baumgarten, an "exculpatio" and an "excusatio" are "exceptiones in iure", or exceptions to the rule of an otherwise certain application of a law in its entire force.

Indeed several years before publication of Baumgarten's *Initia* Joachim Georg Daries had already recognized that the systematic problems connected with the notions of justification and excuse do not lend themselves to analysis

[26] A. A. 19, 88, line 2: "Rechtfertigung". – Naturally Kant was familiar not only with the concept of excuse but also with the terminology corresponding to that concept which was in use at the time he wrote. In a passage contained in notes taken of Kant's lectures, and completely in accordance with Kant's theory in "The Metaphysics of Morals", which will be discussed infra, one finds: "The fragility and infirmity of mankind can only be considered in judging other people's actions. I myself, with regard to my actions, need not rely on them (i. e. on the fragility and infirmity of mankind), in order *to excuse* them (i. e. my actions)." ("Die Fragilitas und Infirmitas humana kann nur blos um andrer Menschen Handlungen zu beurtheilen in Betrachtung gezogen werden, ich selbst muß in Ansehung meiner Handlungen nicht auf dieselbe rechnen, und dadurch dieselbe *entschuldigen.*") A. A. 27.1, 295 (Moralphilosophie Collins; emphasis added). For almost identical language, see A. A. 27.2.2., 1443 (Moral Mrongovius). Both passages refer to Baumgarten's § 198. See also Paul Menzer, Eine Vorlesung Kants über Ethik, 81 (II. ed. Berlin 1925); A. A. 27.2.1., 570 (Metaphysik der Sitten, Vigilantius). The extent to which Kant used language in his lectures similar to our own, although not as terminologically entrenched as our's, can also be seen from the following: "Blameworthiness presupposes an unlawful action." ("Eine Schuld sezt immer ein Unrecht zum voraus.") A. A. 27.1, 155 (Praktische Philosophie, Powalski).

[27] Berlinische Monatsschrift, 22, 257; A. A. 8, 300. On Kant's treatment of the Plank of Carneades cf. also A. A., 19, 268 - 69; 27.1, 191 (Praktische Philosophie, Powalski) and 378 (Moralphilosophie, Collins); A. A. 27.2.1, 513 - 14, 516 and 599 - 600 (Metaphysik der Sitten, Vigilantius); A. A. 27.2.2, 1353 (Naturrecht, Feyerabend); 1509 (Moral, Mrongovius); Menzer, supra note 22, 196 - 7.

[28] See supra note 16 and accompanying text.

on the basis of a mere division between "imputatio facti" and "imputatio legis" as Baumgarten thought. In his *Observatio* on necessity of 1754,[29] Daries refers to Cicero and his differentiation between "necessitas simplex seu absoluta" and "necessitudo cum adiunctione", simple or absolute necessity and limited necessity. For Daries a status necessitatis simplicis is defined through the actual exclusion of every possible resistance and, consequently, through the impossibility of choice. On the other hand, in status necessitatis cum adiunctione the possibility of choice is presupposed. Consequently, the rule "necessitas non habet legem" (necessity has no law) in its strict sense is valid only for the first status, while for the latter status it has no validity, except perhaps in a very restricted sense.

Subsequently, Daries differentiates between two possibilities of necessitas cum adiunctione. He proceeds from the principle that those duties are to be fulfilled both in normal life and in situations of necessity which best serve the highest goal of human actions[30] (whatever that may be). Accordingly, the first group of cases of necessitas cum adiunctione consists of those acts in necessity which violate a particular law, but still correspond with this highest principle. The second group of cases consists of those acts in necessity which not only violate a particular law, but also contradict the highest principle. In the first group, an "exceptio secundum leges instituta" is granted to the actor because his act is in accordance with the system of law. Whereas in the latter cases it is only an "exceptio contra leges instituta" which can be granted since the act is in opposition to the system of law.[31] Daries then refers explicitly to Grotius' distinction between "defensio" and "excusatio".[32] His own reflections imply that two different "defensiones" can be raised in a situation of necessity. A necessitas simplex provides such a defensio. The same is true of a necessitas cum adiunctione, when the deed accords with the highest goal of human actions. On the other hand, a necessitas cum adiunctione provides us with an "excusatio" when the deed is contrary to that goal, but is committed out of momentary fear. In this respect, Daries' division is more differentiated than Barbeyrac's and Baumgarten's. He in fact recognizes a total of three types of cases: (1) cases of necessitas simplex which provide a "defensio" because resistance was physically impossible, (2) cases of necessitas cum adiunctione which provide a "defensio" – not because resistance was impossible, but rather because the deed complies with the highest principle of human actions, and (3)

[29] Joachim Georg Daries, Observationes Iuris Naturalis, Socialis et Gentium, II, Observatio LI (Ienae 1754). On the text to follow, cf. in particular § I, IV, V, X, XV, XX, XXI, XXII, XXV.

[30] On the highest principle, see id. Observatio L § L and Observatio LI § XV.

[31] Id. Observatio LI §§ XX - XXII.

[32] Id. Observatio LI § XX: "Duos esse favoris necessitatis generatim sumti effectus, aut enim, ut cum Grotio loquar, nos defendit aut excusat."

cases of necessitas cum adiunctione which do not provide the perpetrator with a "defensio", but rather with only an "excusatio".

The trichotomy of the concepts "imputatio facti", "adplicatio legis ad factum" and "imputatio iuris": "imputation of the deed", "application of the law to the deed" and "imputation of the law"[33] provides the background for these considerations. According to Daries imputation of the deed, or "the declaration that someone is the author of the deed", precedes the application of the law to the deed whereas imputation of the law, or "the judgment as to the merit or demerit of the deed", succeeds the application of the law.[34] The sequence entails that imputation of the law is not identical with, but rather different from the application of the law to the deed and its possible result. Consequently, the judgment that an act is contrary to duty is not identical with, but different from the assumption of demerit. The former is indeed a necessary condition for the latter.[35] In this respect Daries' concept of imputatio iuris differs from Baumgarten's concept of imputatio legis. Whereas Baumgarten equated the imputation of the law with the application of the law to the deed, Daries clearly distinguished the two. In current terminology, Daries' two levels of imputation correspond to two types of decision rules, one indicating when to attribute an act to a particular actor and the other indicating when to attribute blame to that actor for his unlawful act. On the other hand, Daries' concept of law that is applied to a deed, in contrast to the rules of imputation, corresponds to the system of conduct rules, telling us what is prohibited and permitted under the law.

Employing this trichotomy, one sees that a defensio in necessitas simplex cases indicates that the imputatio facti, or imputation of the deed, is impossible. The person involved has not "committed" the act in question, and consequently nothing exists to which the law can be applied. A defensio in necessitas cum adiunctione case signifies that the deed is in accordance with the highest principle of law. It is equivalent to a justification and hence excludes the applicatio legis ad factum. An excusatio in necessitas cum adiunctione case presupposes the applicability of the law to the deed and simultaneously requires that the deed be freed from the consequences of its unlawfulness. Accordingly, an excusatio raises the issue of imputatio iuris, or more exactly, that of the judgment as to the demerit or blameworthiness of the deed. Daries drew a previously neglected distinction between three basically different groups of necessity, thereby differentiating between three possible defenses to

33 Daries, Institutiones Iurisprudentiae Universalis, Pars Generalis, § 225 scholion (Jenae 1740); id., Observatio XLII § XXI.

34 Daries, Institutiones, Pars Generalis § 213 and § 218.

35 On this distinction generally, see my 'Anhang II. Zur Entdeckungs- und Rezeptionsgeschichte der Unterscheidung von imputatio facti und imputatio iuris', Zeitschrift für die gesamte Strafrechtswissenschaft 96, 692 (1984), and my 'Imputation', Brigham Young Univ. L. Rev. 1986, 669.

a criminal charge, namely the two types of defensio and the possible excusatio. This differentiation was made possible through two more fundamental distinctions, the distinction between the two levels of imputation on the one hand and the distinction between both levels of imputation and the application of the law to the deed on the other.

IV. Kant's Analysis of the Plank of Carneades Case

One must be aware of Daries' contribution when interpreting Kant's renewed and elaborate comments on "ius necessitatis" in *The Metaphysics of Morals* of 1797.[36] "This imagined right", Kant says, is supposed to "be permission to take the life of another person when my own life is in danger, even if he has done me no harm." Clearly "a jurisprudential self-contradiction must be involved here," since the point in question "has nothing to do with an *unjust* assailant on my life, which I defend by taking his (ius inculpatae tutelae)," but rather "with the permission to use violence against someone who himself has not used it against me." Therefore, it is quite obvious that the "allegation" of a right based on necessity "is not to be understood objectively according what the law prescribes, but rather subjectively as the sentence would be cast before a court of justice." Namely, "no *penal law* can exist that awards the death penalty to a man who, having been shipwrecked and finding himself suspended in the same life threatening situation as another, pushes the other off the plank in order to save himself." "For the threat of punishment in the law could not be greater than the threat of loss of life." "Such a penal law", he continues, "can never have the intended effect, for the threat of an evil (being condemned to death by a court) that is *uncertain* cannot exceed the fear of an evil (namely drowning) that is *certain*." "Thus the act of violent self-preservation is not to be judged as *inculpable* (unsträflich) but only as *impunible* (unstrafbar), and this *subjective* impunity, through the astonishing confusion of legal scholars, is held to be *objective* (according to the law)." "The motto of the right of necessity is 'necessity has no law' (necessitas non habet legem); but still there cannot be any necessity that will make what is unjust, lawful",[37] even though

[36] Immanuel Kant, Die Metaphysik der Sitten, A.A. 6, 203.

[37] Id. at A.A. 6, 235 - 36: "Dieses vermeinte Recht soll Befugnis sein, im Fall der Gefahr des Verlustes meines eigenen Lebens, einem anderen, der mir nichts zuleide tat, das Leben zu nehmen. Es fällt in die Augen, daß hierin ein Widerspruch der Rechtslehre mit sich selbst enthalten sein müsse: – denn es ist hier nicht von einem *ungerechten* Angreifer auf mein Leben, dem ich durch die Beraubung des seinen zuvorkomme (ius inculpatae tutelae), die Rede, . . . sondern von einer erlaubten Gewalttätigkeit gegen den, der keine gegen mich ausübte. Es ist klar, daß diese Behauptung nicht objektiv, nach dem, was ein Gesetz vorschreiben, sondern bloß subjektiv, wie vor Gericht die Sentenz gefällt werden würde, zu verstehen sei. Es kann nämlich kein *Strafgesetz* geben, welches demjenigen den Tod zuerkennte, der im Schiffbruche, mit einem anderen in gleicher Lebensgefahr schwebend, diesen von dem Brette, worauf er sich gerettet hat, wegstieße, um sich selbst zu retten. Denn die durchs Gesetz angedrohte

that which one "must judge as unjust in itself may be treated with indulgence in a court of justice".[38]

This passage essentially distinguishes between justification and excuse, albeit without using this terminology. Moreover, it explains clearly enough that an excuse does not, in the language of Gentz, belong to the "system of Law". Lastly, it gives reasons why a court of justice pardons the perpetrator in the plank case.

First of all Kant, using a term common at the time: "ius inculpatae tutelae", recognizes self-defense as a justification. From the context it follows that a deed committed in self-defense would be "inculpable". In the legal discourse immediately preceeding Kant, the Latin equivalent of this word – "inculpabile" – was used to express the lawfulness of an act. In a lecture on Achenwall's *Ius Naturae,* Kant himself explained[39] that "a Factum", or a deed, is either "culpabile or inculpabile". It is "culpabile when it is not in accordance with the law", and thus it follows that it is "inculpabile" when it is pursuant to the law. Kant, therefore, understandably translated Baumgarten's "exculpatio" as "justification".[40] Accordingly, someone acting in self-defense would have an "exculpatio". On the other hand, in the plank case the perpetrator does not have an "exculpatio", instead his deed is a "factum culpabile". However, Kant does provide an argument for him that leads to the exclusion of criminal punishment. An argument of this kind is equivalent to an "excusatio", or an excuse.

According to Kant, a justification is "to be understood objectively", which means that it is part of "what the law prescribes". "To prescribe" must be understood here as indicating prescriptive language, and thus is meant in the broadest sense of the word to include not only laws of command or prohibition, but also laws of permission.[41] In the retrospective, a justification corres-

Strafe könnte doch nicht größer sein als die des Verlustes des Lebens des ersteren. Nun kann ein solches Strafgesetz die beabsichtigte Wirkung gar nicht haben; denn die Bedrohung mit einem Übel, was noch *ungewiß* ist (dem Tode durch den richterlichen Ausspruch), kann die Furcht vor dem Übel, was *gewiß* ist (nämlich dem Ersaufen), nicht überwiegen. Also ist die Tat der gewalttätigen Selbsterhaltung nicht etwa als *unsträflich* (inculpabile), sondern nur als *unstrafbar* (impunibile) zu beurteilen, und diese *subjektive* Straflosigkeit wird durch eine wunderliche Verwechslung von den Rechtslehrern für eine *objektive* Gesetzmäßigkeit gehalten. Der Sinnspruch des Notrechts heißt: 'Not hat kein Gebot (necessitas non habet legem)'; und gleichwohl kann es keine Not geben, welche, was unrecht ist, gesetzmäßig machte." (emphases in the original).

[38] Id. at 236: "Was er selbst an sich als unrecht beurteilen muß, von ebendemselben (i.e. von dem "Gerichtshofe") Nachsicht erlangen kann." (Parenthetical information added to the original.)

[39] A.A. 27.2,2, 1333 (Naturrecht, Feyerabend).

[40] See supra note 26 and accompanying text.

[41] On the relationship, particularly the logical relationship, between the concepts "law of prescription", "law of proscription" and "law of permission" ("Gebots-", "Ver-

ponds to a law of permission. On the other hand, nothing of this sort, and above all not a law of permission, corresponds to an excuse. That is why every excuse, and consequently also that claimed by the perpetrator in the plank case, lies outside of the system of norms of command, prohibition and permission, and thus outside of the system which includes justifications. According to Kant, rules of excuse form a separate system. Daries' differentiation between exceptiones secundum and exceptiones contra leges institutae is easy to recognize here; it is plainly impossible that the latter exceptions, as opposed to the former, belong to the system of leges. It is indeed most probable when viewed historically that Kant's differentiation between the facta inculpabilia and the facta impunibilia is founded upon Daries' differentiation.[42]

Of course Kant surpasses Daries by also giving a reason why the perpetrator in the plank case is to be excused. Similiar to Baumgarten, Kant sees an excuse as an argument valid only before the forum externum, namely in the judgment of others, but not within the forum internum, namely in the actor's conscience, which still "must judge the deed as unjust". It would be absurd for a court of justice to convict the perpetrator for a deed that could never have been deterred by the criminal law. The execution of punishment presupposes the threat of punishment, and the goal of this threat is to prevent possible perpetrators from undertaking the punishable deed. In a situation in which the specific goal of the threat of punishment cannot possibly be achieved, it is "inconsistent"[43] as Kant writes in 'Theory and Practice' to subsequently act as though the criminal law was not inhibited in its effectiveness,[44] and convict the actor. It is not mere chance that a deed, for which, in the prevalent language of the time, there was an "excusatio", is characterized in *The Metaphysics of Morals* as factum "impunibile".

---

bots-" und "Erlaubnisgesetz") see Kant in The Metaphysics of Morals, A. A. 6, 223. For an analysis of the correlating concepts of that which is prescribed, proscribed and permitted, particularly regarding Kant, see my Das deontologische Sechseck bei Gottfried Achenwall – Zur Geschichte der deontischen Grundbegriffe in der Universaljurisprudenz zwischen Suarez und Kant, 45 et seq. (Hamburg 1986), and my 'The Hexagonal System of Deontic Concepts according to Achenwall and Kant', Estudios de Historia della Logica, 277 (Ignacio Angelelli & Angel d'Ors eds., Pamplona 1990).

[42] In the Nova Dilucidatio of 1755 Kant, expressly referring to the author by name, relies on Daries' Elementa Metaphysica of 1743; cf. A. A. 1, 390, line 17 and A. A. 1, 398, line 34.

[43] "Ungereimt", Berlinische Monatsschrift, 22, 257; A. A. 8, 300.

[44] In this regard and generally on Kant and excuses, in light of all the relevant material, cf. B. Sharon Byrd, 'Kant's Theory of Punishment: Deterrence in its Threat, Retribution in its Execution', Law and Philosophy, 8, 151 et seq., 188 et seq. (1989). In former times Kant's analysis of the plank case was often misunderstood. It may be noted, however, that Rudolf Stammler recognized the meaning of Kant's "inculpabile" to be "not unlawful"; see Stammler, Darstellung der strafrechtlichen Bedeutung des Nothstandes, 37 (Erlangen 1878).

V. Conclusion

When reconsidering the initial Gentz text, one is struck not so much by Gentz's position on the plank case, which mirrors Kant's own, but rather by the particular language used by the author. Not because Gentz's language diverges so remarkably from our's (which is much more true of the relationship between our language and Kant's in *The Metaphysics of Morals*) but on the contrary because Gentz's language resembles our own. Gentz is most probably one of the first to expressly apply the relationship between justification and excuse, which was developed in the middle of the eighteenth century, to the Plank of Carneades case in a terminology common today. It is the obvious linguistic ease for today's reader in analysing Gentz's text which shows us how much our own language, and its corresponding theoretical insight, owes to the reflections of the practical philosophy of that time.

Without Daries' conceptual insights into the difference between rules of law and rules of imputation, upon which Gentz's comments are based, the real nature of the justification-excuse distinction would indeed be perplexing. Once one realizes that justifications are rules of law, whereas excuses are rules of imputation, worlds of "accoustic separation" are in fact defined. Permissions and hence justifications are rules of conduct addressed to the general public telling them what they may do. They are part of the system of law, just as a prohibition, such as that against killing, is a part of the system of law. An excuse, on the other hand, is a decision rule. It tells one who judges an actor's conduct what to do when the law has been violated. Namely, it tells us when not to impute blame to an individual who has failed to follow the rules of conduct imposed upon him. Daries' insights, however, give us more than the justification-excuse distinction. They also show us that excuses have something in common with those rules of imputation that prevent us from attributing the causation of harm to someone who had no control over the situation. In not attributing this harm we do not recognize that the person's conduct was in accordance with the law. Instead we recognize that it would be inconsistent to apply the law to what only superficially appears to be a violation. Admittedly, the occurrence in question caused harm. But it cannot be attributed to the person involved as his deed. Similarly, in the case of excuses, although an act can be attributed to someone as his deed, still we cannot lay blame upon him for that act. Both sets of rules relate to the fair treatment of the actor as opposed to sober determinations of what is and is not permitted under the law. This distinction, although available since the middle of the eighteenth century and even applied at that time to different cases of necessity, still is the subject of modern discussions of criminal responsibility.

Form and Substance in American Criminal Law: The Constitutionalization of Proof Burdens

By Laird C. Kirkpatrick, Eugene*

Throughout American legal history, it has been established that the prosecution has the burden of proving the guilt of a criminal defendant beyond a reasonable doubt. A higher standard of proof is viewed as necessary in criminal cases because of the more serious consequences of an erroneous verdict, which include loss of liberty and even life itself. Because this higher proof standard was so widely accepted by case law, statutes and state constitutions, the question seldom arose whether it was also required as a component of due process guaranteed by the federal constitution. In the 1971 decision of *In re Winship,* the United States Supreme Court finally addressed this question and held that "the Due Process Clause protects the accused against conviction except upon proof beyond a reasonable doubt of every fact necessary to constitute the crime with which he is charged".[1]

This fundamental constitutional principle has generated an enormous number of difficult and often conflicting cases during the last two decades. These cases address two primary issues. First, what issues in a criminal prosecution are subject to the government's proof burden and cannot be shifted to the defendant? Second, are there any constitutional limits on the instructions that can be given to the jury explaining this proof burden? With respect to both of these questions, the Supreme Court has given answers that have been criticized as highly formalistic. However, at least with respect to the constitutional standards governing jury instructions, it can be argued that the Court's approach eliminates the formalism of pre-existing practice and instead helps insure that juries are more clearly informed of the jury's powers and responsibilities in determining whether the "beyond a reasonable doubt" standard has been satisfied.

Scope of the government's proof burdens. Because the government has the burden of proving guilt beyond a reasonable doubt, it might be thought that the government also has the proof burden with respect to any factor having a

---

* This essay is dedicated to Professor Robert S. Summers – teacher, mentor, friend. It is based on portions of a forthcoming treatise on Federal Evidence by Christopher B. Mueller and Laird C. Kirkpatrick to be published by Little, Brown & Co., Boston.

[1] 397 U.S. 358, 364 (1970).

significant bearing on the extent of punishment or stigma resulting from conviction. Some viewed the Supreme Court as leaning toward such a position in *Mullaney v. Wilbur,*[2] a case decided five years after *Winship. Mullaney* was an appeal of a Maine murder conviction where the defendant claimed that he acted in the heat of passion which (if established) would reduce murder to manslaughter. The *mens rea* element of the murder statute was "malice aforethought," and under Maine law malice aforethought and heat of passion were viewed as two inconsistent things. By proving heat of passion, the defendant would negate malice aforethought. Therefore, the defendant argued that under *Winship* the government had the burden of *disproving* his heat of passion defense. The trial court disagreed and instructed the jury that defendant had the burden of proving that he acted in heat of passion. A unanimous Supreme Court reversed, finding constitutional error in placing the burden of persuasion on the defendant.

On a narrow view, *Mullaney* is completely unsurprising, because it means only that the state cannot constitutionally shift the burden of persuasion to the defendant to *disprove* an element of the charged offense, like *mens rea.* On a broader view, *Mullaney* could be read to mean the prosecutor must not only bear the burden on central elements like *mens rea,* but on *every* factor that makes a difference in punishment or stigma, including defenses raising new matter. After all, heat of passion does not seem to be *only* the absence of malice (or *only* the negation of *mens rea*), since it carries as well a broad idea of being excusably out of control. And not everyone would agree that heat of passion necessarily disproves the requisite intent, although the Maine criminal code apparently adopted that theory. Hence a holding that the defense cannot be burdened with proving heat of passion might also mean the defense cannot be burdened with proving any new matter that serves as a defense or lessens the seriousness of the offense, whether or not such matter is broader than an element in the charged crime or necessarily tends to refute such an element.

In the subsequent decision of *Patterson v. New York,*[3] the Court confirmed that the narrow reading of *Mullaney* is right. *Patterson* was brought under a trim and modern statute requiring the state to prove "intent to cause the death of another person" and "caus[ing] the death". The New York scheme let defendant raise the affirmative defense of being "under the influence of extreme emotional disturbance", which would (like "heat of passion" in Maine) reduce the offense to manslaughter. *Patterson* approved allocating to the defense the burden of persuasion on this point, because under the New York statute the defense did not negate any element of the crime. The Court noted that the New York judge (unlike his Maine counterpart) told the jury that intent to cause death could coexist with extreme emotional disturbance.

---

2 421 U.S. 684 (1975).

3 432 U.S. 197 (1977).

Taken together, *Mullaney* and *Patterson* are tantalizing but unsatisfying decisions. *Mullaney* held the promise of a protective jurisprudence that might limit legislative and judicial freedom to allocate proof of elements bearing on culpability but adopted no principle or standard to recognize or describe the limits. *Patterson* drew back from this enterprise and instead adopted a formalistic approach deferring to legislative choice in defining the elements of the crime. The Court expressed concern that if the prosecution had to bear the burden to disprove every factor that might mitigate or diminish the offense, the legislature might be reluctant to recognize such factors at all.[4]

Patterson raises the danger that a legislature could circumvent *Winship* by simply rewriting its criminal code to transform elements of an offense into affirmative defenses and shifting the burden of persuasion to the defendant.[5] Thus, a criminal statute with elements A, B and C could be redrafted so the state had to prove only A and B with C being converted into an affirmative defense to be proved by the accused. For example, rape could become merely the act of sexual intercourse, with consent being transformed into an affirmative defense, or larceny merely the act of taking another's property, with absence of mens rea being left as a defense for the accused to prove. The *Patterson* majority did say "there are obviously constitutional limits beyond which the States may not go in this regard",[6] but failed to explicate any such limits.

The Eighth Amendment prohibition against "cruel and unusual punishment" is one source of constitutional limitation on the ways that legislatures (and courts) can define elements of crimes. If a legislature were to eliminate traditional elements of culpability from a penal statute, it would be criminalizing conduct that was previously innocent, and such "new" crimes might be vulnerable to constitutional challenge. The Eighth Amendment embodies the principle that crimes normally require act, blameworthy mental attitude, and proportionality in punishment,[7] and these notions necessarily limit the permissible definitions of crimes and defenses.[8] But Eighth Amendment jurispru-

---

[4] See 432 U.S. at 207 - 208 (noting that the New York criminal code has 25 affirmative defenses "which must be established by the defendant to be operative" and nothing in the Due Process Clause should put the state "to the choice of abandoning those defenses or undertaking to disprove their existence in order to convict of a crime which otherwise is within its constitutional powers to sanction by substantial punishment").

[5] Patterson v. New York, 432 U.S. at 223 (Powell, J., dissenting) (criticizing majority opinion as ignoring "the constitutional values for which Winship stands" because it "allows a legislature to shift, virtually at will, the burden of persuasion with respect to any factor in a criminal case, so long as it is careful not to mention the nonexistence of that factor in the statutory language that defines the crime").

[6] 432 U.S. at 210.

[7] Jeffries and Stephan, Defenses, Presumptions, and Burden of Proof in the Criminal Law, 88 Yale L.J. 1325 (1979) (Eighth Amendment bar against cruel and unusual punishment limits legislative capacity to define criminality in three different ways – by requiring an act, a blameworthy mental attitude, and proportionality in punishment).

dence is not well developed, and it has shown little "bite" in limiting legislative prerogative to define criminal conduct or impose severe punishments.[9]

Under the theory that "the greater includes the lesser", some commentators have argued that a state should be prohibited from shifting the burden of persuasion on an element to a defendant only where it would be unconstitutional to eliminate such an element from the definition of the offense.[10] But this view is even less satisfactory than *Patterson,* because it ignores the important policy advantages of requiring legislatures to address directly what factors should be included as elements of crimes[11] and the burden and inappropriateness of requiring courts to play a vastly expanded role as constitutional referees deciding the permissible boundaries of the substantive criminal law.[12]

Thus, *Patterson* remains as the controlling standard, even though it appears to abdicate any significant judicial role in regulating legislative allocation of proof burdens. It requires only that the legislature use the proper means (i.e., redefining the crime and recognizing an affirmative defense).

---

[8] See Moran v. Ohio, 469 U.S. 948 (1984) (Brennan and Marshall, JJ., dissenting from denial of certiorari) (arguing that a state could not repudiate the defense of self-defense because "both the Due Process Clause and the Eighth Amendment restrict the State's ability to punish a defendant whose 'crime,' for example, consisted in an immediate response to a murderous attack upon him").

[9] Harmelin v. Michigan, 111 S. Ct. 2680 (1991) (upholding against Eighth Amendment challenge a mandatory life sentence without possibility of parole for a first-time drug offender); Rummel v. Estelle, 445 U.S. 263 (1980) (upholding imposition of life sentence under Texas habitual offender statute for defendant convicted on three occasions for fraudulently obtaining money and goods worth a total of $229.11).

[10] See Allen, The Restoration of In re Winship: A Comment on Burdens of Persuasion in Criminal Cases After Patterson v. New York, 76 Mich. L. Rev. 30 (1977) (arguing that if a state would constitutionally by permitted to eliminate a particular element from its definition of a crime it should be allowed to keep it as an element and yet shift the burden of proof to the defendant, because the "greater power should include the lesser"); Allen, Structuring Jury Decisionmaking in Criminal Cases: A Unified Constitutional Approach to Evidentiary Devices, 94 Harv. L. Rev. 321 (1980); Allen, More on Constitutional Process-of-Proof Problems in Criminal Cases, 94 Harv. L. Rev. 1975 (1981); Allen & DeGrazia, The Constitutional Requirement of Proof Beyond a Reasonable Doubt in Criminal Cases: A Comment Upon Incipient Chaos in the Lower Courts, 20 Am. Crim. L. Rev. 1 (1982).

[11] See Saltzburg, Burdens of Persuasion in Criminal Cases: Harmonizing the Views of the Justices, 20 Am. Crim. L. Rev. 393, 407 (1983) (greater-includes-lesser theory "must be rejected because it permits the imposition if stigma without requiring the government to prove that there is a difference between greater and lesser offenders"); Underwood, The Thumb on the Scales of Justice: Burdens of Persuasion in Criminal Cases, 86 Yale L. J. 1299 (1977) (criticizing the "greater includes the lesser" argument because it encourages legislative avoidance of difficult policy issues that should be faced directly; also noting that selected, unpopular defendants may be denied the benefits of a defense if they have to bear the burden of persuasion).

[12] See Sundby, The Reasonable Doubt Rule and the Meaning of Innocence, 40 Hastings L. J. 457 (1989) (criticizing as impractical and undemocratic the view that the Supreme Court should be required to develop detailed constitutional standards governing minimum elements of crimes and limits of punishment).

Constitutional limits on jury instructions. Another significant line of cases addresses the manner in which juries can be instructed regarding the proof burdens imposed by *Winship* and specifically focuses on the use of presumptions. Until recently, it was a common practice in American criminal trials to instruct the jury that a particular element of the prosecution's case could be "presumed" from proof of other facts. Such presumptions were used to help the government establish critical elements of its case. Consider, for example, the element of *mens rea.* Often it is hard to prove because there is no direct evidence, and yet intent may be strongly suggested by what the defendant apparently did – shooting and killing someone at close range is likely to suggest intent to kill, and setting fire to a building with a can of gasoline is likely to suggest intent to burn the building to the ground. Hence many jurisdictions recognized a presumption that a person intends the natural and probable consequences of his voluntary acts.[13] However, particularly after *Winship,* it was questioned whether such use of presumptions conflicts with the government's constitutional obligation to prove each element of the crime beyond a reasonable doubt.

The issue was squarely faced in the 1979 case of *Sandstrom v. Montana.*[14] In *Sandstrom,* the trial court told the jury the law "presumes that a person intends the ordinary consequences of his voluntary acts." Defendant was convicted of murder on facts indicating a particularly brutal attack with a knife and shovel, but the Supreme Court reversed because it found that the quoted phrase was ambiguous and could have been interpreted in four different ways, at least two of which violated defendant's Due Process rights. First, the jury could have thought it had no choice on the issue of intent – that the presumption embodied in the instruction was conclusive. Second, it could have thought the presumption shifted to defendant the burden of persuasion – that it was to find intent unless defendant proved lack of intent. Third, the jury could have thought the presumption shifted to the defendant the burden of production – that it was to find intent unless defendant offered evidence that he lacked intent. And fourth, the jury could have thought the instruction invited an inference of intent – that it was being told it could find intent on the basis of defendant's behavior. When viewed in either of the first two ways (conclusive or shifting the burden of persuasion) the presumption instruction violated the *Winship* requirement of proof beyond reasonable doubt of every element in the offense, so the Court in *Sandstrom* reversed the conviction.[15]

Sandstrom sends a clear warning that ambiguities in presumption instructions can be costly, and that they violate defendant's Due Process rights when

[13] See Agnew v. United States, 165 U.S. 36, 51, 53 (1896) (common law presumption that one intends the natural and probable consequences of voluntary acts is "of ancient vintage").

[14] 442 U.S. 510 (1979).

[15] Sandstrom v. Montana, 442 U.S. 50 (1979).

they bear on elements in the offense and seem either to be conclusive or to shift the burden of persuasion to the defendant. Several years later in *Francis v. Franklin,*[16] the Court reached the same result in another murder prosecution that generated a similar instruction, even though the trial judge had emphasized that the presumption may be rebutted and that the prosecutor bore the burden of proving intent beyond a reasonable doubt. And both the Supreme Court and many lower courts have reversed convictions on account of similar ambiguities in presumption instructions,[17] even where the presumption terminology is taken directly from the language of the underlying statute.[18] Not only have courts condemned the use of "presume" or "presumption" in criminal jury instructions, but also other strong terms and phrases like "require" or "mandatory",[19] or legal-sounding mumbo-jumbo like "the law implies"[20] or "prima facie evidence",[21] which suggest that some high authority has already made the decision and that it is cloaked in special dignity meriting great respect.

---

16 471 U.S. 307 (1985).

17 Yates v. Evatt, 111 S.Ct. 1884 (1991) (reversible error to instruct that "[m]alice is implied or presumed by the law from the willful, deliberate, and intentional doing of an unlawful act without any just cause or excuse"); Hill v. Maloney, 927 F.2d 646 (1st Cir. 1990) (error to instruct that "malice is implied from any deliberate and cruel act against another" because not worded in permissive form); Doncelle v. Vose, 842 F.2d 538 (1st Cir. 1988) (error to instruct that "when the killing is caused by the intentional use of a deadly weapon there arises a presumption that the killing was with malice aforethought"); Hyman v. Aiken, 824 F.2d 1405 (4th Cir. 1987) (condemning instruction that "malice is presumed" from use of deadly weapon as relieving state of burden to prove malice); Engle v. Koehler, 707 F.2d 241, 245 (6th Cir. 1983) (instruction that "the law gives us a rule of thumb that a person is presumed to intend the natural consequences of his acts" violates Sandstrom); Phillips v. Rose, 690 F.2d 79, 81 (6th Cir. 1982) (Sandstrom violated by instruction that malice can be presumed from the use of a deadly weapon); Hammontree v. Phelps, 605 F.2d 1371 (5th Cir. 1979) (error to give instruction that violation of a statute or ordinance is "presumptive evidence" of negligence); Brackeen v. State, 763 P.2d 59 (Nev. 1988) (error to give jury instruction that person is possession of stolen credit cards is "presumed" to have knowledge that they were stolen); See generally Note, Improper Use of Presumptions in Recent Criminal Law Adjudication, 38 Stan. L. Rev. 423 (1986).

18 Carella v. California, 491 U.S. 263 (1989) (constitutional error to use presumption terminology even though taken directly from statute).

19 See State v. Short, 88 Or. App. 567, 746 P.2d 742 (1987) (error to tell jury that it was "not required to draw this inference" unless it found all the facts giving rise to it have been proved beyond reasonable doubt).

20 Hill v. Maloney, 927 F.2d 646 (1st Cir. 1990) (error to instruct that "malice is implied from any deliberate and cruel act against another" because wording is not permissive in form).

21 See State v. Jasper, 467 N.W.2d 855 (Neb. 1991) (constitutional error to tell jury that prima facie evidence means "evidence sufficient in law to raise a presumption of fact or establish the fact in question unless rebutted," which shifts the burden of persuasion to the defendant; the term is intended to be a sufficiency standard for courts and does not belong in jury instruction); State v. Matamoros, 89 N.M. 125, 547 P.2d 1167 (1976) (instruction that one who willfully conceals merchandise is "prima facie pre-

However, subsequent decisions have approved jury instructions inviting the jury to "infer" rather than "presume" one fact from proof of another,[22] at least where the inference is rational under the circumstances of the case.[23] Thus, if in *Sandstrom* the trial judge had instructed the jury that it could "infer" (rather than that the law "presumes") that a person intends the natural and ordinary consequences of his voluntary acts, the instruction would have survived constitutional challenge.

Not surprisingly, a number of commentators have questioned whether a one-word change in jury instructions is significant enough to justify the number of reversed convictions and the volume of constitutional jurisprudence generated by the *Sandstrom* decision. It is certainly open to question whether lay jurors are sufficiently attuned to semantic nuance that the milder term "inference" would by itself achieve the intended purpose of informing the jury that the inference is not mandatory, the burden of proof remains on the government, and the jury is responsible for making the ultimate determination.[24]

For *Sandstrom* to accomplish more than merely replacing one equivocal instruction with another, trial judges should be required not merely to use inference terminology but to explain clearly the permissive nature of the suggested finding. The instructions should highlight the basic facts giving rise to the inference, while referring to all the evidence in the case and gently inviting the jury to accord them their probative worth. At the very least, the instruction should stress that the suggested conclusion is not required.[25] Probably the best approach is to tell the jury essentially that it is often possible to draw the indicated conclusion from the basic facts, while emphasizing context

---

sumed" to have concealed it "with the intention of converting it without paying" violates state rule because jury was not told that it need to make that finding).

22 United States v. Graham, 858 F.2d 986, 992 (5th Cir. 1988) (approving instruction that jury "may draw the inference" that defendant intended "all the consequences which one standing in like circumstances and possessing like knowledge" would expect); United States v. Vreeken, 803 F.2d 1085 (D.C. Cir. 1986), cert. denied, 484 U.S. 963 (1987) (upholding instruction that it is "reasonable to draw the inference and find that a person intends the natural and probable consequences of acts knowingly done"); United States v. Silva, 745 F.2d 840, 851 - 52 (4th Cir. 1984), cert. denied, 470 U.S. 1031 (upholding instruction that "it is reasonable to infer that a person ordinarily intends the natural and probable consequences of his acts"); Kelly v. Commonwealth, 382 S.E.2d 270 (Va. App. 1989) (upholding instruction that "you may infer that every person intends the natural and probable consequences of his acts").

23 County of Ulster v. Allen, 442 U.S. 140 (1979).

24 See Harris, Constitutional Limits on Criminal Presumptions as an Expression of Changing Concepts of Fundamental Fairness, 77 J. of Crim. Law & Criminology 308, 356 (1986) (criticizing Sandstrom as accomplishing little; jury unlikely to understand "you may infer" as being "substantially less coercive" than "the law presumes").

25 See Uniform Rule of Evidence 303 and proposed Federal Rule of Evidence 303 (requiring instruction that would tell jury that it "may" but is "not required" to find the suggested conclusion).

of the case, the evidence presented at trial, and the beyond reasonable doubt standard.[26]

Conclusion. Undoubtedly the most distinctive feature of American criminal law is the extent to which it has become constitutionalized. The Supreme Court's decision in *Winship* to add proof beyond a reasonable doubt to the constitutional requirements applicable to criminal prosecutions is unremarkable and merely reaffirms a rule applied throughout centuries of Anglo-American law. However, the ramifications of *Winship* raise much more interesting and difficult jurisprudential questions. The approach taken in *Patterson* suggests that legislatures might be able to undermine *Winship* and *reduce* the prosecution's traditional proof obligations merely by rewriting their penal codes.

While *Patterson* can be criticized as unduly formalistic, *Sandstrom* should be viewed as an attempt by the Court to focus more on the substantive effect of jury instructions explaining the allocation of proof burdens in criminal cases. If *Winship* truly means that the prosecutor must *prove* all elements of a crime, then the jury cannot be instructed to *presume* an element exists. However, for *Sandstrom* to accomplish its intended purpose, it should be interpreted as requiring more than mere substitution of "infer" for "presume" in criminal jury instructions. Given how critical proof burdens can be to the adjudication of guilt, there is no excuse for continuing confusion in the minds of jurors regarding how those burdens are allocated.

---

[26] See Nesson, Rationality, Presumptions, and Judicial Comment: A Response to Professor Allen, 94 Harv. L. Rev. 1574, 1589 (1981) (suggesting the following example for wording of an inference instruction: "It is often possible to infer from the presence of loaded firearms in an automobile that the occupants of the automobile possessed the weapons. You must decide whether, in the context of this case, such a conclusion is justified as to each defendant. You should consider all the facts. For example, consider where the guns were found, whether they were in plain sight, how easy they were to reach. Based on your consideration of all the evidence, you must decide whether the prosecution has proved beyond reasonable doubt that each defendant is guilty as charged.").

Robert S. Summers and Legal Process at Cornell

By Russell K. Osgood, Ithaca

Many articles in *festschrifts* begin with a nod to the honored person and then launch into a topic that interests the author but is only obliquely related to the honoree. My effort will be different, and more personal, for it will describe how a very fine idea of Robert S. Summers, the William G. McRoberts Research.Professor in the Administration of the Law at Cornell Law School, which I opposed implementing as a faculty member, has turned out to be probably the most significant intellectual development in my own life as a lawyer and legal scholar.

I. History of the Adoption of the Legal Process Requirement

In the Spring of 1983, after considerable study the Cornell Law School faculty adopted a requirement, to be implemented two years later, that each first year law student take a mandatory second semester, three credit hour course, entitled "Legal Process". Cornell had previously experimented with a legal process course in 1969. No one worked harder than Bob Summers during the intervening period to get the school to reconsider the idea.

This course was to be modeled after and generally intended to follow some version of the materials[1] for a course of the same name developed by the late Professors Henry M. Hart and Albert M. Sacks of Harvard Law School. It was planned that the course would be taught at Cornell for the first year after adoption as an elective upperclass course but thereafter would be placed in the first year curriculum.

As preparation for the implementation of the Legal Process requirement, James A. Henderson, the Frank G. Ingersoll Professor of Law, taught the course as an upperclass elective the next year (1983 - 84). In addition, Professor Summers worked on the Hart and Sacks materials and spent a January

---

[1] Henry M. Hart and Albert M. Sacks, The Legal Process: Basic Problems in the Making and Application of Law (tent. ed. 1958). One of the great curiosities of American legal education is why these very highly respected materials were never reedited or put into final form for they remain to this day in a mimeographed binder. It is a recurring rumor at law professor conventions that these materials are about to appear in a final edition in book form.

intercession at Harvard attending a course of a similar type taught by Professor Norman Dorsen of New York University.

In the Spring of 1985 and thereafter each spring the course has been taught at Cornell to a mixed reception by our students. A number of instructors have been involved but in the third year of the course's existence I volunteered to the then dean, Peter W. Martin, now the Jane M. G. Foster Professor of Law, to teach a section. Dean Martin taught the other section.

I had opposed the Legal Process requirement originally,[2] but after the faculty vote, had spent some time reading the Hart and Sacks materials and had found them intelligent, interesting, and worth further disciplined study. At the same time, the various instructors in the course had found that the materials were outdated and unteachable without significant alterations. Thus, after I decided to teach the course I endeavored to put together a fresh set of materials comprised (generally) of more recent cases[3] and law review articles organized along lines or themes prominent in the Hart and Sacks' materials. In addition, I decided to use a few short excerpts from the Hart and Sacks materials that reflected their main points about, for instance, the process of "reasoned elaboration",[4] statutory interpretation,[5] and the meaning and significance of "rights" in the law.[6] I originally considered attempting to develop some hypothetical problems along the lines of those in the original materials but I have never successfully done this in large part because I have found that my cases and other materials served my pedagogical purposes.

The other major innovation[7] I introduced into the course materials was greater explicit exposure to significant jurisprudential writings by H. L. A. Hart, Lon Fuller, Ronald Dworkin, and representative spokesmen for the law and economics movement, critical legal studies, and, more recently, feminist jurisprudence. Because of his closeness at many points to Hart and Sacks[8] and also because of his lucid prose and fecundity as a scholar, I decided to use Dworkin more often (and frequently as a foil) than any other legal theorist.

---

[2] I am not sure why I opposed it except out of a sense that I was unsure what the course was intended to accomplish and I found the title, at that time, meaningless.

[3] I still use a few cases that were included in the original materials. E.g. Norway Plains v. Boston and Maine RR Co., 67 Mass. 263 (1854).

[4] Henry M. Hart and Albert M. Sacks, supra note 1 at 162 - 79.

[5] Id. at 1410 - 17.

[6] Id. at 599 - 613.

[7] In fact, both Professors Summers and Henderson introduced other jurisprudential thinkers into the course the first year they taught it. In his second year, Professor Henderson took his students on what he called a "bus-trip", e.g. a quick (back-to-back) review of major recent jurisprudential materials.

[8] For instance, in his seminal article, "The Model of Rules" Dworkin follows the Hart and Sacks' distinction between principles and policies and uses as an illustrative case, *Riggs v. Palmer*. Hart and Sacks use a similar case to illustrate the same point. See Ronald M. Dworkin, "The Model of Rules," 35 U. Chi. L. Rev. 14 (1967).

My goals in the course (together with some conclusions about it) can be summarized as follows: (i) Students need a solid introduction to jurisprudence but the typical American course on jurisprudence has been too abstract. (ii) Hart and Sacks make basic jurisprudence interesting and "fun"[9] by making it more concrete but also by constantly tying theory to more practical considerations related to the process of law application and to how legal institutions function. (iii) The original Hart and Sacks materials were unsatisfactory insofar as they contained important jurisprudential claims but did not expose students to competing points of view.[10] (iv) The presentation of a theoretical, first year law school course like the one Cornell has undertaken is extraordinarily difficult but even if it fails in part it sends exactly the right signal to students about the role of law and about how the school and its faculty view law. (v) The course should cover enough "practical" material, like that traditionally covered in the basic English course on jurisprudence, for instance on topics like *stare decisis,* etc, to be seen as a course with some immediate value. (vi) The topics covered in the original Hart and Sacks materials can not all be covered so some choices have to be made.[11] (vi) The course attempts to use cases[12] previously encountered in the Cornell first year curriculum and articles, where relevant, written by Cornell faculty on jurisprudential topics.[13] (vii) Various jurisprudential thinkers should be compared, if possible, in writ-

[9] Honesty compels me to admit that many (most or maybe even the overwhelming majority) of my students would not agree with the use of this term.

[10] Hart and Sacks did refer to formal jurisprudential scholarship in their materials on occasion. For instance, in their note on "jural rights" they described the work of Arthur L. Corbin and Wesley Hohfeld, as well as H. L. A. Hart's critical response. See Henry M. Hart and Albert M. Sacks, supra note 1 at 599 - 613.

[11] In a memorandum to the faculty, circulated at the time the Legal Process requirement was adopted but written earlier, Bob Summers correctly identified the main themes in Hart and Sacks and in the proposed course, as follows: (i) the doctrine of precedent, (ii) the reasons judges give when not appealing to precedent or to other forms of authority, (iii) the nature and limits of the adjudicative process, (iv) the basic relations between courts, legislatures, and administrative agencies, (v) the kinds of reasoning lawyers and others engage in when making new written law, (vi) the limited efficacy of law, (vii) general techniques for the interpretation of written law, (viii) the diverse and complex relations between law and fact, (ix) why change and reform in the legal system are necessary and how the system specifically institutionalizes processes for change and reform, (x) private ordering v. official action, and (xi) of "windows" and links". Robert S. Summers, "Notes on Possible Legal Process Course in First Year (Spring Semester)", dated February 24, 1977.

[12] E.g. Yania v. Bigan, 397 Pa. 319 (1959).

[13] For instance, the students in the 1993 spring term course read the following faculty articles in their order of appearance: (i) James A. Henderson, "Process Constraints in Torts," 67 Cornell L. Rev. 901 (1982), (ii) Robert S. Summers and Geoffrey Marshall, "The Argument from Ordinary Meaning in Statutory Interpretation," 43 No. Ireland Leg. Q. 213 (1992), (iii) Jonathan R. Macey, "Promoting Public-Regarding Legislation Through Statutory Interpretation: An Interest Group Model," 86 Colum. L. Rev. 223 (1986), and (iv) Robert S. Summers, "Statutes and Contracts as Founts of Formal Reasoning," in Essays for Patrick Atiyah at 71 (P. Cane and J. Stapleton, eds., 1991).

ings directly responsive to each other or that discuss the same phenomenon.[14] (viii) The course develops in several contexts, including the treatment of precedent, a comparative treatment of the British and American legal order. The use of Dworkin and Fuller on the one hand and Hart on the other facilitates this.[15] (ix) The course explores in a variety of different contexts the arguments about indeterminacy or certainty in the law, comparing Dworkin, Hart, Joseph Singer, and others.

II. Outline of the Course as it is Currently Being Taught

I. Introduction

II. What is law and how does it function?

A. Source of law: legal rules and "principles"

B. Design of law: the genesis and consequences of legal norms

III. Adjudication

A. Adjudicating novel legal questions

B. Stare decisis: evaluating, overruling, and distinguishing precedent

IV. Legal interpretation: statutes, contracts and other legal texts

A. Statutes: plain or ordinary meaning versus purposive construction and the canons of construction

B. Statutes: legislative intention, discernment and application, and statutory desuetude

C. Contract v. statutory interpretation

V. Rights in the law

A. Scope of rights

B. Theoretical basis of rights

VI. Legal certitude

VII. Conclusion

III. My Debt to Robert S. Summers

There have been a lot of doubters about the Legal Process enterprise at Cornell, including many serious and capable students and faculty whom I respect.

[14] For instance, students in the spring of 1993 read two cases on the alleged general common law tort doctrine of no duty to rescue and relevant articles by a legal process scholar (Henderson), two law and economics proponents (William Landes and Richard Posner), and a feminist scholar (Leslie Bender).

[15] My thinking in this regard has been assisted by P. S. Atiyah and R. S. Summers, Form and Substance in Anglo-American Law: A Comparative Study in Legal Reasoning, Legal Theory and Legal Institutions (1987).

I believe now that Bob Summers was correct and that the Hart and Sacks approach provides the best format for an introduction to legal theory in the first year of law school. I also know that in the process of thinking about, preparing for teaching, and teaching this course I have learned and developed more as a lawyer and a legal scholar than as a result of anything else in my professional life.

Bob Summers has of course been greatly influenced by his exposure to the course's themes while a student at the Harvard Law School in the 1950s.[16] This is not to say that he has slavishly followed what Hart and Sacks said in their materials. Recently, for instance, he has criticized them for not placing enough emphasis on the way that ordinary meaning interpretation generally leads to satisfactory statutory interpretation as opposed to constant recourse to a "purposive" approach in interpretation.[17]

Nevertheless, Bob Summers has obviously absorbed many of the major messages of Hart and Sacks and most importantly their careful, contextual approach to law. It is not an accident that Hart and Sacks never wrote general articles about topics, such as whether citizens have a moral obligation to obey the law. They had views on these topics and were no doubt affected by the rich debate about them, but their approach was always tied to the concrete functioning of the Anglo-American legal order.

Some, no doubt, see Hart and Sacks and Bob Summers as apologists for that order. It would be fair to say that all three see or saw admirable things in it. But whether or not Hart and Sacks admired every feature, their materials demonstrate that jurisprudence is an applied science. Many of the most important insights of jurisprudence are to be found only after careful, contextual observation of the functioning of a legal order.

Apart from the excellence of the Hart and Sacks' approach, a major contribution of the legal process course is that it rises above the furious and frenetic subject matter focus of virtually all other courses in the American first year curriculum. While it would be possible to make many jurisprudential points in first year constitutional law, students come out of that course more cognizant of constitutional law doctrine (or its contradictoriness depending on the faculty member teaching it) than of the deeper rhythms of the law.[18] In addition,

---

[16] Bob Summers took criminal law from Henry Hart. Hart used that course as a vehicle to develop many points later found in the Legal Process materials. Professor Henderson took the Legal Process course taught by Henry Hart while a student at Harvard. At least three other Cornell faculty members, Robert B. Kent, Professor of Law, Emeritus, Kevin M. Clermont, the James and Mark Flanagan Professor of Law, and Peter W. Martin took courses, including the legal process course, or were exposed to the work of Henry M. Hart.

[17] See Robert S. Summers and Geoffrey Marshall, supra note 13 at 229 - 35.

[18] I say this as a former teacher of constitutional law.

for two reasons constitutional law is probably not a good place to raise and discuss the issues properly raised in a legal process or basic jurisprudence course. First, students tend to have very strong (and perhaps unsophisticated) views on constitutional law topics which frequently lead them to subordinate their study of the legal materials to those views. Second, many legal doctrines – the doctrine of precedent is a good example – operate in a special (and limited) way in this the highest domain of public, as opposed to private, law.[19]

Another broad insight of the Hart and Sacks materials is the constant emphasis on how structure, function, and outcomes are closely interrelated in law. Classical Anglo-American adjudication functions best when given relatively few choices and when standards are relatively determinate and objective.[20] This is not to say that Hart and Sacks believed the legal order should be confined, either in description or operation, to situations in which classical adjudication works well. They, like Lon Fuller, were sympathetic before its time to the movement for alternative methods of dispute resolution. They were careful students of the difficulties and promise of administrative agencies and law. Finally, Hart and Sacks distinguished in their work between legislative, executive, and judicial functioning. They employed a term, "general directive arrangements," designed to show that all three branches of government function at points in a legal fashion but they also treated the functions as separable and believed that courts should respect "the principle of institutional settlement".[21]

One of Hart and Sacks' themes in the course and materials that I have not made much of in the current course, largely because of time constraints, is the description of the domain of private ordering and its relationship to the legal system. Obviously, this theme should be covered in a well taught contracts course but it is important to Hart and Sacks because of their beliefs about the limited efficacy of law and the concomitant limits on classical adjudication.

The subject of what we mean by the term "right" or "rights" is given serious but abbreviated attention in Hart and Sacks. Currently, I am giving it more attention both at the taxonomic level and also with some exposure to Dworkin and his fight with the utilitarians over the theoretical underpinnings of rights.

The question of whether a legal process course should be placed in the first year has generated considerable debate at Cornell. Some feel as though the students are not yet prepared to absorb the messages of the course. I agree that the course should not be placed in the first semester of the first year and might go even better later in a student's law school experience. But the reality of American legal education is that schools are extremely reluctant, except on

---

19 See generally Frederick Schauer, "Precedent", 39 Stan. L. Rev. 571 (1987).

20 See James A. Henderson, supra note 13.

21 Henry M. Hart and Albert M. Sacks, supra note 1 at 1.

the urgings of their accreditation authorities,[22] to add upperclass requirements. In addition, I think the course goes well enough in the second semester of the first year to justify its retention there. Students are hungry for an overall look at the legal order and for a discussion of core principles and concepts. They are ready to escape the compartmentalization endemic to American legal education.

Besides all of these arguments my debt to Robert S. Summers is actually more personal. It is relatively easy in American legal education to get into a niche, in my case tax and legal history, and not be required to confront basic theoretical issues important even to being a good tax teacher or legal history scholar. Preparing for and teaching the legal process has not made me a superb scholar and thinker but it certainly has made me a better one. And for that I thank Robert S. Summers.

---

[22] This is why a required upperclass course in legal ethics was added to most law school curricula in the last twenty years.

Ectopia, Formalism, and Anti-Avoidance Rules in Income Tax Law

By John Prebble, Wellington*

Ectopia *Pathol.* ... Displacement or anomaly of situation or relation ... (OED)

1. Statutory general anti-avoidance rules

Governments attack tax avoidance in a number of ways. Statutory anti-avoidance rules are one means. Such rules come in two forms: specific and general. By 'specific' rules one refers to provisions that are contained in a particular regime within a tax statute, and that are specific to that regime. For example, a regime that permits a company to carry losses forward from one year to the next may include rules that limit this right to cases where the company maintains a certain minimum continuity of shareholding, or where the company continues to carry on the business where the losses were incurred.

General anti-avoidance rules, on the other hand, potentially apply to any kind of transaction that may result in tax avoidance. A typical example is section 99 of the New Zealand Income Tax Act 1976, which reads:

> Every arrangement made or entered into, ... shall be absolutely void as against the Commissioner for income tax purposes if and to the extent that, directly or indirectly, –
> (a) Its purpose or effect is tax avoidance; or
> (b) Where it has two or more purposes or effects, one of its purposes or effects (not being a merely incidental purpose or effect) is tax avoidance, whether or not any other or others of its purposes or effects relate to, or are referable to, ordinary business or family dealings, –
>
> whether or not any person affected by that arrangement is a party thereto.

Section 99 contains broad definitions of 'arrangement' and 'tax avoidance', the latter including 'avoiding, reducing, or postponing any liability to income tax.' The section empowers the Commissioner of Inland Revenue to reconstruct transactions if, after the section has taken effect and avoided an

---

* BA, LLB (hons) Auckland; BCL Oxon; JSD Cornell; of the Inner Temple, London; Barrister; Professor of Law in The Victoria University of Wellington, New Zealand. The help of the author's assistant, Mr David Plunkett, in preparing this chapter is gratefully acknowledged, as are discussions with Mr Ian Macduff and Mr B. V. Galvin, which aided in refining the author's ideas.

impugned arrangement, the facts do not disclose a liability on the part of the taxpayer.

With the notable exceptions of the United States of America and the United Kingdom, similar rules are contained in the tax legislation of many common law jurisdictions, including:

- Australia: Income Tax Assessment Act 1936 Part IVA
- Canada: Income Tax Act 1952 section 245
- Hong Kong: Income Tax Ordinance, section 61A
- Malaysia: Income Tax Act 1967 section 140
- Singapore: Income Tax Act section 33.

It is sometimes helpful to think of a statutory general anti-avoidance rule as a kind of rule of interpretation. It is a rule of interpretation that borrows from both the English style of strict interpretation and the American style of free interpretation. These two approaches to statutory interpretation are discussed by Atiyah and Summers in *Form and Substance in Anglo-American Law*. Atiyah and Summers consider the case where the draftsman has made an error, with the result that the plain meaning of the words of a statute fails to give effect to the intent of the legislature. They point out that the American lawyer would argue that the statute should be interpreted according to its substance and policy, in order to correct the error, whereas the English lawyer, while not denying that injustice will sometimes ensue, will hew to the plain meaning of the words. For the English lawyer, to start from the assumption that the draftsman is less than competent is likely to lead, in the long run, to more error.[1]

As mentioned, a general anti-avoidance rule may be seen as incorporating elements of both approaches. To the American it says: seek out the substance and do justice. To the English lawyer it says: the draftsman has indeed captured the intention of the legislature in the specific rules of the income tax legislation, but there is a more fundamental intent that must prevail. This fundamental intent is that people must not be permitted to avoid tax by exploiting the strict forms of the legislation.

2. The United States of America

The United States Internal Revenue Code contains no general anti-avoidance provision. This vacuity does not leave a deficiency in the weapons of the United States revenue authorities of the same magnitude that a similar omis-

---

[1] P. S. Atiyah and R. S. Summers, Form and Substance in Anglo-American Law (Oxford 1987) 106.

sion might leave in some other common law countries. The reason is that, by the standards of other common law judges, United States judges take a relatively anti-formalist approach to law in general and to tax law in particular.

American judges are more willing to hold documents to be shams or to take a substance over form approach to tax cases than are their counterparts in other common law jurisdictions. Consequently, American judges are willing to ignore the strict legal form of documents and the strict rights of the parties to them, and to levy tax on the basis of the substance of the transaction in question. That is, when American courts act to frustrate tax avoidance transactions, or to tax a transaction according to its economic effect, they rely on their inherent powers as courts and not on statutory authority to that effect.[2]

3. The United Kingdom

The United Kingdom lacks a general statutory anti-avoidance rule in its income tax legislation, but, at the same time, its judges take a relatively formal approach to law. One result is that transactions that would in other jurisdictions be brushed aside as artificial and avoidance-driven are apt to be tolerated in the United Kingdom. A celebrated example is *Inland Revenue Commissioners v Duke of Westminster,*[3] where the House of Lords upheld an arrangement whereby the Duke contrived to pay his gardener out of before tax income. By covenant, the Duke diverted income from investments direct to the gardener. The alternative was for the Duke to derive the income, to pay tax on it, and to remunerate the gardener out of after tax income. The House of Lords held that the Duke should be taxed according to the legal form of the transactions, and not according to their economic substance.

A more modern example is *Inland Revenue Commissioners v Bowater Property Developments Ltd,*[4] which concerned development land tax. At the time, this tax applied to the realised development value of land above a threshold of £50,000. The taxpayer was concerned about the vulnerability to the tax of a certain plot of land. The taxpayer formed a number of subsidiaries and divided the land among them and itself as tenants in common. That is, the land was not divided into separate titles. It was common ground between the taxpayer and the tax inspector that the transfers were made solely to avoid development land tax. Nevertheless, the taxpayer argued that there was a separate value threshold for development land tax purposes in respect of the beneficial interest in land held by each company. The House of Lords agreed.

---

2 The United States form-over-substance doctrines as applied in tax cases are usefully summarised in B. J. Arnold and J. R. Wilson, 'The General Anti-Avoidance Rule – Part I' (1988) 36 *Canadian Tax Journal* 880, 881.

3 [1936] AC 1; sub nom *Duke of Westminster v IRC* 19 TC 490.

4 [1989] AC 398 HL.

The formalism of the English approach is these days somewhat bluntened by a judge-made rule known as the 'fiscal nullity' doctrine. The extent and limits of this doctrine are still in the process of being worked out but, broadly speaking, the doctrine takes a preordained series of transactions that contains a step that is inserted only in order to avoid tax and treats the series as a single transaction for tax purposes, in effect ignoring the avoidance step. Generally, for the doctrine to apply it must be practically certain at the time of one transaction that the others would follow.[5] The fact that the taxpayer in the *Bowater* case successfully navigated the shoals of the fiscal nullity doctrine gives some indication of its limitations as a weapon in the hands of the revenue authorities.

A second recent development in the United Kingdom is for the courts to examine very carefully the actual legal effect of transactions, or of a series of transactions, in order to determine precisely the legal rights and obligations to which they give rise. That is, the courts are not bound by the labels that parties give to their transactions, nor by the form of the transactions, if name and form do not correspond with legal effect. This approach is not new, but it is nowadays taken further than formerly. For example, and over-simplifying somewhat, in *Ensign Tankers (Leasing) Ltd v Stokes*[6] the House of Lords analysed a transaction that was in form a non-recourse loan, and came to the conclusion that in legal effect it was a joint venture. Their Lordships held that the transaction should be treated for tax purposes as a joint venture and not as a non-recourse loan.

4. The rule of law

The development of the fiscal nullity doctrine has attracted considerable criticism in the United Kingdom. The burden of the criticism is that the doctrine substitutes uncertainty and judge-made law for the rule of law as enacted by Parliament.[7] General anti-avoidance rules contained in statutes, such as section 99 of the New Zealand Income Tax Act, attract similar criticism.[8] A fundamental problem is that whether a general anti-avoidance rule is statutory or judge-made its scope is uncertain. As Lord Templeman said in a New Zealand

---

[5] For a useful summary of the doctrine and an examination of the leading cases see J. Tiley (ed.), *Butterworths UK Tax Guide 1992 - 1993,* 6 - 23.

[6] [1992] 2 All ER 275; [1992] 2 WLR 469 HL.

[7] See, e.g., Revenue Law Committee of The Law Society, *Tax Law in the Melting Pot* (The Law Society 1985) 19ff., and 'The Discourse of Resistance' in Doreen McBarnet and Christopher Whelan, 'The Elusive Spirit of the Law: Formalism and the Struggle for Legal Control' (1991) 54 *Modern Law Review* 848, 856ff.

[8] See, e.g., G. J. Harley, 'Legislative and Judicial Anti-Avoidance Rules', in Asian-Pacific Tax and Research Centre, Singapore and Institute of Policy Studies, Wellington, *Anti-Avoidance and Tax Treaty Policies in the Asian-Pacific Region* (1989) 18 - 28.

appeal to the Privy Council, *Challenge Corp Ltd v Commissioner of Inland Revenue:*

> In the first place, even the [Commissioner] concedes that section 99, albeit expressed in the widest possible terms, has to be read subject to some limitation as regards transactions permitted or authorised by other legislative provisions if it is not to produce results that are absurd.[9]

The reason for this limitation is that some transactions that clearly have a tax-limiting effect are equally clearly envisaged, even promoted, by Parliament. Therefore, they should not be frustrated by an anti-avoidance rule. For example, many jurisdictions encourage savings by affording tax preferences to life insurance premiums or superannuation contributions. A taxpayer who takes advantage of such a preference is clearly liable neither to a statutory nor to a judge-made general anti-avoidance rule, but where does one draw the line? The answer is that it is not possible to draw the line. The law is worked out on a case-by-case basis, with all the uncertainty that this entails, whether the anti-avoidance rule in question is statutory or judge-made.[10]

The disfavour in which lawyers tend to hold statutory general anti-avoidance rules in particular is further explained by factors identified by Atiyah and Summers in *Form and Substance in Anglo-American Law.* Typically, statutes draw clear lines that are easily discoverable and known to all, whereas precedent is by nature less definite and more flexible. Further, statute law is embodied in a fixed, canonical form. It is the paradigmatic type of formal law, and is susceptible to a high degree of interpretive formality.[11] Statutory general anti-avoidance rules not only fail to comply with the paradigm; they unashamedly reject these typical properties of statute law. General anti-avoidance rules direct the courts to adopt a substance-over-form approach, and avowedly introduce uncertainty into a regime (income tax law) that is in most countries highly formalistic and already complex enough. The reaction of the lawyer, who is trained to respect the merits of form, is not surprising.

---

[9] [1986] 2 New Zealand Law Reports 555, 564 (PC).

[10] But see Lon Fuller, who contended in 'American Legal Realism' (1934) 82 *University of Pennsylvania Law Review* 429, 434 - 435 that formalistic rules create more uncertainty than open-textured, informal rules. Fuller's argument was that, in a formal system, judges first decide a case on its merits and then torture the case into compliance with a more-or-less appropriate formal rule, whereas a judge who is governed by open-textured directives can rely on policy justifications, which enable a more logical system of rules to be built up. One could regard the development of the United Kingdom fiscal nullity doctrine as a vindication of Fuller, in that the doctrine is arguably a systematic refusal by English judges to observe the formal rules that governed them. See further, Jason Scott Johnston, 'Uncertainty, Chaos, and the Torts Process: an Economic Analysis of Legal Form' (1991) 76 *Cornell Law Review,* 341.

[11] P. S. Atiyah and R. S. Summers, *Form and Substance in Anglo-American Law* (Oxford 1987) 96 - 97. See also R. S. Summers, 'The Formal Character of Law', (1992) *Cambridge Law Journal* 242, 248, for a list of reasons for, or benefits that flow from, the formal aspect of law.

5. The demands of a taxation system

The existence of general anti-avoidance rules is contrary to the values of certainty, form, and the primacy of the rule of law. But there is a competing value: the need to ensure that a country's tax system works effectively, and is not subverted by ingenious tax planning. In most of the countries mentioned in this chapter this competing value has prevailed, and general anti-avoidance rules have been enacted as legislation.

To put the matter another way, the simple explanation for the desirability of a general anti-avoidance rule is that the forms of business transaction and of investment are infinite and cannot all be predicted by the makers of tax policy. Consequently, governments cannot predict, and cannot comprehensively guard against, the measures that people may adopt to avoid tax. Formal, certain, focused anti-avoidance rules will inevitably have loopholes, which will inevitably be exploited. A general rule acts as a back-stop to narrow, regime-specific rules.

There must be some sympathy for any government that is faced with the problem of minimising tax avoidance and trying to achieve some sort of equity between taxpayers in respect of the effective tax rates that they suffer. Scholars and practitioners in the tax area are very familiar with the way in which expertly-advised citizens are able to minimise their tax burdens, to the detriment of the taxpaying public in general.[12]

Be that as it may, a general anti-avoidance rule *does* erode the the rule of law in the manner that has been described here. In other areas, we are unwilling to see the rule of law give way to practical requirements of the state. One has to think only of the procedural safeguards that protect people charged with criminal offences, or the principles developed in the common law whereby the courts are able and willing to review administrative actions of the government.

The existence of a general anti-avoidance rule of uncertain scope is defended by reference to practicalities, but is that enough? More fundamentally, is the argument even morally or intellectually respectable? A telling consideration is that the argument is an example of 'ends justify means', which is an unfortunate basis for an erosion of the rule of law.

This reflection leads to the questions: is there some other argument that might justify the adoption of general anti-avoidance rules? More specifically, is there some characteristic of tax law that relevantly distinguishes it from the law in general and that justifies the resort to uncertainty that is inherent in a general anti-avoidance rule? The thesis of this chapter is that the answer is yes.

---

[12] See, e.g. Doreen McBarnet and Christopher Whelan, 'The Elusive Spirit of the Law: Formalism and the Struggle for Legal Control' (1991) 54 *Modern Law Review* 848.

Tax law, or, at least, income tax law, has several characteristics that distinguish it from most other areas of law. These characteristics justify a substance over form approach in at least some areas of tax law.

6. Fundamental flaws in the foundations of income tax law

It is basic to income tax law that there must be a concept of income. Taxpayers, the tax authorities, and the courts, must be able to say that a particular receipt or profit is income, and therefore taxable, or that it is not. Further, it is basic to income tax law that some income items are taxable and that some are not. For example, states do not attempt to tax foreign income derived by foreigners. For a tax system to work fairly and efficiently the rules that determine which receipts are income, and, of those, which are taxable, should be logical and consistent with one another.

This basic requirement for rules that can identify receipts that are income and that can determine which income items are taxable can never be perfectly satisfied, even in theory. The problem is that income, in the sense that the term is used in income tax law, is an artificial creation of that law. It is not something that one meets in nature or in the world of reality. This proposition may be illustrated by reference to the connection of income on the one hand with space and time on the other hand.

7. Space

The public law of a state operates within the frontiers and upon the citizens or residents of that state. Thus, with a few exceptions in respect of crimes like piracy, states do not attempt to use their criminal laws to regulate behaviour that takes place beyond their frontiers. Nor will a court of one country attempt to review the actions of an official of another country. In private law, the rules are different. One state will, for example, enforce a contract made somewhere else, or enforce the inheritance rules of another state.

Income tax law is part of a state's public law. No state purports to tax *any* income. All states have rules to determine what income they will tax, and what income they will leave alone. Most states tax income that arises within their borders. Many states also tax income of residents that arises abroad. Some tax income of citizens that arises abroad. But states do not purport to tax the foreign source income of foreigners.

The statement of the rule contains within itself the statement of the problem: for purposes of income tax law it is often necessary to determine whether an item of income has a foreign source or a domestic source. Here lies the difficulty. If the analogy is not over-strained, income tax law is part of public law, but income itself has more the features of something that is related to private law.

Take interest. The earning of interest is something that citizens arrange for themselves, by virtue of rules of private law, and something that they could arrange perfectly well (indeed, more easily) if there were no national frontiers. But what is the source of interest that is paid by a resident of France to a resident of Germany, in respect of a loan that is secured over land in Canada, where the contract was negotiated and signed in England, where the physical payment of the interest takes place by automatic transfer between two Hong Kong banks, and the loan monies are used as circulating capital in a business that is carried on in the United States of America?

None of the jurisdictions mentioned would have much difficulty in enforcing a judgment for the interest, and they would have little more difficulty in adjudicating a dispute on a more fundamental question about whether the interest was payable in the first place. But when it comes to the question of *taxing* the interest problems of principle arise for any country that taxes income on the basis of source.

The problem is that intangible, abstract things like interest cannot have a source in the sense that, for example, a river has a source somewhere in the physical world. Nevertheless, tax law has no alternative but to treat the source of interest as if it were a physical place that can be located in space, geographically. The reason is that national frontiers are a feature of the physical world: they divide it into physical parts; and the existence of national frontiers forces us to identify the source of interest as if it were a physical phenomenon. That is not possible, if only because money is not a physical phenomenon. (Bank notes and other tokens of money exist physically, but only primitive tax systems would answer questions of derivation of interest by reference to the time or place at which bank notes pass from one person to another. Such systems are particularly vulnerable to avoidance.)

The same difficulties arise in respect of business profits. What is the source of the profit derived by an airline that carries a passenger between Bombay and Bangkok, being one leg of a journey from Frankfurt to Sydney? Does it make any difference where the passenger's ticket was bought, or where the airline is incorporated? What is the source of profit from a contract to manufacture goods in Italy and to export them to the United States? Does it make any difference where the contract was concluded, or where property in the goods passes?

Again, there is no logical answer to these questions. The profits are derived not *because of* but *in spite of* or *ignoring* national frontiers. As in the case of interest, the frontiers are an artificial, man-made matrix that are imposed ab extra. Be that as it may, any country that taxes income on the basis of its source must have laws that identify the source of income. For the reasons mentioned, such laws are inherently flawed in the same sense that a rule that purports to measure, say, anger, in terms of centimetres or kilograms is flawed. That is, when one takes into account the manner in which income tax rules must cope with problems of space or geography it becomes clear that there are inherent flaws in the very foundations of the discipline.

These flaws open the way to tax avoidance. There are an infinite number of ways in which people can exploit the spatial limitations of the concept of income in order to avoid tax, but one example will suffice here. Suppose a taxpayer has one million dollars with which to build a factory. The obvious approach is simply to pay a builder to erect the factory, and to move in. An alternative is to use the million dollars to capitalise a company in a tax haven (that is, a country that charges no income tax) and to borrow the capital back at interest, and then to pay the builder, thus creating an artificial deduction for the benefit of the taxpayer. Whether this scheme is worthwhile depends on whether, or on how much, tax is charged on the interest that flows outward to the company in the tax haven. But it is not uncommon for tax planners to be able to achieve a low or zero tax rate on outward flowing interest by one technique or another.

8. Time

The problem of time is similar in kind to the problem of space. The income of a typical business is a stream that continues from year to year without reference to the calendar. But an income tax regime cannot operate in this manner. For there to be income tax, income must not only be identified, but it must be divided into manageable portions. The government cannot wait until a business winds down in order to see what income the business has derived over its life. Rather, the life of the business must be divided into periods and the income of each period must be assessed and taxed.

The period chosen is invariably 12 months, because the year is a duration that people are comfortable with, and that is used for other purposes, including the reporting of profits to owners. Because the year is used in so many contexts its use for taxation is hardly a cause for thought, let alone for comment. But governments could just as well have opted for longer or shorter periods had they so chosen, without making much difference to the rules of income taxation.

Be that as it may, once a government has decided to measure income by reference to time, no matter what length of time, there must immediately be whole codes of rules that are calculated to ensure that people do not contrive to defer their income to a later period, or to accelerate their expenses to an earlier period. Take the taxpayer who lends $ 500 for two years at 12 per cent interest, payable monthly, a total of $ 120. Assume that the 24 months correspond to two fiscal years of the tax regime to which the lender is subject.

From an economic point of view, the monthly payments received by the taxpayer are the same as receipt of all the interest on day one (with an actuarially-calculated decrease in the $ 120 to account for the time value of money) or of receipt of the total sum on day 731, the first day of year three (with a corresponding increase in the $ 120). But in a simple system that assesses income to tax annually on a receipts basis, there will be a considerable difference between the three situations as far as tax consequences go.

Where the interest is all received on day one the taxpayer will pay all his tax in year one. Where the interest is paid monthly tax will be divided equally between years one and two. Where the interest is paid on day 731 tax will be paid in year three. The taxpayer's position is worse in the first case because his fiscal liability is accelerated, and better in the third case because it is deferred. Because of the time value of money, tax deferred is tax saved.

For this sort of reason, most tax systems have rules of greater or lesser sophistication that endeavour to force taxpayers to report their income on an accruals basis that spreads profits evenly into each tax year. As time goes by and as governments learn from one another, tax systems become increasingly mature and such rules become increasingly effective. But the very essence of the rules is that they must treat transactions as if they were different from their factual form, and as if the legal rights of the parties were different from the rights that are set out in their contracts. That is, for example, they must treat the third case in the example given as if interest was spread over 24 months and not in fact received on day 731, and the actual sums deemed to have been derived for tax purposes must be adjusted to allow for the time value of money.

There are other problems with time. Take the farmer who, like most farmers, is prey to the cycles of the market. She enjoys five good, profitable, years, followed by five bad years, where she incurs losses. Suppose that her net result over the ten years is to break even. In most tax systems the farmer will lose, because the tax that she has paid in the first five years will not be refunded in the second five years. To cope with this kind of problem some tax regimes allow farmers, and others whose income is notably lumpy, to pay tax on an average basis rather than on the basis of actual profits.

9. Capital

One timing problem dwarfs all others. This is the distinction between capital and income, a distinction that virtually all regimes that purport to tax 'income' attempt to make. The problem is that there is no clear line that distinguishes capital from income and, even worse, it is relatively easy for taxpayers to convert income into capital, and thus to avoid tax. Of course, most tax regimes have rules that are designed to frustrate this kind of activity, but they are not always successful.

The difficulty, and ultimate illogicality, of distinguishing capital from income is illustrated by considering the question of business premises. If a business leases its premises it will deduct the rent that it pays, along with other expenses, from its receipts in calculating its taxable profits. If the business buys its premises it will not take a deduction for the price, because the price is a capital item, though the law may make the taxpayer an allowance in calculating profits to compensate for depreciation of the premises from year to year. If one form of expenses on premises is capital, and another form is income, what is the difference? To over-simplify, capital expenses relate to things that constitute enduring benefits for the taxpayer, and income items relate to benefits that are more temporary. But business premises perform precisely the same function whether they are rented or purchased.

The lack of a true distinction between capital items and income items may be illustrated more graphically by considering some simple transactions that are postulated to take place in the absence of a tax regime. Suppose a retailer, a sole trader, sells up her business. To her, there is no difference between the cash received for the various components: premises, fittings, and trading stock. In this context, the distinction between capital and income is meaningless for her purposes.

Alternatively, a retailer may consider improving her sales both by increasing her stock and by renovating her shop. For tax purposes she must treat the expenses differently. Admittedly, for the purposes of calculating her profits on an annual basis (if she is so disposed even in the absence of a tax system) she must also categorise the expenses differently. But if it is a question of determining profits over the long haul (say 20 years) both items are simply expenses that have been repeated a number of times, though one more often than the other.

This similarity of function between capital items and income items is fundamental to the ability of taxpayers to change income into capital. Take, for example, a portfolio of shares that is pregnant with profits, held by a private investor. The shareholder who wants to realise and to use the profits has two options. First, she can wait for a dividend to be declared. But a dividend is an income item and is taxable. Alternatively, she can sell the shares, and the proceeds will reflect both the capital value of the shares and the potential dividend. If the taxpayer is a private investor, the proceeds will be capital in her hands and not subject to income tax.

Of course, the benefits to the shareholder of this characterisation of the proceeds may be limited in jurisdictions where there is a capital gains tax, and the income tax rules of the jurisdiction may also have something to say on the matter. But these considerations do not detract from the fundamental point that, by its very nature, an income tax mandates a distinction between capital and income, a distinction that does not have a basis in economic reality.

10. The ectopia of tax law

Preceding sections of this chapter have explained that it is fundamental to an income tax that there should be a definition of 'income' and a delimitation of the geographical scope of the tax, and that both of these rules should be logical and internally consistent. At the same time, it has been argued that the need to fit the concept of income into the dimensions of space and time means that these fundamental requirements can never be perfected.[13] This paradox is a manifestation, or perhaps a consequence, of a more general phenomenon that may be called the 'ectopia' of income tax law.

This term is used by the author to refer to a characteristic that distinguishes tax law from most other areas of law: the fact that tax law is in a sense detached and dislocated from its subject matter. The phenomenon is particularly apparent in rules that relate to the taxation of business profits. Tax law clearly *refers* to business profits, but it does not describe the phenomena by which business profits arise, and its objective is not to regulate profits or the methods by which they are won.

Compare the way that tax law works with, say, criminal law. Criminal law defines certain actions as crimes and provides penalties for them. That is, criminal law is closely related to its subject matter, which is criminal activity. Similarly, laws that regulate business activity describe certain activities that are unlawful, or prescribe procedures for certain kinds of transaction. Antitrust laws, for example, proscribe behaviour that is characterised by the law as monopolistic, and Statutes of Frauds require writing and a signature before certain kinds of contract are able to be enforced.

All this is not surprising; in fact, were it not for the contrast that obtains in respect of tax law the fact that law is usually closely related to its subject matter would hardly be worth mentioning. After all, if one sets out to write a law about crime it is to be expected that the result will indeed relate closely to criminal activity. There is a symbiotic relationship between criminal law and crime, just as there is a symbiotic relationship between most law and its subject matter. To use Weinrib's words, '. . . the distinctive rationality of law is immanent to the legal material on which it operates'.[14]

---

[13] The problems that space, time, and capital pose to the legislator who composes income tax law are explored further in J. Prebble, *Why is Tax Law Incomprehensible?* (1993) IX Victoria University of Wellington Inaugural Addresses (New Series).

Tax law is different. In the business area we start with business activity, an activity that exists independently of tax law. Furthermore, the aspect of business in which tax law is most interested, profit, also exists independently of tax law. Tax law is imposed from above on phenomena that already exist, business and profit. Moreover, far from attempting to describe, mould, or influence business and profit, tax law is most efficient when it is neutral between different forms of business association or investment, between different kinds of transaction, or between different industries.

The purpose of tax law is to raise taxes, not to regulate or to promote business. In order to promote administrative efficiency and to minimise compliance costs, and, indeed, to increase the chances of taxes' working at all, governments ensure that tax legislation is as much in sympathy with the forms of business that the legislation is designed to tax as is possible. But in the end, as has been mentioned, tax law is an alien matrix that is imposed upon existing economic activity that, in the nature of things, it cannot fit exactly. As has been explained, because tax law must classify and delimit income by reference to space and to time, and because income is inherently not apt to be subjected to these measures, there is a dislocation, or ectopia, between tax law and its subject matter.

The ectopic nature of tax law may not be unique, but finding analogies in other areas of law is difficult.[15] One that occurs to the author is the imposition by a conqueror of its family law on a subject people. Suppose that a nation whose family law is based on monogamy conquers a people for whom polyan-

---

[14] Ernest J. Weinrib, 'Legal Formalism' (1988) 97 *Yale Law Journal* 949, 953, and see id., 955 and passim, and at 974: 'Intelligibility involves the interpretation of content and its immanent form. One achieves a complete understanding when the form is exhibited and the content is seen as adequate to it. If the elements initially identified have the truly fundamental significance that legal experience claims for them, they will be constituents in the distinctive unity that makes the juridical relationship what it is. The immediate understanding of legal experience is only provisional until form becomes explicit. Then juridical intelligibility emerges from a mutually reinforcing movement between form and content: form is the organising idea latent in the content of a sophisticated legal culture, and the ultimate test for legal content is its adequacy to the form it expresses.' A major thesis of this chapter is that income tax law cannot pass this 'ultimate test' because of fundamental conceptual inconsistencies in its makeup.

[15] It is emphasised that by 'ectopic' law one refers to law that, logically, can relate only imperfectly to its subject matter. From ectopic law should be distinguished law that, on examination, appears to be incoherent and lacking in principle. The cause of such incoherence and lack of principle may be ectopia. But it may alternatively be that although there is no general agreement on fundamental principle, law makers and scholars treat the law as if it were a coherent matrix. Application of the law may show that there is in fact inconsistency and incoherence, but it is at least conceptually possible that the law might be re-written in a manner that is coherent. Income tax law, on the other hand, can never be wholly coherent because of the impossibility of rationalising rules about time and space. An example of an examination of an area of law said to be incoherent is John W. Van Doren, 'Private Property: A Study in Incoherence', (1986) 63 *University of Detroit Law Review* 683.

dry is the norm, and imposes its family law on the conquered. How are the courts to deal with a dispute between a wife and one of her husbands? Even more difficult, how will the courts cope with a dispute between two husbands of one wife? In short, there will be an ectopia between the law and its subject matter. No doubt partly for that reason, conquerors much more commonly impose their public or commercial law on the conquered than their family law.

The ectopia of tax law is never as apparent as the hypothetical ectopia of family law described in the previous paragraph. One reason is that parliaments try as best they can to fit tax laws to the structures and transactions of the businesses to which the laws apply. This process masks the problem and, be it said, over large areas of tax law solves it. An analogy is a circle (tax law) that covers a square (business) with sides of the same length as the circle's diameter. Coverage is effective over most of the square, but the corners escape.

11. Ectopia and formality in tax law

Not surprisingly, the greatest opportunities for tax avoidance tend to occur where the ectopia of tax law is most apparent – at the corners of the square, as it were. Thus, diverting income to a foreign country to take advantage of the factor of space, or deferring the recognition of income, or converting income to capital, in the latter cases to take advantage of the factor of time, describe in general terms a large proportion of all the techniques of avoidance that are available to the taxpayer. In response, large parts of the income tax legislation of most countries are given over to specific rules that are calculated to frustrate these methods of avoidance.

Typically, these specific anti-avoidance rules are highly formal, which is another feature of tax law. One reason for this formality is the ectopia of tax law; there is a fundamental discontinuity between tax law and its subject matter. Consequently, tax law must rely on form rather than on substance. The substance that it deals with (business) is not the substance of its raison d'être (raising money).

The thesis of the previous paragraph is more familiar when expressed in another manner: for the courts, there is no policy content in tax law. The most frequently quoted judicial statement to this effect is probably this passage from Mr Justice Rowlatt's judgment in *Cape Brandy Syndicate v Inland Revenue Commissioners:*[16]

[16] [1921] 1 King's Bench 64, 71. The lack of policy content in tax law is highlighted by a comparison of tax law with other areas of law. In other areas, it is not so hard for a judge to escape formalism because she generally has some criterion other than the plain language of the statute to which to refer; that is, the policy of the statute can be made out, and the judge can refer to principle, either general or specific. Cf Frederick Schnauer, 'Formalism' (1988) 97 *Yale Law Journal,* 509, 518 - 519.

> ... in a taxing Act one has to look merely at what is clearly said. There is no room for any intendment. There is no equity about a tax. There is no presumption as to a tax. Nothing is to be read in, nothing implied. One can only look fairly at the language used.

So deeply ingrained is this habit of thought that courts will sometimes decline to interpret tax legislation purposively even when directed to do so by statute. For example Section 5 (j) of the New Zealand Acts Interpretation Act 1924 provides that:

> 'Every Act ... shall be deemed remedial, whether its immediate purport is to direct the doing of anything Parliament deems to be for the public good, or to prevent or punish the doing of anything it deems contrary to the public good, and shall accordingly receive such fair, large, and liberal construction and interpretation as will best ensure the attainment of the object of the Act ... according to its true intent, meaning, and spirit ...'

In *Commissioner of Inland Revenue v International Importing Ltd,*[17] Mr Justice Turner, President of the Court of Appeal, said that the approach enjoined by section 5 (j):

> '... is normally of little material assistance in the construction of revenue statutes. The 'object of the Act' which the section designates as a key to questions of statutory construction is often only too clearly the collection of funds to swell the general revenues of the State; and Courts of construction have consistently declined to read implications into such statutes to catch a taxpayer who in his business dealings has relied upon the text of the statute, by some extension of the wording accepting the notion of a moral duty to pay a 'proper' amount of tax. The taxing provision is read as prescribing the tax for which its text plainly provides, no more and no less.'

12. An illusory face of formalism

A modern tax statute is a complex construction of intricate, interlocking, formal rules. Superficially, it appears, as it were, to be aware of its mission and to be carrying out that mission in a businesslike and purposeful manner. There is some truth in that impression. As Summers points out, the highly formal rules of the tax system do in fact function relatively smoothly most of the time, and do in fact enable the state to raise huge sums of money in revenue.[18] To use again the metaphor employed earlier, in the area of the square that is covered by the circle tax laws operate with some certainty. Elsewhere there is an elusive substance of, say, profit, the essence of which cannot adequately be captured by rules that relate to a matter that is external to the profit, that is, rules that are part of an income tax regime that attempts to locate the profit in

---

[17] [1972] New Zealand Law Reports 1095, 1096, CA.

[18] R. S. Summers, 'The Formal Character of Law', (1992) *Cambridge Law Journal* 242, 250.

time and space. In short, the surface appearance of an apparently robust, integrated regime is belied by foundations that are elusive and shifting.

The result can only be a failure of the income tax system to capture gains that its authors intended that it should capture (or would have intended, had they thought of the matter), as lacunae are discovered between formal rules.

This situation lends weight to, and may even justify, an argument for a general anti-avoidance rule. A general anti-avoidance rule is in essence anti-formalist and substantive. But its role is to extend the coverage of an income tax regime to areas that, almost by definition, an income tax regime cannot reach, being areas that elude the law because of the impossibility of ever fitting the naturally occurring phenomena of business and profits into a regime that can operate only within the boundaries of artificial constructs: national frontiers and the calendar.

To put the conclusion another way, the concept of profit is not amenable to definition in terms of rules that fix the profit of a particular taxpayer in time and space. And yet any income tax regime requires such rules to be used for just that purpose. Consequently, such rules can only be formal and, in the end, arbitrary. Being arbitrary, they tend to leave substantive lacunae that escape their grasp. These areas of substance can be reached only by a rule that itself is anti-formalist, namely a general anti-avoidance rule.

[To digress briefly, the fact that a jurisdiction adopts a general anti-avoidance rule, and the arguments that may justify that adoption, do not inevitably lead to the the rule's being applied in the liberal manner that its authors no doubt intend. McBarnet and Whelan usefully list and discuss a number of techniques whereby open-ended anti-avoidance and similar anti-formalist rules sometimes become refined and formalised (the techniques include, for example, self-restraint and the issuance of guidelines by government authorities, and the narrowing of precedents by the courts).[19] The emasculation of a previous form of the Australian anti-avoidance rule (section 260 of the Income Tax Assessment Act 1936) at the hands of the Australian High Court is notorious.[20] Not so dramatically, in the late 1980s the United Kingdom fiscal nullity doctrine was limited and formalised by the courts[21] to such effect that nowadays it is more often called simply the 'New Approach' (ordi-

[19] Doreen McBarnet and Christopher Whelan, 'The Elusive Spirit of the Law: Formalism and the Struggle for Legal Control' (1991) 54 *Modern Law Review* 848, 860ff.

[20] E.g., *Cridland v Commissioner of Taxation* (Cth) (1977) 140 Commonwealth Law Reports 330, 77 ATC 4538; *Slutzkin v Commissioner of Taxation* (Cth) 140 Commonwealth Law Reports 314, 77 ATC 4076; *Mullens Investments Pty Ltd v Commissioner of Taxation* (Cth) (1976) 135 Commonwealth Law Reports 290, 76 ATC 4288. See generally, G. Lehmann, 'Judicial and Statutory Restrictions on Tax Avoidance', in Richard E. Krever (ed.) *Australian Taxation, Principles and Practice* (Melbourne 1987) 295 - 313.

[21] See generally J. Tiley, ed, *Butterworths UK Tax Guide 1992 - 1993,* 6 - 23. In the early 1980s the New Approach appeared to be likely to develop into a true substance-

narily with the capital letters appropriate to a proper name), the label 'fiscal nullity' perhaps being thought to promise more to the revenue authorities than the courts deliver. But the *fate* of a general anti-avoidance rule, as opposed to the reason or justification for its existence, is not germane to the thesis of this chapter.]

It is an interesting irony that the reason for the relative formality of tax regimes is that there are substantive requirements of a tax system that cannot be framed in terms of coherent rules. These requirements cannot, therefore, reasonably be left to the judges, because judges are expected to systematise their decisions in a logical, consistent manner. The rules must therefore be framed as statutes, which can be arbitrary and inconsistent but nevertheless good law.[22] A further irony is that income tax law, that most formal of areas of law, is at bottom incapable of satisfying the indispensable theme of formalism: the internal intelligibility of law.[23] As will have been appreciated, this fundamental lack of internal intelligibility, this substantive incoherence that is an inherent characteristic of income tax law, is different in kind from the general indeterminacy of law that is described by members of the critical legal studies school, and is not an example of that indeterminacy (to express no view on whether those who adhere to the indeterminacy doctrine are correct).[24]

As has been mentioned, in many regimes the formal rules of income tax law are reinforced by a highly informal general anti-avoidance rule, a rule that is so informal that it might even be said to lack the 'essence of law'.[25] But this lack of formality is explained by the fact that income tax law in general lacks something that might also be called an essence of the law: a symbiotic relationship between the law and its subject matter.

---

over-form doctrine, but it became formalised in, particularly, *Craven v White* [1989] AC 398, 62 TC 1, [1988] 3 All ER 495 HL.

[22] Cf P. S. Atiyah and R. S. Summers, *Form and Substance in Anglo-American Law* (Oxford 1987) 96 - 97.

[23] See Ernest J. Weinrib, 'Legal Formalism' (1988) 97 *Yale Law Journal* 949, 952.

[24] For a discussion and evaluation of the idea of indeterminacy, see Ken Kress, 'Legal Indeterminacy', (1989) 77 *California Law Review*, 283, and see generally, Kelman, *A Guide to Critical Legal Studies* (Cambridge, Mass, 1987).

[25] R. S. Summers, 'The Formal Character of Law', (1992) *Cambridge Law Journal* 242, 260.

Involvement and Detachment in the Presentation of Evidence

By Michele Taruffo, Pavia

1. Involvement and Detachment

In one of his most important essays concerning the sociology of knowledge, Norbert Elias sketches out a fundamental distinction between two basic attitudes towards reality. The former attitude is of involvement. The knowing subject is *involved* when he is interested in the outcome of the process of knowledge not only because he aims at knowing a reality, but mainly because he shares the culture, the values, the purposes of the social reality he wants to know. The main criterion to be used in order to identify situations of involvement is the *degree of danger* involved in the situation in which the knowing subject in interested. The latter attitude is of detachment. The knowing subject is *detached* when he acts with a high degree of neutrality and self-restraint with reference to the reality. He is interested in knowing such a reality, but he is not personally involved in it, and he does not run any risk connected with the outcome of his knowledge.

Both involvement and detachment are idealization and extreme descriptions of attitudes affecting the *direction of knowledge*. As opposite idealizations, they should be taken as the opposite poles of a scale on which several mixed attitudes can be found. In fact every actual attitude in knowledge is a mix of involvement and detachment: the distinction between the two extreme ideas is useful in the analysis of such attitudes, but the main problem is to establish how much involvement (and of which kind) and how much detachment are present in any given situation. Of course the quantity and quality of the mix of involvement and detachment in a given concrete situation depend on social and cultural factors, and on the context of that situation. The processes of knowledge are not stiff and fixed once and forever: they vary according to several factors, as for instance the starting conditions of knowledge in a given situation. Among these factors the degree of involvement and/or detachment is extremely important.

According to whether the attitude of the subject is more involved or detached, his approach to the reality, or in general to the matter of knowledge, is different. The detached attitude means a knowledge that, at least in principle, is more coherent to the reality: here the obvious model is given by the natural sciences. Although the knowledge of non-human nature is culture-laden, theory-laden and even value-laden, nevertheless the typical approach of the natural scientist tends to be detached, and therefore coherent to the reality. The higher the personal involvement of the subject in the outcome of knowledge (mainly in terms of danger and fear), the less coherent is this knowledge to the reality.

Elias outlines and discusses the distinction between involvement and detachment mainly with reference to the sociological knowledge, but it is clear that also in his own perspective this distinction has a much wider scope. In order to explain the distinction, in fact, Elias himself draws examples from epistemology and even from painting. Probably, therefore, such a distinction is general, and it can be used in order to analyse any situation where someone has to know some reality, that is when a subject has to build up and state a judgment concerning anything that is taken as an "object" of judgment.

2. The Legal Process

The legal process, civil and criminal, can be described and analysed in a very large number of ways, according to several theories, methods, ideologies, legal cultures and social or political ideals. So for instance the question of the purposes of the legal process is a very complex and neverending issue in the legal culture of every country, and also at the comparative level.

But inside this extremely complicated and varying panorama one point can be assumed as rather common to the several perspectives (although not to every possible perspective). This point is that always the legal process aims at building up and stating a judgment about a case. In order to do so, the process must be structured so that a neutral subject (court, judge, jury) considers the case, determines its subject matter, gets acquainted with the facts of the case and with the relevant legal rules, and therefore states his own judgment on the case. An important feature of the legal process (at least in modern and developed system) is that the opposing parties of the case must be allowed to present their own opposite sides of the case in a dialectic and adversary trial, so that the final judgment stems also from this adversary presentation. At the core of this complex and sophisticated machinery there is in most cases, when the so called *facts in issue* must be established, the *presentation of evidence,* that is the procedure by which the relevant items of evidence are selected, presented, analysed, discussed and evaluated in order to find the basis for a reliable judgment about the facts of the case.

We should be aware of the fact that we are dealing with extremely dangerous, fuzzy, disputable and complicated ideas. So, for instance, the idea of "facts in issue" is disputed from several points of view: one can say that the legal process never deals with *brute* facts, because only *institutional* or *legal* facts are taken into account in the legal process. Someone denies any possibility of speaking of "facts" in any sense of the word, because the legal process should deal only with rules and stories, but never with facts. At any rate, the connection between facts and legal rules is extremely difficult to understand, specially for those who do not have any sensitivity towards the reality of the legal process, and think only of abstract theories concerning what happens in court. Moreover, the procedural machineries for the presentation of evidence are very different in the several legal systems, according to the different structures of the legal process as a whole, to different historical traditions, to different legal cultures, and so on. Correspondingly, significant variations can be found in theories concerning the purposes of the legal process, the kind of judgment that it is expected to produce, and the role of evidence inside the machinery aimed at producing judgments. Another important problem deals with the "search for truth" concerning the facts of the case: the concept of truth is puzzling in the theory and practice of the legal process no less than in philosophy and epistemology, and the concept of "judicial truth" is directly affected by extra-legal problems. Moreover, it is disputed, in several legal systems, *whether* the truth of the facts (in any meaning of the word) should be considered as a purpose of the legal process, and also which kind of truth should or could be reached in the judicial context. More generally, someone denies that any kind of truth can be found in the judicial process, so that the whole problem of facts, evidence and judgment on facts, should be completely overlooked.

Notwithstanding all this, the undeniable fact is that courts state judgments about cases, that such judgments usually contain statements concerning the facts in issue, that these statements are usually founded upon evidence, and that evidence is usually presented by the parties in the legal process, in order to provide for the basis of the judgment on the facts of the case. Therefore, nobody can meaningfully say that all this is devoid of any relevancy, or that it is nothing but sheer nonsense. Of course one may say that, but in so doing he prevents himself from understanding the basic functioning of the administration of justice in any system.

A much more fruitful approach to this cluster of problems is to consider the legal process as a machinery aimed also at building up a reliable judgment concerning the facts of the case, as a necessary condition for a correct decision of the case itself. The main features of this machinery concerning the judgment on the facts in issue are two: a) items of evidence are collected, by means of legally established procedures, in order to find out a proper cognitive basis for the judgment on the facts. This judgment is expected to be founded upon relevant and admissible evidence; it is aimed at providing a reliable picture of the concrete situation from which the case arose. b) evidence is presented in a procedural context where several persons play their own different roles. These roles depend on the structure of the proceedings, and on the functions these persons perform inside this structure. These roles, and the way they are played by the several subjects, directly affect the presentation of evidence, and therefore also the outcome that is drawn from evidence in the final judgment. In order to understand and to analyse these roles, one does not need to go to the smallest details of every legal system. Some significant achievements can probably by reached from a general and functional viewpoint.

This approach assumes only that it is meaningful to consider the legal process as a machinery aimed at yielding reliable judgments concerning the concrete situation involved in a case. Perhaps it implies a cognitive theory of evidence and of the search of truth in the legal process (and it is more deeply consistent with such a theory), but probably it can be maintained even without such an implication. This approach is meaningful also in the strict semiotic perspective, according to which the legal process can be viewed as a context of speeches or as a dialogue played by several subjects about a disputed situation. In fact, even when the philosophical or cognitive problem of judicial truth is left aside, and only the semiotic perspective is taken into account, it cannot be denied that the legal process is a complex semiotic situation that develops according to a legal procedure, and that ends up with the statement of a judgment based upon evidence and concerning the facts of the case.

If one wants to understand some relevant features of such a complex situation, he must take into account that this situation develops *procedurally,* and that its development is based upon the interaction of several subjects performing different roles. The procedural side of the legal process must be taken into account because it provides the institutional framework of the judicial litigation, but it concerns mainly lawyers and legal scholars; therefore, it can be overlooked here. The side that will be considered here is the one concerning the different roles played by the several subjects interacting in the legal process, and particularly in the presentation of evidence. From a formal and legal point of view, these roles are determined by the law, and particularly by the legal rules concerning the proceedings and the several moves that can be made at each step of the proceedings. From a substantial and functional point of view, these roles can be analysed in terms of attitudes, behaviors, speeches and cognitions, evaluations and judgments.

The legal process can be viewed, therefore, as a semiotic situation, and the same holds for its core, that is for the presentation of evidence. But when one thinks of such a situation as a dialogue or a context of speeches or stories, one must consider that the dialogue is complex, that the speaking people play different roles, and that they have different attitudes depending upon their different institutional functions. From this point of view, the very general distinction between involvement and detachment, outlined by Norbert Elias, appears as a useful means in the analysis of the dynamics and interactions of the subjects involved in a legal process. Presenting the evidence means to provide for the cognitive basis of the judgment of fact, and *processing* the evidence, in view of its final evaluation, is a machinery that works by means of semiotic interactions. These interactions can be analysed in terms of involvement and detachment of the interacting subjects.

3. Involvement in the Presentation of Evidence: the Lawyer

The role that is most typically based upon involvement is that of the lawyer. This holds generally in the whole legal process, and particularly with regard to the presentation of evidence. According to the definition proposed by Elias, involvement is connected to a danger existing in the situation that is dealt with by the subject. The lawyer is in a situation of danger because of the inherent risk of loosing his case, as a consequence of an insufficient presentation of evidence. Therefore, the lawyer has a personal, immediate and concrete interest in the outcome of such presentation.

On the other hand, it must be stressed that the functional role of the lawyer in the legal process is essentially one of being the advocate of a party, and of defending zealously his client's interests. Insofar as it concerns the problem of evidence and of the judgment on the facts in issue, the lawyer's role is to present a *side* of the case, and to show that this would be the most truthful and reliable version of the facts. Usually this means also that the lawyer must contest an opposed version of the facts, advanced by another party. The lawyer, therefore, plays a *partisan role* in a situation where the main dynamics is that of an adversary contest. His role cannot be defined in terms of neutrality, of objectivity or of self-restraint: correspondingly, this is in no way a *detached role*. Consider that the lawyer has a duty of candor and of zeal, but no duty of truthfulness. He is not obliged to be coherent with the reality of the facts in issue: he must assert the case of his client, not the case of truth. His attitude cannot be independent and umpireal with reference to the dispute, but partisan and adversary.

From the point of view of the facts of the case and of the presentation of evidence, this role is rather clear in the several moments of the action of the lawyer inside the legal process.

First of all, when the lawyer builds up the claim or the defense in behalf of his client he does not make an impartial and objective narration of the facts of the case. The aim of the statements of facts in the pleadings is not of telling a truthful story; it is of telling a story that should be favourable to the client's position, and able to support the claim or defense alleged in the client's behalf. Therefore, the facts to be stated are selected according to a double criterion: relevancy according to the legal theory of the case advanced by the party, and fitness to support a favourable verdict. The story told by the lawyer is no more that one of the possible stories concerning the facts of the case: theoretically it is the story that is most advantageous for the party's interests. Then this story is not an objective and fair description of facts; it is a strategic means, aiming at fixing premises for a final victory. Stating a favourable version of the facts of the case entails also denying any other version submitted by anyone else, because otherwise the lawyer's case would be impaired. Of course all this holds for the lawyers of both parties, because both of them are in the same functional position with reference to the facts of the case. Therefore, the ideal (and strongly simplified) starting position is that both lawyers advance two different and opposed sides of the case, stating opposed versions of the facts in issue. Theoretically, and in the starting situation, both of these stories claim to be true, although it is clear that none of them is *a priori* truthful. In fact they are nothing but possible hypotheses concerning the facts of the case: being different and opposed, they raise the typical situation of a dispute, that needs to be solved by a choice concerning a reliable story about the facts in issue.

On the basis of the facts initially stated, the second move of the lawyer is to select the items of evidence he will present at the trial. This is a real *selection* because the lawyer does not present every evidence he knows or he has at hand. The lawyer cannot forge evidence or use evidence he knows to be false, but he is not obliged to present evidence that will be unfavourable to his client's case. Therefore, the lawyer will choose to present only the items of evidence that will probably have a favourable impact upon the final judgment. This means that he will submit only the evidence supporting his own version of the facts. The selection of favourable evidence has an evident negative side: if the lawyer knows some items of evidence that may be dangerous he will omit such evidence and ignore it pleadings. Selecting favourable evidence can also mean two other moves in opposition to the other party's moves: one is objecting against the relevancy and admissibility of the other party's evidence; the other is submitting further evidence against the other party's evidence, with the purpose of counterbalancing it.

When the evidence for both parties is admitted by the court, the further problem the lawyers must deal with concerns the *order of presentation* of evidence. It is well known that the order of presentation has some significant impact of the final judgment. In any case, it is an important strategic factor in the management of the case: the lawyer will choose the order that seems to be more advantageous in support of his case.

The core of the presentation of evidence, and a sort of ideal-typical situation, is the examination of witnesses at the trial. Moreover, this is the moment when the main judicial dialogue occurs, and the dialectic interaction among the several subjects takes place in its clearest way. However, one must consider that the examination of witnesses does not start from nothing, nor is it the initial moment of the proceedings. Witnesses are examined with reference to the facts previously stated by the parties' lawyers; only witnesses previously selected by both parties are examined in the order that the parties themselves have chosen, and they are examined in an adversary and partisan context. The examination of witnesses has several features that seem significant from the semiotic viewpoint, and that can show how the lawyer's engagement works affecting the presentation of evidence. One feature deals with the technique of examining witnesses, that is the way of putting questions, the order of questions, the way of managing the sequence questions/answers, the psychological interaction between lawyer and witness, but also between lawyer and judge, and lawyer and lawyer. This is the real *dialogical dimension* of the examination of witnesses. Another important feature deals with the purpose of the examination (that is served by the technique of examination). The purpose is of obtaining from the witness a story that supports and confirms the favourable version of the facts that has been previously submitted by the lawyer. In fact the witness very seldom tells a continuous tale; instead, the story is built up piece by piece by the lawyer, through the sequence of question/answer of which the examination is composed. The examining lawyer tends to extract from the witness a mosaic of answers, that should give a consistent picture of the facts, or of some facts of the case. But the cartoon of the mosaic is not the truth of these facts: it is the version of the facts that the lawyer has previously stated as the basis of his own version of the case. Therefore, the examination of witnesses is oriented to build up, piece by piece, a story that corresponds to the story upon which the position of the party is founded. When this happens, and to the extent that is happens, the lawyer succeeds in proving his case.

Another important feature of the examination of witnesses can be seen in the cross-examination. Here the main task of the lawyer is to fight against an unfavourable story told by an adverse witness. Once again, the role of the lawyer in the cross-examination is not to search the truth, but to react against evidence that could impair his client's position. The cross-examining lawyer does not contest untrue versions of the facts because they are untrue; he contests those versions of the facts that are unfavourable to his own story. This can be done in several ways: one can try to show that the witness is generally incompetent, or that some parts of his deposition are unbelievable, or that some answers are not relevant or are inadmissible. It should also be stressed that also in the cross-examination that there is a complex interaction between lawyer and witness, lawyer and judge, and lawyer and lawyer.

We cannot consider analytically all the sides and moves of the complex and multifaceted dialogue that occurs in the examination of witnesses. But one thing should be clear: the role performed by the lawyers is partisan and adversary in its inherent essence and function. Both lawyers play with stories concerning the facts of the case, and use the examination (and cross-examination) of witnesses as a means to find evidentiary support for their own stories. The final purpose is to show, on the basis of things told by witnesses, that one's own story finds some confirmation, and then that it is a reliable version of facts. But, so to say, the task of the lawyer is somehow circular: he starts stating a favourable hypothesis, that is telling a favourable story about the facts of the case, and then he works in order to show that this story is the best one, and that the other stories told in the same context are not reliable. Then his final aim is to come back to the story he told at the beginning, and to show that the judgment should be delivered on the basis of this story.

This is what the lawyer tries to do when the whole evidence has been presented, and he delivers his final argument. This is the moment for summing up the outcome of the presentation of evidence, and for building up again a consistent and narratively coherent story concerning the facts of the case. But once again the lawyer's task is not to tell a true story, but rather to present as "the judicial truth" the most favourable story he is able to extract from the outcomes of the presentation of evidence. In fact both lawyers present their own versions of the "judicial truth", which means that no judicial truth is actually presented.

4. Other People Involved. Mixed Situations

The situation of involvement is particularly clear in the role performed by the lawyer inside the legal process, but this is not the only example of involvement. There are other situations, or roles, in which a significant involvement can be found, although not in its pure version. Considering these other situations one should speak of mixed roles, because involvement is usually combined, in different and varying ratios, with some measure of detachment.

One interesting example is given by the party, when he or she takes part in the legal process. Usually this happens when the party is examined as a witness, in order to obtain some evidence from his deposition. In such a case there is a puzzling mix of involvement and detachment: on the one side the party is directly interested in the final outcome of the process, and then he is involved in the presentation of evidence, because he runs the risk of loosing his case when the unfavourable evidence is overwhelming. On the other side, being examined as a witness the party has the same duties of any other witness, and particularly the duty of telling the truth under the risk of committing perjury. Therefore the party is in a double conflicting danger, and therefore he is personally involved in a double way. If he tells the truth, and the truth is unfavourable, the danger is he will lose his case: the involvement is then in the sense of not telling the truth. If he tells the story that is favourable to him, but his story is false, the danger is to be punished for perjury: then the involvement is in the sense of telling the truth. The dilemma does not arise only when the story favourable to the party is also true; this is only one of the possible situations.

A somewhat similar example, but with a balance in clear favour of detachment rather than involvement, is that of the nonparty witness. Here the possibility of an involvement depends on the connection between the witness and the party who presents him. In many legal systems, as the civil law ones, this connection is very weak: the witness is presented by a party, but he is supposed not to be partisan in favour of that party. His main and prevailing duty is to be truthful. In other legal systems, as the common law ones, the witness is a *party's witness:* he is selected and presented just because he is expected to provide a story that is favourable to that party, and he is examined by the same party's lawyer just in order to let him tell this favourable story. There is then a rather strong connection between the witness and *his* party, and between the party and *his* witness. This connection can easily produce some personal involvement of the witness, although the danger he runs is placed only at the level of his personal relationships with the party. But the common law witness is also obliged to tell the truth, that is to be neutral and detached, and coherent with the reality of the facts in issue. This obligation should override the personal relationship the witness has with a party: therefore, the attitude of detachment should be the main feature of the witness.

Very similar remarks can be made also for a special type of witness, that is the expert witness. In civil law systems the expert is always "of the court": he is chosen and appointed by the judge, and his function is to give an independent and impartial advice about some issues requiring technical or scientific knowledge. Therefore, the main feature of his function is to be neutral and detached. In common law systems, on the contrary, expert witnesses are usually chosen and appointed by the parties, and they act "in behalf" of the parties themselves, as it happens with nonexpert witnesses. Then the expert witness is expected not to give neutral and objective advice, but to support the case of the party who appointed him, providing the technical or scientific knowledge needed in order to show that this case is well founded. This expert has a personal relationship with the party, that is very similar to that of the ordinary witness; moreover, the expert witness is paid by the party, so that he supports the case of "his" party. This produces a personal involvement of the expert in the outcome of the evidence he provides, since he is somewhat interested in the success of the party who appointed him. On the other side, since the expert witness is a witness, he has the same duties of the ordinary witnesses, and he must be fair and truthful. From this point of view, he is obliged to be detached, although he is not neutral and objective. Only when the expert is appointed by the court does this contradiction not arise, and the common law expert witness is quite similar to the civil law expert, from the point of view of his detached attitude about the matter in issue.

It should be stressed that all these persons (parties examined as witnesses, witnesses and expert witnesses) have the obligation of being fair and truthful about the facts of the case. This means that they should be detached from the matters in issue, and that they should be coherent to the reality while they tell their stories to the court. But it should also be stressed that in fact their situation is seldom one of pure detachment: rather frequently they have some personal interest in the outcome of the dispute, and therefore they are involved in the evidence they give. When this happens, and to the extent that it happens, this attitude affects the stories they tell, because the involvement influences the version of the reality of the involved person. Therefore, the stories they tell pretend to be truthful, but the problem whether they are actually reliable remains open, and it has to be solved by the judge in his final judgment.

5. Detachment: the Judge

If one looks for an ideal situation of detachment inside the legal process, the most important example he finds is the judge. In fact, in every legal system the judge has to be neutral and umpireal, just and objective, independent and fair. Moreover, these obligations of the judge are usually stated as fundamental principles of the administration of justice, and sometimes they are written in the Constitution. It can be said, therefore, that detachment is one of the most important functional features of the judge. The same holds, in the legal systems where it exists, for the jury: the function of the jury is to decide the issue of fact with fairness, independence and impartiality.

These general principles are valid also with reference to the problems concerning the presentation of evidence and the judgment about the facts in issue. The main function of the judge (and of the jury) is to state a final judgment concerning the facts in issue, in the context of the whole judgment about the case. It was mentioned above that many doubts and disputes, starting from different theories and ideologies, concern the features this judgment should have. It is often discussed whether judicial truth should be sought or not, whether some truth can be found inside the legal process, whether the legal process should be oriented or not to establish the truth of the facts in issue, and even whether it is meaningful to speak of truth in the context of litigation. However, one point seems rather clear among all these disputes: it is that the role of the judge is at any rate of *judging,* that is of choosing, among the several stories that are told in court, the one that seems to be the most reliable. It seems no less clear, moreover, that such a choice should not be made at random, or by throwing dice, but according to some reasonable and checkable criteria. In every legal system the criterion is given by the outcome of admissible and relevant evidence fairly and legally presented in court. Therefore, there is no reasonable doubt that the judge must make a rational choice, finding the story of the case that can be considered as the most reliable (that is: the most truthful) on the basis of the evidence at hand. One can wonder whether the judgment of facts can or must be true in any meaning of the word, but nobody can reasonably say that this judgment can or should be founded on error, falsehood or bribery. Likewise, one can discuss the proper meaning of "fairness" or "impartiality", but nobody can reasonably maintain that the judgment on facts should be partisan, one-sided, or prejudicially favourable to one party or to the other.

Therefore, the judge should start from the evidence presented, and on this basis he should find the version of the facts in issue that is mostly supported by proofs. This version should be stated as "truthful" and provide the factual contents of the final judgment. But from this point of view many problems arise. They cannot be even sketched here, since they involve the whole theory of the evaluation of proof and of the judicial decision. In a semiotic perspective it can, however, be underlined that the judge has a quite peculiar role in the context of the judicial dialogue and in the sequence of judicial stories.

In a sense, it is true that the judge takes part in the dialogues that are made in court, and that he too tells a story in his final judgment on the facts. But all this is quite trivial and hasty, if the analysis stops here. The really important problems are: which role the judge performs in the judicial dialogues concerning evidence and the facts in issue, and which story the judge tells in his final judgment.

As to the role of the judge inside the judicial dialogues, that is in the presentation of evidence, one obvious remark is that this role is quite different from the lawyers' role. To use again the distinction made by Elias, the main feature of the judge's role is detachment, while the main feature of the lawyer's role is involvement. Detachment means that the judge has no personal interest in the outcome of the proceedings, and that his attitude is in no way one-sided. This means that he has no ready-made stories to tell, no *a priori* version of the facts to support. In a sense, he is an impartial speaker among partisan speakers. Then the dialogue between the lawyers and the judge is not homogeneous: the lawyers speak partisanly in behalf of their clients, but the judge speaks independently in behalf of nobody.

Consider that detachment and independence do not mean necessarily inertia or passiveness. The problem of the active/passive role of the judge in the legal process is a very important and a well known topic of civil and criminal procedure, but it is not directly relevant in this context. In fact, a passive and umpireal judge is more obviously detached and independent, or at least he more easily appears to be detached and independent. But not necessarily an active judge is involved (in the Elias' sense), and therefore he is partisan and unfair. The widely shared experience of the European legal systems, and partly also of the American system, shows that having an active and "managerial" judge, just with reference to the presentation of evidence, does not mean *a priori* that this judge loses his detachment and fairness. The judge can be active and detached, managerial and fair, without any theoretical or practical contradiction. The idea that an active judge is a partisan judge is an old bias of the legal culture, that should be removed from scientific analysis.

Therefore, one can think of a judge who takes an active part in the presentation of evidence (that is: a judge who speaks actively and independently in the judicial dialogue), without loosing his detached attitude. Moreover, it can also be said that a function of the judge is also to ensure a necessary degree of fairness and balance in a dialogue mainly carried on by lawyers. Even when the judge plays an active role in the presentation of evidence (for instance: when he takes part in the examination of witnesses, or when he calls a witness or an expert witness for the court), he can and should do it without loosing his detached and impartial attitude. Therefore, the judge's main function is just to act as a detached pivot, although not necessarily a passive one, at the center of the complex dialogue performed in the presentation of evidence.

When the legal process comes to the final judgment, the judge tells a story about the facts in issue, in his opinion supporting the *dictum* of the court. This story has some important features that need to be stressed here. First of all, this story does not (should not) contain a partisan version of the facts of the case. Of course it can happen that the story told by the judge corresponds to a story told by a lawyer, but still it is not the same thing. When this story is told by a lawyer, it is by definition partisan; when the same story is told by the judge in his judgment, this is because the judge finds it reliable, truthful and supported by the relevant evidence. Moreover: when a story is told by a lawyer, at the beginning it is an hypothesis to be verified, and a proposal for a possible judgment at the end of the proceedings. When the same story is told by the judge, it is the outcome of an independent choice, oriented to find out which version of the facts can be rationally taken as "the truth". However, in most legal system the story told by the judge does not necessarily correspond to the story told by one or the other party: when it is necessary the judge tells *his own* story about the facts of the case, that is a *third story* concerning these facts. The judge can use pieces of this or that story told by parties, but he builds up his own story. This final story is never comparable to the other stories told in the legal process: it is just the *final* one, that is the story that ends up the procedural dialogue and states the "proper and truthful" version of the facts in issue.

Another important feature of the story told by the judge in his final judgment is that it is usually *justified* (when the judgment is supported by an oral or written opinion). The judge does not confine himself to utter his own version of the facts in issue: he states arguments supporting his own story. Usually these arguments start from premises given by evidence presented to the court, drawing inferences from such premises to the final statements of fact. Therefore, the story of the judge is not a simple narrative tale: on the contrary, it has a justificatory structure. In fact, the judgment states a version of the facts in issue presenting it as a rational conclusion drawn from evidentiary premises and reliable arguments. The styles of judicial opinions are very different in the judicial practice of the several legal systems (and also of the several courts in the same system), but in any case the fundamental structure of the judgment on facts is that of an argumented justification founded upon the relevant evidence. One can say, therefore, that the story told by the judge pretends to be true not only because it is stated as a final version of the facts in issue, but specially because it contains in itself the reasons why it should be considered as truthful and reliable.

The topic of justification deserves some further remarks. Someone speaks of a "judicial rhetoric" besides a "lawyer's rhetoric", mainly in order to show that everything in the judicial context is nothing but a rhetorical performance made by some people making speeches. This is a very good way to bundle all things together, and to fall into the Hegelian night where all cows are black. There is on the contrary an important difference, that cannot be overlooked, between the lawyer's rhetoric and the judge's rhetoric. The lawyer uses rhetorical means and strategies aimed at persuading the judge: the purpose of the lawyer is to win his case, independently of any truth of the facts. If the truth is useful to win, then it is good; if the truth is unfavourable, it has to be overlooked. The judge, in his opinion, can use also rhetorical arguments, and his opinion can be read also in a rhetorical perspective. But the judge does not have to persuade any concrete person, nor must he induce any person to believe or to do anything. Instead of that, the judicial opinion aims at justifying the judgment on the basis of evidence, showing that the judgment is supported by good reasons.

6. Some Differences in Comparative Perspective

The above remarks are based upon a theoretical framework of an ideal legal process, that had to be used just in order to avoid the analysis of an unlimited range of details. Therefore, abstract and idealized concepts of the roles of the lawyers, of the judge and of witnesses, were used just for sake of simplicity.

However, these subjects perform their typical roles in procedural contexts, and these contexts are organized according to different structures in the several legal systems, and even in the several proceedings belonging to the same legal system. Sometimes these differences do not affect significantly the basic attitudes and the fundamental roles played by persons acting inside the judicial process. Sometimes, on the contrary, the structure of the legal process influences some aspects of these attitudes and roles. At any rate, every general analysis needs to be adjusted to some extent, when referred to a given legal system. A comparative panorama of the relevant matters cannot be outlined here, but some examples can be useful.

With regard to the role of the lawyer from a general point of view, no important differences can be found in the several systems. The basic idea is always that the lawyer is by definition involved in the outcome of the litigation, and that therefore his fundamental duty is to act in behalf of his client. Involvement, partisanship, adversariness, and so on, are the typical features of the lawyer's role in every procedural system. The rules of professional ethics sometimes state some duty of fairness and candor towards the court and the other party, but the core of the lawyer's obligation is the interest of the client. From this point of view, the above remarks concerning the role and attitudes of the lawyer can generally hold in every procedural system.

The same holds substantially for the above remarks concerning generally the role of the judge, although some interesting variations can be found. On the one side, in fact, in every system the judge has to perform an independent, impartial, fair and detached role, and he is expected to decide finally the case choosing the most reliable and supported version of the facts in issue. But some differences exist with reference to the choice of the final story to be used as a basis for the judgment, and also with reference to the structure of the story finally told by the judge. In many legal systems (and specially in the European ones), it is commonly said that the judge has the power and the duty to choose the version of the facts that he believes to be the most reliable and truthful on the basis of evidence, even when in order to do so he must build up his own version of the facts, and this version is in part or totally different from the stories told by the parties. In these conceptions, the judge is completely independent and autonomous in stating his own judgment about the facts of the case. On the contrary, in some systems (as f.i. the American and the English civil procedure) it is commonly said that the judge should choose the final version of the facts in issue, but only *between the version submitted by the parties*. Therefore, the judge should never build up his own "third" story about the facts, and he should always take for good either the story of the plaintiff or the story of the defendant. This judge can still be detached, but it is clear that he performs a different role, in comparison with the Continental judge.

The structure of the story finally told by the judge about the facts of the case is very different according to the several judicial practices. When the final judgment on the facts is only a short *dictum* without any justificatory argument (as it is for the verdict of a jury, and for a judge's judgment when no opinion is delivered), there is no real "story". Facts are simply stated as true in a short form. When the judgment on the facts is supported only by the so called "findings", things are quite similar. The facts are stated as true in short, and the "findings" give only a sketchy description of the relevant outcomes of the presentation of evidence. They aim at giving some synthetic and mostly implicit support to the final *dictum,* but they are not a real story about the facts of the case (and sometimes they are not written personally by the judge). Therefore, a full story on the facts of the case can be found only when an extensive opinion is delivered by the court: but in this case the justificatory structure of the opinion tends to prevail on the narrative contents of the judgment. Consider however that judicial practices are very different: sometimes the justification of the judgment of fact on the basis of evidence is detailed, but sometimes the opinion does not contain a sufficient set of arguments supporting this judgment.

The most important differences among systems are however those concerning the proceedings for the presentation of evidence, this is the real core of the judicial dialogues about evidence and facts. Such an analysis cannot be developed here, but two significant and connected factors need to be stressed: one deals with the roles of judges and lawyers in the presentation of evidence, and the other deals with the techniques of the examination of witnesses.

The respective roles of judge and lawyers are defined on the basis of the general principles and the fundamental models of the legal process. In some cases the judge plays the main role in the presentation of evidence, because it is to him to examine the parties and the witnesses, and to put questions to the experts appointed by the court. The dialogue occurs mainly between the examining judge and the examined person; the lawyers are allowed to interfere, but only in order to ask the judge to put some questions to the witness. The tone of the dialogue is therefore neutral and official. The scope of the examination is strictly limited to the relevant facts. The aim of the examination is obtaining clear, objective and coherent answers. The story that is extracted from the witness tends to be truthful, controlled and impartial. Therefore, the outstanding attitude is of detachment.

The situation is quite different when the examination of parties, witnesses and expert witnesses is made by the parties' lawyers. In such case the main dialogue is between the partisan lawyer and the examined person. Then the examination is partisan, its aim is to obtain a favourable story about facts, and the dominant attitude is involvement (as it was said above, in point 3).

The techniques in the examination of witnesses vary according to the procedural context of examination. Sometimes the witness is asked to tell a full story of the facts he knows, in the way and with the order he prefers. In that case the witness is ordinarily allowed to make his own evaluations concerning the facts: very often the story he tells is not only a description, but a real "reconstruction" of the facts. A quite different technique is used when the judge or the examining lawyer proceed putting a sequence of short and detailed questions, each dealing with a little part, a single aspect or a specific circumstance of the situation of fact. In this case the examination proceeds step by step, and it is led by the examiner: the witness must only follow the way of the examination, answering each time to the specific questions. The text of this type of examination is not a story in the common meaning of the word: it is a dialogue, where the dominant role is of the examining person. The answers are not a tale with a continuous and coherent development: they are little pieces of a mosaic built up by the person who puts the questions. The difference is even more evident when cross-examination is considered: here the context is more complex, and the structure of the dialogue is twofold. The first part is the direct examination, where a lawyer carries on a partisan examination aimed at obtaining supporting evidence for his own version of the facts; the second part is a counter-examination, where an opposing lawyer carries on an opposite partisan examination of the same witness, aimed at showing that he is not reliable and that his previous answers were not truthful, or even at obtaining some support for a contrary version of the facts in issue. The text of this complex examination is neither a story nor one consistent dialogue: it is made of two dialogues, each going in different directions aimed at opposite outcomes.

If one considers these variations concerning the roles of lawyers and of the judge on the one side, and the several procedural models on the other side, he can get some ideas about the different contexts of the presentation of evidence. In each context the role of every person taking some part in the proceedings can be analysed in terms of combination between involvement and detachment, and of interaction with the other persons involved. The measures and proportions of this combination vary according to the different situations, and the structures of the interaction vary according to the models of legal process and the techniques used in the presentation of evidence. At any rate, the basic distinction between involvement and detachment seems to be fruitful as an analytical means for the study of procedural dynamics, and particularly for the understanding of the dynamics of the presentation of evidence, and of the judgment on the facts in issue.

References

Damaška, Mirjan R.: The Faces of Justice and State Authority. A Comparative Approach to the Legal Process, New Haven/London 1986.

Elias, Norbert: Engagement und Distanzierung. Arbeiten zur Wissenssoziologie I, Frankfurt am Main 1983.

Interpreting Statutes. A Comparative Study, ed. by D. N. MacCormick / R. S. Summers, Aldershot 1991.

Taruffo, Michele: La prova dei fatti giuridici. Nozioni generali, Milano 1992.

Twining, William: Rethinking Evidence. Exploratory Essays, Oxford 1990.

The Influence of American Legal Realism on Article 2 of the Uniform Commercial Code

By James J. White, Ann Arbor

Introduction

This paper focuses on the most prominent member of the American Legal Realist Movement, Karl Llewellyn, and upon his magnum opus, Article 2 of the Uniform Commercial Code.

Although Llewellyn was not one of the founders of the American Legal Realist Movement, he soon became the most prominent and successful member of the movement. He was the Realists' spokesman in the 1931 debate with Dean Pound conducted in the Harvard Law Review.[1] Although its spokesman, Llewellyn was a comparative moderate within the Realist Movement. Some of the Realists, known as the "scientists," disdained all "paper rules" – whether in statutes or in cases – as having almost no impact on courts' decisions. These radicals found the "law" only in the facts surrounding a controversy and perhaps in the judge's own experience, but not at all on paper.

No "scientist" could have been an honest drafter of Article Two of the Uniform Commercial Code. Disagreeing with the most radical Realist thought, Llewellyn disagreed even more with the legal conceptualists. In that disagreement, Llewellyn embraced the central tenent of the Realists' Movement, namely that judges' decisions arise not merely from the rules they state in their opinions, but at least as much from unstated reasons – from the facts before them, from the expectation of the parties in the trade, and from the judges' own judgment about fairness.

In this most conservative form, American Legal Realism could be called merely a demand for judicial honesty. This honesty would enhance certainty and predictability by allowing judges to state their true reasons, reasons that arise partly from precedent, statute and the like, but also from the judge's conscience, the facts and other "extra-legal" experience. Professor Fuller[2] describes this Realist goal as improving predictability and certainty in the law

---

[1] Llewellyn, Some Realism about Realism – Responding to Dean Pound, 44 Harv. L. Rev. 1222 (1931); Pound, The Call for a Realist Jurisprudence, 44 Harv. L. Rev. 697 (1931).

[2] Fuller, American Legal Realism, 82 U. Pa. L. Rev. 429, 437 (1934).

by giving the judge more "grazing room." Using the analogy of a horse made unruly by being kept in too tight a pen, Fuller suggests that a larger pen (the Realists arena) would make the horse more tractable and its behavior more predictable. Professor Fuller suggests that Legal Realism's principal contribution was to give judges more "grazing room" and so make them behave in more tractable and predictable ways.

While Llewellyn believed that legal rules are found in and derived from the behavior of the actors, he never completely rejected written law as a prescriptive device. By examining various sections of Article 2, I hope to trace some of those sections' Realists' roots and to stimulate the reader to think about how the Realists' teachings apply to "paper law."

The Realist as Legislator

Because there never was any Realist manifesto, scholars who seek the core of Realist thought often identify different qualities as this core. Some might say that empiricism, the need to examine law in action at the street level, is the core idea of Legal Realists. Others might find the core to be a complete rejection of written rules and judicial reasons without any necessary suggestion that the truth is to be found in empirical examination. Yet others might identify the core as a milder version of the latter, namely an open recognition that things formerly regarded as extralegal are "legally relevant." To some extent these differences among current-day observers track the differences that actually existed among the Realists themselves. For the purpose of this paper I need not identify the "core" and I understand that the most radical Realists and their most fervent followers might regard the idea of a Realist as a legislator as an oxymoron.

Turn now to Llewellyn's work on the Uniform Commercial Code. The most prominent and self-conscious Realist, Llewellyn accepted the label, however ambiguous, for himself. Because Llewellyn is the principal drafter of Article Two, we would expect to find some of his Realist ideas there.[3] From Article

---

[3] An account of Llewellyn's involvement with the Code begins in 1937, when the Conference on Uniform States Laws (Conference) took note of Llewellyn's criticisms of the Uniform Sales Act and approved of his intention to revise the Act. Llewellyn immersed himself in the project during the summer of 1940, and in September of that year presented the Conference with a First Draft and Report on a revised Uniform Sales Act. Llewellyn was the principal drafter; while he drew on the second Federal Sales Bill and other materials, he made significant revisions and additions to earlier works.

After considering the draft, the Conference appointed a committee to produce a second draft based on the first, which would become the sales article in the projected Uniform Commercial Code.

"[I]n the summer of 1941, Llewellyn worked intensively on the draft for two months and by the end of August had produced a report ... containing a very detailed

Two and from some of the cases under it, I make some tentative judgments about the influence and success of the Realists' ideas here.

As a starting point one might ask what a Realist could hope to accomplish in a code.[4] Conflicting answers suggest themselves. First, the Realist's interest in and insistence upon finding facts and understanding how institutions work would lead the Realist to squeeze rules out of stereotypical transactions and to codify those rules. To do so is to conform to Fuller's description, namely to allow society to form law, not vice versa.[5]

Second, one might expect the Realist to be acutely aware of the weakness of paper rules. If nothing else, the Realist knew that judges were motivated by many things other than such rules. One mindful of such matters might hope only to encourage judges to state their true reasons so that their decision could be understood and applied even by unsophisticated lawyers and judges. This is Fuller's suggestion, that Realists really wished to give judges more grazing room, to the end that their behavior would be more predictable.

But the two goals are inconsistent. Certainly one can squeeze a rule out of a stereotypical transaction and set that rule down in print. Yet that rule may form a pen even more tightly around a judge than the case law or a conventional statute might. The second goal is to do the opposite, to enlarge the pen.

---

critique of the Uniform Sales Act and the case law surrounding it, an analysis of the problems of producing a semi-permanent code and a complete new draft, backed by extensive annotations and comments."

W. Twining, Karl Llewellyn and the Realist Movement (1973) note 1, at 280. (Where this account of Llewellyn's work on Article Two does not quote Twining, it relies on his information. See id. at 270 - 301 for complete account of Llewellyn's involvement with the entire Code).

In 1942 the American Law Institute agreed to cooperate with the Conference to produce a uniform act on sales. Llewellyn was made chief reporter of the joint committee, which used the second draft of the Revised Uniform Sales Act (RUSA) to produce the first Proposed Final Draft in 1944.

The various drafts of the RUSA and the UCC have been compiled in a twenty-three volume set, E. Kelly, Uniform Commercial Code: Drafts (1984).

[4] A thought that might occur to one drafting a code, particularly one who is sensitive to the disingenuousness of judges' reasons, is to state clearly and honestly one's purpose. This, too, we might expect Llewellyn to do if he drafted a code. Indeed, he did, through the Official Comments to the Uniform Commercial Code. The comment to § 1-A of the Second Draft of the Uniform Revised Sales Act explains the comments' function. They give "the reasons for choosing one expression rather than another, . . . the matters intended to be included, and . . . those intended to be left out." 1 E. Kelly, supra note 3, at 330. See also W. Twining, supra note 3, at 326 - 30 (discussing Llewellyn's views of the role of Official Comments to the Uniform Commercial Code).

[5] One who completely rejected the idea that paper rules ever prescribe behavior or are followed by any relevant actors would find the idea of codifying to have little or no significance, for, by hypothesis, neither judges nor those compelled to follow the rules would do so because of the rules. They would follow the rules only because external factors made them do so. Thus even to speak of a legislator as a realist implies some watering down of the ideas of realism and some recognition that paper rules in certain circumstances have prescriptive value.

Here we see the dilemma faced by all drafters of codes,[6] but a peculiarly acute one for the Realists whose writings had attacked paper rules and had been particularly scornful of attempts to control judicial behavior by narrowly written rules.[7]

Which of these goals did Llewellyn follow? In fact, he followed both; he rode across sales in both directions. On the one hand he included such narrow, explicit, and substantive rules as sections 2-319, 2-320, 2-509, 2-706 and 2-712. On the other, he provided such open-ended rules as section 2-204 on agreement and section 2-302 on unconscionability. The former seemed to come from the pen of a scientist, who having studied the underlying transactions determines its contours and draws a rule from the parties' expectations. The latter draw no specific rule from the underlying transactions, but appear merely to be an acknowledgment that the court must decide these matters on a case by case basis.

Consider first 2-319, 2-320, and 2-509. The symbols F.O.B., CIF, and FAS had long been used in commerce.[8] By the middle of the twentieth century they had acquired relatively fixed and widely understood meaning. The use of the term "F.O.B. seller's place" determined who had the risk of loss during shipment and who was to bear the cost of shipment. By sections 2-319 and 2-320

---

[6] For a nineteenth century expression of the arguments for and against codification, see the Carter-Field debate on the topic of codification of New York State common law. 1 D. Field, Speeches 323 - 38 (A. Sprague ed. 1884); J. Carter, The Proposed Codification of Our Common Law (1884). Both are excerpted in S. Kimball, Historical Introduction to the Legal System 374 - 82 (1966). Field argued that written codes offer greater relative certainty than common law decisions, that they make the law more accessible than when it is to be found in reported decisions, and that they ensure that the legislature – the only governmental organ with the law-making prerogative – promulgates laws. Carter responded that codified law is rigid, absolute law, and that whatever certainty codes do ensure comes at the price of a sacrifice of justice in particular cases.

[7] The drafters of the Second Draft of the Revised Uniform Sales Act, Article Two's precursor, addressed hazards of codification from the realists' point of view in their 1941 report to the Conference of Commissioners on Uniform state laws.

> Any semi-permanent Act on "Code Chapter" must reckon with the danger on the one hand, of remaining remote from life and intelligibility by reason of over-abstractness, or, on the other, of becoming rapidly "dated" by reason of reliance on "practical" "modern" patterns of thought and action which may then prove to be passing ones.

1 E. Kelly, supra note 3, at 28 (308).

[8] The C.I.F. term had been invented by merchants in overseas trade, and the merchants' usage eventually became the term's legal meaning in the Code. See 2 E. Kelly, supra note 3, at 155 (167) (comment to section 45 of the Uniform Revised Sales Act, Proposed Final Draft No. 1, April 27, 1944). As to F.O.B. and F.A.S. terms, it is clear that they had also been used in commerce for a considerable time before the 1940's, and that they too had taken on fairly settled meanings. These terms had tended to produce relatively more confusion than C.I.F., however, because of the variety of situations to which F.O.B. and F.A.S. were applied. 1 E. Kelly, supra note 3, at 208 (488) (Comment to sec. 51 of the Uniform Revised Sales Act, Second Draft, 1941).

Llewellyn transformed this set of practices and expectations into a rule of law.[9] These rules replaced particularly murky and troublesome set of rules under the Uniform Sales Acts where risk of loss and other matters turned on the place of "title."[10] Where title rested was often unclear and subject to much judicial discretion. By the enactment of sections 2-319 and 2-320 Llewellyn was limiting the courts' power to allocate the risk by manipulation of the title concept.

A second place where Llewellyn seems to elevate commercial behavior into the law is in sections 2-706 and 2-712.[11] Prior to the Code some courts had used

---

[9] In a memorandum to the New York Law Revision Commission in support of Article Two, Llewellyn used C.I.F. contracts as an example to show how the Code extracts legal rules from actual transactions.

> No portion of our law is more obscure or uncertain or indeed misleading to the ordinary lawyer or businessman than is the present law in regard to sales of goods. Yet one small portion of that law is relatively clear: that is the law of the overseas contract for sale, typified by the C.I.F. contract. What the Code does is to take this one small clear portion of the law of sales, and to use the methods there developed to make all the rest equally clear. Article 2 moves in terms which any person can understand: from the facts of the contract to the facts as they happened on into a clear statement of the legal result.

1 State of New York, 1954 Law Revision Commission Report, Hearings on the Uniform Commercial Code 5 (69) [hereinafter 1954 N.Y. Law Revision Comm'n Hearings].

[10] See Llewellyn, Across Sales on Horseback, 52 Harv. L. Rev. 725, 728 - 36 (1939); 1 State of New York, 1955 Law Revision Commission Report, Study of the Uniform Commercial Code 18 - 19 (352 - 53) [hereinafter 1955 N.Y. Law Revision Comm'n Study].

[11] See 1955 N.Y. Law Revision Comm'n Study, 225 (559). (Section 2-706 "adds to and strengthens" seller's remedies for breach of contract under the Uniform Sales Act); see also id. at 569 - 70 (2-712 was an "innovation," as the Uniform Sales Act had not recognized cover).

Llewellyn criticized the contract-market damage provisions of the Uniform Sales Act of 1906, as they had been applied by American courts, for being removed from the actual needs of aggrieved buyers and sellers.

> The damage remedies provided under the Sales Act of 1906 were taken in the main almost without verbal change from the English Sale of Goods Act, 1893. The English damage remedies had worked, and still work, very well. The equally satisfactory working of the Sales Act damage remedies was dependent on their being implemented and supplemented by the same type of merchantile and flexible rules and court-practice in regard to measurement of damages which the English courts have been using to work justice under the Sale of Goods Act.
>
> This presupposition of the Uniform Sales Act of 1906 has failed to work out. That Act has in consequence suffered severely in adequacy; in uniformity; in providing merchants with a clean-cut basis for movement or for litigation. The rules of damage-law which have been actually used to supplement the Act have not been uniform, they have been often unfortunately rigid, and even their rigidity has been unreckonable and uncertain in its incidence.
>
> Litigation of an *hypothetical* market price in an *hypothetical* market is indeed always expensive and always uncertain; and as interpreted, the rule of 'time and place where the goods *ought to have been* delivered' too commonly forces the issue to turn on an hypothetical market; and to, too often, an unexpected ruling chooses a market on which counsel is not prepared; or even results in a reversal, in addition to giving inadequate damages.

seller's actual resale or buyer's actual cover as the basis for measuring the plaintiff's damages in a contract action, but in most states a plaintiff who covered or resold could not be confident that he would recover the difference between that and the contract price.[12] Rather, he would face the prospect of being forced to take a different and smaller contract market differential. Intuitively, Llewellyn knew that a disappointed buyer who wanted the goods would cover and a disappointed seller would resell. He also understood that most would recognize resale or cover as the fairest and most appropriate measure of damages, at least if it were done in a reasonable manner.

Not only do these rules in sections 2-319, 2-320, 2-706 and 2-712 limit the "legally relevant" reasons that the judge can bring to bear, they also set out an explicit substantive rule. Not merely do they determine the procedure by which the court is to arrive at the result, they prescribe the result. If the contract is F. O. B. seller's place of business, the risk is on the buyer as soon as the goods are put in the hands of the carrier. If, after breach, the buyer covers in a more or less sensible way, the measure of damages is the difference between the cover price and the contract price.

Consider Llewellyn riding now in the other direction across sales. Here we come to sections like 2-302 and 2-204. These are as undetailed and imprecise as sections 2-319 and 2-320 are specific and certain. They grant the judge the authority under 2-204 to find a contract if the facts are "sufficient to show

---

1 E. Kelly, supra note 3, at 242 - 43 (522 - 23) (emphasis in original).

In the introductory commentary to the new cover provisions in the Second Draft of the RUSA (1941) Llewellyn explained the need to put damage provisions in line with commercial practice. (Note that in the quoted passage, the term "cover" is used to mean both buyer's purchases of substitute goods and seller's resale of refused goods).

> [Cover makes] it possible, in transactions between professionals in the market, for the justified claimant, be he buyer or seller, to fix his rights with speed, after a breach, and then to *move* with safety, in such manner as to get in fact the agreed benefit under the contract, or so much of it as is still available. ... It not only steps up the certainties which the law can provide to help contractors, fitting into mercantile need and mercantile practice; but it also lays a foundation for cheaper and more adequate administration, at law, of the other remedies. ...
>
> These sections incorporate the long standing practice of the English courts to give the aggrieved party reasonable time, on discovering breach, to cover himself in any reasonable way. Any litigation *after cover has been actually sought and had* is thus made to turn first on a fact easy to prove: to wit, what loss was actually suffered.

Id. at 522 - 23.

[12] See 1 1955 N.Y. Law Revision Comm'n Study 225 (559) n. 398 (decisions had occasionally given weight to seller's resale as evidence of market price, citing cases); L. Vold, Cases and Materials on the Law of Sales 215 n. 69 (1958); C. McCormick, Handbook on the Law of Damages 660 n. 10 (1935) (citing cases where resale price was evidence of the market price); id. at 660 n. 11 (citing cases where because of circumstances such as unavailability of market price, the difference between resale and contract price is the appropriate damage measure); id. at 668 n. 35 (where buyer gives notice of intention to purchase substitute goods, purchase price may be evidence of the market value, citing case); id. at 669 n. 37 (if no available market for measure of damages, repurchase price gives the best measure, citing cases).

agreement." Section 2-302 authorizes the court to invalidate a contract or clause in a contract found to be "unconscionable." What is unconscionable is left to the imagination of the parties and the judge.[13] What a remarkable contrast between these sections and those discussed above. Here there is neither channeling for the judge nor any substantive rule. Presumably the judge can listen to the testimony of the parties, of experts, of economists, sociologists, and others. Nothing is excluded; everything socially, morally, economically, and politically relevant is, ipso facto, "legally relevant." Once everything that is legally relevant has been admitted, the court is free to establish the substantive rules of unconscionability and contract formation on an ad hoc, common law basis.

In section 2-302 Llewellyn seems concerned exclusively with method. Llewellyn was particularly suspicious of "covert tools."[14] As a teacher of sales

---

[13] The Code nowhere defines"unconscionability." While § 2-302 makes it clear that the determination of unconscionability is for the court, it does not tell a court how to distinguish an "unconscionable" contract from an acceptable one. Subsection (2) of 2-302 ensures the parties the opportunity to present evidence of commercial setting, purpose and effect of suspect contract provisions, but the court is not limited to this evidence. Neither does the Official Comment to 2-302 confine the court's inquiry. Indeed, the Comment consistently returns to the word "unconscionability" as if to avoid constraining the court's discretion.

> This section is intended to allow the court to pass directly on the unconscionability of the contract ... and to make a conclusion of law as to its unconscionability. The basic test is whether, in the light of the general commercial background and the commercial needs of the particular trade or case, the clauses involved are so one-sided as to be unconscionable under the circumstances existing at the time of the making of the contract.

UCC 2-302 comment 1 (1977).

Critics of § 2-302 have noted that due to its "troublesome vacuity" it "tells a court almost nothing save that unconscionability is bad and that it exists." Danzig, A Comment on the Jurisprudence of the Uniform Commercial Code, 27 Stan. L. Rev. 621, 627 (1975) (footnote ommitted). For an early and leading analysis of 2-302 and its drafting history, see Leff, Unconscionability and the Code – The Emperor's New Clause, 115 U. Pa. L. Rev. 485 (1967).

[14] Llewellyn identified three hazards of "covert tools" in particular.

> A court can "construe" language into patently not meaning what the language is patently trying to say. It can find inconsistencies between clauses and throw out the troublesome one. It can even reject a clause as counter to the whole purpose of the transaction. It can reject enforcement by one side for want to "mutuality," though allowing enforcement by the weaker side because "consideration" in some other sense is present. Indeed, the law of agreeing can be subjected to divers modes of employment, to make the whole bargain or a particular clause stick or not stick according to the status of the party claiming under it: as when, in the interest of the lesser party, the whole contract is conditioned on some presupposition which is held to have failed. The difficulty with these techniques of ours is threefold. First, since they all rest on the admission that the clauses in question are permissible in purpose and content, they invite the draftsman to recur to the attack. Give him time, and he will make the grade. Second, since they do not face the issue, they fail to accumulate either experience or authority in the needed direction: that of marking out for any given type of transaction what the *minimum decencies* are which a court will insist

and contracts Llewellyn doubtless shared the discomfort that most of us experience in teaching concepts such as consideration, mutuality and the like. Ultimately we defend these concepts as obscure, bizarre ways of explaining why certain contracts should be enforced and others should not. Llewellyn would have placed many consideration or mutuality cases under 2-302. He would have encouraged a frank admission that certain contracts are unenforceable because the judge thinks them unconscionable. He would argue that both student and lawyer are less likely to be misled by a bold finding of unconscionability than by the same decision hidden under the skirts of mutuality or contract interpretation.

It is not obvious then that Llewellyn intended section 2-302 to change the substantive law at all, at least the law as it existed in the heads of clever lawyers and clever judges.[15]

Section 2-204 carries more substance. Here, doubtless Llewellyn intended to eliminate some of the common law rules on offer and acceptance that would have kept a common law court from recognizing a contract long after the parties thought they had a binding agreement.[16] Of course the courts are left free to decide what is "sufficient to show agreement," but it is clear that Llewellyn would have the courts find contracts in circumstances where no contract would be found under a proper interpretation of the pre-Code common law.

Returning to the first question posed above, I would argue that the Realist, albeit the schizophrenic Realist, in Llewellyn has contributed to all of the sections described above. The fixation on the facts, on the actors' behavior and

> upon as essential to an enforceable bargain of a given type, or as being inherent in a bargain of that type. Third, since they purpose to construe, and do not really construe, nor are intended to, but are instead tools of intentional and creative misconstruction, they seriously embarrass later efforts at true construction, later efforts to get at the true meaning of those wholly legitimate contracts and clauses which call for their meaning to be got at instead of avoided. The net effect is unnecessary confusion and unpredictability, together with inadequate remedy, and evil persisting that calls for remedy. Covert tools are never reliable tools.

Llewellyn, Book Review, 52 Harv. L. Rev. 700, 702 - 03 (1939) (reviewing O. Prausnitz, The Standardization of Commercial Contracts in English and Continental Law (1937)) (footnote omitted) (emphasis in original).

15 After studying Llewellyn's explanation of the proposed § 2-302, the New York Law Revision Commission understood the purpose of 2-302 as "not to enlarge the area in which agreements of the parties will be defeated by judicial action on the ground of unfairness or undue harshness, but to require that the question of unconscionability be dealt with directly. ..." 1 1955 N.Y. Law Revision Comm'n Study 396 (730).

16 In the comments to § 2-204's precursor, in the Second Draft of the RUSA, the drafters explained the proposed section's relationship to prior law.

> [The section] seeks to make explicit the view of the better case-law that no rules of Offer and Acceptance are ends in themselves, or are too rigid to yield to plain contrary intent, but that they have a purpose; and that the purpose is not to be drowned in the form.

1 E. Kelly, supra note 3, at 68 - 69 (348 - 49) (Revised Uniform Sales Act (2d Draft, 1941) comment to alt. sec. 3-A).

on their expections, and the belief that rules can be extracted from those facts and that behavior produced sections 2-319, 2-320, 2-509, 2-706 and 2-712. On the other hand, sections 2-204 and 2-302 nicely fit Fuller's description of the admirable Realist goal – to give grazing room.

To say that legal realism has spawned these sections does not fully answer the question, how has realism affected contract law? Many statutes have crossed the legislative threshold never to be cited by a court, never read by a relevant actor. Recognizing that thorough knowledge of the impact of Article Two demands that one poke his nose not merely into appellate volumes but also into trials, into arbitration, into negotiations and even into the lawyers' and laymen's offices, I offer far less than that. I speculate on the effect of these sections from the examination of the reported decisions in six volumes of the UCC Reporting Service.

Cases under sections 2-319, 2-320, and 2-509 are both few and unremarkable. In the six volume survey there were only ten cases in which the dispute focused on any of the three sections.[17] A representative example is Ladex Corp. v. Transporters Aereos Nacionales.[18] There thieves stole a cargo of shrimp along with the carrier's delivery truck. Buyer sued the carrier for the value of the shrimp; carrier defended on the ground that the buyer had not yet paid the purchase price and, having incurred no loss, was not entitled to recover. The trial court agreed with the carrier and granted summary judg-

---

[17] Commonwealth Propane Co. v. Petrosol Int'l Inc., 818 F.2d 522 (6th Cir. 1987) (Under 2-509 (2) (c), merchant Buyer assumed risk of loss for propane gas kept in independent storage tanks upon receipt of a "confirmation of distribution" from Seller, but the court reached that conclusion in part by analyzing Buyer's resale of the gas as "acceptance" under 2-606); Jason's Foods, Inc. v. Peter Eckrich & Sons, Inc., 41 UCC 1287 (7th Cir. 1985); Schock v. Ronderos, 394 N.W. 2d 697, 2 UCC2d 1302 (N.D. 1986); Ladex Corp. v. Transporter Aereos Nacionales, S.A., 476 So.2d 763, 42 UCC 133 (Fla. Dist. App. 1985); Emery v. Weed, 41 UCC 115, 120 n.4 (Pa. Super. 1985); Kumar Corp. v. Nopal Lines, 462 So.2d 1178, 41 UCC 69 (Fla. Dist. App. 1985) (reversing a summary judgment that had held for carrier based on "title" analysis, and holding that Seller bore risk of loss under C.I.F. term either because the parties expressly so agreed or because Seller had failed to obtain shipping insurance as required by "C.I.F." term, 2-320); Paramount Supply Co. v. Sherlin Corp., 16 Ohio App.3d 176, 40 UCC 447 (1984) (remand for trial on whether "C.F. Kuwait" term had been modified to authorize shipment to New Jersey port); United States ex rel. Trans-Colorado Concrete, Inc. v. Midwest Constr. Co., 653 F. Supp. 903 (D. Colo. 1987) (parties modified "F.O.B. jobsite" term to put additional cost of transport to a new, more distant jobsite on Buyer); Phillips Puerto Rico Core, Inc. v. Tradex Petroleum Ltd., 41 UCC 1678 (2d Cir. 1985); Buenger v. Pruden, 713 P. 771, 42 UCC 859 (Wyo. 1986) (holding that under § 2-319 "F.O.B. destination" means Seller must pay freight).

My six volume survey figures do not take into account every case which cites the Code sections under examination. Cases which give only a passing mention to a section, or which easily find a section to be inapplicable, are not included. Cases are included wherever the opinion indicates that the court considers the arguments even slightly meritorious.

[18] 476 So.2d 763, 42 UCC 133 (Fla. Dist. Ct. App. 1985).

ment. The appeals court reversed and instructed the lower court to assign the risk of loss between the seller and buyer by determining whether the sale contract had a typical CIF term or an F. O. B. destination term or a CIF term modified by the course of dealing between the parties. Determining the particular term and thus allocating the risk at a second trial should not be a particularly difficult task for the court. If the Uniform Sales Act applied to this transaction and the risk had to be allocated according to rules set out there,[19] the legal

---

[19] The applicable rules under the Uniform Sales Act, were as follows:
Sec. 18. Property in specific goods passes when parties so intend. – (1) Where there is a contract to sell specific or ascertained goods, the property in them is transferred to the buyer at such time as the parties to the contract intend it to be transferred. * * *
Sec. 19. Rules for ascertaining intention. – Unless a different intention appears, the following are rules for ascertaining the intention of the parties as to the time at which the property in the goods is to pass to the buyer.

Rule 1. Where there is an unconditional contract to sell specific goods, in a deliverable state, the property in the goods passes to the buyer when the contract is made and it is immaterial whether the time of payment, or the time of delivery, or both, be postponed.

Rule 2. Where there is a contract to sell specific goods and the seller is bound to do something to the goods, for the purpose of putting them into a deliverable state, the property does not pass until such thing be done.

Rule 3. (1) When goods are delivered to the buyer "on sale or return," or on other terms indicating an intention to make a present sale, but to give the buyer an option to return the goods instead of paying the price, the property passes to the buyer on delivery, but he may revest the property in the seller by returning or tendering the goods within the time fixed in the contract, or, if no time has been fixed, within a reasonable time.

(2) When goods are delivered to the buyer on approval or on trial of on satisfaction, or other similar terms, the property therein passes to the buyer –

(a) When he signifies his approval or acceptance to the seller or does any other act adopting the transaction;

(b) If he does not signify his approval or acceptance to the seller, but retains the goods without giving notice of rejection, then if a time has been fixed for the return of the goods, on the expiration of such time, and, if no time has been fixed, on the expiration of a reasonable time. What is a reasonable time is a question of fact.

Rule 4. (1) Where there is a contract to sell unascertained or future goods by description, and goods of that description and in a deliverable state are unconditionally appropriated to the contract, either by the seller with the assent of the buyer, or by the buyer with the assent of the seller, the property in the goods thereupon passes to the buyer. Such assent may be expressed or implied, and may be given either before or after the appropriation is made.

(2) Where, in pursuance of a contract to sell, the seller delivers the goods to the buyer, or to a carrier or other bailee (whether named by the buyer or not) for the purpose of transmission to or holding for the buyer, he is presumed to have unconditionally appropriated the goods to the contract, except in the cases provided for in the next rule and in section 20. This presumption is applicable, although by the terms of the contract, the buyer is to pay the price before receiving delivery of the goods, and the goods are marked with the words "collect on delivery" or their equivalents.

Rule 5. If the contract to sell requires the seller to deliver the goods to the buyer, or at a particular place, or to pay the freight or cost of transportation to the buyer, question would be substantially more complex. Whether property passed was a complex legal conclusion based not merely on the F.O.B. terms, but on other questions such as time of payment, transfer of possession and a variety of other terms in the contract concerning control and the like.

Cases under sections 2-706 and 2-712 in the six volumes total a mere nine.[20] As with the risk of loss cases, none suggests particular difficulty. Representative of the utterly conventional nature of these cases is Mason Distributors' Inc. v. Encapsulations, Inc.[21] There the appellate court affirmed the trial court's holding that buyer's claimed cover ("as needed" purchases of commodity vitamins in a volatile market) was unreasonably delayed where the buyer made a purchase more than a month and a half after the seller had breached.

---

or to a particular place, the property does not pass until the goods have been delivered to the buyer or reached the place agreed upon.

Sec. 22. Risk of loss. – Unless otherwise agreed, the goods remain at the seller's risk until the property therein is transferred to the buyer, but when the property therein is transferred to the buyer the goods are at the buyer's risk whether delivery has been made or not, except that –

(a) Where delivery of the goods has been made to the buyer or to a bailee for the buyer, in pursuance of the contract and the property in the goods has been retained by the seller merely to secure performance by the buyer of his obligations under the contract, the goods are at the buyer's risk from the time of such delivery.

(b) Where delivery has been delayed through the fault of either the buyer or seller the goods are at the risk of the party in fault as regards any loss which might not have occurred but for such fault.

Reprinted in K. Llewellyn, Cases and Materials on the Law of Sales 987 - 88, 990 (1930).

[20] City Univ. of New York v. Finalco, 514 N.Y.S.2d 244, 3 UCC2d 1742 (N.Y. App. Div. 1987) (seller's resale of used computer system commercially reasonable where seller gave buyer notice of resale, extended buyer an opportunity to reconsider repudiation, and presented evidence of falling market to explain $ 303,000 difference between resale and contract price); Islamic Republic of Iran v. Boeing Co., 771 F.2d 1279, 41 UCC 1178 (9th Cir. 1985) (trial court properly diminished seller's gross resale proceeds by the amount of credit seller extended to resale purchaser of aircraft in calculating resale damages); Sprague v. Sumitomo Forestry Co., 104 Wash. 2d 751, 42 UCC 202 (1985) (denying resale damage award for a technical reason – seller resold privately and failed to first notify Buyer as required by 2-706 (3)); Afram Export Corp. v. Metallurgiki Halyps, S.A., 592 F. Supp. 446, 40 UCC 911 (E.D. Wis. 1984), aff'd in relevant part, rev'd in part on other grounds, 772 F.2d 1358, 41 UCC 1709 (7th Cir. 1985); Hudson Feather & Down Products, Inc. v. Lancer Clothing Corp., 513 N.Y.S.2d 173, 3 UCC2d 1804 (N.Y. App. Div. 1987) (buyer's failure to cover does not bar its right to claim lost profits and other consequential damages); Watson v. Tom Growney Equipment, Inc., 721 P.2d 1302, 1 UCC2d 1523 (N.M. 1986) (Supreme Court affirmed summary judgment that buyer's subsequent purchase of smaller backhoe did not constitute cover, but corrected the award calculation according to 2-713's formula); Consolidated Aluminum Corp. v. Krieger, 1 UCC2d 46 (Ky. App. 1986) (buyer's refusal to "mitigate damages" by passing price increases on to its customers did not affect its action for cover damages); Mason Distributors, Inc. v. Encapsulations, Inc., 42 UCC 1307 (Fla. Dist. App. 1986); Fertico Belgium S.A. v. Phosphate Chemicals Export Ass'n, 3 UCC2d 1812 (N.Y. 1987).

[21] 42 UCC 1307 (Fla. Dist. Ct. App. 1986).

Of course there are many possible explanations for the absence of significant appellate litigation. A plausible explanation, and one I choose to believe, is that the sections are working as they were intended to work. By adopting the reasonable expectations of the parties as the law, the Code has narrowly restricted potential area of conflict. By using quite straightforward rules the Code has reduced the area of conflict about their meaning. Even when reported opinions deal with these sections, one does not find raging controversies over policy that underlies the rules nor radical differences about interpretation of them. I would argue, therefore, that this is a success of the Realists. Here they have found the behavior of the parties and sensibly codified it.

Turning to sections 2-204 and 2-302, one has greater difficulty measuring consequences. These sections have not produced great deal appellate litigation either,[22] but here one might argue that appellate litigation, at least under

---

22 Although the number of cases discussing § 2-302 cases is high – there are twenty-eight in the six-volume survey – the courts often are able to dispose of the unconscionability claims with minimal discussion (or remand for a finding). In only nine cases do the courts uphold the possibility of an unconscionable clause or contract. Irving Leasing Corp. v. M & H Tire Co., 16 Ohio App. 3d 191, 40 UCC 381 (1984) (remand for determination of unconscionability); Martin v. Joseph Harris Co., 767 F. 2d 296, 41 UCC 315 (6th Cir. 1985) (seed seller's disclaimer of warranty held to be unconscionable); Langemeier v. National Oats Co., 41 UCC 1616 (8th Cir. 1985) (contract clause placing risk of early freeze on farmer unconscionable); Bernstein v. Sherman, 497 N.Y.S. 2d 298, 1 UCC2d 375 (N.Y. Justice Ct., Town of Ossining 1986) (alternative ground, unconscionable disclaimer of warranty); John Deere Leasing Co. v. Blubaugh, 636 F. Supp. 1569, 1 UCC2d 658 (D. Kan. 1986) (terms of seller's remedies for default on lease unconscionable); Gianni Sport Ltd. v. Gantos, Inc., 151 Mich. App. 598, 1 UCC2d 1433 (1986) (see text accompanying note 23); Ferens v. Deere & Co., 1 UCC2d 1096 (W.D. Pa. 1986) (insufficient evidence to grant defendant's summary judgment on unconscionability argument); Latimer v. William Mueller & Son, Inc., 386 N.W. 2d 618, 1 UCC2d 1128 (Mich. App. 1986) (limitation of liability to purchase price of seed unconscionable, alternate ground); Esquire Mobile Homes, Inc. v. Arrendale, 182 Ga. App. 528, 356 S.E. 2d 250, 3 UCC3d 1798 (1987) (exclusion of warranties unconscionable as to mobile home buyer).

In nine other cases the court rejects the unconscionability argument but devotes more than a page of its opinion to explaining its reasons. Fotomat Corp. v. Chanda, 40 UCC 795 (Fla. Dist. App. 1985) (limitation of liability clause not unconscionable); Chemical Bank v. Rinden Professional Ass'n, 41 UCC 1035 (N.H. 1985) (waiver of defenses against assignee not unconscionable); Union Exploration Co. v. Dowell Div., Dow Chem. Co., 41 UCC 759 (D. Kan. 1985) (exculpatory clauses not unconscionable as between commercial parties); Best v. United States Nat'l Bank, 78 Ore. App. 1, 714 P. 2d 1049, 1 UCC2d 6 (1986) (2-302 gives no affirmative cause of action); Hunter v. Texas Instruments, Inc., 1 UCC2d 1473 (8th Cir. 1986) (disclaimer of warranty not unconscionable); Lecates v. Hertrich Pontiac Buick Co., 515 A. 2d 163, 2 UCC2d 865 (Del. Super. Ct. 1986) (disclaimer against used car buyer not unconscionable); Zepp v. Mayor and Council of Athens, 180 Ga. App. 72, 348 S. E. 2d 673, 2 UCC2d 1179 (1986) (price charged for water supply not unconscionable); Pacific American Leasing Corp. v. S.P.E. Building Systems, Inc., 2 UCC2d 1516 (Ariz. App. 1986) (contract placing risk of failure of computer's performance on commercial buyer not unconscionable); Maxon Corp. v. Tyler Pipe Indus., 497 N. E. 2d 570, 3 UCC2d 52 (Ind. App. 1986) (indemnification clause unconscionable even in commercial setting, alternate ground).

2-302, represents an advance. If, for example, a party would have escaped from a contract because of "lack of consideration" in the past, the world might be made better and not worse by a subsequent appellate opinion that adopts a section 2-302 rationale in lieu of lack of consideration. To conclude that Llewellyn achieved his purpose by replacing covert tools such as consideration with overt tools such as 2-302 and the doctrine of unconscionability, one would have to examine hundreds of disputes. Assuming one could determine how these cases had been decided in lawyers' offices and in the trial and appellate courts, he would then have to imagine how the same cases might have been decided in the lawyers' offices and in the courts under the former regime with the use of covert tools. Only by comparing these outcomes can one be sure that Llewellyn had succeeded or failed. I have done none of that and cannot make such claims.

In ten cases the courts reject the unconscionability argument with scarcely more than a mention. Computerized Radiological Services v. Syntex Corp., 595 F. Supp. 1495, 40 UCC 49, 68 - 69 (E.D.N.Y. 1984) (summary dismissal of unconscionability argument); Carboline Co. v. Oxmoor Center, 40 UCC 1728, 1733 (Ky. App. 1985) (limitation of liability clause not unconscionable); Salt River Project Agric. Improvement & Power Dist. v. Westinghouse Corp., 143 Ariz. 368, 694 P. 2d 198, 40 UCC 418, 424 (1984) (warranty disclaimer not unconscionable as against commercial buyer); Konicki v. Salvaco, Inc., 16 Ohio App. 3d 40, 474 N.E. 2d 347, 41 UCC 103, 109 (1984) (disclaimer not unconscionable); Goldstein v. S & A Restaurant Corp., 42 UCC 81 (D. D.C. 1985) (exercise of ten-day termination clause not unconscionable); Galvin v. First National Monetary Corp., 42 UCC 379 (E.D.N.Y. 1985) (§ 2-302 does not give rise to a cause of action); Hall v. Fruehauf Corp., 179 Ga. App. 362, 2 UCC2d 435 (1986) (limitation of liability not unconscionable); Dubbe v. A.O. Smith Harvestor Products, Inc., 2 UCC2d 1532 (Minn. App. 1987) (disclaimer not unconscionable between commercial parties); World Enterprises, Inc. v. Midcoast Aviation Services, Inc., 713 S.W. 2d 606, 3 UCC2d 137 (Mo. App. 1986) (commercial limitation of liability not unconscionable); First Security Bank v. Mountain View Equip. Co., 730 P. 2d 1078, 3 UCC 3d 180 (Idaho App. 1986) (no unconscionability involved in secured creditor's sale of collateral).

The six-volume survey included 15 cases involving § 2-204. Flowers Baking Co. v. R-P Packaging Co., 329 S.E. 2d 462, 40 UCC 1631, 1636 (Va. 1985) ("It is true that the UCC had greatly modified the rigors of common-law rules governing the formation of contracts. ... [but the parties did not intend to conclude a contract]"); Carolina Builders Corp. v. Howard-Veasey Homes, Inc.,, 40 UCC 73 (N.C. App. 1985) (existence of contract shown by buyer's expressed willingness to buy seller's output and a series of completed deliveries and payments); Bethlehem Steel Corp. v. Litton Industries, 488 A. 2d 581 (Pa. 1985); Ernst Steel Corp. v. Horn Constr. Div., Hallibarton Co., 104 App. Div. 2d 55, 481 N.Y. S. 2d 833, 40 UCC 145 (1984); Continental Grain Co. v. Followell, 475 N.E. 2d 318, 40 UCC 1232 (Ind. App. 1985) (no agreement found); National Controls, Inc. v. Commodore Business Machines, Inc., 209 Cal. Rptr. 636, 40 UCC 12 (Cal. Dist. App. 1985) (buyer telephoned seller with terms and its purchase order number, thereby forming a contract according to their established course of dealing for reaching agreements); Apex Oil v. Vanguard Oil & Service Co., 40 UCC 1221 (2d Cir. 1985) (seller's representation to its creditor that it had secured a contract for resale of oil shipment confirmed existence of an oral contract for resale); Industrial Fiberglass v. Jandt, 40 UCC 133 (N.D. 1985) (buyer's previous payments of finance charges described on invoice showed that the invoice formed the parties'contract); Mid-South Packers, Inc. v. Shoney's, Inc., 761 F. 2d 1117, 41 UCC 38 (5th Cir. 1985) (buyer

However, there are at least a few cases that suggest sections 2-204 and 2-302 are producing overt and therefore better decisions. Consider, for example, Gianni Sport Ltd. v. Gantos, Inc.[23] In this case a New York manufacturer of women's clothing, Gianni Sport Ltd., agreed to sell a large holiday shipment to be delivered in October to Gantos, a buyer located in Grand Rapids, Michigan. The contract contained a clause that gave the buyer the right to "terminate by notice to Seller all or any part of this Purchase Order with respect to goods that have not actually been shipped by seller . . ."[24] In September buyer cancelled the order. Later the seller agreed to ship the goods to the buyer at one-half the original price. Seller then sued buyer for the original price. The goods under this order comprised more than twenty percent of the seller's business for 1980, and they were made specially for Gantos. Ultimately the Michigan court held that the cancellation clause was unconscionable, that the subsequent agreement was invalid as not necessary and allowed the seller to recover $ 27,290 as the remainder on the original purchase price. The case is full of innuendo about how the buyer chiseled the seller and about how much more powerful the buyer was in the trade than the seller. The facts must have been truly appalling, for a New York seller is surely not a favorite of the Kent County Circuit Court in a suit against a local buyer.

It is possible that the case would have come out differently had section 2-302 not been on the books. Conceivably, in those circumstances the court would have said the buyer had the right to cancel the order and having done so, had the right to negotiate to purchase the goods at any price. It seems more likely that a pre-UCC court would have been stimulated by the same underlying fac-

accepted seller's price increase each time it acknowledged the increase on its own purchase order, notwithstanding buyer's professed intent to withhold the sum of the increases from its last payment): Barclaysamerican/Business Credit, Inc. v. E & E Enterprises, Inc., 697 S.W. 2d 694, 42 UCC 706 (Tex. App. 1985) (exchange of purchase order and acknowledgments showed agreement); Chicopee Concrete Service Inc. v. Hart Eng'g Co., 20 Mass App. 315, 479 N.E. 2d 748, 42 UCC 375 (1985) (general contractor's use of subcontractor's bid in calculating principal bid showed existence of contract; alternatively, contractor's purchase order to sub showed agreement); Consolidated Aluminum Corp. v. Krieger, 1 UCC2d 46 (Ky. App. 1986) (seller was bound where parties agreed upon price and delivery date, and where seller demonstrated intent to be bound by providing buyer with costly production blueprints and sample parts); City Univ. of New York v. Finalco, 514 N.Y.S. 2d 244, 3 UCC2d 1742 (N.Y. App. Civ. 1987); Quaker State Mushroom Co. v. Dominick's Finer Foods, Inc., 1 UCC2d 365 (N.D. Ill. 1986) (although parties'shipment and receipt of goods appeared to recognize agreement, no contract existed because the parties had intended to become bound only upon agreeing to a price, which they failed to do); City of Salem v. Clearwater Constr. Co., 84 Ore. App. 674, 3 UCC2d 936 (Or. App. 1985) (seller's deliveries of partial amounts under buyer's purchase order did not recognize a contract to provide entire amount; instead the shipments were only acceptances of buyer's unilateral offer to supply partial amounts).

[23] 151 Mich. App. 598, 1 UCC2d 1433 (1986).

[24] 1 UCC2d at 1434.

tors that stimulated the Kent County judge and that the case would have come out the same.

A common-law judge might have found that the seller detrimentally relied upon the buyer's promise by manufacturing the dresses and thus that the buyer became bound under section 90 of the Restatement to pay the purchase price. Once a common-law court found the buyer to be bound, it could easily conclude that there was no consideration for the proposed modification and that it was not binding. The second possibility would be to find that the cancellation clause was intended by the parties only to be used if some catastrophe or other specific event rendered buyer's purchase onerous. A common-law court might in effect torture the language to find some condition to the cancellation right.

If without the aid of section 2-302 a court would have arrived at the same outcome by manipulation of the language or by the use of the consideration doctrine, here section 2-302 has done us a favor. Whatever one thinks of the analysis by the court in *Gianni* and whatever one's view of unconscionability, the court's decision is clear and its message is not likely to mislead another lower court or the parties themselves in a similar circumstance.[25] It is more honest than one based on fictional contract interpretation and more comprehensible than one explained in the words of the mysterious consideration doctrine.

In view of the small number of cases, it is hard to say that section 2-302 accomplished its purpose. Conceivably section 2-302 and its cohort section 2-204 have done so. Conceivably trial judges are now willing routinely to set aside contracts or clauses where they should be set aside based on their unconscionability, not on some theory such as consideration. So, too, it is possible that contracts are recognized where they would not have been formerly by trial courts. Given the limited number of appellate decisions, that conclusion is not demanded by the data that I can present. Of course, it is also possible that 2-302 has allowed for development of the law in a way that Llewellyn would have thought appropriate simply because the judges are now freed to deal honestly with the cases before them. None of this can I prove.

It seems plausible that courts are now recognizing contracts where the parties believe contracts existed, but where the English common law would not have recognized them. Likewise it seems plausible that contracts that should

---

[25] If one does not agree with me, and believes instead that a Michigan court would have come to the opposite conclusion but for § 2-302, that presents the possibility for an argument for or against § 2-302 on substantive grounds, an argument that I do not make. I believe that the judge's frank refusal to enforce a contract that he finds to be unfair resting squarely on the unconscionability doctrine is more understandable to students, lawyers, and judges than some mumbo, jumbo about illusory contracts, or twisting of the language to find imaginary conditions.

not be enforced, but might have been formerly, and yet could have been avoided only by torture are now not enforced because of the open admission that they are unconscionable under 2-302. If those two things are true, then Llewellyn has succeeded by granting the courts more grazing room; he has both made the law more fair if we can rely upon the judges to determine that, and has made it more predictable by encouraging honest judicial admission of reasons.

Thus far we have examined only the polar extremes in Article Two, 2-319 (where the Legal Realist factfinder would dig out the rule and the practice and make it law) and section 2-302 (an exhortation to the courts to be honest about their reasoning and a legitimation of the exercise of judicial authority in doing so). There are Realist failures too. The most obvious candidate is section 2-207. That section appears to have been drafted for two types of transactions.[26] First, it was meant to reverse the outcome in cases like Poel v. Brunswick-Balke-Collender Company.[27] There the parties exchanged nearly identical documents (orders and acknowledgments) yet the court found no contract because of insignificant deviations in the acceptance. Second, it was intended to protect an oral agreement from surprise alterations when one or both parties send "confirming" forms containing terms added to or different from those already agreed upon. As originally drafted section 2-207 might be regarded as a subset of section 2-204, concerning contract formation.

Here the Realists went astray.[28] First, they grossly overestimated their knowledge of the underlying transactions. The model transactions con-

---

[26] See Murray, The Chaos of the "Battle of the Forms"; Solutions, 39 Vand. L. Rev. 1307, 1319 (1986). See also 1954 N.Y. Law Revision Comm'n Hearings, supra note 9, at 119 - 20.

[27] 216 N.Y. 310, 110 N.E. 619 (1915).

[28] It would be unfair and inaccurate to attribute the present 2-207 wholly to Llewellyn or even to the realists. Many drafters had a hand in writing 2-207 and its comment, and they contributed to it at various times and probably with various purposes. See Letter from Professor Grant Gilmore to Professor Robert Summers (Sept. 10, 1980), reprinted in R. Speidel, R. Summers, and J. White, Commercial Law Teaching Materials 467 - 68 (4th ed. 1987).

It is possible, however, to look at Llewellyn's early work on 2-207's precursors and see that he originally meant the section to deal with two basic transactions, the purchase order, acknowledgment exchange and the documentary confirmation of oral agreements. Consider the approach taken in the Second Draft of the RUSA to revising the rules on contract formation. Llewellyn chaired the committee which proposed the Draft, and he was heavily involved in the drafting. See note 3 supra. The Draft proposed two alternative sets of rules on offers and acceptances, the first a brief section on the "effect of certain offers" (section 3); and the second a much-expanded range of rules, many of which dealt with specific kinds of contract formation problems which had not been separately treated in the 1940 Draft (Alternative sections 3A - 3J). Among the alternative rules are two antecedents to the present 2-207. These two sections survived the Code's various drafts and drafters to become in somewhat altered form, parts of 2-207. Their presence in 2-207 connects Llewellyn, and his judgment about what kinds templated in 2-207 occur when only two documents, an order and acknowledgment, are exchanged, or when the parties follow their oral agreements with printed acknowledgments. In fact the transactions are much more varied and complex. In the six-volume survey alone, I found cases with three documents, a solicitation, a purchase order, and an acknowledgment;[29] where one party signed the other's documents;[30] and where a party's behavior appeared to indicate assent to materially different terms in the other's responsive form.[31]

---

of transactions should be addressed with rules on business-form contract formation, with the present 2-207.

Alternative Section 3-H. Interpretation of New Terms in Alleged Acceptance. (New to Sales Act.) An expression of definitive acceptance in substance, accompanied by additional terms, shall be construed, in case of doubt, as constituting an acceptance accompanied by an offer of a modification which the other party is free to accept or reject.

***

Comment on Alternative Section 3-H. Where terms are changed in a purported acceptance, the absence of agreement is patent. But where further terms are suggested, and especially where such terms go to arrangements for facilitating performance, the better case-law has tended strongly to read them according to the section.

***

Alternative Section 3-I. Confirmations Containing New Terms. (New to Sales Act.)

(1) This section applies between merchants where a contract has been concluded orally or by wire, and a letter of confirmation contains additional language proposed for inclusion in the agreement, or treated in the letter as being included.

(2) In the absence of express objection by the other party within a reasonable time after his receipt of the letter, the additional language shall be construed as included in the agreement if it satisfies the following conditions –
  (a) If it is of a character reasonably connected with the agreement; and
  (b) If it does not unreasonably depart from the provisions of law which would otherwise govern; and
  (c) If it does not negate or unduly modify the particularized terms of the agreement as made; and
  (d) If it is so placed and printed as reasonably to force attention from the addressee.

(3) If there is express objection by the addressee within a reasonable time, or if the language does not meet the requirements laid down in subsection 2, the original contract stands as made, and the additional language operates only as an offer to modify it.

***

Comment on Alternative Section 3-I. There is no adequate case-law on the subject of this section, although the problem is of daily occurrence when oral or wired deals are confirmed on "our form." Some cases have tacitly read the clauses in; some have forgotten the oral deal, looking only at the letter of confirmation; none have presented a clear and workable general attack on the situation.

The base-line taken here is that the deal is closed, and that both parties know it. Such a phrase as "letter follows" is not to be read as meaning "a letter containing different terms."

1 E. Kelly, supra note 3, at 360 - 61.

[29] Salt River Project Agric. Improvement & Power Dist. v. Westinghouse Elec. Corp., 143 Ariz. 368, 694 P. 2d 198, 40 UCC 418 (1984).

[30] Wyandotte Indus. v. E. Y. Neill & Co. (In re First Hartford Corp.), 63 Bankr. 479, 2 UCC2d 465 (Bankr. S.D.N.Y. 1986).

Unlike "F.O.B., FAS," where the transaction is ossified, here is a young, mutating transaction. The transaction the Realists examined and the rule they attempted to draw from it turned out to be not one transaction, but hundreds of transactions, calling not for one rule but for many rules.[32]

Section 2-207 cases[33] in the last six volumes are in contrast to the cases under the other sections. There are 28 cases in those volumes dealing with section 2-207, but that is not all. These are hard cases; these are cases where 2-207 is not merely an incidental matter, but in which the parties are fighting hammer and tongs over its meaning. Consider Daitom, Inv. v. Pennwalt Corp.[34] a 1984 tenth circuit case. As with almost all of the section 2-207 cases, *Daitom* arose when goods that were accepted and used by the buyer never worked to buyer's satisfaction. Daitom sold industrial dryers to Pennwalt to dry material to be

[31] Twin Disc, Inc. v. Big Bud Tractor, Inc., 772 F. 2d 1329, 41 UCC 1627 (7th Cir. 1985).

[32] For other criticisms of UCC 2-207 see White & Summers, Handbook of the Law Under the Uniform Commercial Code, 3d ed., ch. 1 (1988). See generally the articles of Professor John E. Murray, The Standardized Agreement Phenomena in the Restatement (Second) of Contracts, 67 Cornell L. Rev. 735 (1982); The Article 2 Prism, 21 Washburn L.J. 1 (1981); The Chaos of the Battle of the Forms, 39 Vand. L. Rev. 1307 (1986). Professor Murray has proposed a specific revision of § 2-207 in his article in 6 J.L. & Com. 337 (1986).

[33] Diamond Fruit Growers, Inc. v. Krack Corp., 794 F. 2d 1440, 1 UCC2d 1073 (9th Cir. 1986); Therma-Coustics Mfg. Co. v. Borden Inc., 213 Cal. Rptr. 611, 40 UCC 1640 (App. 1985); Standard Structural Steel Co. v. Bethlehem Steel Corp., 597 F. Supp. 164, 40 UCC 1245 (D. Conn. 1984); Continental Grain Co. v. Followell, 475 N.E. 2d 318, 40 UCC 1232 (Ind. Ct. App. 1985); St. Paul Structural Steel Co. v. ABI Contracting, Inc., 40 UCC 789 (N.D. 1985); Salt River Project Agric. Improvement & Power Dist. v. Westinghouse Elec. Corp., 694 P. 2d 198, 40 UCC 418 (Ariz. 1985); National Controls, Inc. v. Commodore Business Machines, Inc., 209 Cal. Rptr. 636, 40 UCC 12 (App. 1985); Alliance Wall Corp. v. Ampat Midwest Corp., 17 Ohio App. 3d 59, 477 N.E. 2d 1206, 41 UCC 377 (1984); Twin Disc, Inc. v. Big Bud Tractors, Inc., 772 F. 2d 1329, 41 UCC 1627 (1985); Occidental Chem. Corp. v. H & W Indus., Inc., 41 UCC 756 (E.D. Pa. 1985); Custom Roofing Co. v. Alling, 146 Ariz. 388, 706 P. 2d 406, 42 UCC 63 (App. 1985); Chicopee Concrete Service, Inc. v. Hart Eng'g Co., 20 Mass. App. Ct. 315, 479 N.E. 2d 748, 42 UCC 375 (1985); Resch v. Greenlee Bros. & Co., 42 UCC 830 (Wis. App. 1985); Mace Industries, Inc. v. Paddock Pool Equip. Co., 42 UCC 825 (S.C. App. 1986); Quaker State Mushroom Co. v. Dominicks' Finer Foods, Inc., 1 UCC2d 365 (N.D. Ill. 1986); Phillips Petroleum Co., Norway v. Bucyrus-Erie Co., 1 UCC2d 667 (Wis. 1986); Consolidated Aluminum Corp. v. Krieger, 1 UCC2d 46 (Ky. App. 1986); Wyandotte Indus. v. E.Y. Neill & Co., (In Re First Hartford Corp.), 63 Bankr. 479, 2 UCC2d 465 (Bankr. S.D.N.Y. 1986); Diskin v. J.P. Stevens & Co., 2 UCC2d 1502 (D. Mass. 1987); Egan Mach. Co. v. Mobil Chem. Co., 2 UCC2d 69 (D. Conn. 1986); Skyline Steel Corp. v. A.J. Dupuis Co., 648 F. Supp. 360, 3 UCC2d 475 (E.D. Mich. 1986); Wiencken v. Mill-Rite Sash & Door Co., (In re Empire Pacific Indus., Inc.), 3 UCC2d 1337 (Bankr. Or. 1987); Diamond's Run Ltd. v. Rebel Fabrics, Inc., 511 N.Y.S. 2d 996, 3 UCC2d 499 (N.Y. Civ. Ct. 1987); Maxon Corp. v. Tyler Pipe Indus., Inc., 497 N.E. 2d 570, 3 UCC2d 52 (Ind. App. 1986); United Coal & Commodities Co. v. Hawley Fuel Coal, Inc., 525 A. 2d 741, 3 UCC2d 1744 (Pa. Super. Ct. 1987); Continental Can Co. v. Poultry Processing, Inc., 3 UCC2d 31 (D. Me. 1986); Brevel Motors Inc. v. Vendo Corp., 3 UCC2d 1347 (D.N.J. 1986).

[34] 741 F. 2d 1569 (10th Cir. 1984).

made into pills. The dryers could not be made to work properly and buyer sued the seller for breach of warranty. Seller responded that the one-year statute of limitations that had been contained in its response to the request for proposals was a part of the contract and cut off the buyer's claim.

The opinion consists of the usual application of section 2-207's various parts to parties' behavior. In this case buyer solicited bids, seller submitted a response, buyer issued a purchase order and the dryers were shipped and paid for. The dryers sat idle for a year while buyer built its factory. Part of the appeal of buyer's argument was that it would be unfair to apply a one-year statute of limitation clause when the goods had not even been put in use until the time for suit had run out. Seller argued persuasively that its response to the original request for a proposal was the offer, and that the buyer's purchase order was an acceptance which resulted in a contract that included the one-year statute of limitations from seller's form. Buyer prevailed on a clever and incorrect interpretation of 2-207. Buyer maintained that its purchase order should be treated as though it contained an explicit four-year statute of limitations of the kind that would have governed under 2-725. If the response (acceptance) had contained a specific provision of that kind, most would say that the two conflicting statutes of limitations knocked one another out and the statute of limitations would be as provided in the UCC. By treating the acceptance as though it contains an explicit term that would otherwise be implied in the UCC, the court distorts the prior decisions and greatly strengthens the offeree's hand.

The case is representative of the kind of complexity that 2-207 has brought to the interpretation of such contracts. Worse it is an exhibition of exactly the kind of statute torturing that Llewellyn and the other Realists most despised. To think the Realist's own statute has reduced a smart judge to such dishonest behavior would embarrass Llewellyn's ghost.

Unfortunately *Daitom* is not the exception; it is the rule.[35] The sample of cases even in the limited six volumes shows how miserably the drafters failed to segregate and identify particular transactions, much less comprehend the real expectations of the parties. Were one to redo Article Two, section 2-207 would be at the top of the list. Surely it is a failure.

But how did legal realism fail the drafters here? It failed them because the Realists were incapable of understanding the underlying transaction. Although many of the Realists had non-legal training, they were fundamentally lawyers whose research constituted looking at appellate cases. It is ironic that Llewellyn in his later years ridiculed the minuscule output of Underhill Moore,[36] the one Realist who doggedly stuck to looking at the facts to deter-

[35] For an expert's discussion of § 2-207's failure, see Murray, The Chaos of the "Battle of the Forms": Solutions, 39 Vand. L. Rev. 1307 (1986).

mine how law worked. The lesson that Llewellyn should have learned from Moore's experience is not that Moore was a fool, but rather that finding out how law worked is far more complicated and difficult than Llewellyn or any of the other Realists ever realized. The work of the other Realists, Oliphant, Yntema and Cook, was meager fare.[37] Even today those who exhort others to find out how the law works far exceed those who attempt to make their names by doing so.

We have examined three separate areas of Realist effort in Article Two, section 2-319 and the others which extract rules from commercial practice; sections 2-204 and 2-302, which encourage overt explanations of judicial decisions; and section 2-207, with all its difficulties. Should one conclude that Article Two is the apotheosis of legal realism or its damnation? I conclude that it is more nearly the former than the latter. On the one hand is what I regard as an unqualified success, 2-319, 2-320, 2-706 and 2-712. These are additions for which Llewellyn deserves the credit. They are additions one would expect the Realists to bring to a Code. To the extent we can tell, they are working as well as any private law can.

Whether the grazing sections, 2-302 and 2-204, are wholly successful is less clear. I am certainly not ready to condemn those sections. The idea of Article Two as a "common law statute" may yet prove quite workable. I suspect that we are better for having 2-302, 2-204 and the like than we would be without them. I believe that the Realists were right in encouraging judges to abandon covert tools and in expanding the scope of the "legally relevant." Although the

---

[36] In a 1955 article entitled "On What Makes Legal Research Worth While," Llewellyn reviewed Moore's behavioristic, empiral approach to law study.

> [H]e faded into pure behaviorism in regard to the effects of men's behavior on appellate decision. His base-approach, on this, sounds almost insane and was certainly perverse. Moore was so set against taking the impact of words of authority as being in themselves solely determinative that he insisted on studying behavior without reference to the words and configuration of pre-existing rules of law at all, and even without reference to whether any knowledge of the supposedly relevant behavior was brought home to the judges whose deciding was under inquiry; and he insisted on further assuming that these unknown patterns or semi-patterns or non-patterns of often obscurely technical lay-behavior could have significantly measurable and provable determinative impact on the appellate decisions. Be it remembered that the planner of such an amazing project was himself a trained lawyer and one whose high legal art in setting up and coloring a *communicated* background and then playing *communicated* words against that background was the sole important cause of the successive decisions of various groups of people to let him have, over years and years, money and more money with which to get magnificantly into nowhere.

Llewellyn, On What Makes Legal Research Worth While, 8 J Legal Ed. 399, 403 (1956) (footnote ommitted) (emphasis in original).

[37] See Verdun-Jones, Cook, Oliphant and Yntema: The Scientific Wing of American Legal Realism (pts. 1 & 2), 5 Dalhousie L.J. 3, 249, 16 - 17, 42 - 43, 280 (1970); F. Beutel, Some Potentialities of Experimental Jurisprudence as a New Social Science 105 - 113 (1957); Currie, The Materials of Law Study, (pt. 3), 8 J. Legal Ed. 1, 77 n. 344 (1955) (Oliphant's disappointing output in particular).

cases and discussion above hardly prove it, I also believe that the presence of these sections will make the law more knowable, certain and predictable, not less so.

The real difficulty in determining whether the Code will ultimately damn Realist thought or exalt it, lies in the problems presented in section 2-207 and the like. If the world with which the legislature must deal is necessarily so complex, disorganized and changing that it is impossible to make a sensible and reliable taxonomy of the underlying transactions and of the parties' expectations – if the world is as 2-207 seems to make it – then the scientists' wing of realism holds out a false hope. If, on the other hand, better tools will enable scholars to turn disorganized and complex transactions into those that can be made to behave like 2-319, 2-320 and 2-706, the Realists hold out real hope.

I am uncertain about the answer to those questions. It is possible that the Realists were lucky in stumbling upon 2-319 and 2-706 and that they are aberrations and not the usual. Surely it is true that the Realists in general and Llewellyn in particular were far more sanguine than they should have been about the ease with which one can identify specific transactions and determine what the parties to those transactions expect the rules should be. From those engaged in the law and society movement we know how laborious, expensive and time consuming is the study of law in action. Because of the variety among our courts, the differentiation of the economy from state to state and because much law in action is private, drawing the law out of society is going to be much more difficult than the Realists believed. Certainly we will continue to have substantial study that will enable the legislature to tune a statute, possibly even to enact one, and occasionally entirely to change the statutory course, but none of those things will be done routinely.

I conclude that Article Two of the UCC was a noble and probably successful Realist experiment. Part of its success arises not just from the fact 2-319 and 2-320 show us that law can be drawn from society, but also from 2-207, which shows us how difficult it will be to do so in these circumstances, and from sections 2-204 and 2-302, as a way of opening up grazing room for the judges and of making honest persons out of them.

V. Interpretive Formality in Different Social Contexts: The Structure of Normative Reality

The Curious Role of Interpretive Formality in American Constitutional Law

By Dan T. Coenen, Athens*

"[T]he provisions of the Constitution are not mathematical formulas having their essence in their form . . . Their significance is vital, not formal; it is to be gathered not simply by taking the words and a dictionary, but by considering their origin and the line of their growth."[1]

Dedication

It happened in the autumn of 1978, during my first semester of law school. Our contracts professor, Robert S. Summers, had been subjecting us for weeks to obscure hypotheticals, unanswered questions, and a level of intellectual intensity not one of us had encountered in the past. After we had taken our seats on that particular day, one of my classmates raised his hand. In a tone that conveyed a dazed dismay, he openly proclaimed his frustration with the study of law under our professor's tutelage. "I feel," the student said, "like I am banging my head against a wall." Professor Summers' reaction was so memorable I recall it to this day. He paused and then, with a smile creeping across his face, exclaimed: "That's good!"

Bob Summers understood that it is the law teacher's duty to communicate the extreme, but exciting, difficulty of the law. Through my years at the Cornell Law School, he brought that lesson home to me time and time again, subtly teaching me how to teach myself the skills of legal reasoning. After leaving Cornell, I worked for one of this country's leading federal circuit court judges, for a genuinely great Supreme Court justice, and for a number of practicing lawyers of enormous talent and depth. None of these persons, however, made more of a mark on my development as a lawyer than did Bob Summers. It is for this reason that I dedicate this paper to Bob. I do so filled with gratitude for his priceless gifts of endless encouragement, inspired teaching, and enduring friendship.

---

* Associate Professor, University of Georgia School of Law. J.D. 1978, Cornell Law School. B.S. 1974, University of Wisconsin.

1 Gompers v. United States, 233 U.S. 604, 610 (1914) (Holmes, J.).

Introduction

In their seminal book, *Form and Substance in Anglo-American Law,* Professors Atiyah and Summers contrast "formal" and "substantive" approaches to legal reasoning.[2] Although formal reasoning differs from substantive reasoning in a number of ways, one important difference lies in what Atiyah and Summers call "interpretive formality".[3] Their point is that judges asked to interpret a legal text will approach that task with varying styles. In systems that tend toward interpretive formality, the decisionmaker typically will focus on the language of the text in an effort to extract its most linguistically satisfying construction.[4] In systems that tend toward substantive reasoning, the decisionmaker looks instead at such matters as "the underlying substantive reasons which influenced the lawmakers" or "his own background political morality, or ... a political morality which he attributes to the legislature or to the public".[5]

In this paper, I explore interpretive formality (and informality) in American constitutional law. I make three main points. First, the Supreme Court of the United States often eschews interpretive formality in constitutional cases. Second, a wide range of reasons explains this tendency. Third, notwithstanding the "substantive" character of much constitutional decisionmaking, interpretive formality remains an important force in many cases.

In a final section, I offer some tentative thoughts on why the Court sometimes tends toward formal reasoning and at other times tends toward a more substantive style. I also suggest that the Supreme Court has not carried over to constitutional interpretation a key attribute of statutory interpretation – namely, that reasons of interpretive formality generated by text often shut out all consideration of countervailing substantive reasons. I suggest instead that, in the constitutional setting, the Court almost always perceives arguments of interpretive formality as only factors to be put in a balance with other formal and substantive considerations brought to bear in the case.

I.

"Any species of valid law generating a formal reason may require some interpretation, but precisely what is (or should be) involved in such interpretation is a highly controversial question."[6] Less controversial is the proposition

---

[2] P. S. Atiyah and R. S. Summers, Form and Substance in Anglo-American Law (Oxford 1987).

[3] E.g., id. at 14 - 16.

[4] See id.

[5] Id. at 15 (footnote omitted).

[6] Id. at 14.

that, in some legal systems, interpretation focuses on "the verbal expression of the law."[7] By and large, however, this approach has not marked the modern American Supreme Court's interpretation of the Constitution.

As Atiyah and Summers note, the tendency toward substantive reasoning in constitutional cases is in large measure the inevitable consequence of the highly indeterminate language of the constitutional text.[8] One of the most important provisions of the Constitution, for example, requires states to afford persons "equal protection of the laws."[9] Such open-textured language leaves courts with little choice but to draw on substantive considerations in deciding concrete cases. The Equal Protection Clause says nothing about considering the strength of the government's interest in adopting a challenged classification or the fit between the classification and the purpose of the governmental policy. Courts, however, routinely consider these matters in applying the clause.[10] After all, they have to consider something.

The equal protection cases illustrate how courts of necessity often go beyond "the verbal expression of the law" in interpreting the Constitution. There is, however, much more than that to the matter of interpretive informality, for the Supreme Court has in many cases eschewed constitutional interpretations that are supported strongly, if not overwhelmingly, by constitutional text. Indeed, three of the most important constitutional principles developed by the modern Court typify this tendency: incorporation, due-process-based equal protection, and substantive due process.

Incorporation. The first Ten Amendments of the Constitution, or so-called "Bill of Rights," were adopted shortly after the Constitution's ratification. These amendments, which place limits on only the *national* government, include some twenty-three different safeguards of life, liberty, and property. Those safeguards include freedom of speech, freedom from cruel and unusual punishments, the right to a speedy trial, the right to counsel, the right to just compensation upon the taking of property, and the right to a jury trial in both civil and criminal cases. Following the Civil War, the states ratified the Fourteenth Amendment to the Constitution, which provides that: "No state shall make or enforce any law which shall abridge the privileges or immunities of citizens of the United States; nor shall any State deprive any person of life, liberty, or property, without due process of law; nor deny to any person within its jurisdiction the equal protection of the laws."[11]

Once this Amendment became law, the question arose whether it rendered applicable to the *states* the various protections afforded against the *national*

---

[7] Id. at 15.

[8] Id. at 45.

[9] U.S. Const. amend. XIV, § 1.

[10] See, e.g., Craig v. Boren, 429 U.S. 190 (1976).

[11] U.S. Const. amend. XIV, § 1.

government by the Bill of Rights. Early on, the Court blocked claims that these protections were incorporated into the Fourteenth Amendment by way of its first clause, concerning privileges and immunities.[12] Nor did it make any sense to say that the uniformly and automatically applicable protections of the Bill of Rights extended to the states by the way of the third clause, which mandated only the *equal* treatment of persons in the adoption and application of state law. Thus the only possible mechanism for rendering the various protections of the Bill of Rights applicable to the states became the Fourteenth Amendment's Due Process Clause.

Those interested in reading the Bill of Rights into the Due Process Clause, faced a formidable formal obstacle, however, because one of the Fifth Amendment's own five clauses declares that no person shall be "deprived of life, liberty or property without due process of law."[13] In other words, an incorporation of the Bill of Rights into the Fourteenth Amendment's Due Process Clause would require the Court to assign the verbal formula in that amendment a meaning necessarily different from (indeed, extraordinarily different from) exactly the same verbal formula used in the Fifth Amendment.[14]

This formal complexity did not stop the Court. As early as 1925,[15] and at an accelerating pace through the 1960s, the Court read virtually every protection embodied in the Bill of Rights into the Fourteenth Amendment's Due Process Clause.[16]

Due-Process-Based Equal Protection. In *Brown v. Board of Education,*[17] the Supreme Court held that racial segregation of state-run public schools violated the Equal Protection Clause of the Fourteenth Amendment. In a companion case, *Bolling v. Sharpe,*[18] the Court confronted a trickier question: whether the segregation of schools operated by the District of Columbia – an arm of the national government – also was unconstitutional. The difficulty of the case arose because no provision located in the Bill of Rights or elsewhere in the Constitution commands the *national* government to afford persons "equal protection of the laws." In other words, while the Fourteenth Amendment required states to afford both due process and equal protection, the rights-creating sections of the Constitution (at least on their face) required the national government to afford due process, but not equal protection. Hence,

---

[12] See The Slaughter-House Cases, 83 U.S. 36 (1872).

[13] U.S. Const. amend. V.

[14] Alternatively, it would require the Court to read the Fifth Amendment's Due Process Clause so capaciously as to render all provisions of the first eight amendments, except the Due Process Clause itself, mere surplusage.

[15] See Gitlow v. New York, 268 U.S. 652 (1925).

[16] See, e.g., Duncan v. Louisiana, 391 U.S. 145 (1968). See generally Laurence Tribe, American Constitutional Law § 11 - 2 (Foundation Press 2d ed. 1988).

[17] 347 U.S. 483 (1954).

[18] 347 U.S. 497 (1954).

the equal-protection-based holding of *Brown* did not seem applicable to *Bolling*.

This formal difficulty, however, once again did not stop the Court. To be sure, the text of the Fourteenth Amendment indicated that the right to "due process" did not ensure "equal protection." (After all, if it did, the Fourteenth Amendment's framers would not have had to include a separate Equal Protection Clause.) According to *Bolling* and its progeny, however, the principle of due process as set forth in the previously enacted Fifth Amendment did and does ensure equal protection – a legal rule of extraordinary significance in large numbers of constitutional cases.[19]

Substantive Due Process. By its terms the due process clause deals with "process." Applying the ordinary meaning of this term, the Court has had no difficulty finding that the Constitution imposes *procedural* restrictions on the states and national government.[20] Through the years, however, litigants have urged the Court to hold that the Due Process Clause also imposes *substantive* limits on government's power to act – that is, limits based on the *content* of government policy regardless of the degree of procedural regularity with which such policy was adopted and pursued. Again, such arguments face grave difficulties of interpretive formality. As Professor Ely puts it: "[T]here is simply no avoiding the fact that the word that follows 'due' is 'process' ... [W]e apparently need periodic reminding that 'substantive due process' is a contradiction in terms – sort of like 'green pastel redness.'"[21]

The Court, however, has not been deterred by this linguistic difficulty. Indeed, some of the Court's most far-reaching decisions – including its landmark decision invalidating state abortion laws[22] – have rested on the principle of substantive due process.[23]

Other examples of interpretive informality. There are many other examples of the Court's willingness to stretch the constitutional text. For example, the First Amendment safeguards freedom of "speech" – a term normally under-

19 See Tribe, supra note 16, § 16 - 1, at 1437. Put another way, while the incorporation decisions established that Fourteenth Amendment due process was in one sense broader than Fifth Amendment due process, the principle of *Bolling* meant that Fourteenth Amendment due process was in another sense narrower than Fifth Amendment due process. In the end, Fourteenth Amendment due process came to mean Fifth Amendment due process minus equal protection plus most of the non-due-process protections of the first eight amendments. Conversely, Fifth Amendment due process came to mean Fourteenth Amendment due process plus Fourteenth Amendment equal protection minus all of the protections of first eight amendments incorporated into the Fourteenth.

20 See, e.g., Goldberg v. Kelly, 397 U.S. 254 (1970) (requiring that welfare recipient receive notice and hearing before benefits are terminated).

21 John Hart Ely, Democracy and Distrust 18 (Harvard 1980).

22 Roe v. Wade, 410 U.S. 113 (1973).

23 See generally Tribe, supra note 16, §§ 15 - 1 to - 21.

stood to mean communicating with words. The Court, however, has read the word "speech" to cover essentially all forms of conduct intended to be communicative or expressive. Many would be surprised to learn, for example, that "speech" includes burning flags,[24] sleeping in parks,[25] and dancing with no clothes on.[26] A particularly important example of the Court's willingness to range beyond the confines of constitutional text is provided by the so-called "dormant Commerce Clause."[27] Although the Commerce Clause by its terms does nothing more than grant to *Congress* the *power* to regulate interstate and foreign commerce,[28] the modern Court repeatedly has read the clause to invalidate many forms of state regulation even in the absence of congressional action.[29] Moreover, the Court has interpreted this dormant Commerce Clause principle to permit a broad-gauged balancing of state and federal substantive interests in deciding whether state action is unconstitutional.[30]

These examples show that the Court has not hesitated to sidestep constitutional text in an effort to expand constitutional rights. It is equally important to see, however, that the Court also has eschewed interpretive formality in ruling against persons who seek to invoke federal constitutional protections.

The modern Court, for example, has rejected strong text-based claims for an absolutist reading of the First Amendment.[31] In similar fashion, the Sixth Amendment recognizes the right of an accused "to be confronted with the witnesses against him."[32] The Supreme Court has noted that, "[i]f one were to read this language literally," it would eradicate all exceptions to the hearsay rule, since those exceptions necessarily envision prosecutorial use of accusatory statements by person not present at trial.[33] The Court has rejected this interpretation, however, as "unintended and too extreme."[34]

---

[24] Texas v. Johnson, 491 U.S. 397 (1989).

[25] Clark v. Community for Creative Non-Violence, 468 U.S. 288 (1984).

[26] Schad v. Mt. Ephraim, 452 U.S. 61 (1981).

[27] See generally Tribe, supra note 16, §§ 6 - 1 to - 20.

[28] See U.S. Const., art. I, § 8, cl. 3.

[29] See, e.g., Chemical Waste Management, Inc. v. Hunt, 112 S. Ct. 2009 (1992).

[30] In particular, courts are to invalidate even a "statute [that] regulates even-handedly to effectuate a legitimate local public interest" if "the burden imposed on [interstate] commerce is clearly excessive in relation to the putative local benefits." Pike v. Bruce Church, Inc., 397 U.S. 137, 142 (1970).

[31] See infra notes 65 - 68 and accompanying text.

[32] U.S. Const. amend. VI.

[33] Ohio v. Roberts, 448 U.S. 56, 63 (1980).

[34] Id. For an even more pointed example of a non-textual approach to the Confrontation Clause, see Maryland v. Craig, 497 U.S. 836 (1990). In that case, the issue was whether the confrontation clause permitted a State to introduce, via closed circuit television, testimony subject to cross-examination but elicited outside the presence of the defendant from a child who would face serious emotional distress if forced physically to confront her alleged abuser. The Court upheld this procedure, rejecting the claim that

The Court also has declined to read the seemingly absolute language of the Contracts Clause as imposing an absolute prohibition. Again, according to the Court, the clause "is not to be read with literal exactness like a mathematical formula."[35]

In a "conservative" vein, the Court has looked beyond the Constitution's text to recognize doctrines protective of state autonomy. Illustrative of this tendency are the jurisdictional abstention doctrines developed by the Court,[36] as well as its recognition of nontextual state regulatory immunities.[37] The starkest example of the Court's embracing a counter-textual interpretation to protect state interests is provided by its treatment of the Eleventh Amendment. That amendment provides that: "The Judicial power of the United States shall not be construed to extend to any suit in law or equity, commenced or prosecuted against one of the United States by Citizens of another State, or by Citizens or Subjects of any Foreign State."[38] Despite the seemingly unmistakable implication that the federal judicial power *does* extend to suits brought against a state by *its own* citizens, the Supreme Court has held just the opposite.[39] The Court, in short, has read the Eleventh Amendment as though its final fourteen words did not exist.[40]

The foregoing discussion highlights how, in many ways, American constitutional law has eschewed interpretive formality. Some commentators have been critical of this reality,[41] but that is not the point here. Indeed, one can offer many reasons that tend to explain and legitimate the substantive character of American constitutional law. It is to that business that we turn in Part II.

---

the clause gives defendants "the *absolute* right to a face-to-face meeting," id. at 844 (emphasis in original), and finding a need in this setting for an exception to "the irreducible literal meaning of the clause," id. quoting Coy v. Iowa, 487 U.S. 1012 (1988). Justice Scalia in dissent chided the majority for applying "'interest-balancing' analysis where the text of the Constitution simply does not permit it." 497 U.S. at 870.

35 Home Building & Loan Ass'n v. Blaisdell, 290 U.S. 398, 428 (1934).

36 See generally Tribe, supra note 16, at §§ 3 - 28 to - 30.

37 See, e.g., New York v. United States, 112 S. Ct. 2408 (1992); see also Helvering v. Gerhardt, 304 U.S. 405 (1938).

38 U.S. Const. amend. XI.

39 See Port Auth. Trans-Hudson Corp. v. Feeney, 495 U.S. 299 (1990); Pennhurst State School & Hosp. v. Halderman, 465 U.S. 89, 100 (1984); Pennsylvania v. Union Gas Co., 491 U.S. 1, 29 (1989) (Scalia, J., concurring in part and dissenting in part); Welch v. Texas Dep't of Highways & Pub. Transp., 483 U.S. 468 (1987) (plurality opinion).

40 See generally Tribe, supra note 16, § 3 - 25, at 175 ("[T]he Supreme Court, in deciding eleventh amendment cases, has focused not on the language of the eleventh amendment, but on the concept of sovereign immunity of which it is a reminder and 'exemplification.'").

41 See, e.g., Robert H. Bork, The Tempting of America (Simon & Schuster 1990).

II.

In *McColluch v. Maryland,*[42] the Supreme Court confronted the question whether Congress had the authority to charter a national bank as "necessary and proper" to carrying out its enumerated powers to raise revenues, spend money, regulate commerce, and wage war.[43] Opponents of the bank argued that establishment of the bank was impermissible because not "indispensable" – and therefore not "necessary" – to exercising these powers. Rejecting this view, Chief Justice Marshall found that establishment of the bank was "necessary" because "appropriate" to carrying out Congress's enumerated powers.[44] In reaching this result, Justice Marshall relied – albeit with a noting selectivity – on a number of formal reasons.[45] More important for the future course of American law, however, he rested his broad and purposive interpretation of the Necessary and Proper Clause on the ringing declaration that "it is a *constitution* we are expounding."[46]

This proclamation invites the question: So what? What *is* special about the Constitution as a legal text? And why, in particular, should the Constitution invite interpretation based on purposive reasoning channeled little by ordinary meaning and linguistic structure? Why, in short, should courts feel free to downplay interpretive formality in applying the Constitution's commands?

Marshall himself identified one reason when he observed that the Constitution does not "partake of the prolixity of a legal code."[47] Although one might again ask why this fact matters, at least three responses seem at hand. First, given the Constitution's treatment of a wide-ranging subject matter, its brevity necessitated such terse and open-textured commands that courts have had no choice but to range beyond the words of the text to give the document meaning.[48] Second, the very fact that the Constitution is not written like a Code designed to deal comprehensively with a particular subject matter implies that

---

[42] 17 U.S. 316 (1819).

[43] See U.S. Const. Art. I, § 8.

[44] See McCulloch, 17 U.S. at 423.

[45] In particular, Justice Marshall emphasized that, while the Articles of Confederation provided that the states retained all powers not "expressly delegated" to the national government, the Tenth Amendment omitted the word "expressly." Id. at 405; see also id. at 414 (contrasting use of term "necessary" in necessary-and-proper clause with the term "absolutely necessary" in import-export clause); id. at 419 (making argument that strict interpretation of term "necessary" renders companion term "proper" meaningless). Justice Marshall did not deal with the argument that the Constitutional Convention had refused to empower Congress to charter corporations in part on the ground it unwisely would empower Congress to charter banks. See Gerald Gunther, Constitutional Law 84 (Foundation Press 11th ed. 1985) (quoting opinion of Secretary of State Jefferson to President Washington on constitutionality of chartering national bank).

[46] 17 U.S. at 407 (emphasis in original).

[47] Id.

it need not be interpreted like such a Code. Thus, rules devised to deal with other forms of legal texts – for example, the rule that the specification of certain things excludes others – may simply carry less weight in constitutional adjudication.[49] A third and related point is that the profoundly non-Code-like character of the Constitution suggests that (at least in the main) it is not properly seen as a set of rules at all, but instead as an embodiment of principles from which courts are to derive rules.[50] The Court, moreover, may see itself as having a particularly free hand in this enterprise because of the distinctive difficulty of discerning the intentions of the Constitution's enactors.[51]

In *McCulloch,* Chief Justice Marshall also emphasized that the Constitution was "designed to endure for generations to come."[52] His point is simple, but critically important. If the Constitution is to endure in meaningful form, it must be adaptable to changing conditions. Moreover, if the Constitution is to be adaptable, it must be construed in light of underlying purposes conceived at a high level of generality, with limited stress on the Framers' precise choice of verbal phrasing.[53]

The appropriateness of adaptive interpretation may be reinforced by the difficulty of securing constitutional amendments. As Atiyah and Summers have noted: "[T]he federal Constitution is not easily subject to formal amendment, so that change in American constitutional law has to take place through some form of interpretation... [T]hese factors exert continuous pressure for rela-

---

48 See Atiyah and Summers, supra note 2, at 153, 238 ("highly purposive interpretation ... and so of low interpretive formality ... was rendered a practical necessity by the vague and broad language of the Constitution itself").

49 See McCulloch, 17 U.S. at 413 (stating that Court should not "change, entirely, the character of the [Constitution], and give it the properties of a legal code").

50 See id. at 406 ("nature [of constitution] requires, that only its great outlines should be marked, its important objects designated, and the minor ingredients which compose those objects, be deduced from the nature of the objects themselves"); see also William A. Kaplin, The Concepts and Methods of Constitutional Law 25 (Carolina Academic Press 1992) ("The drafters, moreover, may have made deliberate use of language's open texture, using vague words with no precise and fixed meaning, so as to allow future interpreters a range of discretion in attributing specific meanings to words in unforeseen circumstances.").

51 See id. at 84 (questioning "whether the framers had a collective state of mind capable of ascertainment"; noting also "that the framers include not only those who participated in the drafting and approval process but also those who participated in the ratifying conventions" and that "theoretical and practical difficulties involved in the search for the framers' intent increase with this broadened definition of the group").

52 17 U.S. at 415.

53 This is so in part because the Framers' choice of phraseology inescapably reflected their own time-tied circumstances. For example, the Fourth Amendment, by its terms, extends to searches of "persons, houses, papers and effects" – and not to the interception of electronic signals carrying vocal communications. U.S. Const. amend. IV. Focusing on the *purpose* of the Fourth Amendment, however, the Court has held its proscriptions applicable to the many forms of modern-day electronic surveillance. See, e.g., Katz v. United States, 389 U.S. 347 (1967).

tively low interpretive ... formality."[54] In other words, the difficulty of amendment not only may help to assure the *legal* survival of core constitutional principles by making it hard to amend them away; it also may help assure their *practical* survival by justifying adaptive interpretation by the federal judiciary.

An adaptive, and therefore substantive, approach to constitutional interpretation also finds support in the fact that some constitutional clauses openly invite consideration of contemporary conditions. So it is, it would seem, with deciding whether a punishment is "unusual" for purposes of the Eighth Amendment. Even more important, some of the Constitution's broad phrases may be viewed as permitting, if not requiring, consideration of contemporary *values*. Whether a punishment is "cruel," for example, seems intrinsically contingent on prevailing moral norms.[55] The same might be said about whether particular procedural protections are "due" or a particular form of compensation is "just."[56] In other words, "the language of many individual rights clauses ... can be read to leave much developmental work to future generations"; "these clauses might be termed 'invitational clauses.'"[57]

Most striking among those clauses that invite consultation of substantive values is the Ninth Amendment. Without further elaboration, that amendment provides that: "The enumeration in the Constitution, of certain rights, shall not be construed to deny or disparage others retained by the people."[58] The meaning of the Ninth Amendment has been much disputed, and it is not my purpose now to enter that fray.[59] At the least, however, the amendment contributes to a spirit of non-technical rights-mindedness that cuts against a fixed judicial focus on the "verbal expression of the law."[60] The tendency away from textbound interpretative formality also finds support in widely shared perceptions that the Constitution embodies "great outlines,"[61] "tacit postulates,"[62] "great silences,"[63] and a "spirit ... to be respected."[64]

[54] Atiyah and Summers, supra note 2, at 76.

[55] See, e.g., Trop v. Dulles, 356 U.S. 86, 101 (1958) (plurality opinion) (holding that Eighth Amendment embodies "evolving standards of decency that mark the progress of a maturing society").

[56] U.S. Const. amends. XIV, V.

[57] Kaplin, supra note 50, at 131; see, e.g., Harper v. Virginia State Bd. of Elections, 383 U.S. 663, 669 (1966).

[58] U.S. Const. amend. IX.

[59] See Gerald Gunther, Constitutional Law 503 n. 2 (Foundation Press 12th ed. 1991) (collecting literature); Tribe, supra note 16, at 774 - 77.

[60] Atiyah and Summers, supra note 2, at 15. So too, it might be added, does the natural-rights theory of law that coursed through American political thought in the days of the Constitution's adoption. See id. at 229 - 39.

[61] Davis v. Passmann, 442 U.S. 228, 241 (1979) (Brennan, J.) (quoting McCulloch, 17 U.S. at 407).

[62] Nevada v. Hall, 440 U.S. 410, 433 (1979) (Rehnquist, J., dissenting).

A substantive approach to constitutional interpretation also has been driven by practical experience and common understandings. During Justice Black's tenure on the Court, for example, debate raged about whether the First Amendment imposed an absolute prohibition on laws that abridge freedom of speech and of the press.[65] Justice Black persistently urged that "no law" meant "no law," and some commentators advanced theories supportive of this view.[66] To most of us, however, Justice Black's outlook was irreconcileable with self-evident premises of life in organized society. Government *could* sanction the person who falsely shouted "Fire!" in a crowded theater.[67] Government *could* punish perjury. Government *could,* at least in certain cases, criminalize verbal threats of harm or award damages for defamation.[68] In short, "no law" did not mean "no law," at least in the ordinary sense.

The rejection of Justice Black's literalist vision of the First Amendment invited non-literalist approaches to other constitutional provisions as well. After all, if the First Amendment means something other than what its language says, why should we not feel free to reach the same conclusion about the Fifth Amendment Due Process Clause,[69] the Fourteenth Amendment Due Process Clause,[70] and other important constitutional provisions as well?[71] More generally, the rejection of an absolutist view of the First Amendment opened the door to a constitutional discourse built around "balancing."[72] The ascendancy of balancing – with its overriding focus on "practical effect"[73] and "capaciously conceived" governmental interests[74] – brought with it an emphasis on substantive, rather than formal, legal reasoning.

The foregoing discussion is not designed to provide a full explanation of the highly substantive inclinations of the modern Supreme Court. The discussion suggests at least, however, that many forces favor this orientation. In light of this reality, it is not surprising that modern constitutional discourse is not predominated by arguments of interpretive formality.

---

63 H. P. Hood & Sons v. DuMond, 336 U.S. 525, 535 (1949) (Jackson, J.).

64 Sturges v. Crowninshield, 17 U.S. 122, 202 (1819) (Marshall, C. J.).

65 Compare, e.g., Konigsberg v. State Bar of Cal., 366 U.S. 36 (1961) (Harlan, J.) with id. at 56 (Black, J., dissenting).

66 E.g., T. Emerson, The System of Freedom of Expression (1970).

67 Schenck v. United States, 249 U.S. 47 (1919).

68 See, e.g., New York Times Co. v. Sullivan, 376 U.S. 254 (1964) (recognizing availability of claim for defamation of public official upon showing of actual malice).

69 See supra notes 17 - 19 and accompanying text.

70 See supra notes 11 - 16 and accompanying text.

71 See supra notes 24 - 40 and accompanying text.

72 See generally Alienikoff, Constitutional Law in the Age of Balancing, 96 Yale L.J. 943 (1987).

73 E.g., Mobil Oil Corp. v. Commissioner of Taxes of Ver., 445 U.S. 425, 443 (1980).

74 Fallon, Individual Rights and the Powers of Government 7 (unpublished manuscript on file with author; to be published at 27 Ga. L. Rev. 343 (1993)).

III.

Based on what has been said so far one might conclude that the Supreme Court pays no attention to formal reasons in deciding constitutional cases. Not so. Although no comprehensive taxonomy is attempted here, the following examples suffice to show that interpretive formality remains an important ingredient in the Court's constitutional work notwithstanding its receptiveness to substantive reasoning.

In some cases, the Court relies on the plain language of the constitutional text.[75] *Buckley v. Valeo,*[76] for example, presented the issue whether the President pro tempore of the Senate and Speaker of the House could appoint a majority of members of the Federal Election Commission. The Court invalidated this scheme based on the "plain language" of the Appointments Clause.[77] Under that provision, even "inferior officers" could be appointed only by "the Courts of Law" or "the Heads of Departments,"[78] and "neither the Speaker of the House nor the President *pro tempore* of the Senate comes within this language."[79] The Court in *Buckley* went on to note the substantive argument "that Congress had good reason for not vesting in a Commission composed wholly of Presidential appointees the authority to administer the Act, since the administration of the Act would undoubtedly have a bearing on any incumbent President's campaign for re-election."[80] This argument, however, was overridden by considerations of interpretive formality. As the Court put it: "such fears, however rational, do not by themselves warrant a distortion of the Framers' work."[81]

The Court also relies on familiar principles of textual construction in interpreting constitutional provisions. In *Immigration and Naturalization Service v. Chadha,*[82] for example, the Court invalidated a one-house legislative veto based in part on the fact that the Constitution enumerates specific situations in which one congressional house properly can act, without making any reference to a one-house power to overturn executive branch action pursuant to a congressional delegation of authority.[83] The Court has relied on negative implica-

---

[75] e.g., Maxwell v. Dow, 176 U.S. 581, 602 (1900) (suggesting that purposive interpretation is not properly available to give effect to a constitutional provision "in a manner which the plain and unambiguous language used therein would not justify or permit").

[76] 424 U.S. 1 (1976).

[77] Id. at 127.

[78] U.S. Const. Art II, § 2.

[79] 424 U.S. at 127.

[80] Id. at 134.

[81] Id.

[82] 462 U.S. 919 (1983).

[83] Id. at 995.

tions of constitutional text in other settings as well. Thus in *Bowsher v. Synar*[84] the Court reasoned that the Constitution's express provision for congressional removal of federal officers by impeachment negated an authority to remove such officers by other means.[85]

Contrasts in the language of clauses also may count with the Court. For example, while the dormant Commerce Clause and the Article IV Privileges and Immunities Clause stem from a "shared vision of federalism,"[86] the Court has held that only the former contains a "market participant" exception.[87] The key reason why is that the Commerce Clause by its terms focuses on market "regulation" – as opposed to market participation – while the Article IV clause speaks sweepingly of "privileges or immunities."[88]

The Court also looks to context and companion clauses in giving constitutional provisions meaning. A key question in *Roe v. Wade,*[89] for example, was whether the unborn fetus is a "person" within the meaning of the Fourteenth Amendment. In answering this question in the negative, the Court noted:

> The Constitution does not define 'person' in so many words. Section 1 of the Fourteenth Amendment contains three references to 'person.' [The term 'person' also] is used in other places in Constitution . . . But in nearly all these instances, the use of the word is such that it has application only postnatally. None indicates, with any assurance, that it has any possible prenatal application.[90]

It also bears emphasis that the Court – even when not utilizing textual arguments – frequently invokes reasons that are "formal" in the sense that they differ greatly from appeals to fairness and sound policy. In particular, the Court may focus on traditional practice,[91] actions taken at the Constitutional Convention,[92] the teachings of the Federalist Papers,[93] or other focused indications that a specific activity was or was not intended by the Framers to be constitutionally protected.[94]

---

[84] 478 U.S. 714 (1986).

[85] Id. at 722 - 24.

[86] Hicklin v. Orbeck, 437 U.S. 518, 532 (1978).

[87] See generally Coenen, Untangling the Market Participant Exemption to the Dormant Commerce Clause, 88 Mich. L. Rev. 395 (1989).

[88] See United Bldg. & Constr. Trades Council v. Camden, 465 U.S. 208, 220 (1984).

[89] 410 U.S. 113 (1973).

[90] Id. at 157.

[91] E.g., Burnham v. Superior Court, 495 U.S. 604 (1990) (plurality opinion).

[92] E.g., New York v. United States, 112 S. Ct. 2408 (1992).

[93] E.g., Garcia v. San Antonio Metro. Transit Auth., 469 U.S. 528 (1985).

[94] One common form of such reasoning involves reliance on the actions of the first Congress, many of whose members were involved in drafting the original Constitution. See, e.g., Myers v. United States, 272 U.S. 52, 174 - 75 (1926); Bowsher v. Synar, 478 U.S. 714, 724 (1986).

In *Marsh v. Chambers,*[95] for example, the Court considered whether a state legislature's practice of beginning sessions with a chaplain's invocation violated the First Amendment's Establishment Clause. Under the Court's then-prevailing Establishment Clause test it seemed clear that this practice was unconstitutional.[96] The Court, however, upheld the legislative prayer based on the historical fact that "[f]rom colonial times through the founding of the Republic and ever since, the practice of legislative prayer has coexisted with the principles of disestablishment and religious freedom."[97] Even more pointedly, legislative invocations had been "authorized by First Congress," the very Congress that adopted the First Amendment.[98]

All these forms of analysis differ greatly from highly substantive reasoning, which emphasizes "moral, economic, political, institutional or other social consideration[s]."[99] Indeed, an overarching purpose of relying on text, tradition, or the focused treatment of a particular practice by the lawgiver is to block (or at least temper) resort to the decisionmaker's own views of morality and utility.

The important point to be drawn from these examples is that the use of reasons of interpretive formality remains prevalent in the argument and disposition of modern constitutional cases. Indeed, the remarkable resilience of this style of reasoning should do much to refute the claim that constitutional interpretation is nothing more than a thinly disguised brand of politics.

IV.

It should now be clear that the Supreme Court sometimes gives great weight to arguments of interpretive formality, while at other times it pays such arguments very little heed. Although I shall not attempt to articulate a full-blown theory as to why this is the case, there may be merit in taking a few halting steps toward systematically explaining this curious phenomenon.

To begin with, the role of interpretive formality varies from case to case because "the enlightenment gained from the [constitutional] text will vary from clause to clause."[100] There can be no doubt, for example, that the Court has liberally poured meaning into the Due Process Clauses in part because of their stark and amorphous phrasing.[101] In addition, some justices are more for-

---

95 463 U.S. 783 (1983).

96 See id. at 795, 796 - 801 (Brennan, J., dissenting).

97 Id. at 786.

98 Id. at 790. For a general discussion of the use of history in interpreting the religion clauses, see Tribe, supra note 16, § 14 - 3.

99 Atiyah and Summers, supra note at 2, at 5.

100 Kaplin, supra note 50, at 202.

101 See supra notes 8 - 23 and accompanying text.

mality-minded than are others.[102] The make-up of the Court thus will have an impact on how strong a role interpretive formality plays in the decision of constitutional cases.[103]

The subject matter of cases also may bear on the Court's inclination to embrace or eschew arguments of interpretive formality. The Court, for example, probably deems itself at greater liberty to move from formal to substantive reasoning in cases that involve controversies within the particular expertise of the judiciary. This factor may help explain the Court's willingness to incorporate into the Fourteenth Amendment most of the Bill of Rights (which largely treats matters of judicial procedure),[104] as well as the Court's particularly substantive orientation toward disputes over federal-court jurisdiction.[105]

Another consideration that *could* drive the Court toward interpretive formality is suggested by Professors Atiyah and Summers. As they put it, "basic and fundamental constitutional structures are almost by necessity highly formal."[106] Thus, formality is associated with "core rules ... relating to the basic structure of government."[107] While it is true that many structural rules are inherently formal,[108] these comments are misguided if meant to suggest that the *Court* tends toward heightened *interpretive* formality in the area of structural law. The Court, for example, has read the Constitution to authorize widespread rulemaking by unelected federal administrators[109] even though Article I states that "[a]ll legislative Powers herein granted shall be vested in a Congress of the United States."[110] The Court also has upheld the exercise of adjudicative authority by executive agencies,[111] notwithstanding the Constitu-

---

102 Chief Justice Warren, for example, was widely perceived as a "substantive" judge. Justice Scalia, in contrast, is widely perceived as "formal." See generally Scalia, The Rule of Law as a Law of Rules, 56 U. Chi. L. Rev. 1175 (1989). At the same time, it is important to recognize that justices perceived as "liberals," no less than justices perceived as "conservatives," may tend toward interpretive formality. Justice Black provides a striking example. In addition, justices perceived as formal-minded sometimes will vote in ways that seem counter-formal. Justice Scalia, for example, endorsed a non-textual view of the Eleventh Amendment, see supra note 39, and he also joined the majority opinion that deemed flag-burning speech, see supra note 24. Of course, formality-based reasons unrelated to text-based interpretive formality might help explain these results; in the eleventh-amendment context, for example, Justice Scalia relied heavily on longstanding Supreme Court precedent.

103 See Atiyah and Summers, supra note 2, at 336 - 37.

104 See supra notes 11 - 16 and accompanying text.

105 See supra notes 36, 38 - 40 and accompanying text.

106 Atiyah and Summers, supra note 2, at 72.

107 Id.

108 For example, the Constitution requires that there be a legislative, executive and judicial branch, that there should be one president and two houses of Congress and that each state should have two senators.

109 E.g., Yakus v. United States, 321 U.S. 414 (1944).

110 U.S. Const. Art. I, § 1.

111 E.g., Crowell v. Benson, 285 U.S. 22 (1932).

tion's vesting of the judicial power in the federal courts.[112] These decisions – like other counter-textual Supreme Court rulings – reflect the Court's attentiveness to changed conditions. In particular, they respond to the increased practical need for specialized government regulation in light of the complexity of modern society. In short, important Court rulings in the area of governmental structures, no less so than in the area of individual rights, have sprung from substantive concerns vindicated in the teeth of strong arguments of interpretive formality.

One factor that bears on the Court's style of reasoning in any particular case is the strength of the formal and substantive reasons at hand. In *Bolling v. Sharpe,*[113] for example, the Court was well aware that a powerful argument of interpretive formality cut against judicially imposed desegregation of the District of Columbia public schools.[114] This reason, however, was simply outweighed by extremely powerful substantive reasons that cut in the other direction. In particular, "in view of [the] decision that the Constitution prohibits the states from maintaining racially segregated public schools, it would be unthinkable that the same Constitution would impose a lesser duty on the Federal Government."[115]

A recognition that substantive reasons may outweigh formal reasons in this way may aid understanding of the Court's constitutional work. Some commentators, for example, have criticized the Court on the ground that it has moved erratically between so-called "formal" and "functional" approaches to separation-of-powers problems.[116] If the depiction of reason-weighing decisionmaking offered here is correct, the criticisms of these commentators may be overdrawn. Thus, rather than being perceived as schizophrenically shifting between incompatible approaches in deciding separation-of-powers cases, the Court more accurately may be seen as responding in different cases to reasons of differing weights. In particular, the Court has given decisive weight to very strong reasons of interpretive formality in cases like *INS v. Chadha*[117] and *Bowsher v. Synar.*[118] On the other hand, it has given far more play to substantive reasons in cases like *Morrison v. Olson*[119] and *Mistretta v. United States,*[120] where reasons of interpretive formality were not nearly so compelling.

---

[112] U.S. Const. Art. III.

[113] 347 U.S. 497 (1954).

[114] See supra notes 18 - 19 and accompanying text.

[115] 347 U.S. at 500.

[116] See generally Strauss, Formal and Functional Approaches to Separation-of-Powers Questions – A Foolish Consistency?, 72 Cornell L. Rev. 488 (1987); Fallon, supra note 74, at 6 n. 11.

[117] 462 U.S. 919 (1983).

[118] 478 U.S. 714 (1986).

[119] 487 U.S. 654 (1988).

[120] 488 U.S. 361 (1989).

A broader point lurks beneath the surface of this discussion. Professors Atiyah and Summers have suggested that a key attribute of *statutes* is that they sometimes generate formal reasons that shut off all resort to arguments of substance.[121] The persistent overriding of strong appeals to interpretive formality in constitutional cases, however, suggests that, at least in general, this conception of the role of a legal text does not extend to the American Constitution. Instead, formal reasons generated by the Constitution's text – even if very powerful – seem only to "tip the scales in one direction" in such a manner that they may "be overridden by contrary substantive arguments."[122]

Notably, this counter-formal conception of reason-weighing in constitutional cases finds support not only in the Court's practice, but in broader theoretical pronouncements as well. Most important, in its foray into constitutional theory in the *Carolene Products* case,[123] the Court stated that "[t]here may be a narrower scope for operation of the presumption of constitutionality when legislation appears on its face to be within a specific prohibition of the Constitution."[124] The structure of this statement is telling: even if the law "on its face" falls within a "specific" constitutional prohibition, that fact does not render the law unconstitutional; rather, it merely "narrow[s]" the "presumption of constitutionality." In other words, even the most powerful formal reasons generated by constitutional text are not dispositive; rather, they may be put in a balance with countervailing reasons of form and of substance.[125]

---

121 Atiyah and Summers, supra note 2, at 8.

122 Id. This sort of "everything is in the balance" orientation toward formal and substantive reasons is illustrated by the Court's decision in Reeves Inc. v. Stake, 447 U.S. 429 (1980). In that case the issue was whether South Dakota's decision to sell cement produced by the state itself solely to South Dakota residents violated the anti-discrimination principle of the dormant Commerce Clause. In finding the anti-discrimination principle inapplicable the Court focused on the linguistic distinction between market "regulation" (dealt with in the Commerce Clause) and market "participation" (not dealt with in the Commerce Clause). Constitutional history reinforced this distinction since the Court found "no indication of a constitutional plan to limit the ability of the States themselves to operate freely in the free market." Id. at 437. Broader substantive considerations also came into play; for example, the Court emphasized that fairness favored the claim of state residents to enjoy the benefits of resources generated through their own investment and risk. Id. at 446. To be sure, countervailing formal and substantive considerations were in the picture, but these considerations were outweighed by the amalgam of formal and substantive reasons brought to bear by the Court. See id.

123 United States v. Carolene Prods. Co., 304 U.S. 144 (1938).

124 Id. at 152 - 53 n. 4.

125 It is important to note that, while interpretive informality pervades American constitutional law, this fact does not mean that all constitutional rules are informal in all respects. For example, although the Court may downplay arguments of text-based interpretive formality in constructing constitutional rules, those rules, once formulated, may partake of a high level of *mandatory* formality by excluding reference to substantive considerations at the point of application. See, e.g., Coenen, Rights as Trumps, 27 Ga. L. Rev. (1993). By way of example, the Court has held that the discontinuance of a benefit that is removable only for cause under subconstitutional rules constitutes a

Conceiving constitutional decisionmaking as entailing a broad-gauged weighing of formal and substantive considerations, even when constitutional text seems clear, invites the perennial criticism that the Court illegitimately has invaded the legislative domain. It is important to see, however, that the *type* of decisional balancing documented in this essay highlights a key *difference* between judicial and legislative processes. Under this form of constitutional "balancing," after all, the Court does and must put weight (and sometimes very heavy weight) on formal reasons, including text-tied reasons of interpretive formality. Legislatures, in contrast, seldom take any account of such formal considerations in enacting laws.

Conclusion

I noted at the outset of this article Professor Summers' abiding respect for the complexity of law. Professor Summers' life work has been to untangle that complexity by plumbing the nooks, crannies, and essential nature of judicial reasoning. In this essay, I have sought to build on Professor Summers' work by examining interpretive formality in American constitutional law. While I offer no grand theory, my hope is that this essay casts light. My deeper hope is that it bears witness to the sort of careful and caring inquisitiveness that Bob Summers so generously strove to instill within me.

---

deprivation of property or liberty that triggers due process protections. See, e.g., Cleveland Bd. of Educ. v. Loudermill, 470 U.S. 532 (1985); Vitek v. Jones, 445 U.S. 480 (1980). This principle, although defensible on substantive grounds, is hardly discernible from the constitutional text and thus is not marked by interpretive formality. Court majorities, however, have applied the principle with unwavering consistency, thus lending it a high level of *mandatory* formality. For a discussion of mandatory formality, see Atiyah and Summers, supra note 2, at 16 - 17.

Legal Reasoning in the Conflict of Laws: An Essay in Law and Practice

By Richard Fentiman, Cambridge

A *festschrift* is no place for an epitaph, for the finality and solemnity an epitaph implies. In thinking of Robert Summers, however, and his contribution to legal learning, an epitaph comes to mind, a famous one, one located fittingly in his beloved Oxford. 'Inter homines philosophus inter philosophos homo'. These words, in Balliol College chapel, commemorate Lord Lindsay, Balliol's one-time Master. 'Among men a philosopher, among philosophers a man'. To vary the theme only slightly, Robert Summers is at once a philosopher among lawyers, a lawyer among philosophers, his work bringing the insights of the one group to bear on the problems of the other, enriching and educating both.

The following remarks, taking their lead from Robert Summers' twin concerns, merge matters of substantive law with reflections on their jurisprudential implications. Their first purpose is to identify some of the characteristic features of the culture of the English Conflict of Laws – a term interchangeable with Private International Law in English legal parlance. Their second, and broader, task is to use that distinctive, perhaps peculiar, culture to illustrate more general conclusions about common law legal reasoning. Although hinging on technical aspects of Private International Law, what follows has much to do with the analysis of legal reasoning and the nature of the common law legal process. In that sense, as an essay in legal method which draws much on the distinctions between form and substance, formalism and instrumentalism, its debt to Robert Summers will be manifest.

1. English Conflicts Culture

The conflict of laws, like any branch of law, is driven by tactical and economic, not purely legal, considerations. This is true especially of the high-grade, protracted, commercial litigation which looms so large in the practice of English conflicts lawyers. Invariably involving corporate litigants, often substantial enterprises, sometimes sovereign states or their agencies, such transnational litigation is far from being an exercise in seeking legal truth, still less justice in some abstract sense. It is, rather, an investment, a calculated commercial risk taken only if the benefits in view outweigh the likely costs. It is moreover, in the English context, an investment of a high-risk sort. The expense of resolving international disputes in London's Commercial Court is high and the absence of a contingent-fee charging system, familiar to American lawyers, makes litigation an economically harzardous, potentially crippling, business. More precisely, the English rule that costs follow the cause, whereby the loser at trial bears not only his own costs but those of the winner as well, gives special focus to the need for the parties to balance the pros and cons of going to court. The prize for victory, however, is correspondingly high. The winner wins all, sacrificing nothing to his lawyers in settlement of their fees, and gaining the considerable bonus that follows from the United Kingdom's membership of the Brussels and Lugano networks for the execution of judgments;[1] for all practical purposes an English judgment is instantly enforceable against a defendant's assets wherever in Western Europe they may be.

Such economic realties constantly inform the thinking and tactical decision-making of English litigation lawyers. They are given special impetus, moreover, by another feature of the conflict of laws in England, its surprising indeterminacy. This indeterminacy, reflected as one would expect in a common law system, by a dearth of decided cases, was captured by the late Dr Cheshire with characteristic aptness:

> [English Private International Law] ... is not overloaded with detailed rules; it has been only lightly touched by the paralysing hand of the Parliamentary draftsman, at least as regards its fundamental structure and basic tenets; it is perhaps the one considerable department in which the formation of a coherent body of law is in course of process; it is, at the moment, fluid not static, elusive not obvious; it repels any tendency to dogmatism.[2]

Written in 1935, this observation remains almost as true now as it undoubtedly was then. Granted the Brussels and Lugano Conventions have codified much of English law's rules of jurisdiction, true that the 1980 Rome Convention[3] has harmonised and, in the process, crystalised the law on choice of law in Contract, but much remains in flux. Extraordinary as it seems English law still lacks clear direction on the vexed matter of choice of law in marriage; if a French woman marries an Englishman in Spain with the intention of residing in Germany it remains alarmingly unclear what law should decide whether they are validly married.[4] Take again the case of tort. Although conventional wisdom has probably come around to an acceptable view of what law governs claims in English courts based on foreign torts, there is no definitive authority

---

[1] The 1968 Brussels Convention on Jurisdiction and the Enforcement of Judgments; the 1988 Lugano Convention on Jurisdiction and the Enforcement of Judgments.

[2] Cheshire /North, *Private International Law* (12th ed. 1992), p. vii, reproducing the Preface to the First Edition (1935).

[3] The 1980 Rome Convention on the Law Applicable to Contractual Obligations.

[4] See Cheshire / North, op. cit., pp. 586 - 603.

on what England's choice of law rule in such cases ought to be.[5] Again, taking a more technical example, suppose a Dutch corporation sells goods to an English buyer subject to a retention of title clause. Asked which law governs the clause's proprietary aspects an English lawyer would have no answer, none at least based upon decided cases.[6]

The case-sparseness of English private international law, the subject's open-texture and its striking uncertainty, have immense implications. Pragmatically viewed, it shapes the thinking of lawyers and judges alike, depriving them not only of clear law, of the raw material with which to work, but of the experience and confidence to handle the subject. Jurisprudentially, it makes the conflict of laws in England a veritable laboratory in which to see the common law in action, its worst excesses and its greatest achievements. For in a legal environment where nothing, or little, is certain, where fundamental questions of policy and principle remain unanswered or unasked, all cases are hard cases.

2. Case-Sparseness Explained

Why should the conflict of laws in England be so peculiarly lacking in decided cases? It is not that there are none, of course; there are quite enough that the subject yields some sizeable textbooks. Moreover, some sub-departments of the subject, like that dealing with rules of jurisdiction, are replete with authority. Indeed, it is important to emphasise that, in speaking of the case-sparseness of English conflicts law what is meant, more precisely, is the lack of cases on choice of law questions, cases concerning which law shall govern the substance of a dispute. With this proviso, however, it is fair to say that the subject as a whole lacks the weight of caselaw one might be used to in other major sectors of English law, like contract, for example, or the law of tort. Certainly, there are many central areas of the subject, notably concerning choice of law in tort and in marriage, where decisions are surprisingly few. Although the case-sparseness of the conflict of laws in England is only relative, however, it is enough to be worthy of remark, enough to make an impact on the subject and shape its culture.

In one sense, the conflict of laws is bound to yield fewer cases than the major departments of domestic law. Only a small proportion of cases will have the foreign element necessary to transform them into conflicts cases. Moreover, notwithstanding that the United Kingdom comprises three law areas, England and Wales, Scotland and Northern Ireland, English courts face nothing like the volume of internal conflicts with which the courts in, say, the United States, are so familar. The conflict of laws in England is primarily concerned

[5] Ibid. at pp. 528 - 550.
[6] Ibid. at pp. 802 - 803.

with international conflicts, hence the fact that English lawyers often refer to it as Private International Law.

Such first impressions are readily contradicted, however, by other factors which imply that international conflicts ought to occur regularly in English courts. On the one hand, the ethnic diversity of English society, born of significant immigration from former colonies with different cultural traditions, suggests that personal conflicts, principally concerning the validity of marriages or the recognition of divorces, should be frequent. Again, London's almost unique status as a worldwide commercial centre, especially in the areas of shipping, banking and insurance, suggests that commercial disputes with an international flavour should be commomplace.

The truth is that factors such as these indeed create the potential for large numbers of conflicts cases. The intriguing fact, however, is that numerous other factors control the number of disputes which arise, disputes, at least, concerning choice of law questions. Some are general, affecting the subject in all its branches, others relate only to specific areas. Three factors of general importance are especially significant in explaining why many potential conflicts cases never become conflicts disputes. The first is just the simple truth that in many respects, as comparative law surely teaches, the legal systems of the world yield remarkably similar results to particular legal problems, whatever the differences in their juridical traditions, legal idiom and conceptual assumptions. This overwhelming similarity robs many choice of law questions – questions about which nation's law should govern the substance of an issue – of any practical necessity. The parties to a contractual dispute, for example, will hardly make an issue out of which law governs their agreement if in the end, each of the alternatives yields the same result (or a result so similiar that the cost of arguing the point outweighs the benefit of doing so). Nor, for instance, will the beneficiaries under a will contest the deceased's domicile – domicile in English law determines which law regulates the distribution of property on death – if the possible laws are significantly similar.

The second general consideration, which militates against potential conflicts of law becoming actual, concerns English procedural law's distinctive approach to pleading foreign law. In English law this is a purely voluntary matter.[7] It is for each party, not for the court, to decide whether to plead foreign law in a given case, thus activating the foreign element in a dispute and turning it into a matter for the conflict of laws. This principle is sufficiently strong that even in a case, for example, concerning a contractual agreement that a given foreign law should govern, an English court would think nothing of applying English law, were neither party to allege that the agreed law actually governed. The similarity, just noted, between the results obtained in different legal systems, is an obvious reason for choosing not to plead foreign law; why do so if nothing

[7] Fentiman 'Foreign Law in English Courts' [1992] 108 *Law Quarterly Review* 142.

turns on it? In other cases, however, it may be that considerations of cost, convenience and delay weigh against pleading foreign law. Where, for example, the content of foreign law is obscure or controversial, such that its proof in English proceedings would be protracted, expensive and, above all, unpredictable, neither party is likely to invoke it.

Such considerations as these provide the backdrop against which the case-sparseness of the English conflict of laws might be explained. Essentially, it is for the parties to decide whether to introduce the foreign element in a case. Often, as where each of the systems of law which might be applied yield the same result, they will have good reasons not to do so.

There is, moreover, a third general factor influencing the dearth of English conflicts case-law, the tendency of litigants to settle their differences before trial, at least in commercial matters, where the need for an essentially declaratory judgment will be less than in cases concerning personal status. Thus, in commercial cases at least, settlement on favourable terms is almost invariably the real object which disputants have in view. The litigation process, whether or not in conflicts cases, is merely the framework within which the parties can position themselves so as to display their case in its best light. Once an English court decides it has jurisdiction, for example, or when it decides otherwise, the parties often settle because, once it is known where the trial will occur, a number of questions, concerning the remedies available and the choice of law rules to be applied will become clear. In the light of such information the parties' relative strengths and weaknesses come into focus, allowing them to judge whether to settle or not, and on what terms. The process of discovery, whereby each party discloses documentary evidence to the other, is another watershed, a natural break, in the litigation process which allows a similar assessment of the balance of power, as is the distinctively English process of exchanging witness statements before trial.

The fact is, therefore, that many cases with a foreign element never become choice of law disputes, however likely it is that a jurisdictional contest will ensue. Either the parties will settle before trial, obviating the need for any choice of law dispute, or the case will proceed to trial, not as a conflicts dispute but, because neither side pleads foreign law, as a purely domestic case.

These general features of the conflicts litigation process help to explain the dearth of decided cases, at least on matters of choice of law. It should be emphasised, however, that, by contrast, jurisdictional disputes are very frequent in England, especially in commercial matters. Indeed, it is worth stressing that they are probably more frequent than in many countries, owing to English law's distinctively discretionary approach to jurisdiction. Roughly speaking, the recent European conventions on jurisdiction aside, English courts have considerable discretion whether or not to entertain proceedings, a discretion which invites, indeed requires, litigation. It is, however, with choice of law issues that we are largely concerned and, in that area, as we have seen, the paucity of authority is striking.

The general features of the English conflicts process, which account for the reduced importance of choice of law matters in practice, are augmented by factors special to particular situations, all of which contribute to the same phenomenon. Take marriage for example. Conflicts cases traditionally have concerned the essential validity of marriage. This is an issue bearing upon whether a marriage should be annulled, however, annulment proceedings now being a rarity with the growth of divorce as the standard means of terminating a marriage. Divorce in the English courts, however, is always a matter for English law, no conflicts issue arising. The upshot is that most matrimonial proceedings now concern cases where no choice of law issue is involved. And what of tort? Here the English conflicts rule, the so-called double actionability test, is a notorious deterrent to a plaintiff's suing in England in such a case. For, uniquely perhaps, a plaintiff must demonstrate not only that the wrong is actionable under English domestic law, but under the *lex loci delicti* as well.[8] Given that such a plaintiff would almost certainly be able to sue in the *lex loci* it is perhaps unlikely that he would rather do so in England, given the double hurdle in his way.

What, again, of contract cases? Here the paucity of choice of law cases is attributable to three main factors. First, many contractual disputes are submitted to arbitration, a process which might yield choice of law disputes but not reported cases. Secondly, many, if not all, commercial contracts, contain express selections of the governing law, such a selection invariably being respected in the English courts, thereby removing any room for a choice of law dispute. Thirdly, and most simply, contract may be an area where a great degree of similarity exists, in result if not of form, between the domestic laws of trading nations; where laws are the same no conflict of laws exists.

Such considerations as these are part, at least, of what may be a more complex phenomenon, the case-sparseness of the English Conflict of Laws, at least in choice of law matters. They suggest, in any event, and partly explain, the existence of that phenomenon. It remains to track its implications.

3. Conflicts Cases as Hard Cases

The sparser the case-law, the less determined the law is by authority, the harder cases become. The more opaque the legal sources to hand, the easier it is, within the law's open-texture, to provide very different but equally plausible versions of what the law requires. Conversely, the thinner a line of authority, the harder it is for courts to discern a clear shape and direction in the law,

---

[8] *Phillips v. Eyre* (1869) L.R. 4 Q.B. 225.

the harder it is to adjudicate between contrasting images of the truth. Behaviourally, this generates in courts and lawyers alike a range of techniques for coping with indeterminancy and the cost it entails. Conceptually, the dearth of decided cases on the English conflict of laws throws into unusually sharp relief the distinctive and more general features of common law reasoning. It illuminates, in particular, the two principal modes in which such reasoning operates, the formalist and the instrumentalist.

The relative merits of formalism and instrumentalism are much discussed in contemporary legal theory, as are the meanings of the terms themselves.[9] For now it is enough to adopt an uncomplicated definition of each, one which fights shy of the ideological baggage sometimes associated with both. Formalist legal reasoning, therefore, is simply that which is conducted without regard to the purpose of legal rules or to the consequences of their application in a given case. Such reasoning proceeds, or tends to, on the assumption, usually unstated, generally unconscious, that the law is a closed body of doctrine capable of yielding right answers to contested legal questions. Certainly, it tends to take for granted that the internal consistency of legal rules is the sole important measure of their worth. Instrumentalism is formalism's polar opposite, instrumentalist reasoning being that in which the law is deployed in the service of other, wider goals than consistency alone, sometimes involving considerations of policy or general principle, sometimes calling for no more than just or efficacious results in particular cases. Instrumentalism implies a different image of the law, assuming it to be flexible, mutable, a tool in the court's or lawyers' hands.

The reasoning of practising lawyers is, in a sense, invariably instrumental, their role being to deploy the law in their client's interests. The approach of judges is more mixed and may depend on factors as elusive as temperament, intellectual calibre or the type of case involved. For both groups, however, the tendency to reason instrumentally tends to increase the more able, experienced and confident the lawyer or judge becomes. A tyro lawyer, for example, might be more inclined to cleave to the textbook view, the conventional wisdom, on a point, as might a judge unused to a given kind of question. Those with a better grasp of the law, however, those more aware of its limits, might take a bolder line.

Paradoxically, the complexity of English conflicts problems, stemming from the subject's doctrinal transparency and its lack of cases, encourages both formalism and instrumentalism, though not of course simultaneously. Faced with a truly hard case, assisted only by opaque authority, or contradictory authority, or none at all, lawyers and judges alike are apt to take shelter in for-

[9] Summers *Instrumentalism and American Legal Theory* (Ithaca and London, 1982), Chapter 6; Atiyah / Summers, *Form and Substance in Anglo-American Law* (Oxford, 1987), Chapter 1.

malism. To do so gives, perhaps, the falsely comforting sense that things are clearer than they are. To do so also serves as a refuge when, faced with a case of first impression, a judge or lawyer necessarily – and forgivably, of course – lacks the experience, the confidence, the feel for a topic's nuances and purposes, to reason more creatively.

Take, as an example, *I. R. C. v. Bullock,*[10] the English decision which, perhaps, represents the high-watermark of the English courts' notorious formalism in the area of domicile. Though not strictly a case of first impression – domicile cases are not infrequent – the case had something of that quality, being one in which the Court of Appeal had a rare opportunity to resolve some long-standing problems regarding the meaning of domicile.

The English courts have long experienced difficulty in defining precisely the requirements for a change in personal domicile. Defined as a combination of someone's actual residence and their intention the doctrinal difficulty concerns which of the two elements to favour most. What is more important, the place where someone resides or the place they intend to be their home? The trial judge reasoned plausibly that, as Mr Bullock's matrimonial home had been in England for more than forty years, England was his domicile. The Court of Appeal, however, unaware, apparently, or unconcerned, about the effects of so doing, quite refused to accept the simple equation between home and domicile. Instead, in an effort to give content to the requirement that a party must intend any change in domicile, they resorted to technicalities. Mr Bullock's intention, they said, was to return to Nova Scotia, his birthplace, should his wife predecease him. They found that there was a substantial possibility of her doing so as, although younger than he, she was as likely to predecease him as the he to predecease her. As a result of that entirely abstract exercise in probabilities he was held never to have acquired an English domicile notwithstanding forty-four year's residence there. It is hard to resist the conclusion that such a counter-intuitive result was brought about by the Court of Appeal's desire to lend some semblance of certainty to the domicile enquiry, a degree of precision to ameliorate the difficulty of identifying the place with which someone is best connected.

Formalism then is a response to the difficulty of the conflict of laws, a difficulty bred in part by its case-sparseness. But so is instrumentalism. In a legal environment where authority is sparse there is an opportunity for lawyers to take the initiative in a way they might not do, or could do as easily, in more settled, doctrinally stable areas. Not only does it allow them to so, however, it may require it, in so far as it may be necessary to look outside the law, to extrinsic policies and purposes, to give the reason for decision which an impoverished case-law cannot provide. Indeed, a case-sparse subject provides

[10] [1975] 1 W.L.R. 1346 (Brightman J.); [1976] 1 W.L.R. 1178 (C.A.).

a very licence for instrumentalism; all answers become right answers or, at least, acceptable answers, where the law's seamless web is only loosely woven.

The *locus classicus* of instrumentalism in the English conflict of laws may be the legendary decision of Cumming-Bruce J. in *Radwan v. Radwan (No 2)*.[11] Certainly, it exemplifies the opportunities case-sparseness provides for judicial creativity. The case concerned a marriage in polygamous form between an English-domiciled woman and an Egyptian-domiciled man. Strictly speaking, the marriage should have been invalid. Certainly, the orthodox view, sanctioned by conventional wisdom and some authority, was then overwhelmingly in favour of the so called dual domicile test, whereby marriages will only be valid in English law if each party has capacity to marry the other by his or her domiciliary law. The husband in *Radwan* was capable of marrying, as the Muslim law of Egypt favours polygamy, but the wife was not. She was English and English domestic law does not countenance polygamous marriages. The judge neatly side-stepped orthodoxy, however, and found the marriage to be valid, precisely by exploiting the absence of decisions in the area. There was no authority, he said, bearing on the question which law governs capacity to contract a polygamous marriage. Absent such authority it was for him to decide which of the prevailing academic theories to accept. He chose the so called intended matrimonial home test, not the more commonly favoured dual domicile test, a choice which allowed him to apply Egyptian law, the law of the couple's intended matrimonial home, a law which treated the marriage as valid.

The instrumentalism of Cumming Bruce J.'s decision was quite deliberate. He was certainly aware that he was flying in the face of orthodoxy and it is hard to avoid the conclusion that his decision was aimed partly at avoiding English law's somewhat ethno-centric hostility towards polygamous marriage, partly at ensuring a just result on the facts; after all, the couple had lived as man and wife for some years in Egypt and their legitimate expectation must have been that they were married. As Cumming Bruce J. seems to have acknowledged it would have been wrong to have applied the dual domicile test, in formalistic fashion, to polygamous marriages in general and on the facts of *Radwan* in particular.

4. Legal Reasoning and Abstentionism

A particular response to conflicts questions, to disputes in cases with foreign elements, is to avoid the conflicts elements in such cases. Litigants sometimes do this by failing to plead foreign law at all. Courts do so by deciding such cases in such a way as to minimise or jettison their foreign elements.

[11] [1973] Fam. 35.

a) Abstentionism and the Parties

We have seen how the English rules of pleading permit the parties to ignore a case's foreign element by allowing them not to plead foreign law at all. In the nature of things, examples are hard to discern, but there are numerous reasons why they might thus eschew foreign law, arguing the dispute as a purely domestic one. Proving foreign law, for example, often requiring costly expert evidence and protracted examination at trial, is expensive, time-consuming and unpredictable. So too might be the solution to the choice of law question which the pleading of foreign law necessarily attracts in a given case. Given the surprising uncertainty of the conflict of laws, the nature of such a question, what the choice of rule is, is often profoundly unclear. So too might be the process of applying such a rule, of identifying what the governing law is; maybe a couple's domiciliary laws should govern their capacity to marry, but where are they domiciled? Against this background, the cost implications of pleading foreign law can be serious and there are often good reasons why the parties might abstain from pleading foreign law, from posing the conflicts question in a case.

The voluntarism of English law's approach to pleading foreign law, indeed to pleading generally, has distinct advantages, not least that it minimises the cost of litigation. But the principle can be taken to extremes. Take, for example, *Re O'Keefe,*[12] a case notorious for its luminously absurd result, in which the distribution of an estate was held to be governed by Irish law, although the deceased had never lived in Ireland and, indeed, died domiciled in Italy, Ireland having been her domicile at birth. The strangeness of this result is perhaps explained by Crossman J.'s passive acquiescence in two curious aspects of the pleadings. It had been argued that the doctrine of *renvoi* applied, by no means a foregone conclusion as a matter of law, and, oddly, it was never alleged that Italian law might apply. As to the first point, it is alarming that the judge simply accepted that *renvoi* was relevant when the scope and status of that curious doctrine was then, and remains, profoundly unclear. True it is that a judge should decide a case as pleaded, but only when the pleadings correctly reflect the law. As to the second point, it is equally true that pleading foreign law is for the parties, and thus the decision to introduce a conflicts element into a case. But what if the manner of the pleading, the way the conflicts question is put, is so plainly in error? The truth is that the dearth of conflicts cases, their infrequency, and the inexperience that breeds in conflicts matters encourages mistakes, something hardly conducive to the subject's health.

---

[12] [1940] Ch. 124.

b) Abstentionism and the Courts

The voluntary nature of the English rules of pleading underwrites party abstentionism in the conflicts of laws, ensuring that litigants will only plead foreign law where the benefits of doing so, judged against the costs, so require. We should turn next to abstentionism on the judge's part. This is abstentionism of a different, subtler sort, for judges can hardly refuse to decide questions put to them by the parties. Judges can, however, answer such questions in a fashion which distorts, minimises, even avoids their conflicts implications.

It is often unclear whether the courts' abstentionism, the failure to put potential conflicts questions, is conscious or unconscious, whether, we might say, it is instrumentalist or formalist. For now, however, nothing is won by pressing such a distinction. It is enough to identify cases in which the courts have avoided posing conflicts questions, or have answered them in a particular way, arguably because the subject's indeterminacy make such questions hard to resolve.

A formalist judge might avoid the complexities of a given conflicts question by sheltering behind, for instance, technical requirements as to the burden of proof. It has been known, for example, for a court to avoid wrestling with the definition of personal domicile, a troubled issue in English law, by declaring that, whatever the nature of the test for domicile, the burden of proving a change of domicile has not been discharged. As one English judge put it, with disarming frankness:

> ... I cannot say that I can come to a satisfactory conclusion either way [as to the domicile of the propositus]; but then the law relieves me of the embarrassment which would otherwise condemn me to the solution of an insoluble problem, because it directs me in my present state of mind to consider upon whom is the burden of proof.[13]

An example of abstentionist instrumentalism, rich in its implications, is the Court of Appeal's decision in *Lawrence v. Lawrence.*[14] A husband and wife, both domiciled in Brazil, divorced in Nevada. Was the wife's later remarriage to another husband valid in English law? That depended on how the question was put. If the issue for the English court was whether it recognised the divorce the remarriage would be upheld as long as it did so. As English law undoubtedly recognised the divorce the remarriage was certainly valid according to such an approach. If, however, the question was whether, by the usual English rules on the validity of marriage, the remarriage was valid there was a real risk that the remarriage would fail. Certainly, that would have followed had the dual domicile test applied, whereby each party to a marriage must have capacity under his or her domiciliary law to marry the other. That was

---

[13] *Winans v. Attorney-General* [1904] A.C. 287, 289.

[14] [1985] 3 W.L.R. 125.

because the wife's Brazilian domiciliary law regarded her as still married, not recognising the divorce.

Unsurprisingly, perhaps, the court in *Lawrence* favoured asking the 'recognition' question, an approach which ensured the remarriage's validity. One explanation for thus abstaining from putting the 'validity' question is only indirectly connected with the subject's indeterminacy. It is perhaps possible that in doing so the court hoped to avoid having to apply the dual domicile test for validity, a test prized in the conventional wisdom of the subject, the power of the conventional wisdom itself attributable to the lack of conclusive authority on the point. Another explanation for the court's position owes more, or more directly, to the subject's undeterminacy. Might the Court of Appeal have hoped to save the marriage in *Lawrence,* to avoid the dual domicile test, without having to address head-on the vexed question of the essential validity of marriage? No doubt they could have done the same, had they posed the 'validity' question, but at what cost in terms of delay, worry and expense to the parties and the court? It is in the nature of the subject, given what we have seen, that such hard cases will be relatively common, and it is in the nature of lawyers and the courts to make such cases easier.

Abstentionism in the English conflict of laws has, therefore, a special status. It is both a response to the subject's case-sparseness, allowing courts to minimise the difficulty that the subject's uncertainty engenders, and a cause of such case-sparseness, ensuring that the subject's uncertainty is sustained. The spiralling, self-replicating indeterminacy of the subject both produces, and is produced by, abstentionism in conflicts matters.

5. Conventional Wisdom and the Conflict of Laws

So far we have charted the effect of case-sparseness on the reasoning of lawyers and the courts. A particular response to that phenomenon in conflicts cases, probably a species of formalism, is the tendency of both groups to rely on conventionally approved solutions to intractable conflicts problems. In the absence of clear guidance in the cases, courts and lawyers alike often take refuge either in conventional wisdom, in prevailing assumptions amongst practitioners as to what the solution ought to be, or in the views of textbook writers. Such reliance is no doubt inevitable. The dearth of cases makes solutions hard to discern, offering either little information with which to work, or too wide and baffling an array of possible answers. Moreover, the infrequency of choice of law cases prevents courts and lawyers from acquiring the necessary experience and confidence, the elusive 'feel' for the subject, the unarticulated sense of its principles and purposes, upon which legal reasoning in hard cases so much depends. Faced with such difficulty, orthodox opinion, or the pronouncements of writers, provides an identifiable, comforting prop.

a) Orthodox Opinion in Conflicts Cases

Any legal subject is partly the product of its conventional wisdom, the prevailing view, typically within the bench and bar, but extending also to scholars, as to what is right and wrong, what is arguable or not. This is especially so, at least in England, for three main reasons. First, it is advocates who shape and package the law on which courts decide cases. It is a trusim of the adversarial process that judges judge not upon the law, but upon the law as pleaded to them. Any preconceptions on the part of counsel as to what the law might be are, in such a system, communicated at once to the court by the terms in which cases are argued. Counsel, not the courts, set the agenda for decision. Secondly, if paradoxically, the views of the bar as to what is right – or acceptable – or not are in turn shaped by an appreciation of what judges themselves regard as right, or acceptable. Thirdly, in the English system, only counsel, experienced counsel, the best of the bar, become judges. Advisers become law-makers, thereby turning the conventional wisdom of the bar into the wisdom of the bench.

Each of these factors explains the existence of a body of knowledge and experience, of assumptions and predelictions, of prejudices and preferences, shared alike by bench and bar. Such conventional wisdom is, moreover, a potent element in structuring the terms of legal argument. As Pollock and Maitland said:

> So soon as there is a legal profession, professional opinion is among the most powerful of all the forces that shape the law.[15]

This view is echoed by a leading judge:

> The climate of legal opinion percolates through to ... the judges. I think they get the idea that there is a feeling amongst lawyers, barristers, solicitors and lower judges that something should be done, and that does percolate.[16]

This conventional wisdom takes many forms. Sometimes it affects the form of legal rules, as with the unstated assumption of English judges in many areas of law that legal rules should be tightly drawn, not open-ended. At other times it provides a recurring policy which underpins and orientates the law, such as the assumption in matrimonial conflicts cases that courts should generally favour the validation of marriages. Again, the conventional wisdom is sometimes quite specific, favouring the use of a given legal rule, even when the rule lacks any firm warrant in the cases. Although, interestingly, a feature more of the conventional wisdom amongst academics more than judges, the preference of orthodoxy for the dual domicile test for a marriage's validity is an example.[17]

---

[15] *History of English Law* (Cambridge, 1898), i, 196.

[16] Lord Guest, interview quoted in Patterson, *The Law Lords* (London, 1982), p. 31.

[17] See e.g. *Law Commission Working Paper No. 89* (1985), pp. 69 - 104.

Arguably, this view is sustained, as it were, by its own momentum, the fact that it is orthodoxy by itself ensuring that it is orthodoxy, although the case-law on the point is, at best, equivocal, at worst, hostile to such a rule.

A strong instance of the self-sustaining, self-replicating nature of conventional wisdom in English conflicts law, almost the *reductio ad absurdam* of the potency of a prevailing view, concerns choice of law in tort. English law's difficulty in this area stems in part from the 1969 decision of the House of Lords in *Chaplin v. Boys.*[18] There is no doubt who won in that notorious dispute, the plaintiff did, an Englishman injured by another Englishman in a motor accident in Malta. There is equally no doubt that the basis of choice of law in tort was left intact in *Boys.* The rule remains that claims on foreign torts are possible in England only if the wrong complained of is actionable both in English domestic law and by the law of the place of the wrong. Beyond that, however, obscurity reigns, largely because, although all five Law Lords found in the plaintiff's favour each did so for difference reasons. What then is the exact *ratio decidendi* of the case? Strictly speaking it is hard to discern a genuine majority in favour of any one reason for decision, although alternative views abound. For present purposes, however, the interest of the case is that the conventional wisdom holds that one Law Lord's speech, that of Lord Wilberforce, represents the holding in the case. Put differently, Lord Wilberforce's views, those of one judge in a tribunal of five, have come to be regarded as defining the English choice of law rule in tort.

The gradual mutation of Lord Wilberforce's speech into settled law offers an instructive lesson in the power of the familiar, of the conventional. The first step was taken by the Court of Appeal some seven years after *Boys.* They accepted that Lord Wilberforce's speech was to be used, not because they reasoned that it should, but because counsel for both parties had assumed that it should.[19] (English judges, it should be recalled, seldom if ever depart from the terms on which the parties' lawyers have put the case.) In another case, this time at first instance, some seven years on again, the trial judge in effect felt himself bound by the Court of Appeal's acceptance that Lord Wilberforce's views expressed the law, although all the Court of Appeal had done was to aquiesce in counsels' position.[20] Most recently, in a decision which is widely regarded as definitive, another trial judge has endorsed Lord Wilberforce's view.[21] He did so, however, in a somewhat indirect fashion. Speaking of the statement of the law in Dicey and Morris' *Conflict of Laws,* the subject's leading textbook, which was in itself a summary of Lord Wilberforce's view,

---

18 [1971] A.C. 356.

19 *Church of Scientology v. Commissioner of Metropolitan Police* (1976) 120 Solicitors Journal 690.

20 *Coupland v. Arabian Gulf Oil Co.* [1983] 1 W.L.R. 1136.

21 *Johnson v. Coventry Churchill* [1992] 3 All E.R. 14.

the judge remarked with revealing frankness that '[c]ounsel have conducted this case on the basis that this accurately reflects the law and I see no reason to depart from that acceptance'.[22] In other words, a court adopted Lord Wilberforce's speech in *Boys,* not because authority or principle actually compelled such a view, but because several judges had accepted it, a leading textbook had endorsed it and counsel had taken the textbook to be correct.

The transformation of Lord Wilberforce's speech into legal doctrine, the passage of opinion into law, is entirely explicable and laudable. However much litigants might take advantage of legal uncertainty to score against each other there comes a point at which cases become utterly unwieldy unless some common foundation can be found. Total incommensurability does not foster argument, it hinders it. In less extreme terms, it is unlikely that either party, in any of the cases just described, would have wished to guarantee for themselves a hearing before the House of Lords, with all the delay, expense and uncertainty that would entail. To have made an issue about the *ratio* of *Boys* would, however, surely have ensured such a result. Most importantly, there is no doubt that most discussions of *Boys* do proceed as if Lord Wilberforce's speech is the law and that the conventional wisdom holds this to be true, something the parties in subsequent cases have simply endorsed. In any event, however explicable, the story of Lord Wilberforce's judgment is illuminating: it reveals how counsel, not the courts, are sometimes, in effect, the law makers; it shows how a proposition, whatever its doctrinal warrant, can become true by repetition; and it shows how conventional wisdom is a potent source of law.

b) Scholarship and Conflicts Cases

Resort to legal scholarship is another response to resolving hard cases. Traditionally sceptical, even dismissive, of the academic study of law, stoutly pragmatic in their attitudes and prizing legal skills over legal learning, English lawyers have begun only recently to draw on scholarly writing for assistance or, at least, to acknowledge the fact. More generally, in a tradition in which many practitioners have never studied law, learning it only for professional examinations, law schools and law teachers have never enjoyed the influence, overtly at least, of their civilian or American counterparts. In truth, however, any law school, by alternately reproducing and questioning the orthodoxy of one generation of lawyers, fashions that of the next. Law teachers mediate in the classroom between the law's past and its present, influencing its practice, if only in a diffused, vicarious way. Scholars also enjoy the luxury of time to reflect on the law, identifying its trends and tensions, logging the tides of judicial opinion, to a degree which busy practitioners cannot match. The scholar's capacity to influence legal practice is, moreover, all the more pronounced in a

---

[22] Ibid., p. 17.

subject as open-textured as the conflict of laws where academic opinion, or the remembered lessons of the law school, are often all there is to resolve hard cases.

If the conflict of laws in England is thus uniquely receptive to academic influence, the academic tradition in this area, responding to demand, has been signally influential. It cannot be coincidence that a prominent textbook on jurisprudence offers the conflict of laws as an example of a subject which has been profoundly affected by juristic writing,[23] or that a recent study of judicial behaviour in general dwells on a notable example of such influence.[24] It is also noteworthy that Dicey, the great Victorian scholar, whose writings once dominated the subject and still rule us from the grave, was acutely self-aware about the textbook writer's power. He credited Story, his American precursor, with having created the Conflict of Laws as a branch of English law and said approvingly of Westlake, another American writer of legendary influence, that 'his work is traceable in whole lines of cases'.[25]

In practice, it is not unusual for practitioners, even judges, to seek the views of scholars on contested conflicts questions. And, as we shall see, the English courts in conflicts cases have been unusually ready to acknowledge their debt to academic literature. This influence of conflicts scholarship on conflicts practice may be attributable to several factors. First, as will now be clear, there is often little else to go on, certainly in choice of law matters, given the subject's scant supply of cases. Secondly, again as we have seen, few lawyers and fewer judges acquire real expertise in conflicts matters. Certainly, they seldom acquire a real sense of the subject's overall structure and operation, their acquaintance being confined to specific types of case, concerning marriage, contracts or whatever, where conflicts points are, in any event, merely parasitic upon the real subject matter of the dispute. Arguably, only academics have prolonged exposure to the subject and a general picture of the connection between its parts, which transcends the narrow specialism of legal practice. Thirdly, whatever the state of the subject, but especially in the light of its underdeterminacy and the forgivable inexperience of many practitioners, the influence of scholarly writing on the conflict of laws was bound to be profound because of the power of its leading textbook; Dicey and Morris', *Conflict of Laws*[26] enjoys a unique position as a codification of the subject which gives it a special status in forging it. Perhaps, by extension, its authoritative nature lends credence to scholarly conflicts writing generally.

---

[23] Paton, *Jurisprudence* (Oxford, 4th ed., 1972), p. 265.

[24] Patterson, op. cit., p. 16, discussing *Oppenheimer v. Cattermole* [1976] A.C. 249; see *infra.*, text to n. 32.

[25] *Law and Opinion in England* (London, 2nd. ed. 1914), p. 365.

[26] (London, 12th ed., 1993).

Such is the influence of Dicey and Morris, increasing in inverse proportion to the scarcity of cases, that it is worth detailing some examples. The tendency for counsel and the courts to rely on its views, even where there are pertinent cases, certainly where there are not, is a familiar feature of English conflicts practice. If nothing else, argument may take the form of enquiring whether Dicey and Morris' rule is correct which, often, presumptively it is assumed to be. In one case at least the Court of Appeal even considered that a trial judge's decision was unsafe because the relevant part of Dicey and Morris had not been cited to him.[27] On occasions the book's role, tantamount to being a source of law, has been acknowledged.[28] On others a judge has indicated concern that his decision should have to depart from Dicey's rule.[29] Dicey and Morris, therefore, enjoys a special status in English conflicts reasoning, a status reflecting the nature of the subject. It is, in effect, a *de facto* Restatement of the Conflict of Laws in England, an analogy only inapt because in so many ways the subject has never been stated at all.

A final point should be made about the influence of Dicey and Morris, concerning the book's distinctive form. It is noteworthy, given the subject's uncertainty, that, echoing Dicey's own avowed positivism, it adopts a formulaic, canonical style of presentation, reducing the law to a series of carefully devised rules. What could be more useful, more tempting for counsel to argue for, and judges to apply, in a vague and open-textured subject, than a crisp and well-defined rule? As Dicey himself put it, with considerable insight, and some premonition of Professor Dworkin's work:

> If an author of ingenuity has reduced some branch of the law to a consistent scheme of logically coherent rules, he supplies exactly the principles of which a court is in need.[30]

The status of English conflicts writing in general has been acknowledged in several ways. In one famous case the judge overtly decided the conflicts point by choosing between the competing views adopted, on the one hand, by Dicey and Morris and, on the other, by its illustrious competitor, Cheshire and North's, *Private International Law*.[31] Again, when the 1980 Rome Convention on the Law Applicable to Contractual Obligations came to be introduced into English law by the Contracts (Applicable Law) Act 1990 it was necessary to provide in the Act that English judges might have regard to the official report on the Convention in interpreting it. This was so because scholarly writing, which in a sense the Report was, is not strictly admissible in England as a source of interpretation. Following some discussion, Parliament phrased the

---

27 *The Parouth* [1982] 2 Lloyd's Rep. 351.

28 *The Hollandia* [1982] Q.B. 872, 884.

29 *Radwan v. Radwan (No. 2),* supra., n. 11.

30 *Law and Opinion in England* (London, 2nd. ed., 1914), p. 365.

31 (London, 12th ed., 1992).

relevant instructions to the courts in such a way as to allow them to refer to the Report but '[w]ithout prejudice to any practice of the courts as to the matters which may be considered' apart from the Report. The purpose was to ensure that the courts could refer to English scholarly writing in interpreting the Convention.

Such examples of juristic influence on the conflict of laws could be multiplied. In one case, for example, an article by Dr F. A. Mann, commenting on a case, prompted two re-hearings before the House of Lords, and an acknowledgement by that court that their Lordship had changed their minds on reading it.[32] In another, Lord Goff took time to thank those writers whose work had influenced his decision, famously referring to legal academics as 'pilgrims with us on the endless road to unattainable perfection'.[33] Whatever the position in other subjects, in many of which the scholar's imprint is usually more feint, it seems in the conflict of laws that lawyers and courts alike show a marked preparedness to employ juristic writing to answer the many questions which remain unanswered or, in view of the subject's case-sparseness, have simply gone unasked.

6. Conclusion

The foregoing reflections have several implications. They suggest, for example, that the stress of traditional conflicts courses on issues of choice of law is scarcely realistic. They underscore, moreover, the influence that litigants enjoy, by their lawyers, in the common law tradition. Judges, the conflict of laws reminds us, as it operates in England, decide cases not according to the law *per se,* but according to the law as pleaded. Most importantly, the conflict of laws in England, its choice of law aspect relatively bereft of cases, undetermined by authority, short on legal material, illuminates how much the common law, and common law reasoning, depends on the quantity of caselaw, on the density of material with which to work. Case-sparseness, we have seen, makes all cases hard cases and, in so doing, exaggerates the law's tendency to formalism on the one hand, instrumentalism on the other. The former is some relief from the difficulty of decision, the latter a response to the freedom an open question offers a creative judge.

More precisely, the English conflict of laws exhibits several specific features, the existence of which is attributable to the subject's paucity of decided cases. One is abstentionism, the tendency of lawyers especially, courts somewhat, either to avoid conflicts questions altogether, or to pose them in the least troublesome way. The very difficulty of such questions, caused by the

[32] *Oppenheimer v. Cattermole,* supra., n. 24.
[33] *The Spiliada* [1987] A.C. 460, 482.

lack of material with which to resolve them, is a reason for this, exacerbated by a widespread lack of confidence and experience in conflicts matters. Certainly, the tendency to avoid conflicts issues, sometimes not to notice them at all, is an arresting feature of the subject, bred of a system in which choice of law questions seldom arise. Ironically, however, the more abstentionist lawyers and judges are in conflicts cases, the fewer conflicts decisions there are, and the greater is the desire to abstain in future cases. Case-sparseness is thus a self-fulfilling prophecy; the fewer conflicts cases there are, the fewer there will be.

Another reflection of case-sparseness is the tendency of English conflicts lawyers to rely on conventional wisdom, on the orthodoxy of bench and bar, whether or not strictly sanctioned by authority. Such deference to the familiar is closely allied to the habit, visible in other areas but almost invariable in conflicts cases, of relying on commentators to formulate the law.

Such phenomena are intriguing in themselves, and important for conflicts scholars, but they speak to wider themes as well. They suggest why it is never enough for lawyers to content themselves with legal doctrine alone. Legal doctrine is forged in practice and it is only by appreciating the realties of such practice that legal doctrine assumes its full meaning. More importantly, perhaps, the conflict of laws in England illuminates an important truth: the study of law in its fullest sense, the proper understanding of legal experience, is as much about gaps in the law as the law itself. Decided cases matter, but so do those that were never decided at all.

The European Internal Market and the Law

By Peter-Christian Müller-Graff, Trier

Prescriptive formality and normative rationality in modern legal systems as well as form and substance in legal reasoning are subjects *Robert S. Summers* ponders on intensively.[1] Cooperation and conflicts between these two elements might be discovered in almost any field of law, at least in modern western legal systems.[2] European Community law should be no exception to that. Although the idea of analysing form and substance in the legal reasoning of the Court of Justice of the European Communities seems likely to pose an appealing challenge to any attempt to explain in depth the development of Community law in terms of methodology, I will concentrate this contribution in honour of my revered teacher, adviser, colleague and friend to the rather broad question what basic aspects the legally prescriptive objective to establish and to maintain the European internal market, a "goal reason", implies for the legal order in the European Community.

Hence the topic to deal with herein is the relationship between the European internal market and the law.

A. To scrutinize this question first of all it might be useful to ask what the term "internal market" means, and to ask even more precisely, if the objective of the internal market implies a change of the hitherto existing aim of the market integration in Europe. The reason for this question is evident: the insertion of the objective "internal market" into the European Community law took place in 1987, but that was not the beginning of the market integration. Market integration in the framework of the European Community had already begun some thirty years ago in 1958 with the foundation of the European Economic Community (EEC) and its objective to create a common market. Does the objective of the "internal market" imply a change? As always it is useful to distinguish public opinion and legal situation.

I. Viewing the public opinion it is evident that the discussion about the proper way to market integration has become more controversial since the objective of the "internal market" was inserted into the Treaty.

---

1 See R. S. Summers, Two Types of Substantive Reasons: The Core of a Theory of Common-Law Justification, 63 Cornell L. Rev. 707 (1978); P. S. Atiyah / R. S. Summers, Form and Substance in Anglo-American Law (1987).

2 For other systems see W. Fikentscher, Methoden des Rechts, Vol. I (1975).

1. On the *economic* level very optimistic expectations of advantages for the general welfare exist – documented for example by the famous expert report of Cecchini.[3] It is especially expected that free movement of goods and services promises a positive effect on the prosperity of all concerned[4]: "more production and more prosperity, through better allocation of production factors, each country specialising in the products for which they have a comparative advantage; more efficient production thanks to scale economies and keener competition".[5] Advantages are also expected from the free movement of labour[6] as well as from integrated capital markets.[7] But on the other hand there also exist unanswered questions concerning the costs of adopting to the enlarged market for enterprises, for certain national branches and regions, and moreover questions concerning the ecological costs of increased economic growth and the potential loss of welfare in case the internal market leads to a withdrawal of European economic activities from the world market.[8]

2. On the *political* level there also exists a broad scope of positive expectations in view of the internal market: the deepening of the peaceful symbiosis of the participating states ("economic integration reduces conflicts between nations"[9]), a strong push towards even closer European integration and the strengthening of the position of the Member States in their union on the level of world politics. On the other hand the political costs are increasingly articulated: especially the impairment of the traditional freedom of action and competences of the Member States – a concern particularly expressed by the British government, the Danish Parliament and the states of the Federal Republic of Germany. The latter are only parts of a Member State, but not Member States themselves with the right to take part in the decision-making process of the Community. This implies that the states of the Federal Republic have no active part in the decision-making of the Community on the Community level till now even if their legislative competences – for example in education (schools, universities) and culture – are involved.[10] In addition there are

---

[3] P. Cecchini, Europa '92. Der Vorteil des Binnenmarktes (1988).

[4] W. Molle, The Economics of European Integration – Theory, Practice, Policy – 10 (1990).

[5] Id., 15, 18.

[6] Id., 21.

[7] Id., 24.

[8] See F. Franzmeyer, Economic, Social and Political Costs of Completing the Internal Market, in: R. Bieber / R. Dehousse / J. Pinder / H. H. Weiler (eds.), 1992: One European Market? A Critical Analysis of the Commission's International Market Strategy 55 (1988); for the effects for third countries see K. M. Meessen, Europe en Route to 1992: The Completion of the Internal Market and Its Impact on Non-Europeans, The Int. Lawyer 359 (1989).

[9] W. Molle note 4 at 9 reporting the result of an analysis of S. W. Polachek, using data for 30 countries in the 1958 - 1967 period, that showed that doubling the trade between two countries leads to a 20 per cent decline in the frequency of hostilities.

concerns in the United Kingdom and in Germany that in economic policy the liberal ideas of trade as outlined by *Adam Smith* or *Walter Eucken* might be superseded by a more intervening and administrative philosophy in the sense of the French mercantilistic tradition of *Colbert*.[11] Also there are fears (in Denmark[12] and among German trade unions) that the present high level of consumer protection and of social security in some countries might be diluted. And finally there is concern that the elimination of controls at the borders inside the Community will encourage the uncontrolled immigration of people coming from Non-Member States and will promote the free movement of crime, drugs and terrorism. Most of these aspects of market integration are not really new but the public perception that European market integration now is seriously and consequently put into practice gives all these considerations an actual weight.

II. Does the objective of the internal market also imply a change in the legally binding perspective of market integration?

1. This question is not without controversies among scholars. They are rooted in the wording of Art. 8 A EEC-Treaty. Art. 8 A reads: "The internal market shall comprise an area without internal frontiers in which the free movement of goods, persons, services and capital is ensured in accordance with the provisions of this Treaty." This formulation has caused some brain-racking. Does it mean that the hitherto existing objective of the Treaty, the objective of the common market, has been changed?

a) Especially the former judge at the Court of Justice of the European Communities, *Pierre Pescatore,* has criticized the new provisions and given a partly shared assessment that the notion of the internal market is only a fragmentary description of the objectives of the EEC-Treaty and thus less than the concept of the common market and a stepback.[13] Indeed: the quoted provision seems to comprise only a part of the matters that are traditionally associated with the concept of the common market: namely the removal of frontiers between Member States by means of the so-called four fundamental freedoms: the free movement of goods, of services, of capital and of persons. However,

---

10 For this problem see e.g. A. Weber, Die Bundesländer und die Reform der Gemeinschaftsverträge, Deutsches Verwaltungsblatt 800 (1986); G.-E. Zur Hausen, Die deutschen Länder als Souffleure der Brüsseler Bühne, Europarecht 322 (1987); E. Haas, Die Mitwirkung der Länder der EG-Vorhaben, Die öffentliche Verwaltung 613 (1988).

11 See e.g. H. Giersch, Europa nicht auf dem Verordnungswege, in: FAZ Oct. 8. 1988, p. 15; see also Europäische Integration, Wieviel Wettbewerb – wieviel Bürokratie? (1989).

12 See e.g. Memorandum from Danish Government Concerning Article 100 A of the EEC-Treaty (Jan. 22, 1987; PE 113. 064/Ann.); C. Gulmann; The Single European Act – Some Remarks from a Danish Perspective, CMLRev. 31 (1987).

13 See P. Pescatore, Some Critical Remarks on the "Single European Act", CMLRev 9 (1987).

in Art. 8 A EEC-Treaty there is no reference to the free movement of payments and above all there is no express reference to some other basic elements of the concept of the common market such as a system ensuring not only that competition in the common market is not distorted, but also ensuring the elimination of tax barriers or the common customs and trade policy. Nevertheless, in my opinion, Art. 8 A EEC-Treaty implies no reduction of the objectives of integration. The very wording aims at guaranteeing the free movement "in accordance with the provisions of this Treaty". In other words it does not understand the free movement in an isolated way, but in the context and under the conditions of all other provisions of the EEC-Treaty, thus especially in the context of a system ensuring that competition in the common market is not distorted. Moreover the quoted provision says that the internal market shall *comprise* an area of free movement. "Comprising" means "including" without necessarily excluding other aspects. Thus Art. 8 A EEC-Treaty names only the minimum content of the internal market anyhow, namely the center piece of the whole concept of integration. This center piece is not the creation of a Community of administration, of a state or of a federation but the guarantee of free border-crossing private economic initiatives.[14]

b) Does this mean that the notions of "internal market" and "common market" are synonyms? Against such an interpretation[15] stands the pure fact that the new term has been inserted into the Treaty without dropping the older one. Moreover the new term has been linked to a deadline of establishment and additionally to a better suited procedure of Community legislation. It also was the general understanding that the idea of the common market[16] is only internal-market-*like,* but not identical.

c) Above all, the wording "area without internal frontiers" provokes the question if the content of the internal market does exceed the objectives of the common market. Surely this wording can not mean an area without frontiers of law and public authorities. If it is, however, read in the light of the so-called White Paper of the Commission of the European Communities concerning the establishment of the internal market[17] it becomes clear that its main target is

[14] For this concept of integration see P.-C. Müller-Graff, Privatrecht und Europäisches Gemeinschaftsrecht – Gemeinschaftsprivatrecht, 2nd. ed. 17 (1991).

[15] For this notion see e. g. J. de Ruyt, L'Acte unique européen 150 (1987); B. Langeheine, Article 100 A notes 21, 23, in: Kommentar zum EWG-Vertrag (ed. by E. Grabitz) (1987).

[16] See e. g. Court of Justice of the European Communities Case 15/81, Gaston Schul (1982) E. C. R. 1409, 1431.

[17] See White Paper note 11 (June 1985); H. Schmitt von Sydow, The Basic Strategies of the Commission's White Paper, in: R., Bieber / R. Dehousse / J. Pinder / H. H. Weiler (eds.), One European Market? A Critical Analysis of the Commission's Internal Market Strategy 79 (1988); M. Petite, Le programme législatif pour la réalisation du marché unique, in: J. Schwarze (ed.), Legislation for Europe 1992, 23 (1989); P.-C. Müller-Graff, Die Rechtsangleichung zur Verwirklichung des Binnenmarktes, 24 Europarecht 107 (1989).

the abolition of the border-controls at the internal frontiers. In other words: the area without internal frontiers has to be understood as an area of free movement without border controls at the internal frontiers, at least as far as the crossing of the border happens during the use of one of the mentioned basic freedoms.[18] There was no such perspective in the hitherto existing provisions of the common market law.

2. Summing up the objective of the internal market contains a threefold enrichment of the hitherto existing objective of European market integration: abolition of border controls, deadline for establishing the market integration and facilitation of the necessary legislation.

B. Thus the main question of our topic as mentioned at the beginning can be raised: what does the objective of the internal market imply for the legal order in the European Community? "Legal order" in this context will be understood as the totality of law in force within the Community. This means Community law as well as the different national laws.

The relation between the objective of the internal market and the legal order can be discussed from three points of view: Firstly it can be asked what the function of the legal order is for the objective of the internal market. Secondly the opposite question can be posed: which changes of the legal order are necessary in view of the objective of the internal market? Eventually and thirdly we can ask in which way internal market and legal order are linked in terms of the legal system.

I. 1. When asking firstly what function the legal order is to exert towards the objective of the internal market one quickly encounters an economic approach of thinking favoured especially by the British Bruges-group[19] that holds that the establishment of competition in Europe should not be entrusted to the law. On the contrary it holds that the law should be entrusted to the competition. Thus this philosophy suggests for the realisation of the internal market to abstain from legal regulation, and – instead of regulation – it encourages free movement together with a so-called competition of the national legal orders.[20] It is not yet the moment to evaluate this approach thoroughly but it cannot be neglected that the European market integration is hardly to be achieved without the socle and pedestal of law. This results from the necessity that the legal order has to render possible and to stabilize the

---

18 See P.-C. Müller-Graff note 10, p. 123. This happens to a large extent considering the broad scope of the free movement of services; see Court of Justice of the European Communities Case 286/82 and 26/83, Luisi and Carbone (1984) E. C. R. 377; P.-C. Müller-Graff, Dienstleistungsfreiheit und Erbringungsformen grenzüberschreitender Dienstleistungen, in: Festschrift für Rudolf Lukes 471, 488 (1989).

19 For the "Bruges Group" see FAZ Feb. 10, 1981, p. 9.

20 See e. g. H. Giersch note 11.

opening of the markets against the inconstancy of the politics of the Member States and their pressure groups.

The law has to *render possible* the market integration, because – in the light of historical experience – it is not very likely that the national controls of market entry will be given up without a mutual agreement between the participating states on the basic principles and their effective judicial enforceability.

At the same time the legal order *stabilizes* the market integration, because it creates durability of the mentioned agreement and gives reliability to all parties. Without a legal frame there would be an even greater danger of the erection of new entry barriers by the Member States at every politically opportune moment.

The legal order also has the task to *link* together the market integration with the whole political and social order, because it makes its contribution that the free wheeling and dealing does not injure major needs of public interest and that no situation emerges in which the economics of the market develop without any correction by the public interest and public authority. In this way the legal order serves, for example, the protection of health of children against dangerous toys,[21] the protection of the environment against harmful emissions of exhaust gas[22] or the protection of a free and undistorted competition against private restrictions[23] or public intervention.[24]

2. If one accepts these tasks of law in the market integration, the question has to be raised on which level of the legal order they have to be accomplished. Especially the British government has opposed repeatedly the necessity of binding rules of Community law. It is, however, not imaginable that the mentioned tasks could be mastered *only* on a national legal level. On the other side it is not cogent that they can be mastered by Community legislation alone. As long as the legal integration has reached only a limited scope, a cooperation between Community law and national laws is inevitable anyhow: a cooperation in form of a division of tasks in a way that can be observed in its rough outlines for some time already.

a) In such a division of tasks the *national law* has to provide the general legal frame, especially the basics of private law, of the legal protection of public goods and of the judicial system of enforcing legal rules.[25] For example, if an enterprise acts in violation of the prohibition of cartel agreements as laid

---

[21] See Directive 88/76/EEC, O. J. 1988 L 36/36.

[22] See e.g. Directive 83/851/EEC, O. J. 1983 L 197/1.

[23] See Articles 85, 86 EEC-Treaty.

[24] See Article 92 EEC-Treaty; P.-C. Müller-Graff, Die Erscheinungsformen der Leistungssubventionstatbestände aus wirtschaftsrechtlicher Sicht, 152 Zeitschrift für das gesamte Handelsrecht und Wirtschaftsrecht 403 (1988).

[25] For the realization of Community law by means of national private law see P.-C. Müller-Graff note 14, 24.

down in Article 85 EEC-Treaty, the question if a competitor can sue it succesfully for damages has to be answered by the applicable national law.[26] The Treaty contains no special rules for this problem. Thus, e.g., the British courts have developed a new type of tort to cope with this question.[27]

b) In the mentioned division of tasks *Community law* has to guarantee the free movement across the intra-Community borders of law and national authorities and also a system ensuring that competition in the market is not distorted. How far has Community law come by now to mastering these two tasks?

aa) As far as the free movement is concerned, the realisation achieved can be best seen in the decisions of the Court of Justice of the European Communities dealing with the free movement of goods as laid down in the Articles 9 to 36 EEC-Treaty.

(1) The guarantee of free movement of goods is marked by two prohibitions: the prohibition of customs duties on imports and exports and of all charges having an equivalent effect and the prohibition of quantitative restrictions on imports and exports and all measures having an equivalent effect between Member States. The prohibition mentioned last – measures having an equivalent effect – has gained outstanding importance as a means of fighting subtle legislative and administrative obstacles to market entry caused by a Member State. This is due to the Court's precedents giving the prohibition the most extensive interpretation possible. According to the Dassonville-case a measure having equivalent effect is every measure taken by a Member State suitable to restrain trade between Member States directly or indirectly, actually or potentially.[28] This formula implies that imports are not only protected against discriminating provisions and practices such as prohibitions against advertisement for foreign products.[29] In principle they are also protected against inhibitions that result from requirements valid for imported goods and home-made goods in the same way without any distinction;[30] for example, the German interdiction to sell beer with additives such as rice or other stuff not compatible with the old Bavarian recipe for brewing pure beer. This interdiction had been enacted for all beers, not only for imported beers.[31]

---

[26] See e.g. J. Pipkorn, Article 85 sec. 2 notes 105 - 106, in: H. von der Groeben / H. von Boeckh / J. Thiesing / C.-D. Ehlermann (eds.), Kommentar zum EWG-Vertrag, 3rd ed. (1983); for Germany see § 823 sec. 2 BGB.

[27] See Lord Denning in Application des Gaz S. A. v. Falks Veritas LTD, 3 Weekly Law Reports 235 (1974); For Ireland see Cadbury Ireland v. Kerry Cooperative Creameries, Dublin University 335 (1981).

[28] Case 8/74, Dassonville (1974) E. C. R. 837, 847; for the subsequent cases see P.-C. Müller-Graff, Article 30 notes 22 - 35, in: H. von der Groeben / J. Thiesing / C.-D. Ehlermann (Eds.), Kommentar zum EWG-Vertrag, 4th ed. (1991).

[29] Case C 362/88, GB-INNO BM v. CCL, Judgement of the CJEC of March 7, 1990.

[30] See P.-C. Müller-Graff note 28, Article 30 note 23.

However, not every restraint of imports is covered by the prohibition of measures having an equivalent effect. Certain obstacles are held compatible with the internal market by an exception clause of the Treaty (Article 36), namely obstacles caused by those measures that are justified to protect certain public interests, herein especially public morality, public security, health and life of humans, animals or plants, national treasure possessing artistic, historic or archeological value, industrial and commercial property. Moreover the Court of Justice has added some other exceptions in its so-called Cassis-de-Dijon-jurisprudence.[32] However, not every public interest can justify a restraint of trade and not every measure is justified on the grounds of a recognized public interest as the practice of the Court shows. For example, the mentioned interdiction of additives in beer was held as being unjustified by the Court because of its undifferentiated ban of all additives.[33] The same was true for the interdiction to sell those liquids under the name "beer" that had not been brewed in accordance with the Bavarian purity rule. Rightly the Court held that protection of consumers against misguidance could be achieved by appropriate labeling.[34] This is a method that does not impede sales from the very beginning.[35] If however an obstacle is justified by these standards – and many are justified – they can be overcome only by legislative action.

(2) A comparable exhaustive degree of interpretation has been reached for the rule of free movement of services (Articles 59 - 66 EEC-Treaty).[36] Therefore the German requirement of a national establishment for certain insurances had to yield to this rule.[37] The same happened to the requirement of territorial exclusivity for lawyers services in courts.[38] On the other side the requirement of admission for services in labour exchange was upheld as justified.[39] The border-crossing movement of capital (Articles 67 - 73 EEC-Treaty) has been liberalized recently.[40] Also the furthest-reaching extension of

[31] See Case 178/84, Commission of the European Communities v. Germany (1987) E. C. R. 1227, 1262.

[32] See as leading case Case 120/78, Rewe-Zentral-AG v. Bundesmonopolverwaltung für Branntwein (1979) E. C. R. 649; see also Case 220/81, Robertson (1982) E. C. R. 2349; Case 261/81, Rau (1982) E. C. R. 3961; see as survey P.-C. Müller-Graff note 28 Article 30 note 77 - 81.

[33] See above note 30.

[34] Id.

[35] See P.-C. Müller-Graff, Ordnungspolitische Divergenzen und wettbewerbliche Lauterkeit in der Verfassung des Gemeinsamen Marktes, in: Festschrift für Karl Carstens 227 (1984).

[36] See above note 18.

[37] Case 205/84, Commission of the European Communities v. Germany, 40 Neue Juristische Wochenschrift 576 at 52 (1987).

[38] Case 427/85, Commission of the European Communities v. Germany, Judgment of the CJEC of Feb. 25, 1988 at 40.

[39] Case 279/80, Webb (1981) E. C. R. 3305, 3325.

[40] See especially Directive 88/361/EEC, O. J. 1988 L 178/5.

the right of establishment in another Member State as laid down in the Treaty (Articles 52 - 58) seems to have been reached by now. The French interdiction for lawyers[41] and for physicians[42] to have two offices has been declared as incompatible with the common market by the Court. In a similar way the freedom of movement for workers (Articles 48 - 51 EEC-Treaty) is secured to a large extent. Here delicate questions exist as to the access to the public service of another Member State.[43] Until now the Court has opened the access for persons with the nationality of another Member State step by step, for example for nurses in a Brussels hospital and for construction workers in the Belgian public railway.[44]

bb) How far has Community law come by now to mastering the second task, the institution of a system ensuring that competition in the common market is not distorted? In this respect Community law has also been developed very far in important areas, but some loopholes also exist.

(1) As far as competition rules applying to undertakings are concerned, the instruments against collective restrictions of competition as well as against the abuse of a dominant position within the common market have proven highly effective both in the hands of the Commission and the Court of Justice.[45] Eventually after 18 years of tough negotiations especially between Germany and the United Kingdom on one side and France on the other with her different philosophy of economic policy, a painful gap of the whole system was closed when a European merger control was put into force.[46] It seems that the new provisions will not easily enable the Commission to pursue and to realize objectives of discrete industrial policy instead of guarding the structure of competition.[47]

(2) A system ensuring that competition is not distorted also needs instruments against distortion by public intervention. The Treaty itself contains an important and more and more enforced basic prohibition of aids granted by Member States in case they distort or threaten to distort competition by

---

41 Case 107/83, Klopp (1984) E. C. R. 2971.

42 Case 96/85, Commission of the European Communities v. France (1986) E. C. R. 1475.

43 See Case 225/85, Commission of the European Communities v. Italy, Judgment of the CJEC of June 16, 1987.

44 Case 149/79, Commission of the European Communities v. Belgium (1980) E. C. R. 3881 and (1982) E. C. R. 1845, 1852 at 9; see also Case 307/84, Commission of the European Communities v. France (1986) E. C. R. 1725; Case 66/85, Lawrie Blum (1986) E. C. R. 2121.

45 As a survey see P.-C. Müller-Graff, Wettbewerbsregeln des gemeinschafteuropäischen Binnenmarktes (1991).

46 Regulation 4064/89, O. J. 1989 L 395/1.

47 See Th. Janicki, EG-Fusionskontrolle auf dem Weg zur praktischen Umsetzung, Wirtschaft und Wettbewerb 194 (1990).

favouring certain undertakings or the production of certain goods, as far as it affects trade between Member States (Art. 92 sec. 1).[48] However, exceptions exist in the Treaty itself (Art. 92 sec. 2 and 3), and their conditions are open for different interpretations.[49] Until now no comparable instrument exists against state-measures distorting competition that do have not the form of an aid like – for example – the French decree that retailers of books have to observe tied prices and publishers have to tie prices.[50] An open flank of the whole system is the absence of enforceable rules against distortions of competition by aids and other actions of the European Community itself.

Leaving the first question that asked for the functions of the legal order for the objective of the internal market it is now appropriate to move on to the second question posed above.

II. The second question was based on the opposite view: the legal order seen not as an active subject in the process of establishing the internal market, but as an object shaped by the legally prescriptive objective of the internal market.

1. The Commission of the European Community considers changes in law as inevitable and links the establishment of the functioning of the internal market to the condition that the Member States abolish all kinds of barriers, harmonize their technical standards and approximate their legal provisions and structures of taxation.[51] But this is only one side. The objective of the internal market requires also changes of the Community law and legislative policy itself.

2. As far as the national legal orders are concerned one question is at hand: what form should the requirements of the functioning of the internal market on national law take? Should it be deregulation of national provisions, approximation of national law according to a Community directive or mutual recognition of national provisions as being equivalent?

a) The demand for deregulation stands at the center of the above mentioned economic approach to the internal market.[52]

---

[48] See above note 24.

[49] For regional policy in the new states of the Federal Republic of Germany see P.-C. Müller-Graff, Regionalförderung im vereinigten Deutschland vor dem Hintergrund des Beihilfenrechts der EG, in: W. Zippel (ed.), Deutsch-deutsche Wirtschafts-, Währungs- und Sozialunion im Rahmen der Europäischen Gemeinschaften 37 - 65 (1991).

[50] See Case 229/83, Leclerc, Europarecht 158 (1985); P.-C. Müller-Graff, Wettbewerbsbeschränkung durch Gesetz, Preisbindungspflicht bei Büchern, Europarecht 295 (1985); Unternehmensinvestitionen und Investitionssteuerung im Marktrecht 302, 440 (1984).

[51] See above note 17: White Paper p. 1 at 1.

[52] See above note 11.

aa) This demand discards as misguiding the questions how many legal provisions should still be enacted until the internal market is established and exerts its functions. Instead it is asked how many legal provisions still have to be abolished in order to transform Europe into a great market.[53] The starting-point of this reasoning is quite simple. It is the idea that European integration should be propelled like all market-processes by the spontaneous forces of competition and its invisible guiding hand in the sense of *Adam Smith* and *Friedrich von Hayek*. Therefore this philosophy heads explicitly against the so-called constructivists, thereby meaning those, who prefer as many approximations and harmonisations of legal provisions and technical standards as possible for the establishment of the internal market.[54] On the contrary this approach trusts in the principle of the country of origin; this means in the idea that – for example – a product that is brought legally into trade in one Member State according to its provisions is suitable to circulate in the whole internal market and may not be barred by national law from doing so. The principle of the country of origin is based on the recognition of the legal and technical rules of the Member States as being equivalent, thus on the mutual confidence of the Member States in the standards, quality and efficiency of legal orders of the other Member States. The consequence is sometimes described as a *competition of the legal systems*.[55] With this metaphor it is meant that, for example, not only certain kinds of food – e.g. yoghurt – are competing for the favour of the English consumer but with it also the different standards of the Italian or the Danish regulations for food quality. Thus it is up to those who have a demand to decide on the preferred standards of quality, security and compatibility of goods or on the preferred qualification of persons in liberal professions coming from different systems of education or on the preferred reliability of banks and insurances controlled by different systems of supervision.

bb) How does this approach have to be assessed? First of all, the demand to use the forces of competition for the European integration is not new at all. On the contrary it is the basic idea as laid down in the Treaties more than thirty years ago.[56] Thus on the pedestal of the Treaty we can observe a process of deregulation for a long time as, e.g., the mentioned decision on the purity of beers shows[57] representing a huge bulk of similar decisions.[58] However, it would be wrong to assert that the consequence of the basic freedoms is a total

---

53 Id.

54 Id.

55 See above B I 1 at note 20.

56 See e.g. W. von Simson, Die Marktwirtschaft als Verfassungsprinzip in den Europäischen Gemeinschaften, in: Zur Einheit der Rechts- und Staatswissenschaften 59, 62 (1967).

57 See above note 31.

58 See P.-C. Müller-Graff note 28 Article 30 note 47 - 74.

flattening of public regulation in the economy. There are two limits in particular.

The first limit to deregulation can be seen in the fact that the provisions guaranteeing free movement do not abolish the binding authority of national rules for "purely state-internal" events and transactions. This can cause the problem of reverse discrimination[59] as in the beer case. Different from importers, German breweries still have to fulfill the requirements of beer purity if they want to sell their product on the German market.

This problem has not yet been solved. The Court of Justice of the European Communities holds that the competence to cope with this question cannot be found in Community law but rests solely with the national law. However, considering Article 3 lit. f (Objective of a system ensuring that competition in the common market is not distorted), Article 5 sec. 2 (obligation of Member States to abstain from any measure which could jeopardize the attainment of the objectives of the EEC-Treaty) and Article 8 A (objective of the internal market) EEC-Treaty this is a doubtful assumption. In Germany the Federal Court of Civil Law (Bundesgerichtshof) has seen no violation of the principle of equal treatment (Article 3 of the Constitution) until now.[60] However, this assumption is even more doubtful.[61]

A second limit to deregulation is that not every national measure that restrains trade is deprived of its binding force, since all measures can be upheld that are justified by the necessary protection of certain public interests.

This limit is obviously essential in the interest of the people of the respective country into which goods or services are imported and cannot be superseded by the principle of the country of origin. The obstacles to free movement inherent in those national rules can be overcome only by means of Community action: approximation of national laws obliging Member States to recognize provisions applied by other Member States as being equivalent for the protection of the involved public interest.

b) This leads now to the second possible approach. How much approximation of national laws is needed and should be conceded in establishing the internal market?

aa) After all that has been said above it is obvious that in order to enable free movement the fixation of a Community standard and in consequence of it the approximation of national laws is inevitable, if national barriers of market entry cannot be abolished by the bearing of the Treaty provisions on basic

---

[59] See e.g. M.-A. Reitmaier, Inländerdiskriminierungen nach dem EWG-Vertrag (1984), U. F. Kleier, Freier Warenverkehr (Art. 30 EWG-Vertrag) und die Diskriminierung inländischer Erzeugnisse, Recht der Internationalen Wirtschaft 626 (1988).

[60] BGH, Recht der Internationalen Wirtschaft 589 (1985).

[61] See e.g. U. F. Kleier note 59 at 628 - 629.

freedoms or by the mutal recognition of national provisions as being equivalent. There are many such barriers. Thus the national law systems in the Community are unavoidably exposed to permanent pressure and to legal obligations to harmonize their market-relevant provisions according to a Community standard.

bb) This pressure, however, is not without limits. It is justified only to the extent required for the proper functioning of the internal market. Thus the EEC-Treaty does not provide for unlimited powers for the Community to harmonize. It only contains different competences for the approximation of market-related law.[62] For example the new Art. 100 A EEC-Treaty[63] reads: "The Council shall, acting by qualified majority on a proposal from the Commission ..., adopt the measures for the approximation of the provisions laid down by law, regulation or administrative action in Member States which have as their object the establishment and functioning of the internal market." Thus it seems hardly conceivable to found on this basis, for example, a European law of domestic relations, succession or the execution of sentences. On the other side a clear-cut limitation of the powers of the Community along the traditional lines of certain fields of law or according to a principle of subsidiarity (as in Article 130 r sec. 4 EEC-Treaty for evironmental protection[64]), is not possible. It is not possible along the traditional lines of certain fields of law because the causes for trade restrictions are not confined to those lines, but are rooted in many fields; to pick only some examples: in regulations for the quality of food as well as in the code of conduct for practising lawyers, in the law against unfair competition as well as in the law for the insurance business. A clear-cut limitation of the powers of the Community is not possible according to a "principle of subsidiarity" either as in the policy relating to the protection of environment, because the establishment of the internal market by approximation of law does not imply the question if this objective can be attained better at the Community level than at the level of the individual Member States since its genuine purpose is the abolition of state restrictions of trade.

c) All these possible influences on national laws make it evident that the decision for market integration cannot work without consequences for the traditional order and balance of legislative powers. More and more this is considered to be a problem by the national parliaments and the states of the Federal Republic with regard to the far-reaching directives of the Community.[65] A

---

[62] See Articles 43 sec. 2, 49, 54 sec. 3 lit. g, 56 sec. 2, 57 sec. 1 und 2, 69, 70 sec. 1, 75, 84 sec. 2, 99, 100, 100 A, 101 EEC-Treaty.

[63] For its function and interpretation see P.-C. Müller-Graff note 17 at 121.

[64] See D. H. Scheuing, Umweltschutz auf der Grundlage der Einheitlichen Europäischen Akte, 19 Europarecht 152, 164 (1984).

[65] See K. Hailbronner, Die Rechtsordnung der Europäischen Gemeinschaften: Hemmschuh unserer Politik – Gefahr für unsere Rechtsordnung? in: Ausbau der Europäischen Rechtsgemeinschaft – Ausverkauf unserer Rechtsordnung? 71 (1988).

directive is binding, as to the result to be achieved, upon each Member State to which it is adressed, but shall leave the national authorities the choice of forms and methods (Article 189 sec. 3 EEC-Treaty). Though this does not mean a loss of competences in a formal sense, in reality the autonomous range for free action of the national legislative body is limited by the obligation to transform their own law according to the directive and by the obligation to stick to the remodelled provisions in the future.[66] The political complaints about this situation are one side. The fact that the Member States have agreed on the powers of the Communities when ratifying the Treaties is the other.

3. It was said that the objective of the internal market requires not only changes in national laws but also changes of the *Community law* and the legal policy on this level itself. This implies two questions: how far does the Treaty law (called primary law) have to be adopted? And in which manner does the Community have to handle its powers to create secondary law (this is namely regulations and directives)?

a) As far as the adaptation of the *primary law* is concerned there has already been the mentioned reform by the Single European Act of 1986.[67] By it the mandate for the Community to establish the internal market has been flanked by several modifications of the hitherto cumbersome system of legislative decision-making on the Community level. Has this goal been achieved? For this question only four remarks shall be made.

aa) Firstly: the simplification of the decision-making process seems to be a successful reform.[68] Especially in the scope of the mentioned Art. 100 A EEC-Treaty, the basic competence for harmonization, the Council can now act by a qualified majority. This change was over-due, since the traditional principle of unanimity had blocked many proposals from the Commission in the past. As a method for political decision it could no longer satisfy the challenges of a dynamic common market. In fact, the decision-making process of the Community has been considerably sped up since this reform. There had not been as many harmonization directives in ten years before as in the last five years. Interestingly enough the sheer possibility of acting by qualified majority has caused a hitherto unusual pressure on the Council to come to terms.[69]

bb) Secondly: On the reverse side the easier way to come to action has created a new problem. It is the problem that a decision taken by a qualified majority is not accepted politically in a Member State that voted against it

[66] See H. P. Ipsen, Europäisches Gemeinschaftsrecht 701 (1973).

[67] For the origin see J. W. de Zwaan, The Single European: Conclusion of a Unique Document, CMLRev. 747 (1986).

[68] See Commission of the European Communities, Fourth Report of the Commission with Regard to the Realisation of the White Paper of the Commission Concerning the Establishment of the Internal Market, 3 at note 7 (1989).

[69] Id.

because it wanted a higher level of protection of the involved public interests such as health or the environment. To my mind this problem is fairly mitigated in a realistic way by several clauses of Art. 100 A EEC-Treaty. First of all some matters assessed as especially sensitive or intricate are excluded from the qualified majority rule: namely fiscal provisions, provisions relating to the free movement of persons (therein included the law of immigration and sanctuary and the provisions against crime and drugs) and moreover the provisions relating to the rights and interests of employed persons (Art. 100 A sec. 2 EEC-Treaty). Secondly: As far as the majority rule is applicable the Commission is bound by the Treaty to take into its proposals concerning health, safety, environmental protection and consumer protection "a high level of protection" as a base (Art. 100 A sec. 3 EEC-Treaty).[70] If the Commission fulfills this obligation the state interested in a high level of protection is secured against any weakening by the requirement of unanimity to deviate from the proposal.[71] The most discussed means of relieving the problem of acceptance (in the case of a harmonization measure adopted by a qualified majority) is the clause of opting out (Art. 100 A sec. 4 EEC-Treaty). This clause guarantees the right of a Member State to apply national provisions different from the Community standard on grounds of major needs referred to in Art. 36 EEC-Treaty or relating to the protection of the environment or the working environment. This means that except for the protection of the consumer and the rules against unfair competition the Member States still hold sufficient competences for a policy favouring a high level of protection of the cited values. Moreover, the possibility to opt out enables the interested state to negotiate with rigour for high standards on the Community level itself. Whether it turns out to be only a hypothetical possibility will be seen in the future. For after the fixation of a Community standard it looks uncertain if it remains feasible for an outvoted Member State to hold on to a higher and usually more expensive level of protection. Eventually Art. 100 A sec. 5 EEC-Treaty grants the additional possibility to include a safeguard clause in harmonization measures authorizing the Member States to take, for one or more of the non-economic reasons referred to in Article 36, provisional measures subject to Community control procedure.

cc) Thirdly: Great attention will have to be directed to the ability of the decision-making system for reforms of directives and regulations of the Community in order to keep pace with the dynamic developments of the market and to avoid any torpidity of rules.

---

[70] The legal enforceability of this obligation is doubtful; for this problem see C.-D. Ehlermann, The Internal Market Following the Single European Act, CMLRev. 366 (1987).

[71] See P.-C. Müller-Graff note 17 at 135.

dd) Fourthly only one sentence: the rules of participation of the directly elected European Parliament in the decision-making process of the Community[72] are still not sufficient.[73]

b) The simplification for taking legal action on the Community level has furthered the question which direction and what extent the enlargement of *secondary law* should have.

aa) The massive harmonization policy of the Community has caused a variety of critical attacks: complaints about uniformity, criticism of special projects, allegations of over-regulation.[74] These objections cannot simply be discarded, since it is far from clear that all measures of the Commission as, e.g., laid down in the White Paper[75] are really necessary for establishing the internal market.

bb) As it was said before the Treaty empowers the Community to adopt measures of harmonization only if they are required by the market-objective.[76] Naturally this criterion leaves the Council with a wide prerogative of assessment to identify the fields of action. Thus it is mainly a political challenge to cope with the danger of over-harmonization.

(1) Thus one has to applaud the so-called new approach of the Commission.[77] For it takes as a principle to draw a clear line between those fields in which harmonization is inevitable, and those in which the mutual recognition of national provisions can be relied upon. This means conceptually a combination of the principle of Community standard and the principle of the country of origin. However this general approach does not exclude that concrete measures of harmonization remain problematic in terms of their necessity.

(2) Apart from those problems it can not be overlooked that most measures are unavoidable only because the Member States themselves insist on the necessity of regulation. Complaints about regulations adopted by the Community do not seldom ignore that those regulations have been provoked by state-caused market-entry-barriers. For example: the proposal to harmonize the legal provisions for the seats of saddle tractors was provoked by a regulation that had been introduced by the German professional association to protect the farmers against damaging their backbones.[78] If this objective is considered

---

[72] See H.-J. Glaesner, Das Verfahren der Zusammenarbeit (Art. 149 Abs. 2 EWGV), 23 Europarecht 121 (1988).

[73] For the problem of a parliamentarian-democratic legitimary see P.-C. Müller-Graff, Direct Elections to the European Parliament 11 Case Western Reserve Journal of International Law 1, 19 - 36 (1979).

[74] See e.g. K. Hailbronner note 65 at 70; H. Giersch note 4.

[75] See above note 17.

[76] See Articles 3 lit. h., 8 A sec. 1 EEC-Treaty; P.-C. Müller-Graff note 17 at 128.

[77] See White Paper (above note 17) at note 61.

as justified in the interest of the protection of health, therefore saddle tractors that are constructed differently are not admitted for sale in Germany, consequently the question of harmonization gains attention.

III. Thus the concluding third question can be raised: in which way do the legally prescriptive internal market-objective and the legal order cooperate in terms of the legal system? The basic answer is that a new field of law has evolved and still is evolving on the level of Community law that can be labelled as "market law" (Marktrecht)[79] and is developing into an "internal market law". To characterize it only seven concluding short statements shall be given.

1. Firstly: Though Community law is a separate legal order, the internal market law is not foreign to the national legal systems, but a common descendant of their basic principles.

2. Secondly: the substantial legitimation, function and definition of the internal market law derives from the objective to establish a common market, not a state or a federation.

3. Thirdly: The internal market law is rooted in the basic preference of Community law for a free market and for the free coordination of economic activities by competition instead of public economic planning and intervention.[80]

4. Fourthly: The internal market law contains a reformatory potential for the law. Oriented towards the market it can work as a means of examining and reforming the law in other areas.[81] Thereby it implies even the chance to further the self-determination of persons.

5. Fifthly: In the interest of a uniform application of the internal market law in all Member States the authority of the Court of Justice of the European Communities and an interpretation of national law in conformity with the legally prescriptive internal market objective of the Community law are required.

6. Sixthly: The legislation of the secondary market law needs more parliamentarian-democratic participation.

7. Seventhly: The effects of the internal market law on the economic activities will provoke demands for more cooperation of the Member States as well as for more competences of the Community with respect to flanking policies to stabilize the internal market. This can be seen now in the efforts

[78] U. Everling, Gestaltungsbedarf des Europäischen Rechts, 22 Europarecht 214 (1987).

[79] For the grounds of market law see P.-C. Müller-Graff, Unternehmensinvestitionen und Investitionssteuerung im Marktrecht 280 (1984).

[80] Id.

[81] See as example Case 178/84 above note 31.

to create a European Monetary Union (Maastricht Treaty) and a European Social Charta and to shape a coherent policy of regional developement and of environmental protection on Community level.

C. This brings me to a concluding remark. The most important potential for the development of the legal order in Europe that is implied in the objective of the internal market is the chance to strengthen the awareness of a common European legal system. It might be that this again will further the spirit of a closer solidarity and unity in Europe. *Ludwig Raiser* once characterized the German developement in the 19th century, that the political unity in 1871 was supplemented by the legal unity later on.[82] Today, in a reverse way, we witness and experience the rediscovery and growth of a European legal community and of a European jurisprudence that will perhaps further a stronger political community. In this perspective a word of the French politician, *Jean Monnet,* one of the founding-fathers of the European Community, should be remembered: "The real task is not to form coalitions between states but to unite people".[83] And this again is an eminent task of law.

[82] See L. Raiser, Die Aufgabe des Privatrechts 162 (1977).

[83] See J. Monnet, Erinnerungen eines Europäers IV (1988).

Kelsen and the Marburg School: Reconstructive and Historical Perspectives

By Stanley L. Paulson, St. Louis

Introduction

A great deal of confusion persists over the question of the neo-Kantian dimension of Hans Kelsen's Pure Theory of Law. In Kelsen's texts, there are many, many references to Kantian doctrines. For example, Kelsen addresses a transcendental question to the law,[1] and he refers to the "ought" as designating a "relative *a priori* category for comprehending empirical legal data",[2] to the basic norm as "revealing the transcendental logical conditions" of legal cognition,[3] and to the "constitutive" character of legal science.[4]

And there are striking structural parallels between Kelsen's Pure Theory of Law and Kant's critical philosophy. For example, Kant resolves the first of the mathematical antinomies, posed by the juxtaposition of dogmatic rationalism and sceptical empiricism, by arguing that the notion of "a world of the senses existing of itself"[5] – existing absolutely – amounts to a self-contradiction, and must be replaced by the notion that the world exists not "of itself" but only in relation to mind.[6] Kant works up the latter position, his "middle way", in the Transcendental Analytic of the *Kritik der reinen Vernunft*. Similarly, Kelsen resolves the jurisprudential antinomy, posed by the juxtaposition of natural law theory and traditional legal positivism, by arguing that the law cannot be understood strictly in terms of either morality or fact. In works such as his *Philosophical Foundations of Natural Law Theory and Legal Positivism*

[1] Kelsen, consciously following Kant, poses his own transcendental question: "How is positive law *qua* object of cognition, *qua* object of cognitive legal science, possible?" Kelsen, Philosophical Foundations of Natural Law Theory and Legal Positivism (first published 1928), trans. Wolfgang H. Kraus, as an appendix to Kelsen, General Theory of Law and State (Cambridge, Mass. 1945), 389 - 445, at 437; see also Kelsen, Reine Rechtslehre, 2nd edn. (Vienna 1960), § 34 (d).

[2] Kelsen, Reine Rechtslehre (Leipzig/Vienna 1934, repr. Aalen 1986), § 11 (b).

[3] Ibid., § 29.

[4] Kelsen, Reine Rechtslehre, 2nd edn. (fn 1 above), § 16.

[5] Kant, Prolegomena to any Future Metaphysic, § 52 (c), at 107 in the translation by Peter G. Lucas (Manchester 1953).

[6] On the mathematical antinomies generally, see Kant, Kritik der reinen Vernunft, at A426 - 38/B454 - 66, A490 - 567/B518 - 95.

(1928), and in the first and second editions of his *Pure Theory of Law* (1934, 1960), Kelsen hints at some of the details of his "middle way". The key concept in his venture is the basic norm, or – to turn to alternative idioms – the "ought" *qua* relative *a priori* category, or the category of normative imputation.[7]

Despite, or perhaps because of, the abundant references in Kelsen's texts to Kantian doctrine, there is no consensus on how, exactly, the neo-Kantian dimension is to be understood. Many commentators on Kelsen presume that he was in fact influenced by the Marburg School of neo-Kantianism;[8] Kelsen himself, as we shall see, indicates as much.[9] My own thesis is two-fold. *First,* while granting that Marburg neo-Kantianism, and Hermann Cohen's theory in particular, may well be suggestive as a basis for a *reconstruction* of Kelsen's theory,[10] I question the general presumption of a *historical* influence stemming from Marburg. I argue that a rebuttal of the presumption is supported by Kelsen's own texts, in so far as they bear on the question of historical influence. *Second,* I argue – again by way of textual analysis – that in so far as the historical influences on Kelsen are neo-Kantian at all, they stem in fact from Heidelberg, not Marburg.[11]

---

[7] Of course these do not have to be seen as mere "alternative idioms". To illustrate the point, there is an interpretation of the "ought" *qua* relative *a priori* category that distinguishes it significantly from the other two concepts mentioned here. See Alf Ross, Towards a Realistic Jurisprudence, trans. Annie I. Fausbøll (Copenhagen 1946, repr. Aalen 1989), at 39, 41 - 2, 48; Ross, Kritik der sogenannten praktischen Erkenntnis. Zugleich Prolegomena zu einer Kritik der Rechtswissenschaft, trans. Hans Winkler and Gunnar Leistikow (Copenhagen / Leipzig 1933), 418 - 21; Wilhelm Windelband, Präludien, 1st edn. (Freiburg/Tübingen 1884), 280 - 311, at 283 - 6; 9th edn. (Tübingen 1924), vol. 2, 161 - 94, at 164 - 7.

[8] For example, William Ebenstein writes: "In respect of the issue of method, a decisive influence has been exerted on the Pure Theory of Law by the extreme idealism of Hermann Cohen..." Ebenstein, The Pure Theory of Law, trans. Charles H. Wilson (Madison 1945, repr. New York 1969), 38; see also Robert Walter, "Hans Kelsen", Neue Deutsche Biographie, vol. 11 (Berlin 1977), 479 - 80, at 479. This, so far as I can tell, is the majority view among commentators.

[9] See section II below.

[10] For reconstructive efforts that reflect something of Marburg, see Renato Treves, "Il fondamento filosofico della dottrina pura del diritto di Hans Kelsen", Atti della Reale Accademia delle Scienze di Torino, 69 (1933), 52 - 90, repr. in Hans Kelsen and Renato Treves, Formalismo giuridico e realtà sociale, ed. Stanley L. Paulson (Naples / Rome 1992), 59 - 87; Helmut Holzhey, "Kelsens Rechts- und Staatslehre in ihrem Verhältnis zum Neukantianismus", in Untersuchungen zur Reinen Rechtslehre, ed. Stanley L. Paulson and Robert Walter (Vienna 1986), 167 - 92. These writers suggest that Cohen's philosophy may well be promising from the standpoint of a reconstruction of Kelsen's Pure Theory of Law; they do not claim that Cohen in fact influenced Kelsen significantly.

[11] I should perhaps note that my use of "neo-Kantian" is limited, here, to the fin de siècle movements in Marburg and Heidelberg. I am not addressing nineteenth-century influences of a Kantian nature – for example, whatever influences there may have been on Kelsen stemming from his reading of Schopenhauer.

I can only argue here for bits and pieces of a two-fold thesis that is, I know, audacious in scope. References in Kelsen's texts to Kantian doctrine, such as those I listed at the outset of the paper, can be supported by appropriate arguments, and may well establish a historical influence on Kelsen that stems from Kant or from particular neo-Kantians. The structural parallel, however, between Kant's mathematical antinomy and a Kelsenian jurisprudential antinomy, suggesting that the resolution of each of the respective antinomies points to a "middle way", to each thinker's alternative to the tradition, does not reflect any straightforward historical influence. The parallel is, rather, the upshot of a reconstruction.

The distinctions between historical and reconstructive enquiry in philosophy are of considerable significance.[12] I believe it is the failure to appreciate such distinctions that explains in part the confusion over the question of the neo-Kantian dimension of Kelsen's Pure Theory of Law, and I offer, in section I, some remarks on historical and reconstructive enquiry generally. I then turn, in section II, to the question of historical influences on Kelsen, arguing against the proposition that a significant historical influence stems from Marburg, and alluding, in the last part of section II, to historical influences stemming, rather, from Heidelberg.

I. Reconstructive versus Historical Enquiry

The parallel between Kelsen and Kant that I drew at the outset, the "middle way" emerging in both thinkers' work from their respective resolutions of jurisprudential and mathematical antinomies, is reconstructive in nature, not historical. Similarly for Kelsen's employment of the regressive version of the Kantian transcendental argument, a version familiar from the work of, *inter alia,* Hermann Cohen, the leading writer in the Marburg School.[13] I am not

---

[12] On reconstruction in philosophy generally, see Wolfgang Stegmüller, "Towards a Rational Reconstruction of Kant's Metaphysics of Experience", in Stegmüller, Collected Papers on Epistemology, Philosophy of Science and History of Philosophy, vol. 1 (Dordrecht/Boston 1977), 66 - 136, at 66 - 71. I am grateful to Mario G. Losano for pointing out, in connection with my own work, the importance of the distinctions between reconstructive and historical enquiry; see his paper, "The Periodization of Kelsen Proposed by S. L. Paulson", in Hans Kelsen's Legal Theory. A Diachronic Point of View, ed. Letizia Gianformaggio (Torin 1990), 111 - 21. The fundamental distinction at issue is captured in agreeably brief compass by Chandran Kukathas, writing on Friedrich A. Hayek: "I am interested in the presuppositions of Hayek's argument in defence of liberalism, rather than in its origins." Kukathas, Hayek and Modern Liberalism (Oxford 1989), p. viii.

[13] On Cohen's own language, and for references to further literature, see my essay, "The Neo-Kantian Dimension of Kelsen's Pure Theory of Law", Oxford Journal of Legal Studies, 12 (1992), 311 - 32, at 330.

pretending that Kelsen worked up details of either a jurisprudential antinomy or something resembling Cohen's regressive argument. In fact he did not. Rather, I am suggesting that it may be instructive to develop and evaluate Kelsen's theory by appeal to such doctrines, drawn *per analogiam* from Kant and from Cohen.

Reconstruction might be understood in terms of two steps. *First*, a theoretical "ideal type" is constructed – that is, a theory reflecting the basic ideas of the philosopher in question,[14] but in a form that the theory might take if it were developed rigorously and in some detail. *Second*, the doctrine in question is evaluated by appeal to the theoretical ideal type. Thus, in Kelsen's case a neo-Kantian or regressive version of Kant's transcendental argument would provide one theoretical ideal type, and, I believe (though there is no consensus here), Ernst Mach's principle of economy might well provide another.[15] Then, the doctrine in question – Kelsen's basic norm and the normativity thesis associated with it – is evaluated by appealing, in turn, to each of the ideal types. In effect, one is asking: How would Kelsen have fared if he had developed, say, the regressive version of Kant's transcendental argument in some detail, and had then appealed to it in support of his normativity thesis?

Such reconstructions are to be sharply distinguished from historical and textual questions about actual influences.[16] The difficulties of determining whether and how philosopher *A* was influenced by philosopher *B* are notorious, but such claims are nevertheless made. And some of them have been well established in the history of philosophy – a significant Cartesian influence on John Locke, a profound Lockean influence on Berkeley, and so on. Leszek Kolakowski writes that a philosopher is "intelligible only in contrast to, and

---

[14] Stegmüller, "Towards a Rational Reconstruction" (fn 12 above), 67.

[15] On Kelsen's use of Mach, see Das Problem der Souveränität (Tübingen 1920, repr. Aalen 1981), § 24, at 99; and Leonidas Pitamic, "Denkökonomische Voraussetzungen der Rechtswissenschaft", Österreichische Zeitschrift für öffentliches Recht, 3 (1918), 339 - 67. For illuminating commentary, see Wilhelm Jöckel, Hans Kelsens rechtstheoretische Methode (Tübingen 1930, repr. Aalen 1977), 68 - 73, 181 - 8. Günther Winkler rightly remarks that it would be instructive to compare Kelsen's orientation toward Mach's principle of economy with Husserl's notion of logic qua normative discipline. Winkler, Rechtstheorie und Erkenntnislehre (Vienna 1990), 17. Giuliana Stella has taken steps in the direction of such a comparison; see her paper "Hans Kelsen, Ernst Mach, Edmund Husserl", in Kelsen e il problema della sovranità, ed. Agostino Carrino (Naples/Rome 1990), 143 - 53.

[16] I am not suggesting that there is in fact a bright line of demarcation between the historical and reconstructive enterprises. There are, however, paradigmatic cases of each. In philosophy one thinks, for example, of the reconstructive work of Wilfred Sellars, and of the historical work of Richard Popkin. See, e.g., Sellars, Science and Metaphysics. Variations on Kantian Themes (London 1968); and Popkin, The History of Scepticism from Erasmus to Spinoza (Berkeley 1979). Here the differences between the two enterprises are profound.

against the background of, the philosophical culture" he attacks[17] and, by the same token, the philosophical culture upon which he draws. This applies to Kelsen no less than to such seminal figures in the history of modern philosophy as Descartes, Locke, and Berkeley. And it applies, in particular, to the question of the neo-Kantian dimension of Kelsen's Pure Theory.

The arguments below speak to historical influences, not to reconstructive evaluations. In the case of the Marburg School, the burden of my argument is to show that despite Kelsen's claim of indebtedness to Hermann Cohen vis-à-vis certain doctrines in the theory of knowledge, a debt mentioned by Kelsen in the Preface to the second printing of the *Hauptprobleme der Staatsrechtslehre,*[18] these doctrines were in fact adopted by Kelsen independently of Cohen, and were used in a way that presupposes nothing whatever of Cohen's philosophy. In the case of the Heidelberg School, the burden of my argument is to show that in addition to such well-known Heidelberg neo-Kantian doctrines as the distinction between causal and normative methods or points of view (which Kelsen draws from Wilhelm Windelband), and the distinction between "is" and "ought" (in the form in which Kelsen draws it from Georg Simmel),[19] there is a significant link to Heidelberg, too, in Kelsen's normative counterpart to Heinrich Rickert's theory of concept formation in the social sciences.

II. Kelsen and Marburg neo-Kantianism

In the Preface to the second printing of his *Hauptprobleme der Staatsrechtslehre,* appearing in 1923, Kelsen refers to several central doctrines in the theory of knowledge, attributing them to Hermann Cohen of the Marburg School. These doctrines, Kelsen writes, represent "the decisive epistemologico-theoretical standpoint" of his work on public law; indeed, Kelsen continues, absent this standpoint, the view of the concepts of state and law that he had adopted in work published after the *Hauptprobleme* would not have been possible.[20] Repeating my statement of the thesis I want to defend:

17 Leszek Kolakowski, Husserl and the Search for Certainty (New Haven 1975), 5.

18 Hauptprobleme der Staatsrechtslehre (Tübingen 1911, second printing, 1923, repr. Aalen 1960). The second printing contains, at p. xvii, the point in the Preface to which I am referring. For essentially the same allusion to Cohen, four years later, see Kelsen's first autobiographical sketch (February 1927), in Hans Kelsen and Renato Treves, Formalismo giuridico e realtà sociale (fn 10 above), Italian text: trans. Agostino Carrino, 27 - 32, at 28; German original: 33 - 7, at 34. And for still another suggestion of indebtedness to Cohen, see Kelsen's letter to Renato Treves (3 August 1933), in ibid., Italian text: trans. Agostino Carrino, 51 - 4, at 52; German original: 55 - 8, at 56.

19 See references at fn 51 below.

20 Hauptprobleme (fn 18 above), Preface to second printing (1923), p. xvii.

If Kelsen's claim is evaluated historically and textually, that is, in terms of the extent to which he actually draws on Cohen and the Marburg School in his writings, it cannot be regarded with anything but scepticism. I shall provide reasons for my sceptical stance.

First, however, I should like to back up a step and consider how the Marburg neo-Kantian view came to Kelsen's attention in the first place. The standard account, which Kelsen himself provides in the Preface to the second printing of the *Hauptprobleme,* invites the reader's attention to a book review of this work shortly after its first printing, in 1911. In the review, Oscar Ewald describes Kelsen's work as an attempt "to introduce the transcendental method into legal philosophy". In Ewald's words:

> As a convincing sign that the methodological principles of modern epistemology are beginning to find their way into other fields of enquiry, one may refer to Kelsen's work, *Hauptprobleme der Staatsrechtslehre*. This book is an attempt, carried out with logical rigour and energy, to introduce the transcendental method into legal philosophy. The author takes as his starting point the distinction between norm and law of nature, between what ought to be *(Sollen)* and what is *(Sein),* between normative and explicative points of view, in order to bring out what is unique among the properties of the legal norm. This unique factor is to be sought not at the level of what is, but at the level of what ought to be. ... Comparing a norm with the facts of the external world, in so far as the latter can be linked to those persons subject to the norm, gives rise to the concept of imputation *(Zurechnung)*. Here the question is not what the subject has done or forborne from doing, but simply what the obligation was, and who was obligated. The will plays a role in the problem of imputation that goes well beyond its psychological meaning. Here the will is not a concrete, real process, but rather a conceptual construction; it represents the endpoint of imputation, shifted, so to speak, to within the human being. As a means of demonstrating this, Kelsen turns to cases of liability for negligence, where the element of will is missing – indeed, it is precisely this lack of will that establishes such liability. Legal science cannot, therefore, resolve the liability problem in psychological terms. And so, opposition to psychologism becomes the cornerstone of a method that is essentially the transcendental, Kantian method. Looking to Cohen's interpretation of Kant, and to Cohen's *Ethik des reinen Willens,* one sees that his concept of will coincides in a most remarkable way with Kelsen's. The charge of formalism, leveled against work of Kelsen's that is fundamentally concerned with the objective and subjective forms in which the legal norm appears, has no justification, for it is precisely the *cognitive forms* specific to the theory of public law that are being analysed. The introduction of the transcendental method into a field that was hitherto partially closed to it, and rigorous adherence to its principles, together constitute the great merit of Kelsen's book, which one can only hope will have a far-reaching influence on the development of the philosophy of law.[21]

---

[21] Oscar Ewald, "Die deutsche Philosophie im Jahre 1911", Kantstudien, 17 (1912), 382 - 433, at 396 - 8. My translation. (Although there is an English translation, by William A. Hammond in the Philosophical Review, 21 (1912), 499 - 526, at 507 - 8, it contains many errors and omissions.)

A number of points in Ewald's review alerted Kelsen to "broad parallels between [his] own analysis of legal will and Cohen's view"; earlier, Kelsen adds, Cohen's view had not been familiar to him at all.[22]

How, then, do these thinkers' respective analyses of will compare? Cohen writes that the legal act is "nothing other than the self-development *(Selbstentfaltung)* of will",[23] which is to say, *inter alia,* that legal will functions as a criterion for identifying legal acts. This concept of legal will cannot, however, be equated with its naturalistic or psychological counterpart. For, as Cohen argues, it would be *"fundamentally false to equate* [*legal*] *person and human being."*[24] And on this point Kelsen's view is indeed comparable. As he writes, it would be impermissible to argue from the psychical will to the validity of a legal transaction in which this will has found expression. Rather, it is the other way around: "A transaction is willed in so far as, or because, it is valid."[25] This radical inversion of the relation between psychical will and the validity of the corresponding legal transaction is not to be understood as a reinterpretation, let alone as a denial, of psychical will. Rather, just as with Cohen, Kelsen's inversion counts as a rejection of psychical will *for legal purposes* and, to replace it, the introduction of a new, peculiarly legal concept of will.

Since, as Kelsen notes, he was not familiar with Cohen's view at the time he wrote the *Hauptprobleme,* published in 1911, the similarity in their respective concepts of will looks like a coincidence. Still, there is no reason to believe it was solely a coincidence. Kelsen's acquaintance, before 1911, with the work of the Heidelberg School of Neo-Kantianism clearly played a role in developing his concept of will.[26] And there was, too, his deeply held conviction, from the beginning, that the various forms of reductivism evident in the legal science of his day were utterly wrong-headed.[27]

---

22 Hauptprobleme (fn 18 above), Preface to second printing (1923), p. xvii.

23 Hermann Cohen, Ethik des reinen Willens, 2nd edn. (Berlin 1907, repr. Hildesheim 1981), 223.

24 Ibid., 230 (Cohen's emphasis).

25 Hauptprobleme (fn 18 above), 133; see also my paper, "Kelsen's Legal Theory: the Final Round", Oxford Journal of Legal Studies, 12 (1992), 265 - 74, at 165 - 6.

26 On the role of the Heidelberg theorists vis-à-vis Kelsen generally, see sub-section 3 of the present section, below.

27 Although Kelsen's view of reductivism scarcely requires documentation, the following references are of special interest. In the Hauptprobleme (fn 18 above), Preface to the second printing (1923), at p. ix, Kelsen refers approvingly to Husserl's arguments against psychologism; in "Rechtswissenschaft und Recht", Zeitschrift für öffentliches Recht, 3 (1922), 103 - 235, at 104, repr. in Fritz Sander and Hans Kelsen, Die Rolle des Neukantianismus in der Reinen Rechtslehre, ed. Stanley L. Paulson (Aalen 1988), 279 - 411, at 280, Kelsen writes, speaking for himself, Rudolf Stammler, and others, that in taking cues from "Kant's transcendental philosophy", we are combating a "naive empiristic naturalism".

After 1912, Kelsen and others in the Vienna School of Legal Theory apparently made an effort to absorb something of Cohen's philosophy.[28] And, a decade after the appearance of Ewald's review, Kelsen in the Preface to the second printing of the *Hauptprobleme* reflects on Cohen's influence. In particular, as I remarked at the outset of the present section, he writes that he is in Cohen's debt where several central doctrines in the theory of knowledge are concerned. The status of these doctrines in Kelsen's legal theory is the first of three issues that I wish to consider on the question of Cohen's influence on Kelsen.

1. *Kelsen's Alleged Debt to Cohen for Central Doctrines in the Theory of Knowledge*. The doctrines in question are, *first,* the idea that "the method of cognition determines the object of cognition", and, *second,* the notion that "the object of cognition is logically constituted by a source *(Ursprung)*".[29] *Third,* there is an important corollary[30] of the first two doctrines: "the state, in so far as it is the object of legal cognition, can only be law."[31] The corollary, in other words, gives expression to the thesis that state and law are identical.[32]

It is these doctrines that together represent the "decisive epistemologico-theoretical standpoint" of which Kelsen speaks, and without which, he claims, he could not have arrived at a correct view of certain issues in public law. On

[28] See Kelsen, Hauptprobleme (fn 18 above), Preface to second printing (1923), p. xvii; Kelsen, Das Problem der Souveränität (fn 15 above), Foreword at pp. vii - viii; Alfred Verdroß, "Alfred Verdroß", in Österreichische Rechts- und Staatswissenschaften der Gegenwart in Selbstdarstellungen (Innsbruck 1952), 201 - 10, at 201. In his autobiographical sketch, Verdroß refers to Kelsen's private seminar, first organized in 1912 or 1913; early participants included, along with Verdroß, Adolf Merkl, Leonides Pitamic, and Fritz Sander. Verdroß remarks that the participants considered such problems as the relation between constitution and statute, and between international law and state law. He then continues: "Consideration of these formal problems soon led us to a closer study of neo-Kantianism, which was truly thriving at that time; we studied, above all, the works of Hermann Cohen and Paul Natorp."

[29] Hauptprobleme (fn 18 above), Preface to second printing (1923), p. xvii. Compare Cohen, Logik der reinen Erkenntnis, 2nd edn. (Berlin 1914, repr. Hildesheim 1977), 35 - 8, 79; see also Verdroß's reading, at fn 38 below. On the notion of *Ursprung* in Cohen's philosophy, see generally Helmut Holzhey, Cohen und Natorp, vol. 1 (Basel 1986), 175 - 201.

[30] I speak, here, of a "corollary", since this third doctrine is not, stricto sensu, an epistemological tenet. On the other hand, it is arguably derivable from one or the other of the first two doctrines, above, and they of course are epistemological tenets. (Kelsen argues that the third doctrine is derivable from the first, see my text at fn 42 - 3 below; he does not himself, however, make any distinction among the three doctrines with respect to their epistemological status.)

[31] Hauptprobleme (fn 18 above), Preface to second printing (1923), p. xvii. Compare Cohen, Ethik des reinen Willens (fn 23 above), 63.

[32] For Kelsen's own views on the identity of law and state, see, above all, his treatise Der soziologische und der juristische Staatsbegriff (Tübingen 1922, repr. Aalen 1981). For other dimensions of Kelsen's concept of the state, see Kelsen, Dio e stato, ed. and trans. by Agostino Carrino (Naples/Rome 1988).

the basis of a textual analysis, I contend in response that these three doctrines – which, to be sure, do play an absolutely fundamental role in Kelsen's theory – were adopted by him independently of Cohen's philosophy, and do not, as he uses them, reflect anything peculiarly Cohennian. I shall take up, then, each of the doctrines in turn, this time with an eye to its origin and to the role each plays in Kelsen's own work.

The first doctrine, that "the method of cognition determines the object of cognition", simply flags the Kantian or neo-Kantian approach to the theory of knowledge generally. It does not delineate anything peculiar to the Marburg School, let alone anything peculiar to Cohen as a figure within the Marburg School; indeed, it is prominent in the work of the Heidelberg School.[33] In so far as Kelsen himself uses a version of this doctrine in his early work, most prominently in his sharp reply to Georg Jellinek's (and Kistiakowski's) "two-sides theory" of law,[34] he simply assumes as true by definition a certain link between method and object, ruling out in effect Jellinek's claim that distinct methods may be brought to bear on one and the same object.[35] Nothing in Kelsen's counterargument to Jellinek requires any appeal to the Marburg philosophers, and Kelsen makes no such appeal.

The terminology of the second doctrine – to the effect that "the object of cognition is logically constituted by a source *(Ursprung)*" – is clearly Cohennian.[36] It is much less obvious, however, that Kelsen's understanding of the doctrine, as distinct from the terminology in which he couches it, is in any clear sense Cohennian. For in so far as this second doctrine counts as a notion that is distinct, in Kelsen's work, from the first doctrine, the reference to source (or *Ursprung*) has to be understood as a reference to the basic norm, albeit in the nomenclature of *"Ursprungsnorm"*.[37] Kelsen's own colleagues in the Vienna School, Alfred Verdroß and Felix Kaufmann, interpret *"Ursprung"* in precisely this way – as a reference to the basic norm.[38] And finally, the immediate

33 For example, Heinrich Rickert writes: "We identify the concept of the object on the basis of the concept of the science that investigates it". Rickert, Die Grenzen der naturwissenschaftlichen Begriffsbildung, 2nd edn. (Tübingen 1913), 225; 5th edn. (1929), 228. The neo-Kantian Bruno Bauch writes that the "correlation between cognition and object", stemming from a single reference in the work of Rudolf Lotze, is fundamental in Rickert's work. See Bauch, "Das transzendentale Subjekt", Logos, 12 (1923-4), 29 - 49, at 30.

34 See Kelsen, Staatsbegriff (fn 32 above), at 106 - 40.

35 Georg Jellinek, Allgemeine Staatslehre, 3rd edn. (Berlin 1914), 11 - 12, 74, 137 - 9, 174 - 83, et passim.

36 See references at fn 29 above.

37 Kelsen himself uses the nomenclature of "Ursprungsnorm" in early writings; see, in particular, Das Problem der Souveränität (fn 15 above), Foreword at pp. vii - viii; § 24, at 98n, 100; § 26, at 107; et passim.

38 Alfred Verdroß, interpreting the Cohennian terminology of *"Ursprungsnorm"* and *"Ursprungshypothese"*, writes: "The fundamental idea of modern legal theory is the

historical influences that shaped Kelsen's basic norm are reasonably clear: Walter Jellinek,[39] and on the other hand, Alfred Verdroß.[40] There is no obvious Cohennian influence.[41]

As for the third doctrine, the corollary that "the state, in so far as it is the object of legal cognition, can only be law", I have already touched upon it above, in connection with the first doctrine.[42] State and law must be identical, Kelsen contends, and their identity is shown by appeal to the doctrine that the

---

hierarchical system of legal norms in a unitary system based on a unitary basic norm. Because it is the state constitution (in its material, Aristotelian sense) that specifies, for the state legal systems, this highest basis of the law, from which ordinary legal norms derive their legal force *(Rechtskraft),* the basic norm *(Grundnorm)* is also characterized as the constitution or, in neo-Kantian terminology, as the source norm *(Ursprungsnorm)* or source hypothesis *(Ursprungshypothese).*" Verdroß, "Die gesellschaftswissenschaftlichen Grundlagen der Völkerrechtstheorie", Archiv für Rechts- und Wirtschaftsphilosophie, 18 (1924-5), 413 - 31, at 423, repr. in Die Wiener rechtstheoretische Schule, ed. Hans Klecatsky et al., vol. 2 (Vienna 1968), 2079 - 95, at 2088. This link between the nomenclature of *"Grundnorm"* and *"Ursprungsnorm"* in the Cohennian sense of the latter is unmistakable in Verdroß's text, for in a footnote to the lines quoted above, he attributes the *"Ursprungsnorm"* nomenclature to Cohen's Logik der reinen Erkenntnis (fn 29 above), at 36, 79.

Similarly for Felix Kaufmann in his book, Die Kriterien des Rechts (Tübingen 1924, repr. Aalen 1966), at 129; Kaufmann, in indicating his preference for the terminology *"Grundnorm"* over *"Ursprungsnorm",* refers expressly to Cohen as the originator of the latter. For the reference to Kaufmann, I am indebted to Agostino Carrino; on both terminology and substantive issues of *Grundnorm* and *Ursprungsnorm,* see his Kelsen e il problema della scienza giuridica (Naples/Rome 1987), at 70 - 6.

39 Walter Jellinek, Gesetz, Gesetzesanwendung und Zweckmäßigkeitserwägung (Tübingen 1913, repr. Aalen 1964), 26 - 9. For a brief statement on Kelsen's use of Walter Jellinek's notion of *Ursprung,* see my essay, "Toward a Periodization of the Pure Theory of Law", in Hans Kelsen's Legal Theory. A Diachronic Point of View (fn 12 above), 11 - 47, at 30 - 3.

I speak, here, of the immediate historical origins of Kelsen's basic norm; they can be established with some confidence by appeal to the texts. The question of the philosophical underpinnings of the basic norm is, of course, far more difficult; see generally Werner Krawietz, "Grundnorm", Historisches Wörterbuch der Philosophie, vol. 3 (Basel 1974), columns 918 - 22.

40 See Alfred Verdroß, "Zum Problem der Rechtsunterworfenheit des Gesetzgebers", Juristische Blätter, 45 (1916), 471 - 3, 483 - 6, repr. in Die Wiener rechtstheoretische Schule (fn 38 above), vol. 2, 1545 - 57, and compare Kelsen, Hauptprobleme (fn 18 above), Preface to second printing (1923), p. xv, where Verdroß is credited with the distinction between the "constitution in the juridico-logical sense" and the "constitution in the sense of positive law"; the former is a surrogate for the basic norm.

41 It is significant, too, that in the only paper in which Kelsen considers Cohen's theories at any length, he at no point discusses the basic norm in a way that reflects Cohennian doctrine; see "Rechtswissenschaft und Recht" (fn 27 above), at 156, 161 - 2, 214 - 15, 231 - 3, repr. in Die Rolle des Neukantianismus (fn 27 above), at 332, 337 - 8, 390 - 1, 407 - 9. On Kelsen's treatment of Cohen in "Rechtswissenschaft und Recht" generally, see sub-section 2 of the present section, below.

42 See text at fn 34 above. A brilliant discussion, in brief compass, of Jellinek and Kelsen on the identity of state and law is Kurt Sontheimer, Politische Wissenschaft und Staatsrechtslehre (Freiburg 1963), esp. 18 - 22.

method of cognition determines the object of cognition. Thus, if Georg Jellinek[43] considers the state from the legal or juridical point of view – as he must, Kelsen thinks – then the method in question is *ex definitio* juridical and, *eo ipso,* determines a juridical object. What appears to be the state is, from the juridical point of view, the law; state and law are identical. A sociological concept of the state is not possible, Kelsen is arguing, for it is only by appeal to legal or juridical criteria that the state can be identified *qua* state.[44] Here, too, Kelsen adduces arguments that turn in no way whatever on Cohen's philosophy.

I do not mean to suggest that Kelsen's effort to acquaint himself with Cohen's philosophy is irrelevant. No doubt even a passing acquaintance with Cohen lent support to the three doctrines that Kelsen lists in the Preface to the second printing of the *Hauptprobleme*.[45] The fact remains, however, that an evaluation of these doctrines by appeal to what Kelsen actually wrote produces overwhelming textual evidence that his use of the doctrines – his adoption and application of versions of them – does not reflect any use of Cohen.

This concludes my remarks on the status of the ostensibly Cohennian doctrines that Kelsen mentions in the Preface to the second printing of his *Hauptprobleme,* the first of the three issues that I wish to consider on the question of Cohen's influence on Kelsen. The second issue turns on Kelsen's only substantive discussion of Cohen, and the third, on Kelsen's own attribution of sources other than Cohen.

My own position, briefly, on the second issue is that Kelsen's only substantive discussion of Cohen, a lengthy reply to the *enfant terrible* of the Vienna School, the brilliant Fritz Sander, offers no support for the assumption that Kelsen had a working knowledge of Cohen's philosophy. And on the third issue, my position is that if one lends credence to Kelsen's own attributions of

---

43 See references at fn 35 above.

44 In reply, one can argue that Kelsen confuses meaning with criteria of identification. Even if it is true that one must appeal to legal criteria in order to identify the state, it will not follow that "state" means the same as "law". This question remains open.

45 Mario G. Losano gets it right, or nearly right, when he says: "Cohen receives generous acknowledgement in the second printing of the *Hauptprobleme* because Kelsen did not consider him so much a source as a reinforcement and confirmation of what had already been stated in the first edition." Losano, "The Periodization of Kelsen" (fn 12 above), at 120. My only quarrel here is with the application of Losano's remark to the three doctrines that Kelsen lists in the Preface to the second printing of his *Hauptprobleme*. Kelsen, in acknowledging a debt to Cohen in the Preface to the second printing, is acknowledging a debt for what he, Kelsen, had incorporated into his theory – thanks ostensibly to Cohen – *after* the appearance of the first printing of the *Hauptprobleme,* in 1911. What is important in Losano's remark, however, deserves to be emphasized: Kelsen feels that Cohen's theory lends "reinforcement and confirmation" to positions that he, Kelsen, had adopted independently. Kelsen's remarks in the documents to which I refer at fn 18 above can be squared, I think, with this interpretation.

sources, as virtually everyone has done vis-à-vis his reference to Cohen in the Preface to the second printing of the *Hauptprobleme,* then in so far as the question is that of historical influence, one has to consider all of Kelsen's attributions of sources. And then things appear in a different light, with the representatives of the Heidelberg or "South-West" School of neo-Kantianism figuring prominently. I offer support, now, for my position on each of these issues.

2. *Kelsen's Sole Substantive Discussion of Cohen.* In his long paper, "Rechtswissenschaft und Recht" (1922),[46] the only article in which Kelsen considers Cohen's philosophy on the merits, he appears to be ambivalent, even uncertain, on the subject of Cohen. For example, with an eye to "constituting ethics transcendentally", Cohen had used as his base a *Faktum der Wissenschaft,* that is, a fact of science – here, the fact of legal science. Kelsen chooses not to pass judgment on the success of Cohen's enterprise, not generally, and not on the specific question of "constituting ethics transcendentally" either.[47] This uncharacteristic reaction of Kelsen's is neither fish nor fowl, neither an endorsement of Cohen, nor the outspoken criticism for which Kelsen was famous.

At another point in the same work, Kelsen positively endorses Fritz Sander's criticism of Cohen. An important document on the role of neo-Kantianism in the Vienna School generally, Sander's "Die transzendentale Methode der Rechtsphilosophie und der Begriff der Rechtserfahrung" (1920) considers various objections to Cohen's construction of ethics. The critique of legal science, Cohen had argued, is provided by ethics, and Sander's objection turns on the question of whether legal science can have a single unified object of cognition:

> The problem of pure cognition arises from the specification of the natural sciences; each of them – mathematics, mechanics, physics, chemistry – has as its task *(Aufgabe),* however, the unity of nature, the unity of the object of cognition, nature. ... The inevitable question arises, namely, whether those sciences whose critique is supposed to be ethics regard and can regard as their object of cognition *(Gegenstand)* a single unified object. If the *idea of nature* is the unity of the task *(die Einheit der Aufgabe)* in the natural sciences, then the *idea of humanity* should characterize the unity of the task in the social sciences *(Geisteswissenschaften).* But how [is this possible] when there are sciences that are outside the natural sciences, but whose idea has never been and cannot be that of humanity? In what sense is it claimed, then, that the ideal object of cognition for legal science is the idea of humanity? Does this claim not turn up against a background of natural law? If, as Cohen claims, legal science is the mathematics of the social sciences, then there would have to be a showing that just as mathematical judgments find their reference to existence in the mathematical natural sciences, so likewise the judgments of legal science, more than anything else, are concretely applied in the other social sciences. *Such a showing, however, cannot be*

---

[46] Kelsen, "Rechtswissenschaft und Recht" (fn 27 above).

[47] Ibid., at 128, repr. in Die Rolle des Neukantianismus (fn 27 above), 304.

made. To give just one example, there is no internal connection [of the required kind] between legal science and economics.[48]

In a word, Sander is sceptical of Cohen's view that the social sciences – among them, legal science – lend themselves to a single unified object of cognition, the idea of humanity. And Kelsen endorses Sander's criticism.[49]

Kelsen's reluctance to engage Cohen is remarkable, for Kelsen examined other thinkers' texts with notable confidence, and pursued criticism with a vengeance.[50] It would be mistaken to infer from this that Kelsen had no working knowledge of Cohen. I am only suggesting that one cannot support, by appeal to Kelsen's texts, the claim that he did have a working knowledge of Cohen.

3. *Kelsen's Attributions to Other Writers*. In the text of the *Hauptprobleme*, and alongside his acknowledgement of Cohen in the Preface to the second printing of that book, Kelsen speaks of an influence on his work stemming from the interpretation of Kant developed by Wilhelm Windelband and Georg Simmel.[51] Curiously, this reference to other major thinkers in the neo-Kantian tradition has been ignored by most commentators.[52] In a major essay of 1916, Kelsen discusses at length the Heidelberg neo-Kantians Heinrich Rickert and Emil Lask.[53] In the same essay,[54] as well as elsewhere,[55] Kelsen discusses the early work of the legal philosopher Gustav Radbruch, who was profoundly influenced by the Heidelberg neo-Kantians.[56] And in the preface to his treatise

---

[48] Fritz Sander, "Die transzendentale Methode der Rechtsphilosophie und der Begriff der Rechtserfahrung", Zeitschrift für öffentliches Recht, 1 (1920), 468 - 507, at 474 - 5 (Sander's emphasis), repr. in Die Rolle des Neukantianismus (fn 27 above), 75 - 114, at 81 - 2.

[49] This critique of Cohen had already been made, albeit in somewhat different terms, by Paul Natorp in "Recht und Sittlichkeit", Kantstudien, 18 (1913), 1 - 79, at 21 - 6.

[50] See, e.g., Kelsen, "Eine Grundlegung der Rechtssoziologie", Archiv für Sozialwissenschaft und Sozialpolitik, 39 (1915), 839 - 76, repr. in Kelsen und die Rechtssoziologen, ed. Stanley L. Paulson (Aalen 1992), with pagination of original. This paper is Kelsen's scathing critique of Eugen Ehrlich's treatise in legal sociology.

[51] Kelsen's adoption of Windelband's causal and normative points of view, and of Simmel's distinction between "is" and "ought" in the early pages of the Hauptprobleme (fn 18 above), is clear; see esp. 4 - 8, 12 - 13, 20 - 4; see also the Preface to the second printing (1923), p. vi.

[52] Renato Treves, "Il fondamento filosofico della dottrina pura del diritto di Hans Kelsen" (fn 10 above), is an important exception.

[53] Kelsen, "Die Rechtswissenschaft als Norm- oder als Kulturwissenschaft", Schmollers Jahrbuch für Gesetzgebung, Verwaltung und Volkswirtschaft im Deutschen Reiche, 40 (1916), 1181 - 239, repr. in Die Wiener rechtstheoretische Schule (fn 38 above), vol. 1, 37 - 93.

[54] See ibid., at 1225 - 39, repr. in Die Wiener rechtstheoretische Schule (fn 38 above), vol. 1, 80 - 93.

[55] See Kelsen, "Eine Grundlegung der Rechtssoziologie" (fn 50 above), at 840 - 1.

[56] See Radbruch, Grundzüge der Rechtsphilosophie (Leipzig 1914), 29 - 42 et passim. Radbruch's later work, Rechtsphilosophie (Leipzig 1932, repr. in Radbruch, Gesamt-

of 1925, the *Allgemeine Staatslehre,* where there is no mention of Cohen, Kelsen invites special attention to Carl Friedrich Gerber, Paul Laband, and Georg Jellinek as the leading figures in nineteenth-century German public law, adding that he identifies "more closely than before" with their "strictly *juridical,* that is, *politically* unbiased theory". Kelsen goes on to describe the method of this theory as having been

> determined – more or less consciously, more or less rigorously – by Kant's critique of reason: the dualism of "is" and "ought"; the substitution of transcendental categories, as the conditions of experience, for the metaphysical postulates and hypostases [of the philosophical tradition]; the transformation of absolute – because qualitative – and transsystemic antitheses, within one and the same discipline, into relative, quantitative, intra-systemic differences; the move away from the subjectivistic sphere of psychologism and into the field of logico-objective validity – these are some of the essential elements of this method. And they are the guiding principles *(Richtlinien)* that have been decisive in my work in legal theory."[57]

Kelsen's references to Windelband, Simmel, Rickert, Lask, and Radbruch, his adoption of their doctrines, his substantive discussion of their work, further, his references to the tradition in German public law theory, especially to Jellinek, and, finally, his allusion to leitmotifs in Kant's own theory of knowledge – all of these are significant as a counterthrust to his reference to Cohen.[58] Windelband, Rickert, and Lask form the core of the Heidelberg School of neo-Kantianism. Simmel, the philosopher and sociologist, and Georg Jellinek, the public law theorist, were sympathetic to Heidelberg neo-Kantianism, and influenced by it. Indeed, if one were to distinguish the single most important influence on Kelsen, Georg Jellinek would no doubt be named. And although he is best known for the extraordinary role he played in the theory of public law, Jellinek also reflects a philosophical persuasion – Heidelberg neo-Kantianism.

My conclusion is that a significant historical influence on Kelsen is not evident when one looks to Marburg, but can be found by looking to Heidelberg instead.

---

ausgabe, ed. Arthur Kaufmann, vol. 2 [Heidelberg 1993]) reflects the same influence; see esp. §§ 1 - 2, 4, et passim.

57 Kelsen, Allgemeine Staatslehre (Berlin 1925, repr. Bad Homburg v. d. Höhe 1966), p. vii; see also pp. viii - ix.

58 These references do not, of course, somehow cancel out Kelsen's reference to Cohen in the Preface to the second printing of the *Hauptprobleme;* however, they must be considered a counterbalance alongside the reference to Cohen. I underscore the point as a way of acknowledging Mario G. Losano's welcome corrective to my earlier effort; see his paper "The Periodization of Kelsen" (fn 12 above), at 120.

The Context of the Judicial Application of Norms

By Csaba Varga, Budapest

Prescriptive formality? normative rationality? mastering the actual working of the law?[1] Or, rather, characterizations of an ideal type, standing for the ambiguities of any conceptual description? No final answer can be done to perplexing questions like these and the dilemmas raised by them without the clarification of the paradigms that stand behind and define the overall frame of the workings of the law, paradigms which relate partly to the user's operation with both norms and facts,[2] and partly to the background and the genuine contexture in which any operation with norms and facts can at all realistically take place.[3] In the present paper dedicated to Professor Robert S. Summers, only some aspects of one of the conceivable contextures will be delineated.

---

[1] Cf., as magisterial contributions through the juxtaposition of which the gradually developing theory of Robert Samuel Summers have been built, his 'Two Types of Substantive Reasons: the Core of a Theory of Common-Law Justification' Cornell Law Review 63 (1978), pp. 77 - 35; Instrumentalism and American Legal Theory, Ithaca/London 1982, chapter 6; [with P. S. Atiyah] Form and Substance in Anglo-American Law A Comparative Study of Legal Reasoning, Legal Theory, and Legal Institutions, Oxford 1987, chapters 1 - 7; 'On Why Courts in Cases not Governed by Binding Law Seldom Need to Assess Closely the Relative Justificatory Force of Conflicting Substantive Reasons' in Reason in Law I, ed. Carla Faralli/Enrico Pattaro, Milano 1987, pp. 207 - 223; Interpreting Statutes A Comparative Study, ed. with D. Neil MacCormick, Aldershot/Brookfield/Hong Kong/Singapore/Sydney 1991, particularly chapters 1, 11 & 12 [Applied Legal Philosophy]; 'The Formal Character of Law' The Cambridge Law Journal 51 (1992) 2, pp. 242 - 262.

[2] Cf., as to my own attempts at theoretical explanation, Csaba Varga A Theory of the Judicial Process The Establishment of Facts, Budapest 1994 [in press], including as first versions for part chapters, 'The Judicial Establishment of Facts and Its Proceduralty' in Sprache, Performanz und Ontologie des Rechts Festschrift für Kazimierz Opałek zum 75. Geburtstag, ed. Werner Krawietz/Jerzy Wróblewski, Berlin 1993, pp. 245 - 258 and 'On Judicial Ascertainment of Facts' Ratio Juris 4 (1991) 1, pp. 61 - 71, and, as a methodological frame, 'Judicial Reproduction of the Law in an Autopoietical System?' in Technischer Imperativ und Legitimationskrise des Rechts, ed. Werner Krawietz/Antonio A. Martino/Kenneth I. Winston, Berlin 1991, pp. 305 - 313 [RECHTSTHEORIE Beiheft 11]. As to an approach similar in several respects, cf. Law, Interpretation and Reality Essays in Epistemology, Hermeneutics and Jurisprudence, ed. Patrick Nerhot, Dordrecht 1990, section 1, 'Legal aspect of "Reality"' [Law and Philosophy Library, volume 11].

[3] Cf., for a further element of the paradigm, Csaba Varga 'Law and Logic: Societal Contexture Mediated in Legal Reasoning' abstracted in Law, Justice and the State, compiled by Eyja Margét Brynjarsdóttir, Reykjavík 1993, p. 99 [IVR 16th World Congress].

1. Presuppositions

If we apply the *presuppositions of modern formal law* concerning its own operation[4] to the actual process of legal reasoning, we reach the following conclusions: *(1)* in judicial decision-making, norms – similarly to facts – constitute a given element. *Both the facts and the norms are at the judge's disposal as given:* the former from outside the laws, the latter from inside. Consequently, the judge has no other task but to *(2) establish the facts* of the case, and then to *apply the norms* at his disposal to the facts. It logically follows from the nature of this process that all this is *(3)* predominantly *theoretical* an activity. Accordingly, no significant role is played in this process (at least in average situations) by the judge's personality, his individual choice, his practical status or his commitment to values. *The judge's job is essentially cognitive as far as the facts are concerned, and logical as far as the norms are concerned.* All these factors guarantee and predict not only the objectivity and relative impersonality of the judicial process, but at the same time also *(4)* render the *conclusion necessary and inevitable.* After all, the cognitive procedure aimed at establishing the facts can have no other end result but the truth itself. And similarly: in the case of due procedure, the logical application of the norms to the facts *cannot result in anything but proper conclusions.*

In the judicial process, these presuppositions are enframed by our natural inclination to describe the processes at issue as a *deductive syllogism.* In this process, the personality who passes the judgment becomes a replaceable automate, or "verdict machine." His personality through which he participates in the process is hardly anything more or different than a context in which a given case is linked to a similarly given proposition of law,[5] this linkup inevitably leading to and producing a statutorily determined result. Consequently, the intellectual developments within the personality (or *any* individual) who passes the judgment are completely independent from *his* personality. This is nothing but sheer logic, which, according to these presuppositions, is known to assert itself in all circumstances.[6]

---

[4] Cf. Csaba Varga 'The Fact and Its Approach in Philosophy and in Law' in Law and Semiotics 3, ed. Roberta Kevelson, New York/London 1989, pp. 357 - 382, in particular para 1.

[5] "The judges of the country [...] are but mouths that utter the words of the law; [they are] inanimate creatures [...]" Montesquieu De l'esprit des lois [1748], book XI, chapter VI.

[6] "Die konkrete Rechtsfolge ergibt sich [...] syllogistisch aus dem Rechtssatz und dem konkreten Tatbestand nach der ersten aristotelischen Figur Modus I." [The given legal consequence results syllogistically from the norm-proposition and the facts constituting the case according to Modus I of Aristotle's First Form.] Lorenz Brütt Die Kunst der Rechtsanwendung Zugleich ein Beitrag zur Methodenlehre der Geisteswissenschaften, Berlin 1903, p. 39, quoted by Jerzy Wróblewski 'Legal Syllogism and Rationality of Judicial Decision', RECHTSTHEORIE 3 (1974) 1, pp. 33 - 46 at 39.

The degradation of the "legal event" into sheer syllogistic application postulates such a *naive realistic epistemology,* which considers man's conceptual world to be a *reflection of external reality,* the complexity of these concepts to be a *reflection of the structure of the reflected reality,* and the internal conceptual distinctions he makes to be the mirroring of the *discrete entities of reality.* From this it follows that this approach considers language to be the vehicle of this reflection.

Moreover, this approach views the meaning of language as a reflection of the very linguistic expression which it employs in the mirroring process. Accordingly, it is hold to have been organized in such a way that it takes pattern from the reality which it mirrors. In other words, naive realism seeks in social reality the *imprints of a tough, unchanging and unchangeable message,* just as the factors of natural existence are alleged to leave (or mediate through their notional representations) such imprints on natural reality.[7] This renders complete the evolution of law into an *independent factor.* As a result of these processes, law becomes a medium created by man, but which still remains *independent* of him. *In law, the rule of the general is enforced and becomes reality.* At the same time, law – which is hoped to get distributed among people in a blind, unbiased and egalitarian way – *brings the general to perfection in the individual in an impersonal way.*[8]

I must note that what we are talking about here is not only that modern statehood – alongside with modern formal law that has been established in conjunction with it[9] – have formed a peculiar complexity, complete with rules, institutions, positions peculiar to the social division of labor, specific practices, special skills, fundamental sets of values, and last but not least with professional training, mediating traditions, all these within the framework of a professional ideology.[10] Also, it is not just that the process of institutionalization conceptually postulates – and, through a subsequent institutional differentia-

---

[7] Cf., e.g., George Lakoff Cognitive Science And The Law [a paper presented at Yale Law School, Legal Theory Workshop, on 27 April 1989] [manuscript] 49 p.

[8] Although indirectly, this concept can be traced back to those *utopias* which consider the world the result of a unifactorial operation and, at the same time, the product of a single unrestrained operating agent. In these utopias, a fetishistically unified and homogeneous aggregate of rules manifests itself as the radiation of a single thought, and appears within a single order. In these utopias, mankind's innocence as projected into a dreamed Golden Age of yore manifests itself as a yearning for a similarly undifferentiated and automatically tendered symphony (because it shrinks back even from the need to overcome disharmony). Cf. Csaba Varga Codification as a Socio-historical Phenomenon [1979], Budapest 1991, viii + 391 p. at chapter VIII, point 3.

[9] Cf. Csaba Varga 'Moderne Staatlichkeit und modernes formales Recht' Acta Juridica Academiae Scientiarum Hungaricae 26 (1984), 1 - 2, pp. 235 - 241.

[10] This ideology is not just a kind of false consciousness, but also an ingredient of ontological nature and significance as an existentially functioning element of the given social complex. Cf. Csaba Varga The Place of Law in Lukács' World Concept, Budapest 1985, 193 p.

tion, demands to realize – that the making of the law *(law-making)* become separated from its concretization in individual cases *(law-application)*. And, as a result of this, the forms of activity covered by law-making differ from those covered by law-application.[11] From a theoretical point of view, this may well be considered the product of mere wishful thinking.

What we are talking about here is more like the circumstances – crucial in the present context – that once theory slavishly subscribes to the ideological presuppositions outlined above, it promotes law itself to be a *unifactorial phenomenon*. In other words, it renders law to be completely *immobile and static* a manifestation. By doing so, it ultimately reduces law into a kind of product that offers to be defined by its static and permanent state, and which therefore assumes a *quasi-material substance*.

What I have in mind here is not so much the inclination of the *policy-making legal positivism* to generate seemingly tautological simplifications. I do not refer here to the principle of *"das Recht ist das Recht,"* according to which the ultimate criterion of "the law" cannot be laid down independently of "the law" itself. In this context, I think more of the fundamental tenet of the *ideological legal positivism,* which ultimately eliminates the freedom and alternativity of scholarly thought. This approach is suitable for presenting the most diverse wishes as if they were facts. For this end, it employs conceptualization in a theoretical disguise.

For example, one such tenet of ideological legal positivism declares that the *ius is but a mass of such enacts which have been promulgated as lex*. Accordingly, law is but the cover for anything which *specific organs through specific procedures have produced as laws*. This, of course, is one possible definition for law. However, if we accept this as a starting point in theory, we are bound to also accept that the creation and emergence of laws cannot be separated (no matter how exactly) and cannot differ from the normative definition of law. Now if we agree that the law is but the mass of such phenomena which become associated with the law through their specific genesis, we cannot indeed conceive law as anything else but a static, factual and even material substance, which does no motion by itself, but can be made to move from the outside only. This means that law is made to be a *unitary phenomenon, identical with itself,* and also *unchanged and unchangeable* from the very beginning. In this interpretation, law is but an instrument, which gets applied in various situations to various situations.

The underlying problem as formulated by Kelsen[12] is especially intriguing because if we describe the law as unchanged and unchangeable – in which all

[11] Cf. Peter Sack 'Law and the Social Sciences' The Academy Law Review 11 (1987), pp. 133 - 147, in particular at 138 - 141.

[12] Cf. Csaba Varga 'Hans Kelsens Rechtsanwendungslehre: Entwicklung, Mehrdeutigkeiten, offene Probleme, Perspektiven' Archiv für Rechts- und Sozialphilosophie LXXVI (1990), pp. 348 - 366.

forms of dynamism are bound to be illusory only and can only be considered the mere reprojections of applications extraneous to the law –, well, in such a case the ideological image inherent in the problem (whose paradoxes and contradictions we have to gradually identify) is bound to evolve into the methodologically consequential conclusion according to which the law – contrary to what was said above – is incomplete, and is theoretically as well as practically impossible to complete. After all, at this stage law itself becomes the product of a kind of *intellectual reconstruction.* It looks as if it were seen from the perspective of the consequential processes, built up from the retrospective view of further construction. In other, and perhaps simpler, words: the perception of law as an immanent system, in which *the logical connections of the legal enactments define themselves as law,* leads us to a conception according to which *the law itself is process-like* (that is, built from the separate phases of the endless flow of consecutive legal acts). According to this concept, *the last actual procedural step marks out the boundaries of the law* and, simultaneously, it also determines the probable coherence and internal structure of the laws.

Let me refer here to a statement, which qualifies as a basic tenet of modern legal positivism: "Codified law [...] is meant to provide a basis for judgment, but it is not meant to be judged. There is nothing superior to law [...] and nothing can be more rational or just than the rationality and justness of the law."[13] In fact, the belief that the *lex* is exclusive and that it is vested with the characteristics of the *ius,* has been challenged by a number of schools since the late 19th century. (The schools in question included theoretical and practical ones alike. Suffice it to recall Magnaud's distinction of "le bon juge," the free-law movement, the post-World War Two revival of the doctrine of natural law, or the contemporary German or American interpretations of the Constitution.) At the same time, it was only two to three decades ago when the first theoretical refutations appeared of the preconception that law has only the officially recognized enactments as its ingredients, and that the enacted norm-statements can themselves lead to conclusions on their application. Of course, here I left out of considerations the few scattered precursors to these refutations (such as the early realization of the contestability of the decisive role of the judicial logic,[14] or Carl Schmitt's criticism of democracy based on the concept of "concrete order").[15]

[13] Mourlon Répétitions écrites sur le Code civil contenant l'exposé des principes généraux, leurs motifs et la solution des questions théoriques, 1 - 2, Paris 1864, viii + 903, viii + 901 p., as quoted by Léon Husson Nouvelles études sur la pensée juridique, Paris 1974, 521 p. [Collection "Philosophie du Droit" 14] at p. 183.

[14] M. Polydore Fabreguettes La logique judiciaire et l'art du juger, Paris 1914, 570 p. at 482 – quoted by Wróblewski, p. 36 – believes that the reference to judicial syllogism is but a subsequent rationalization.

[15] Carl Schmitt's basic tenet – Über die drei Arten des rechtswissenschaftlichen Denkens (Hamburg: Hanseatische Verl. Anst. 1934) 67 p. [Schriften der Akademie für

Of these refutations, Chaïm Perelman's so-called "new rhetorics"[16] was the most far-reaching. Having followed a methodologically well-mapped path, Perelman managed to prove that *(a)* those inferences which are essential in the decision-making process are in fact *not logical,* and by virtue of a formal necessity they are *not reconstructible* either; and that *(b)* those inferences which are essential – i.e., the premises of the decision that can be reconstrued from reasoning – cannot be described as rules of a universal application, since they are always *tied to concrete situations in the judicial process.* And these situations, as we know, can never be separated from the *auditorium* that participates in the process.

Perelman has broken new ground with his theory. His works have fertilized all the thinkers who succeeded him. Remarkably, Perelman has never abandoned the relatively narrow path of his initial interest, namely the methodological reconstruction of the judge's reasoning process. In fact, he was not in search of any comprehensive socio-theoretical explanation, and he also avoided other recent methodological traditions (hermeneutics, semantics, semiotics). The climax of his œuvre has thus occurred in the synthesis of that very methodologically renewed and high-level approach whose denial had once served as his own starting point. This synthesis is known as *Legal Logic.*[17]

What we have identified as ideological legal positivism manifested itself most markedly in the continental European schools of our age. It is therefore no accident that the need for a breakthrough was the strongest there. The *Common Law* traditions were perhaps not different theoretically, but they were definitely more flexible. For example, they were *averse to all doctrinaire solutions,* and promoted the stronger presence of pragmatic approach, common sense and practicalness in law. And their pattern of thought, which was far removed from the axiomatic rigor of deductive legal syllogism, and which reckoned on the existence of conflicting alternatives in judicial solutions, could also call for a theoretical renewal only in ways different from Continental traditions.

In the Common Law world, the breakthrough came with the question *"Is law a system of rules?"*[18] However, as the still continuing debates reveal, the radical criticism inherent in Dworkin's approach aimed to surpass positivism

Deutsches Recht] – holds that *"concrete order"* is the only realistic concept. But because it is concrete, it can be the product only and exclusively of men, and *not* of the supremacy of the law.

[16] Ch[aïm] Perelman & L[ucie] Olbrechts-Tyteca La nouvelle rhétorique Traité de l'argumentation, I - II, Paris 1958, 734 p.

[17] Ch[aïm] Perelman Logique juridique Nouvelle rhétorique, Paris 1976, 193 p. [Méthodes du Droit].

[18] Ronald M. Dworkin 'Is Law a System of Rules?' [reprinted from 'The Model of Rules' University of Chicago Law Review 35 (1967) 14] in The Philosophy of Law ed. R. M. Dworkin, Oxford 1974, pp. 38 - 65 [Oxford Readings in Philosophy].

primarily from within. Accordingly, while in the light of the theoretical reconstruction of judicial reasoning he pointed to the internal contradictions in the traditions of the English-typed rule-positivism (from Austin to Hart) and to its ensuing inadequacies, he nevertheless failed to touch the very spirit of these traditions. And although the contemporary upshots of these traditions go far beyond the original points of controversy, and point toward the emergence of a new type of argumentative theory and reasoning practice and tradition (along with other kinds of theoretical experience), they do not affect those very problems which concern us in the present study. After all, their aim is not to reconstruct actual processes and then to reconsider the nature of law on that ground. Instead, upon the acceptance in a given social context of certain social values as fundamental values, they want to make proposals concerning the conditions of a rational discourse.

And yet, in perhaps the most paradoxical development (which also gives evidence of the embeddedness of the presuppositions above in our legal culture), the validity of the presuppositions at issue was confirmed (albeit indirectly) precisely by that trend which (although from legal-political considerations) was the loudest in demanding the surpassing of these presuppositions. The trend I have in mind is the *social policy* one of American legal sociology. This trend strives to surpass the legal arrangements that enforce themselves in the present through a clear-cut change of legal formations – by depicting past, present and future in historical typologies (in which ideology and the underlying institutional frames serve the typological set-up in an inseparable unity)[19] – and, simultaneously, they implicitly reveal that the ideological goals at issue are realistic, i.e., they are backed by reality. They do not even ponder over the fact that the functioning of any system is as a matter of course the function of the system's components. In other words, if we change any of these, the system itself is also bound to change.

Let me remind the reader here that all the previous shakings of or attempts to shake the modern formal legal establishment (the emerging ethos of "le bon juge," the free-law movement, the dilution of the formal system of law with so-called general clauses, administration of justice with reference to the "nature of the thing," or the stealing back into the legal system of natural legal reasoning as a source of law) equally had their roots in the criticism or rejection of the ideological presuppositions of law. Only the temporary substitution of these could lead to the acceptance of such ethoses of the administration of justice, or of such situations, which held out the promise of some kind of alternatives.

---

[19] Cf., e.g., Roberto Mangabeira Unger Law in Modern Society Toward a Criticism of Social Theory, New York 1977, ix + 309 p. at chapter II and Philippe Nonet & Philip Selznick Law and Society in Transition Toward Responsive Law, New York etc. 1978, vi + 122 p. In theoretical review, see Csaba Varga 'Átalakulóban a jog? [Law in Transformation?]' Állam- és Jogtudomány XXIII (1980) 4, pp. 670 - 680.

2. Context

The ideal functioning of the law as described above postulates the raising of further presuppositions regarding the nature of both law itself and the activities that can be performed through it. More specifically, law is usually seen as a *system with definite make-up and clear-cut structure* which, because of its orderly or systemic nature, lends itself to be applied any time and to any case. In other words, law is organized in a way which provides propositions for both simple and complex situations in life. Through its conceptual structure, law enables its users to apply it to any kind of situation. It provides a basis for such conclusions to be drawn through logical inference which the legal profession (sanctioned by society) believes it contains. Through this, law guarantees with a conceptual directness and internal necessity that the result is *objective, impersonal and last but not least foreseeable.*

Theoretical research, however, does not substantiate the veracity of the presuppositions of this kind.

2.1 Actualization in concrete meaning

How do we define law when we approach it as a subject of cognition? What is our definition for law when we comment on an argument that law provides a basis and at the same time sets the limits? After all, it seems self-evident that we cannot take law in our hands as if it were an object in our natural environment, and we cannot observe it as we do, say, the blue skies. If we gaze on our variegated world, we find that law is not possible to create out of its elements even through such an analysis which we use to detect the presence of oxygen in the atmosphere. The more questions we ask, the closer we get to the perplexing realization that law should not be sought there, that we should not expect law to be simply a part of our environment. Law somehow exists *in me, in us.* In other words, the law *originates from and from within me, from and from within us, it has eventually been alienated from within all of us,* despite the fact that we believe it to be extraneous and alien to us.

"Every *law* or *rule* (taken with the largest signification which can be given to the term *properly*) is a *command.*"[20] Well, at first glance, this quasi-classical statement may appear fully acceptable. But once the above doubts take effect on us, we are bound to ask the question: how should we construe "command" and the act of commanding, and what meaning should we attach to the statement that its result appears as a "rule"? Should we identify "command" and "rule" with whatever we objectify in or through them? Should we identify them in the way they are delivered, or perhaps in the way they appear in con-

[20] John Austin Lectures on Jurisprudence Or the Philosophy of Positive Law, London 1861, p. 88.

text? Or should we perhaps consider "command" or "rule" simply an aggregate of symbols?

The more questions we ask, the more obvious it becomes that there is no potential *definiens* that could properly define or explain the *definiendum* in an unambiguous way. We cannot attach a definition to law without including in it our personal and collective relationship to it. What does that mean if, for example, I give this answer: the only consideration that specifies any of the potential definitions of "command" and "rule" is that they are characteristically normative? But let's ask further questions: is law a text? If yes, is this text characteristically normative? What differentiates it from other texts? Is this normativity a result of the condition that, say, the law is promulgated first in a serial that has the words "Official Gazette" or "Journal officiel" as its title?

The rejection of the above arguments amounts to the admission that we have become bogged. However, if we subscribe to these arguments, we find ourselves confronted with yet another question: how does this difference become manifest (if it becomes manifest at all) if the text is not promulgated under such a heading for the first time? What difference does it make for the text if I make a copy of it first, and then rely on it as a law? What happens to the differences if I subsequently promulgate a differing text and describe it as a replacement for the original?

Normativity, as well as the peculiar quality that it creates, are thus associated with *our relationship to them,* with the role they play in the practices of society, and with the purposes they serve. "The essence of the norm is not that it is a rule for judgment, but that it must be such a rule for judgment which is conceived as an approving or disapproving verdict during the rendition of a *judgment,*" *Kelsen* said in his first major work.[21] Consequently, whatever our approach may be to the criterion – we can identify it either with the act of derivative commanding (this is the so-called *expressivist* concept) or with its conceptual manifestation (this is the so-called *hyletic* concept)[22] –, we are bound to find that law differs from all the other (for us mute) phenomena and can thus address us, because the law is *addressed to us, and has a meaning and message which we accept.*

In other words, what we have identified as a norm and defined as the framework of legal reasoning is *in itself but an abstract concept.* It cannot provide a foundation for more detailed analyses. On the level of abstraction where law is identified as a norm, in a non-metaphoric usage or sense we cannot even say that we "apply" the "norm". After all, abstract concepts cannot be "applied," or more specifically, an abstract concept has no applicable ele-

---

[21] Hans Kelsen Hauptprobleme der Staatsrechtslehre entwickelt aus der Lehre vom Rechtssatze, Tübingen 1911, xxvii + 709 p. at 17.

[22] E[ugenio] Bulygin 'Norms and Logic (Kelsen and Weinberger on the Ontology of Norms)' Law and Philosophy 4 (1985) 2.

ment. The declaration of a general-abstract norm *can at most be treated as one of the elements of a rather general logical action.* Accordingly, I can use it, say, as a starting point in my quest for individual norms. And of course there is nothing to prevent me from using it as an argument in any kind of reasoning. But what I believe to be its "application" – i.e., the attempt to establish its message as reflected to any concrete individual situation – is prevented by its very general nature.

At the same time, recent research appears to prove that meaning cannot be identified as a self-contained, satisfactory and clear field of reference, just as concept is not a closed field with clear-cut boundaries. Only naive realism can postulate a conceptual world which would directly correspond to a kind of external reality, which could directly reflect the movements, articulations and formations that occur in external reality, or which would in itself lead us to logically inevitable conclusions. Similarly, the remnants of naive realism manifest themselves in all those conceptual representations and logically treated conceptions of the world, according to which the meaning they offer may appear within the framework of a previously defined set of unambiguous contents and scope.

Meaning, as we know, is *concrete* by definition. Even if we conceive it as generic, we can only do that through the generalization of the individual characteristic of a concrete manifestation. Other research has proved that answers to the questions of what becomes typical for us and what can represent the conceptually created generic in a specific and concrete way, are *conditional primarily on human experience.* For this reason, it changes by historical period, social circumstances and our preferences of cultural values. Consequently, we do not need to answer the questions of whether the difference would be manifest in the conceptually circumscribable contents and scope, and if so, what would this difference be like – well, irrespective of the answers the word 'chair' would still have different connotations in a modern European society, and in a traditional neighborhood in Africa. Similarly, the connotations of the words 'color' and 'white' would be different in an equatorial area than in an Arctic community. "A term like 'religion' gets its meaning through being applied to certain 'paradigm' cases like Roman Catholicism; it is then extended to other cases that do not differ from the paradigm in too many respects. But it is impossible to say exactly how many respects are too many."[23].

Furthermore, and also following from what has been said above, meaning is not a kind of substance that is peculiar to the aggregate of signs itself, or which is inherent in the written text or in any other vehicle for the sign. The meaning

---

[23] William P. Alston Philosophy of Language, Englewood Cliffs/New Jersey 1964, xiii + 113 p. [Prentice-Hall Foundations of Philosophy Series] at 89.

which we eventually gain *can only be the product of a communication process.* In other words, it is the result of our efforts to decipher a message communicated to us by someone else. "[T]he meaning of a text or utterance is inferring what a writer or speaker *was or is doing* with language and not what some linguistic object essentially was or is."[24] Consequently, meaning is socially conditioned. Furthermore, it is also dependent on linguistic and communicative coherence. And finally, it is also determined by our value-choices.

The development and formation – or, more specifically, determination – of meaning can be construed only and exclusively within the context of social communication, as an element of the historical process of communication. Meaning is *process-like* by definition. And within this process, meaning appears as a kind of "continuant with changing states or contents."[25] All those factors which can potentially appear as elements of meaning are but the products of earlier processes. And all those elements of meaning which are subjective or contingent in any concrete situation are themselves the results of previous subjective or contingent choices. "[T]he contexts, while they are productive of interpretation, are also the products of interpretation."[26]

Accordingly, the process of the determination of meaning is in every respect rooted in the past, in the retention in human memory of the experiences of the past, and in the continuous and permanent application of these memories to present situations.

Let me give an example: *categorization* and *ideation* – even though they may seem to be the end-results of cognition, i.e., the products of a highly developed and abstract intellectual activity – may on a given level become exclusive and determinative themselves. Consequently, they function as switch-levers even in the seemingly elementary act of cognition. "What can be seen will be a function of the categories of vision that already inform perception, and those categories will be social and conventional [...]. [N]eutral vocabulary [...] in terms of angles, movements, tendons and joints [...] would itself be possible only under a *theory* of movement, ligatures, etc., and therefore would be descriptive only of what the theory (that is, the interpretation) prestipulates as available for description."[27]

Those various models – primarily *metaphors* and *metonyms* – which enable man to construct diverse linguistic and conceptual schemes, appear as *cognitive* (and quasi-cognitive) *models* through their interaction with reality. These

---

24 Gerald Graff "Keep off the Grass," "Drop Dead," and Other Indeterminacies: A Response to Sanford' Texas Law Review 60 (1982) 3, pp. 405 - 413 at 400.

25 L. Jonathan Cohen The Diversity of Meaning, London 1962, xi + 340 p. at 268.

26 Stanley Fish Doing What Comes Naturally Change, Rhetoric & the Practice of Theory in Literary and Legal Studies, Durham, N.C./London 1989, x + 613 p. [Post-contemporary Interventions] at 53.

27 Ibid., p. 82.

cognitive models are *idealized.*[28] Quite often they appear as cultural phenomena which *mould social experience into normative forms.*[29] (For example, if I utter the word 'mother,' the semantic space is filled not only with the biological and social functions of the conception of the fetus as a reproduced human being, its birth, nursing and raising. As a function of all these, and through their context, all those backgrounds, divisions of work and roles, and biological and later purely socially enabled surpluses appear simultaneously, which our culture and intellectual development have created. Accordingly, the word also carries the notions of patriarchy that replaced matriarchy, grand motherhood, legal motherhood, adoptive motherhood, substitute and hired motherhood, genetic motherhood, and so on.)

All these, however, do not render language a mere requisite. As a result, language will not become the repository or mere residuum of bygone facts and inherited situations only. After all, every single element, reference and association of language is tied to concrete situations, that is, it is *situational.* Through this, language is always and fully shaped by the present. All those historical memories or experiences of the past which language retains in the collective or individual memory, can assume a role *only through selection and revival by the present, only through the filter of the present, and only in a present context.*

Consequently, there is an inextricable interrelationship between what has been and what will emerge. "[The] line between the making and the made is never clear."[30] Each and every element of language is created, defined, adopted as linguistic element or identified as the building block of some configuration in the course of speech or writing, i.e., while the act of communication.[31] From this it follows that *language is not a self-contained entity.* Through theoretical terms, language can hardly be described as "an abstract formal sys-

---

[28] "*[Idealized cognitive models]* are like [...] 'folk theories' by which humans in a given culture organize the diverse inputs of daily life into meaningful *Gestalts* that relate that which is 'relevant' and ignore that which is not." Steven L. Winter 'The Cognitive Dimension of the Agon Between Legal Power and Narrative Meaning' in [Michigan Law School Symposium on Story-Telling 1988] [manuscript] 70 p. at 11.

[29] Cf., primarily, George Lakoff Women, Fire, and Dangerous Things What Categories Reveal about the Mind, Chicago/London 1987, xvii + 614 p., as well as Winter, pp. 54 - 55.

[30] James Boyd White 'Thinking About Our Language' The Yale Law Journal 96 (1987), pp. 1960 - 1983 at 1964.

[31] To confer a *meaning?* "Indeed, 'confer' is exactly the wrong word because it implies a two-stage procedure in which a reader or hearer first scrutinizes an utterance and *then* gives it a meaning. [...] [O]ne hears an utterance within, and not as preliminary to determining, a knowledge of its purposes and concerns, and [...] to so hear it is already to have assigned it a shape and given it a meaning. In other words, the problem of how meaning is determined is only a problem if there is a point at which its determination has not yet been made, and I am saying that there is no such point." Stanley Fish Is There a Text in This Class? The Authority of Interpretive Communities, Cambridge, Mass./London 1980, p. 310.

tem which, in John Searle's words, is only used incidentally for purposes of human communication."[32] This is why we cannot speak about language in general terms, and we cannot treat it as independent of its actual use. We cannot ignore the past or present factors of the use of language, and we cannot disregard either the events and memories associated with it, the possibility of repetition, etc.[33]

If our aim is to compile a comprehensive theoretical description, and within that a so-called analytic deconstruction, we cannot but establish that there is no kind of external limitation for us to refer to, which we could refer as an obstacle to human practices. On the level of society and in the last analysis, *human practices can be delimited by human practices only.* In absence of any kind of external compelling authority, *only we ourselves can discipline, influence or control our own practices.*

2.2 Linguistic undefinedness

The realization that the qualities which are identified as linguistic elements exist only in an actualized form in the concrete use of language, and that at best they can be but the products of abstract generalizations based on the observation of the coherence in the use of language, obviously makes itself manifest also in our ability to use language as a vehicle for definitions. More specifically, if meaning is but a kind of continuum and at the same time one of the concrete-specific aspects of the actual use of language, then *linguistic definition has to remain relative.* It will be hardly more or other than *definition by means of the undefined.*

What specifically is the problem here? Our dilemma is rooted in our inability to determine whether certain denotations or objects are included in, or excluded from, the coverage of linguistic meaning.[34] In other words, there are situations in which language does not give us clues to decide whether a linguistic term is applicable or not.[35] This means that linguistic definition is by defini-

---

[32] Fish (1980), p. 106; similarly James Boyd White 'Law and Literature: No Manifesto' Mercer Law Review 39 (1988), pp. 739 et seq., in particular at 750 - 751.

[33] The concreteness of being is only an ontological statement here. It is therefore not a question of transcendental logical presuppositions, like, e.g., the neo-Kantian methodological question that queries the qualities the objects must exhibit in order to make their scientific analysis possible. The simultaneous parallelism of the statements at *Saussure* and *Kelsen* are analysed by Peter Goodrich 'Law and Language: An Historical and Critical Introduction' Journal of Law & Society II (1984) 2, pp. 173 - 206 at 179 - 180.

[34] Willard Van Orman Quine Word and Object, Harvard and New York/London 1960, xv + 294 p. at 126.

[35] Paul Edwards The Logic of Moral Discourse (Glencoe, Ill.: The Free Press 1955) 248 p. at 150 - 151; William P. Alston Philosophy of Language, Englewood Cliffs, New Jersey 1964, xiii + 113 p. [Prentice-Hall Foundations of Philosophy Series] at 84.

tion characterized by a permanent field of undefinedness *[Unbestimmtheitszone]*.[36] In order for us to see clearly on this point, it must be emphasized that our main question here is not whether there could be, or are, deficiencies or obstacles in language. After all, we must be aware of the fact that the breakthrough of modern linguistic philosophy, which has shaken the philosophy of science and the sciences at the beginning of our age, occurred with the realization that the puzzling facts in question – namely that the definitions in our everyday life are but definitions by way of the undefined – are not the results of occasional deficiencies or the improper use of language, but fundamental elements of linguistic mediation, prime characteristics of linguistic definition.

According to a definition which has become classical by now, "[A] proposition is vague when there are possible states of things concerning which it is intrinsically uncertain whether, had they been contemplated by the speaker, he would have regarded them as excluded or allowed by the proposition."[37] The point is that *there are extreme cases,* and that *it is not possible to choose from them.*[38] That a concept is not congruent with anything else but itself has been known practically since the dawn of linguistic philosophy, as the basic philosophy of science tenet of the limited (i. e., culture-mediated) cognizability and describability of reality. Of course, this means only that *describability is limited theoretically.* At the same time, however, it also means the *blurring to a certain extent of the dividing line between the exclusive duality of truth and falseness,* and thereby the relativity of this division.[39] And as we know, each concept has a measure of indefiniteness in it. This sometimes applies to mathematical concepts as well.[40]

Furthermore, indefiniteness and undefinedness do not only exist perforce, but they are also theoretically impossible to eliminate. In other words, both *indefiniteness* and *undefinedness* are fundamental structural characteristics of the language. These characteristics manifest themselves in the general effect of the way language functions, and simultaneously also in each element, aspect

---

[36] Cf. Richard Von Mises Kleines Lehrbuch des Positivismus Einführung in die empiristische Wissenschaftsauffassung, The Hague 1939, xii + 967 p. [Library of Unified Science, vol. 1] at 23 - 25.

[37] C. S. Peirce 'Vague' in Baldwin's Dictionary of Philosophy and Psychology 2, London 1902, p. 748, quoted by Max Black Language and Philosophy Studies in Method, Ithaca/London 1949, p. 30 and Claudio Luzzati 'Discretion and "Indeterminacy" in Kelsen's Theory of Legal Interpretation' in Hans Kelsen's Legal Theory A Diachronic Point of View, ed. Letizia Gianformaggio, Torino 1990, pp. 123 - 137 [Analisi e Diritto 2] at 126.

[38] Black, p. 30.

[39] Bertrand Russell 'Vagueness' Australasian Journal of Philosophy 1 (1923), pp. 84 - 85.

[40] Charles Sanders Peirce Collected Papers I: Principles of Philosophy, ed. Charles Hartshorne/Paul Weiss, Cambridge 1931, xvi + 393 p. at 6.496; quoted by L. Jonathan Cohen The Diversity of Meaning, London 1962, xi + 340 p. at 266.

and relationship in linguistic usage. This is why "by removing the first, we have made visible other vaguenesses that were there all along – even if we could decide just which combination of conditions was necessary and sufficient for the application of the term [...], the terms in which these conditions are stated are themselves more or less vague – the removal of all vagueness from a given term is an unrealistic goal; the most we can hope to do is to approach it asymptotically."[41]

From all this it follows that the categories (as well as the internal structures) of *perception and meaning enable us, as a matter of course, to define our relationship to them only gradually*. This means that the veracity of any such statement that contains categorization can (at best) be gradual only.[42]

Underlying all this is our age-old dilemma concerning the basic understanding (emergence, criteria, role, and function) of the concepts. The school, which we have identified above as *naive realism,* considered the concepts the intellectual representation of the discrete – i.e., separately and individually existing – elements of reality. According to it, the concepts are *patterned on the structure of reality* and, as a result of this, their *criteria are clear and unambiguous*. Since they correspond to reality, they also represent a context which enables them to objectively describe reality.

However, the expectation that the concepts themselves should be discrete and objectively separated entities with clear-cut dividing lines and unambiguous boundaries, and that in their capacity as representation of reality they should simultaneously be neutral to the values, objective and also realistic – well, such an expectation can result only and exclusively from the presupposition outlined above. Now the problem is that none of these traditions is supported either by formal-logical reconstruction completed within the sphere of modern philosophy of science, or by the numerous linguistic, psychological, sociological or historical analyses made by linguistic philosophers, experts of cognitive sciences, the sociology of knowledge and other relevant branches of the humanities.[43] On the other hand, those aspects which have been reasserted by today's scholarship do not run counter to such a conclusion. In

---

41 Alston, p. 91. From a purely semantic point of view, this is the same as what Friedrich Waismann 'Verifiability' in Essays on Logic and Language ed. Antony Flew, Oxford 1951, pp. 117 - 144, in his pragmatic approach, established as the paradox of the *open texture*. Cf. Varga (1992), pp. 100 and 166. Consequently, continuing with the original reasoning, "when we form a concept, we only have certain kinds of situations in mind; as a result, the concept is armed only against certain contingencies. [...] There will always be an indefinite number of other conceivable cases with respect to which the concept is still not delimited." Alston, p. 94.

42 Eleanor Rosch Heider On the Internal Structure of Perceptual and Semantic Categories [manuscript], Berkeley 1971, quoted by George Lakoff 'Hedges: A Study in Meaning Criteria and the Logic of Fuzzy Concepts' Journal of Philosophical Logic 2 (1973), pp. 458 - 508 at 491.

43 Cf. Lakoff (1989), pp. 2 - 4.

other words, what we have here is not a manifestation of subjectivism. It is not discretion or arbitrariness. It is not the acceptance of a kind of solipsism that eventually disowns cognition and the ability to cognize. Instead, it is an intermediate stance, which simultaneously rejects both extremes. It is thanks to such a realism that it can make cognition conditional on social practices (i. e., human practices, orientations towards needs, social contextures, cultural presuppositions), as, at the same time, also embedded in the same practices.

Seen from this angle, it is a crucial realization that uses of the language – and also the formation of concepts – have their roots in human necessities, that is, in the ideation of these necessities and in the efforts aimed at satisfying these necessities. The evolution of the use of language, and of the individual choices made, can be explained only in this very context.[44] At the same time, the reality to which it refers is itself impossible to gaplessly conceptualize. For *reality is such a totality of endless relationships that theoretically precludes all forms of conceptually separated and clear-cut structures to fully describe them in depth.* Furthermore, it also precludes all such exclusive or gradual processes which are marked by conceptual conclusions on the succession of the stages of its process-like being. In other words, the unlimitable complexity of both its references and potential configurations in any given situation prevents us from realistically reflecting anything in our conceptual world (except, of course, temporary and single aspects of it). All that we can do is to simplify our approaches to our finite goals.[45]

This is why linguistic philosophy draws a clear-cut distinction between linguistic undefinedness as discussed above, conceptual generalizations, as well as conceptual ambiguities. From a language philosophy point of view, *conceptual ambiguity* belongs to the realm of phonetics. Here the question is whether the same form (sign, expression etc.) can or does convey alternative meanings, or cover or stand for more than one concept. *Conceptual generalization,* on the other hand, concerns the scope or volume of the concept. And the same

[44] Cohen, p. 268; Black, p. 31. "Every common noun, every concept is essentially merely an affective grouping. In a plurality of objects, differing from the point of view of perception even very widely from one another, we discover the same capacity to satisfy some given affectivity, some given need or desire of ours, and through this capacity we reduce this very plurality to a unity." Eugenio Rigano Psychology of Reasoning (New York 1923), p. 109, quoted by Black, ibidem. Approaching the issue differently: if we ignore the peculiar human interests associated with the objects, we have to reach a paradoxical conclusion, like for example that – to quote *Wittgenstein* – in games there is nothing in common except for the fact that the games are all games. In other words: in principle there is no need for two members of the same family to have similar qualities in order to belong to the same family and to exhibit similar facial features. Renford Bambrough 'Universals and Family Resemblances' in Proceedings of the Aristotelian Society New Series, vol. LXI (London: Harrison 1961), pp. 207 - 222 at 208 - 218.

[45] "The inexhaustible concreteness of particulars is just as much part of the indefinite changeability of concepts, and the non-existence of any single norm-setting or ideal language, as is the open texture of descriptive terms." Cohen, p. 275.

applies to *linguistic undefinedness* as well. But while conceptual generalization refers to one potential feature of the scope of the concept (i.e., its general state), linguistic undefinedness signifies a structural aspect of the scope of the concept (i.e., the undefined and undefinable nature of its boundaries).[46]

The duality described above – i.e., the conditionality on man's interests and the relative undefinedness – accounts for the fact that *there is no such conceptualization which, when confronted with reality, could assume a kind of exclusive position.* When confronted with reality, concept and the act of conceptualization become powerless. From all this it follows that however logically correct or otherwise convincing a formula may be, we cannot accept it as the only one probable or verifiable. And all that has been said so far equally applies to the individual components of the conceptual world, and to the operations carried out with them. *There is therefore no such point where our given formula could become simultaneously necessary and exclusive.*[47]

It remains a fact beyond dispute that in real life each human step can only be temporary, transitional and experimental, and can become or seen as definitive, final and perfect only through – and because of – man's faith, determination and vocation. Through this and to an extent involuntarily, we also elevate the routine gesture of acceptance from the eternal temporary level which beautifies and confirms human qualities, into the autonomous world of absolute perfection.[48] In short, the mere fact that our activities are inevitably imperfect does not necessarily render us unpractical. Although in principle all our conclusions are right concerning the limited nature of truth, the openness of contextures and the impossibility of their closure, we still have to admit that language – seen as it is practiced and considering the aim for which we use it – is reliable in its entirety.

This in turn means that from a practical point of view, our reservations outlined above do not make much sense. Or more precisely, they either make sense in their entirety, or they do not make sense in their entirety. After all, the elements discussed above tend to crop up anywhere, and at any moment – and so they may as well accompany our attempt at a formal reconstruction. They may also come up in practical contexts, though only exceptionally, like

---

[46] Black, p. 29.

[47] "Under no circumstances can we be compelled to choose from among the competing systems of the genuine classification of various objects in the sense that any of them – and for whatever purpose – should be accepted as *the* only chance for classification. The potential classification of objects are limitless." Bambrough, p. 221.

[48] We are now about to prove how weak this ideological manifestation is – contrary to the expectations generated by itself and suggested through ideologies. After all, "while we struggle for coherence in our expression, this coherence will always be tentative, always incomplete, for all that we say, all that we are, is in part a function of the context in which we live, always imperfectly perceived and always changing." White (1987), p. 1981.

for example when the question concerns an extreme situation. Since these extreme situations are mostly typical from a social point of view, and notwithstanding that in theory it is not possible to preclude the element of obscurity, the theoretical uncertainties can in most cases be traced back to practical certainties. The very same pattern applies to truth as well. After all, in the last analysis, the criteria for the concept of truth used for qualifying the descriptive statements are determined by the very same practice. Consequently, the standard of truth applicable to human practice (primarily in average cases) is generally reliable (notwithstanding the fact that man's potential to establish truth remains limited and conditional on his prevailing social presuppositions).[49]

Indicative of the decisive extent to which language is determined by practice and to which it serves to satisfy human needs is the fact that all questions and criteria relevant to the language make sense and have justification only and exclusively *within their own circle* – that is, *in the light of linguistic conventionality*. In other words, while all those doubts and limitations inherent in language which are laid down by linguistic philosophy are in principle valid to all forms of linguistic usage, they appear in practice only in those specific – in particular, scientific (mathematical, logical, etc.) – languages and usage which aim for the utmost accuracy and which take pattern from the ideal language of formal symbols. These doubts and limitations are normally not raised whilst the routine, everyday use of language. After all, a claim for distinct conceptual boundaries there would indeed be artificial, transcending practical expectations. We, players of everyday life games, are all aware that the everyday formation of concepts and their application to average situations are adjusted to average acts of communication, and "indeed the demand to perform this operation is felt to be inappropriate *in principle*."[50]

---

[49] Cohen, pp. 271 - 273. "The description is judged by the relevant standards of completeness operative at the time, not by some metaphysical standard of absolute completeness that would make all finitely long descriptions incomplete and thus put complete descriptions beyond the reach of mortal beings." Ibid., p. 274.

[50] Black, p. 32.

The Significance of History for Legal Philosophy and Positive Law*

By Dieter Wyduckel, Dresden

I.

Despite increasing attention to historical issues vis-à-vis the law,[1] the question of the role of history in legal philosophy and the positive law remains open. Doubts arise in legal circles on whether, for example, historical arguments are to be qualified as "merely" historical, and whether history is neglected for being "only" or "solely" history. In this context the historical dimension suddenly gets an antiquarian, even antiquated character. Moreover, history seems to be considered as a matter of individual and contingent facts of the past, opposed to a kind of timeless realm of rules presumed to be particular to law and jurisprudence.

This may show us that until now the position of history in legal thought has not been given sufficient attention. Generally, and seen from the standpoint of an ideal classification, one can distinguish three different ways in which history

* This paper is a slightly modified version of my German contribution delivered at the XVth World Congress of the International Association for the Philosophy of Law and Social Philosophy, in 1991, in Göttingen and published under the title: "Zur Bedeutung der historischen Dimension in der Rechts- und Sozialphilosophie", in: Archives for Philosophy of Law and Social Philosophy, Beiheft 44, Stuttgart, pp. 394 - 410. I would like to thank Franz Steiner Verlag, Stuttgart, for the kindly granting permission to publish a version of the paper in English. I dedicate this contribution, with special pleasure, to my colleague Bob Summers, whose collegiality I have been privileged to enjoy over the last decade. I should like to thank my colleague, Stanley L. Paulson, of Washington University (St. Louis), presently in residence in Göttingen, for very kindly revising and reworking the English-language version of my text.

[1] On first glance, history seems to be of considerable significance to legal and social philosophy. Sensitivity to historical questions is no doubt increasing, and the number of publications pertaining to historical issues is vast. The growing importance of history becomes apparent, too, when one considers that two recent World Congresses of the International Association for the Philosophy of Law and Social Philosophy were devoted to questions of historical import. The rubric of the 12th World Congress, held in Athens in 1985, was "Law, Man, and History" (see Philosophy of Law in the History of Human Thought, ed. S. Panou, et al., Stuttgart 1988 [Archives for Philosophy of Law and Social Philosophy, Supplement]). And the rubric of the 14th World Congress, held in Edinburgh in 1989, concerned "Enlightenment, Rights and Revolution", with attention to the Glorious Revolution of 1688, the French Revolution, and the American Constitution (see Enlightenment, Rights and Revolution, Essays in Legal and Social Philosophy, N. MacCormick and Z. Bankowski, (eds.), Aberdeen 1989).

has been treated in legal and social philosophy: first, a manifest-explicit way, second, a latent-implicit way, and third, a self-referential manner, that is to say, one directly reflecting upon history as a problem of law and legal thought.

(1) The manifest approach of history consists in selecting a special subject of the past for legal and philosophical research. This can be a legal author, special aspects of his work, or some other topic of legal relevance that can be treated from a standpoint of legal and social philosophy. If we leave it at that, we can say that all questions concerning the past are both capable and worthy of being discussed, without making any distinctions. Under these circumstances, it would make no difference whether we turned to Aristotle, to Kant, or, for example, to Dante and his work. The last mentioned author is of special interest, for *Kelsen* wrote his very first book on Dante's theory of the state.[2] Kelsen justified his choice with the argument that this subject had not hitherto been treated from a legal point of view in a systematic and critical manner.[3] That sounds familiar enough, without any indication of specific deliberation. Indeed, Kelsen is in the end obliged to admit that his subject of research had not been very important. For he comes to the conclusion that Dante's theory of the state, based on imperial dignitiy, was already out of date, as the final expression of an obsolete and fruitless idea.[4]

Even a result such as this may, however, be of significance. One has to ask, however, whether Kelsen would not have been better off from the beginning with a different, possibly more fruitful subject of research. Still, his choice becomes understandable, at least to some degree, if we take into consideration the fact that his book on Dante dates from the period of historicism, according to which every historical subject is deemed to be of equal value. The German historian *Leopold von Ranke* justified this historical conception by pointing out that every period of history possesses a specific value grounded in itself.[5]

It is beyond question that history, no more than a legal philosophy founded on history, cannot forbear from inquiring into the peculiarities of a certain historical epoch, that is – speaking in the words of Ranke – how men of a special epoch have thought and lived, or, more generally, "what it was really like".[6] This cannot, however, suffice. For in this case history would be reduced to a kind of relativistic and positivistic antiquarianism directed at best at simply collecting or accumulating the material at hand without any regard for a greater perspective or standard. Historicism, precisely owing to these deficien-

---

[2] Kelsen, Die Staatslehre des Dante Alighieri, Wien 1905.

[3] Ibid., p. 1.

[4] Ibid., p. 149.

[5] Ranke, Über die Epochen der neueren Geschichte (On the Periods of Modern History), ed. by Th. Schieder and H. Berding, München 1971, pp. 59 et seq.

[6] See Ranke, Preface to: Geschichte der romanischen und germanischen Völker von 1494 bis 1514 (History of the Latin and Teutonic Nations), 2. ed., Leipzig 1874, p. VII.

cies, was therefore already being criticized at its most flourishing moments. So, *Nietzsche* in the nineteenth century warned of the dangers of an untamed use of history,[7] and at the beginning of the twentieth century *Ernst Troeltsch* criticized historicism for being arbitrary and going along with a lack of productivity for the sake of the present.[8] But the main criticism was expressed by *Karl R. Popper,* who from the middle of our century has been attacking historicism in a fundamental way.

Popper's criticism can be summarized in the following way: History as a science must be selective lest it be choked by a flood of poor and unrelated material. It is therefore necessary to introduce into history a preconceived, selective point of view.[9] Popper thus points out the deficits of a concept of history that makes arbitrariness a principle of science and that fails to differentiate between what is important or unimportant, essential or inessential. He only partially succeeds, however, in dealing with these difficulties, for the point of view that he introduces vis-à-vis history is claimed not to be testable in a scientific manner.[10] This does not mean that criticism is to be precluded. On the contrary, Popper plainly demands a critical attitude based on his broader concept of Critical Rationalism.[11] Scientifically, however, such criticism is less than adequate for want of a sufficiently elaborated basis. Thus, Popper criticizes Plato's legal and social philosophy for being speculative and totalitarian, but he is unable to give other than political arguments for his own position, aimed at an open society based on liberty and reason.[12] Thus, the problem of the arbitrariness of history and the historical sciences is not solved but only shifted to another level. This is all the more serious since Popper, along with historicism, rejects in a wholesale manner the philosophy of history as well as social philosophy from Plato to Hegel and Marx and even beyond them, as scientifically indefensible. After all, Popper takes a view seen by himself as old-fashioned, namely, that history is characterized by its interest in topical, singular, or specific events, rather than in laws or generalizations.[13] Certainly, Popper's Critical Rationalism, as far as history is concerned, is

[7] Nietzsche, Vom Nutzen und Nachteil der Historie für das Leben (On the Use and Abuse of History), published at the second part of "Unzeitgemäße Betrachtungen" (Thoughts Out of Season), Leipzig 1874.

[8] See Troeltsch, Der Historismus und seine Probleme (Historicism and Its Problems), Tübingen 1922; Troeltsch, Der Historismus und seine Überwindung (Historicism and How to Overcome), Berlin 1924.

[9] Popper, The Poverty of Historicism, 2nd ed., London 1960, p. 150.

[10] Because there is necessarily a plurality of interpretations which are fundamentally on the same level of both suggestiveness and arbitrareness, ibid., p. 151.

[11] See his Preface of the German version of "The Poverty of Historicism", 5th ed., Tübingen 1979, p. IX.

[12] Popper, The Open Society and Its Enemies, esp. vol. I: The Spell of Plato, Princeton, New Jersey 1963 (first published in 1944).

[13] Popper, The Poverty of Historicism (note 9), p. 143.

more than a revival of antiquarian historicism: at the end, however, it does not go substantially beyond a historical positivism enlarged by a critique of ideology. The same is true of *Kelsen,* who in a second historical approach turns to ancient Greek philosophy with special attention to Plato, whose legal and social ideas Kelsen severely criticizes owing to their presumed irrational and ideological character.[14]

Still, seen from the standpoint of critical historicism alone, the historical dimension of law and legal philosophy cannot be adequately grasped, in particular, for the reason that in such cases a great many philosophers and philosophical schools of thought would be excluded. In order to avoid this precarious state of affairs, it is necessary to reestablish philosophy historically as well as history philosophically. If we do so, critical reflection on the presuppositions of historical research is indispensable. It cannot, however, be enough simply to appeal to a diffuse sort of historical interest or to an arbitrarily selected point of view without further reasoning. On the contrary, we have to keep in mind that the criteria of selection and the interests that guide knowledge are to be examined, and what is more, that they have to be justified with respect to their legitimacy. This stems from the fact that problems of legal philosophy are related to the context of the social and cultural lifeworld in so far as they refer to human beings living together in a community. Epistemologically, legal and social philosophy are, therefore, not to be isolated from social and political interaction.[15] This leads to the conclusion that the relevance of a historical or philosophical problem is not simply given, but has to be shown, namely, by referring to its legal, political and social context. Thus, we are able to distinguish between those questions which are of genuine relevance and those which are merely interesting. Unlike the latter, the former are focused on the solution of specific problems of legal and social philosophy. The relevance of a historical theme, therefore, is a function of the extent to which it contributes to the solution of a question of legal and social philosophy and, thus, to the solution of the underlying legal and social problem.

A methodological position such as this can be characterized as a historical and philosophical realism that has passed through historicism in order to go beyond it. Realism understood in this manner aims at legal and social philosophy within the framework of its institutional, structural and systemic context over a greater period of time. Consequently, it allows for a higher degreee of generalization than a theoretical approach could provide, dealing as it does with merely particular and individual data. In the following, this concept will be developed further by drawing on historical, philosophical and legal thought with an eye to critical reflection on the foundations of law and society.

---

[14] Kelsen, Aufsätze zur Ideologiekritik, ed. by E. Topitsch (Contributions to the Critique of Ideology), Neuwied 1964, pp. 198 et seq.

[15] This has been emphasized, in particular, by Habermas, Knowledge and Human Interests, transl. by J. Shapiro, Boston 1972 (first published in German in 1968).

(2) Still, the historical dimension of legal philosophy and positive law should not be confined to its manifest-explicit form. History is also present where it is not explicitly dealt with. In order to understand this, one must imagine, for example, that a legal thought or act belongs to the past at the very moment it comes into being. The same applies to a legal or philosophical work which, as soon as it has been published, becomes part of the past. In this way the past is continually augmented.[16] We are not always aware of this fact, in particular, if we consider authors of the recent past as belonging to a presumed present. This does not, however, alter the fact that *Kelsen,* for example, is an author of the past like *Kant,* or, to go further back, like *Thomas Aquinas* or *Plato*. The difference between them, seen temporally, is not a matter of principle, but a gradual difference. This is also true if we consider a single author and his work. In this case, too, we can distinguish different levels of time so that, strictly speaking, we are not allowed to refer to it in general without further reasoning. So, for instance, we have to differentiate between the thought of *Rudolf von Ihering* before and after his so-called "conversion" from legal constructivism to an interest-oriented jurisprudence in the early sixties of the nineteenth century, or the attitude of *Gustav Radbruch* to legal positivism before and after World War II. Recently, particular attention has been directed to different temporal phases in the work of *Kelsen,* whose Pure Theory of Law has passed through a development over a number of decades and, therefore, cannot be referred to as a kind of timeless doctrinal system.[17]

Finally, in a latent form, the historical dimension is present where legal or philosophical orientations are said to carry other, earlier orientations forward in a new way. The historical dimension, in this case, is a latent one, since history is referred to not in its proper sense but for other purposes. This use of history manifests itself in numerous "neo"-schools of thought, reaching from neo-Platonism and neo-Aristotelianism to neo-Thomism and on to neo-Kantianism and neo-Positivism. The same phenomenon can be observed in reverse, namely, the tendency to place one theoretical movement after another once the direction of the continuum has emerged, thanks to a post-metaphysical, a post-positivistic or, more generally, a post-modern form of thought.[18]

---

[16] Karl-Georg Faber, in particular, has invited attention to the quantitative augmentation of the past. See his Theorie der Geschichtswissenschaft (Theory of the Science of History), 5. ed., München 1982, p. 39.

[17] See Stanley L. Paulson, Toward a Periodization of the Pure Theory of Law, in: Hans Kelsen's Legal Theory. A Diachronic Point of View, ed. by L. Gianformaggio, Torino 1990, pp. 11 et seq., with critical discussion of his suggestions following his own paper.

[18] See, for example, Habermas, Nachmetaphysisches Denken (Post-Metaphysical Thinking), Frankfurt a. M. 1988; Arthur Kaufmann, Rechtsphilosophie in der Nach-Neuzeit (Legal Philosophy in the Post-Modern Period), 2nd ed., Heidelberg 1992.

There is no reason to argue against those classifications, not, at any rate, where the epistemological premises and historical implications have been elucidated. Usually, however, this is not done, with the result that the historical dimension which is to be brought to light remains obscure. This is all the more problematic when the reference to the categories of "before" and "after" implies that to some extent a temporal orientation is indispensable.

(3) The problems raised thus far become fully evident only if we take a look at a third way of considering history with regard to law and legal philosophy. This consists of posing the question of for the historicity of law, state and society along with its theoretical reflection. It would, however, be inappropriate to confine history only to the past. History and historicity in their theoretical dimension represent more than that. Passing beyond a merely retrospective view, they are directed to the phenomena of development and change, of socio-cultural evolution as well as of continuity and, therefore, aim not only at the past but, at the same time, at the present and the future.

From a more general and abstract standpoint, we can say that history is decisively characterized by time. History and historical knowledge are actually made possible by the existence of time and temporal structures. The factor of time, therefore, is constitutive of the historical dimension and, along with this, of what is or can be of historical interest.

In this context, it is neither necessary nor possible to enter into a detailed discussion of time and the concept of time; however we try to define it – as an a priori, an empirical or as a relative factor – it would be, in any case, more than a mere analytic category applied at will to legal norms, facts and circumstances.[19] All events, all knowledge, even cognition and logic are related to time and closely linked to it. That means, referring to law as a normative order: Every existing legal, political and social structure is, just like our legal and philosophical reflection on it, the result of historical developments and, therefore, of temporal processes which do not lose their relevance even if we neglect them or try to put them aside. All of the past was once part of the future, just as the future will, one day, be past. Seen against this background the present is but an assumed bridge between what is no longer and what is yet to come. In other words: The present seems to be a mere construct which serves the function of symbolizing the continuous growing of the past on the one side, and of the future on the other.

All these questions are too important to be treated merely as a matter of the history of legal and social philosophy. The history of law, state and society,

---

[19] As to time and the concept of time, see Wolfgang Deppert, Zeit. Die Begründung des Zeitbegriffs, seine notwendige Spaltung und der ganzheitliche Charakter seiner Teile (Time. The Foundation of the Concept of Time, Its Necessary Division, and the Integral Character of Its Elements), Stuttgart 1989, who critically examines theories and models of time stemming from Kant.

conceived as the expression of humans living together within the framework of time, and time as a decisive element of legal, political and social structures, represent fundamental phenomena, the impact of which is evident in all positive law and legal thinking. Considering this state of affairs, we have to ask ourselves how we can come to terms with the problem of time in law and legal science. An adequate solution is to be expected not on the basis of a legal standpoint alone, but from an interdisciplinary approach as well as from a multi-level approach, which in dealing with the problems at hand has to consider all germane aspects and all relevant levels of law and society. Theoretical reflection on the historical dimension of law, therefore, should not be restricted to its genesis but ought to be extended to its validity, too, which is always validity within time. This is not to deny the idea of law, however conceived, but only its presumed existence outside of or beyond time.

It may be that time, as a factor of law, is sometimes neglected for practical reasons of legal argument. If such neglect should persist, however, it will lead first to inadequate questions, second to wrong solutions, and finally to self-delusion – this for the reason that time-oriented legal insights, consciously or unconsciously, are considered and dealt with as timeless, valid truths. We have to turn now to the further question of whether and to what extent a historically minded reason is able to overcome deficits such as these, owing to neglect or the disregard of time in legal and social thought.

II.

The historical dimension, in a naive or ingenuous sense, seems to be a reconstruction of how law was practised and reflected upon in more or less remote times. Yet, on closer inspection epistemological and methodological problems become apparent, and their solution raises considerable difficulties. On the one hand, we have to consider the problem of the temporal difference between the observer and the subject observed, on the other, the crucial question that the history of law and legal thought is not immediately accessible but has to be reconstructed through its textual configuration. In addition, we have to ask how the historical dimension is to be founded methodologically.

(1) As for the problem of time, the question arises of how far it is possible to reduce or even to eliminate the temporal difference between the observer and the subject of observation. Usually, this is accomplished by trying to understand a period of the past through its own preconditions and circumstances.[20] This, however, will be successful only up to a certain point, for it seems to be almost impossible to escape the prevailing ways of thinking and

[20] This method has been demonstrated, in particular, by Otto Brunner in his work on "Land und Herrschaft" (Land and Reign), first published in 1939.

acting in the observer's own world. But even if this problem were to a certain extent resolved, the present conceptions and patterns of thought would still continue to form, consciously or unconsiously, a kind of horizon or background for what is identified as belonging to the past. Moreover, due to the effort of eliminating present categories of thinking, the past might be conceived as being far more different than it actually is. Thus, medieval law is usually thought of in a way that disregards its rational aspects; these exist no less for that.[21] A medieval concept of positive law as the expression of human law-making has, therefore, been denied, and so has a medieval concept of state and sovereignty – but without sufficient reason. A corresponding constellation can be observed with regard to pre-revolutionary legal thinking, that is, legal thought before the French Revolution, which notwithstanding its early modern aspects is sometimes characterized as old-European (in the sense of belonging to the Ancien Régime), that is to say, as inadequate to the modern period and its legal and social thinking.

Of course, periodizations can be justified. However, they must not be misinterpreted as representing sharp breaks, lest periods preceding such a break not only be identified as "old" or "remote" but even be excluded as without relevance. Thus, legal and social structures belonging together would be separated and regarded as utterly different from each other. This distortion of perspective is not, however, inevitable. It can be avoided if the past is not done away with as a matter of history but is considered as lasting and continuing in the present. Thus, the view on what is coherent must be reopened. Legal authors, works, and orientations are no longer to be considered as incomparably isolated from each other solely because they are separated by a presumed time barrier. The temporal difference between past and present cannot be eliminated in this way. It is necessary, however, to redefine it. Granted that it is impossible to return to the past for the reason that time is an irreversible category, it is only consistent to approach past legal and social action and thought from the present horizon of time in order to study its development. Nevertheless, detailed studies that are directed at a particular, narrowly defined period of time are indispensable. Still, they will remain precarious if not inserted into a greater temporal context. From this, I would like to suggest a *first thesis:* The historical dimension of law and legal thought is not to be restricted to the perspective of the past. From the standpoint of the fundamental phenomenon of time, it refers to the inner connection of past, present, and future. Studying the historical and philosophical foundations of positive law, therefore, will be productive to the extent that its temporal structures are elucidated.

---

[21] For a critical discussion of this position, see D. Wyduckel, Princeps Legibus Solutus. Eine Untersuchung zur frühmodernen Rechts- und Staatslehre (The Prince is Not Bound by the Laws. A Study of Early Modern Theories of Law and State), Berlin 1979, esp. pp. 120 et seq.

(2) In addition to the problem of time, another difficulty arises from the fact that law and legal thinking generally find expression in written texts. It is hard to say, however, whether and to what extent we are allowed to draw conclusions from a given text with regard to its original meaning. Usually, we refer to hermeneutics and its method of interpretation – the process of understanding. Still, the so-called "hermeneutic circle" shows that all interpretation is related to some pre-existing sense, so that understanding texts of earlier times seems hardly conceivable without reference to present connotations. Nevertheless, *Quentin Skinner,* taking modern philosophy of language as his point of departure, and following, in particular, *J. L. Austin,* points out that the original meaning of a text can be reconstructed by referring to its contemporary framework – that is to say, to the context of ideas and patterns of thought in of the author's own time.[22] The basic problem of interpretation cannot, however, be solved in this way. To be sure, Skinner is able to reduce the extent to which present connotations figure in the course of understanding and interpreting texts of the past, but he cannot exclude them. Furthermore, he is compelled to pin down the author and his text to individual problems of the period in question, and therefore fails from the beginning to get a sense which goes beyond them.

Taking the historical dimension seriously, legal and social theory cannot restrict themselves to such an attitude: rather, they will ask for the possibility of relations and connections betweeen different horizons of texts and times. For that purpose it is necessary to refer to a certain level of abstraction on the one hand and to temporal elasticity on the other.[23] Only in that way can long-term structures of law and society be discovered and reformulated on a theoretical level.

This does not mean that the present conceptions of law, state, and society are to be transposed, unexamined, to the past. They are suited, however, to serve as reference points from which legal and philosophical texts of the past can be analyzed and developed within a broader theoretical framework. This is accomplished by looking for legal concepts that are valid over a long span of time. Thus, historical arbitrariness focusing on individual events and thoughts can be avoided and the understanding of history will be enhanced. Proceeding

---

[22] Cf. Quentin Skinner, Meaning and Understanding in the History of Ideas, in: History and Theory 8 (1969), p. 3 sqq. For the pros and cons of Skinner's thesis see: Meaning and Context. Quentin Skinner and His Criticis, ed. by James Tully, Oxford 1988. Further Jean-Fabien Spitz, Comment lire les textes politiques du passé? In: Droits. Revue française de théorie juridique 10 (1989), pp. 153 et seq.

[23] For the reconstruction of historical processes see Niklas Luhmann, Geschichte als Prozeß und die Theorie sozio-kultureller Evolution (History as Process and the Theory of Socio-Cultural Evolution), in: Historische Prozesse, ed. by Karl-Georg Faber and Christian Meier, München 1978, pp. 413 et seq. Cf. further Luhmann, Weltzeit und Systemgeschichte (World-Time and the History of Systems), in: Kölner Zeitschrift für Soziologie und Sozialpsychologie, Beiheft 16, 1972, pp. 81 et seq.

in this way would no doubt be legitimate, in particular, for the reason that the legal conceptions and ideas of the present are the result of a process of differentiation that is in itself historical and therefore dependent on time. In addition, a mere reproduction of legal texts and thoughts of the past without any kind of interpretation would be neither wise nor possible. Moreover, those ideas and thoughts of a period that appear to be most profound may well not be given expression in the period itself, but are instead reconstructed at a later point in time.[24]

Naturally, we have to ask to what extent legal and philosophical concepts can be extended into time. This question cannot be answered from the standpoint of hermeneutics or the philosophy of language, let alone from the horizon of a single author. Rather, one must consider the underlying basic problems as well as the corresponding legal, political, and social structures, all of which necessarily go beyond a mere individual-oriented view. This is not to be understood in the sense of a causal nexus between legal conceptions on the one hand and their socio-political context on the other. Yet we may assume that there are correlations between these two levels, in particular, for the reason that the semantic framework cannot vary arbitrarily with regard to the society making use of it.[25]

None of this aims at a *philosophia perennis* purporting to give valid answers to the eternal questions of legal and social philosophy. Attention, however, is to be directed to a structural and institutional approach taking into account long-term developments of law and legal theory that are not accessible from a merely individualistic or short-term perspective. This view is familiar in historical research under the rubric of "longue-durée structures", and it has been developed, in particular, in French historical and social science.[26] Those structures are not to be considered as static alone, for they, too, are dependant on time and are therefore related to change. Hence, structural and developmental approaches do not stand in contrast to one another. Moreover, legal and social structures, whether past or present, can be conceived as a kind of congealed or frozen development. Thus, legal philosophy, seeing itself as social philosophy, cannot close its eyes to a long-term structural and institutional

---

[24] See Fritz Kern, Recht und Verfassung im Mittelalter (Law and Constitution in Medieval Times), 2. ed., Darmstadt 1958, p. 8. In this sense also Thomas Würtenberger, Zeitgeist und Recht (The Spirit of the Time and Law), Tübingen 1987, pp. 45 et seq.

[25] See Luhmann, Gesellschaftsstruktur und Semantik (Social Structure and Semantics), vol. I, Frankfurt a. M. 1980, pp. 13 et seq., esp. p. 17.

[26] See Fernand Braudel, Geschichte und Sozialwissenschaften. Die "longue durée" in Geschichte und Soziologie (History and Social Sciences. The "longue durée" in History and Sociology), ed. by H.-U. Wehler, Köln 1972, pp. 189 et seq. For an application to public law, see Wyduckel, Ius Publicum. Grundlagen und Entwicklung des Öffentlichen Rechts und der deutschen Staatsrechtswissenschaft (Foundation and Development of Public Law and German Constitutional Law), Berlin 1984.

approach without diminishing its epistemological perspective. This yields a *second thesis:* The historical dimension of law and legal thinking is limited neither to the understanding or interpretation of legal texts and conceptions of the past nor to a mere reproduction of attitudes and ways of thinking in earlier times. Rather, it tries to present the reflection of law and society within the framework of time-oriented dynamics, thereby contributing to the history of legal and social theory as well to its position in the present day.

(3) The question remains in which way the historical dimension of law and legal thinking can be founded from a methodological point of view. This question cannot be solved along the lines of historicism, unable, as that view is, to make a substantiated selection or to establish priorities. In that case, untheoretical research on arbitrary matters would in fact become a scientific virtue. It seems, however, to be easier to point out what not to do than to give positive directions for a methodological inquiry. In any case, it would be problematic to concentrate too much on single authors even where the so-called classics are concerned. On the one hand, the great questions of legal and social philosophy can, to be sure, hardly be answered without reference to their outstanding thinkers. On the other hand, one should not be tempted to draw the conclusion that particular problems and their solution by particular authors, however renowned, might simply be generalized or regarded as representative of the whole of legal and social thought. Thus, *Popper,* not without reason, has warned against the habit of yielding to the great figures of the history of philosophy.[27] The fact that this warning has not become obsolete can be observed again and again in the history of legal and social philosophy, which is far more author- and authority-guided than is warranted. Thus, problems and perspectives are often personalized and individualized without taking into account their greater context. What is more, the selection of the legal and philosophical authors considered is a reflection of value-oriented categories that have not been adequately considered in their own right. Against this background, it may not be without interest to note that in the German tradition of legal and social philosophy, the extraordinarily high regard enjoyed, for example, by *Jean Bodin* or *Thomas Hobbes* stands in remarkable contrast to the regard shown, for instance, to *John Locke* or *Jean-Jacques Rousseau.* It is quite obvious that differentiation such as this does not, or at any rate does not only, originate in value-free cognition.

It would be inaccurate, however, to eliminate guiding values from reflection on matters legal and social, for they are part of the reality of law and society, and of legal science, too. Nonetheless, values and interests guiding research should not remain unexplained but, rather, should be incorporated into legal and philosophical thought, thereby facilitating a critical analysis at their legiti-

[27] Popper, The Open Society (note 12), vol. I, Preface to the first English edition, p. VII.

macy. Considering the historical dimension of legal and social philosophy, this is to be done with reference to the temporal dimension of law and society. From this standpoint, scientific objectivity is not to be identified with an abstention from questions of values. Rather, objectivity should be considered as the faculty of reflecting upon and discussing the conditionality of the observer's own point of view within the framework of a historically based legal and social theory. It may be true that under these premises, false assessments and judgments cannot be excluded. Still, the wider the selected temporal perspective, the smaller this risk will be – and this for the very reason that the material and information available on the basis of long-term studies is far greater than that dealt with in short-term studies, thereby making possible a comparison of different levels of law and society, and also a more broadly based empirical solution to the problems at hand. From this, a *third* thesis can be derived: The historical dimension of law and legal thought cannot be exhausted by reducing it to individual authors and their particular perspectives. It will develop its full potential only if these authors and perspectives are examined according to their specific contribution to long-term problems of legal and social science. This implies reference to values and interests that have to be explicated and legitimated within a temporal dimension.

III.

Finally, the question arises: For what purpose is history considered in law and legal thought? More precisely: What kind of contribution to legal and social thinking can be expected from reflections on law and society that are historical in nature? In the present section, this problem will be examined from three different standpoints: First, that of knowledge, second, that of enlightenment, and third, from the standpoint of optimizing legal reasoning.

(1) Every science deserving of the name aims at cognition as well as at the acquisition of knowledge. Given that this is so, then with regard to time, science qua cognition would appear to be valid only for the brief continuum of time constituting the present.[28] Thus the horizon of cognition and knowledge would from the beginning be restricted. Legal history and legal theory try to extend this temporal horizon in order to achieve insights into a deeper dimension of the law which would otherwise not be easily accessible.

It would not be enough, however, to understand history in its narrative function alone. Rather, if scientific insights are to be obtained, it is necessary to formulate specific goals of cognition. This can be done in different ways.

[28] See Hans-Ulrich Wehler, Soziologie und Geschichte aus der Sicht des Sozialhistorikers (Sociology and History from the View of Social History), in: Kölner Zeitschrift für Soziologie und Sozialpsychologie, Special issue 16, 1972, pp. 59 et seq., esp. p. 63.

Legal theory can turn to the history of ideas on the one hand, to social history on the other, or it can appeal to a combination of both.

Law and legal thinking, seen from the point of view of a history of ideas which expects insights into ideal legal entities, would hardly be taken into serious consideration today. Still, a history of legal ideas has not therefore become obsolete. Rather, it can be pursued epistemologically as a history of legal *theory* that raises the question of the historical implications of law and society, in order to pursue them in a critically and systematically reflective manner within the dimension of time.[29]

Legal theory, when referred to social history, is confronted with the same problem, albeit at another level. It requires that one focus on the social conditions and circumstances of law and legal thought – without, however, running the risk of neglecting the specific character of law, let alone depriving it of its relevance through undue concentration on its social and political framework. It is obvious, then, that the two views should be combined. This can be achieved either by means of a history of legal concepts that inquires into their social and political extension within a given period of time,[30] or by means of a history of political ideas that examines positive law from the perspective of its institutional context,[31] or, finally, by means of a sociology of knowledge, based on systems theory that analyzes legal and social structures with attention to their semantic tradition.[32] Approaching law in this manner is imperative lest legal theory and legal science be isolated or be forced to adhere to a position of epistemological self-restraint. A post-positivistic realism, conceiving positive law as a variable normative structure of society can be useful in this context as a means of developing a suitable design of theoretically reflective research.[33]

---

[29] See, from the standpoint of political theory, Günter Trautmann, Hat Theoriegeschichte Sinn? (On the Meaning of the History of Theory), in: Politische Vierteljahresschrift, Special issue 15, 1984, pp. 250 et seq.

[30] See Reinhart Koselleck, Begriffsgeschichte und Sozialgeschichte (The History of Concepts and Social History), in: Historische Semantik und Begriffsgeschichte (Historical Semantics and the History of Concepts), ed. by Koselleck, Stuttgart 1979, pp. 19 et seq.

[31] See Gerhard Göhler, Politische Ideengeschichte – institutionentheoretisch gesehen (The History of Political Ideas Seen from the Perspective of the Theory of Institutions), in: Göhler, Lenk, Münkler and Walther (eds.), Politische Institutionen im gesellschaftlichen Umbruch (Political Institutions and Social Change), Opladen 1990, pp. 7 et seq.

[32] See Luhmann, Gesellschaftsstruktur und Semantik (Social Structure and Semantics), Frankfurt a. M. 1982 - 1989, 3 vols. See also Luhmann, Die Wissenschaft der Gesellschaft (The Science of Society), Frankfurt a. M. 1990, esp. pp. 549 et seq.

[33] See Wyduckel, Recht und Rechtswissenschaft im nachpositivistischen Rechtsrealismus (Law and Legal Science in the Light of a Post-Positivistic Legal Realism), in: RECHTSTHEORIE Beiheft 9, 1986, pp. 349 et seq., at 363.

The problem of whether there is any meaning in law and history must not, however, be forgotten. The concept of meaning ist not, however, to be understood as an absolute category but as a relative one, dependent on space and time, and, therefore, manifesting itself only if specific epistemological goals have already been formulated.[34] Irrelevant questions will lead to irrelevant results unless a problematic "ruse of history", even unquestioned, were thought to reveal a presumed hidden meaning. Thus, the meaning of law and legal thought is not absolutely certain, but has continually to be reconstructed in an ongoing process of socio-philosophical reflection.

(2) The historical dimension of law and legal thought is of significance not only because of its epistemological function but also under the aspect of enlightenment. If we understand enlightenment, in the *Kantian* sense, as man's release from his self-incurred tutelage,[35] and further, if we take into consideration the fact that Kant distinguishes between the Age of Enlightenment and an enlightened age, then enlightenment is not simply given or bound to a particular epoch but is rather a perspectival process that necessarily remains unfinished. This process of enlightenment, essentially shaped by the traditional Kantian understanding, is usually contrasted with history. This is due to a particular Hegelian-oriented view attributing enlightenment to the neglect of history, even to historical blindness. This does not mean, however, that enlightenment cannot be conceived as a historical category expressing itself and finding its own language in the course of a historical process that would otherwise not be communicated.[36] History and enlightenment, therefore, are not necessarily opposed; rather, they stand in a relation of mutuality to each other. Thus, an enlightened history is as justifiable as a historical enlightenment that aims at a critical revision of law and legal thinking in the light of time and temporal experience.

This is to say that one must criticize pretended claims to truth and validity formulated without temporal reference, querying strategies of immunization directed to the elimination of history, or dogmatized doctrines passing themselves off as scientifically founded and, linked therewith, the attitude of admitting only those questions that exclude time as a relevant factor from the very beginning. Accordingly, historical enlightenment would have to insist, first, on

---

[34] That is, in so far, as Popper, The Open Society (note 12), vol. II, p. 278, is right when he thinks it is possible to give history a meaning.

[35] See Kant, Beantwortung der Frage: Was ist Aufklärung? (Answering the Question of What is Enlightenment), Works, vol. VIII, Berlin 1923, pp. 35 et seq., at 40.

[36] See Jürgen Mittelstraß, Kant und die Dialektik der Aufklärung (Kant and the Dialectic of Enlightenment), in: Aufklärung und Gegenaufklärung in der europäischen Literatur, Philosophie und Politik von der Antike bis zur Gegenwart (Enlightenment and Counter-Enlightenment in European Literature, Philosophy and Politics From Antiquity to the Present), ed. by Jochen Schmidt, Darmstadt 1989, pp. 341 et seq, esp. p. 353, with insights into Kant's historical thought.

disclosing what is concealed, second, on reflecting upon systematic contexts with a view to their synchronous and diachronic structure, and, on opening up temporal perspectives in order, in a third step, to try to inform legal thinking about itself under the aspect of time continously passing. That may be inconvenient, even very difficult. It would nevertheless be preferable to a state of historical un-enlightenment which time, sooner or later, would catch up with.

(3) However important critical enlightenment on behalf of history may be, the crucial question is whether there is a species of historical reason that can guide legal thought and legal practice. In our time, of course, we are not inclined to answer this question in the manner of Hegel or Savigny and the Historical School of Law. The claim to which Hegel gives expression, namely, "that *reason* be in history" has however by no means lost its import.[37] Yet up to now, legal theory has failed to conceptualize historical reason in an adequate way.[38] Naturally this cannot be done in the present paper. Still, some suggestions may be put forward.

Historical reason, first, should contribute to the improvement of the concept of meaning in the world of law, that is, it should contribute to a mediation between the potentiality and the reality of law with respect to the constant transition from past to present and present to future. Futhermore, historical reason itself should be conceived as a historical category that has to be reconsidered continually in the light of temporal development. From this angle, legal argumentation could claim rationality only in so far as it can be justified in the light of its historical and temporal implications.

To be sure, we cannot expect that a historical reason, thus understood, will offer concrete solutions to particular legal problems, even if this is possible in special cases. Historical reason, however, can make an essential contribution to optimizing theoretical and practical legal reasoning.

Conceiving the historical demension of law and legal thought as historical reason will no doubt have consequences for the concepts of law and legal validity. In particular, separating legal genesis and legal validity under these circumstances is hardly to be maintained in its current form. The positivity of law,[39] understood as the expression of law being laid down by a lawgiver as well as its variability, would in fact be misinterpreted if it were limited to a unique historical act. Law as positive law is valid only if it is perceived in relation to time as a temporary selection from among other persistent possibilities,

[37] See Hegel, Enzyklopädie der philosophischen Wissenschaften im Grundrisse (1830), ed. by F. Nicolin und O. Pöggeler, Marburg 1959, § 549, p. 430.

[38] From the view of historical science, however, see Jörn Rüsen, Historische Vernunft. Gundzüge einer Historik I: Die Grundlagen der Geschichtswissenschaft (Historical Reason. Outlines of a Theory of History I), Göttingen 1983.

[39] The positivity of the law is, of course, a phenomenon to be reckoned with quite apart from whether or not one regards oneself as a legal positivist.

that is, "if it is experienced as changeable at any time".[40] This temporal mobility is decisively curtailed if legal validity is reduced to an ideal normative sphere from which the temporal and social basis of law has been separated. Separating law from its temporal implications is, at the same time, to isolate it from its social and political context. This is the deeper reason why Kelsen's Pure Theory of Law, notwithstanding its apparent dynamics, produces the impression of a static system. Indeed, his concept of law and legal positivity, in the sense of a normativistic legal positivism, is distorted in such a way that society, in the end, is locked out and time locked in.[41]

At present, it is hard to say what consequences a concept of law that seriously embodies the factors of history, development and time might have. We cannot, however, simply leave the matter to the conception of variant social, political and legal structures by means of analytical categories, which are thought of as invariant. How far an evolutionist approach might be able to conceptualize the problem of positive law with regard to its temporal structures must in the present context be left undecided.[42]

---

[40] This is emphasized by Luhmann, Positivität des Rechts als Voraussetzung einer modernen Gesellschaft (The Positivity of Law as a precondition of a Modern Society), in: Luhmann, Ausdifferenzierung des Rechts, Frankfurt a.M. 1981, pp. 113 et seq., esp. p. 124.

[41] For the "dynamic" character of Kelsen's Pure theory of law, see Andrés Ollero, Zum Verhältnis von Positivität und Geschichtlichkeit im Recht (On the Relation between Positivity and the Historicity of Law), in: Philosophy of Law in the History of Human Thought (note 1), pp. 150 et seq., esp. p. 152, who characterizes Kelsen's concept of positivity, despite its formal flexibilization, as "radically ahistorical".

[42] See for further consideration Ernst-Joachim Lampe, Genetische Rechtstheorie. Recht, Evolution und Geschichte (Genetic Legal Theory. Law, Evolution and History), Freiburg and München 1987, pp. 41 et seq.

VI. Democratic Stability, Social Solidarity, and Constitutional Rights

Publicly-Funded Civil Legal Assistance for Poor People in the United States

By Roger C. Cramton, Ithaca[1]

I am honored to contribute to this Festschrift celebrating the work and achievements of a great American legal scholar whose work in jurisprudence and legal theory is known throughout the world. Bob Summers, it can be said, has lent distinction to the Cornell Law School and has put Halfway, Oregon on the world map. As a colleague of Bob's for nearly twenty years, I have benefitted enormously from his example of intellectual integrity, analytical rigor, wise practical judgment and focused effort. Bob's gift of friendship has been expressed in countless measure during this period. I have learned so much from him that I can no longer separate my own ideas from what he has taught me.

Civil legal assistance for the poor in the United States[2] has departed from patterns developed in Europe and elsewhere in the world.[3] Since 1974, when the Legal Services Corporation Act[4] was enacted, the provision of civil legal aid has been carried on by staff attorneys employed by non-profit organizations that receive most of their funding from the federal government. The staff-attorney organization has made poverty law a lifetime professional specialization of several thousand lawyers and has encouraged an activist mentality that has resulted in the politicization of the legal services program.[5] Fund-

[1] Roger C. Cramton is Robert S. Stevens Professor of Law, Cornell University, Ithaca, N.Y. 14853. A portion of this paper is derived, with permission, from material included in a longer essay, Delivery of Legal Services to Ordinary Americans, prepared for the National Conference on the Legal Profession in the 21st Century, held at Case Western Reserve University School of Law, Cleveland, Ohio, on June 1 - 3, 1993.

[2] The reader should know that I served as the first chairman of the board of directors of the Legal Services Corporation, the federal instrumentality which funds local programs and has rule-making and monitoring authority over the recipients. President Ford appointed me in 1975 and I served as chairman until 1978 when Hillary Rodham Clinton succeeded me. Thus I was an active participant in the early development of the national program.

[3] For a comparative assessment, see Mauro Cappelletti, James Gordley & Earl Johnson, Jr., Toward Equal Justice: A Comparative Study of Legal Aid in Modern Societies (1975).

[4] Pub.L. 93 - 355, 88 Stat. 378, codified as 42 U.S.C. § 2996 et seq.

[5] See Carrie Menkel-Meadow, Legal Aid in the United States: The Professionalization and Politicization of Legal Services in the 1980s, 22 Osgoode Hall L.J. 30 (1984) (arguing that development of the legal services program created a professional cadre of

ing limitations flowing at least in part from the ensuing political controversy have limited legal assistance to a fraction of poor people needing legal help. Faced with this situation, staff lawyers, who control the deployment of resources, follow a *triage* approach justified on utilitarian grounds. The ideological commitment and professional rewards of the staff lawyers lie primarily in pursuit of law reform and test cases that raise legal issues broader than the concerns of a poor individual.[6] The purpose of this paper is to explore in brief compass some implications and problems of the American model.

I. Development of Federal Legal Services Program[7]

Until the 20th century, poor people depended on the charity of private lawyers for legal assistance. In small communities in which general practitioners had face-to-face contact with all sectors of the community, including poor people, this approach occasionally worked well. Lawyers were urged by bar associations to devote a portion of their time to free or reduced-fee work for those who could not afford to pay. Many lawyers did so. Whatever its merits at the time, voluntary pro bono cannot be relied on to meet the needs of poor people under today's conditions of urbanization, specialization and social stratification.

Legal aid in a more organized form began around 1900, sometimes as self-help associations of worker and immigrant groups, sometimes as local charitable organizations. Through the 1950s legal aid programs were funded almost entirely by charity and subscription of members of the bar. The programs usually had a small staff, often one person, assisted by volunteers and law students. The agencies were few in number, located almost exclusively in major cities, thinly funded, relatively passive, concentrating on individual cases and having the aura of a charity. In 1962 236 local legal aid organizations had a total national budget of less than $ 4 million.

In the 1960s the Ford Foundation made legal aid a major undertaking and infused it with new money, new stature and new assertiveness. In 1964, the Economic Opportunity Office (OEO) of President Lyndon Johnson's "Great Society" program contemplated and provided funding for a quantum leap in

---

specialized poverty lawyers ("professionalization") and involved the program in partisan political controversy because of its perceived role as an instrument of social and legal change).

[6] See Jack Katz, Poor People's Lawyers in Transition (1982).

[7] For general and historical background, see Earl Johnson, Jr., Justice and Reform: The Formative Years of the OEO Legal Services Program (1974); Reginald Heber Smith, Justice and the Poor (1919); Emery A. Brownell, Legal Aid in the United States (1951); Elliot Cheatham, A Lawyer When Needed (1963); Jerome E. Carlin, Jan Howard and Sheldon L. Messinger, Civil Justice and the Poor (1966); Barlow F. Christensen, Lawyers for People of Moderate Means (1970).

civil legal assistance. Lawyers who enrolled in the legal aspect of the "War on Poverty" were committed to a law reform agenda that made aggressive use of the armory of substantive and procedural arguments available to the most creative American lawyers. The judicial activism of the Warren Court years, in which many federal judges responded with enthusiasm to claims that existing law oppressed the poor, was a parallel development.

The federal legal services program originated in this OEO initiative. The visionaries and activists who started the legal services movement in the turbulent 1960s had three missions in mind: (1) the individual client-service mission of traditional legal aid, (2) law reform and institutional change, and (3) empowering poor people by creating organized groups that might engage in direct action such as boycotts, demonstrations and political activity. The activists in the legal services movement deprecated individual-client assistance as "band-aid" work that failed to get at fundamental problems.[8] They sought to direct the program's resources into social advocacy and organizational activity. The provision of lawyers for otherwise represented persons in dealing with public or private institutions resulted in numerous decisions requiring more elaborate procedure or establishing new substantive law. The ultimate objective – a substantial redistribution of societal wealth and power – proved to be too large and too politically controversial to be accomplished by lawyers through the mechanism of the courts.

The social reform potential visualized in the 1960s for the federal legal assistance program excited hopes of reformers and fears of conservatives, both probably exaggerated. The result was a political struggle for control of the program, involving the organized bar at various levels, political action groups, factions in Congress and various agencies in the Government. Broadly speaking, the reformers sought to make legal aid programs a vehicle for structural legal reform, through test cases, class actions and legislative activity, in such areas as housing, civil rights, education, women's rights and regulation of the workplace. The conservatives sought to maintain legal aid as a service program for needy individuals in such traditional matters as child support and custody, landlord-tenant disputes, debtor-creditor disputes and securing welfare benefits.[9]

In 1974, a detente of sorts was reached. The federal legal services program was established on a permanent basis through the Legal Services Corporation

---

8 See Stephen Wexler, Practicing Law for Poor People, 79 Yale L.J. 1049, 1053 (1970) ("If all the lawyers in the country worked full time, they could not deal with even the articulated problems of the poor. ... In this setting, the object of practicing poverty law must be to organize poor people, rather than to solve their legal problems").

9 For one view at the time, see Carlin, Howard and Messinger, supra; for another, see Geoffrey C. Hazard, Jr., Social Justice Through Civil Justice, 36 U. Chi. L. Rev. 242 (1970); Hazard, Law Reforming in the Anti-Poverty Effort, 37 U. Chi. L. Rev. 242 (1970).

Act.[10] The statutory objectives are stated in politically neutral terms of "equal access to justice" and "high-quality legal assistance" for the poor. Political and organizational activities on the part of legal services lawyers are largely excluded by specific restrictions: a ban on political activity by lawyers in the field, a prohibition on participation in organizational activity (as distinct from legal advice concerning it) and procedural constraints on the use of class actions. These restrictions suggest that individual-client service and test-case litigation arising out of it constitute the central statutory mission.

The structure of the national program involves the Legal Services Corporation (LSC) as a funding agency for local programs that actually represent clients and deliver legal services. The Corporation is forbidden to provide legal services to others, but it has an uncertain extent of regulatory authority over the operation of the local programs. Restrictions on the matters that could be undertaken by the local programs were included in the original Act (e.g., abortion and school desegregation cases). These restrictions have since been modified, elaborated and fought over, each time in highly political battles. Parallel struggles over the level of funding occur annually.

The purpose of the Legal Services Corporation Act was to depoliticize legal services by stressing the goal of "equal access to justice." This goal had a neutral political ring that picked up the legal profession's concern about the provision of legal assistance to poor people who could not afford to retain lawyers. Use of the existing staff-attorney system was defended on grounds of efficiency and specialized competence. Controversy over the law reform orientation of the staff attorney system was muted by requiring that the specialized "backup centers," which had carried on much of the most controversial litigation, be limited to cases arising out of the representation of eligible clients. Statutory limitations on political activity by lawyers in the field (e.g., electioneering), a ban on participation in organizational activity (as distinct from legal advice concerning it), and procedural restrictions on class actions attempted to mute the political aspect of the staff-attorney framework.

Beginning in 1975, the Legal Services Corporation developed a rationale for the program (access to justice), an operating principle (high-quality lawyering) and a national goal (availability to many poor persons by providing a legal services lawyer for every 5,000 eligible poor people). This approach provided the national legal services program with a politically neutral posture, the strong support of the legal profession and a practical goal for its growth into a substantial national program. Federal funding of the program grew from $ 71 million per year in 1975 to over $ 300 million in 1981. At that time the legal services program had been extended throughout the country (in 1975 it was concentrated in major cities and in a few regions) and was staffed by 6,000 fulltime

---

[10] Pub.L. 93 - 355, 88 Stat. 378, codified as 42 U.S.C. § 2996 et seq.

lawyers. Although the Corporation did not attempt to exclude a more aggressive posture on the part of local programs who received funding, the Corporation's public rhetoric was limited to the politically neutral messages of access, high quality and efficiency.

The effort to mute the political aspect of the program did not persuade President Reagan, who persistently sought to abolish the program in the 1980s. Reagan opposed the law reform orientation of the staff-attorney system and favored treating civil legal assistance as a private charitable activity which was the responsibility of the private sector generally and especially of lawyers. Major bar associations, led by the American Bar Association, in company with various civil rights and other activist groups, fought hard for the program. An uneasy compromise emerged in which, Reagan, unable to eliminate or drastically modify the program because of congressional opposition, accepted its survival on funding diminished by budget cuts and inflation. The stalemate continued under President Bush, who was unwilling or unable to take any initiatives on the subject.

The Reagan-Bush concern about the political activism of the program probably did influence local programs to reduce the proportion of resources devoted to group representation. The Corporation, controlled by Reagan-Bush appointees, also pushed the local programs into greater reliance on the volunteered services of private lawyers. The decrease in federal funding also drove local programs to develop state, local and private funding that in the 1990s has the effect of somewhat reducing their dependence on national funding.

The federal legal aid program has emerged from this period of strife with modest funding and a relatively traditional program, but on a more or less permanent basis. About 4,000 staff lawyers, down from the 1981 figure of 6,000, work fulltime on civil legal aid, augmented by the pro bono efforts of thousands of private lawyers. Periodic disputes over restrictions on program activities as well as funding levels are likely to recur.[11]

Today the U.S. legal services program has the following characteristics: (1) It is funded primarily by annual congressional appropriations. (2) Legal services are provided primarily by employed lawyers who work fulltime for local non-profit programs. (3) Because the demand for legal assistance is much larger than can be provided at current funding and staffing levels, most poor people who have a legal problem go unrepresented. The decisions as to who is represented are made primarily by the staff lawyers of local programs, although they are required to formulate priorities in consultation with local

[11] See generally Roger C. Cramton, Crisis in Legal Services for the Poor, 26 Villanova L. Rev. 521 (1981); Carrie Menkel-Meadow, Legal Aid in the United States: The Professionalization and Politicization of Legal Services in the 1980s, 22 Osgoode Hall L. J. 28 (1984).

representatives of the poor. And (4), although most of the day-by-day effort of staff lawyers is spent on individual-client service, the ideological commitment of staff lawyers favors an approach that would promote distributive justice by empowering groups of poor people, enhancing their legal rights and shifting social resources to them.[12]

II. Recurring Policy Issues

1. Staff-Attorney System vs. Judicare

The United States is distinctive in that civil legal assistance to the poor is provided primarily by organizations that employ "poverty lawyers" – lawyers who are employed full time by local non-profit organizations engaged in delivering legal services to eligible poor persons (generally defined as persons whose household incomes are below 125 percent of the federal "poverty line"). In other countries eligible poor persons are referred to members of the private bar, who are then paid by the state at rates fixed by statute or regulation.[13] The latter system, by analogy to a U.S. program of health care for the poor, Medicare, is referred to as "judicare" in the United States.

The staff-attorney system, which is favored by nearly all insiders in the U.S. legal services movement, provides a cadre of lawyers who are intellectually and personally committed to serving the poor; the delivery of service may be organized so that clients are served by experienced specialists in various areas of poverty law, such as welfare, housing, or education; and it permits more aggressive pursuit of institutional reform that benefits groups of poor people rather than merely an individual client.

Proponents of judicare as a replacement of or alternative to the staff-attorney system argue that use of private lawyers permits a more normal lawyer-client relationship (the client chooses the lawyer and controls the objectives of the representation) and leads to greater client satisfaction.[14] Some proponents favor judicare for precisely the reasons that those enamored of law reform litigation prefer the staff attorney system: Judicare is more likely to stick to individual-client service. Studies performed by the Legal Service Corporation, as well as the experience elsewhere in the world, indicate that both systems are feasible, the existence of some staff component is essential in controlling costs,

---

[12] See Marie Failinger and Larry May, Litigation Against Poverty: Legal Services and Group Representation, 45 Ohio State L.J. 5 (1984).

[13] See Cappelletti, Gordley and Johnson, supra note 3.

[14] Samuel J. Brakel, Judicare: Public Funds, Private Lawyers, and Poor People (1974); Brakel, Styles of Delivery of Legal Services to the Poor, 1977 Amer. Bar Found. Research J. 219.

and the staff system offers a potential of having a larger impact on the legal rights and living conditions of eligible clients.[15]

2. Social Advocacy vs. Individual Client Service[16]

The activist vision is one in which lawyers improve the lives of poor people by redistributing power to them to influence decisions that will affect them. Professor Gary Bellow, for example, criticized the tendency of most legal service organizations to devote most of their effort to individual client service.[17] Poorly trained and inexperienced lawyers were thrown into frustrating and tension-laden situations that resulted in minimal service and did little to ease the larger problems of the poor. The program's potential for social change, he argued, could not be achieved unless its priorities were reversed, so that political organization of the poor would come first, followed by aggressive pursuit of strategic priorities in a way that would apply maximum pressure in favor of institutional and legal changes that affect large numbers of poor people.

> A massive expansion of minimal, routinized legal assistance throughout the low-income areas of the country, mediated by selective efforts at "law reform", is potentially a powerful system of social control, capable of defining and legitimating particular grievances and resolutions and ignoring others. Legal aid lawyers, unwilling or unable to respond to client concerns in ways which link them to a larger vision of social justice, can readily become purveyors of acquiescence and resignation among the people that they are seeking to help. Clients can be literally "taught" that their situations are natural, inevitable, or their own fault, and that dependence on professional advice and guidance is their only appropriate course of action; that is, legal assistance for the poor can become a bulwark of existing social arrangements. To echo a now familiar phrase, a profession that is not part of the solution can soon become part of the problem. The legal aid experience may soon be a troubling illustration of the modern homily.[18]

---

[15] Legal Services Corporation, The Delivery Systems Study: A Policy Report to the Congress and President of the United States (1980).

[16] See generally Marshall J. Breger, Legal Aid for the Poor: A Conceptual Analysis, 60 No. Car. L. Rev. 282 (1982); Marie A. Failinger and Larry May, Litigating Against Poverty: Legal Services and Group Representation, 45 Ohio State L. J. 1 (1984).

[17] Gary Bellow, Turning Solutions Into Problems: The Legal Aid Experience, 34 N. L. A. D. A. Briefcase 106, 122 (1977). See also Gary Bellow, Legal Aid in the United States, 14 Clearinghouse Rev. 337 (1980).

[18] Id. at 122. See also Jack Katz, Poor People's Lawyers in Transition (1982). Katz's study of the legal services program in Chicago finds that during the 1970s "law reform" activities replaced an earlier emphasis on organizing and community education. The result was what Katz calls the "legalization of poverty." Legal services lawyers helped create government programs for the poor that were professionally administered, confined by formal procedures and limited by rules and standards. Poverty lawyers became poverty managers and "helped rationalize the state's organization of the poor as a homogeneous segregated social class."

David Luban provides an elaborate philosophical defense of a vision of politicized legal services.[19] A specific example of the kind of services he favors, graphically raises all the important objections to politicized public interest law practice:

> ... The center's lawyers manipulated clients, took sides in a dispute within the client community (over whether the development should be built in an integrated neighborhood), spent public money to take a partisan stand on several divisive and politically controversial issues, switched from a general legal services practice to a politicized legal campaign, and used the courts to take control of a political institution. All of these are highly debateable tactics. ...[20]

Luban's conclusion, however, is that, choice of tactics aside,

> There is absolutely nothing illegitimate about impact work being done by legal services lawyers, even highly politicized legal services lawyers. On the contrary, law reform of this sort is at once an admirable attempt to further social justice and a professional responsibility to help more clients rather than fewer. It is precisely what lawyers ought to be doing.[21]

Luban argues that successful law reform solves the problems of many poor people at once and is therefore the most efficient use of scarce legal resources. Although client control and manipulation are sometimes involved, he concedes, "one cannot succeed in political action without dirtying one's hands."[22] Moreover, the people and groups served by the lawyer's political use of legal machinery are aware of what is going on. Their free and mutual commitment to the lawyer's cause justifies the unusual degree of lawyer control. Winning the battle in the courts rather than in the legislatures does not violate democratic principles because the courts are intervening on behalf of groups that are under-represented in the legislatures. Luban concludes that public interest lawyers, by helping "fragmented constituencies to organize themselves, ... serve the highest goal of democracy: to engage citizens in responsible deliberation about the ends of action."[23]

Luban's argument may have some force when applied to the litigation activities of privately-funded interest groups such as the NAACP, the Sierra Club, Planned Parenthood or a trade association interested in a particular matter. The use of a representative action or test case to raise a larger question on which many persons have an insufficient interest to litigate avoids free-rider problems and prevents under-enforcement of law. Even in this context, however, the supposed underrepresentation of the various groups in legislative bodies does not justify countering political injustice with another injustice.

---

[19] See David Luban, Lawyers and Justice (1990).

[20] Id. at 297 - 98.

[21] Id. at 302.

[22] Id. at xxiv.

[23] Id. at xxv.

"Democracy" is being used in a very special sense when interest groups within the larger society rely on unaccountable, life-tenured officials (federal judges) for social change. Whatever the limitations, the constitutional assignment of legislative authority to the elected representatives of the people has much to be said for it, especially when weighed against the shortcomings of other alternatives.

One need not reach these issues of judicial activism, however, to conclude that publicly-funded legal services raise very different social and political issues than the voluntary and private activities of private groups that resort to the courts for social change. Why should the general taxpayer support this partisan political activity?

The critical fact is that Congress has not appropriated funds for the purpose of organizing "fragmented" and otherwise unrepresented groups of poor people for political action or to support test-case manipulation of clients on behalf of the social activism of legal services lawyers. The Legal Services Corporation Act prohibits such activity and permits grants only for the purposes of "furnishing legal assistance to eligible clients."[24] The legal assistance is to provide "equal access to the system of justice," be of "high quality," and must be "kept free from the influence of or use ... of political pressures." Legal services lawyers are commanded to "protect the best interests of their clients" in accordance with "the high standards of the legal profession." The substantive restrictions included in the Act and the procedural constraints on the use of class actions reinforce the political neutrality of the basic scheme.

3. Who Should Be Served?

The demand for free goods, even if their use involves time and inconvenience, is likely to exceed the available supply. The result is an inevitable rationing problem. Because lawyers cannot and will not be provided to all people who feel aggrieved and who lack the resources or capacity to seek relief on their own, someone must decide who will be served. Local legal services programs are required to establish priorities after consultation with representatives of client groups but it is recognized that staff lawyers play a dominant role in shaping and then administering priorities. The establishment of a priority in one area, such as public housing issues, may lead to refusing service in categories of other cases. A number of legal services programs, for example, refuse to accept divorce cases. Critics of the current program suggest more neutral principles, such as queuing or some effort to replicate the private market, as with a voucher system or client copayments.[25]

---

[24] For a discussion of the Legal Services Corporation Act and its legislative history, see Warren George, Development of the Legal Services Corporation, 61 Cornell L. Rev. 681 (1976).

Defenders of current arrangements rely on utilitarian arguments of *triage:* Because funding is so limited, scarce resources must be devoted to the most serious problems that will do the most good for poor people as a whole. This argument places group interests above the right of individuals to obtain access to justice to defend or enforce their legal rights. Inevitably, it places authority in staff lawyers who decide what cases to take and, in doing so and in handling the subsequent representation, make decisions as to what is in the best interests of poor people. Finally, it departs from the traditional lawyer-client relationship in ways that should be avoided if possible.

a) Individuals are entitled to minimal legal service on vital matters.

The United States at present fails to provide its poor citizens with a minimal access to justice. The Legal Services Corporation estimates that only about 20 percent of poor people needing legal help get it. Even if this figure is much exaggerated (many of those below the eligibility line have sufficient resources to pay the relatively low fees required for some routine legal services, such as an uncontested divorce), a much larger emphasis on caring for individuals in need is desirable. Perhaps we cannot afford to do so; but the problem appears to be one of mistaken social priorities. Given the political opposition to the current program, a gradual shift to one on the European model – reimbursing at low rates members of the private bar who provide legal services on meritorious matters – is warranted.

I do not make this argument as one of constitutional entitlement, but as a basic social provision that a legislature concerned with social justice should implement.[26]

b) What are the interests of the poor?

The "interests of the poor" are not easily determinable. Luban's view, resting on a claim that legal services lawyers know what these group interests are,

---

[25] See Douglas J. Besharov, Legal Services for the Poor: Time for Reform xiv, xvi (1990) (staff lawyers, who dominate priority setting, devote little effort to the problems associated with family breakdown, which are the most critical problem of poor people today; client copayments would force clients to choose among their needs); and Marshall J. Breger, Legal Aid for the Poor: A Conceptual Analysis, 60 No. Car. L. Rev. 282 (1982) (utilitarian justifications of a lawyer-centered rationing of service should be replaced by an individual-rights approach).

[26] See Breger, supra n. 25. Breger argues, persuasively in my view, that the claims of poor people of access to justice are best protected through allocation and litigation procedures that give equal weight to each person's complaint, not by procedures that turn on the group impact of a given poor person's case. Failinger and May, supra n. 12, responding to Breger's argument, dispute his claim that access rights are more important than welfare rights.

is limited and elitist. The interests of the poor are complex and variegated. To assume the right to take steps on their behalf is paternalistic. It is not obvious that the highly educated, middle class lawyers who make those decisions on behalf of poor people are well qualified to do so. Moreover, the rewards and incentives within the legal services program flow from establishing new rights and procedures, though it is not clear in many cases whether legal victories on these matters really serve the interests of the poor as a whole. Thus the systematic efforts of many legal services programs to convert residence in a subsidized public housing project into a legal right that can be terminated only by formal procedures is thought by many (perhaps most) residents of public housing projects to be harmful to their interests. Effective means of eliminating violent and drug-pushing tenants have been eliminated, with adverse results on the living environment. Similarly, successful efforts by legal services lawyers to require more elaborate procedures for school discipline are thought by many informed individuals to have worsened educational opportunities in central city public schools.

Evidence is lacking that the law reform and political action models of the legal services movement have actually produced beneficial results for poor people. Every action, such as increased enforcement of building codes in low-income housing, leads to a counter action, such as reduction of the housing supply or increased rents. Although the strategy of the legal services movement – to use the courts to establish rights that would benefit poor people – was well-meaning, a high price in political support has been paid for dubious returns in the form of distributive justice.

c) Departure from a normal lawyer-client relationship

In most cases of private representation there is no problem of identifying the client or who speaks for the client. If an individual is represented, that person decides on the objectives of the representation and, even as to tactics and methods, must be consulted.[27] The client makes the decision whether or not to settle, determines how much should be expended on the representation and is free to discharge the lawyer at any time. The relationship is different with poor

---

27 See ABA Model Rules of Prof. Conduct 1.2 and 1.4 (1983 as amended) (allocating decision-making authority in the lawyer-client relation and stating a lawyer's duty to communicate with a client). The ABA Model Rules have been adopted with various changes in 37 states. For discussion of the lawyer-client relationship, see Barbara A. Curran, Surveying the Legal Needs of the Public: What the Public Wants and Expects in the Lawyer-Client Relationship, in Gibson and Baldwin (eds.), Law in a Cynical Society: Opinion and Law in the 1980's 107 - 19 (1985); Douglas E. Rosenthal, Lawyer and Client: Who's in Charge? (1974) (study of relationship between personal injury clients and their lawyers); Austin Sarat, Lawyers and Clients: Putting Professional Service on the Agenda of Legal Education, 41 J. Legal Educ. 43 (1991); Robert A. Burt, Conflict and Trust Between Attorney and Client, 69 Geo. L. J. 1015 (1981).

clients, who are more dependent on their lawyers and who have nowhere else to go for legal representation.[28] When a lawyer is representing a corporation, identifying the client is more complicated if there is an internal fight for control, but in the more usual situation in which the corporation is opposing third persons or the government, the managers of the corporation are in a position to make decisions concerning the direction, methods and cost of representation.[29] In short, the private client is in charge, with the lawyer acting as the client's agent.

The deployment of the scarce time of lawyers in a legal services office is a very different situation in which the private-representation analogy is not fully applicable. The private-client analogy most fully applies when a legal services lawyer is representing an individual client in a matter that has few implications beyond the individual case, whether the matter is a divorce, a bankruptcy or a welfare benefits problem. Even here, however, the priority-setting process may lead the program's lawyers, who as a practical matter control the timing and outcomes of this process, to reject entire categories of cases, such as those dealing with family problems, in order to deal with what the lawyers feel are more fundamental problems of poor people.[30] As lawyers develop specialized competencies, these priorities are resistant to change.[31] Any candid discussion of client participation in the setting of priorities reflects the truth that no good method of reflecting the interests of all eligible clients in a service area has yet been devised.[32] Nor is it clear that there is any way to replicate in the distribu-

---

[28] Once the attorney-client relationship has been formed, either by appointment of a court or, more likely, by acceptance of a case by a legal services office, the lawyer and client are essentially in a deadly embrace. The lawyer cannot easily withdraw from the representation; the client has no other choices other than the lawyer assigned. If personalities conflict, a legal services program may assign a different lawyer to the matter. The lawyer, who possesses superior information and skill and is balancing the interests of one client against those of others in what is usually a heavy caseload, is in control.

[29] See ABA Model Rule of Prof. Conduct 1.13 (lawyer for an organization represents the entity not its agents or employees). For discussion of the duties owed to a lawyer when the client (an organization) owes duties to others (e.g., shareholders), see Geoffrey C. Hazard, Jr., Triangular Lawyer Relationships: An Exploratory Analysis, 1 Geo.J. Legal Ethics 15 (1987).

[30] See Paul R. Tremblay, Toward a Community-Based Ethic for Legal Services Practice, 37 U.C.L.A.L. Rev. 1103 (1990), arguing that the legal services lawyer faces the dilemma of choosing between "allegiance to the individual client" and making choices and imposing limits that serve interests of groups of poor people. Tremblay states:

> Legal services offices must engage in a form of triage, or "screening of [clients] to determine their priority for treatment [i.e., representation]. They cannot allocate their services according to the usual method of price, so they must choose other means to decide between potentially eligible clients.

Id. at 1111. See also M. Lipsky, Street-Level Bureaucracy: Dilemmas of the Group and Individual in Public Service 3 (1980).

[31] Social programs tend to conform over time to the interests of the staff who run them. The legal services program has been criticized as a "lawyers' program" run by lawyers. Empirical studies provide some report. See Katz, supra note 18.

tion of a public good the consumer sovereignty provided by free markets in goods and services.

When cases in a legal services program arise that raise larger issues, there is a temptation to shape the case, not in the interest of the individual client, but to raise the larger issue that, in the view of the program's lawyers, will advance the strategic interest of a class of poor people.[33] A lawyer for a private client must withdraw when faced with a conflict of interest between that client and other clients, but the legal services client has no other options and may be induced to consent to a more limited or representative litigation.[34] The problem arises both in selection of cases and issues, framing the objectives of litigation and deciding whether and on what terms to settle. At the extreme end of the spectrum is the class action in which the legal services lawyer may have constructed the legal theory, constituted the class, selected its representatives, and made all of the decisions along the way, including a decision to settle that may not accord on the merits or in remedy with the interests or desires of a majority of the represented class. Here, as in the kindred situation of representative suits brought on behalf of amorphous classes of shareholders or consumers, it is a fiction to think of the client class as being in control of the litigation.[35] The lawyer for the class is primarily in charge and the principal check comes from the requirement that the judge approve any settlement. Thus the analogy to private representation must take account of the fact that client control of litigation becomes suspect in legal services litigation involving broad issues; at the extreme of a class action seeking injunctive relief, control by clients is usually fictitious. In those situations the lawyer should be viewed as either lacking a client or as his or her own client.

---

[32] Alan Houseman, one of the most experienced and knowledgeable observers of the legal services movement, has stated that client participation had not achieved its goals and good solutions to the problem do not exist. See also Tremblay, supra note 34, arguing that legal services lawyers must make choices among their present clients in much the same fashion that they make choices among prospective clients:

> The process of client representation is an elastic one; absent some control on demand such as billing in the private sphere, the subsidized client will continue to compete with his fellow clients for the scarce time, energy, and funds available to his lawyer.

Id. at 1115. Tremblay, a former legal services lawyer, defends the practical reality that "a legal services lawyer must make normative choices among her clients in distributing the scarce funds." Id. at 1120.

[33] This proposition is conceded and defended by Luban and Tremblay. See Luban, supra note 19; Tremblay, supra note 30.

[34] See Fiandaca v. Cunningham, 827 F. 2d 825 (1st Cir. 1987) (conflict between two groups of eligible clients simultaneously represented by a legal services organization).

[35] See Greenfield v. Villager Industries, Inc., 483 F. 2d 824, 832 n. 9 (3d Cir. 1973): "Experience teaches that it is counsel for the class representatives, and not the named parties, who direct and manage [class] actions. Every experienced federal judge knows that any statement to the contrary is sheer sophistry." See also Deborah L. Rhode, Class Conflicts in Class Actions, 34 Stanford L. Rev. 1183 (1982).

Restructuring the legal services program to provide individual-care service through private lawyers, reimbursed by public funding at rates specified by regulation (e.g., so much for a personal bankruptcy or an uncontested divorce), would provide poor people with a relatively normal lawyer-client relationship to poor people. A staff-attorney component would remain to provide screening of cases for eligibility and merit, to refer the cases to an appropriate private lawyer and to maintain quality control and to provide payment. In addition, a central legal services organization in major cities or on a statewide basis would provide necessary functions: (1) training for private lawyers who desired to give pro bono assistance on a part-time basis and (2) back-up support on specialized poverty-law matters for private lawyers handling cases.

4. Standard of Service

Ordinary people who desire a lawyer to prepare a will, get a divorce or facilitate a transaction must pay the customary charge of lawyers for that service. Numerous studies indicate that many of them forego the use of legal services because of cost, inconvenience or fear of becoming involved in the legal machinery. Those with little choice, who are cast as defendants in a proceeding brought by someone else, reluctantly hire lawyers, but generally push them to handle the matter as cheaply as possible. The result is a world in which most people "lump it" on many legal matters and get low-cost or minimal representation on many others. That is the reality of the legal market place in which most private persons make their decisions.

The most ambitious vision of legal services for the poor, however, looks to the representation provided to wealthy individuals and large corporations in high-stakes matters as the appropriate analogy. Earl Johnson, who headed the OEO legal program in the 1960s, states that he learned what full-servicing lawyering for a client really meant from a partner at Covington & Burling who represented American Airlines. Poor people, Johnson concluded, are entitled to the same quality and extent of legal service that is provided to a wealthy client in a high-stakes matter: aggressive advocacy at every stage, including appeals; representation in administrative and legislative matters, including lobbying; and use of representative or class actions when in the interest of the client. The implication is that eligible clients of publicly-funded legal services offices are entitled to what only a few wealthy persons and large corporations actually receive: Unrestricted full-service lawyering that leaves no stone unturned and is not as restrained by considerations of cost as would be true of most other persons and entities.

The premises of the argument, however, are fallacious. Upper income people, let alone people of lesser means, do not employ a "full court press" in litigation except where it appears cost effective and often not even then. Such a commitment of legal services may be warranted where the existence of a wealthy organization is threatened, but it is not warranted, even with wealthy people, in a dispute over repairs on a Mercedes. A scheme of misdirected policy flows from a false assumption about what the non-poor do regarding use of legal services, which is then used as a predicate for a demand for equal treatment of the poor.

Moreover, if society was committed to giving the poor an income supplement equal in value to the "full court press" which is urged on their behalf by lawyers, why should it be provided in the form of lawyers' services rather than in the form of a welfare check?[36] Individual poor persons would undoubtedly prefer the freedom of choosing how much they wanted to spend on legal services and other wants. Knowing that this is the case, defenders of providing assistance only in prescribed forms (i.e., lawyers, not money which poor people might use for their own purposes) assert that "the full court press in this case will redound to the benefit of other poor people." But we are now back to the class-suit fallacy, in which optimistic, if not absurd, claims concerning its beneficial consequences are advanced to rely on its use in the judicial arena. The class-suit strategy is appealing because it provides interesting employment for capable lawyers with an intense concern for the poor. This is not the first time that a social benefit program has been captured by the professionals who administer it.

One caution is warranted: The stakes involved in some test cases or class actions clearly justify full-service lawyering. The aggregation of small, related claims may collectively constitute a major claim that justifies a substantial commitment of legal resources whether the case is pursued by a legal services lawyer, without fee, or by a class-action lawyer who anticipates a fee award from a successful action.

Other matters, however, present issues of proportionality and fairness as well as those of effectiveness that have already been discussed. A private litigant ordinarily will not pursue a $ 1,000 matter by expending more than some fraction of that amount on legal services. But a publicly-funded lawyer is not similarly constrained in litigation on behalf of a poor client. As Gary Bellow and others have recognized, this fact confers enormous leverage on legal services lawyers in dealing with private persons and some leverage in dealing with government agencies. Because the costs of litigation from the point of view of a private person may be larger than the amount at stake, the possibility of

[36] Some critics of the federal legal services program argue that it is a lawyers' program that primarily benefits lawyers: providing interesting employment to a substantial number of politically concerned lawyers and requiring private interests who oppose the legal services lawyers to spend much larger amounts in hiring lawyers to defend their interests. In this view, the decision to provide poor people not with money but with lawyers is what the program is really about: a subsidy of lawyers.

extortionate settlements exist. The constraints on this behavior on the part of legal services lawyers are the practical ones of heavy caseloads and limited staffs, constraints that advocates of full-service lawyering on behalf of the poor vigorously lament and want removed.

Shift to a Judicare model would eliminate most of the fairness problems of disproportionality in civil legal assistance. Poor people would receive by state funding the same standard of service normally provided to middle-class and lower middle-class Americans who pay their own way.

III. Conclusion

A fundamental dilemma of the U.S. legal services program is that political opposition, resulting in funding limitations, is directly related to the law reform, institutional change and social advocacy aspects of the program. Individual client service receives almost universal acceptance from the public and its elected representatives as well as from the legal profession. Some law reform activities command the support of political liberals but intense opposition from many interests faced with such litigation, including state and local governments. Larger-scale institutional reform in which clients become nominal plaintiffs selected and controlled by staff lawyers are viewed with considerable hostility and suspicion, not only by those on the political right but by many in the center. Finally, taxpayer support of political organization and direct action (e.g., picketing, demonstrations) are viewed with great public hostility and opposition.

The crucial point is that there is large bipartisan support for a politically neutral legal services program primarily concerned with individual client service. The organized bar will give strong support to such a program and defend limitations on its activities with great vigor. Yet if the program is perceived as following an ideological approach, retaliation inevitably results. Political interests adversely affected by institutional reform litigation will fight back in the legislative and executive corridors. Limited funds, inconsistent direction and chronic instability will tend to cripple the program.

On the other hand, an exclusive focus on the routine problems of individual poor persons leads to minimal service and is inefficient in that it neglects the greater bang for the buck produced by vigorously pursuing targeted priorities by use of representative actions. Perhaps the best solution is one that utilizes the neutral rhetoric of access and quality, primarily devotes itself to individual client service, but pursues aggressively broader issues arising out of individual-client service when the client wants the lawyer to do so.

The federal legal services program should be restructured by amendment of the Legal Services Corporation Act. To assure that poor clients get the same representation as those who can afford to pay, the program should be shifted largely to a Judicare model in which the eligible client picks a lawyer from those enrolled in the program. The present legal services organizations would screen clients for eligibility and a preliminary assessment that a meritorious claim was involved, refer clients to lawyers enrolled in the program, and provide training, support and specialized substantive assistance to lawyers participating in the program either on a volunteer basis (pro bono) or as paid participants. Legal fees to private lawyers handling poor people's matters would be restricted to relatively modest statutory schedules (e. g., $ 200 for an uncontested divorce). Class actions and social advocacy would be left largely to private groups under current fee-shifting statutes, although existing legal services specialists would provide expert assistance on significant poverty law matters raised by individual cases referred to members of the private bar. These changes would create a more traditional lawyer-client relationship in publicly-funded legal services, treat poor people in much the same way as middle class clients are handled by the private bar and eliminate most of the political controversy from the legal services program.

Constitution and Stability in Latin America

Ernesto Garzón Valdés, Mainz

Introduction

One of the oldest, and yet still one of the most urgent questions in politics is that about the factors responsible for the stability or instability of a political system. In the last few decades, the conditions of democratic stability have been a recurrent focus of interest for political scientists investigating transition processes in Southern Europe, in Latin America, and currently in Eastern Europe. Judgements of stability or instability are often, rather intuitively, based mainly on the observation of constitutional continuity or disruption. Although this approach may seem plausible at first sight, I think it does not survive closer scrutiny. Instead, I will argue in this paper, the constitution is certainly one, but not the only, and not even necessarily the most important characteristic of a political system to be taken into account in assessing system stability. In all this, obviously, the concept of political stability is of crucial importance.

In what follows, therefore, I intent to:

I. Propose a definition of "stability" of a political system in general;

II. Provide some examples of constitutional history in Latin America which show the rather limited relevance of the constitutions as a factor of stability; and

III. Present some tentative conclusions on the basis of the examples.

I. The Concept of Stability of a Political System

First of all, I propose to define the stability of a system in general as follows:[1]

Definition 1: A system (S) is stable iff, under certain circumstances (C), it has the tendency, or disposition, to react in a way enabling it to maintain its identity (R_i).[2]

---

[1] For a more detailed presentation see Ernesto Garzón Valdés, Die Stabilität politischer Systeme. Analyse des Begriffs mit Fallbeispielen aus Lateinamerika, Freiburg/Munich 1988.

[2] Ibid., p. 35.

Now, if we want to look at political systems and their stability in particular, what we need is a criterion for the identity of such systems. This criterion must be both more flexible than mere recourse to constitutional provisions and less vague than that to psycho-sociological elements – as, for example, the political culture of a country – and, at the same time, it must offer a framework of reference whithout which it cannot even be determined which political system's stability or instability is at issue in any specific case. In my opinion, H. L. A. Hart's notion of "rule of recognition" has all the required properties and is uniquely well suited to lead to a promising approach in this respect.

Using Hart's concept of "rule of recognition", then, the general definition proposed above can be transformed into:

Definition 2: A political system (S_p) is stable iff, under certain circumstances (C), it has the tendency, or disposition, to react in a way enabling it to maintain its rule of recognition (R_r).[3]

Since the rule of recognition contains the criteria for the validity of norms and their membership in the respective system, it is indeed the basis for the system's identity and unity. Every political system has exactly one rule of recognition – which, of course, may be more or less complex. The existence of more than one rule of recognition in a society indicates that the system is in a pathological state; in that case, the system cannot be described, it has, so to speak, a "split personality". And since, on the other hand, any system necessarily does have some rule of recognition – whose determination is basically an empirical problem –, Def. 2 has the advantage over Def. 1 of clearly not being analytical.

It is also important to remember that the existence of a political or legal system is closely related to the existence of an "internal point of view": Such a system exists only if at least the dominant group accepts the rule of recognition from the internal point of view.

Obviously, for the existence of a political or legal system, it is not enough that a smaller or larger group of persons adopt the internal point of view with respect to a particular rule of recognition; in other words: the internal point of view is a necessary, but not a sufficient condition for the corresponding system's existence. Those who adopt it must, in addition, also have the power to impose their rule of recognition on the respective society.

At this point, I think it is important to note that the actual imposition of the rule of recognition must take place in accordance with the norms valid in the system, for the simple reason that the existence of a particular rule of recognition means precisely the application of, and compliance with, the valid system norms. A departure from these norms endangers the identity, and that means: the stability of the system.

---

[3] Ibid.

On the other hand, this does not mean that a system has to be static in order to maintain its identity; not every alteration poses a challenge to its identity or stability. Identity remains intact, of course, when a system is changed in accordance with its rule of recognition. Therefore, the validity of the rules of change, and of the changes carried out with their help, cannot be determined exclusively on the basis of their constitutionality; additionally, one also has to take into account the – possibly complex – criteria for the identification of valid system norms embodied in the rule of recognition.

Using Kurt Hübner's concepts of "explication" and "mutation",[4] one can say that every political system, even a dictatorial one, does have explicatory rules of change.

With the criterion of explication or mutation, the definition of stability proposed above thus transforms into:

Definition 3: A political system (S_p) is stable iff, under certain circumstances (C), it has the tendency or disposition to react in such a way that the changes it experiences are explications of its rule of recognition (R_r).

There is, of course, at least one more factor which is relevant in judgements of stability, and that is the factor of time. We do not say that a political system that has kept its rule of recognition for just a few months is stable, but we do tend to predicate stability of systems that haven't changed their rule of recognition for many decades. The question is only how many decades this must be: four, six, ten, or even more? If one agrees that stability or instability is something like the "good or bad weather" of a political system, it may be useful to recall Thomas Hobbes' famous observation about the state of war:

> "For war, consisteth not in battle only, or the act of fighting; but in a tract of time, wherein the will to contend by battle is sufficiently known; and therefore the notion of time, is to be considered in the nature of war; as it is in the nature of weather. For as the nature of foul weather, lieth not in a shower or two of rain but in an inclination thereto of many days together: so the nature of war, consisteth not in actual fighting; but in the known disposition thereto, during all the time there is no assurance to the contrary."[5]

The same applies to the case of stability. There too, the necessary "track of time" cannot be stated precisely. And there too, the question can be answered only by refering to the "inclination" or "disposition" to R_r during "many years together". Thus, the concept of stability is relative to the historical and regional context of the respective system S_p.

Venezuelan democracy, for example, is more or less of the same age as democracy in the Federal Republic of Germany; the fact that judgments about the stability of these two systems possibly differ shows that what counts is not

[4] Kurt Hübner, Kritik der wissenschaftlichen Vernunft, Freiburg/Munich 1979.

[5] See Thomas Hobbes, The English Works, 10 vols., Aalen 1966, vol. 3, p. 113.

merely the duration of reactions of type R_r but also the contextual circumstances of each system.

On the basis of all these considerations, I propose the following working definition of the concept of stability of political systems:

Definition 4: A political system (S_p) is stable iff, in cases related to the institutionalized exercise of violence – be they "normal" or "hard" cases –, it has the tendency, or disposition, to react in such a way that the changes it experiences are explications of its rule of recognition (R_r), and it manifests this disposition during a period of time which, considering its historical and geographical context, is significant.

Keeping in mind the definition of stability just proposed, I will now defend the following thesis:

> Reference to the constitution is not only of little help in determining the identity of a political system, it can even lead to a mistaken view with respect to this identity and, consequently, the interpretation of changes in terms of stability or instability.

In order to support my thesis, I will advance three empirical arguments, and then take a closer look at the last one of them.

1. Identifying the rule of recognition with the written text of the constitution is insufficient even in those cases where the constitution is fully implemented, that is, cases of what could be called "constitutional order". The written text of the U. S. Constitution, for example, does not tell us much if we don't take into consideration the interpretation it has been given by the Supreme Court.

2. There are cases where the constitution stays formally in force, i. e., is not derogated, and where, nevertheless, it would be absurd to say that there has not been a fundamental alteration of the system.

The most notorious case of this type is probably the transition from the Republic of Weimar to the Nazi regime. It is precisely for this reason that it is possible to use the paradoxical expression of "legal revolution" for it. A number of authors have underwritten the thesis that the constitution of Weimar "continued to exist, but had to be interpreted according to the spirit of the new order".[6] Others have maintained that there was a "superposition of constitutions", i. e., there existed "two constitutional layers which were simultaneously valid" *(zwei Verfassungsschichten nebeneinander in Geltung)*.[7] Bernd Rüthers' seminal work *Unlimited interpretation. On the alteration of*

[6] Cf. Gerhard Dannemann, Legale Revolution, Nationale Revolution, in: E.-W. Böckenförde (ed.), Staatsrecht und Staatsrechtslehre im Dritten Reich, Heidelberg 1985, pp. 3 - 22, here p. 15.

[7] Ibid.

civil law under national-socialism[8] contains countless examples of how a legal system can be altered by way of "interpretative elimination".

3. Finally, there are those cases that could be called "constitutional chaos", i.e., where the constitution is of little help in identifying even the valid legal order. This is the situation in most Latin American countries, and I think it may be useful to take a closer look at these cases.

II. System Stability and Constitution in Latin America

In order to illustrate the Latin American situation with respect to the relationship between constitution and stability, it may be useful to recall that from 1958 to 1984, only four countries – Colombia, Costa Rica, Mexico and Venezuela – have experienced an uninterrupted succession of political power according to the respective constitutional requirements.[9]

In looking at the role of the constitution for the socio-political configuration of Latin American countries, two fundamental aspects should be kept in mind:

(i) Although there are differences between the legal order as it has been enacted and the legal order as it is in fact implemented in European countries too, nowhere are they as large as they have always been in Latin America.

Therefore, when we analyze Latin American constitutional law, we must always explicitly state whether we are talking about the letter of a constitution or about its real efficacy. It is no exaggeration to say that the legal orders of a substantial number of countries in Latin America suffer from what H. L. A. Hart once called the "pathology of law".

(ii) Another source of problems is the existence of two contradictory attitudes with a long tradition in Spanish America: on the one hand, an enormous faith in the constitution as a main factor for regulating social reality, and, on the other, the conviction that the gap between legal order and social reality is nothing one needs to worry about. The gap is taken, instead, to be a more or less unfortunate, but rather irrelevant fact, and jurists tend to dedicate themselves to the study of enacted norms *as if* they were effectively in force.[10]

---

[8] Die unbegrenzte Auslegung. Zum Wandel der Privatrechtsordnung im Nationalsozialismus, Frankfurt a. M. 1973.

[9] See Alain Rouquié, Amérique latine – Introduction à l'Extrême Occident, Paris 1987, p. 110.

[10] For some authors – for instance, Howard J. Wiarda, Law and Political Development in Latin America, in: idem (ed.), Politics and Social Change in Latin America, University of Massachussetts Press 1974, p. 283 – this divergence even constitutes a positive element since it would show a certain "flexibility with respect to reality".

In order to take a closer look at these phenomena, I will now concentrate on three cases which I think are paradigmatic: the Bolivian, the Mexican, and the Argentinian case.

1. The Case of Bolivia

In the 132 years from 1825 until 1957, Bolivia has had 14 constitutions, and in the 100 years between 1825 and 1925, it has suffered 190 seditious movements – conspiracies, revolts, "pronouncements", uprisings, and revolutions.[11] The constitution currently valid is from 1967, but

> "[b]ecause of the uninterrupted sequence of military dictators between 1969 and 1979, the latest constitution of the country has been practically irrelevant".[12]

The Bolivian constitutionalist Ciro Félix Trigo affirms:

> "Even the most superficial examination of constitutional theory and reality clearly reveals a notorious imbalance between the two. The discrepancy between what the law says, and what is done in its name or without invoking it [is enormous]. Old customs, inveterate habits, and a low or inexistent civic culture conspire against the correct and faithful application of basic norms. Also, there is the weight of the tradition of conduct observed by the authorities with respect to the laws dictated by the king of Spain for the Indies which can be resumed in the following maxime: 'It is accepted, but not complied with'. Unfortunately, we can still say today that the constitution is accepted, but only partially and sporadically complied with.
>
> This is why the struggle for implanting a constitutional regime in Latin America permits a generalized classification: Those who govern and who see in the constitution an obstacle to their purposes of uncontrolled power, infringe and violate its norms in order to stay in power; and those who are governed and who call for the effective validity of the constitution often surpass the limits of the permissible, make exaggerated claims, and provoke de facto situations which constitute new violations of the constitution. These constitutions which have been ten times sworn allegiance to [...] and a thousand times abused, these abuses of authority and the people, that is what Bolivian history is all about."[13]

Without too high a risk of error, one can say that

> "[c]onstitutions in Bolivia, whether good or bad, have been neither a wall of authority nor a revolutionary impulse; governments have fallen, one after the other, through the schemes of social, political or military forces carried out by passing underneath, passing overhead and even going right through the Fundamental law".[14]

The case of Bolivia illustrates the irrelevance of the constitution as a factor of stability, and it is a good example for the conceptual importance of distin-

[11] See Ciro Félix Trigo, Las Constituciones de Bolivia, Madrid 1958, p. 61.

[12] See Leon E. Bieber, Bolivien, in: Peter Waldmann et al., Politisches Lexikon Lateinamerika, Munich 1980, p. 46.

[13] See Ciro Félix Trigo, op. cit., pp. 48f.

[14] Ibid., p. 100.

guishing between rule of recognition and constitution. In order to judge the validity of an alteration, the rule of recognition is decisive; therefore, changes that would be a manifestation of chaos in one system may perfectly well be the "normal way" in another. To keep this in mind is especially important if one wishes to compare political systems.

An excellent example of an application of the criterion just proposed is Howard J. Wiarda's study *Critical Elections and Critical Coups* where, among others, the following theses are sustained:

> "[. . .] that clear and discernible 'systemic' political patterns exist in a continent [Latin America, E. G. V.] that to North Americans often seems to be characterized by chaos and anarchy;
>
> [. . .] that these patterns tell us a great deal about the Latin American change process, about the periodicity and stages of Latin American development, and about class and structural shifts and fundamental socio-political realignments".[15]

To what extent military coups may be considered the "normal way" of political change in Latin America is illustrated by the fact that Rigoberto Paredes, a Bolivian politician, once made the proposal to enact "regulations for revolution".[16] That would, of course, make for some strange "rules of change", but whether they should be accepted or rejected depends ultimately on the rule of recognition one accepts.

Now, someone might think that in a country affected by so many revolts and *coups d'Etat* there is hardly any use in talking of a relationship between constitution and stability, and that it would therefore be wise to look for a country with great political stability and an unaltered constitution.

2. The Mexican Case

In Latin America, the best example in this sense is Mexico: its constitution, enacted in 1917 and in force until today, at the time of enactment was one of the most modern constitutions in the world, considering that it established the system of a welfare state under the rule of law, and since 1930 all presidents have completed their terms as prescribed in the constitution. However, a closer look at Mexico's constitutional and legal reality brings to light some rather surprising phenomena.

A few data may serve to document the way Mexican democracy works. Between 1920 and 1982, the official presidential candidate never won less than 70% of the vote:[17]

---

[15] See Howard J. Wiarda, Critical Elections and Critical Coups: The Processes of Sociopolitical Realignment in Latin American Development in: idem (ed.), The Continuing Struggle for Democracy in Latin America, Boulder, Col. 1980, p. 28.

[16] See Ciro Félix Trigo, op. cit., p. 59.

Year	Official candidate	% of vote
1920	Obregón	95,8
1924	Calles	84,1
1928	Obregón	100,0
1929	Ortiz Rubio	93,6
1934	Cárdenas	98,2
1940	Avila Camacho	93,9
1946	Alemán	77,9
1952	Ruiz Cortines	74,3
1958	López Mateos	90,4
1964	Díaz Ordaz	88,8
1970	Echeverría	86,0
1976	López Portillo	92,3
1982	de la Madrid Hurtado	71,0
1988	Salinas de Gortari	48,8

With respect to the relationship between executive and legislative power, it is interesting to note that in 1935, 1937 and 1941 100% of the bills sent to Congress by the executive were unanimously approved by the House of Representatives. The percentage of unanimously approved executive bills in later years was:

1943: 92%
1947: 74%
1949: 77%
1959: 95%
1961: 82%.

As for the judiciary, Pablo González Casanova stated in 1965 that "by and large, it follows the politics of the executive, and serves to strengthen his stability".[18] In 1988, Alejandro M. Garro observed with respect to the binding force of the jurisprudence of the Mexican Supreme Court in *amparo* sentences:

> "Mexican *amparo* law exempts the administrative and legislative authorities from the obligation to respect the jurisprudential theses which for the judiciary are binding. When the Mexican constituent assembly thus limited the effects of *amparo* sentences, it assumed that once a law were declared unconstitutional by the judiciary it would lose its prestige and would no longer be applied [...] But this hope of the constituent did not materialize, and it is instead in the discretion of the administrative authorities to decide when and in what cases they will not apply a law that was repeatedly

[17] See José María Cartas, Orden político y orden económico en México: dilemas y alternativas, Buenos Aires 1990, p. 7.

[18] See Pablo González Casanova, La democracia en México, Mexico-City 1965, p. 25.

declared unconstitutional by the Supreme Court of Justice of Mexico [...] Neither does the legislature seem to have the obligation to accept the decisions of the Mexican Supreme Court on the constitutionality of laws [...] The insecurity created by the fact that there is no certainty about an eventual application of a norm that may have been repeatedly declared unconstitutional by federal courts has given rise to criticism [...] in favor of giving *amparo* sentences force *erga omnes*."[19]

This does not mean, of course, that the Mexican Constitution does not recognize the principle of division of powers. On the contrary, article 49 says: "The supreme power of the federation is divided in its exercise into legislative, executive and judicial power." And one should not forget that in Mexico we are concernced with a democracy *sui generis* that has no similarity whatsoever, for example, with the case of Nicaragua under the Somozas where articles 316 and 320 - 324 of the Constitution prescribed a system of party pluralism and the government, despite its dictatorial reign, repeatedly alleged that it was loyally respecting the constitution.

Pablo González Casanova's observation about legislative power in Mexico applies to all these cases as well:

"The legislature apparently has only a symbolic function. It sanctions the acts of the Executive. It gives them validity and a foundation of a traditional, metaphysical kind, such that executive Acts acquire the status of laws, or rest on and are supported by the legal order, and thus obeys a very ancient, although secular symbolic mechanism."[20]

Now, someone may object that the Mexican problems are irrelevant since, because of the heterogeneity of its population (according to anthropologists, there are 56 ethnic groups), it is a very special case requiring special treatment. In that case, the Argentinian Republic, with a population that is much more homogenous racially and ethnically than that of the United States, could possibly be a more interesting case. As I will try to show, unfortunately, the Argentinian panorama does not turn out to be much more encouraging.

3. The Case of Argentina

In Argentina, the so-called period of national organisation began with the defeat of Juan Manuel de Rosas in the battle of Caceros in 1852. This was the end of an era in Argentinian history marked by violent rivalries between pro-

---

[19] See Alejandro M. Garro, Eficacia y autoridad del precedente constitucional en América Latina: las lecciones del derecho comparado, in: Revista Española de Derecho Constitucional No. 24 (sept. - dec. 1988), pp. 117 and 119. What has been said here about the Mexican case applies to other countries in Latin America as well. For the Argentinian case, see Roberto Bergalli, Jueces e intereses sociales en Argentina, in: idem, Crítica a la criminología, Bogotá 1982, pp. 245ff.

[20] See Pablo González Casanova, op. cit., pp. 32f.

vincial *caudillos* and the struggle between two competing political ideologies: unitarianism and federalism.

From the legal-institutional perspective, the most important consequence of this development was the promulgation in 1853 of the constitution which is still in force today. Nothing would be better suited to illustrate the discrepancy between the newly enacted constitutional order and the real situation in the country at the time than a look at the theoretical foundation of this constitution and the proceedings of the constituent assembly.

The most important theoretical document is Juan Bautista Alberdi's study *Bases and points of departure for the political organization of the Republic of Argentina, derived from the law which governs the development of civilization in South America.*[21] Alberdi never conceals that the institutional model he proposes does not fit the social reality of Argentina. The options, therefore, are either to give up the model or to change the country. Alberdi chooses the latter: Since the ethnic structure in Argentina, in his view, was not suited to handle an advanced institutional model, and such a model had to be implemented in order to fulfill the "capital and supreme law of the development of a christian and modern civilization"[22], it was necessary to further the modernizing effect of the constitution with the corresponding demographic change. In Alberdi's own words:

> "It is utopia [...] to think that our Spanish-American people, as it has emerged from its dark colonial past, can implement today a representative republic. [...] It is not the laws we need to change: it is the people, the facts. We must exchange our people, incapable of liberty, for others who can handle it."[23]

And he adds:

> "With three million indians, christians and catholics [...] you will surely not create the republic. You will not create it with four million Spaniards either. [...] If we must fit our population to the system of government, if we should rather fit the population to the proclaimed system than the system to the population, then we must encourage an anglo-saxon population on our soil. This is the kind of population identified with the steamboat, with commerce, and with freedom, and we will not be able to establish these things among ourselves without the cooperation of this people of progress and civilization."[24]

Alberdi's disbelief in the fitness of Spaniards and *criollos* – and indios, of course – for modern development was shared by another great Argentinian writer and statesman, Domingo Faustino Sarmiento, who repeatedly gave

---

[21] Juan Bautista Alberdi, Bases y puntos de partida para la organización política de la República Argentina, derivados de la lei que preside al desarrollo de la civilización en la América del Sud (1852), reprint Buenos Aires/Madrid 1913, p. 12.

[22] Ibid.

[23] Ibid., p. 178.

[24] Ibid., p. 180.

voice to it in his book *Facundo – Civilization and Barbarity*, one of the first sociological studies of Latin America.

And even in Esteban Echeverría's *Socialist Dogma,* despite the democratic aspirations of the author, it cannot be overlooked that the proposed institutional order is condemned to be effectively valid only for a limited part of society:

"Sovereignty is the greatest and most sublime act of reason of a free people. But how could those who do not understand its significance possibly participate in that act? People who for their lack of mental powers are unable to distinguish good from bad in public affairs? People who, out of ignorance about the issue to be decided, do not have their own opinion and are therefore exposed to the manipulations of malevolent contemporaries? People who, with their imprudent judgement, could endanger the liberty of our fatherland and the existence of our society? [...] He whose well-being depends on the will of another and who does not enjoy personal independence will even less be able to enjoy his sovereignty; because he will most certainly not sacrifice his interest to the independence of reason. Therefore, the ignorant, the vagabond, he who has no personal independence, needs tutelage. The law does not generally prohibit them to exercise sovereign rights, but only insofar as they are mentally under age: It does not rob them of these rights but only establishes a condition for their possession which is the condition of emancipation."[25]

Reading the proceedings of the constitutional debates, one easily comes to the conclusion that – with only a few exceptions, the most notable being Facundo Zuviría – this attitude was widely shared by the fathers of the Argentinian Constitution.

And what has been said for the case of Argentina also applies, *mutatis mutandis,* to other countries in Latin America. Thus, for example, José Galvao de Souza observes:

"The constitutional design of Brazil and the countries of Spanish America [...] very eloquently shows the conflict between the law as it has been drafted by the ruling minorities, and the relationships experienced by the people in the course of each nationality's historical progress. [...] From the very first political leaders at the time of independence – as Miranda in Venezuela or Maia in Brazil – to the creators or reformers of constitutions – as the Argentinian Alberdi or the Brazilian Ruy Barbosa – all were imbued with anglo-saxon democratic formulas and did not know enough about the life of the people in their own country. The constitution thus became the work of men guided by external influences, detached from their respective native countries, and linked to the interests of the dominant social class. They were marginal elites. [...] The constitution assumed the character of an ideological charter composed to serve certain political conceptions, and ceases to be a pragmatic instrument designed to preserve specific liberties, as the British *Magna Charta* [...]".[26]

---

[25] Esteban Echeverría, Dogma socialista de la Asociación de Mayo, reprint Vaduz 1978, pp. 60ff.

[26] See José Galvao de Souza, Remarques sur l'idée de constitution et la signification du droit constitutionel, in: Jahrbuch des öffentlichen Rechts (Tübingen) vol. 10 (1967), p. 63.

Undoubtedly, those who dictated these constitutions possessed unshakeable faith in the law; but there is also no doubt that reality did not fit these constitutions, and that the abyss between the normative order and reality did become a source of serious political and social trouble.

As can easily be shown, in cases of conflict between the text of the constitution and the necessities of political and social reality, it was usually the constitution whose implementation was relaxed. For the purpose of this paper, it may suffice to recall the long periods of emergency rule: In the case of Argentina, the state of emergency was upheld during 35 of the 53 years between 1930 and 1983. Consequently, faith in the constitution has degenerated into an empty formula, although, surprisingly, this has not deprived it of its force, as manifested by the still frequent invocations of this faith by constitutional and even *de facto* governments.

In fact, even though the Argentinian Constitution which is still in force today was first enacted in 1853, almost one third of the life of this republic after independence has been marked by the rule of *de facto* governments. The interesting aspect for our purpose is that the Supreme Court has granted these *de facto* governments a legal status similar to that of *de jure* governments, a fact which has caused considerable confusion with respect to the role of the constitution as the supreme norm. A few examples may illustrate this:

On September 6, 1930, a military coup put an end to the first liberal democracy in Argentina. The attitude taken by the Supreme Court of Justice toward the coup is quite interesting: On September 10, the Court acknowledged receipt of a written message by the new government. In its note, the Court recognized the *de facto* government, announcing only that it would control its compliance with the constitution (invoked by the new government itself) just like it would in the case of a constitutional government. A few years later, in 1933, the Court extended the powers of the *de facto* government, granting it the right to dictate law-decrees, that is, the competence to assume legislative functions.[27]

This tendency to endow *de facto* governments with extensive competences was maintained in Argentina during almost half a century. When there were doubts about the "trustworthiness" of the Supreme Court, the option wisely adopted was to exchange all its members. This was done in 1943, in 1955, and in 1966.

In 1947, the Supreme Court decided that

"insofar as it is necessary to legislate in order to govern, a *de facto* government has the necessary legislative powers, and the determination of this necessity – concerning

[27] See Carlos S. Nino, Fundamentos de derecho constitucional – Análisis filosófico, jurídico y politológico de la práctica constitucional, Buenos Aires 1992, p. 131.

its extension or convenience –, being part of political prudence, cannot be subject to judicial review . . .",

and in another sentence of the same year, it sustained that

"the law-decrees dictated by the *de facto* government are valid because of their origin, and since they are equivalent to laws they subsist, even if they have not been ratified by Congress, as long as they are not derogated in the only possible way for laws, that is, by other laws".[28]

In 1949, under the Peronists, the constitution was changed without observation of the requirements established in article 30 concerning the calculation of the necessary parlamentary majority. This new constitution was derogated by decree in 1955 (under the military *de facto* government). A Constituent Assembly which put the constitution of 1853 back into force – with only slight modifications like those of article 14 *bis* concerning social rights – was convened by decree and excluded the Peronists, which meant the exclusion of a large sector of the Argentinian electorate.

In 1966, there was another military coup. The new government enacted the so-called "Statute of the Argentinian Revolution" by which it authorized itself to take on the role of the legislative power. Military rule was ended through the elections of 1973 which were held on the basis of a *de facto* constitutional revision, namely, the so-called "Fundamental Statute" enacted by decree in 1972.

The "legislative" activity of the military government, however, had created a situation that shows how difficult it is to identify the "valid legal system" in more than one period of Argentinian history. *La Nación* – one of the country's leading newspapers – wrote about it under the telling headline "State of insecurity".[29] For the sake of illustration, let me quote a few passages from this article:

"[T]he country is living in a state of extreme constitutional uncertainty. In some legal respects – for example, the validity of legislation enacted by *de facto* governments since 1966 – chaos could hardly be worse. The three branches of power of the Republic, in fact, have different positions in this crucial matter. [. . .] First of all, the National Supreme Court of Justice [. . .] has upheld that this legislation has ceased to exist together with the governments that enacted it [. . .] Second, the executive has shown its predilection for ambiguity in this matter: in some cases, it has repealed law-decrees, or, as they used to be called before, 'laws' of the revolutionary government, by simple decree [. . .]; in other cases, it turned to Congress, sending bills derogating 'laws' enacted between June 28, 1966, and May 25, 1973. [. . .] Third, the National Congress seems to underestimate the significance of this question since it has, on the one hand, silently accepted the repeal by decree of law-decrees issued by the

[28] Ibid., p. 136.

[29] See Carlos S. Nino, Notas de introducción al derecho, Buenos Aires 1974, Vol. 3, pp. 43 ff.

revolutionary government and, on the other, accepted to derogate legal dispositions of equivalent rank through law [. . .]".

The problem mentioned in the article was, of course, not a purely theoretical, but also a practical matter. The question was what was to be understood by "law" for the years 1966 - 1973. In accordance with art. 5 of the Statute of the Argentinian Revolution, the military government that had taken power in 1966 had taken over the functions of Congress. It therefore claimed that the norms it enacted were not decrees or law-decrees, but laws. While in 1972, Tilman Evers could still call this new terminology "legally irrelevant",[30] in 1973 it became apparent that this was not the case.

To give an example: According to the constitution of 1853 whose partial validity the military government had recognized,[31] the nomination of generals, admirals, major generals, judges, ambassadors and envoys requires the approval of the Senate. Because of the above-mentioned art. 5, the military government believed the nominations it had carried out in these three areas – armed forces, judiciary, and foreign service – to be perfectly valid.

After the change of government on May 25, 1973, the validity of these nominations was not judged according to uniform legal criteria: neither were they declared void, nor was their validity generally accepted. Instead, eminently political criteria were adopted, taking into account the actual distribution of power: the promotions in the armed forces were not contested at all; those in the judiciary were accepted, but it was decided that some judges whose loyalty to the executive could not be sufficiently guaranteed would be sent into early retirement; the promotions in the foreign service, however, were considered incomplete acts requiring the confirmation of the Senate.

In this case, as in other, similar ones – after all, a great number of these so-called "laws" had been issued during the time of military rule – the law no longer fulfilled one of its main functions, i.e., that of directing the expectations of the people whose behavior it is supposed to regulate. This certainly justifies the label "State of insecurity" employed in the newspaper-article quoted above.

During the same time, it was just as difficult to determine the hierarchy of the sources of the prevailing normative order. Art. 3 of the Statute of the Argentinian Revolution established three main sources: the Statute itself, the Constitution of 1853, and the objectives of the Argentinian Revolution as stated in Appendix 3 of the Revolutionary Act.

As for the hierarchical relationship between the Statute and the Constitution, two opposing theories emerged: one of them saw a vertical relationship

[30] See Tilman Evers, Militärregierung in Argentinien. Das politische System der "Argentinischen Revolution", Hamburg 1972, p. 79.

[31] See Article 3 of the Statute of the Argentinian Revolution.

between them, with the Statute being of higher rank; the other asserted a horizontal relationship and maintained that the dispositions of the Statute and those parts of the Constitution compatible with them constituted one single body of law.[32]

Similar problems arose with respect to the significance of the "objectives of the Revolution", and especially to the question of whether they were directly valid or merely constituted sources of judicial interpretation.

For all these reasons, it was anything but easy to identify precisely which was the normative system valid in Argentina between 1966 and 1973.

And again, what has been said with respect to the case of Argentina applies to other countries in Latin America as well. The difficulty of identifying the valid legal order in Peru, for example, has been underlined by Hans-Jürgen Brandt:

> "[T]his legal order is particularly complex and not very well known even to those who belong to the dominant social sectors. This is true even for experts who are trying to come to grips with the approximately 25 000 legal provisions issued since 1904 and unable to say which of them are still in force. An avalanche of laws and decrees (the annual legislative output oscillates between 300 and 500 legal provisions), a disorderly and often inconsistent legislation, and the inexistence of systematic, periodically revised editions of the valid legal texts have created enormous chaos. In this situation, it is rather difficult for the average citizen to adapt his behavior to the legal order, as the constitution commands."[33]

The military dictatorship established in Argentina in 1976 and lasting until 1983 promulgated an act listing the purposes and objectives of the so-called "Process of National Reorganisation", derogating the supreme rank of the constitution, and establishing the Military Junta, the National Executive Power and a Legislative Advisory Commission as governmental organs.

Strangely enough, however, at the same time the fiction of the validity of the constitution was maintained, and thus, when General Reynaldo Bignone assumed the office of President of Argentina, General Nicolaídes asked him to swear "to observe and make observe the Constitution of the Argentinian Nation".[34] The request was nonsense, but it was not at all original: on March 29, 1976, General Jorge Rafael Videla also had sworn "to faithfully observe and make observe [...] the Constitution of the Argentinian Nation".[35]

---

[32] See Tilman Evers, op. cit., pp. 74ff.

[33] See Hans-Jürgen Brandt, Justicia popular – Nativos y campesinos, Lima 1986, pp. 169f.

[34] See El País (Madrid), July 2, 1982.

[35] See Helio Juan Zarini, Historia e instituciones en la Argentina, Buenos Aires 1981, p. 364.

In this context, it is interesting to note that the proclamations invariably accompanying a military coup almost always explicitly state that the constitution is and will be respected. Some examples may illustrate this:

In the military proclamation of 1930 – the first in a long series – we read: "The provisional government [...] proclaims its respect of the Constitution and valid law." Curiously, however, it goes on to confirm "its desire to return to the normal way of things as soon as possible [...]".[36] This can only mean that they proclaim to have created a situation at once in accordance with the constitution and constitutionally irregular.

The protagonists of the military coup of June 4, 1942, who then brought to power Juan Perón, stated: "We will maintain our institutions and our laws."[37]

On March 28, 1962, the constitutional government of Arturo Frondizi was ousted by another military coup whose leaders declared:

> "We hold on to the Constitution as the only straw of salvation for all Argentinians. [...] In taking the decision to promote the deposition of the President, we believe to be protecting the Constitution and to restore faith in its principles."[38]

This is, indeed, an excellent example of a method which could well be called "restoration of faith through sin".

The military junta which on March 24, 1976, initiated one of the bloodiest dictatorships in 20th century Latin America, swore "by God and the Holy Scriptures [...] to firmly observe and make observe [...] the Constitution of the Argentinian Nation".[39]

Preoccupation with "legality" was also shared by the soldiers who ruled Guatemala from 1982 until 1986: In an interview published in the *New York Times* (July 15, 1982), dictator Ríos Montt declared: "I thus had to create the legal framework which permitted entering another's house without leaving the ground of legality [...] now, I can kill on a legal basis."[40]

III. Some Tentative Conclusions

On the basis of the aforesaid, and taking into account also more recent developments in the political and legal culture in Latin America, I think one can conclude, at least, the following:

---

[36] Cf. Horacio Verbitsky, Medio siglo de proclamas militares, Buenos Aires 1987, p. 45.

[37] Ibid., p. 48.

[38] Ibid., p. 91.

[39] Ibid., p. 143.

[40] See Jennifer Schirmer, Zur Sicht des guatemaltekischen Militärs über Gesetz, nationale Sicherheit und Menschenrechte, in: Lateinamerika – Analysen, Daten, Dokumentation (Hamburg) No. 14 (July 1990), pp. 53 - 60.

1. In important countries in Latin America, the legal order promulgated either in accordance with constitutional provisions or by *de facto* governments does not inform the behavioral expectations of institutions and individuals in large areas of social interaction. Not only is the deontic status of an action often unclear; even in cases where there are no severe doubts about what is legally obligatory, permitted, or prohibited, the efficacy of the respective provisions is, at best, imperfect.

2. In many Latin American countries, the constitutional legal order has not been a relevant source of legitimation for the acts of the political powers.

The difference between the political and legal evolutions in Latin America and in Western European countries can be seen very clearly if one performs the mental exercise of using Max Weber's idea of belief in the legitimacy *(Legitimitätsglaube)* as the foundation of a legitimate type of domination, and analyzes the attitudes of large sectors of Latin American populations towards the way power is exercised in their respective country. As a result, one will hardly be able to speak of "rational domination" or of the subordination of governments to the "impersonal order of the law".[41]

While one can say that in Europe the law has acquired, in the course of a long development, the function of a source for the legitimation of power, a similar judgement can hardly be made with respect to constitutional order in Latin America.

Certainly, the return to democracy of almost all Latin American countries gives reason to hope that the valid constitutional orders will also be put into effect. In many cases, however, the return of the armed forces to their barracks does not mean that they have given up the ambition of exercising political power (as has been shown by a number of incidents in recent years, in Argentina as well as in other countries). In the area of human rights – with its enormous importance for the effectiveness of constitutional guarantees – Amnesty International's annual report for 1989, e.g., registered severe violations in formally democratic countries as Colombia, Guatemala, El Salvador and Peru. In this context, Rodolfo Stavenhagen reminds us that:

> "Observers consider these human rights violations to be even more serious than those that occurred during the last stages of several military dictatorships, not only for their specific content but because they are carried out in the context of democratic legal systems, and because they underline the ineffectiveness of weak civilian governments in adequately protecting the rights of their citizens. These violations take place in the context of severe internal conflicts, a general spreading of crime and violence, and the disintegration of State structures."[42]

---

[41] See Max Weber, Wirtschaft und Gesellschaft, Tübingen 1976, pp. 124ff.

[42] See Rodolfo Stavenhagen, América Latina: Derechos humanos y desarrollo, in: ifda dossier (Nyon) No. 79 (Oct./Dec. 1990), p. 46.

3. Since it cannot satisfy functions 1. and 2., the constitutional order is usually unable to offer sufficient reasons for the actions of individuals and institutions alike. To what has been said about the confusion and uncertainty with respect to the identity of the valid legal order, one has to add the effects of the disintegration of the State apparatus brought about in some countries by criminal organizations related to the drug business. The best-known example for this is, of course, Colombia. In a book published in 1989,[43] Marcos Kaplan has analyzed in detail the socio-political consequences of the drug business in such countries as Colombia, Peru and Bolivia. He coined the expression "drug-State" *(narco-Estado)* to indicate the predicament the State of Colombia has been thrown into by the *mafia* of drug dealers. A few quotes from the book may illustrate how serious the situation is:

"The confidence of individuals and groups in the authority of the State has vanished. [...] The drug dealers [...] seem to be omnipotent, and untouchable in their display of violence [...]. More and more, they are turning into a clear and threatening challenge to the sovereignty of the State, the legitimacy and efficacy of public administration and the viability and effective legal force of democracy and its institutions."[44]

"Because of continous murder threats, and actual assassinations, many judges have had to leave the country. Those remaining in the country are intimidated or corrupt, they do not prosecute or sentence drug criminals, or set them free after legal proceedings have been initiated against them; they declare extradition treaties unconstitutional and revoke extraditions. The judiciary is suffering a severe ethical and functional crisis, and has stopped functioning; it threatens to collapse, and contributes to the general impotence and weakness of the government."[45]

And Henry Oporto Castro's observations about the Bolivian case sound very similar:

"All this economic power [of the drug dealers, E. G. V.] has certainly penetrated the decision-making mechanisms of the executive, parlament, the judiciary, the police, the armed forces, the political parties, the mass media, and other areas of the society and the State in all of which drug trafficking is being protected. This is the only explanation possible for the total inactivity displayed so far by the official side in the struggle against the mafia."[46]

4. Because of the frequency of military coups and the often long duration of the state of emergency, the constitutional order rarely has fulfilled the function of regulating the procedures for the modification of the law and the functioning of the institutions assigned to implement them. In a number of important Latin American countries, these functions were taken over instead by so-

---

[43] See Marcos Kaplan, Aspectos sociopolíticos del narcotráfico, Mexico-City 1989.

[44] Ibid., p. 185.

[45] Ibid., p. 190f.

[46] H. Oporto Castro, Bolivia: el complejo coca-cocaína, in: D. García-Sayán (ed.), Coca, cocaína y narcotráfico – Laberinto en los Andes, 2nd ed. Lima 1989, pp. 171 - 190, here p. 178.

called "institutional" or "constitutional acts". This precisely is the reason why the relevance of the constitutional order as an obstacle or a stimulus for social development is, at best, very reduced.

In any case, the renewed preoccupation with constitutional revision in several South American countries expresses once again the belief in the legitimating power of the constitution.[47] In November 1990, the Colombian government published a document entitled *Reflections on a new Constitution*. The observations to be found there about the role of the constitution as an instrument to prevent the "erosion of legitimacy" are correct. It is an indisputable fact that a constitutional order fixing the framework of a participatory democracy is a necessary condition for the peaceful development of Latin American societies. Given the social and economic realities of these countries, the question is, however, whether it is also a sufficient condition. The document just mentioned is aware of this when it states (p. 4):

> "Obviously, spelling out the rights of Colombians in a legal text does not guarantee their effective protection. But it is the first step if Colombians are ever to begin to identify with this constitution that today seems so unfamiliar and incomprehensible to them."

This type of problems is taken up by authors like José Matos Mar who, in a book with an illustrative titel that could be translated as "Popular Incontinence and Crisis of the State",[48] has proposed a comprehensive restructuring of the State, taking into account with respect to the legal order the "unusual dynamics affecting the entire social, political, economic and cultural structure"[49] of Peru.

5. Those who have taken a more skeptical position with respect to the actual role of the constitution, on the other hand, claim that it serves only the following functions:

a) The almost "metaphysical" function (to use the expression of González Casanova) of an ideology available and dismissable *ad libitum*, depending on the need of the moment. The constitution thus becomes something like a "last fund of arguments" governments and political parties can invoke, with the additional advantage of the emotive charge of the expression "constitutional law".

b) The function of a programmatic declaration of duties to be fulfilled in a more or less remote future. This immunizes the constitution against any

---

[47] Among the extensive literature on this topic, for the case of Argentina see especially the publications of the Consejo para la Consolidación de la Democracia: Reforma Constitucional, 2 vols, Buenos Aires 1986 and 1987, and Presidencialismo vs. Parlamentarismo, Buenos Aires 1988.

[48] J. Matos Mar, Desborde popular y crisis del Estado, 7th ed. Lima 1988.

[49] Ibid., p. 17.

possible violation, for example on the level of fundamental citizens' rights, because it can always be argued that one is still "in the process of" implementing the program embodied in the constitution.

c) As a consequence of these functions, the constitution is converted into a special element of the political mythology of each country. It is used, mainly in times of crisis, with the intention of reconciling the discrepancies existing between professed values and actual behavior; its principles have no significant practical relevance.[50]

Good arguments can be found for both positions: On the one hand, the starting point for any legitimate democratic order certainly has to be set by constitutional norms; on the other hand, the implementation and stability of such an order presupposes the correction of current circumstances. The satisfaction of both sets of conditions is probably one of the biggest challenges Latin Americans are facing today, at a time when the regional and global situation does not exactly seem favorable to such undertakings.

6. Besides the more formal or theoretical aspects already mentioned, with respect to what Joseph Raz has called the indirect social functions of the law,[51] it should not be forgotten that especially in very heterogeneous societies (as in Mexico or the Andean countries), if the constitution – which almost invariably resembles those designed for homogeneous societies – were in fact generally applied, this would lead to a consolidation and deepening of social inequalities. On this point, I think Hans-Jürgen Brandt is right when he observes:

> "The constitution establishes equality before the law as a fundamental human right. While in the abstract this disposition guarantees non-discriminatory treatment, and therefore a benefit, what happens in practice is that through the establishment of the equality of rights and duties for socially, economically and culturally dissimilar social groups inequalities are reinforced."[52]

In the case of regimes belonging to the category of so-called "modern authoritarianism",[53] instead of being an indirect and unintended side-effect, this was obviously one of the pursued objectives. But whether it was intended or not, the consequence was that the legal order did not fulfill one of the func-

---

[50] On this conception of political myth see Kenneth M. Coleman, The Political Mythology of the Monroe Doctrine, in: John D. Martz and Lars Schoultz (eds.), Latin America, the United States, and the Inter-American System, Boulder, Col. 1980, pp. 95 - 114.

[51] See Joseph Raz, On the Functions of Law, in: A. W. B. Simpson (ed.), Oxford Essays in Jurisprudence, Second Series, Oxford 1973, pp. 278 - 304, esp. p. 299.

[52] See Hans-Jürgen Brandt, op. cit. p. 169.

[53] On the concept of "modern authoritarainsm", see especially David Collier (ed.), The New Authoritarianism in Latin America, Princeton University Press 1979, with more references.

tions Carl J. Friedrich has considered fundamental in Western countries, i.e., the reduction of social tensions.[54] This has led to substantial deficits in the satisfaction of the most basic principles of justice, and thus makes the ethical justification of such law impossible. Until recently, this has been one of the favorite topics of social and political scientists analyzing the functioning of the State in Latin America.

7. The properties of the law, as a normative system, obviously affect the situation of jurists too. If, as I believe to have shown with the examples given, it is true that Latin American legal systems suffer from almost permanent uncertainty about the criteria of validity for their norms, that there is an enormous gap between constitutional and applied order, and that there are structural anomalies in legal institutions, then it does not seem very adventurous to assume that jurists in these systems are in constant danger of committing the following major "sins":

a) To describe a law with no effectiveness at all for all practical purposes, not in a way a historian could certainly do this, but rather pretending to refer to actual reality. This is the case of many constitutionalists in Latin American universities. In this way, legal scholars, under the guise of an alleged respect for the constitution, contribute to cover up reality and keep citizens misinformed;[55]

b) To try to harmonize the *de facto* legal system with the constitutional system, glossing over the contradictions between the two. This has been a very common attitude of many judges;[56]

---

[54] See Carl J. Friedrich, Die Verfassungsproblematik der Entwicklungsländer im Hinblick auf die Aufgaben des modernen Staates, in: Theo Stammen (ed.), Vergleichende Regierungslehre, Darmstadt 1976, pp. 451 - 476.

[55] Cf. M. Miranda Pacheco, Crisis de poder y poder ejecutivo en América Latina, in: Instituto de Investigaciones Jurídicas de la UNAM (ed.), El predominio del Poder Ejecutivo en Latinoamérica, Mexico City 1977, pp. 351 - 364, here p. 355: "Conceptionally, Latin American constitutional dogmatics identifies, describes and functionalizes an abstract political power that has no connection to the specific facts arising from socio-historical reality. This is not an argumentum ad hominem directed against legislators and theorists, but the constitutive characteristic of a social science looked down upon as second-rate." Obviously, to describe the valid constitutional law as if it were actually effective is also a favorite method of those who wish to gloss over the dictatorial character of some "constitutional" regimes in Latin America. A very good example of this is the book by Hubert Krier, Tapferes Paraguay, Würzburg 1979, esp. the references to the civil rights that were guaranteed during the Stroessner regime and that "could be compared to the corresponding norms of any constitution in the free world" (p. 51).

[56] For the relationship between the judicial system and the armed forces, cf. A. Palma Fourcade, Poder Judicial – Fuerzas Armadas, in: Universidad Menéndez Pelayo (ed.), La lucha por la democracia en América Latina, Guadalajara (no year), pp. 153 - 160. I cannot analyze here the reasons for this accomodating attitude of the judiciary towards *de facto* governments. Palma Fourcade mentions among other factors the conservatism of the judges, the way they are appointed, and their social background. Enrique Varsovi, El predominio del poder ejecutivo en América Latina, in: Instituto de

c) To trivialize the discrepancies between valid constitutional law and its actual implementation (in countries that are not under *de facto* rule); jurists this way create a sort of "ideological cement" as a substitute for the inexistent homogeneous social and economic structure.[57]

With the first two "sins", jurists have been an important social group contributing to the stabilization of *de facto* regimes. Besides, if one admits that the classification of a regime as "legal" is not a mere description according to given criteria, but an act of recognition and consent with clearly prescriptive connotations, there can be no doubt that the behavior just mentioned has been a very effective way of proclaiming such legality.[58]

8. In this context, it may also be worth noting that, as Emilio García Méndez correctly observed,[59] in regimes belonging to the category of so-called "new authoritarianism", the difference between promulgated and actually applied norms has tended to be rather small. This was due to

a) a greater concentration of legislative power,

b) the firm will to implement the promulgated norms, and

c) command over the necessary means of coercion.

A good example for the first aspect is article 182, introduced into the Brazilian Constitution of 1967 through the reform of October 17, 1969. The text of this article is as follows:

> "Institutional Act number 5 of December 13, 1968, and the other Acts issued subsequently remain in effect.
>
> Single paragraph: The President of the Republic, after consultation with the National Security Council, may decree the repeal of any of these Acts in case their provisions are considered unnecessary."

This is an excellent example of what Kelsen once called "supreme competence", that is, the unlimited legal authority to modify the constitution.[60] One could even say that the Brazilian constitution of 1969 consisted of a single article: article 182.[61]

Investigaciones Jurídicas de la UNAM (ed.), El predominio del Poder Ejecutivo en Latinoamérica, Mexico City 1977, pp. 439 - 447, adds the lack of a regulated legal career and the low income of the judges who are directly dependent on executive decisions.

[57] Cf. Norbert Lechner, La crisis del Estado en América Latina, Caracas 1977, p. 160.

[58] On the ascriptive character of the notion "legal government" cf. R. M. Hare, The Lawful Government, in: P. Laslett/W. G. Runciman (eds.), Philosophy, Politics, and Society, Third Series, Oxford 1967, pp. 157 - 172.

[59] See Emilio García Méndez, Autoritarismo, institucionalización y control social, Buenos Aires 1985.

[60] See Hans Kelsen, Das Problem der Souveränität und die Theorie des Völkerrechts, Aalen 1960, pp. 47ff.

As for aspects b) and c), an extensive discussion cannot be attempted here; but it should at least be underscored that the willingness of this type of government to enforce its own norms is closely related to its belief that it possesses sufficient grounds for self-legitimation.[62] As a consequence, these regimes feel a reduced need for declarations ascertaining their legality.[63]

9. On the basis of what has been said so far, projects of constitutional revision – as they are currently proposed by a number of democratic governments in Latin America – should, to say the least, be handled with care. If it is true that in the past the legal and political systems – except in the case of dictatorial regimes – have suffered from notorious ineffectiveness, then the question almost automatically arises to what extent the slogan "The less State, the better" is correct, and whether the expectation that the contradictions mentioned in point 4. will be overcome with a reduction of state intervention is sufficiently well-grounded.

***

I think the Latin American examples demonstrate just how irrelevant the constitution can be as a factor of stability. While the example of Bolivia where military coups have often been accompanied by constitutional revision seemed to point toward a significant relation between the two phenomena, the Mexican case shows that it is possible to have stability together with a very reduced efficacy of the constitution, and the case of Argentina demonstrates that the distinction between *de facto* and *de jure* governments is anything but clear.

---

61 This has been pointed out – correctly, I think – by Senator Paulo Brossard; see Luiz Pinto Ferreira, Predominio del poder ejecutivo en América Latina, in: Instituto de Investigaciones Jurídicas de la UNAM (ed.), El predominio del Poder Ejecutivo en Latinoamérica, Mexico-City 1977, pp. 25 - 64, esp. p. 34.

62 It is precisely this characteristic which makes the regime type of "new authoritarianism" the exact opposite of the liberal State which emerged as a consequence of the Illustration; cf. on this point, e.g., H. Lübbe, Staat und Zivilreligion. Ein Aspekt politischer Legitimität, in: ARSP Beiheft 15 (1981) pp. 40 - 64.

63 This confidence in the self-sufficiency of a legitimating ideology is the reason why these governments generally refuse to look for a legitimating framework beyond their own limits. As an excellent example for this type of attitude, cf. the document of the Argentinian Presidential Office of August 8, 1978, which states among other things: "This entire process [the so-called 'Process of National Reorganization'] is based on a single source of legitimacy: the documents of March 24, 1976 [i.e., the declarations following the military coup]. Therefore, there is never to be any open or indirect transference of legitimacy on any other source. The project is not to be submitted to deliberation by political leaders – since that would mean to ascribe representativity and 'sovereignty' to them – nor to any type of plebiscite that, even if it would result in approval, would restore the demagogical concept of the 'people' and convey sovereignty on something that actually is nothing but a political myth."

These cases reinforce my conviction that it is advisable to maintain the definition of stability proposed at the beginning which, by refering to Hart's concept of the rule of recognition, helps avoid the problems that usually arise if one links the validity of norms to a supreme normative order, as in the theory of Hans Kelsen.

The Small-Coin Right of Resistance

An Admonition to Civil Courage

By Arthur Kaufmann, Munich*

In the recent past there has been a considerable amount of confusion in the discussion about the "Right of Resistance" and the way it has been brought into sheer discredit for quite a few people. It has almost become part of our every day life that house-occupiers, environment-protectors, anti-nuclear-energy-fanatics, and other "alternative people" refer to a Right of Resistance when they fight official orders with intimidation and violence. In this respect it appears more than macaber that there is no hesitation to link these kinds of actions to the resistance of the 20th of July 1944 or the one of the "White Rose" against Hitler. That means a sell-out of the Right of Resistance at dirt-cheap prices. Back in 1968 the philosopher Dolf Sternberger already spoke of "the illtimed resistance": during the Third Reich "there was a tyrant and poor resistance, today there is a strong resistance but no tyrant". In addition to that we are confronted with another awkwardness of the Right of Resistance that was pointed out by the Greek professor of constitutional law, Themistokles Tsatsos, namely the respective temporary relativity of its acknowledgement: the question whether or not there is such a thing as a Right of Resistance at all is either "being put forward at one and the same time with its factual realization or else only after the abolition of the regime whose rules and orders the resistance was built up against".

Actually tragic, however, is the fact that even those who wanted to install and secure the legitimate function of a Right of Resistance in a constitutional political system contributed to an important degree to the process of the growing relativity of the Right of Resistance. That is to speak of those parliamentarians and politicians who in the fateful year of 1968 (above all with the aim to make the new Emergency Powers Act acceptable for the Labor Unions) wanted and achieved that the Right of Resistance was anchored in the German Constitution (Art. 20 IV). That was certainly well meant. But what it did was the squaring of the circle, the normalizing of the merely non-normable. The very same way that a free-conscience-decision cannot be subject to an order, the resistance against injustice caused by the state cannot be ruled by the

---

* English by Reinhard Merkel, Hamburg.

state. Mr. Peter Schneider speaks of a "negative double-effect" as the necessary consequence of a constitutional legalization of the Right of Resistance: "the dramatizing of the normal" and "the trivializing of the unnormal state of affairs".

The tragedy of resistance, its uselessness but also its undeniable dangerousness for the political order of a society is not in the least based on the fact that, up to the present day, there has been no success in trying to give resistance its proper position in the consciousness of human beings. That may seem paradoxical but the paradox vanishes if one considers that the term "resistance" is used here in a twofold sense.

In the traditional "classical" sense the Right of Resistance is a right of social self-defence against a criminal government using its power in a way that leads to physical threat and danger for the people. Only this aspect: right of self-defence in an extreme and exceptional situation makes transparent why the Right of Resistance has been bound to strict conditions from its very foundation in the classical antiquity to the present day. And this again is the explanation why resistance in most cases does not succeed whether for the reason of failure or of not taking place at all. Let us recapitulate those "classical" conditions of the Right of Resistance.

First of all the Right of Resistance requires a drastic abuse of political power. The government must clearly appear to be the aggressor against the common well-being and the main human rights. Secondly, a Right of Resistance comes into question only as a subsidiary one, i.e. after all legal and peaceful means are at their ends – that is to say: it can only be the ultima ratio in a situation of distress that cannot be coped with otherwise. Thirdly, the "Principle of Proportion" must be observed. The means being used – disobedience, violence, in the extreme case: assassination of the tyrant – must be in an adequate relation to the aspired purpose. It always needs to be considered that justified resistance, unlike a revolution, aims for the restoration of the harassed public order and not its overthrow. Closely linked to this is another presupposition: there must be a reasonable hope for a successful outcome of the resistance. This does not mean that resistance can be judged by its factual success, whereby one has to consider that failing resistance can be of a very high moral value. But an a priori hopeless and therefore senseless resistance cannot be accepted.

It is obvious that these presuppositions draw narrow limits for the Right of Resistance. But it can also be overlooked that there is no way of developing exact criteria, and thus the legitimacy of an individual case of resistance can be very questionable. Practically never can one precisely say: From here and now on violent resistance against an unlawful government can be justified. In the end one has to deal with a decision that he is made responsible for by his own conscience. Too often it is the fate of the resistance fighter to appear guilty of high treason under superficial criteria and to remain unheard with his justifications, and all of this for the sake of a constitutional state far away at the moment of his action and still to be restored for future generations.

How to get out of this dead-end road? Above all, how to avoid situations where the fight for justice can be called high treason? How to escape the doom that injustice coming from above can only be fought when it is too late? And how to prevent the escalation of violence that is the usual consequence of violent resistance and its violent oppression?

The Right of Resistance in the traditional classical sense is, as stated, the concept of an extreme ultimate move of self-defence against an already perverted political power that bears, so to speak, its illegitimacy on its forehead. From this point of view the calamitous amalgamation of resistance and assassination of the tyrant becomes transparent, and, if not to talk of assassination, then at least of violence, unrest, rebellion. And only under the aspect of that kind of resistance Dolf Sternberger can speak of an "ill-timed resistance", can the status of a legitimate resistance be denied for today's actions and protests against political measures. For the Federal Republic of Germany is without question no tyranny.

But neither was the Republic of Weimar and yet the most terrible despotism of the history of mankind arose from it. From what moment in the resistance would have been at the right time and therefore justified then? As long as the government remained within the very limits of law and legacy or at least the essential principles of a constitutional state had not been completely abandoned, the kind of obvious situation that the Right of Resistance should be restricted to had not yet occured. The legal safety and consistency was to be put above the fight against injustice with a possibility of social unrest. But after the last residue of the constitutional system had been abolished and the despotism rigidly established, there was no more sense in resistance, because then it seemed hopeless. According to the classical theory it was not even admissible anymore, for part of the legitimacy of resistance is its chance for success, i.e. the perspective of improving things and not making them even worse. That brings up the disquieting question: what time at all can be considered "right for resistance" and thus provide a Right of Resistance. As it looks now: none whatsoever.

But here we are confronted with an essential mistake. The antithesis: here constitutional order – there tyranny contains a wrong concept, at least an inadmissible simplification. The boundaries between a constitutional state and despotism are floating. There is no political order beyond the threat of transforming into the perversity of a tyranny. The mutation of legal systems, as the German law philosopher Fritz von Hippel states, is a constant problem of human existence. The perversion starts at the very point where law and legal order are considered granted, something that is just a given fact, an achieved aim where a society can rest. The consequence of this way of thinking is necessarily a petrification, a numbness, and thus an alienation of the law. For law can only remain what it is meant to be if it is persistently being worked at and developed. Only the non-perfect, the processing subject, is alive.

Under this aspect we can derive a new and different interpretation of the Right of Resistance: A Right of Resistance not of the great heroic and often so fruitless actions, but a Right of Resistance of an everyday practical reason, a "small-coin Right of Resistance", as I want to call it.[1] Resistance in this sense is not the ultimate means against an already completely perverted government, but rather the first medium against upcoming deviations from the correct way. Its function is to resist even the beginnings of perversion. This "small" kind of resistance needs to be practiced constantly in order to make the "great" resistance unnecessary. We have to take care under normal circumstances that the serious and extreme case will not occur. In this interpretation, resistance is an essential element of the law itself, and as such naturally beyond the possibility of being legally fixed.

Because resistance in this form is not directed against an illegitimate order but against a still legal one that is nevertheless threatening the common well-being, the use of *violence* as well as the *exposed disobedience* are forbidden under any circumstances whatsoever. The "small-coin resistance" is not a matter of noisy agitation but a matter of reason, a civic attitude in various shades: doubt towards those in power, courage for an open criticism, unmasking of grievances, a "no" to injustice even, and even the more, if it comes from "above" or is derived from a "leading opinion", no participation in actions that are looked through and recognized as calamitous, even though one may loose sympathies in doing so – there is an unlimited number of possibilities. Richard Hauser, the philosopher and member of the Anti-Nazi-Resistance, names as means against infringements of the legal authority: the legally provided objection, the protest, the secret compensation, the virtue of Epikie (wisdom), and above all, the "suffering obedience" which is – as Hauser properly points out –, according to its inner structure, no real obedience, since this kind of submitting oneself only hides the refusal of the order. It is just this "suffering obedience" whose effect is most often not recognized. If only during the period of dictatorship all those who afterwards claimed to have been opponents had struggled to their feet to just remain passive, to abstain from any kind of endorsement, any acclamation, any opportunistic bow, and to vote "no" at the so-called "plebiscites" – for certain some of the events would have come out a different way. And that would have meant actions of resistance that had not overstrained the "common man", for they might have caused him a few inconveniences, but certainly hat not gotten him into prison or concentration camp.

[1] It is not much different from John Rawls' "Civil disobedience" (A Theory of Justice, 1971).

Resistance in this interpretation therefore has nothing to do with revolution. Revolution is really a twin brother of reaction: as soon as it takes over, it aspires to the securing of the achieved power as irrevocable and therefore prohibits any kind of change. Resistance on the contrary means permanent evolution. It never reaches its goal, like a sailor never arrives at the horizon. But it is the moving force that the law and the constitutional state need for their constant renewing and thus prevent their own deterioration.

Throughout centuries the philosophy and the theology of order have taught us that obedience to the authority, be it the government's or the Church's, was the highest of virtues and that he who obeys is not responsible for what the order requests. That way citizens blindly followed abominable regulations, soldiers criminal orders, judges unjust laws, Christians false doctrines of the Church, without the slightest twinge of conscience, and they did so not only in times of dictatorship. To resist was not their part. Resistance was something abstract, unreal, something that might have been of importance in former times or for other people, but not here and now, and therefore was without personal relevance.

But today's reality seems to show a different scene. In our country – and not only in our's – rebellion against the authorities and against effective laws is part of the every day life. It has practically become impossible to build a highway, an airport, a nuclear power plant without militant groups attempting everything, including violence, to paralyse those projects. To prevent misunderstanding: I believe the vigilance of our citizens towards the various threats facing our natural resources to be a good thing. For the people responsible are forced to reconsider their actions more thoroughly and to justify them more accurately, and in quite a few cases they actually had to revise their decisions.

Those positive forms of civil iniative should not be despised. But one cannot overlook that most of these actions reveal a blind and pernicious actionism that has nothing to do with the concept of resistance as an attempt to improve our legal situation. Whoever dislikes something, whoever is not willing to accept a majority decision or to pay a small contribution to the common well-being, demonstrates in the street to fight for his alleged "right", and be it with violence against people and things. In contrast to that it must be emphasized that resistance can only be justified for the sake of a better law and not as a means to satisfy personal interests and wants, and that violence is – with the only exception of the legally provided cases – never allowed in an intact political system.

The resistance I am talking of has nothing in common with noisy machinations, with riots, and with causing social unrest. I am pointing at something different: at a mental unrest, at the "cor inquietum", and at a kind of thoughtful and responsible acting that does not hide behind the mass. In addition I want to mention another virtue: *patience*. Patience is one of the very important conditions of resistance although it is almost never refered to in this context. The great German philosopher of law, Gustav Radbruch, said: The impatient person cannot wait for something to grow. He wants to be ready and at his goal right away. And because impatience is not able to wait but must have everything as a whole and now and is never pleased with later or partial granting, it is the main cause of violence.

The reader's probably long prepared objection is my own: What I am talking about is not resistance but just practicing the right of free expression of one's opinion, the right of criticism, of opposition, and the right to demonstrate. It is as well the expression of a person's heart and civil courage but – since those are allowed actions within the frame of our legal system – no resistance. Resistance has its place exclusively in an injust political order, i.e. only where it represents a "ius contra legem corruptam". And whoever detaches it from this reference contributes finally to the process of making it harmless and worthless.

Certainly, where civil courage is being practiced as something that's understood, one would not consider it "resistance". But in this country that is not the way things are. The theologian Steinbach regretted that we did not properly use the possibilities for the future opened up by men and women of the resistance: "Resistance did not really find a place in our people's hearts. We have not become a politically aware nation but again are pleased with a purely private existence that corresponds with the ghostly abstractiveness of our political routine." This statement gets exactly to the point of the matter. While resistance (in the traditional sense) is an essential part of the legal consciousness in Latin and Anglo-Saxon, and – at least was in the past – in Eastern European countries, we in Germany are having great difficulties with the 20th of July 1944, because we have a different attitude towards our state. The German constitutional and democratic state between 1840 and 1930 had developed under the aspect of an emphasized averting from the Middle-Ages Right of Resistance. That explains to a certain extent the persistent warnings in our country: not to overlook the status of exception of the Third Reich and the resistance there and then. This remark is certainly plausible considering a constitutional state's claim to obedience. But it also contains an eminent risk: the risk of pushing aside the tradition and the tenets of the Right of Resistance and, above all, to narcotize the consciousness and critical awareness of the citizens. Thus practically the entire literature in the field of constitutional law neglects the idea of resistance as something of only marginal importance.

This fact requires and justifies the attempt to ensure the status of the Right of Resistance and its function in the defence against the abuse of political power. It must be made clear that this is also a way of resisting and objecting which incidentally may take sacrifices but is a debt to the common well-being, though limited by it as well. As far as the development of a democratic consciousness is concerned it can hardly be overemphasized that resistance in this sense must not be put ad acta even in a democratic constitutional state. For the Right of Resistance opens up a way out of the fatal vicious circle of action and reaction, of destructive social unrest and paralysing law-and-order ideology that appears to be significant for our present day situation. Only in the tension of obedience and objection freedom becomes reality.

The Future of Constitutional Free Speech

By Geoffrey Marshall, Oxford

I.

The role of formal free speech guarantees and the difference that is made by introducing them where they do not exist can be seen by comparing the present law of the United Kingdom with that of similar liberal societies that already possess a general free speech guarantee incorporated in a Bill of Rights. We can easily specify some of the ways in which a formal guarantee can make a difference. In the first place it may mention or define particular circumstances that fall within the guarantee. Illustrations can be found from Germany, Japan, Spain or the European Convention. The Spanish Constitution of 1978, for example, mentions literary and scientific production, academic freedom, personal conscience and professional secrecy. The European convention specifies the right to receive, as well as to communicate information as an incident of free expression.[1]

Secondly, a free speech guarantee may encourage consistency between different statutory provisions that may otherwise be treated differently or be subject to different standards: Public order, Race, and Industrial relations law, for example, in the United Kingdom all involve questions of free expression but may be treated as if they raised unrelated problems of statutory interpretation.

Thirdly, a formal guarantee may tilt the balance more presumptively in the free speech direction where the law already acknowledges in some degree the claim of free expression as a value or policy to be weighed in for example contempt, defamation or copyright issues.[2]

Fourthly a guarantee may encourage a wider understanding of what is to count as a free speech issue.

---

[1] Article 10 guarantees "freedom to receive and impart information ... without interference by public authority". In *Gaskin* v *United Kingdom* (Case No. 2/1988/146/200) a distinction was drawn between restricting a person from receiving information that others wish to communicate and a right of access to information that has been refused.

[2] See A. Boyle, Freedom of Expression as a Public Interest in English Law [1987], Public Law 574.

II.

This last point suggests that when we consider the future development of free speech protection, an issue that is likely to have increasing importance is how we are to recognise the existence of a free speech issue? How is it to be established that the issue of free speech protection can properly be brought into the reckoning? Two other general issues upon which there remains scope for debate are the following. Against whom may a generally enunciated guarantee of free speech be deployed? Does it extend protection to everyone from everyone or only to citizens from acts or regulation engaged in by state or public bodies? A further question relates to the internal organisation of the free speech principle. Are there distinctive types or categories of free expression? Do all of them deserve an equal degree of protection? Is there what some have called a 'core' and a 'periphery' of the free speech principle? We can sketch out these difficulties under three heads that we might label the 'Area', 'Depth' and 'Anatomy' of free speech.

Area and Boundaries

The term 'constitutional speech' is notoriously a complex one, since unlike speech in the ordinary sense it excludes a number of things that literally consist in speaking or writing but also includes a number of activities that literally are not forms of speech or writing. Thus a map of the free speech terrain contains two distinct segments. One segment plots the traditional category of cases that most free speech theory since Mill has been concerned to analyse, namely those cases in which limits or qualifications may be placed on the written or spoken word. The second segment is needed to delineate the uncertain non-speech area and to identify non verbal activities that qualify for protection under the free speech principle, or at least qualify for consideration for protection. Consider the following fact situations – a conflation of some historical and hypothetical examples.

a) A refusal to license a satellite broadcasting channel.

b) A ban on the use of puppets or caricatures representing members of the royal family.

c) A ban on the membership of any organisation any of whose objects involve violence or illegality.

d) A law forbidding the posting of election leaflets or notices on public property.

e) A law forbidding the advertising of abortion facilities.

f) A criminal conviction for the publication of a book called 'Seven Ways to Commit Suicide'.

g) A ban on the publication of any photograph of a person holding judicial office.

h) A law compelling all motor vehicles to carry the national or state watchword or slogan on their numberplates.

i) A requirement that the police be given one week's advance notice of any procession or public meeting.

j) A refusal to issue passports to a football team intending to play in South Africa.

The image of the map with its two segments is problematic in this sense. When we discuss the area covered by the free speech principle we may have in mind a distinction that has been suggested between the 'coverage' of a right (in this case the free speech right) and the degree or amount of protection that is offered by the right.[3] If so, we seem to need for each segment two maps, one superimposed on the other. On the first map will appear those acts that fall within the area, or ambit or coverage, of the free speech principle, and therefore qualify to be considered for protection. On the superimposed map we can then plot those acts that actually qualify for and deserve protection. Let us label the two segments of the map or maps the *S* (acts of speaking and writing) *Segment,* and the *Non-S* (other forms of communicative or allegedly communicative action) *Segment.* How do we determine what goes on the initial map in each segment? Is it that all acts that literally involve speaking or writing qualify for inclusion on the initial *S-Segment* map whilst only a selection of non-speech acts appear on the initial *Non-S Segment* map? Or is it that in the *S-Segment* map too some speech acts do not even get included on the initial map, as not qualifying or not within the coverage of the map?

In Professor Frederick Schauer's account of the coverage protection distinction, it does not seem that all forms of speaking or writing would be included on the initial *S-Segment* map. Perjury and extortion for example though they involve speech are held to lie outside the *scope* of the free speech right on the ground that they 'have nothing to do with what free speech is all about'.[4] This is contrasted with defamation committed in the course of criticising public officials, which whilst not deserving protection may fall within free speech coverage. On the *Non-S Segment* map, clearly, not all *non-S* acts appear. But is it possible to separate the criteria for appearing on the initial *Non-S coverage map* from those that determine inclusion on the final *Non-S protection map?* Can we determine the first independently of the second? And what are the criteria that we appeal to in excluding speech acts from the *S-Segment coverage* map on the ground that they do not involve the idea or purpose of free speech?

---

[3] See Frederick Schauer, *Free Speech; a Philosophical Inquiry* (1985), Chapter 7.

[4] At p. 89.

Whatever the answers, the coverage/protection, or dual mapping procedure, involves approaching free speech issues (indeed all rights issues) in two stages. Obviously, if it can be clearly determined that an act or fact situation does not fall within the area, coverage or map boundaries at all, the question of its being protected does not arise and need not be argued. The importance of this in constitutional litigation as a preliminary point is obvious. The importance of a conclusion that the free speech right is in play is also clear since a higher standard of proof or burden of argument may be required to disallow an activity, even if it is disallowed or overruled by other claims, if that activity is held to lie within the free speech sphere.

Perhaps there are some non-speech acts that can be seen intuitively and obviously to have no connection with the free speech principle. The same is true – though perhaps less obviously so – in the speech-act segment. Speech that involves fraud, deception or blackmail might provide examples. A difficulty is that there will be many cases in which the distinction between what free speech rights do not cover, and what they cover but fail to protect, will be less clear or admitted. The distinction implies that a newspaper whose free speech argument has been overruled by a finding that it has committed defamation, contempt or breach of confidentiality must conclude that all it has lost is the *protection* of the free speech principle, not the right to free speech or the right to speak freely, even though in that case they are not able to speak freely.

There is also a possibility that difficulties may be legislated away, or further argument about the nature of the activities in question sidestepped. The suggestion that particular words or utterances are outside the concept of constitutionally protected speech has played some part in American First Amendment history as when 'fighting words'[5] or obscenity[6] have been said not to be speech. It is true that pornography or violence are not what free speech is all about. Neither is free speech about the destruction of reputation or the usurpation of fair trials. But those conclusions can hardly operate as premisses when what is in issue is whether particular utterances or writings are to count as contemptuous or defamatory or obscene.

In the *non-speech segment* the supposition that some activities can be uncontroversially observed to be outside the coverage of the free speech principle is threatened by the not infrequent occurrence of instances in which judicial protection is given to novel cases that previously might have been thought to raise no free speech issue (as with some forms of bodily display or politically motivated crimes). In this area the arguments for coverage and the arguments for protection do not seem to have been consistently separated and perhaps cannot be.

---

[5] *Chaplinski* v *New Hampshire* 315 U.S. 568 (1942).

[6] Roth v U.S. 354 U.S. 476 (1957).

Depth of Protection

It is in many cases unclear (when constitutional instruments simply declare the existence of rights) who the appropriate correlative duty-bearers are intended to be. In the United States, under the First and Fourteenth Amendments, it is, on the face of it, Congress and the states that are forbidden to abridge the freedom of speech. In practice the extension of free speech obligations to others has involved rights of access for the purposes of speaking or demonstrating on private property (such as shopping centres). In the 1960s Mr Justice Black asserted that the First Amendment did not guarantee a general right to use other people's or government property as a stage for ideas.[7] That view has been supported in decisions such as *Hudgens* v *NLRB*,[8] though it has also been held that a state constitution might properly require such access to be given in certain circumstances.[9]

In Canada the Charter of Rights and Freedoms lays down as a general principle that it applies to the Parliament and Government of Canada and to the legislatures and governments of each province in respect of all matters that come within their respective authority.[10] At the time of enactment it was argued that private activity was not intended to be covered by the Charter. Such actions as an employer restricting an employee's freedom of speech or assembly could not be breaches of the Charter because no action by federal or provincial legislatures or governments would be involved.[11] That position seemed to be accepted in *RWDSU* v *Dolphin Delivery Ltd.*[12] In that case it was held that an injunction obtained by a private employer to restrain picketing did not involve any breach of the Charter's free speech guarantee. The lines between matters involving private and public issues or matters within the authority of governments or legislatures are however not easy to draw with confidence. The common law under which a remedy may be sought (if a statute is not involved) is a matter within the authority of Parliament. Is there always a public issue when a law that the legislature has made (or could alter) permits a citizen's right to be restricted even if the restriction is at the instance of another citizen? Does a free speech guarantee place limits that would not otherwise exist on the extent to which private employment or contractual relationships can legitimately limit the right to speak or communicate?

---

[7] *Brown* v *Louisiana* 383 U.S. 131 (1961).

[8] 424 U.S. 507 (1976).

[9] *Pruneyard Shopping Center* v *Robins* 447 U.S. 74 (1980).

[10] Canada Act S. 32.

[11] See P. W. Hogg, *Canada Act 1982* Annotated at p. 76 and *Constitutional Law of Canada* 2nd ed at pp. 674 - 8.

[12] (1986) 33 D.L.R. (4th) 174.

An issue raised by recent United Kingdom legislation designed to protect free speech in Universities[13] is whether the obligations of publicly supported institutions can legitimately be made co-extensive with those of non-publicly supported institutions. It is not easily explicable why a private body of persons should not choose for themselves those to whom they wish to offer facilities for speaking, or to deny such facilities.

Anatomy of the Principle

One way of describing the development of the free speech principle in recent years, particularly in North America, is to say that courts have discovered or invented a number of new categories of constitutionally protected speech. Examples are:

Commercial Speech

This category is potentially a wide one as it may include not merely advertising but a wide range of business communications between entrepreneurs and between entrepreneurs and consumers. In both Canada and the United States it has been recognised that Commercial speech comes within the boundaries of free speech protection, but it may be regulated provided that there is a substantial governmental interest in the particular regulation, that the regulation directly serves that interest and the limitations are no wider than are required to serve it.[14] In *Posadas de Puerto Rico Ass.* v *Tourism Co of Puerto Rico*[15] a majority of the US Supreme Court upheld restrictions on the advertising of gambling facilities to local residents. Discriminatory restrictions of this kind (which occur in various parts of the world) sound as if they ought to raise equal protection as well as free expression issues.

Corporate Speech

Under this heading the communication of information (sometimes subsidised by the taxpayer) by public or private bodies may be protected. The corporate boasting of the water and sewage authorities of England and Wales prior to privatisation provides a British example. If there is a difference between the communication of commercial and political information, it may be

[13] Education (No. 2), Act 1986. See Eric Barendt, 'Free Speech in the Universities' [1987], *Public Law* 344.

[14] *Virginia State Board of Pharmacy* v *Virginia State Citizens' Consumer Council Inc.* 425 U.S. 748 (1976); *Central Hudson Gas and Electric Corp.* v *Public Service Commission* 447 U.S. 557 (1980); *Ford* v *AG Canada* [1988], 2 S.C.R. 712.

[15] 106 St.Ct. 2968 (1986).

difficult to classify the information transmitted in this area, which may contain commercial, political and ideological elements. If the case for regulating political communication has to be greater than that for controlling commercial information, does it make a difference that political messages may be transmitted by commercially interested bodies?

Electoral Speech

A category with this label can be constructed from the protection given in the United States and Canada to the activities and in particular the financial expenditures of political parties and groups raising and spending money to support candidates in elections.[16]

Solicitatory Speech

Perhaps both electoral and commercial speech are a sub-category of a wider phenomenon. The activity of soliciting popular support, financial or otherwise, for a product or a cause, or a charitable or allegedly charitable enterprise, is one that frequently attracts public regulation in the interest of avoiding fraud, deception or exploitation. How far should fund raising in general be protected as thus involving the expression and communicating of ideas? A door to door collection by an environmental protection group was treated as within First Amendment protection in *Village of Schaumberg* v *Citizens for a Better Environment,*[17] as was solicitation of legal business by the NAACP, which might otherwise have been restricted by state regulation aimed at the suppression of barratry.[18]

Industrial and Economic Speech

Picketing is an obvious communicative activity blending speech and action. If it is constitutional speech it is none the less so when the picketing is secondary picketing (though secondary picketing is often penalised).

Artistic or Aesthetic Speech

Speech blended or brigaded with action might equally describe many theatrical or filmed performances, though some American decisions take the view

---

[16] *Buckley* v *Valeo* 424 U.S. 1 (1976); *National Citizens Coalition* v *A.G. Canada* (1984) 11 D.L.R. (4th) 481 (Alberta).

[17] 444 U.S. 620 (1986).

[18] *NAACP* v *Button* 371 U.S. 415 (1963).

that staged sexual performances brigaded with the consumption of alcohol may properly be subjected to regulation.[19] The boundaries of what constitutes an artistic performance are somewhat uncertain. Could athletic performances such as weight-lifting or all-in wrestling qualify, even though lacking aesthetic appeal? Perhaps the category is simply that which outwardly expresses some inward endeavour.

Symbolic action

With the miscellaneous category of what has been called 'symbolic' speech we reach a species of activity that can be exemplified more easily than it can be defined. Examples of it include the display of symbols or uniforms,[20] and the destruction of significant objects. One such has been the American flag. Other national flags seem to have escaped the attentions of symbolic communicators. Alternative significant objects are however conceivable. The removal of the coronation stone from Westminster Abbey or the seizure of the mace in the House of Commons might provide British examples (though when Mr Michael Heseltine took hold of the mace, on a particular demonstrative occasion, he did not claim to be exercising the freedom of speech, debate and proceedings in Parliament mentioned in Article 9 of the Bill of Rights). In those legislative assemblies where physical objects are on occasion thrown in the course of debate it is equally unclear whether ideological motivation is felt to confer any degree of immunity from censure.

There does not seem to be much consensus about what entitles allegedly symbolic acts to appear on the speech map or to come within the coverage of a free speech guarantee. The widest definition of such an act would perhaps be that it should be motivated by some general idea or belief and be intended to convey that idea to others. Some have in fact been prepared to contemplate the possibility that any ideologically motivated action should be entitled to some degree of free speech protection provided that it is the expression of sincerely held views and does not result in substantial physical damage, or more than minor or remediable social inconvenience. This might be thought an excessively tolerant view since substantial harm can be caused to the rights of others even by damage or inconvenience that could not be classed as physical.

A narrower view has been taken by the United States Supreme Court in relation to the destruction of draft cards as distinct from symbolic flag-burning. The Court has refused to contemplate the proposition that a 'limitless variety of conduct can be labelled speech whenever the person engaging in it

---

19 *California* v *La Rue* 419 U.S. 109 (1972).

20 *Colin* v *Smith* 578 F.2nd. 1197 (7th Cir. 1978) (display of Nazi armbands and flag by American Nazi Party members).

thereby intends to convey an idea.[21] These cases do not offer any clear idea as to how it may be decided as a preliminary issue whether the First Amendment is in play. They merely lay down the conditions on which limits may be placed on acts that combine speech and conduct even on the assumption that constitutional speech is involved. In *Clarke* v *Community for Creative Non Violence*[22] the Court was prepared to assume that sleeping in tents in a Washington Park to demonstrate the plight of the homeless was 'expressive conduct protected by the First Amendment'. The protection did not extend very far in this instance, since the overnight sleeping that they wished to engage in was forbidden and the prohibition upheld as a regulation of time, manner and place, and in the interest of preserving the condition and attractiveness of the park. It is not clear exactly what it was about the nature of the conduct that justified the assumption that it might in principle attract First Amendment coverage. Was it the message and its character? Would the message have enjoyed any status as speech if the related conduct had been different? Suppose the protesters had uprooted all the trees in the park as a sincere gesture of contempt for the City's political priorities. Would that have made a difference? Would it have excluded the conduct and its purported message from the category of constitutional speech altogether, so that it could be forbidden without the ban having to meet conditions held appropriate for speech regulation? Two of those conditions were similar to the conditions prescribed for the regulation of commercial speech, namely that there should be a substantial government interest in the regulation in question and also that regulation should be narrowly tailored or no wider than necessary to secure the interest. Two further criteria were that the regulation should be neutral in its impact and not directed at the content or subject-matter of the ideas communicated[23] and also that the regulation should leave ample alternative channels of communication.

The interpretation of these tripartite and quadripartite tests for the validity of restrictions placed upon speech rights (as also on other rights) is a matter of difficulty. In some respects they are undesirably vague. The existence of alternative channels of expression, for example, could be interpreted in a large number of ways. There are almost never no alternatives. But whether they are adequate is something about which the proponents of symbolic action and those they oppose are likely to find little in the way of a common measure of agreement. The choice of a medium of expression and the inadequacy of the alternatives is frequently felt by protesters to be an essential feature of their right to express themselves.

---

[21] See for example Franklyn S. Haiman, *Speech and Law in a Free Society*. E.g. in US v O'Brien 391 U.S. 367 (1968).

[22] 468 U.S. 288 (1984).

[23] *Police Dept* v *Mosley* 408 U.S. 92, 95-6 (1972) (Prohibition on picketing in terms of subject matter).

It is also the case that differences of opinion about the application of the criteria are likely to come down to fine or sometimes fairly minor or technical differences of opinion. In *Clarke* for example the two sides were divided on the question whether the incremental benefit to the park was sufficient to justify the overnight sleeping. Whether the ban advanced the public object of park preservation and whether it was precisely tailored to that objective seemed to come down to uncertainly based technical judgments in which the court had to second guess the assessments of the park service. Is it likely that judges will be impartially determined in their conclusions by such inquiries? Are they not likely to find their judgments about what is urgent or substantial or proportional or reasonable shaped by rawer and more general attachments and sympathies?

A rapid tour of the controversial areas of free speech protection in North America shows us where the future difficulties lie for any jurisdiction formalising its free expression principles into the shape of a general guarantee. Perhaps the main anatomical question about free speech is whether the various categories of speech should be arranged in any order of priority, so as to be subject to greater and lesser degrees of protection. If it is true that a free speech guarantee such as the First Amendment is not confined to protecting political speech it becomes harder to apply the central insight that liberals believed themselves to have about the free speech right, that 'government has no power to restrict expression because of its message, its ideas, its subject matter or its content' so that 'our people are guaranteed the right to express any thought free from government censorship'.[24] On the extended anatomy or map of free speech protection there are a number of areas in which the right to express any thought without regard to its content or to its truth or falsity is not so keenly felt. Some may be pushed to the conclusion that economic or commercial speech should be placed outside the range or coverage of the free speech principle in order to maintain the integrity of its central inspiration.[25] This seems a mistaken strategy. It would be very odd if the most obvious location in which Mr Justice Holmes's theory about the marketplace of ideas could not be allowed to operate freely were to be in the marketplace itself.

---

[24] *Police Department* v *Mosley* 408 U.S. 92, 95-6 (1972).

[25] A question raised by Professor Frederick Schauer in Commercial Speech and the Architecture of the First Amendment 56 *University of Cincinnati Law Review* 1181 (1988). Compare C. Edwin Baker, *Human Liberty and Freedom of Speech* (1989), Chapters 1 and 9.

The Interpretation of the Declaration of Human Rights by a Constitutional Judge

By Michel Troper, Nanterre

Adjudicating means applying prexisting rules for the settlement of conflicts. It is common knowledge that in modern societies, such rules are set out in written texts. Because they are written in ordinary language, they are often – some even say always – vague and ambiguous. Therefore, they need to be interpreted. But how should they be interpreted, and how are they interpreted in fact? Among all the questions which arise in constitutional law, this is probably the most important and difficult one. Theories of interpretation are of two kinds: in the one view, interpretation consists mainly in finding the meaning contained in the texts; in the other, it consists in determining this meaning freely, of one's own free will. The first theory implies that the interpreter is bound, the second that he is free. If the interpreter is a judge, the first theory implies that he is primarily a technician, deprived of any effective power. On the contrary, the second theory implies that the judge has all the power, since he can reformulate the norm which he is supposed to enforce.

The aim of this paper is not deal with this problem as a whole. We shall only inquire how it relates to the interpretation of the 1789 Declaration of the Rights of Man and of the Citizen, due to the ancientness and of the importance of this text. This document represents indisputably a landmark in the history of mankind. It reflects not only a new conception of constitutional law – it is not even limited to law as such –, but also a revolutionary conception of man's relationship to power and society; a conception that has now been spread, at least in principle, over the surface of the earth. A close examination of the way in which it is interpreted can help clarify the issue of interpretation, particularly the type of relationship and interaction that one finds between the interpreter and the text. Above all, it can help clarify what interpretation is about. It is generally said that to interpret is to find or determine the meaning of a text. But the word *meaning* can itself have several meanings, or one could say that there are several levels of meaning. For example, one can speak of the meaning of the Declaration of 1789 in three different ways:

a) One can refer to its meaning either as a text, endowed with legal value, imposing obligations on individuals and State authorities, or as a philosophical doctrine or political position, lacking specific legal value.

b) If the Declaration has legal value, one can say that it has either the meaning of a declaration of natural law, as the title seems to indicate, or that of an act of will of those people who happened to be in power at a certain historical moment.

c) Finally, one can refer to the meaning of the various provisions of this document. If one has accepted under b) that they are prescriptive, what do they actually prescribe?

Regarding these questions, a general theory of interpretation will not bring us very far. Such a theory, for one, will tell us nothing about the first level of meaning. Even, if we assume that the Declaration of the Rights of Man is a binding document, we run the risk of seeing the topic disintegrate, because its interpretation will not differ from the interpretation of texts in general and we may very well be tempted to say about the interpretation of the Declaration the same things which we would say about the interpretation of any document. For example, from the point of view of a general realist theory of interpretation, we would say that no application is possible without interpretation, that interpretation is a function of the will as opposed to a function of knowledge, that it is necessary to distinguish the context of creation from that of justification, or that legal theory cannot specify any interpretative method. But these are precisely the issues for a particular discussion of the interpretation of the Declaration and this type of answer from the realist's point of view would be tantamount to begging the question.

If a general and abstract approach does not lead to any result, we can turn to the document itself and look for some characteristics, from which we can attempt to infer its meaning in one or all the meanings of that word. We can take into account not the nature of interpretation but its object and formulate the issue in a totally different way. Clearly, interpretative methods are not identical, when the object to be interpreted is a statute, an administrative regulation, a contract or an international treaty. It is a matter of indifference whether we consider these methods from a strict positivist point of view, i.e. from a descriptive point of view or rather from a prescriptive one: it is also a matter of indifference whether such methods have effectively been applied in determining the meaning of the text or whether they are displayed in a showcase when justification is needed. It suffices to stress that these methods differ according to the characteristics of the text that is being interpreted.

The most obvious of the characteristics of the Declaration is that it is universal. Yet, for several reasons, it does not follow that it has – or that it lacks – the meaning of a legal document, that it is endowed with legal value.

Firstly, universality does not square well with the notion of legal validity. If a text is endowed with legal validity, it means that it is integrated in the positive law of a given country, its domestic law as opposed to universal law.

Therefore, it can only be asserted as a political doctrine, not as a legal proposition that the Declaration has universal value.

Secondly, the legal value of a text depends on an effective act of will, inserting it in the positive law of a given country: whether it is the enactment of August 1789, the will of a later Constitution maker to refer to this deed of foundation, the legislator's will ordering that it should be enforced, or even the opinion of a judge justifying a decision and mentioning the text as its legal basis. The question of the legal value of the Declaration of the Rights of Man can thus only be given a contingent answer. We should note that in the third hypothesis, when a judge refers to the Declaration, he interprets it as legally binding. In other words, the legal nature of the Declaration is the result of an interpretation, even before being the object of an interpretation.

Thirdly, the legal value of such a text – its binding quality – is not necessarily the same for all. It is convenient and practical – even if this does not square with the historical truth[1] – to regard this text as a set of prescriptions. But prescriptions may be classified according to their addressees and it is far from easy to identify the addressees of the Declaration of the Rights of Man – legislator, judge, citizens, constitutional assembly. Whom is it directed at? In other words, on whom is it binding, provided it is binding? The question may also be formulated as follows: with regards to whom may it be asserted that the Declaration has legal value?

The question of the legal value of the Declaration may thus only be given partial and local answers. Moreover, these answers are questionable and much debated because positive law is subject to contradictory interpretations. It is quite clear that the Declaration of the Rights of Man in France, and the Bill of Rights in the United States carry legal value and that they are especially binding upon the legislator. Are they also binding on a constitutional court? And if so, does the binding quality have the same meaning for the legislator and the constitutional court?

For the same reasons, one cannot from the universal character of the document draw any conclusion regarding its prescriptive or descriptive meaning or the substantive meaning of its various provisions. The same could be said about another characteristic of the text, namely generality. Furthermore, the qualities of the Declaration cannot be regarded as objective, but they themselves are the result of a process of interpretation, rather than its motive. Depending on the interpretation, the Declaration can be seen as having universal scope, or as a document, legally relevant for France only. The generality can mean that every other norm in the system ought to be compatible with

[1] Michel Troper, Qu'est-ce que la déclaration des droits de l'Homme, ds. Eivind Smith (ed.), Les droits de l'Homme dans le droit national en France et en Norvège, Paris 1990, p. 23 - 34.

the words of the text, or simply that the principles it expresses ought to be respected as much as possible but could be weighed against other principles.

There is then only one truly objective quality of the Declaration of 1789: its ancientness. This is an objective quality in the sense that it is not the result of an interpretation, but an undisputed historical fact that it has been adopted in 1789. What can therefore be attempted then is to examine if – and to what extent – the age of the Declaration plays a role in the process of its interpretation, i. e. of the determination of its meaning.

One can think of two ways in which age could affect interpretation: an indirect and a direct one. Firstly, many ancient documents are repeatedly interpreted over a long period of time, and an interpretive tradition is established, with a superpositioning of several layers of meaning, or, by a different metaphor, with a succession of interpreters, each taking into account what previous interpreters have done. This influence of age is only indirect. The real influence is that of tradition. Age only has an effect because it takes time to establish a tradition. The French case is special and offers a pure laboratory situation, because there is age without tradition. With some simplification, it can be said that the Declaration has not been considered a true legal document and has not been subject to judicial interpretation until very recently. It is only in 1971 that the *Conseil Constitutionnel* has decided that the Declaration was part of the Constitution and that a statute contrary to the Declaration was therefore unconstitutional. If then, age has an influence on the process of interpretation, it is a direct influence and not through tradition.

The problem can now be looked at in the following way: how does age influence the determination of the meaning of the Declaration on the three levels: the general meaning or "nature" of a text endowed or not with legal value; its meaning as a declaration or a prescription; the meaning of its various provisions?

The first problem need not hold us for very long. It is quite clear that, since 1971, the Declaration possesses legal character, that this binding character is the result of the process of interpretation, but that age has nothing to do with it. There are several possible explanations for the interpretation given by the *Conseil Constitutionnel* in 1971 of the nature of the Declaration.

The most likely is that the *Conseil* wished to find some constitutional principle possessing a value superior to that of statutes and could not find in the numbered articles of the Constitution a principle suited for the purpose of deciding that a limitation of the freedom of association was unconstitutional. The Preamble of the Constitution refered to both the Preamble of the previous Constitution and the Declaration of 1789. It is, therefore, the Preamble of 1958 that provided the justification for the decision to consider the Declaration of 1789 as a binding document. Had the Declaration not been mentioned in the Constitution of 1958, it would most probably have been used, as it had been in the past by other French courts as a source of inspiration, but never as a source of law. It would not have been interpreted as a binding document.

On the contrary, age is a weak argument in the process of justifying such an interpretation: the Declaration can only be part of the Constitution, if the constitution-making power has played a role in its enactment. This cannot be the case if the Declaration is older than the Constitution itself.

This leaves us with two types of questions:

What is the influence of the age of the Declaration on its interpretation as a declaration or as an act of will, on the interpretation of its nature?

What is its influence on the interpretation of its substance?

I. Nature of the Document

The problem of the nature of the Declaration of the Rights of Man is important both for the justification of its legal quality and for the choice of methods of interpretation. Once it has been decided that the Declaration has constitutional value and is binding on all, the question arises of the justification of this binding character. Either we ought to abide by it, because we think that it has a descriptive character, that it is the expression of a supreme natural law, which the National Assembly did not will but merely declared in 1789, or we ought to abide by it because we regard it as the will of the sovereign.

For a positivist, none of these answers is fully satisfactory. If one does not believe in the objective existence of a natural law and if one considers the law to be only a function of the will, as opposed to knowledge, the first answer must be rejected. As far as the second answer is concerned, it is also inadequate even for positivists: if the document expresses its authors' will, there is still need to explain why people should conform to the will of men who have been dead for so long.

Nevertheless, even if it is impossible to find a satisfactory answer, the question cannot be escaped, because the answer has important consequences for the methods of interpretation. If the statute of the Declaration is held to be prescriptive and if it is interpreted in such a way that it expresses the will of the men of 1789 and that complying with this text is obeying these men, then the meaning of the text is none other than the author's intention. Interpretation consists in analyzing this intention. Because it is presupposed that the linguistic form was chosen on purpose in order to express this intention, linguistic interpretation should be regarded as the most adequate interpretation method, and the main arguments should be drawn from the meaning of the words of the text.

On the contrary, if the nature of the Declaration is regarded as indicative, if one thinks that the men of 1789 merely stated a theory of natural law then the power and the meaning of the text only depend on the truth value of this theory. In this case, the linguistic form does not matter much and the most important arguments will be drawn from the function that the principles stated in the document can exercise in our time, regardless of the intentions of the men of 1789.

Regarding this dilemma age is a very important factor. It has often been stressed that the *prima facie* appearence of the Declaration – first of all its title – is that not of a set of regulations, but of a series of assertations. Discussions focus on whether the text is truly a declaration of natural rights, or on the contrary, if the reference to natural law is merely a showcase presentation designed to disguise the political will prevailing in 1789. This question may be dealt with from two different points of view: the historical one and from what we could name the semiotic point of view. The former is indifferent with regard to the issue of interpretation, because it is always possible to interpret a text which was regarded as a declaration by the authors themselves, as if it were the expression of a will. Conversely, it is always possible to interpret a text seen as the expression of a political will, as the presentation of a doctrine of natural law. We should bear in mind for example that civil law scholars have sometimes interpreted the code Napoléon not as if it reflected the French legislator's will in 1804, but as if it were a necessary law, resulting from human nature.

The semiotic approach consists in considering that the prescriptive or descriptive statute of the text does not result from the mental state of the author, but from an interpretation. A text is a Declaration if it is interpreted as such. Likewise, it expresses a political will if it is interpreted as such.

It should be noted that one cannot settle the question by pointing to the fact that it is the Constitution of 1958 which refers to the Declaration of the Rights of Man, because this does not suffice to justify obediance. True, one could say that, when complying with the Declaration, people do not conform to the will of the men of 1789, but to that of the men of 1958. But, even if we presuppose that the men of 1958 were fully aware of the importance of the reference to 1789 – which is not the case – there is no reason why people should obey them more than their ancestors of 1789. One cannot accept the objection that the basis of obedience is then the same as for the other provisions of the 1958 Constitution. Compliance with the other provisions of the 1958 Constitution is not unconditional: it is always possible to adopt a law held to be contradictory to the Constitution by means of the constitutional amendment procedure. Submission to the Constitution then does not really mean obeying the original constitutional convention's will, but that of the derived constituting power. This power is always capable of amending the Constitution. If he decides to keep it as it is, it means that he wants it to be enforced according to the terms with which it is expressed.

However this analysis does not apply to the Declaration of the Rights of Man, because it is impossible to imagine how this text could ever be modified. According to a common positivist justification of judicial review, when a constitutional court decides that a statute is unconstitutional, all it does is determine that this particular decision cannot be passed in the form of a statute, but can be passed in the form of a constitutional amendment. Yet, as Dean Vedel puts it, in the case of a statute contrary to the Declaration, the decision cannot be viewed "as an invitation to the representatives of the nation to amend the constitution in order to limit liberties".[2]

If an interpretation of the Declaration as an act of will is not a satisfactory justification for obeying it, one is understandably tempted to view it as a declaration of natural rights. But it is not only a negative reason that leads to such an interpretation. There is also a positive reason related to age. The fact that the Declaration is old and that it has been complemented by later documents leads to the necessity to harmonize these texts and this harmonization, in turn, can only be justified by the idea that they are not separate acts of will, but that they contribute to the piecemeal revelation of the treasure of natural law.

It is very striking that a prominent jurist, like Dean Vedel, who as a scholar has always written as a positivist, declares, as a member of the *Conseil Constitutionnel,* that it is impossible to consider rights without accepting the idea that they are transcendent.[3] This does not mean of course that one cannot become a constitutional judge without adhering to a natural law doctrine. It reflects the specific rationality of legal discourse. What Dean Vedel call's the transcendent character of the Rights of Man correspond to what Vaihinger called a fiction. A fiction is different from a hypothesis, in that sense that one does not believe in its reality, but one needs them as a concept without which reasoning is impossible. Fictions are not verifiable, because one knows that they are faulse. One uses them because of their utility. Thus, when some material resists direct examination, fiction enables to reach knowledge "indirectly".[4]

Thus, even if it were true that the Declaration had been adopted in 1789 or mentioned in 1958 as an act of will, its application by the constitutional judge inevitably leads to the idea that the rights it proclaims are transcendent.

---

[2] Georges Vedel, Le Conseil constitutionnel, gardien du droit positif ou défenseur de la transcendance des droits de l'Homme, ds. Pouvoirs, 1988, n° 45.

[3] Ibid.

[4] Hans Vaihinger, Die Philosophie des als ob, trad. angl. The philosophy of as if, London 1935. The most important application of Vaihinger's philosophy in the field of Legal Theory is Kelsen's later version of the concept of the Grundnorm, cf. Die Funktion der Verfassung, Forum (1964) II, n° 132ff., 583ff.

This solution also has the very great advantage of allowing an interpretation independent of the intentions of the fathers of the Declaration. Anyway, intentions would be hard to discover and if discovered hard to accept.

It is true for every type of legal document: when one speaks of the intentions of its author, it is not clear what the reference of this term can be. One does not always even know who the author is: those who took an intellectual part in the drafting, or those who voted it? If we consider the latter only, how do we know what their intent was? In a political assembly, most of the people who vote do not take part in the discussion, those who speak do not always reveal their true motives; they may give contradictory explanations; some may vote for a given provision without knowing what they are voting for, mistaking it for another one, or in order to gain some political advantage in exchange for their ballot.

Studying old texts such as the Declaration of the Rights of Man involves another difficulty: at the time it was drafted and adopted, there was no full Record of the proceedings; the minutes of the debates are incomplete; speeches printed by order of the Assembly or on the authors' initiative do not always correspond to the actual speeches such as they were delivered. They were delivered among the audience's shouts and tumult in a room which had not been conceived to house an assembly, and it is likely that almost no one heard them, in addition it seems that some of the provisions (among the most important ones, such as article 16) were adopted without any debate.

Besides, even if we managed to know the exact intention unanimously followed by the National Assembly, what should we do about it? There is no clear evidence that this intention merges with the meaning of the text, as it does with the interpretation of laws, particularly recent laws. In this case the justification for the enforcement of a statute is compliance to the will of a lawmaker, because he is supposed to have expressed the general will and he can always change the law. Searching the meaning is looking for his intention, more precisely his present intention. However, refering to the Declaration of the Rights of Man does not mean that we wish to abide by these men's wills. The question of what they really wanted is only interesting from an historical point of view.

On the other hand, the "true", historical meaning of such an ancient document may well be perfectly repugnant to us. For example, it is probable that, according to that 1789 intention, in the phrase "all men are born free and equal in rights", "men" only referred to white males. It is, therefore, preferable for the court to be able to interpret the text, without being bound by its formulation, i.e. to assume that it is the expression not of an intention, but of some principle, capable of being "true". The text has the meaning, which, when given to it, makes it "true". For example, the *Conseil Constitutionnel* has repeated several times that the principle of equality means "in similar situations, similar rules, in different situations, different rules".[5] The same goes with the provision concerning fiscal equality. It is perfectly clear that in the state of mind prevailing in 1789, this principle excluded progressive taxation. However, it may be interpreted as compatible – or even as implying this progressive quality – if, instead of refering to the constituent's aim, we take into account the "truth value" of the principle.

This is the reason why the decisions often take the form of philosophical statements, as in the famous 1982 decision, in which the judge wrote that

"in spite of the evolution in the finality and conditions of exercise of the right of property . . . the conservation [of this right] constitutes one of the aims of society . . . ".[6]

Yet, the phrase "truth value" gives rise to various problems if, as it is the case with positivists, a principle is considered to be a norm: therefore it cannot be either true or false. On the other hand, if the indicative conception of the Declaration is rejected, we do not have the opportunity to resort to a comprehensive interpretation method.

An intermediate solution, which also seems to be used by the *Conseil Constitutionnel,* consists in adhering to the prescriptive conception while considering terms in a strictly formal meaning. This is precisely what is done in the process of interpretation of the provisions of the Declaration.

II. Meaning of the Provisions

It is generally said that the necessity to interpret arises from several factors: conflicts with other texts, lack of clarity of the text. But deciding that a legal document conflicts with another or that it lacks clarity is also an interpretation.

Beside the Declaration of the Rights of Man, the constitutional deposit includes other texts: the Constitution, along with its preamble, as well as the preamble to the 1946 Constitution. Since one and a half centuries separate these texts they naturally reflect different ideologies, so that a statute may be seen as contradicting one but not the other.

One of the most striking example is the relation of the law of nationalization to article 17 of the 1789 Declaration and to the preamble of the 1946 Constitution: according to the former *"property being inviolable and sacred, no one may be deprived of it, unless when public necessity, legally established, requires it"*, whereas the latter sets out that all companies acquiring the character of a monopoly have to be nationalized. But, the contradiction is not evident in itself.

---

[5] Cf. Favoreu, L. et Philip, L., Les grandes décisions du Conseil constitutionnel, Paris 6ème édit., 1991, p. 277.

[6] Conseil constitutionnel, 16 janvier et 11 février 1982, in: Favoreu et Philip, op. cit. p. 473.

There is a conflict only if the first text is interpreted in a restrictive way, if it is considered for example that what is meant by "public necessity" is something different from the political desire to prevent a corporation from having a monopoly. In other words, the observation of conflicts between texts as well as the need to reconcile them result from a spontaneous and preliminary interpretation of texts, which have been given such meanings that make them incompatible. In that case the conflict has to be settled in accordance with one of the usual principles *lex posterior derogat* or *specialis generalibus derogant.*

It is also possible to consider that the conflict does not exist if the first text is interpreted in the light of the second one. This is exactly what the *Conseil Constitutionnel* has done in 1982, when he decided that the purpose of the law of nationalization is "to favour economic growth and fight unemployment", and that this purpose is a public necessity in the sense of the Declaration of 1789.[7]

The choice between interpreting the two texts as conflicting or not conflicting is greatly influenced by the age of the Declaration and by the fact that this document is considered as a declaration of natural law and not as an act of will. If it were an act of will, it would be perfectly understandable that a recent political will is different from an older one, that there are conflicts and that the newer will carry more weight than the older. But, if it is a true statement about natural law, it remains true, in spite of every aspect of economic or social evolution. It must be respected without any qualification and cannot conflict with any other document. This does not mean that the judge in that case has no discretion. It only means that in order to regard the document as not conflicting, he has to interpret it as general and vague.

Natural language is said to be characterized by fuzziness or vagueness and ambiguity, and that the need to interpret legal texts exists precisely because they are written in natural language.[8] In addition, they increase with the degree of generality: texts which set out detailed regulations – such as tax regulations or technical standards for buildings or machinery – are much more accurate than the Declaration of the Rights of Man, although obscurity cannot be avoided totally. It is also commonly said that, for all legal texts both characteristics are either intentional or non-intentional.[9] Vagueness and ambiguity, therefore, are viewed as qualities of certain texts.

But, just as clarity, fuzziness and ambiguity are not empirical qualities and before starting to interpret a document, because it is fuzzy, one has to interpret it as fuzzy rather than clear. Whether that fuzziness is intentional or not is

[7] Ibid.

[8] Jerzy Wróblewski, Meaning and Truth in Judicial Decision (edited by Aulis Aarnio). Helsinki 1979; D. Neil MacCormick / Robert S. Summers (eds.), Interpreting statutes; A comparative study, Dartmouth 1991.

[9] Cf. par ex. Hans Kelsen, Théorie Pure du Droit, 2ème édit. trad. fse par Ch. Eisenmann, Paris 1962, pp. 455 - 456.

then also the result of rather than the cause of interpretation. Now it is important to stress that age is an obvious incentive to interpret a document as vague or ambiguous.

The word citizen provides a good example of how difficult it is to determine whether an ambiguity is intentional or not. It is employed in various contexts and may have three different meanings in the Declaration: *lato sensu,* it refers to man living in society as opposed to nature, regardless of sex, age and nationality; it takes into account all human beings, including women and children. Article 7 states:

> Any citizen summoned or apprehended by virtue of the Law, must give instant obedience; resistance makes him guilty.

Stricto sensu, the word refers to all people living on the territory, who are the citizens of a given society, such as is set out in article 13:

> a general tax is indispensable; it must be equally distributed among all citizens, in proportion to their ability to pay.

Strictissimo sensu, it refers exclusively to the French citizens of adult age, such as is stated in articles 14 or 6:

article 14

> All citizens have the right to ascertain, by themselves, or through their representatives, the need for a public tax, to consent to it freely, to watch over its use.

article 6

> The Law is the expression of the general will. All citizens have the right to take part, personally or through their representatives, in its making.

This distinction leads to two further remarks. First, in order to determine the three meanings set out above, it was necessary to interpret the three articles separately. The interpretations were based on the three contexts and on the prevailing attitude in case law; however different interpretations are conceivable. We might have developed a systemic method of interpretation under which a word would have been given the same meaning for all its occurrences, or at least for several of them. We might decide, for example, that the citizens among whom taxes are shared are the same citizens who possess the right to evaluate their necessity. Therefore the ambiguity lies in the fact that the writer of the document does not know which interpretation method is to be applied. In practice, following a different method from ours, it has been advocated that article 6 should be interpreted so as to give not only nationals but also foreigners, in some cases, the opportunity to take part in the formation of the law.

Second remark, this distinction does not completely eliminate ambiguity: none of the two concepts of citizens examined above refers to sex, so that we have no idea whether citizens are male only or if women too can be citizens. In the case of articles 7 and 13, the answer is yes, since women too have to obey immediately and to pay taxes. But the ambiguity of the word remains in article 6: depending on the circumstances, the word may be interpreted as including women, or not.

Not only are texts ambiguous, they are also vague. A word is considered to be vague if we know what it means without being able to determine with accuracy to which concrete object it refers to. The Declaration provides a good example of a vague term with "necessary punishments". The meaning is quite clear, the sentence should not be either too lenient or too heavy, but it is impossible to know whether a concrete sentence is or is not necessary. Obviously the use of such vague terms is intentional and unavoidable, because it was impossible for the National Assembly to define it more precisely without determining, if not criminal law as a whole, at least the main basis of a criminal policy. The easiest thing to do was then to rely on the future legislator, in such a way that the notion of "necessary punishments" becomes simply formal: a sentence is necessary if it is regarded as such by the legislator, depending on the customs current at the time he legislates. The Declaration is full of examples of this kind of terms which are mostly used in articles refering to the law.

There are fewer examples of non-intentionally vague terms: in 1789, they conveyed a very precise meaning, which does not correspond any longer to our current value system. This is the reason why we consider them to be vague and interpret them as such: article 13 provides that all should contribute to public expenses "in proportion to their ability to pay". At the time, this phrase probably meant "proportional to (capacity to pay)". It was intentionally vague only inasmuch as it did not specify in which proportion every one had to contribute to public spending. If we want to reconcile this requirement and the notion of progressive tax – likely to have been regarded as non-proportional tax – we need to give it an even more vague meaning. The legislator has to set tax rates in a measure considered to be fair according to the values and custom in his society at the time when he legislates. The same goes for the allocation of these contributions for financing public spending. In 1789, it was only necessary to collect the receipts in order to cover the expenditures. Redistribution was not even contemplated, nor was the use of taxes as means of economic policy, and it is not part of the notion of public spending. This notion thus has to be modified made vaguer in order to be reconciled with these aspects of tax allocation.

Thus, age makes it necessary to interpret the Declaration as vague, ambiguous or simply formal in order to avoid conflicts with modern legislation. The provisions of the Declaration of the Rights of Man, like those which prescribe equality or compliance with public interest or justice (article 17 on property for instance), have no specific content. They are mere forms which have to be filled with whatever will be regarded as equality and justice at the time the text is enforced.

VII. Legal Positivism Revised: Anti-Formalism versus Formalism in Modern Law

Legal Change and Legal Theory: The Context for a Revised Legal Positivism

By Tom D. Campbell, Canberra*

Legal theories come in many different modes and modules. Some set out to provide conceptual analyses of basic legal terms, others seek to explain such phenomena as legal change, and there are those which purport to guide and direct positive developments in the law at varying levels of generality.[1] This essay concentrates on the third mode of theorising: theory directed at, or used to formulate, proposals for, legal change and, hopefully, legal progress, something along the lines adopted so successfully by Professor R. S. Summers in his exposition, qualified defence and development of 'pragmatic instrumentalism'.[2]

In current legal scholarship, all areas of legal study are, at their frontiers, explicitly and self-consciously addressing conceptual, moral, political and economic issues at a level of some theoretical sophistication. This may be seen in the language which pervades the pages of the major law reviews and the nature of the issues which divide their authors. Even if we can evade the discourse of deconstruction and 'differance', we cannot be altogether blind to opportunity costs and Pareto optimality, to say nothing of rule-utilitarianism and the prisoner's dilemma. This theoretical infusion of traditionally doctrinal territory – let us call it 'applied legal philosophy' – is noteworthy for the fact that its participants are as much at home in the terminology of preference maximisation as of precedent.

---

* This essay has been developed from a paper read to the annual meeting of the Australasia Law Teachers Association held at the Queensland University of Technology in 1993. I acknowledge gratefully the comments made on a draft of this paper by my colleagues Peter Drahos and Stephen Parker. Elements of Part IV are drawn from Tom Campbell, 'The Legal Contribution to Political Theory' in R. Goodin and P. Pettit, Companion to Contemporary Political Philosophy, Oxford 1993.

[1] Of course, this sort of normative theorising must involve a deal of conceptual analysis and depends on many assumptions about what forces in society cause or divert legal variations, but its interest in such matters is subordinate to the utility of such conceptual schemes and empirical assumptions in serving the prescriptive force of the theory. In the sort of normative theory I want to explore, it is the value goals that set the criteria of theoretical relevance.

[2] Robert S. Summers, Instrumentalism and American Legal Theory, Ithaca 1982; and Essays on the Nature of Law and Legal Reasoning, Berlin 1992, particularly chapter 5 'Pragmatic Instrumentalism and American Legal Theory', which first appeared in 13 RECHTSTHEORIE, 1982, 257 - 66.

The immediate impact of the increasingly theoretical nature of legal research is to render any straightforward legal approach to law reform problematic. Here there is no authoritative doctrinal exposition awaiting only further application or logical extrapolation to new circumstances. Rather we find detailed articulations of deeply conflicting moral, social and political views relating to the interpretation and assessment of the areas of law in question. In contemporary legal scholarship generally, moral and political alternatives – between which there can be no neutral legal arbiter – vie openly for our loyalties.

Consider, for instance, the nature of the debates which arise in current approaches to torts. First, there is the major divergence between utilitarian and deontological approaches, the former looking to the instrumental role of law and the latter searching for a basis in commutative justice.[3] Thus there is the modified utilitarianism of Richard Posner, Guido Calabresi and many others who approach tort law from the point of view of the 'efficient' allocation of resources with respect to the cost of accidents.[4] Contrast this with the views of such as George Fletcher, Richard Epstein and Ernest Weinrib, who emphasise, in one way or another, interpersonal justice or fairness as between injurer and injured in the determination of liability to pay compensation for harms which arise from the conduct of others.[5] That the pursuit of justice may have an economic cost is, for this latter group, no veto on an attribution of tortious liability, while the former subsume justice within wealth maximisation.

---

[3] Utilitarianism as a moral theory states that the rightness of an action is determined solely by its consequences, which are classically evaluated in terms of pleasures and pains. A deontological moral theory analyses right and wrong in terms of a number if distinct duties, which may include the duty of benevolence. See A. C. Ewing, Ethics, New York 1953, p. 61, and B. Williams, Ethics and the Limits of Philosophy, London 1985, p. 16.

[4] R. A. Posner, The Economic Analysis of Law, 2nd Edition, 1972, Boston, Mass; G. Calabresi and A. K. Klevorick, 'Four Tests of Liability in Torts', 14, Journal of Legal Studies, 1985, pp. 585 - 627. Posner distances himself from certain aspects of utilitarianism but his approach is clearly within that tradition.

[5] G. P. Fletcher, 'Fairness and Utility in Tort Theory', 85 Harvard Law Review, 1972, pp. 537 - 73.; R. A. Epstein, 'A Theory of Strict Liability' 2 Journal of Legal Studies, 1973, pp. 151 - 204; E. Weinrib, 'Understanding Tort Law' 23 Valparaiso University Law Review, 1987, pp. 485 - 526. Work of this sort can lead back into historical argument about what constitutes the essence of the traditional common law of torts Such discussions have a comforting doctrinal feel, since they involve teasing out the general principles of particular legal traditions. However, it is evident that such disagreements about the correct interpretation of legal history are not fundamental to the protagonists. Perhaps it is because they are lawyers that they cannot help arguing that their analyses have the support of historical precedent, but it is clear that what motivates them primarily is ultimately a concern with normative questions about the direction in which tort law should now be encouraged to develop. In this prescriptive vein, the theoretical debates within tort law lead us into standard issues within social and political philosophy. Freedom and self-reliance contend with competing conceptions of justice and the demands communitarian values and welfare needs. The details may be embedded in complex legal analyses but they are at base moral and political disputes.

This disagreement does not, however, break down into a simple utilitarian versus deontological split. For instance, a quasi-utilitarian such as Posner, might be expected to support strict liability in tort in order to maximise its deterrent effect, but, in fact, on empirical grounds, he holds that the fault principle may be more efficient.[6] In contrast Epstein, for all his emphasis on individual responsibility, argues that the requirement of fault, in the sense of individual worthiness, weakens everyday notions of responsibility as they are embedded in the conventions of ordinary language which determine when a person may be said to have 'caused' and thus be responsible for an injury.[7]

From yet another perspective, represented by Izhak Englard, all the participants in this debate share a highly individualistic approach which has the disadvantage of separating the discussion of tort law from the broader social concerns of community welfare provision.[8]

No doubt, such fusion of legal and political analysis represents a healthy interconnection between legal and other practical philosophies. Certainly, it is important to realise that all disputes about law reform relate back to conflicting political visions that cannot be resolved within the confines of legal theory itself. Hence the current importance for law reform of the work of political philosophers like John Rawls, and his more legally-oriented compatriots, such as Bruce Ackerman and Jules Coleman.[9]

However, the merging of legal and political analysis renders much contemporary legal theory unmanageable for law-based legal reformers who may well not be in a position to articulate and deploy their own system of values as well as work out their best legal instantiation, or, if they are in a position to do so, may feel that it is wrong for them to use the mantle of legal expertise to further their own social and politicial values.

Moreover, while it is essential to bear in mind that law holds only limited neutral ground between competing visions of the good polity, it remains for legal theorists to discuss what law can and cannot offer to whatever political values and assumptions we ultimately choose to adopt. For instance, we must ask whether law is an instrument which can be made to serve any preferred social goal and how it works most effectively in relation to the chosen objectives, or whether it has deeper functionalist or symbolic roles which shape its

---

[6] R. A. Posner, 'Strict Liability: A Commentary', 2 Journal of Legal Studies, 1973, pp. 205 - 21.

[7] R. Epstein, op. cit., p. 175.

[8] I. Englard, 'The System Builders: A Criticial Appraisal of American Tort Theory', 9 Journal of Legal Studies, 1980, pp. 27 - 69.

[9] J. Rawls, A Theory of Justice, Oxford 1972; Bruce Ackerman, Social Justice in the Liberal State, New Haven 1980; J. L. Coleman, Markets, Morals and the Law, Cambridge 1988.

methods and content. We must also be sensitive to the social side effects, good and bad, which typify characteristic legal approaches to the resolution of human conflicts. In that sense, every complete political philosophy needs an assumed working theory of law, a model of what law is and what it can do, a model which is to some extent detachable from its more controversial moral and political elements, if only by the fact that the value questions it raises are distinct from the ordinary substantive disputes concerning political value and priorities. Not that any theory of law, however second order, is actually above normative dispute; quite the contrary. But we may aspire to a measure of agreement on a working model law which attracts a degree of value consensus within which we can argue out our moral and political disagreements. Perhaps this is what a legal reformer ought to expect from legal theory.

It is clear that we do not have such a consensus. This presents serious problems for the law reform process. There is deep public cynicism about the social value of law and lawyers and the relevance of the legal approach to such matters as commercial disputes, family breakdowns and gender equality. Costly irrelevance, at best; meddlesome and avaricious trouble-making, at worst. Combine this with current forceful scholarly attacks on the vaunted objectivity of the legal process, attacks which are not at present being effectively answered, and we have the makings of a crisis of confidence which has the potential to undermine the motivation to improve our laws and legal system. Discussion already centres as much on alternatives as on improvements to law.[10]

In this debate, costs and delays are but two of the parameters of criticism. There is also an underlying uncertainty arising from the persuasive postmodernist message with its beguiling enhancement of traditional moral and social relativism. Pervasive indeterminacy and all encompassing subjectivism render us vulnerable to the contention that the legal progress for which we strive can never be anything more than a phoney legitimation for de facto economic and political power.[11] It cannot be assumed that such talk is misguided and misinformed. Rather, we need to address the question of whether, despite important political divergencies, we can have an intellectually viable and moral convincing theory of law to take with us into the law reform process.

---

[10] Consider, for instance, the move to commend and adopt various forms of 'alternative dispute resolution' including methods which bypass rule-based adjudication and exclude lawyers. See W. Faulkes, 'The Modern Development of Alternative Dispute Resolution in Australia', 1 Australian Dispute Resolution Journal, 1990, p. 61; M. Thornton. 'Equivocations of Conciliation: the Resolution of Discrimination Disputes in Australia' 52 Modern Law Review, 1989, p. 733; R. Abel, (ed.) The Politics of Informal Justice, New York 1982; and E. Brunet ,Questioning the Quality of ADR' 62 Tulane Law Review, 1987, pp. 1 - 56.

[11] Under 'postmodernism' we may take in the work of a disparate collection of theorists, such as Derrida, Lyotard and the later Wittgenstein. See Dennis M. Patterson, 'Postmodernism/Feminism/Law'. 77 Cornell Law Review, 1992.

There is certainly no lack of theories of law from which to choose, although it is not clear that all of them are at the level of abstraction that suits them for our quest for a framework theory of law. Indeed there is an embarrassment of contenders: Economic Analysis of Law (EAL), Critical Legal Studies (CLS), Feminist Jurisprudence (FJ), Rights Theory (RT) as we may designate the approach of those who make the idea of fundamental rights basic to their legal analyses, to say nothing of current resurgences of various styles of Natural Law (NL), Pragmatic Instrumentalism (PI) and a not altogether extinct Legal Positivism (LP).

Some of these broad theoretical positions offer radical objections to the whole enterprise of law rather than programmes for legal reform. Their adherents would certainly baulk at the idea that the purpose of theory can be to improve rather than destruct law. For them, the question – 'what can legal theory offer the proponents of legal change?' – smacks of a conniving instrumentalism which marginalises radical criticism and closes the door on significant change.

At least some CLS scholars suggest that the traditional goals of legal regulation of society are hopelessly contradictory and serve, if anything, merely to cloak the operation of class, racial and gender power. At least some FJ theorists suggest that law is, in its form as well as its substance, a male method of going about the business of making human relationships work, and one, therefore, that is more often than not better abandoned rather than utilised to better effect. And, at least some exponents of EAL, in almost Marxian terms, see the economic approach as a replacement of a previously supposed independent realm of human decision making – the autonomous legal sphere – by a higher form of discourse: the economic.[12]

It is a worrying feature of our current responses to such movements of thought that we see them, according to our point of view, as deeply threatening or as refreshingly liberating. On either view they present as opening up a gulf between currently dynamic theory and the practicalities of the law reform process. Moreover, there is a need to sort out, within these broad theories, the relatively detachable moral and political values from the underlying assumptions about law, and its particular moral significance, and then subject these to anlysis and criticism. Hopefully, this can be done in a way which finds a limited and subordinate place for EAL and accommodates the undoubted force of current destabilising theories, such as FJ and CLS, without wholly embracing their non-reformist implications.

This essay is a modest attempt to start in on this job. Its strategy is to offer, first a critique and partial rehabilitation of two leading contending theories

[12] R. A. Posner, 'The Decline of Law as an Autonomous Discipline: 1962 - 1987', 100 Harvard Law Review, 1987, pp. 761 - 80.

(RT and EAL) in order to curb their imperialistic tendencies and expose their limitations; second, to outline a new Positivist theory which offers some common ground to contending theoretical parties; and third, to consider how this approach ('the legal theory of Ethical Positivism') might take on board in a open-minded way the critiques of CLS and FJ.

I. The Insufficiency of Rights

Lawyers in search of an ego-boosting general theory of law could do worse than adopt the politically popular and more or less intellectually rehabilitated Rights approach to law according to which the prime and distinctive feature of law is its protection and furtherance of fundamental moral rights. Perhaps they might adopt the version of the Rights Theory (RT) in which matters of policy are surrendered to the economically minded and hopefully democratically controlled policy makers, while the lawyers' input is to insist on and if possible entrench some set of independently ascertained moral or human rights. Politics is about goals, law is about rights.[13]

This Rights-commitment can be exciting, even ennobling, as well as flattering enough to bolster the self-image of a profession that faces diminution of its own influence and public esteem. It is, however, highly doubtful whether the distinction between rights and goals can bear the weight that is required to make it an effective fence against the intrusion of the certain aspects of politics into 'law's empire'. Any policy statement in terms of goals can readily be rewritten as a claim of right, and a commitment to protect and further rights can easily be seen as an important political and social goal. In other words, not only may respecting rights be our goal, we may also demand the right to pursue certain goals. In general the terminology of rights and goals would appear to be interchangeable.[14] Thus, if there are not enough beds in the local hospital, is this a matter of a deficiency in the policy objectives of government or a violation of the basic rights of those on the waiting lists for elective surgery? On such conceptual conundrums would issues of social and political contention fall into the provenance of legislatures or courts, with the prospect that the courts could choose to intervene in the democratic process when and where they chose to do so, with no great intellectual gymnastics being required to justify their prononcement.

---

[13] For a forceful reassertion of the significance of right-based law as against modern managerialism, see B. A. Ackerman, Reinterpreting American Law, Cambridge, Mass. 1984.

[14] For this standard criticism of Dworkin's conceptual schema see T. D. Campbell, Justice, London 1988, p. 13 and K. Greenawalt, 'Judicial Decisions, Policy and Rights', 11 Georgia Law Review, 1977, pp. 993 - 1053; also J. L. Mackie, 'The Third Theory of Law', 7 Philosophy and Public Affairs, 1977, pp. 3 - 16.

Moreover, if we are looking for a consensual theoretical position on law, a Rights approach is unhelpful because proponents of CLS and FJ often view rights as verging on bogus universals protecting class or gender interests.[15] Moreover, rights occupy only a subordinate position within EAL as the defeasible preconditions of efficiency in market exchanges.[16] Compromises are difficult to achieve in this sphere.

The fact that RT is highly controversial in relation to the divisions of economic class may not worry us so much in the current stage of world politics, but this does not enable us to evade in practice the problems which emerge when rights, as an assumedly individualist concept, clash with the manifest needs of groups, even the interests of that group of groups, society itself.[17] Even if we can learn to live with these difficulties, RT cannot generate specific visions of legal change without some philosophical foundation to give substance to rights and proposals for concrete implementation to give them effect.

As to philosophical foundations we can hardly rest content with the appeal to moral intuitions, given the cultural variables that appear to determine the workings of this 'faculty' and their apparent imperviousness to reasoned criticism. We could opt for some version of the new classical Natural Law approach which reasserts what John Finnis and other see as the proper interpretation of Aquinas,[18] but this lacks general appeal in a pluralist and secular age, even if we can muster the necessary personal convictions. There are similar problems with the more Protestant or Kantian path, with its over-emphasis on rational autonomy and its evident naivety as to the power of the universalisability technique of practical reasoning to settle substantive moral questions. You do not need to be a postmodernist to be sceptical about how far we can get towards agreement on basic moral principles by asking what maxims we, as rational agents, are prepared to adopt as universal laws.[19]

However politically successful it may be in some jurisdictions to give to unelected judicial officers the power to overturn legislative enactments on the basis of highly general entrenched rights, this does not vindicate rights as a theoretical foundation for approaching legal change. Almost anything can be intuited as a right of some type or other. Rights are better viewed as objectives than as starting points for law reform. And, in so far as the language of rights may be used to set objectives, it is able to do this not only for promoting autonomy, or for establishing side-constraints on the way we go after our goals, but

---

[15] See C. Smart, Feminism and the Power of Law, London 1989; and R. Unger, 'The CLS Movement' 96 Harvard Law Review, 1983, pp. 563 - 625, at 599ff.

[16] R. A. Posner, Economic Analysis of Law, p. 70ff.

[17] For this communitarian theme see, M. J. Sandel, Liberalism and the Limits of Justice, New York 1982.

[18] J. Finnis, Natural Law and Natural Rights, Oxford 1980.

[19] See M. G. Singer, Generalization in Ethics, London 1963, chapter 9.

may properly enter into the delineation of all the preferred interests that law should serve and protect.[20]

One of the attractions of RT within legal theory is that it does seem to offer some view of the distinctively legal contribution to society, namely instantiating and applying prior existing moral rights. It has to be admitted, therefore, that, if we find a Rights approach to be insufficient to capture the role of law in society, our task of uncovering a consensus meta-theory of law is that much more difficult.

II. Economics in its Place

If the drift of the preceding section is that law reformers should ask 'what laws ought we enact to create the sort of positive rights we wish to have?' (rather than 'what moral rights are there and how can we protect them?'), then the Economic Analysis of Law (EAL) can offer us a basis for selecting our preferred positive rights. In the tradition of radical utilitarianism, EAL theorists can argue that natural rights are nonsense, and inalienable natural rights nonsense upon stilts, and proceed to enter into the calculus of utility to determine which human concerns ought to be raised to the status of legally protected interests according to whatever best serves the general happiness, aggregate preferences or gross national product.[21] Should we have a right to dispose of our bodies? That depends on whether such a right most effectively facilitates the transferral of bodily organs to the persons able and willing to pay most for them. Should we have the right to sell our labour to the highest bidder? Certainly, because that is a prerequisite of the free exchange which constitutes efficient economic relationships.

Of course, in the EAL version of utilitarianism, the allocation of rights is not of theoretical importance. As Coase has taught us,[22] whatever initial allocation is made of any resource, given free exchange and no transaction costs, it will find its way into the hands of those who can use it most profitably. This applies to rights as to all else. It just so happens, according to Posner at least, that it is more efficient to give standard fundamental rights to individuals because 'the wealth-maximizing principle requires the initial vesting of rights in those who are likely to value them most, so as to minimize transaction costs'.[23] It is, in fact, the realities of transaction costs, the costs involved in preparing for, making and carrying through rational and informed exchanges, that gives rise to the need for a great deal of law, law whose function is to

[20] Tom Campbell, The Left and Rights, London 1983, chapter 2.

[21] This is the Benthamite legacy. See D. Lyons, 'Utility and Rights', in J. Waldron, Theories of Rights, Oxford 1984, pp. 110 - 36.

[22] R. H. Coase, 'The Problem of Social Costs', 3 Journal of Legal Studies, p. 1.

[23] R. A. Posner, op. cit., p. 71.

'mimic the market' by placing rights and duties, and other benefits and burdens, in the hands of those who would possess them in a perfectly performing market.[24]

The relevance and force of EAL in relation to commercial law are hard to gainsay, its weaknesses here being largely such as are common to all attempts to apply abstract economic theories to the complexities of actual economies. However, there are both methodological and moral objections to its deployment in non-commercial areas. Methodologically it is hamstrung outside the economic sphere by the absence of monetary values by which to measure prices and costs in the supposed transactions of ordinary social life, be they political, sexual, or whatever. In real life people do not always choose to maximise their wealth, unless we simply assert that whatever they choose to do is what constitutes wealth for them, perhaps measured by the opportunity costs of the activity in question. There is only one difficulty with this assumption, namely that people may then be said to be maximising their wealth whatever they choose to do. In non-economic fields, at least, EAL analysis of human conduct, if it is meant to be explanatory and predictive (which, as a consequentialist theory, it must be, or else it would have no prescriptive force), is a vacuous and unverifiable hypothesis which fits any consistent regularity of activities.[25]

Morally EAL fails not because utility is unimportant, but because it is not all important. EAL is morally incomplete because it does not consider the initial distribution of rights as a matter of justice and humanity beyond the calculation of societal wealth maximisation. The same applies to a purely utilitarian assessment of the eventual results of the operations of any of the many theoretically possible perfect markets, let alone the outcomes of actual markets. This does not mean that we can ignore the substance of much economic analysis of law. At least some form of law and economics study is required for the calculation of the consequences of legal change. What we cannot do is to accept that our policy goals are set by the value assumptions of economists. For this reason alone, law reform issues cannot be left to the unfettered abstractions of EAL.

III. Ethical Positivism

The standard response to the deficiences of EAL is to seek to combine it with a modest number of rights-based principles. However, given the reservations we have noted about the derivation of rights-claims, this is simply to put

---

24 Op.cit., p. 6, etc.

25 See, C. E. Baker, The Ideology of the Economic Analysis of Law', 5 Philosophy and Public Affairs, 1975.

all political evaluations of law back into the original pluralist soup from which we are presumably seeking to escape.

We may, however, seek some common, if less encompassing, ground if we ask whether RT and EAL have any shared conception of law itself, as distinct from the objectives it ought to serve. Dogmatically and summarily, it can be claimed that plausible versions of RT require that law be seen as a set of rules which protect preferred interests and which cannot be overridden by purely utilitarian calculations,[26] while any plausible version of EAL requires that law be seen as a relatively fixed body of rules in the light of which rational individuals govern their conduct according to the incentives on offer. In other words, some form of rule-based Legal Positivism affords a measure of consensual presupposition as to what law is all about.

It may, however, be hard indeed to see how we can retreat to the old consensus around some form of Legal Positivism as the starting point for lawyer-centred programmes of law reform. Surely it is no longer feasible to adopt working assumptions whereby government provides the utility-based policy (perhaps in the modernised guise of EAL although this approach is highly suspicious of any governmentally inspired projects) which lawyers then help to transform into sets of rules which, when enforced in courts, will have the effect that the sovereign desires. Legal Positivism is, after all, the whipping horse of most current lively theoretical movements. Legal Realism put paid to the idea that we can ever have a set of clearly formulated rules which can effectively apply themselves to specific factual instances without passing through the medium of open-ended judicial interpretation and messy fact-finding. Following which, CLS and FJ have made much of the way in which established powers make use of the alleged objectivity of positive rules to get their own way in the supposedly neutral application of sovereign legitimated laws.

Moreover, Legal Positivism as a form of philosophical positivism seems barren of moral insight and is readily blamed for abdicating from moral choice in its unfettered recognition of de facto political power[27] and the blandishments of populist utilitarianism.[28] Further, Positivism is open to sociological analysis which sees it as the jurisprudence of legitimation, whose task is to offer (phoney) justification of legal functions and lawyers' incomes.[29]

---

[26] Tom D.Campbell et al (eds.), Human Rights: From Rhetoric to Reality, Oxford 1986, pp. 1 - 14.

[27] See Radbruch's criticism, discussed in H. L. A. Hart, 'Positivism and the Separation of Law and Morals', 71 Harvard Law Review, 1958.

[28] This is the essence of the Dworkinian critique of Hart. See R. M. Dworkin, Taking Rights Seriously, London 1977, chapters 2 and 3.

[29] See R. Cotterrell, The Politics of Jurisprudence, London 1989, chapter 3.

Intellectually in disarray, morally bankrupt and politically suspect, Legal Positivism seems a discarded ghost of the past rather than a basis for the future of law reform. Indeed the fact that so much legal theory still goes on in terms of the Natural Law-Positivism dichotomy, two positions which seem to lack credibility and relevance in the late twentieth century, seems to indicate that orthodox legal theory has nothing helpful to offer the contemporary theorist let alone the practical law reformer. The archaic terminology simply reflects a moribund orthodoxy.

Despite all this, it may be possible to rehabilitate some version of Legal Positivism, perhaps a new Legal Positivism, but a Positivism none the less. Certainly not a Positivism which denies the role of value judgments in law-making and the political justification of legal systems, or simply expresses the ideology of liberalism, but a Positivism which nevertheless seeks to innoculate the process of rule application to some degree from moral and political influence, while accepting that any law represents a controversial value postulate.

Yet, is this not precisely the discredited 'formalism' that is belied by any sopisticated analysis of the law in action? Positivism does not provide a picture of what law actually is in reality. The challenge of empirical falsification can, however, be countered by a Positivist approach to law and adjudication which supports as an *ideal* (not a description or definition) rules and rule governed procedures which seek to minimise bias between litigants within the limits of liberal social democracy and, in the adjudication, utilises no value presuppositions which are not there in the legislative enactment or in the rationale for adopting a rule-based approach in the first place.

Such a theory need not assume moral scepticism and may accept that law may serve both individual and political moralities.

Nevertheless, it aspires to a process of rule application which is in itself sufficiently value free to ensure that legal judging need not be moral judging, any more than it need be economic or political judging.

Such a theory will not enable us to determine the value of specific substantive laws, but it may provide a framework within which such political issues can be decided by the political process, a framework that sets out consensual standards as to what a technically (and thus, on the theory 'ethically') 'good' law will look like.

The name is a problem. 'Positivism', as defined in opposition to Natural Law, is associated with value scepticism (not in itself a disgrace in postmodernist eyes). It is even more associated with narrow empiricism and the extremities of individualistic liberalism. Since we might wish to dissociate ourselves in varying degrees from all such company, we may be well advised to drop the terminology of Positivism, but there are other associations which are, to my mind, more constitutive of its personality. Perhaps the best we can do in these circumstances is to modify this particular label by adding a qualifying adjective: and call the position the legal theory of 'Ethical Positivism' (LEP).[30]

A good deal of LEP is inherited from the old Austinian Positivism, 'properly understood' (that is viewed as an ideal not a stipulation or deduction from arbitrary definitions and certainly not as a description of legal reality). This ideal does involve certain sociological assumptions. For instance, any Positivism must hold: (1) that general rules can, to an extent, govern human conduct in that human beings are capable of acting as rule-following creatures who can both comprehend what a rule of conduct requires and recognise the requirement to follow a mandatory rule even when this is not what the subject would otherwise wish to do[31]; (2) that some rules of conduct may be couched in terms which make them applicable without resort to the affirmation of moral criteria (in the use rather than the reference mode), so that there is no necessary connection between a rule, be it legal or non-legal, and morality, in that there are rules which can be applied without deploying a moral assessment or judgement; (3) that this makes possible a conceptual and to some extent institutionalisable division between legislation and adjudication; and (4) that a sociological distinguishing feature of law is that it embodies those rules which a society's political authorities present and if necessary enforce as mandatory or non-optional.[32]

Further refinements exhibit what may be called the new Positivism emanating from H. L. A. Hart and developed by Joseph Raz and Neil MacCormick, namely: (1) the sources thesis, according to which 'what is law and what is not is a matter of social fact'[33] and are thus 'publicly ascertainable';[34] (2) the hermeneutic thesis: that assertions can only be understood in terms of the subjective meanings emerging from particular histories and practices. It is therefore

---

[30] See Tom D. Campbell, 'Ethical Positivism' in S. Panou et al. Theory and Systems of Legal Philosophy, Wiesbaden 1988, pp. 67 - 71.

[31] So much may be appropriated from Lon Fuller, but without his fanciful claim that aspirational norms of clarity, consistency, prospectivity, feasibility, and so forth, favour any specific moral quality of rule content.
See, The Morality of Law, New Haven 1969.

[32] For law as mandatory rules within a specific territory, see T. D. Campbell, 'Obligation: Legal, Political and Societal' in P. Harris (ed.), On Political Obligation, London 1990.

[33] J. Raz, The Authority of Law, Oxford 1979, p. 37. As a descriptive claim this is implausible, but as a commendation it encapsules an essential aspect of LEP: that the validity of a law should not depend on what the adjudicaor thinks of its content. This appears to contrast with the view of R. S. Summers that 'an ideal legal system would include many explicit content-oriented tests [of validity]', see 'Toward a Better Theory of Legal Validity', in Essays on the Nature of Law and Legal Reasoning, Berlin 1992, p. 44. However, as Summers acknowledges, a rule identified by its source may set up a content-oriented test as the one which is to be applied. LEP has no difficulty with this provided the content-oriented test does not require the exercise of moral judgment for its application.

[34] Op. cit., p. 52.

acceptable, indeed inevitable, that legal rules be read in the light of at least selected elements of the relevant cultural understandings, including the positive morality and general cultural assumptions of the community. In other words, laws must be addressed to the appropriate cultural relativities and require to be understood through entering into that cultural milieu.

Why should such a collection of sociological assumptions be labelled as 'ethical' Positivism? In part, the adjective 'ethical' is warranted simply to draw attention to those overlooked aspects of classical Positivism which emphasise the value goals which underpin the recommendation of the Positivist model of law, a model which has historically been advocated, not for its own sake, nor to satisfy some neat conceptual scheme, but to further certain moral and political objectives.[35] The broad evaluative thrust of Legal Positivism has always been that mandatory rule-governed relationships are a desirable medium for political organisation. It may be conceded that classical and indeed modern positivists tend to present their theory as descriptively accurate of legal process as it is, indeed as it must be, rather than as a particular type of legal aspiration. However, they all incorporate an underlying value commitment to the purported benefits of law-governed polities. This is the element which I extract and from which we may extrapolate to formulate the theory of Ethical Positivism. To that extent, therefore, LEP revamps the Positivistic model as an ideal rather than a description or explanation of existing legal law and legal systems.

Many of the moral reasons for preferring a Positivist model of law may be found in both the old and the new Positivism, particularly in relation to the standard rationales for their content-neutral version of the rule of law. Thus: (1) technically applied positive law is a prerequisite for democracy without which a majority determination of social practice is not feasible; (2) there is a measure of impartiality to be gained through judicial application of general rules which avoids arbitrary disadvantaging of particular persons; (3) the existence of publicly recognisable and interpretable rules enables individuals and groups to plan their lives so as to maximise their utilities, thus institutionalising a measure of individual and group liberty; (4) the utility of stable co-operation between and within communities.[36]

Beyond (and to an extent in modification of) all this, the Ethical Positivism I would commend is marked by at least six further features:

(1) a firm commitment to the value selectivity of positive law and the full recognition of substantive law as representing a partisan choice which requires political vindication and is, in general, inappropriate for judicial change; (2)

---

[35] See D. N. MacCormick, Legal Right and Social Democracy, Oxford 1982, chapter 2.

[36] See, The Left and Rights, chapter 3.

an acceptance of the desirability of enacting rules which embody no more value commitment than is necessary for the objective in question; (3) a willingness to take account of the reality of a far wider range of morally suspect biases which operate in extant legal systems in relation to the initiation and implementation of legal directives and a commitment to discovering ways of combating such damaging distortions; (4) more particularly, an emphasis on the need for a strong and distinctive legal professional ethic, as an essential aspect of procedural justice in action; (5) a reduction of the emphasis on internal consistency as between different branches of law as a principle of interpretation as distinct from an ultimate aspirational ideal, thus giving more direct and powerful impact to novel legal change, and (6) an emphasis on the fundamental importance for legal reform of empirical information in relation to how laws are actually applied and the resultant social consequences.

To this, we may tentatively add a further ingredient, (7) the recognition that there is an important affinity between the moral and legal points of view which makes legal adjudication an acceptable mode of political decision making within prescribed limitations. This affinity has to do with relative impartiality as between competing parties to a dispute, a defining characteristic of both the moral and the judicial point of view, something on which we can trade when a modicum of judicial law-making is thought desirable or inevitable. This is not the only aspect of Ethical Positivism which is likely to fall foul of the post-modern critiques which are the subject matter of the next part.

IV. Critical Reflections

To suggest that Ethical Positivism presents potential common ground for lawyers of very different political persuasion who are involved in the law reform process, does not imply that we can simply ignore the powerful critiques of CLS and FJ according to which Positivism is a none-too-subtle legitimation of a system in which class and gender are the ruling forces.

LEP need not, however, claim that the ideals commended are adequately realised within any polity. Ethical Positivists may themselves rage at the indeterminacy, contradictoriness and bias of existing legal systems. Indeed, Positivistic failings in actual systems of government provide the basis for deligitimations of the use of power.

Thus, while Ethical Positivists may not see the same homogeneity of forces at work behind false claims to objectivity in actual and particular systems, they may readily take on board many of the insights of critical and feminist theorists relating to the inadequacies of existing law and legal processes.

LEP has no difficulty recognising, for instance, the phenomenon of reification, whereby, on the CLS analysis, laws, which are human artifacts, are mistakenly treated as pre-existing things whose natural facticity limits the choices of their creators.[37] The ontology of this critique of reification accords with the Positivist view that law is made, not discovered, and may be readily changed or annulled by acts of will. The 'pseudo objectivity'[38] associated with false beliefs in the 'naturalness' of laws is potentially as much a prime target for Ethical Positivists as for CLS, since it negates the power of the law-maker and misdescribes the role of the law-applicator. For the Ethical Positivist, however, this does not mean collapsing the distinction between law-making and law-interpretation. That laws are artifacts of human institutions does not prevent them from being a medium of communication.

Serious disagreements do, however arise if the ideals of Ethical Positivism are alleged to be either incapable of being realised or undesirable in themselves. However, even on these issues of feasibility and desirability, Ethical Positivists are not committing to holding that Positivism is equally achievable in all areas or even that it is a desirable system in all areas of social interaction. On the contrary, in contrast to many other theoretical approaches, Positivism is well adapted to mapping the limitations and weaknesses of legal approaches to social problems.

To explore the feasibility issue further we must first make clear that the ideals of LEP are not to be equated with all the elements of the straw formalist model of law with which CLS and FJ are routinely contrasted.[39] For CLS 'formalism' is a multi-faceted collection of errors. It involves the belief that all legal problems can be solved by reference to nothing more than the appropriate valid legal rules interpreted in the light of their plain meanings and read within the larger network of valid principles and concepts of the legal system in question. Thus Kennedy regards formalists as supposing that the contradictions and ambivalencies in liberal law can be resolved by reference to valid laws alone.[40] Ethical Positivism makes no such extravagant claims, and is, indeed, actively hostile to the idea that concrete legal solutions follow from general concepts or vague rules, but holds only that some conflicts can be settled and some objectives achieved by enacting appropriate specific laws and entrusting their application to properly constituted courts within a relatively homogenous culture.

Nor does LEP pretend that laws can be morally neutral, as the formalist is said to maintain. Rather its contention is that the moral choices involved in all

---

[37] P. Gabel, 'Reification in Legal Reasoning', 3 Research in Law and Sociology, 1980, pp. 25 - 51.

[38] D. Kennedy, 'Freedom and Restraint in Adjudication: A Critical Phenomenoloy', 36 Journal of Legal Education, 1986, pp. 513 - 62.

[39] D. Kennedy, 'The Structure of Blackstone's Commentaries' 28 Buffalo Law Review, 1979, pp. 214; ; R. W. Gordon, 'Critical Legal Histories', 36 Stanford Law Review, 1984, p. 69.

[40] Kennedy, 'The Structure of Blackstone's Commentaries', p. 214.

principled law-making can be made politically not legally and that the role of controversial value judgments in the application of law can be significantly limited by good legislation and constrained interpretation. On the other hand, it is evident that a morally committed law does not have to settle all moral disputes in the area to which it applies. It is a feature of a well-formulated law that it takes sides only in so far as is required by the objective of the legislation in question.

Moreover, Ethical Positivists do maintain that some values are protected and enhanced by any legal system in so far as it approximates to the Positivist model, although this can be accomplished without begging the question as to the values that ought to be enshrined in the substance of the law. No doubt it would be inconsistent if Ethical Positivists were to be indifferent as to whether the values which justify the choice of a Positivistic system of law were ignored altogether in the creation of substantive law but they need not hold the view that these legal values should be the sole or even the dominant ones in the determination of substantive law. However, liberal neutrality, as complete indifference concerning the choice of competing ways of life, is not a postulate of LEP.[41]

No more is the ideal of consistency in law as dominant for an Ethical Positivist as it is asserted to be in the straw Formalist scheme. Positivists can recognise that political sources can speak with inconsistent tongues. Indeed political change is usually a piecemeal matter which may involve introducing reforms despite the fact that they are inconsistent with existing law which cannot be repealed simultaneously with the novel enactments. A Positivist, in respecting the will of the sovereign, will urge the enforcement of the new law despite its evident inconsistency with the (as yet) unreformed law. Of course, if the inconsistencies are such as to produce straight contradictions in the statement of legal rights and duties so that a person has a duty both to do and not to do a specific act, then adjudicative resolution is requisite. But many inconsistencies are far from being so blatant and involve no more than the fact that an objective or value which is being promoted in one rule or area of law is being undermined by another rule or branch of law. Such inconsistencies call for political rather than legal resolution.

Nor is there anything incurably liberal in the aspirations of LEP. Indeed, if anything, the Positivist model sets the scene for conceptualising the law as an instrument of a centralised state of a type which is, rather misleading, thought to be typically socialist, at least in the degree of its interventionism. Certainly, it cannot be assumed that LEP is biased towards individualism, although it is certainly compatible with the view that all values, rights and duties should be grounded in the interests and activities of individuals. This itself is compatible

[41] On this topic, see W. Sadurski, Moral Pluralism and Legal Neutrality, Dordrecht 1990.

with the communitarian views that the individual is socially constituted and that individual preferences do not always take priority over community values. Positivistic rules can be viewed as part of the cement of group relationships and both the subjects and the objectives of such rules may as readily be communal as individual.

There are, to be sure, limits to the elasticity of Ethical Positivism, in that it must claim that, to some measure, well formed rules can significantly curtail the discretionary power of adjudicators and decision-makers generally and give effect to politically chosen objectives.

At this point it is easy to make glib counters to the indeterminacy claims of CLS by saying that, in their strong forms they render all communication, including the transmission of the ideas emanating from CLS, impossible, and in their weak forms they represent no more than the platitude that it is always possible to disagree over the meaning of signs which are after all based on human conventions rather then independently ascertainable natural facts.[42] Neither extreme is of much interest here. What is at issue is whether rules can, not in glorious isolation but in certain consensual contexts, provide powerful restraints on the exercise of power, in that they can be used definitively and uncontroversially to say that certain actions are permissible or required while others are not. There is a threshold question here. If any rule has such de facto indeterminacy that it can always be interpreted in a way which allows the power holder to do as she likes, then its residual determinacy is of no use to us. (This is not to say adjudicators cannot choose simply to ignore rules, but that is another type of problem, and one which presupposes that we can tell when this is being done.)

Particularly relevant here is the CLS claim, redolent of Marxist analysis, that there are essential inner contradictions inherent in liberal law. Influential work in this vein has been done by Duncan Kennedy whose structuralist approach to the analysis of legal thought is manifest in the claim that the underlying structure of common law legal tradition is the constant and unrecognised tension between the self and others, or between individualism and collectivism. This tension, for Kennedy, represents a reality inherent in human relationships in which we wish to assert the priority of our individual choices and yet at the same time recognise our dependence on and need for the assistance of others. Law is a matter of collective coercion and is therefore both a requisite and a denial of individual freedom. This genuine social dilemma is, however, masked in the legal realm so as to deny the dichotomy and thereby help with the legitimation of the status quo, making present (oppressive) social structures appear inevitable and natural. Thus there are 'fundamental con-

[42] The weak and strong interpretations of CLS views on indeterminacy are well explored in A. Altman, Critical Legal Studies, New Jersey 1990.

tradictions' which underlie all legal doctrines, all of which represent a 'single dilemma of the degree of collective as opposed to individual self-determination that is appropriate'. Law itself is simply a 'mechanism for denying contradictions'.[43]

Kennedy argues that this mystifying and legitimating process is present in the very organisation of the classic liberal statement of the common law, Blackstone's *Commentaries on the Law of England (1765 - 69)*. He follows this out in his analysis of current law, pointing, for instance, to the way in which contract law both insists on the imposition of the wills of the parties (thus respect the self) and allows for recognition of the necessary altruism of social life in that its standards enable the courts to set aside 'unconscionable' bargains and agreements not entered into in good faith (thus respecting others).[44]

Some of Kennedy's contentions, such as the claim that *the* contradiction is between egoism and altruism, or the view that individualism is expressed in precise rules while altruism comes in via more general standards, are so bold as to be highly vulnerable to empirical criticism. However, the general theme, derived from American Legal Realism, that existing law is a mess of incompatible maxims from which the judiciary can draw such conclusions as they will, is less easily controverted.

Indeed, all that can be done without resorting to straightforward and unconvincing counter dogma, is to take each example individually and to see if the alleged contradiction can be brought into the daylight and resolved in principle. If this can be done in at least some cases, then this undercuts the claim that legal systems *must* fail in the way that Kennedy suggests.

In the example under consideration, it is clear that it is not possible to have a system of contract law which holds parties rigidly to their explicit agreements and, at the same time, allows extensive escape clauses, on such bases as unconscionability, inequality of bargaining power and economic duress, so that it is not possible for stronger parties to enter into agreements with any confidence that they will be enforced. But this does not mean that, even in this spongy area, it is not possible to formulate rules relating to such matters as unconscionability which will enable two parties, simply by examining the relevant rules, to have a pretty good idea what courts will decide where there is contractual default by the weaker party. For instance, loans for which the family home is a security, could be deemed unenforcable.[45] Such rules will result in paternalistic limitations on the opportunities of weaker parties to take on

[43] Kennedy, 'The Structure of Blackstone's Commentaries', p. 213.

[44] Kennedy, 'Form and Substance in Private Law Adjudication' 89 Harvard Law Review, 1976, p. 1685.

[45] Consider: Commercial Bank of Australia v Amadio (1983) 151 CLR 447.

potentially onerous liabilities that they would be in no position to meet without undue hardship, which may be undesirable, but it is not thereby rendered impossible or incoherent to limit the freedom of such contracting parties in a clear and explicit manner. Rather, the situation is that hard political choices have to be made earlier to avoid hard judicial choices arising later from the failure of law-makers to resolve such issues by opting for what they determine to be the lesser evil.

Of course, we cannot easily combat the claim that liberal or any other polities do not have the capacity to resolve such dilemmas, but we can at least see what such resolutions might look like and study the extent to which actual legal systems approximate to the many alternative resolutions that are compatible with Positivism. That we are pushed into seeking some rule defined solution rather than acquiescing in unfounded optimism that we can have our autonomous cake and still eat our humanitarian pie may be something for which we have CLS and a wider range of socialist theorists to thank.[46] We are similarly indebted to them for pointing to patterns of judicial decision making that show how, if we do leave such unresolved choices to judiciaries to be solved on a case by case basis, the resultant discretionary field will be used in a way which favours established economic power.[47] For such reasons, any plausible Positivism must concentrate a large part of its attention on procedural, institutional and cultural phenomena which generate hierarchical bias. Good Positivist rules are clearly not enough without fair legal process and appropriate cultural assumptions on the part of those involved in putting law into action. LEP requires us to put as much energy into studying the 'law in context' as into the tailoring rules to achieve legislative purposes.[48]

In assessing what to make of the contribution of CLS scholars, such as Duncan Kennedy, it is as well to keep a firm distinction between the postmodern philosophy of language thesis according to which there can be no firm interpersonal consensus on meaning, and the neo-Marxist use of this notion of linguistic indeterminacy to expose the underlying inconsistencies of apparently coherent language systems.

Clearly the uncovering of contradictions does not require that these be obfuscated by linguistic flexibilities, and the actual indeterminacy of meaning may mask nothing more than underlying confusion or chaos. Indeed it seems evident that if law were entirely open and indeterminate then it would not be possible to show that it is contradictory. It must therefore be necessary to

---

[46] For instance, H. Collins, The Law of Contract, London 1986.

[47] Thus, Mark Kelman, 'Interpretative Construction in Substantive Criminal Law' 33 Stanford Law Review, 1981, pp. 591 - 673.

[48] As in S. Bottomley, N. Gunningham and S. Parker, Law in Context, Annandale 1991.

moderate Klare's claim that 'Legal reasoning is a texture of openness, indeterminacy, and contradiction'.[49] At any rate, although CLS theorists combine these two strands by the assertion that oppressors protect their legitimacy by exploiting indeterminacy to hide their privileged positions, we may well wish to examine the indeterminacy and the contradiction theses independently.

As far as the 'rule through law' aspect of Ethical Positivism is concerned it is the indeterminacy thesis that is initially the more alarming theme, for its implications would appear to be that there is ultimately no distinction between government by individual whim and government via the enactment and enforcement of general rules, apart, perhaps, from the fact that the idea of the latter enables oppressors to set up a machinery of oppression under the rubric of rule application and enforcement.

Here, the main focus seems to be on the legally typical (but not legally unique) process of applying general terms to particular circumstances, since, routinely, law consists of prescriptions and permissions containing a number of general terms of varying degrees of generality with a paucity of proper names and other particularities.

In this arena the multiplication of legal examples of cases in which decisions involve choices about the scope of general terms which are conceptually arbitrary but are presented as linguistically required does serve to give an inductive plausibility to the contention that rules cannot constrain decisions in particular cases.[50] Often the available rules are not adequate to the instances, but this cannot establish that this must always be the case. No quantity of illustrations can prove the universal claim that rules cannot put meaningful limits on judicial discretion. The device whereby any 'clear' case can be turned into a 'hard' case by pointing to possible alternative interpretations does not establish that some interpretations are not much more predictable on the basis of shared cognitive meaning than others.

Here the confusion seems to be between the claim that, if the local conventions on meanings were different, then the case would be no longer evident, and the claim that there are no local conventions which agreement can ever be relied upon for interpretative purposes.[51] This latter contention, in its extreme form, is, of course, unarguable since it can be used self-referentially to make nonsense of the critical thesis. If words cannot be used to communicate they certainly cannot be used to criticise. In its weaker form it becomes a matter of degree to which there is consensus on the meanings of words or the successful establishment of agreed criteria for the use of technical language. The mere

[49] K. Klare, 'The Law School Curriculum in the 1980s: What's Left' Journal of Legal Education, 1982, p. 32, at p. 34.

[50] On this theme, see P. Drahos and S. Parker, 'Rule Following, Rule Scepticism and Indeterminacy in Law: A Conventional Account' 5 Ratio Juris, 1992, pp. 109 - 119.

[51] 'Freedom and Constraint in Adjudication: A Critical Pheonomnology', passim.

possibility that any such consensus can be undermined by a clever lawyer, a scheming tyrant, a prejudiced judge or an oppressor class does not establish the incoherence of such communicative objectives, although it does point to the reasons for commending a Positivist model in the first place and the need for an effective interpreters ethic.

Kennedy himself accepts that, for an actual judge, some legal arguments are subjectively easier to run than others and that this felt objectivity is inter-subjective in that it is closely related to the individual judge's anticipation of the responses of her peers.[52] He then falls back on philosophical authority more than on the experience of judging to argue that there is in fact no fixed point against which to test such subjectivities[53] so that the judge is not ultimately correct to hold that she cannot argue as she will and reject any or all of the shared assumptions of a common way of life. There is, however, no need to provide for an underlying epistemological bedrock for shared understandings in order to establish the possibility of one person accurately applying what other people have legislated. Indeed the claimed Wittgensteinian approach can be turned around to posit the existence of a public language as a presupposition of successful communication. That successful communication is elusive and can never be guaranteed or definitely validated does not render the Positivist ideal incoherent, although it may turn out to be impracticable in highly pluralistic societies. We may agree that it can be liberating to become aware that the basis of our shared understanding are not fixed by nature but it could be foolish not to use such inter-subjective agreement as we can muster.

Once the indeterminacy debate comes down to the degree to which there is or is not agreement on meanings and the extent to which the lack of agreement is utilised to perpetrate hierarchy, then it is no longer a philosophic dogma which negates the ideal of rule through law, and becomes simply one of the many factors which can intervene to hinder efforts to establish the Positivism model. Rather it sets up hurdles to be overcome on the way to more determinacy. Indeterminacy matters only because determinacy matters. CLS may be, in large measure, descriptively correct as to the factual claims it makes about actual legal systems, but the view that all legal systems *must* be this way can remain an unprovable if sometimes plausible dogma which does not undermine Positivism as an at least partially realisable ideal.

Not surprisingly, given the presence of many feminists within the CLS movement, a similarly qualified welcome can be extended to many of the central tenets of FJ. Feminist thinking about law has moved beyond the study of

---

52 Loc. cit, p. 562.

53 In Kennedy's view, 'The task of criticism is to demystify our thinking by confronting us with the fact that the contradiction is a historical artefact. It is no more immortal than is the society that created and sustains it. Understanding this is not salvation, but it is a help', 'The Structure of Blackstone's Commentaries', p. 221.

law a mechanism for combating sexism to the articulation of a distinctively feminist view of law as such and a genuine theoretical endeavour to identify the core of gender-based domination. In its most contemporary phase FJ offers powerful arguments to the effect that law itself is a masculine enterprise and that the study of male domination through law reveals the sexual core of male violence and gender hierarchy.

Current FJ manifests, at the very least, an ambivalent attitude towards law. There is little desire to decry the importance of the legally oriented victories which have been attained by the women's movement. The long and hard battles to remove legally enforced gender disqualifications in the spheres of politics and employment; the moves to counter male prejudice by requiring formal equality of opportunity and permitting or requiring preference to be given to women in competitive employment situations through affirmative action; the efforts to bring the domestic sphere more fully into the arenas of civil and criminal law; all these achievements are celebrated and defended with more or less enthusiasm.[54]

On the other hand, the realities of continuing gender inequality in employment, economic well-being and political power, together with the general ineffectiveness of legal remedies for matters of most concern to women, such as domestic violence, rape and employment discrimination, excavates a well of scepticism about the relevance of law to the lot of women in modern society. Thus Carol Smart, noting the persistence of gender inequalities, is led to wonder 'why law is so resistant to the challenge of feminist knowledge and critique'.[55] Drawing on Foucault's insight into the connections between the authoritative sources of knowledge and societal power, Smart identifies the 'malevolence' of law in its congruence with masculine culture, a culture which uses law to define social categories and behavioural norms in ways which delegitimise women's perspectives. This is illustrated in various legal processes: by decreeing that certain matters are outside the law, it is made to appear that law is neutral on matters such as prostitution, which involve the exploitation of women; by defining relevance in ways which, for instance, admits in evidence the victim's sexual history but not the accused's, the whole adjudicative procedure is biased against women in rape trials; and requiring that legal argument be presented in terms of case analysis ensures that if the interests of particular women caught up in legal process are to be protected then it is necessary to utilise precedents which embody gender prejudiced outlooks, so that the practicing lawyer has a choice between being a good lawyer or a good feminist. For such reasons feminists are urged to be suspicious of law and seek other avenues for reform. In Smart's terminology, law is to be 'decentred' so

[54] See, N. Naffine, Law and the Sexes, 1990.

[55] C. Smart, Feminism and the Power of Law, London 1989, p. 2.

that at least this one epistemological source of male domination can be bypassed.

Not all feminists take such a negative view of the law's potential and continue to seek radical reform by redrawing the boundaries between 'public' and 'private' and thus between law and non-law so that women can be protected more effectively in their sexual and economic relationships; or by proposing various devices for replacing a male with a female or gender-neutral perspective on legally relevant categories, such as what counts as 'work' for the purposes of compensation.[56]

However, the more exciting, if also the more speculative line, is that these objectives are bound to be illusory because of the masculine nature of law itself. On this view, it is not simply that men have captured law as an ideological weapon for male supremacy, but that the idea of law expresses a masculine frame of mind. This view can be traced to Carol Gilligan's findings that the tendency to see disputes in terms of rights and rules is essentially a masculine phenomenon.[57] In a return to something akin to the much criticised stereotypes of woman as caring and man as combative, Gilligan's thesis concerning the non-individualistic, even loving, approach to problems of human interaction has been taken up and developed into the thesis that a Fuller-style characterisation of law as the 'enterprise of subjecting human conduct to the governance of rules'[58] is a male venture that seeks solutions through dividing lines, creating dichotomies and giving simplistic yes/no answers to complex problems. In Janet Rifkin's words: 'Law is a paradigm for maleness'[59] – 'The historical image of maleness – objective, rational and public – is the dominant image of law'.[60]

Rifkin's own contribution to this line of thought is an historical one, in that she traces women's exclusion from the public sphere in the capitalist world as something that was achieved through the manipulation of developing contract law to express male authority and thereby exclude women from trade and commerce. In the event, it would appear that she seeks to undermine the male paradigm of law as power rather than to reject law itself. Similarly, other theorists look to law adopting a feminist method which will avoid abstract universals and concentrate on the more observable similarities and differences between classes of persons and behaviours. Standard legal abstractions, it is argued, have little to offer those seeking a solution to concrete social

---

[56] R. Graycar and J. Morgan, The Hidden Gender of Law, Annandale 1990, chapter 11.

[57] C. Gilligan, In A Different Voice, Cambridge 1982.

[58] The Morality of Law, p. 96f.

[59] J. Rifkin, 'Towards a Feminist Jurisprudence', 3 Harvard Women's Law Journal, 1980, p. 85

[60] Loc. cit., p. 92.

inequalities. Thus to have a gender neutral law which prevents employers discriminating against women with pre-school aged children but allows job selectors to exclude those who have the duty of caring for children, simply perpetuates the inequality which stems from the social fact that it is women who in practice are the dominant child carers. Such questions, should, it is argued, be solved on the basis of standards which use abstractions only as a method of uncovering the underlying moral issues at stake in the legal dispute in question. In the example cited, the standard commended will be oriented towards eliminating disadvantage. This will enable legislators and judges to see past the abstract concerns about similarity and difference to the social situation which requires women to be compensated for the unfair distribution of the burdens of child care.

The extent to which this is a demand for the improvement rather than the demise of law is opaque. It may be suggesting that we adopt morally relevant distinctions from a women's perspective and embody these within laws. It may be more of a plea for rule-free authority to determine disputes in accordance with the moral vision of the adjudicator. Certainly, it raises in a vivid form whether or not certain areas of social life require that disputes be settled by what an old fashioned Positivist would regard as non-legal means.

The attractions of various forms of alternative dispute resolution as radical alternatives to law reform are hard to deny in an era of escalating legal costs and delays. In so far as LEP can accept this enticing line of development it will wish to do so by an overt withdrawal of law from the sphere in question. The withdrawal will, however, be with a warning, that the field so vacated may become one in which the powerful and persuasive obtain their way in compromises which those at risk have little way of resisting. It is perhaps a terminological matter whether rule-free adjudication is or is not legal process. If mandatory decisions are made by such bodies on the basis of no more than highly generalised standards such as equality, freedom and fairness, then we may be said to have either another form of law or a non-legal approach. What an Ethical Positivist will argue here is that such generalised standards can be manipulated for hierarchical ends, to an even greater extent than specific rules can be interpreted as exclusionary of oppressed group interests. Further, when enforceable decision-procedures are replaced by entirely voluntary conciliation processes, we have clearly left the sphere of law, Positivist or otherwise. Equally clearly, such methods are entirely unrealistic in current social forms where there are entrenched social inequalities that inevitably render such 'voluntary' processes de facto coercive.

This essay has no simple conclusion. It arises from the conviction that much current legal theory, when combined with public scepticism about law, is eroding the basis for confidence in legal change as a source of social progress. Its contention is that, by acknowledging that critical legal theory is drawing attention to real doubts about the credentials of actual legal systems, we are in a better position to work out how to restore justifiable public confidence in law. This does not mean that it can be claimed that our legal systems actually conform to a Positivist model of rule through law, rather that we require to devise new strategies for moving towards that ideal. This entails limiting the pretension of law so that we do not endorse the impression that law can remedy the defects of bad political decisions. On the other hand, lawyers working within an ethics which relates to the ideal type of Ethical Positivism may hope to convince others that it is worthwhile pursuing social objectives through legal change. The hope is that those enthralled with novel critiques of law will take note of the flexibility of Positivism as a battered but necessary ideal form, and ponder the congruence of its moral rationales with those of substantive anti-hierarchical critiques. Conversely, those whose adherence to some form of Positivism is not in doubt may take note of those aspects of current legal theory which undermine any complacency that may remain regarding traditional approaches to legal reform and appreciate the need to be adaptable in the face of endless revelations of hopefully remediable partialities in the administration of law.

Normative Rationality
de lege ferenda and *de lege lata*

By Jan Hellner, Cleveland

The discussion of rationality in law is generally focused on arguments *de lege lata* in a strict sense. The rationality is supposed to depend *inter alia* on the validity of the legal norms. The validity in its turn generally refers to the judge's situation. Some consider the acceptance by the judge or the acceptability to him to be the criterion of the validity of the norm. Others derive the validity of the norm from some other source but assume that the norm is directed to the judge, or at least concerns him if the issue should arise. The direction towards the judge appears most clearly if the norm is supposed to be the will of a legislator who prescribes what the judge should do, or what actions and other facts are relevant to the judge. Examples of such views are so numerous that they need not be mentioned here.

My contention is that this view, even if common, is too restricted.[1] We can examine what rationality is not only with regard to *lex lata* but also with regard to *lex ferenda* in the strict sense, i.e. the activity of the legislator. There is, in other words, a rationality that is at least largely independent of the notion of valid law. Rationality *de lege lata* and *de lege ferenda* have thus much in common, although there are considerable differences.

This is a point of view which, I hope, will appeal to Robert S. Summers, to whom this essay is dedicated. He combines the theoretical insight necessary for dealing with fundamental questions of law, with a deep knowledge of practical legal problems, which is demonstrated in a long line of works on contract law and other parts of what the civilians call the law of obligations.

My arguments will follow three different paths, the first by presenting a fable, the second by a discussion about the arguments that can be considered to be rational *de lege ferenda,* and the third by a comparison between constitutional and non-constitutional assessment of a special issue, the retroactivity of legal rules.

---

[1] The following is based partly on my book "Lagstiftning inom förmögenhetsrätten" (Stockholm 1990), and most of the ideas advanced here are developed further in this book. Cf. also "Rationalitet och empiri i rättsvetenskapen", J. Hellner (ed.) (Stockholm 1985).

1. A Fable

The dance theorist X presents a theory of dance. I do not know whether such a theory exists, but if it does, it is certainly different from what I shall assume here.

The theory of dance that is presented by X contains a number of theses about dance and its rules. The theory is well developed, it contains statements about how dance is actually executed and about how it should be executed, about its structure, about its relationship to music, about what makes a dance good and what makes it bad. X also mentions disputes about what a good theory of dance is and what a bad one is, and about the relevance of the theory of dance to the practice of dance.

Now another person, let us call him Y, presents a criticism of this theory. Y contends that the theory only concerns one special kind of dance, the quadrille, and that, although it agrees well with the rules and practice of the quadrille, it does not fit with dances such as the foxtrot or the rumba.

X replies that all leading theorists of dance refer exclusively to the quadrille when they write of dance. If the object of a theory of dance is discussed explicitly, it is according to X generally agreed that only the quadrille is worth considering as the subject of such a theory. There are distinct and determined rules for the quadrille, and there are generally accepted criteria for what constitutes a good performance of it. Various performances have been skillfully recorded and analysed by experts, and empirical material therefore exists that can be the basis of the theory. It is at least in principle possible to arrive at a consensus among scientists on a theory of dance which is based on the quadrille. The theses have the intersubjectivity that is required for the results of a science. If one also considered the foxtrot and the rumba as relevant for a theory of dance, one would lose these advantages. The general agreement that had been achieved would be lost in exchange for the possibility of results that could be surmised in advance to be dubious. The general theses, if such could be established, would be so vague as to be worthless. At least, the criteria for the validity of theses about dance would be blurred. There would also be great problems in making distinctions between dances and singing games, calisthenics accompanied by music, skating to music and similar matters.

Y then asks what he should do, since he dances not only the quadrille but the foxtrot and the rumba as well and would like to have a theory for them. Is it not possible, he asks, that there might be a theory of dance that also embraces the foxtrot and the rumba, and might not such a theory have some advantages over one that is limited to the quadrille? It might be worthwhile to see what the different dances have in common and how they differ. It is not necessary to try to establish a theory that embraces all the numerous dances that are practised by mankind, but a first step would be to take into account some dances that are common in the Western world. Y maintains that the arguments for the restriction to the quadrille may have been relevant during the 18th century, when the quadrille was the dominant dance, but that the situation is different in the 20th century, when a great number of people dance the foxtrot and the rumba. Although not an expert in the theory of dance, he will try to find some theses for a theory. He finds that he has a number of predecessors who have written on the theory of the foxtrot, although the experts on the theory of dance have chosen to ignore their work, rather than take account of them either favorably or unfavorably.

2. Rationality in Legislation

a) There exists a considerable amount of *literature* on the theory of legislation, although much of it is not concerned with rationality, not even in a broad sense.[2] For instance, works on the practical procedure of legislation cannot in general be considered to relate to rationality. Rationality, as understood here, can be seen from a formal point of view and then concerns the way in which a statute gains legitimacy through the manner in which it is enacted. Rationality can also be judged from a substantive point of view, and the main question then is what material is relevant, what methods are permissible and what arguments can be considered to be valid in preparing and assessing legislation. What I shall deal with is this latter aspect.

In the literature on the theory of legislation there are at least three works that can be said to be classical. The first is Jeremy Bentham's "Nomography" from the first half of the 19th century.[3] In this work Bentham deals with a number of practical questions concerning legislation from the point of view of his general utilitarianism.[4] The second is Robert von Mohl's *"Die Abfassung der Rechtsgesetze"* from 1862.[5] von Mohl summarized various practical experiences from preparing legislation.[6] The third is Peter Noll's *"Gesetz-*

---

[2] A systematic bibliography by E. Baden can be found in "Gesetzgebungslehre", Schreckenberger, König and Zeh (eds.) (Stuttgart 1986), pp. 186 ff. See further H. Schneider, Gesetzgebung (2d. ed. 1991). There are also periodicals devoted to the theory of legislation. Zeitschrift für Gesetzgebung (ed. Beck, München) and Statute Law Review (ed. Oxford University Press) may be mentioned.

[3] This work is published in Vol. 3 of John Bowring's edition The Works of Jeremy Bentham (1838 - 43), pp. 321 ff. Bentham deals more shortly with legislation in several other works, too numerous to be noted here.

[4] Bentham had predecessors in England, among whom Francis Bacon may be mentioned. See De augmentis scientiarum, Book 8, Ch. 3, Title 1, published in translation in The Works of Francis Bacon, Spedding, Ellis & Heath (eds.), Vol. 5 (1889), pp. 88 ff. Cf. D. Liebermann, The Province of Legislation Determined (Cambridge 1989), pp. 181 ff.

[5] R. von Mohl, Die Abfassung der Rechtsgesetze: Ein Bruchstück. Staatsrecht, Völkerrecht und Politik. 2. Bd: Politik. 1. Bd. (Tübingen 1862), pp. 375 ff.

gebungslehre" from 1973.[7] Noll made a systematic analysis of the problems of legislation, on the basis of theoretical insight as well as practical experience, with critical remarks in regard to those legal scientists that ignore the theory of legislation.[8] The present literature in the German language is extensive.[9]

b) None of the works now mentioned, nor indeed any work dealing with rationality in legislation, is independent of the writer's *general views on law*.

For those who adhere to theories of natural law, a theory of legislation does not present any great problems of principle. Natural law prescribes the contents of such parts of legislation for which it is relevant, and positive law should therefore conform with natural law.[10] However, natural law, as understood by those of its proponents who deal with legislation, has proved to be flexible enough to support a number of rules that work well in practice.[11] Another problem might be to draw a line between the area governed by natural law and the area for which natural law does not impose any rules. Even this problem does not seem to have raised any great obstacles.[12]

For adherents to theories of positive law, the problem is quite different. If law is by definition the will of the legislator, the way in which this will arises is not a subject for science, except in so far as regards the forces at work. The empirical facts that should form the basis for legislation are accessible to scientific knowledge but not the conclusions drawn from them, as these latter depend on valuations. As is often the case, the ideas of Hans Kelsen represent

---

[6] von Mohl is strongly influenced by Bentham and deals, mostly critically, with a number of earlier writers on the subject. See footnote on p. 376. It may be noted that among those few that get a favorable mention is the historian T. Macaulay, because of his introduction to a draft penal code for India.

[7] P. Noll, Gesetzgebungslehre (Reinbek bei Hamburg 1973).

[8] Noll ascribes the lack of interest in legislation, characteristic of most legal theory, to the preoccupation with "Rechtsprechungswissenschaft und Rechtspositivismus", see op. cit., pp. 18ff.

[9] Of special interest, because of the approach to questions of theory, are the works of Jürgen Rödig. As Rödig died young, many of his works have been published posthumously. See in particular "Studien zu einer Theorie der Gesetzgebung", H. Kindermann ed., (Berlin 1976).

[10] The Austrian Code of 1811 is particularly illustrative. The principles underlying it have been stated by F. von Zeiller in "Grundsätze der Gesetzgebung" (1806/09), reprinted in Quellenbuch zur Geschichte der deutschen Rechtswissenschaft, E. Wolf (ed.) (Frankfurt am M. 1949).

[11] Both the French "Code civil" of 1804 and the Austrian "Allgemeines Bürgerliches Gesetzbuch" of 1811 still survive, although amended on a great number of points.

[12] A somewhat curious example can be found in the writings of the Swedish 19th century legal scientist E. V. Nordling. He discussed the foundations in natural law of the rights of inheritance of survivors to a deceased person according to the Swedish Code of 1734, which had been in force for more than a hundred years when he wrote. See "Anteckningar efter föreläsningar över ärvdabalken" (1872), pp. 1ff.

the extreme views of legal positivism.[13] In Scandinavia, Alf Ross has expressed similar ideas.[14]

Even a number of writers who cannot be considered to be positivists seem to limit their interests in the same way. As mentioned before, they deal with valid law, and the validity is sometimes considered to be part of the definition of law.[15] The problems that are treated are those with which the judges deal. Law is supposed to be a static system, and the dynamics are included only to the extent that law is developed by the judges' activity. Neither the creation of norms by legislation nor the private creation by such bodies as, e.g., the International Chamber of Commerce are generally taken into account by legal theorists, in spite of their practical and theoretical importance.[16]

c) However, if these limitations are abandoned it can easily be seen that the *problem of rationality is largely the same for the legislator as for the judge.* Admittedly, there are important differences. The judge deals with separate cases, although he may, by making a precedent, create a lasting principle. The legislator, on the other hand, deals with general norms. The judge is bound by rules, more or less strict. Even if the legislator is bound by the rules of a constitution, he has much greater liberty. A judge is generally supposed to exercise his office independently of political considerations. For a legislator, on the other hand, political considerations are often paramount, and the task of the state organ that gives shape to a statute may then be to implement the wishes of the political powers. However, even in such cases there are issues of legislative technique that depend on rationality. For statutes dealing with matters of little or no political importance, the requirements of rationality may be driven further.

In the present context, it is more interesting to look for similarities between legislation and jurisdiction than for differences, because the similarities are those that are most intimately concerned with rationality. It is impossible to treat the subject exhaustively, and only a few examples can be given. I shall be concerned mainly with the field of law with which I have worked, and in which political considerations are relatively unimportant. This field is the law of obligations, which comprises the law of contracts and the law of torts.

---

[13] See H. Kelsen, Reine Rechtslehre (Wien 1980), pp. 79ff., 107ff., 230ff. To some extent Kelsen's ideas appear *e silentio;* see in particular "Allgemeine Theorie der Normen" (Wien 1979), where – as far as I have been able to see – not a single sentence is devoted to any possibility of rationality in the creation of norms.

[14] See Alf Ross, Om ret og retfærdighed (København 1953), pp. 417ff.

[15] See for a recent instance R. Alexy, Begriff und Geltung des Rechts (München/Freiburg 1992), p. 45.

[16] The International Chamber of Commerce is the source of the "Uniform Customs and Practices for Documentary Credits" and of the "Incoterms". Both of these bodies of rules are applied by courts in a way fully comparable to the application of statutes.

d) A number of questions concerning logic in a broad sense, or more particularly the *validity of arguments,* have roughly the same character *de lege ferenda* as *de lege lata.*

The importance of attention to validity is obvious, in regard to both legal literature and decisions by the courts. In most cases in which I disagree seriously with colleagues, I find that the main reason for the disagreement lies in the fact that I cannot accept their arguments as valid, and often my own arguments are not accepted as valid by others. The disagreements that are based on differences of opinion about facts, or about sources of law in the sense usually ascribed to this expression, are much less common. The validity of arguments is important for legislation as well, with the difference that politicians are often uninterested and care more for whether the proposed legislation will satisfy their political aims.

Questions regarding the validity of legal arguments have, at least as far as Scandinavia is concerned, lately fallen into the background in comparison with the discussion of "sources of law", a concept that is closely entangled with that of "valid law".

The simplest kind of logical mistake in arguing about law is the one occurring when a statement that is said to be a conclusion from certain premises does not follow from them. The validity of conclusions regarding normative statements may be different from those relating to statements of fact.[17] But it can hardly be denied that even in normative argumentation conclusions are drawn that must be considered incorrect from a logical point of view. The criteria for correctness are complicated, just as they are when logic is applied to everyday arguments about factual situations, but they need not be discussed here.

There are other requirements of validity, and other failures that make an argument invalid, which are more specific to law. Some of them are well known from discussions about legal method.

Conceptual jurisprudence *(Begriffsjurisprudenz)* has long been a target for criticism in legal theory.[18] Without going into the question of how far this criticism is justified, it should be admitted that if an argument is invalid *de lege lata* as based on conceptual jurisprudence, it is also invalid *de lege ferenda.* If a conclusion concerning a special rule is considered invalid because it is based on the concept of a *"Sachenrecht"* – which can be considered as a standard example of invalid conceptual jurisprudence – the argument has the same character whether it is used *de lege lata* or *de lege ferenda.* Arguments that are appar-

[17] See, e.g., a recent debate in Ratio juris 1991 (vol. 4 number 3), including the "guest editor's preface" by Tecla Mazzarese.

[18] The classical criticism is that of R. von Jhering, Scherz und Ernst in der Jurisprudenz (13th ed. 1924, reprinted 1988, Darmstadt).

ently based on conceptual jurisprudence can sometimes be reformulated as depending on functional connections between rules, and to that extent they should be admitted.[19] It is possible that the functional aspect may be somewhat different in the *lex ferenda* context than in *lex lata*. Such a question cannot be decided without a thorough analysis of the special instances. Essentially the validity or non-validity is the same.

During an earlier period, the validity of legal arguments particularly engaged the proponents of the Uppsala school. In my opinion, the chief importance of the Uppsala school to the analysis of legal method lies in its critical attitude to arguments whose validity is dubious.

Among the legal theorists of the Uppsala school, Karl Olivecrona directed his criticism chiefly against metaphysics in the law, even when this concept was not mentioned explicitly.[20] The criticism may have been partly mistaken, since the concepts and arguments against which he argued were not in fact metaphysical.[21] For those who adhere to metaphysics in the law, Olivecrona's attitude may be irrelevant. However, when criticism for metaphysics in legal argument is admitted to be justified, the criticism has the same force *de lege ferenda* as *de lege lata*.

Another member of the Uppsala school, Vilhelm Lundstedt, devoted much of his work in legal theory to combating circular arguments and the use of fictions for justifying legal rules.[22] Lundstedt was certainly mistaken in a great number of cases, but this fact should not make us overlook the importance of avoiding both circular arguments and fictions, whether *de lege lata* or *de lege ferenda*.[23]

Other criticism relating to the validity of arguments concerns the justification of a rule or a decision by referring to general principles which are irrelevant or insufficient in the context. One such argument is the reference to the

---

[19] Cf. L. Lindahl, Definitioner, begreppsanalys och mellanbegrepp i juridiken, in: Rationalitet och empiri i rättsvetenskapen (supra n. 1).

[20] Olivecrona summarizes his views on legal theory in English in the second edition of Law as Fact (London 1971). His anti-metaphysical attitude to legal arguments appears more clearly in his works on special subjects, such as "Rätt och dom" (Right and judgment) (Stockholm 1960).

[21] In "Rätt och dom" he describes judgments based on the notion of right as belonging to "metaphysical private law" (pp. 146ff.).

[22] Lundstedt's main work in English is "Legal Thinking Revised", published posthumously (Stockholm 1957). However, this work is not a satisfactory presentation of Lundstedt's ideas, and his works in Swedish give a better understanding.

[23] I have analysed some of Lundstedt's main ideas in two essays, "Legal philosophy in the analysis of tort problems", Scandinavian Studies in Law 1958, pp. 149ff. (158ff.) and "Scandinavian Legal Realism in the Law of Contract", in: Essays for Patrick Atiyah (Oxford 1991), pp. 53ff. In these essays I have tried to do justice to Lundstedt's ideas, while maintaining a critical attitude.

principle of *"pacta sunt servanda"*. This principle indubitably functions unobjectionally as a practical rule in a number of cases where it is clear that a contract or a promise should be binding. It can also serve as the compressed summary of a number of rules whose validity has been established by other means. However, a reference to the principle of *"pacta sunt servanda"* is not relevant as an argument when the discussion involves whether or not an exception to the principle should be made.[24] There are a number of exceptions that are beyond dispute, at least for the special system involved. No one contradicts the statement that contracts made by those who are legally minors are generally void. Under most legal systems, contracts resulting from fraud or coercion are void. When the question arises whether a further exception should be made for a certain type of contract, or for a contract entered into under certain circumstances, a reference to the principle of *"pacta sunt servanda"* will not in itself give any guidance. This is as true *de lege ferenda* as it is *de lege lata*. However, it is perhaps most important *de lege ferenda,* since when the rule is enacted and thus belongs to the *lex lata,* it does not matter so much if the argument originally advanced in its favor was logically valid or not.

Another example of a principle that is invoked unjustly in favor of decisions both *de lege lata* and *de lege ferenda* is the one that "no one should be allowed to enrich himself at the expense of another".[25] There are numerous cases in which it is perfectly legal to enrich oneself at the expense of others. The principle is so broad as to be worthless in deciding practical questions. If it is added that the enrichment should be "unjust", the important element will be the circumstance that decides whether it is unjust or not, and as long as it has not been demonstrated what constitutes the unjustness, the reference to the principle will be empty. However, the reference to the principle may sometimes have a heuristic value. By enquiring why an enrichment appears to be unjust, we may, by using our practical experience or imagination, find good reasons for judgments and for legislation.

There are differences in the validity of references to unjust enrichment between various contexts, but these on the whole have no connection with the difference between *lex lata* and *lex ferenda*. In some legal systems, a principle of unjust enrichment belongs to the corpus of accepted rules.[26] The validity of a reference to the principle will then depend chiefly on its relation to this body of accepted rules. The relation is important not only for arguments *de lege lata* but also for arguments that are advanced *de lege ferenda*. In other legal systems, which do not contain any general principle of unjust enrichment, a reference to the principle stands alone. This is the case in Swedish law.

[24] Cfr. my essay "Pacta sunt servanda" in: Samfunn, Rett, Rettferdighet, Festskrift til Torstein Eckhoff (Oslo 1988), pp. 335ff.

[25] I have examined this problem at length in my doctoral dissertation many years ago: Om obehörig vinst, särskilt utanför kontraktsförhållanden (Uppsala 1950).

[26] German law is an outstanding example; see "Bürgerliches Gesetzbuch" sec. 812.

e) There are logical considerations of a different kind that have particular importance for legislation, even if they arise when deciding particular cases as well. These considerations concern the legal *system* as a whole, or partial legal systems, e.g., statutes that cover a special field of law. For such systems the general requirements are those of consistency, completeness and independence.[27] Consistency means that the systems do not contain any rules that contradict each other. Completeness means that all questions that emerge within the field of the system can be answered according to its rules. Independence means that there are no rules that are redundant.

From the point of view of rationality in legislation, the requirements on statutes in the respects mentioned cannot be put very high. In practice, so much must be taken for granted, even if not expressed explicitly in statutes, that the requirement of completeness cannot be fulfilled. The less complete a statute is, the smaller the risk is both of contradiction and of redundancy. Problems caused by legislative failures can to some extent be remedied by decisions of the courts. The courts have well-known techniques for dealing with these problems.[28] Apparent gaps, especially, cannot be condemned universally. But rationality in legislation requires at least attention to the aspects now mentioned. If the failures are such that they cannot be remedied by the courts, they must be considered to be true defects relating to rationality.

f) The sphere of rationality must also be considered to include *factual realism*.[29] This is not only an obvious point but also one on which shortcomings are easily observed. Deterrence is often mentioned as an objective of rules of tort liability, *inter alia* when a rule of liability is to be introduced by legislation. The factual realism of such an argument is generally uncertain, and often the only fact in its favor is that it is as difficult to disprove it as to prove it. Without going into detail, factual realism may be mentioned as an element of rationality.

g) Avoiding defects in logic in a broad sense and satisfying the requirements of factual realism are, however, not sufficient for achieving rationality in legislation. There are substantive aspects as well, relating to the *contents of the decisions,* which are well recognized in discussions about methods *de lege lata* but sometimes overlooked with regard to *lex ferenda*.[30]

Not only the judge but also the legislator is bound by rules. The liberty of the legislator is generally much broader than that of a judge, although it

---

[27] See C. E. Alchourrón and E. Bulygin, Normative Systems (Wien 1971).

[28] Cf. D. N. MacCormick & R. S. Summers, Interpreting Statutes, A Comparative Study (Aldershot 1991).

[29] Cf. T. Eckhoff, "Empiriske metoder i rettsvitenskapen" in: Rationalitet och empiri i rättsvetenskapen. op. cit. supra n. 1.

[30] Cf. MacCormick & Summers, op. cit. supra n. 28.

depends largely on the constitution of the state. The difference, however, is one of degree, not one between being bound and not bound. Just as the liberty given to a judge may differ greatly, depending on a number of circumstances, the liberty of the legislator varies. As a consequence, it is much more common that opinions differ on what is the right decision in regard to legislation than with regard to judgments. On some, perhaps on many, occasions it may be claimed that all competent judges will arrive at the same solution of a problem de lege lata. But even the wisdom of Solon could not make his laws indisputably right. The difference in binding force does not, however, create any substantial difference in the arguments that can be considered relevant. As will be demonstrated in the third part of this essay, questions which in one legal system appear in the form of interpretation of the constitution may in another system appear as general questions of discretion in the exercise of the powers conferred on the legislator.

h) What will be examined next is the rationality of the legislator's activity when he is *not bound by rules* or by paramount considerations of justice, such as occur in the protection of citizens' rights.[31] This rationality can be compared to that of other kinds of system creation, such as the organization of an enterprise, a defense system or a system of electrical communications. The first concern for all such activity will be to decide on a policy.

With regard to the dominant policy for a statute, there are always many demands that cannot all be satisfied at the same time. It is therefore necessary to decide on priorities. The priorities should as far as possible be discussed expressly, not only emerge indirectly from an examination of the rules themselves. The priorities are of different kinds.

Most writings on the theory of legislation have a distinct *teleological* tendency. The three works mentioned here (*supra* a) as classical, however different they may be in other respects, have the teleological character in common. Whereas the role of teleological arguments *de lege lata* may be open to discussion,[32] it seems clear that for legislation rationality must depend on teleological arguments. Litigation occurs because at least one party chooses to bring the matter into court, but legislation depends on the decision of the legislator, and the legislator must have some motive for intervening. Different reasons may lead to legislation and cannot be summarized under any simple headings.

At least within the field now discussed, legislation functions as a method of steering societal activity. There are different ideas of how far the legislator should try to influence such activity. Even if the legislator is prepared to exercise an influence, detailed regulation on the one hand and deregulation on the

[31] I have developed this theme at length in my "Lagstiftning inom förmögenhetsrätten", supra n. 1. particularly in part 3 (pp. 133ff.).

[32] See MacCormick and Summers, op. cit. supra n. 28, pp. 514ff.

other are competing ideals for most fields. Deregulation is also a goal, even if only an intermediary goal for reaching further goals.

Inherent in the teleological attitude is the conviction that a first step should be to analyse what *problems* exist. This analysis must be followed by decisions on the *goals* of the legislation. The analysis of problems and the decisions on goals are closely interrelated. The problems that are found by a preliminary analysis give a first indication of what the goals should be, and the analysis of goals clarifies the problems.[33] Since legislation is not the only means at the disposal of the state, decisions must be taken on whether problems should be solved by other measures, either with the assistance of the state or without it, or perhaps should be left unsolved.

There are two main kinds of goals for legislation on matters of private law (and various other fields of law as well).[34] One concerns the resolution of disputes, the other the long-run consequences of the rules. Reconciling these two aims, or giving priority to one of them, is a major issue in most legislation.

Sometimes it is assumed that the chief means even of achieving long-run effects by legislation is to influence the courts' decisions. As a consequence the courts' decisions should, according to this line of thinking, be appropriate with regard to long-run effects. Obviously, problems of the same type appear in legislation as well as in judicial decisions.

Among goals a distinction can be made between intermediate goals and ultimate goals. Intermediate goals are those that are worth reaching in order to attain goals that lie further away.[35] If the safety of citizens with regard to their property is considered an ultimate goal, it must be examined to what extent it can be reached by establishing the intermediate goal of efficiency in punishing criminals. If indemnifying those who suffer accidents or illness is considered an ultimate goal, it must be decided whether the best intermediary goal is to develop liability in tort or to rely on social insurance. The establishment of intermediary goals is generally the result of compromises between desires to reach various ultimate goals which cannot all be fully reached.

When decisions on goals have been taken, a further step will be to decide what the effects, good or bad, of the proposed legislation will be. Since such

---

[33] Cf. op. cit. supra n. 1, pp. 167ff.

[34] Cf. op. cit. supra n. 1, pp. 159ff.

[35] Many different terms occur for what are here called "intermediary goals" in relation to "ultimate goals", e.g. *"Unterziele"* in relation to *"Oberziele"* (Schäffer, "Rationalisierung der Rechtsetzung", Theorie der Rechtsetzung, Schäffer ed. (Wien 1988), pp. 199ff., "instrumental means" in relation to "final ends" (M. Atienza, Ratio juris 1992 p. 277), and *"instrumentale Ziele"* in relation to *"homeostatische Ziele"* (Wroblewski, Einführung in die Gesetzgebungslehre, 1984, p. 18). The differences in terminology do not seem to be important.

effects will lie in the future, they can only be estimated more or less accurately in advance.

The analysis of problems, goals and probable effects, however skillfully made, can never be decisive for the ultimate decisions. Problems of evaluation will remain. In the discussion of these evaluations a great number of well-known problems emerge, many of which are discussed by professional philosophers as well as by social scientists, including lawyers. As random examples corrective, commutative and distributive justice, economic efficiency and favoring the least advantaged may be mentioned.

It is of course impossible to analyse and take a position on such evaluations here. There are two principal points to be made.

One is that even *de lege ferenda* decisions must depend on the existing legal system. There must be a certain harmony between the new rules and the old ones, in order at least to avoid arbitrary differences in the treatment of similar practical situations. There are other arguments as well that speak in favor of harmony but need not be elaborated here.

The second point is that rationality requires that before any test of the value of proposed rules is applied, the problems, goals and possible effects should be examined. Too often it is assumed that the goal of legislation is simply to bring about the contents of the rules, and that assessments of rationality can be based on the assumption that reality will correspond to these contents.[36] As a consequence, judgments regarding the value of rules are applied indiscriminately to the rules as they appear in statutes or in other similar ways.

i) Having gone this far, the legislator faces the practical problems of *implementing the decisions* which he has taken by creating statutory rules. This activity, which concerns legislative technique, should also be rational, although the kind of rationality required in this field generally has no counterpart in decisions *de lege lata*. The actual, as opposed to formal, liberty accorded to the legislator is often small, in so far as he is bound by the traditions inherent in previous legislation with regard to technique as well as policy.

In some states, there are official "guidelines" for legislative technique.[37] Such guidelines may refer to systematics, concept formation and language. In other states such guidelines do not exist or refer only to peripheral issues, for instance the use of headings for different sections, how many paragraphs a section may contain, what words are permitted and the spelling of some words

---

[36] As expressed by W. Hugger: "Wie bei Gesetzen häufig, wird auf eine klare Zielangabe verzichtet, um – wenn überhaupt – die geregelte Maßnahme selbst als gesetzgeberisches Ziel zu deklarieren." See "Gesetze – ihre Vorbereitung, Abfassung und Prüfung" (Baden-Baden 1983), p. 123.

[37] In German the term is "Legistische Richtlinien". See for an example H. Schneider, Gesetzgebung (Heidelberg 1991) pp. 429ff.

which have different spellings in ordinary writings.[38] To the extent that official guidelines do not exist or do not cover an issue of legislative technique, traditions in the Ministries of Justice and similar bodies will decide what kind of rationality in legislative technique can be expected. However, this kind of rationality has little bearing on the general subject and can therefore be disregarded here.

3. Constitutional Considerations

The issues that bear on the *constitutional background* remain to be discussed. There are considerable differences in this respect among legal systems. Some states have no written constitution, others have constitutions that contain comparatively few rules that bind the legislator, and others have constitutions that lay down a great number of rules that are binding on the legislator. However, even in the absence of explicit rules in the constitution, the legislator must take normative rationality into account and cannot act arbitrarily. There are some limits based on judgments of what is just and equitable.

This general issue can, as far as it refers to normative rationality, be analysed by referring to a special example, that of retroactive legislation in Norway and in Sweden. The Norwegian constitution, *"Grunnloven"* from 1814, contains a general prohibition against retroactive legislation in Sec. 97.[39] This provision binds the legislator, and in addition the courts of law can decide that the application of a statutory provision in a special case would violate it. Retroactive legislation can therefore be considered to be subject to *lex lata* in Norway. The Swedish constitution, *"Regeringsformen"* from 1974, prohibits retroactive legislation in Ch. 2 Sec. 10 with regard to criminal sanctions and taxes but is silent regarding retroactive legislation in other fields. In these other fields, retroactivity in legislation is therefore wholly a matter of considerations *de lege ferenda*. The Swedish legislator has indubitably greater liberty than the Norwegian one in these matters, but the difference is mainly one of extent and degree, not one relating to the arguments that may be advanced.

In Norway the discussion is more formalized, due to the provision in the constitution, as well as more extensive. In Sweden, on the other hand, the discussion is informal, based on general considerations of justice and equity, and there is hardly any general discussion of the problem. The issue appears

---

[38] See for Sweden "Statsrådsberedningen, Myndigheternas föreskrifter" (Ds 1992:112).

[39] This provision has been discussed extensively in Norwegian legal literature, both by public law specialists and by writers who point to the similarity between the provision and rules that occur in private law. See, in the former group particularly F. Castberg, Norges statsforfatning Vol. II (Oslo 1964), pp. 187ff. and J. Andenæs, Statsforfatningen i Norge (Oslo 1990) pp. 483ff., and in the latter group, R. Knoph, Rettslige standarder (Oslo 1939).

mainly when retroactivity is considered in regard to special statutes.[40] In both countries the main underlying policy is considered to be the foreseeability connected with "the rule of law", although a number of other considerations are also invoked.[41] Altogether, the decisions have been based on the special circumstances of each separate case in which the issue of retroactivity is at stake.

The difference and similarity between Norwegian and Swedish law may be illustrated by an example. In both countries statutory rules have been introduced that permit the courts to set aside or modify unfair contract terms (Sec. 36 of the common Scandinavian Contracts Act). When such legislation is introduced, it must be decided to what extent it should apply to contracts that have been entered into before the time at which the statutory provision enters into force.

In Sweden – which was the first of the two States to enact such legislation – it was decided that for various reasons it was necessary to make an exception from the principle of not making new private law retroactive.[42] Sec. 36 of the Swedish Contracts Act thus applies even to contracts that were made before it entered into force.[43] The question of retroactivity did not raise much interest during the legislative proceedings.[44]

In Norway, on the other hand, during the parliamentary proceedings concerning Sec. 36 it was discussed vividly whether its application to contracts made before the enactment might violate Sec. 97 of *Grunnloven*. However, the result was that retroactivity was accepted, although with some reservations.[45] In later Norwegian Supreme Court decisions, Sec. 36 has been applied to revise long-term contracts that were entered into long before this provision was enacted, and Sec. 97 of *Grunnloven* has not been considered to prevent such application.[46]

---

[40] In the field of private law, the issue is specially relevant for family law, where there are numerous examples both of retroactivity and of refusal to introduce new rules with retroactive effects.

[41] See for Norway in particular Castberg, op. cit., pp. 189ff.; cf. Knoph, op. cit., passim. For Sweden, the lack of comprehensive treatment in legal literature makes it difficult to cite similar statements. Cf. U. Bernitz and B. Södermark, Utlåtande angående de rättsliga förutsättningarna för ett avbrytande av det pensionsgrundande allemanssparandet m.m., October 1992 (mimeographed), pp. 17ff., with references.

[42] See "Proposition" 1975/76:81, p. 149, where it is pointed out that special considerations may be necessary in retroactive application. Cf. the report "Generalklausul i förmögenhetsrätten" (SOU 1974:83), p. 199.

[43] An exception was made, however, for law-suits that had been commenced before the entrance into force of the statute.

[44] The so-called Council of Law (three high judges, who examine proposed statutes from points of view of i.a. constitutionality) recommended the limitation mentioned in the previous footnote. See Prop. 1975/76:81 p. 170.

[45] The events and discussion are described in detail by K. Huser, Avtalesensur (Bergen 1984), pp. 55ff.

The issue of retroactivity of legislation may be considered to be a special case, but in my opinion it illustrates that, when we get to practical issues, the difference between *lex lata* and *lex ferenda* appears as a difference between the way in which problems are handled, and not as a difference in the possible rationality of the arguments.

4. Conclusions

The various problems arising when rationality *de lege ferenda* is involved have only been treated very briefly here. However, I hope that it will be clear that such problems do exist and that the legislators' decisions cannot be completely arbitrary or wholly dictated by political considerations. Moreover, I hope that it has appeared that rationality in legislation is not a simple matter, which can be established *a priori* by listening to experts on legal theory, but the sum of a number of complex judgements that are neither completely free of, nor completely bound by, legal, factual and logical considerations.

[46] See the cases in Norsk Retstidende 1988 p. 276 and p. 295. Cf. Norsk Retstidende 1990 p. 284. In the latter case it was stated that sec. 36 of The Contracts Act could not be used for setting aside the consequences of sec. 97 of Grunnloven with regard to a statute on leases. See Andenæs, op. cit. supra n. 39, pp. 499 ff.

Formalism and Anti-Formalism in Modern Law – State Law and Beyond*

By Massimo La Torre, Florence

Summary: 1. State Law and the rule of law. 2. From the State of law to the constitutional State – Towards a new "ius commune". 3. Beyond legal positivism: impossibility of a "pure" theory of law. 4. Interdependency of law and morality: legal argument as a special case of moral argument. 5. The social responsibility of institutions: "reflexive law", corporatism and legal pluralism. 6. Beyond State Law?

1. State law and the rule of law

Modern law in the European countries is the outcome of a specific cultural and political development with at its core the concept and institutional figure of the State. This is what imprints on Continental law its modern features, its (limited) universality and uniformity which are according to Santi Romano a reflection of rationalist natural law, and its (apparent) axiomaticity, which sharply transforms the nature of "legal science".[1] This has to do with a conception of law and with a new legal epistemology: legal positivism. This presented itself as a legal version of philosophical positivism, despite the many differences between them. Legal science is no longer conceived as "iuris prudentia", the art of topical or rhetorical argument, but lays a claim to be a *science,* in the strong sense (that of the English word rather than of *Wissenschaft*), in most cases deductive, but also inductive-deductive with the rise of the empirical sciences like biology or chemistry. Jhering, for instance, compares the dogmatist's work to the chemist's, and the legal "institutions" to the chemical elements of which other materials are composed.

In the new State legal system, judges have no reason to argue or weigh different rights and principles at dispute. All they have to do is apply the law. The

---

* I completed this work during my stay at the University of Münster on a scholarship from the Alexander von Humboldt Foundation. The frequent discussions with my amiable host, Professor Werner Krawietz, strengthened, particularly through the confrontation of my ideas with his skeptical, relativist position on sources of law, my convictions regarding the hypothesis of a law "beyond the State".

[1] On the mutual influence between State and legal science, cf. inter alia D. Grimm, Recht und Staat der bürgerlichen Gesellschaft, Frankfurt am Main 1987, pp. 347ff.

topical or rhetorical paradigm is replaced by the syllogistic one, which affirms not so much the need to argue syllogistically (though this is also present in the rhetorical procedures), as the idea that sole "reason" for the legal decision has to be the law. If we accept the tripartite division proposed by Joseph Raz[2] among three fundamental types of requests that may be made with regard to a case to be decided by a court, namely (i) to decide according to the law, (ii) to decide taking all relevant factors for the case into account, (iii) to decide what the law applicable to the case is, we may say that on the legal positivist paradigm the only legitimate request would be the last one, where just the cognitive aspect, determining the "source", seems to cancel out the volitional element (one's own assessment of the case).

With the modern State, and especially with the codifications, it is less a syllogistic paradigm than a legalist ideology that is imposed; more than a theory of legal argumentation, a theory of the "sources" of law (the *source theory* Joseph Raz speaks about).[3] No further need to use syllogisms can remain, even by such a confused, opportunistic lawyer as Manzoni's *Azzeccagarbugli* (petty-fogger).

This explains why legal positivism – "closely linked with the formation and development of a certain type of political organization, the one characteristic of the type of State customarily called modern"[4] – has developed both theories of the sources of law and theories of legal interpretation (a paradigm case is Hans Kelsen). "It is only with legislatively enacted law – Lon Fuller rightly says – that positivism feels itself reasonably at home and that only [...] so long as problems of interpretation are avoided".[5]

These transformations are possible thanks to a new conception of political society founded on the concept of sovereignty, that is, the monopoly of force and of the production of law. Thus, modern law is essentially *State law,* and the modern State is the *State of law,* the State that regulates and limits itself, to use Georg Jellinek's formula.

However, this formula is in a sense empty.[6] According to the formalist or legal positivist interpretation of it, in which the "law" is regarded as the act through which the State manifests its will, each State constitutes itself as a State of law; as Hans Kelsen, and also Carl Schmitt, repeatedly tell us: "Jede Ordnung ist eine Rechtsordnung und jeder Staat ein Rechtsstaat."[7] In this

[2] See J. Raz, On the Autonomy of Legal Reasoning, in "Ratio Juris", 1993, p. 3.

[3] See J. Raz, The Authority of Law, Oxford 1979, Chapter 3. Cf. J. Raz, On the Autonomy of Legal Reasoning, op. cit., p. 7.

[4] U. Scarpelli, Cos'è il positivismo giuridico, Milan 1965, p. 49.

[5] L. L. Fuller, Anatomy of the Law, Harmondsworth 1971, p. 161.

[6] Compare G. Zagrebelsky, Il diritto mite, Turin 1992, p. 22.

[7] C. Schmitt, Römischer Katholizismus und politische Form, 3rd ed., Stuttgart 1984, p. 41. Cf. F. Neumann, The Rule of Law – Political Theory and the Legal System in

case the principle of legality does not express any substantive qualificatory criterion, nor even any strong formal criterion like the generality and abstractness of the law, but the idea that the law is the supreme legal act to which no other act can legally be opposed. This also implies that, the written law being the supreme legal act, and since it more or less by definition regulates everything that is to be regulated, the judge's role is rather slight and his decision predetermined.

The legality of the norm (its origin in some organ) is the source simultaneously of the *validity* and the *legitimation* of legal norms. This brings us to a continuing confusion between two senses of validity: as the norm's *belonging* to the (State) legal system and as the norm's *bindingness.* The thesis of the juxtaposition of these two concepts of validity is central to Hans Kelsen's "pure theory", to the point that a manifestly unconstitutional or illegal norm retains its juridicality (its validity and bindingness) thanks to a tacit clause (implicit in the "fundamental norm"). This device, as we know, was used by the Austrian jurist also to base the legality of custom, including custom "contra legem". The bindingness of a precept derives from its inclusion in a complex dynamic of referrals and delegations of powers. In a certain sense, the capacity the norm has to motivate conduct and act as a premise in practical reasoning is founded on its belonging to the system (the State). It is the system, which presents itself as single and more or less complete, that holds the monopoly of juridicality.

The principle of legality is identified with the principle of sovereignty: there is only one organ capable of imposing its will, on which no other will is in turn imposed. This is the legal positivist interpretation of the formula "State of law [constitutional State, rule of law]" along the theoretical line from Gerber through Jellinek to Kelsen, a line that has certainly determined public-law doctrine in the Continental European countries.

The following considerations will be developed at two levels, reflecting the vagueness of the term "law", and the ambiguity of the jurist's task resulting from that vagueness and nourished by it. We can understand the term "law" in two fundamental senses: (i) the law as *institution,* as legal system, that is, as a set of valid, effective rules and as the set of corresponding behaviour; (ii) the law as *concept,* as a set of ideas as to what law is or ought to be as an institution. In this second sense, law may be spoken of as a set of theories or ideologies. Thus, discussing the theme of the evolutionary trends in law in our times we must consider separately the law as institution and the law as concept.

The prospects for the development of law as an institution are inextricably bound up with the prospects for evolution in legal theory, so that the latter

---

Modern Society, Leamington Spa 1986, p. 180: "Such a conception is neither right nor wrong; it is simply meaningless".

cannot be understood without taking the former into account. I wish however to emphasize that in this context speaking of "evolutionary trends" does not force me into any compromise with any theory of social evolution or of law (such as those of Jürgen Habermas, Niklas Luhmann or Gunther Teubner).

2. From the State of law to the constitutional State – Towards a new "ius commune"

Among the prospects for the evolution of law, the most relevant seems to me the end of the illusion of being able to regulate by positive norms, State provisions, the whole of social life with all its institutional changes. In a certain sense, this is the collapse of the belief that a few codes can contain the necessary and sufficient norms to guide and solve all social issues. This a crisis in the ideology that affirms that the sole sources of law are the norms promulgated by the State's authorized organs, and that law and State are homologous phenomena.

We might define this as a trend to the "dejuridification" of society, if this term were not still ambiguous. What we are seeing today is on the one hand a process of *dejuridification,* if we take it that juridification means only governmental, centralist regulation. On the other hand, we see a process of *juridification,* if by this we understand the situation where there is a multiplicity of centres charged with issuing or producing valid rules or applicable legal principles.[8]

I think a more appropriate term for this type of development is "rematerialization" of law, making explicit reference to the concept of substantive rationality of law developed by Max Weber.[9] Here "rematerialization" indicates a growing orientation of State norms towards substantive values and their reformulation (as far as content is concerned) as administrative acts, that is, as direct, specific interventions in *all* the areas of social life. Legislation is increasingly presented as "special law". As the Bolognese professor Francesco Galgano writes, "law-making through codes has dwindled in this century [...] legislative output being manifested particularly in the proliferation of *special laws*".[10] "Today's law-making technique," he continues, "has changed. [...] The civil code still retains great importance as a *source of cognition* of the law.

---

[8] Cf. G. Teubner, Verrechtlichung – Begriffe, Merkmale, Grenzen, Auswege, in Verrechtlichung von Wirtschaft, Arbeit und sozialer Solidarität, ed. by F. Kübler, Frankfurt am Main 1984, pp. 289 - 344.

[9] See, e.g., Max Weber, Wirtschaft und Gesellschaft. Grundrisse der verstehenden Soziologie, 5th rev. ed., ed. by J. Winckelmann, Tübingen 1976, p. 397.

[10] F. Galgano, Diritto privato, 4th ed., Padova 1988, p. 38. Cf., inter alia, E. Forsthoff, Rechtsstaat im Wandel, Stuttgart 1964, Chapter 5, and U. Scarpelli, Cos'è il positivismo giuridico, op. cit., p. 140.

[...] However, it has lost its older importance as a *source of production* of law: the new needs of law-making tend today to be met through specific laws that are added to the civil code, rather than by remaking the code entirely."[11]

The materialization, or "rematerialization" if you like, of law, especially in the States of the European continent, is fairly clearly manifest in the transformation of the traditional State of law into the constitutional State. The State is, using Forsthoff's words, reduced to "the relativity of its corresponding constitutional form".[12] In the traditional State of law, the law was self-founding as to its validity and legitimation, that is to say, it was the law which, thanks to its formal prerogatives – above all its origin – justified itself, without recourse to extra-legal sources, special normative contents or strong formal criteria (the generality or universality of its formulation). In the modern constitutional State, by contrast, the law is defined through, and subordinated to, substantive criteria whose explicit formulation is sanctioned by the constitution. The constitutional *Grundnorm* consists not just of delegations of power to the legislature, but itself lays down rules of conduct or at least substantive principles the realization of which the legislator's intervention has to be guided by. Consider, for instance, the radical transformation of the principle of equality in European constitutional systems from a purely formal criterion binding as to the application of the law and therefore particularly upon the judge and public officials, into a substantive postulate binding on the issuing or validity of the law, and therefore chiefly upon the legislator.

In commenting on the first part of Article 3 of the Constitution of the Italian Republic – which states that "All citizens have equal social dignity and are equal before the law, without distinction of sex, race, language, religion, political opinion or personal or social condition" – the majority of legal scholars tell us that this clause is to be interpreted as the list of qualifications that judges and public administration are barred from taking into account in applying the law. With some scholars, one might add: "But the clause has another meaning too. It indicates the descriptions that the law cannot adopt as discriminatory criteria either. In this respect, the bindingness is primarily *upon the legislative power.* And it impinges on the *content* of the law as well as on its effectiveness."[13]

The Italian Constitutional Court, however, accepts the law's using special categories of subject if these are not taken as general classes, and does not find distinctions founded on sex or other personal or social conditions to be unconstitutional if these distinctions are justified *reasonably.* Inequality of normative

---

[11] F. Galgano, op. cit., p. 39.

[12] See E. Forsthoff, Rechtsstaat im Wandel, op. cit., chap. 5.

[13] A. Barbera, F. Cocozza, G. Corso, Le libertà dei singoli e delle formazione sociali. Il principio di eguaglianza, in Manuale di diritto pubblico, ed. by G. Amato/A. Barbera, Bologna 1984, p. 305. Emphasis in original.

treatment is not sufficient reason for a law's unconstitutionality unless another requirement comes in: the "unreasonableness" of the treatment itself (see e. g. the following Italian Constitutional Court rulings: nos. 170 and 264 of 1976, no. 100 of 1977, no. 73 of 1979, no. 72 of 1980).

A judgement on respect for the principle of equality is accordingly converted into an assessment of a law's "reasonableness". This assessment includes consideration of the limits within which the legislator's discretion appears as "reasonable". Here the "unreasonableness" is more or less equivalent to "exceeding the legislative competence" (see Italian Constitutional Court ruling no. 38, 1965). The principle of "reasonableness" ends by absorbing the principle of equality as justificatory basis for normative treatment and by being applied not only when comparing norms that in some way conflict but also in relation to each norm considered individually.[14]

In assessing a law's reasonableness, the constitutional judge assesses its congruency with the object it pursues. "There is, in short, verification [...] of *rationality in relation to the purpose,* which does not question the purpose in itself, determination of which is reserved to the legislator, but the congruency of the means in relation to it, which has justifiably led to the notion of a check on *exceeding the legislative competency.*"[15] The criterion of a law's reasonableness assumes general relevance in the Italian Constitutional Court's case law to the extent that this criterion is untied from any relationship with constitutional principles or values. This means that the criterion of a law's reasonableness, very close, as Gustavo Zagrebelsky stresses, to Weber's criterion of "purposive" rationality, requires not so much that the law be congruent with some constitutional end, but mainly that it be appropriate to its own objective and object, thereby coming close to the criterion of "the nature of the matter".

However, once the law (each law) is subordinated to the criterion of "reasonableness", the law ceases to be a mere manifestation of will. "It has rightly been said that the law, once made subject to the standard of reasonableness, ceases to be the impenetrable manifestation of *voluntas* conceived by French doctrine on legislative sovereignty and becomes an act judicable on the basis of its *ratio.* It ceases to be an "arbitrary" act and becomes a "discretionary" act (and accordingly checkable also from the viewpoint of exceeding legislative competency, not just for specific violation of constitutional provisions). The legislator thus loses portions of sovereignty to the 'rationality of law' and its interpreters."[16] Accordingly, in the modern constitutional State, where there is a developed constitutional jurisdiction that in some way reviews

---

[14] Cf. ibid., pp. 312 - 131.

[15] G. Zagrebelsky, La giurisdizione costituzionale, in Manuale di diritto pubblico, ed. by G. Amato/A. Barbera, op. cit., p. 778. Emphasis in original.

[16] A. Barbera, F. Cocozza, G. Corso, op. cit., p. 313. Emphasis in original.

the legislature's discretion as to the very content of the law (even going beyond its compatibility with constitutional principles), it is hard to go on asserting that *"auctoritas non veritas facit legem"*. Indeed, the opposite will hold: truth, not authority, makes the law. This will, to be sure, be a "truth" in the improper sense of a "normative truth": that is, congruency with rationality criteria going beyond the rather narrow limits of formal validity.

We are further seeing a radical, albeit slow and difficult, shift in the concept of sovereignty. The crisis in this concept, and in the corresponding institutional phenomena, is pointed to by one of the most interesting Italian constitutionalists, Gustavo Zagrebelsky: "The dominant concept in State law, both internally (internal public law) and externally (external or international public law) was accordingly the sovereignty of the State as 'person'. Today, however, this concept is no longer recognizable in its erstwhile clarity as a functioning political reality. Corrosive forces have been powerfully at work since the turn of the century, both internally and externally."[17]

The State of law, the *Rechtsstaat* of German doctrine, *de facto* represented the predominant version of the sovereign State in continental European countries. This type of State did not question the absolutist dogma of sovereignty in any of its central features. This dogma was projected onto institutional life, with two important consequences. (i) Within the society considered, the State was the privileged legal subject, hierarchically superior to any other subject, and all its relations with these other subjects were relations from superior to inferior, from sovereign to subject, relations of domination on the one hand and subordination on the other. (ii) In the context of international relations, the sovereign State appeared as sole legal subject: international law was recognized as valid only to the extent that it was incorporated into State legislation. Finally, State sovereignty was asserted insofar as it constituted the sole source of law in both the national and the international spheres.

(i) "Internal" sovereignty is questioned with the rise of the modern constitutional States, as the concept of public law merges with that of constitutional law, and accordingly can no longer be grounded upon the criterion of "imperium" but on that of public utility or a primordial agreement on the ideals and procedures of political society. The sovereignty of modern constitutional States increasingly connotes a procedure of formation of the public will rather than the power of last resort, that of defining the "state of exception" (or better, of derogation from the constitution), that Carl Schmitt dreams of. Sovereignty is no longer an attribute of any subject, entity or organ ("capacity of the person" as Felice Battaglia defines it).[18] Sovereignty is the procedure for

---

[17] G. Zagrebelsky, Il diritto mite, op. cit., p. 6.

[18] See F. Battaglia, Die Souveränität und ihre Grenzen, now in Volkssouveränität und Staatssouveränität, ed. by H. Kurz, Darmstadt 1970, p. 242. Cf. H. Kelsen, Der Wandel des Souveränitätsbegriffes, now in Volkssouveränität und Staatssouveränität,

arriving at decisions binding upon all the citizens. This transformation is particularly stressed by Jürgen Habermas: "Heute zieht sich die staatsbürgerliche Souveränität des Volkes in die rechtlich institutionalisierten Verfahren und die grundrechtlich ermöglichten informellen Prozesse einer mehr oder weniger diskursiven Meinungs- und Willensbildung zurück."[19] "Sovereignty, now anonymous and without subject, and indeed dissolved intersubjectively, withdraws into the democratic procedure and into the exacting communicative requirements for its exercise."[20]

In a work written shortly before his death, Adolf Merkl pointed to the ambiguity of the term "State of law" and stressed that it could mean either (a) a State that exercises its power through the law or (b) a State that does not only rule through the law but is also ruled by the law.[21] And as Merkl himself reminds us, the latter is the conception of the *Rechtsstaat* adopted by German legal scholars in the 19th century, starting with a famous definition by Julius Stahl. In the words of this Prussian philosopher and jurist, the State of law is not one that regards the law as its objective and foundation, but one for which the law is nothing but the instrument for accomplishing its ends.

In the first version of the State of law, its legitimation is founded merely on the use of the formal instrument of the law, that is its logical and semantic character (generality and abstraction), and the division and delegation of powers among the separate organs of the State apparatus. In the second version of the State of law, its legitimation requires that the law be the outcome of a process of rational public debate. However, the legitimation through procedure spoken of here is not to be identified with the *Legitimation durch Verfahren* described by Niklas Luhmann. According to the Bielefeld sociologist, the procedure that legitimizes the State consists of a specific social system. It is a "procedure" as being a reduction of complexity and selection of possibilities, and not as being a form or structure for a deliberation or decision.[22] The conver-

---

ed. by H. Kurz, op. cit., p. 169: "Das Souveränitätsdogma mit seinem Primat der eigenstaatlichen Rechtsordnung ist Staatssubjektivismus."

[19] J. Habermas, Staatsbürgerschaft und nationale Identität, now in appendix to idem, Faktizität und Geltung. Beiträge zur Diskurstheorie des Rechts und des demokratischen Rechtsstaates, Frankfurt am Main 1992, p. 649.

[20] J. Habermas, Souveränität als Verfahren, now appendix to idem, Faktizität und Geltung, op. cit., p. 626.

[21] See A. J. Merkl, Idee und Gestalt des Rechtsstaates, in Festschrift für Hans Kelsen zum 90. Geburtstag, ed. by A. J. Merkl/A. Verdross/R. Marcic/R. Walter, Vienna 1971, p. 126. Cf. K. Tuori, Four models of the Rechtsstaat, in Öffentliche oder private Moral? Vom Geltungsgrunde und der Legitimität des Rechts. Festschrift für Ernesto Garzón Valdés, ed. by W. Krawietz/G. H. von Wright, Berlin 1992, pp. 451 ff.

[22] "Verfahren werden als soziale Systeme gesehen, die mit Entscheidungsprozessen synchronisiert, aber nicht identisch sind" [Procedures are seen as social systems that are synchronized with decisional processes but not identical with them] (N. Luhmann, Legitimation durch Verfahren, III ed., Frankfurt am Main 1989, p. 3). Luhmann's sociological-juridical theory has little room for considering the normative aspects of

sion of the concept of sovereignty from a quality or attribute of some "body" or "entity" into a quality or attribute of some "procedure" however indicates something different: "procedure" is here a (rationally and morally justified) structure for the formation of a universalizable will. "Procedure" for Luhmann is equivalent to "legality", so that *Legitimation durch Verfahren* is close to the legitimation through legality theorized by Max Weber. "Procedure", from the viewpoint of a normative reconstruction of the constitutional State, is equivalent to "public debate among free and equal subjects".[23]

(ii) "External" sovereignty, in the area of international relations, is questioned by the development of certain communities integrating distinct national legal systems (the most relevant and advanced example being the European Community). Consider what the Maastricht Treaty provides *inter alia* on citizenship. This is somehow untied from subjection to a national State, and makes it possible for someone without the nationality of a given State to exercise certain electoral rights there.

The development of European Community law – as recently pointed out by Neil MacCormick – should not be set in the framework of a traditional view of law as connected with the existence of a (single) sovereign, and of international law as the product of delegations of power and of organs delegated by the sovereign himself. "It seems obvious – he writes – that no State in Western Europe any longer is a sovereign state. None is in a position such that all power exercised internally in it, whether politically or legally, derives from purely internal sources. Equally, of course, it is not true that all the power which is exercised either politically or normatively is exercised by, or through, or on the grant of all or more organs of the European Community. Nor has the Community as such the plenitude of power politically or normatively that could permit it remotely to resemble in itself a sovereign state or sovereign federation of states."[24] Community law, even before Maastricht, was beginning to assert itself as a new "ius commune" of the European countries, recalling situations before the great codifications, when, for instance, Roman law as reinterpreted by the "doctores", or the law of the Holy Roman Empire, were applied to national systems of law without being direct expressions of them.

---

social reality and in practice gives little relevance to the concept of norm. On this undervaluing of norms as conditions for social action see the critique by W. Krawietz, Zur Einführung: Neue Sequenzierung der Theoriebildung und Kritik der allgemeinen sozialen Systeme, in Kritik der Theorie sozialer Systeme. Auseinandersetzungen mit Luhmanns Hauptwerk, ed. by W. Krawietz/M. Welker, Frankfurt am Main 1992, esp. pp. 29 - 32.

[23] For such a normative reconstruction see esp. J. Habermas, Volkssouveränität als Verfahren, op. cit., pp. 600ff.

[24] N. MacCormick, Beyond the Sovereign State, in "The Modern Law Review", 1993, p. 16. Cf. W. Krawietz, Recht ohne Staat? Spielregeln des Rechts und Rechtssystem in Normen- und Systemtheoretischer Perspektive, in RECHTSTHEORIE, 1993, pp. 81ff.

Nor should another aspect of the crisis of sovereignty connected with its "external" aspect be forgotten. We are seeing the rise of forms of legal regulation of international commercial relations developing independently from the primacy of national law. Private international law is increasingly being untied from the protection of any State as far as major economic transactions are concerned, and leading to a sort of new "ius commune": a modern "lex mercatoria".

3. Beyond legal positivism: impossibility of a "pure" theory of law

As far as law as a concept is concerned, at least two major developments can be discerned: (i) the rise of "post-positivist" theories of law, particularly at the level of theory of law *stricto sensu:* (ii) the rise of "responsive" theories of law, at the level of sociology of law. But what does legal "post-positivism" mean?

A distinction should first be drawn between two chief meanings of "legal positivism". In a broad sense, legal positivism is the theory that asserts that law is the work of man, the product – albeit involuntary – of his action. In a strict sense, legal positivism is the doctrine that asserts that the sole producer of law is the State and that there are no other sources of law outside its boundaries. According to this doctrine, "legal" would be equivalent to "of the State".

There are at least two other theses connected with the two senses of legal positivism identified. The first thesis is the exclusion, as far as establishment of the "meaning" of legal rules is concerned, of any reference to factors outside positive law (the written laws). This position implies expelling from the sphere of legal method any considerations of a philosophical, historical or sociological nature.[25] This strategy of isolation can be linked with the thesis of the separation between a descriptive study and a prescriptive study of law. The jurist's task on this second thesis is solely to describe what law is, that is, valid law in force. It would seem there is no need for recourse to normative or prescriptive criteria to establish what law is. However, this thesis is not a necessary condition for a legal positivist position. The "ideological positivism", for which *Gesetz ist Gesetz,* that is, the law takes on an intrinsically strong (moral) normative value, does not count the separation between description and prescription, since the description of valid law is immediately the prescription of what it is right to do. From the thesis (more methodological than moral or political)

---

[25] Cf. D. Grimm, Methode als Machtfaktor, in idem, Recht und Staat der bürgerlichen Gesellschaft, op. cit., p. 349: "Unter Positivismus verstehe ich dabei diejenigen Interpretationsmethoden, welche den Sinn von Normen allein aus rechtlichen Faktoren ermitteln wollen, den Rückgriff auf Rechtsideen, Regelungszwecke und Wirklichkeitsbefunde und damit auch alle Anleihen bei den Sozialwissenschaften, der Philosophie und Geschichte ablehnen."

of the separation between the descriptive and the prescriptive consideration of law, some also derive the thesis of the separation between law and morality (which is more moral and political than methodological). Thus, for instance, for authors like Herbert L. A. Hart and Ota Weinberger, and – polemically – Ronald Dworkin, legal positivism implies the imposition of an uncrossable boundary between law and morality.

A second thesis that can be deduced from the position of law's nature as being of the State is the Utopian notion of the completeness of the legal system. If law is only what emanates from the State, what the State produces is all the law possible, and it is accordingly complete. From this, together with the obligation on the judge to decide always and in every case, there is to a large extent deduced the thesis of the denial of the judge's creative power, and the idea of the judge's decision as mere syllogistic, mechanical application of the rules issued by the State organs. Thus, by contrast with what Ronald Dworkin believes, for legal positivism it is possible and even necessary to conceive the judge's decision as the "one right answer", the only just or proper decision. The judge who confines himself to syllogistically applying the law can do no more than arrive at a conclusion which – from a legal positivist viewpoint – has to be accepted as the sole just decision. As Walter Ott, author of one of the best studies on legal positivism,[26] writes, "the legal positivist approach relies in particular on confidence in the stability of the political situation within the State and *on the guarantee that the 'right' solution will be found by the legislator*".[27]

If, then, while there are no signs of crisis in the concept of legal positivism in the broad sense as the conception affirming the "humanity" of law, there is indeed a crisis in the conception of legal positivism in the strict sense that defends the "statishness" of law. The process of "rematerialization" of law we discussed, however briefly, brings a crisis not only in the conception of the State as the sole source of law but also in the thesis of the completeness of the legal system. The weight of fundamental laws, "principles" and even "values" in modern constitutional States is too great for it to be possible to continue defending a merely legalist theory of judicial decision.

If as sources of law we accept not just State norms but also social rules like, for instance, those laid down by trade unions or private agreements reached outside the traditional scope of law (for instance in the context of private international law), and extra-positive legal principles introduced say through constitutional practice or through the ever-growing recourse to so-called "values", we can end by accepting that State law is not the sole normative system that

[26] See W. Ott, Der Rechtspositivismus, Berlin, 1st ed., 1976; 2nd ed., 1992.

[27] W. Ott/F. Buob, Did Legal Positivism Render German Jurists Defenceless During the Third Reich?, in "Social and Legal Studies", 1993, p. 96. My emphasis.

guides us in regulating the conduct of private individuals as far as judicial decisions are concerned. In this situation, the paradigm of the legal syllogism and the ideology of the judge as a mere repeater of the law, *vox legis* as Paul Laband[28] called it (or "subsumption automaton" in Regina Ogorek's term),[29] are facing a very serious crisis.

However, we can speak of "postpositivist" theories of law in a sense that has nothing to do with the senses of the term "legal positivism" mentioned above. In this other sense, "post-positivism" is the label given to some epistemological theories which – following and developing from Karl Popper – affirm the following thesis, as simple as it is destructive of logical neo-positivism and neo-empiricism: that scientific laws cannot be established without previous theories, that there is no scientific knowledge without theoretical "paradigms". This is a thesis that recalls the ideas of Thomas Mann's Naphta: "Dear friend, pure knowledge does not exist. The legitimacy of the religious concept of knowledge, which can be summed up in St. Augustine's words 'I believe in order to know', is absolutely indubitable. Faith is the organ of knowledge, the intellect is secondary. Your science with no premises is a myth. There is always a belief, a world view, an idea; in a word, a will, and it is for reason to interpret and demonstrate, always and in every case. The point is to arrive at the *quod erat demonstrandum.*"[30] Many "Popperians" might share these words of Naphta's, even though they may fear them to be a bit too mystical and irrationalist. In any case, according to Popper and his disciples any scientific proposition is theory-laden – theoretically compromised.

These post-positivist epistemological theses translated into the terms of legal theories imply according to some that the validity of a law cannot be established nor a legal decision arrived at (especially a judicial decision) without recourse to normative criteria outside those posited by the legal system itself. One further consequence of this latter conclusion is heavy skepticism as to the possibility of a legal science not only without prior epistemological concepts, but also of a value-free legal science, *wertfrei* in Max Weber's sense.

Frome a post-positivist viewpoint, legal science appears as the product of strong, that is political and/or moral, normative positions. This is the thesis defended by, for instance, Ronald Dworkin. That American philosopher believes that in order to interpret a law one must first have a theory about what is the "best" law. Moreover, the interpretation of the law must tend to present it as the best law possible.[31] In the same way, the interpretation of a

[28] Compare L. Prieto Sanchís, Ideología e interpretación jurídica, Madrid 1987, p. 107.

[29] R. Ogorek, Richterkönig oder Subsumtionsautomat? Zur Justiztheorie im 19. Jahrhundert, Frankfurt am Main 1986.

[30] T. Mann, Der Zauberberg, Frankfurt am Main 1989, p. 419.

[31] This second assumption – shared by Alexander Peczenik – seems to me rather problematic since it may have the consequence of barring common types of interpretive

literary work presupposes, according to him, a theory as to what is the best work of art, since the object is to present the literary work in question as the best possible: "Interpretation of a text attempts to show it as the best work of art it can be."[32] This brings down the illusion of a "pure" theory of law, a theory, that is, that does not require, for its explanatory and descriptive task, any prior concept of law or any recourse to extra-legal argument.

4. Interdependency of law and morality: legal argument as a special case of moral argument

One of the points where legal positivism is most attacked by the theoretical developments of recent years is its concept of validity and binding force. Along with the "humanity" and "statishness" of law, another fundamental assumption of the theoretical assemblage known as "legal positivism" is that legal norms constitute *independent* reasons for acting. That is, the norms do not derive their binding force, their capacity to form part of a practical argument, from other types of reasons, for instance moral or prudential reasons. Legal norms are held to be sufficient in themselves to determine the conclusion that some human act ought to be.

However, there are legal positivist theoreticians who recognize that alongside the legal norms, the strongest normative reasons are represented by moral rules. Yet this does not constitute any problem for them, since on the one hand they very clearly separate legal norms and moral norms, and on the other they attribute to the former greater power of motivation, due for instance to the fact that they are accompanied by social sanctions and applied by (coercive) orders that actually exist and are generally effective. Morality, despite its greater normative "force", is held not to have sufficient motivating power, from being anchored in the mere individual conscience or in the best of cases in a free inter-subjective relation.[33] Thus morality, in order to become a concrete, effective rule of social life, is held to need the sanction of law, its recognition and protection.

The other positivist strategy is represented by what Alf Ross would call "ideological" legal positivism, that is, the position that the fact that there is a legal norm is already a sufficient reason to accept as morally valid and obligatory the conduct it prescribes. "Punctually obey and freely criticize" – this say-

---

argument, for instance *reductio ad absurdum* or the so-called "economic argument". To avoid this clearly unacceptable consequence, it would be necessary to understand "law" in Dworkin's formula not as individual law, a particular text or norm, but as law in the holist sense, as "the law" or legal system.

32 R. Dworkin, A Matter of Principle, Oxford 1986, p. 150.

33 See, e.g., the works of one of the classics of modern legal doctrine, Franz von Zeiller, author of the ABGB, the Austrian Civil Code, esp.: Grundsätze der Gesetzgebung, ed. by E. Wolf, Frankfurt am Main 1948, pp. 31ff.

ing of Bentham's, sometimes hailed as the highest expression of the separation between law and morality, lays down the bindingness of legal precepts even where the addressee does not believe that so acting is morally desirable or acceptable. In any case, on both sides, we are seeing an identification between legal bindingness and bindingness *tout court.* Of bindingness there is only one, as of one's mother.

This positivist paradigm has today been repeatedly attacked. John Finnis, for instance, tells us that even for our descriptive concepts of law we need strong normative criteria (therefore *moral* ones). For him it is not methodologically possible to identify a body of rules as belonging to a particular legal system without having an idea of what that system is. This idea could not however be in turn descriptive, since that would presuppose decisions and stipulations as to what criteria are relevant for the end considered. From beginning to end, such criteria would be moral principles.[34]

As we know, Ronald Dworkin writes of the "one right answer" as the outcome of the "best theory", and the latter is supposed to be the one closest to the community's political and moral principles. Legal theory, in order to found and justify itself, would have to cross to the ground of political and moral doctrine. A judicial decision is right (and in this view there is only *one* possible right decision) if and only if it is the best expression of the community's political or moral principals.

For Joseph Raz, every judicial decision is to some extent a moral decision, since it assumes the legal system being in force to be morally desirable. The argument here is not so much that the judge, in taking the internal viewpoint of the norms, has to opt for the legal system in question and take a clear political position in its favour (as maintained by Uberto Scarpelli in his book *Cos'è il positivismo giuridico*). Raz's argument is more that maintenance of the established order has *prima facie* moral primacy over any intent not to apply it. Between the anarchy that could lead to disobedience to legal precepts and the social order considered apart from its intrinsic moral value, the latter ought to be (morally) privileged. Consequently, legal norms would, at least *prima facie,* be moral rules.

Other blows at legal positivism come from major philosophers of law like Carlos Nino and Robert Alexy. Nino's conception starts from the critique of what he defines as the "essentialist" attitude in legal philosophy. Most of its scholars believe there is a need to establish *one* concept of law, a concept that can give an account of the reality of the phenomenon of "law". The concept of law would then correspond to the true reality or "essence" of the law. This position, Nino tells us, is a consequence of the idea that to concepts there correspond specific entities, that there are no concepts, words or utterances with-

[34] See J. Finnis, Natural Law and Natural Rights, Oxford 1980.

out "something" that they correspond or refer to. To "essentialism", Nino opposes a sort of "pragmatism": concepts are regarded as tools for human ends, and accordingly can, in a given area of experience – the law for example – be very manifold. It would then not be correct to speak of *the* concept, but of *concepts* of law.

Accordingly, for Nino, the legal positivist concept of law that refers to particular facts as "sources" of law would be useful and appropriate only as a descriptive concept from the viewpoint of an observer seeking to describe the legal practices of some social group. The legal positivist concept of law as a descriptive concept would thus be incapable of offering independent reasons for action. "If a legal norm – writes the Argentinian philosopher – is a normative judgement that we can accept because of its enactment by a certain authority, or its establishment by a certain social practice, then the legal norm cannot be an operative reason for justifying a decision."[35] This is insofar as one accepts "Hume's law" that from a descriptive statement (in this case that there is a norm, that the legislator has promulgated a certain law) one cannot derive a descriptive or normative statement (in this case the judge's verdict or an individual's decision that he ought to act in a particular way).

A legal norm (that ist, the fact that some prescription has been promulgated by some authority, or that there exists some social practice) gives us, according to Nino, an independent reason for acting if and only if there is a strong normative principle laying it down that we should obey that norm. This principle can be no other than a moral rule, since it cannot be founded on the fact that it derives from some "source", but that it has certain contents. And a normative principle justifying an action founded solely on its "merits", that is, solely on its content, can only be given by a moral rule.

The conclusion of this argument is what Nino calls "the fundamental theorem in philosophy of law": "A legal norm or law only justifies the practical reasoning of judges and other social actors insofar as it is accepted by virtue of a moral judgement that grants legitimacy to certain authority and a descriptive judgement of the prescriptions of that authority."[36] Nino's position can be summarized as a strong thesis of conceptual connection (from the viewpoint of the participant) between law and morality: *no* legal decision is possible without a prior moral decision, that is, without prior acceptance of a moral principle. "A judge cannot justify any decision on the basis of a legal norm [...] if he does not ground the legitimacy of that norm either explicitly or implicitly upon some *moral* principles."[37]

---

[35] C. S. Nino, A Philosophical Reconstruction of Judicial Review, in "Cardozo Law Review", 1993, p. 813.

[36] Ibid., pp. 823 - 824.

[37] Ibid., pp. 814 - 815. Emphasis in original.

According to the Argentinian philosopher, legal validity – once the external (observer's) viewpoint, satisfied with the concept of effectiveness, has been excluded – has meaning only if reformulated as moral validity. Validity as "belonging" to an order is regarded as a typical notion from the observer's viewpoint amounting to the notion of the order's effectiveness, and accordingly incapable of grounding or justifying any practical decision.

Robert Alexy treats the problem of the relation between law and morality differently according to whether the law is regarded as the particular legal norms or as a set of norms, that is, as a legal system. For his theory, this professor from Kiel uses, along the same lines as Carlos Nino, the distinction between "external" (oberver's) viewpoint and "internal" (participant's) viewpoint. From the "external" viewpoint, as far as the particular norms is concerned, it is held not to be possible to establish a necessary classificatory (value-free) connection, and not simply a qualificatory (evaluative) one, between law and morality. From the observer's viewpoint what is needed is a "neutral" concept of law that does not include strong normative elements, that is to say moral ones.[38] Accordingly, since from the external viewpoint the connection between legal rules and moral rules can be no more than classificatory (descriptive, value-free), there is no *necessary* connection between law and morality (as far as its particular norms are concerned). On this point, Alexy concurs with the present great German defender of the positivist thesis of the separation between law and morality, Norbert Hoerster.[39]

As far as sets of norms, legal systems, are concerned, even taking the observer's viewpoint, it must according to Alexy be found that those systems, in order to ground legal decisions or the promulgation of laws arrived at within their framework, contain a claim to rightness of the decision or promulgation. It is this *Anspruch auf Richtigkeit* that distinguishes a legal system from a "meaningless normative order" (say that of a disorganized group of foragers) or a "predatory order" (like that of an organized band of thieves and murderers).

A legal order is held to classify through the claim to legitimacy of its acts. Accordingly, "norm systems that neither implicitly nor explicitly lay claim to rightness are not legal systems. Every legal system lays a claim to rightness".[40] However, since all actually existing normative systems contain this claim to legitimacy or rightness, the practical consequences of this statement are minimal. In any case, as far as legal systems are concerned, and from an "external" point of view, the legal positivist thesis of the separation between law and morality would be only partially correct.

---

[38] See R. Alexy, Begriff und Geltung des Rechts, Freiburg 1992, pp. 56 - 57.

[39] See, e.g., N. Hoerster, Zur Verteidigung der rechtspositivistischen Trennungsthese, in "Archiv für Rechts- und Sozialphilosophie", Beiheft 37, pp. 27 - 32.

[40] R. Alexy, op. cit., p. 62.

The scene changes if we come to take the "internal" viewpoint. Maintaining the distinction between particular norms and legal systems from the participant's viewpoint, as far as particular norms too are concerned, one can, our Kiel professor tells us, establish a necessary classificatory relationship between law and morality. To reach this result, Alexy trusted to Gustav Radbruch's formula that a legal norm is valid and is to be applied if it has been promulgated in accordance with the criteria of the legal system in question and belongs to it. This norm would be valid even if it violated moral principles or rules, except where such violation was so extreme that application of the legal norm would be intolerably unjust.[41]

Robert Alexy offers us the following definition of the concept of law. The law is a normative system that lays claim to rightness *(Richtigkeit)* of its rules. This system is constituted by (I) the set of norms (i) that belong to a constitution *(Verfassung)* that is in general socially effective and (ii) are not extremely unjust. This system is constituted also of (II) the set of norms which, issued in respect for that constitution, possess a minimum of social efficacy (or possibility of being effective) and are not extremely unjust. The normative system of law is further constituted by (III) the principles and other normative arguments that serve (or ought to serve) to found the procedure for applying the law and to fulfil or satisfy the claim to rightness of the system itself.[42]

This definition clearly goes beyond the limits of legal positivist doctrine in at least three directions. Firstly, according to Alexy, principles and other criteria in argument that constitute reasons justifying the *application* of the legal norms are also elements of the legal system. These justificatory reasons largely lie outside the scope of the positive provisions. Accordingly the criteria for legal argumentation, for instance, interpretive methods, or logical rules, have the same dignity as source of law as already attributed to enacted provisions.

Secondly, and here it becomes clear that Alexy's definition is given from the viewpoint of the participant in a given legal system, particular norms that are extremely unjust (Radbruch's criterion) cannot be regarded as valid rules of the system, or, if considered valid, invalidate the system itself by taking away its legality. Here the "justice" of the norm – which is superimposed on its "rightness" – takes primacy over its "validity", a consequence that breaks the splendid isolation of the legal positivist concept of law and introduces moral reasoning (about what is "just") into legal reasoning (about what is "valid" and appropriate to the case).

Thirdly, the principles and criteria for argument elevated to the dignity of basic elements of the legal system retain a strong normative connotation.

---

[41] See G. Radbruch, Gesetzliches Unrecht und übergesetzliches Recht, in idem, Rechtsphilosophie, 8th ed., Stuttgart 1973, pp. 339 - 350.

[42] See R. Alexy, op. cit., p. 201.

These principles and arguments, Alexy tells us, are not just those *de facto* used to justify the procedure of applying the norms, but also and especially those that ought to be used for that justification. Consequently, the legal system is strictly bound up with strong normative considerations, that is, ultimately *moral* ones. Practical reasoning, especially its normative theory, is thus included in the definition of law. Ultimately, here what law is largely amounts to what law *ought to be.*

5. The social responsibility of institutions: "reflexive law", corporatism and legal pluralism

At the end of the 1970s there began to be talk of the crisis of the Social State because growing State intervention was causing all sorts of negative effects: increase in fiscal pressure, increase in public debt, more bureaucratization (or "colonization" as Habermas put it) of social life, growing difficulties in steering an already elephantine State apparatus, growing corporative and interest-group pressures.[43] The machinery of law, loaded with too many tasks, was ending up grinding to a halt. One response to this position has been the reduction in the areas and intensity of State intervention, especially as regards the direct administration of economic centres and the production of social services. However, the solution of reducing law's tasks faced with the complexity of technological society and its many needs and inter-relations has *de facto* been more of an ideology advocated than a viable programme. There are areas that even in the most liberal systems cannot easily be "deregulated": environment, for instance.

The interventionist Welfare State and the instrumentalist conception of law that accompanied it led to what Gunther Teubner has called the "regulatory trilemma", that is, the alternative among (i) the "incongruency" between law and society, their separation and non-communication, and the lack of responsibility of the legal institutions to civil society, (ii) the superlegalization of society, that is, the fact that a large part of social relations go through the loop of law, or are regulated by law or other interventions by legal and administrative institutions, (iii) the super-socialization of law, that is, the fact that the law reflects a large part of the dynamics, organization, values and needs of the active social groups in a given State, showing a significantly passive attitude towards them.[44] This "trilemma" has been responded to by seeking alternative ways to either statism or liberalism. It is in this context that what I would call "responsive" theories of law appear.

---

[43] Cf., e.g., Wachsende Staatsaufgaben – sinkende Steuerungsfähigkeit des Rechts, ed. by D. Grimm, Baden-Baden 1990.

[44] G. Teubner, Das regulatorische Trilemma. Zur Diskussion um post-instrumentale Rechtsmodelle, in "Quaderni fiorentini per la storia del pensiero giuridico moderno", 1984, pp. 125 - 126.

As we know, "responsive law" is a term coined by sociologists Philippe Nonet and Philip Selznick. These two authors identify three main types of law (or better, three stages in the evolution of law) in modern times: (i) repressive law, (ii) autonomous law, (iii) responsive law. These three types of law are responses to, or consequences of, the most relevant question, according to Nonet and Selznick, in the context of legal phenomena: the relation between "integrity" and "openness". There is integrity "where an institution is strongly dedicated to a particular task or can be made responsible for that task by external controls".[45] Openness "presupposes wide extents of discretionality, so that the action of the institutional organs can remain flexible, adaptable and self-correcting".[46]

(i) "Repressive" law is the type that marks the openness and passive and opportunist adaption of legal institutions to the social and political environment. That is, law here takes on a purely instrumental function in relation to the objectives of political and economic power. (ii) "Autonomous" law marks a reaction against indiscriminate openness and further aims at preserving institutional integrity. It makes law close in on itself, reducing its responsibility to the social environment, and accepting as the price of integrity a blind formalism. (iii) "Responsive" law is supposed to seek to resolve the tension caused by autonomous law between formalism on the one hand and the need to adapt legal norms to the environment and its needs on the other. The third type of law, write Nonet and Selznick, "we call responsive, rather than open or adaptable, in order to suggest a capacity for adaptation that is responsible, that is, discriminating and selective".[47]

In "autonomous law" the judge has above all to guarantee the internal consistency of the system, while in "repressive law" the judicial function is supposed to consist in directly promoting certain objectives of relevance to some conception of the public good, that is, some policy. "Responsive law", by contrast, tends to change the judge into a sort of moderator among different normative frameworks, more of an arbiter acting at the same hierachical level as the parties and pursuing a compromise between them than a judge acting more or less autocratically and sanctioning the victory of one party over the other.[48]

---

[45] P. Nonet/P. Selznick, Law and Society in Transition. Toward Responsive Law, New York 1978, p. 76.

[46] Ibid.

[47] Ibid., p. 77.

[48] On the judge's function according to Nonet and Selznick, cf. L. J. Wintgens, Roberto's Crusade, in RECHTSTHEORIE, 1991, p. 107: "According to these scholars, a judge is not the passive instrument in a legal system of preestablished rules and principles. Instead, he actively collaborates in the installment of social and political goals in an environment of political pluralism. This attitude compels judges to a permanent arbitration between concurring values and politics as a target of social change. The judge's task, in their opinion, consists of more than preserving the legal system, without radically smashing the legal context that defines, in the end, his own function."

I personally think that we might define as "responsive" all those theories that propose a type of law that goes beyond formal (or autonomous) law, that is, goes in the direction of rematerializing it without falling into any form of legal instrumentalism, and paying great attention to the value of the formal guarantees offered by the institutions.

As well as Nonet's and Selznick's "responsive law" we find, in the same area of legal sociology, two other theories: (a) of "procedural" law, proposed by Frankfurt professor Rudolf Wiethölter, and (b) of "reflexive" law, whose chief representative, Gunther Teubner, is a Professor at the London School of Economics and Social Science.

Wiethölter portrays an evolutionary theoretical model of law connected with some similarly evolutionary stages in the concept of morality. Here, one may suspect an influence of Kohlberg, and therefore of Apel and Habermas. His scheme is as follows.

(i) First, there is a "rigid" rational morality to which there corresponds law founded solely on formal reasoning, with no relation with any type of social necessity. (ii) Second, there is a "flexible" rational morality. In this stage, the law follows the relativization of the absolute criteria brought about by the "flexible" morality. Thus the law, losing much of its formal security, acquires the capacity to adapt substantially to the interests present in a given society. (iii) Finally, in the third evolutionary stage there comes, according to Wiethölter, a "communicatively" rational morality: this is the law he calls "procedural". This type of law aims not so much at offering social performance or legal guarantees as at establishing the conditions for the possibility of such performance or guarantees through procedural structures. "By proceduralization of the law – writes the same Wiethölter – one may understand the transformation of a social context of legal freedoms [...] into a system of justification of the respective new social contexts of 'ideas' and 'interests'."[49]

"Procedural" law is thus a sort of compromise between the traditional formal law of the liberal State and social needs expressed through sometimes self-managed machinery. "Proceduralization of law – concludes Wiethölter – might be the contemporary manifestation of a bourgeois society which, while it does not (yet?) give up its institutional hopes (synthesis of individual and societal needs, reconciliation of achieved 'culture' and realizable 'interests'),

[49] R. Wiethölter, Materialization and Proceduralization in Modern Law, in Dilemmas of Law, in the Welfare State, ed. by G. Teubner, Berlin 1986, p. 246. Cf. K. Eder, Prozedurale Legitimität. Moderne Rechtsentwicklung jenseits von formaler Rationalisierung, in "Zeitschrift für Rechtssoziologie", 1986, pp. 1 - 30, and K. Eder, Die Autorität des Rechts. Eine soziale Kritik prozeduraler Rationalität, in "Zeitschrift für Rechtssoziologie", 1987, pp. 193 - 230. Cf. also K. H. Ladeur, "Prozedurale Rationalität". Steigerung der Legitimationsfähigkeit oder der Leistungsfähigkeit des Rechtssystems, in "Zeitschrift für Rechtssoziologie", 1986, pp. 265 - 274.

does not start to follow different paths to that institutionalization."[50] "Proceduralization thus aims not so much at social performance guarantees (as 'right of freedom'), nor at concession (as 'political administration'), but at conditions for the possibility (and then organization, procedure, staff for realization) of such guarantees and concessions of integrable reconciliations of interests through legal conduct arrangements."[51]

So-called "reflexive" law, the most prominent theoreticians of which are Helmut Willke and Gunther Teubner, is very similar to Rudolf Wiethölter's "procedural law". In the theory of "reflexive law" too, we meet an evolutionary paradigm of the concept of law. According to these authors, in modern times there are three "stages" of law, expressed in three distinct programmes: (a) the conditional programme, (b) the instrumental programme, and (c) the relational programme.[52]

(a) According to the conditional programme, law establishes a very broad set of rules that act as framework conditions within which specific action and conduct is assigned to decision by individuals, conceived of as abstract subject. As Niklas Luhmann writes – he makes great use, though synchronistically rather then diachronistically, of the opposition between "conditional programme" and "instrumental programme" – the conditional programmes are established "independently of who is to decide".[53] The "conditional programme", if this concept is used diachronically and an evolutionary paradigm is adopted, corresponds to the ideal type of the classical liberal State.

(b) According to the "instrumental programme", the law directly and specifically regulates the conduct and action of concretely determined individuals. Here there is no scope for autonomy left to the subjects. They are mere addressees of the rules, passive subjects of a game played out over their heads. The "instrumental programme" corresponds, if the evolutionary paradigm is

---

[50] R. Wiethölter, Materialization and Proceduralization in Modern Law, op. cit., p. 249.

[51] R. Wiethölter, Proceduralization of the Category of Law, in Critical Legal Thought. An American-German Debate, ed. by C. Joerges/D. M. Trubek, Baden-Baden 1989, pp. 509 - 510. Cf. also R. Wiethölter, Entwicklung des Rechtsbegriffs (am Beispiel des BVG-Urteils zum Mitbestimmungsgesetz und – allgemeiner – an Beispielen des sog. Sonderprivatrechts), in "Jahrbuch für Rechtssoziologie und Rechtstheorie", 1982, pp. 38 - 59, and R. Wiethölter, Zum Fortbildungsrecht der (richterlichen) Rechtsfortbildung: Fragen eines lesenden Recht-Fertigungslehrers, in "Vierteljahresschrift für Gesetzgebung und Rechtswissenschaft", 1988, pp. 27 - 28.

[52] G. Teubner/H. Willke, Kontext und Autonomie: Gesellschaftliche Selbststeuerung durch reflexives Recht, in "Zeitschrift für Rechtssoziologie", 1984, pp. 4ff. Cf. N. Luhmann, Einige Probleme mit "reflexivem Recht", in "Zeitschrift für Rechtssoziologie", 1985, pp. 1 - 18, and I. Maus, Perspektiven "reflexiven Rechts" und Deregulierungstendenzen, in "Kritische Justiz", 1986, pp. 390 - 405.

[53] N. Luhmann, Zweckbegriff und Systemrationalität, Frankfurt am Main 1984, p. 102.

adopted, to the ideal type of the social State in its various versions (democratic, authoritarian, totalitarian). One version of this ideal type is held to be represented by the Italian Republican Constitution of 1948. Here "the law no longer confines itself to providing the general and abstract canons of private action, that is the conditions that allow the individuals' will to pursue freely chosen ends. The *selection of purposes* now falls within the competence of the legislator, who accordingly wills in place of the individuals, or encourages and promotes their will towards specific destinations. The essence of law is radically transformed by this: no longer an 'instrumental' rule offering to individuals procedures and techniques suitable for implementing the decisions, but a 'final' rule, prescribing, suggesting or counselling given purposes".[54] In the social State the law takes on, as it were, the characteristic signs of private contract, or better of an administrative act: it is merely a more or less immediate and effective response to a specific, concrete problem whose solution lies in the law itself and not in any possible subsequent legal acts formed within the framework of the law.

(c) Finally, the "relational programme" is made up of rules that lay down conditions no longer for the action of individuals but of groups and organizations. Here there is what some have defined as "constitutional organization" in a sense opposite to the Constitution (as fundamental law of guarantees) of subjective rights and private contracts, typical of the "conditional programme". The "relational programme" is manifested in "reflexive law". In this type of law "the legislator does not pursue immediate objectives; the procedural norms serve more to put those concerned in a position to regulate their own affairs themselves".[55] (The most typical example of "reflexive" law would be wage bargaining.) "Reflexive" law serves only to bring about legal monitoring of social self-regulation,[56] and to allow enhancement of the pluralism of the sources of law.[57] This new evolutionary stage of law corresponds as ideal type to the liberal-social State, or better the neo-corporatist one.[58]

---

[54] N. Irti, L'età della decodificazione, Milan 1979, p. 15. All this was already pointed out by Giuseppe Capograssi. See, e.g., G. Capograssi, L'ambiguità del diritto contemporaneo, also in idem, Incertezze sull'individuo, Milan 1969, pp. 98 - 99.

[55] J. Habermas, Recht und Moral (Tanner Lectures), now also in idem, Faktizität und Geltung, op. cit., p. 553. Such proposals, I believe, are close to ideas that Italian "communitarian" jurists like Pietro Rescigno were defending over thirty years ago: see P. Rescigno, Persona e comunità, Bologna 1966, see esp. the article Le società intermedie (pp. 29 - 67).

[56] Cf. G. Teubner, After Legal Instrumentalism? Strategic Models of Post-regulatory Law, in "International Journal of the Sociology of Law", 1984, p. 384.

[57] See G. Teubner, The two Faces of Janus: Rethinking Legal Pluralism, in "Cardozo Law Review", 1992, pp. 1443 ff.

[58] For a classification of the meanings of the term "corporatism" see G. Tarello, Corporativismo, in Enciclopedia Feltrinelli Fischer, vol. 27, Scienze Politiche 1 (Stato e politica), ed. by A. Negri, Milan 1970, pp. 68 - 81. Applying Tarello's scheme to "reflexive" law, it might represent a version of corporatism in its "ideological, legal,

6. Beyond State Law?

Summarizing, here are the points where the image of law as State law displays its weakness, at least as far as the States of Western Europe are concerned.

(i) The State can no longer present itself as "sovereign" internally (because of growing social pluralism, extra-judicial procedures for solving legal conflicts and the development of a concept of constitution bound by moral rights and principles), nor externally (with the creation of supra-national legal systems that take over powers of the national system). The "sovereign" presents itself not so much as a subject, an entity, a "body", but more as a network of communications, the object of which is the formation of a universalizable and therefore binding public will, that is, it is presented as a "procedure".

In modern constitutional States the principle that "auctoritas non veritas facit legem" can hardly apply. *De facto* these are legal systems where the legislator's discretion is controlled (and limited) in relation to both the constitutional values and principles and the law's appropriateness to its object, that is, its "reasonableness". In other words, we might say that, at least as far as legal systems where there is judicial review of the constitutionality of law are concerned, what Noberto Bobbio maintains as the supreme principle of judicial interpretation, "dura lex sed lex", no longer applies.[59] This Italian philosopher asserts that this principle is confirmed by the principle that in the States of law, in the event of conflict between the two ideal models guiding legal interpretation, that of the "good legislator" and that of the "loyal judge" (faithful to the law), the second ideal (the "loyal judge") takes primacy. That is to say that where the law cannot be interpreted as an act emanating from a just, reasonable subject, the judge would nonetheless be obliged in virtue of being bound by the law to apply that law even if it were unjust and unreasonable. However, where minimal judicial review of the constitutionality of laws is possible, the "loyal judge" is just the one that defends the ideal of the "good legislator", since one of the constitutive claims of a democratic constitution is that it is a spokesman for ideals of justice and reasonableness. The judge's loyalty is here

---

pluralist" sense: "In this sense, "corporatism" serves to designate the ideology, or conception, or model of legal organization on which standing as sources (exclusive or competing with others) or production of law of the overall system has to be granted to "corporations" of "corporate groups" or (sometimes the preferred term) "institutions", all of them entities that can be identified when recording or describing social facts and at the same time are autonomous "legal" entities insofar as they express both internal legal orders and general norms, which may conflict with each other" (ibid., pp. 70 - 71).

[59] See N. Bobbio, Le bon legislateur, in Legal Reasoning. Proceedings of the World Congress for Legal and Social Philosophy (30. 8. - 3. 9. 1971), ed. by H. Hubien, Brussels 1971, pp. 243 - 249.

exercised not so much in relation to the law (the legislator) as in relation to the *good law,* that is the Constitution and its principles (or, the "good legislator").

(ii) There is doubt of the possibility of a science or descriptive theory of law that does not assume either holistic concepts (for instance a certain concept of law) or cultural concepts (for instance, a notion of subjective rights or of human rights) that cannot be reduced to contents of norms in force (duties, chiefly) in the legal system.[60] To describe or understand what a legal system or even a statute prescribes it does not seem possible to do without extra-legal, and in some way extra-juridical, assumptions. That is, it is doubted that the written law is the sole source for knowing the law, so that there is growing skepticism as to the legal positivist method that from its birth accompanied the political form of the modern State, and contributed to its establishment.

(iii) There is doubt that a merely descriptive concept of law can be capable of constituting a body of reasons for acting without referring to, or presupposing, some normative concept of law. It is doubted that it is possible to go from the "is" of a norm (or better, from the fact that a norm exists in a text, is respected in social custom or is dictated by some authority) to the "ought" of the conduct that the norm prescribes, without having at the top of the legal structure of norms (or of normative reasoning) a basic normative norm; that is, Kelsen's *Grundnorm,* but no longer as a cognitive tool or assumption (serving for the knowledge or description of some law), but as the justificatory foundation for the normativity (the motivating power) of the rules within the system. As we know, Kelsen's *Grundnorm* is a "hypothetical" norm in the sense that it is a norm that must be "assumed" if some system of positive rules is to be known. Kelsen calls it the "logical transcendental assumption". However, as Kelsen admits, there are other ways of knowing law (a system of rules) that are not strictly "juridical". It is possible to have a sociological knowledge of law. But if this is so, the *Grundnorm* no longer has the same rank as a Kantian "logico-transcendental" assumption, since one can "know" even without it. Moreover, a "hypothetical" norm like the *Grundnorm* cannot constitute an independent reason for acting. For this, a "categorical" norm is required.

This theoretical position and the critique of Kelsen's *Grundnorm* it implies to some extent reflects the fact that the modern constitutional State, by clearly distinguishing between Constitution and legislation and structuring the Constitution in terms of fundamental principles and rights, *explicitly* introduces strong moral elements into the system, and subordinates positive law to principles of justice and the fundamental rights of the citizens. These are no longer "subjects", as modern public law dogmatics still defines them (*der Untertan,* from Gerber to Kelsen – not to forget Heinrich Mann), but *citizens.* Their

[60] On the difficulties of reducing laws to duties and to positive norms, see F. Laporta, Sobre el concepto de derechos humanos, in "Doxa", no. 4, 1987, pp. 23ff.

rights are not founded, as in Jellinek's doctrine, on a situation of total subordination to the State power. In fact we are faced in the modern European constitutional State with an opposite procedure. Restrictions on individual freedoms within the constitutional State are justified preferentially with the argument that these restrictions serve to guarantee the fundamental, innate, inviolable freedoms of the individuals. In this connection, contemporary constitutionalism renews the link with the rationalist doctrines of natural law that seemed irreparably dissolved by the illwill of legal positivism. The dynamic between State law and State of Law that support and justify each other breaks down faced with the mistrust of some constitutions (and some judges) who take civil rights and the principles of justice seriously.

(iv) Finally, there is doubt that the programme dominating law is "conditional", without falling into its opposite ("instrumental" programme). The conditional programme and the instrumental programme are both based on the virtues of a strong centralized power which in the first case guarantees the autonomy of the subjects, and in the second directly accomplished the ends regarded as useful or suitable for the development of society and its welfare. "Reflexive" law and the "relational" programme, or "procedural" law, distrust this centrality of the State and may be the motors for an effective legal pluralism where the sources of law are no longer solely those of the State.

These theories of "reflexive law" may be asked at least two questions. The first concerns the meaning of the legal changes that underpin the assertion of an evolutionary trend towards "reflexive law". Recently, for instance, Erhard Blankenburg has stressed the fact that neo-corporatist regulatory strategies, on the birth of which Teubner founded his thesis of "reflexive law" as a delegalizing response, also bring a need to legalize areas hitherto unregulated and left to the vicissitudes of a struggle of conflicting forces. "What Teubner called the 'reflexive law' carries that notion: delegating so far legal conflict regulation to the social institutions concerned and considering law and legal institutions as a last resort only for those cases which resist self-regulation. However, the historical development to institutions of reflexive law has more often been the result of the reverse; to quote some examples forwarded by Teubner himself: the self-regulation of collective agreements in industrial relations or the handling of consumer complaints by informal easy-access institutions do not *replace* former legal regulation, but rather are attempts to formalize formerly unregulated areas of conflict."[61]

The second question is if and in how far it may be asserted that the liberal social State assumed by "reflexive law" actually exists in today's social and

---

[61] E. Blankenburg, Legal Cultures Compared, in Laws and Rights. Proceedings of the International Congress of Sociology of Law for the Ninth Centenary of the University of Bologna, ed. by V. Ferrari, Milan 1991, p. 97.

political reality. Be that as it may, the one thing certain is that if one wishes to avoid on the one hand the incongruency between law and society (a danger inherent in the "conditional programme") and on the other the super-legalization of society and super-socialization of law (risk both typical of the "instrumental programme", the first more of the authoritarian social State and the second more of the democratic social State), then account will have to be taken of the possibilities offered by the model of "reflexive law".

Is Contemporary Law Post-Modern?

By Valentin Petev, Münster

In this paper I will discuss the question as to what extent contemporary legal thought is affected by the post-modern critique. I intend to show that the differing approaches in modern legal theory do not at all offer a heterogenous set of ideas; that theoretical efforts on an international level focus on joint projects which demonstrate that theorists think in concurring patterns. This paper is dedicated to Robert S. Summers, who in many profound analyses has brought to bear the common core in the structure of thought within different legal systems while respecting their particular character.[1]

I will treat this topic under the following three main headings: The post-modern critique of present-day Western society; the attempt to describe this society in other, socio-axiological terms; the rejection of the characterization of law as autonomous, self-regulating, reflexive and subsidiary.

(1) Today's communicatory society offers a multi-facetted set of images and is therefore difficult to describe. Some critics emphasize the inherent crisis-laden momenta in economical development and in the functioning of administration, and underline the dangers and risks associated with the uncontrolled expansion of technology and science. Harsh critics see the basic flaw of this society in the hopeless fracturing of ethical convictions and political concepts that questions the legitimacy of society's foundation. Whereas the differentiation of social structures and the breaking up of the spheres of science, morality and art were still seen by Max Weber[2] as a sign of the rationality of Western culture, contemporary authors qualify the polarization of the social worlds of life as a serious crisis.[3] Postmodern criticism emphasizes the variety and heterogeneity of the social reality of our time and diagnoses a break with previous systems, which purported to offer an explanation of the total system of knowledge and experience. From the perspective of post-modern criticism,

[1] P. S. Atiyah / R. S. Summers, Form and Substance in Anglo-American Law, Oxford 1987; R. S. Summers and M. Taruffo, Interpretation and Comparative Analysis, in: D. N. MacCormick / R. S. Summers (eds.), Interpreting Statutes. A Comparative Study, Aldershot et al. 1991, pp. 461 - 510.

[2] Cf. J. Habermas, Die Moderne – ein unvollendetes Projekt, in: W. Welsch (ed.), Wege aus der Moderne. Schlüsseltexte der Postmoderne-Diskussion, Weinheim 1988, p. 185.

[3] J. A. Hall, Diagnoses of Our Time. Six Views on Our Social Condition, London 1981.

reality is not meant to be homogenous, but heterogenous, not harmonious, but dramatic, not uniform, but diversely structured. Thus, the basic categories of the post-modern worldview are plurality, discontinuity, antagonism and particularity.[4]

I am not convinced that the plurality of contemporary society, as far as social interests, political goals and ethical convictions are concerned, does necessarily imply antagonism and discontinuity; that there is no possibility of comprehensive and expedient designs for shaping society that are borne at least by major social groups; and that therefore particularity is the dominant feature of social life. We cannot deny that in our time some political movements have not only aimed at new goals but have brought about profoundly new political conceptions. One misses with certainty the essential aspects of our time, if one does not grasp the growing demand for respecting basic and human rights and for the widening of the social security system. Some see in this a continuation of the central tasks of classical modernism.[5] But it would be equally appropriate to regard them as the great challenges of our time. Salient features of the present political spirit are also the call for new ethical standards in the sciences, the striving for a clean environment and the prevention of war as well as the integration in larger, supranational political associations.

In our contemporary open society all these claims and desires are introduced into a broadly based, institutionalized discourse. Neither the undeniable differences between the interests of the participants of such a discourse nor the difficulty of the conceptual determination of these interests can be reduced to a *différend* (Lyotard). It would certainly not be correct to deny, because of the differing semantics of the various kinds of discourse, the possibility of mediating between the participants' positions and of finding prospective solutions.[6] To adopt such an attitude would be destructive, for it would ultimately thwart the performance of practical discourse. People only speak to each other under the premise that mutual understanding is possible. In today's open society ethical-political discourse and legal decision-making processes take place constantly. Both are neither without meaning nor without consequence because of the supposed incommensurability of the respective ways of speaking, nor do they lead inevitably to a "totalization", i.e. the foisting of a determinate way of thinking and arguing, which does not give fair due to the

---

[4] W. Welsch, Unsere postmoderne Moderne, 2nd ed., Weinheim 1988, p. 188.

[5] R. Wiethölter, Politik und Aufklärung, in: J. Rüsen / E. Lampert / P. Glotz (eds.), Die Zukunft der Aufklärung, Frankfurt/Main 1988, pp. 36 seq.

[6] Yet this is stated by J.-F. Lyotard, Le différend, Paris 1983, pp. 203, 212, passim; but, on the other hand, there are optimistic variants of the postmodern philosophy, which regard the diagnosed plurality of society not as a symptom of its dissolution, but as an innovative and positive version of the modern understanding of society, which can be observed in the fields of science, philosophy, literature and art (Welsch, s. supra note 4).

particular position of at least one of the participants, and thereby consistently doing him injustice. Therefore, one cannot generally state that the social practice in the open society is characterized by a permanent disregard of the legitimate interest of others, as post-modern critics claim.

Whoever analyses and criticizes today's Western societies, should take into consideration that there is a spirited philosophical discussion on problems of social communication, political action and ethical concerns, which surmounts the narrow metaphysical analysis of the individual self-consciousness as the point of convergence of any philosophical investigation.[7] One should not underestimate the contributions of the *Transzendentalpragmatik,* which is in quest of "ultimate justifications" for norms of social conduct[8] and, in a period of wide-ranging plurality of ethical and political convictions, presupposes the possibility of practical reason and tries to justify those norms rationally. Beyond this, there are influential voices in favour of an "ontology of the present", which focusses on the conception of the unlimited autonomy of the subject as an ethically and politically informed citizen, who draws, on his own behalf, the final consequences of the evaluation of his time.[9] If some claim a "factual powerlessness" or even the "non-existence of an autonomous subject",[10] they should keep in mind that it was exactly this much-slandered citizen who, together with his kind, brought forth in this century democratic political systems of considerable quality and recently effected the collapse of the totalitarian regime in Eastern Europe.

(2) Legal philosophy and the philosophy of State have disclosed in their respective analyses further characteristics of present-day society worthy of criticism. Thus, a crisis has often been diagnosed in the legitimacy of social institutions, the consequences of which are "ungovernability" and "social disintegration".[11] The social controlling and regulating function of law is called into question, and the doubts regarding the capacity of law go so far as to see

---

[7] Cf. J. Habermas, Nachmetaphysisches Denken, Frankfurt/Main 1988, pp. 14 seq.

[8] Cf. K.-O. Apel, Diskurs und Verantwortung, Frankfurt/Main 1988; V. Hösle, Die Krise der Gegenwart und die Verantwortung der Philosophie, München 1990.

[9] For such an approach cf. V. Descombes, Philosophie par gros temps, Paris 1989, pp. 149 seq.

[10] See the detailed analysis of the different approaches within the critique of reason and subject by A. Wellmer, Zur Dialektik von Moderne und Postmoderne, Frankfurt/Main 1985, pp. 70 seq.

[11] Cf. eg., W. Conolly (ed)., Legitimacy and the State, New York 1984, and A. Aarnio / K. Tuori (eds.), Law, Morality and Discursive Rationality, Helsinki 1989; only sporadic publications point out the positive aspects of the contemporary "Rechts- und Sozialstaat", cf., e.g., L. M. Friedman, Legal Culture and the Welfare State, in: G. Teubner (ed.), Dilemmas of Law in the Welfare State, Berlin 1986, pp. 13 seq.; O. Weinberger, Rechtskultur und soziale Effizienz der Jurisprudenz, Archiv für Rechts- und Sozialphilosophie (ARSP), Beiheft 35, 1990, pp. 148 seq.

in it an alien force which destroys the originality of the social world ("colonization of the *Lebenswelt*").[12]

It is with great theoretical effort that deficiencies of modern law are made explicit and referred back to a set of basic causes. It is asserted that modern law is no longer capable of influencing social life positively. Law is shown as an inadequate, "repressive" and "autonomous" system that either serves the oppressive powers or only protects its own integrity as a differentiated institution. In contrast to this, what would be needed here is a "responsive law" which meets social needs and claims.[13] To the previously raised objection regarding the steady growth of legal over-regulation of social phenomena[14] is now added the criticism of a qualitative inadequacy of legal regulation. Law not only provides the framework for social conduct, but also tries to produce rules of substantial content ("materialization of formal law").[15] The latter is judged to be highly disadvantageous.

The image of the law of today's society which thus emerges is not a flattering one. The law is not only accused of exhibiting slight defects but even of a fundamental regulative insufficiency, which cannot be eliminated by minor improvements. This naturally raises crucial questions: What are the basic defects of today's law? and, even more fundamentally: Do we, in the complex contemporary society, need a law of such deficiency? A general answer postmodern critics give to these could be: If we need a law at all, we need another kind of law, a "post-regulatory" law, which works parallel to other mechanisms of regulation and would only be used in a supplementary manner.

This line of questioning is by no means new. Each school of legal philosophy has, so far, attempted to design the specificity of law as a social phenomenon and its resemblance to other normative systems of social conduct, such as morals, religion and custom. The conclusions to which the diverse theories have come on this issue vary. Up to the present, there has been no commonly accepted answer to the crucial questions which the law poses concerning its nature, validity and its effects upon the other social phenomena. The different attributes of law which these schools emphasize serve more as distinguishing criteria for the particular theories than as a substantial characteristic of the

[12] Habermas, Die Moderne – ein unvollendetes Projekt, s. supra, note 2.

[13] P. Nonet / P. Selznick, Law and Society in Transition. Toward Responsive Law, New York 1978, p. 14.

[14] Cf., among numerous publications raising this objection, R. Voigt (ed.), Verrechtlichung, Frankfurt/Main 1980; Id. (ed.), Gegentendenzen zur Verrechtlichung, Opladen 1983; Id. (ed.), Grenzen des Rechts, Pfaffenweiler 1987.

[15] G. Teubner, The Transformation of Law in the Welfare State, in: G. Teubner (ed.), Dilemmas of Law in the Welfare State, Berlin 1986, pp. 4 seq.; concerning a conception of "proceduralization" of law, according to which a "post-interventionalistic-minded legislator should renounce giving material legal norms", cf. G. Teubner, Recht als autopoietisches System, Frankfurt/Main 1989, pp. 83 seq.

phenomenon called law. The novelty in today's post-modern criticism of law is its effort to find the place of law within a general theory of society. Recently the general sociological system theory and the autopoietic theory have become engaged in this issue.[16] Their cardinal thesis is that of autonomy and self-reference of social sub-systems. This thesis has wide-ranging consequences for the understanding of law and its role in society. It emphasizes that there are distinct domains in society – such as politics, economy, science, religion, family etc. – which, functioning as sub-systems, are mainly characterized by their self-reference, self-constitution and self-regulation. Accordingly, the law, also a sub-system, intrinsically reveals these qualities. In this manner, the very nature of law and its functions are purportedly detailed. This prompts us to examine more closely what this thesis holds.

It seems easier and perhaps even more fascinating to speak of "systems" and, in analogy to observable "living systems", to ascribe to them features and regularities in structure and functioning than to deal – taking into account a long philosophical tradition – with conflicts of interests, ethical evaluation, norm-justification, practical information and the motivation to and performance of social acts by individuals and social groups. Yet, the difficult questions which arise from the traditional perspective are not satisfactorily answered but only replaced by specific problems of thinking in terms of "systems". No matter how this approach construes things, the epistemological problems remain the same.[17]

I do not think that it is possible to identify distinct areas of social relations as "closed" and "self-referential". The empirically observable and theoretically emphasized differentiation and complexity of social conditions in modern society has led rather to a pervasion and entangling of social relations – e. g. in economy, politics and law – and not to a closing off and isolation of systems which follow an inherent logic. There are, for instance, hardly any economic branches which are free from legal regulation. All decisions made in the economic field are either linked to legal provisions or have legal consequences of one kind or another. These decisions, whenever they touch upon fundamental social problems in this field, such as employment, wages or social secu-

---

[16] Cf., e. g., N. Luhmann, Soziale Systeme, Frankfurt/Main 1984; H. R. Maturana, Man and Society, in: F. Benseler / P. M. Hejl / W. K. Köck (eds.), Autopoiesis, Communication and Society, Frankfurt/Main, New York 1980, pp. 11 - 31; G. Teubner (ed.), Autopoietic Law: A New Approach to Law and Society, Berlin 1988; Id., Recht als autopoietisches System, Frankfurt/Main 1989; M. van de Kerchove / F. Ost, Le système juridique entre ordre et désordre, Paris 1988; W. Krawietz, Recht und moderne Systemtheorie, in: Rechtstheorie, Beiheft 18, 1986, pp. 281 seq.; J. Nocke, Autopoiesis. Rechtssoziologie in seltsamen Schleifen, in: Kritische Justiz 1986, pp. 363 seq.; S. Tönnies, Ist das Recht ein Biotop?, in: Rechtstheorie 1987, pp. 105 seq.

[17] Social reality as something individual, collective, personified, systemized is always a mental artefact – e. g. individual, people, grand sujet, juridical person, system, cf. J. Baudrillard, A l'ombre des majorités silencieuses. La fin du social, Paris 1982.

rity benefits, become the subject of practical discussion, in which persons from all social branches having a stake in the respective matters are involved, not only the forces of an "autonomous" economic system.

In addition, the impact of law on the economy is not of a somewhat diffuse kind. It takes on rather the shape of a genuine regulation of social conditions and may not be minimized, such as the autopoietic theory does. It is not accurate to regard law solely as a quantitative momentum in economic reasoning. Generally, law here is not primarily considered to be a cost-inducing factor, which is taken into account and whose effects are to be ruled out (e.g. by calculating the payment of damages), but as an obligatory parameter that may not be deviated from in the case of investments, taxes and the taking out of loans. That shows the preponderant role of law over the purportedly "self-regulative" functioning of economic processes.

A similar situation prevails in the field of science: In the open society scientific issues and their solutions are not treated "esoterically" within the scope of scientific investigation. It is true that there are specific implications here such as individual freedom of investigation and the "logic of discovery", but the institutions themselves as well as the results achieved are regulated by and beneficial for the whole of society.

The intertwining of economy, science, politics and law is undeniable, and I do not believe that anything is gained in theoretical, methodological or practical respect by maintaining the thesis of the separation and closedness of social subsystems.

The fallacies of the criticized view become even more obvious in the case of politics. It is misleading to think of politics as an ontologically independent "system", for there are no politics as such, no political relationships which do not stem from a particular social branch. The political discourse is not concerned with "pure" categories of interests and powers; it always deals with notions, which affect distinct social areas where politics unfold their very function. Therefore, we do not merely speak of politics but always of economic policy, of cultural and domestic affairs, education or foreign affairs. Without this reference to a discrete subject matter the political phenomena would not be capable of being subjected to a theoretically sufficient analysis.

(3) Finally, when we focus on the phenomenon of law, we become aware once more how untenable some of the main theses of the autopoietic theory are. We can hardly qualify the law as an "autonomous" system. Both ontologically and epistemologically it is mandatory not to separate law from its societal substrate, i.e. from the actual social relationships regulated by law, even when in the process of interpretation and application law is primarily seen as a system of coherent normative propositions. According to the institutional, realistic point of view, which I hold, law is never solely a construction

of social reality, but at the same time it is – all fallibility of knowledge considered – this reality itself.

In characterizing law as autonomous and self-referential,[18] as the autopoietic theory does, one neglects its regulatory function: it is obvious that this function cannot exhaust itself in a self-regulation of the "system" law. Rather, law by its nature intervenes in the different spheres of society such as economy, technology, science, the environment, culture etc. and gives them a distinctive shape. Moreover, it would not be correct to state that law decides by itself what belongs to its own system, i.e. what can claim legal quality. What law really determines is the way in which acts belonging to the legal system come into existence and become valid. The rules of law creation exhibit their formal character in bringing about the principle of legality. They do not indicate which social matters should be subjected to legal regulation. This is but a political decision. It is ineluctible for a close ontological analysis of law to stress that law does not create itself, but, as I contend, is applied by the political power of a society as a regulating and controlling mechanism.

This can be illustrated by several examples. It is not the law which decides, for instance, whether measures are to be taken to protect the environment, or whether the school system should be changed, whether the length of military service should be shortened, or the child adoption procedure be modified. It is the legitimate political power in an open, democratic society which has these issues at its disposal. The political measures can display various legal forms. In any case, if one wants to effect a certain mode of social conduct, one has to ensure that such conduct is made binding for all. In an open, heterogenously structured society this can only be achieved by legal regulation, for in such a society law is the sole system of norms of social conduct, which – unlike morals and custom – holds general obligatoriness.

Whichever kind of legal regulation is chosen depends on the relevance of the respective matters: Issues of utmost importance, for instance, are usually regulated by statutes. In this case, the parliament does not only operate as the supreme norm-giving body, but also as the leading political instance, which in the final run decides what social relationships should be governed by law. Equally, modifications of the legal system itself – its premises, normative contents and sanctions – are the consequence of political decisions. According to this line of argumentation, law presents itself as an "open" system.

It is, of course, also possible to use here the metaphor of the "cognitive openness" of the legal system. Yet, this metaphor becomes superfluous as

---

[18] Cf. G. Teubner, Recht als autopoietisches System, pp. 29 seq.; N. Luhmann, The Self-Reproduction of Law and its Limits, in: G. Teubner (ed.), Dilemmas of Law in the Welfare State, Berlin 1986, p. 112; N. Luhmann, Die Einheit des Rechtssystems, in: RECHTSTHEORIE 1983, pp. 129 seq., 133 seq., 139; K.-H. Ladeur, Perspektiven einer post-modernen Rechtstheorie, in: RECHTSTHEORIE 1985, pp. 400 seq.

soon as one discards, as I do, the thesis of its "normative closedness". Moreover, it is in itself misleading, because it suggests a process of cognition by the law itself, which does not reveal the intrinsic function of law, i. e. to be an efficient instrument in regulating social affairs. Law does not "learn" as individuals do, it does not seek advantageous knowledge in order to preserve its own integrity, but serves as a normative regulatory mechanism, which fulfills its very function by active intervention in the shaping of society.

The autopoietic theory cannot ignore the fact that law has a decisive impact on society, but it purports that law regulates society by regulating itself.[19] Yet, the full extent of this problem first becomes clear, when one considers that in the perspective of the autopoietic theory the different social spheres are themselves, as systems, autonomous, closed and self-regulating. Here Teubner rightly raises the issue: "How is one to escape, by means of legislation, the closed circle of social worlds?"[20] If this thesis does not completely obscure the regulatory function of law – which would be a regrettable result – it in any case makes the understanding of this function more difficult. If the various social spheres are ultimately not autonomous, in contrast to what the autopoietic theory contends, the question should be asked, whether law may only intervene in a subsidiary way, as "reflexive law" or "context regulation". Yet, this would mean that within these spheres social rules of conduct would be produced which completely satisfy the needs of regulation. But if this were to be the case, what would law have to contribute to the regulation of social relationships?

The thesis of self-regulation within distinct social spheres can easily be refuted empirically. Indeed, in contrast both to non-complex, homogenous societies and to the social order of early capitalism, we do not observe anywhere in our post-industrial society an intense, spontaneous regulation of social relationships from within – neither in the economic sphere nor in the field of personal relationships. This state of affairs can also be explained in theoretical terms. What characterizes complex societies is that here divergent interests of major social groups are at stake, whose comprehensive reconciliation is not to be expected. In particular, it is not easy to find acceptable solutions for the opposing parties, e. g. in the field of economic competition or the protection of the environment. In this respect, the familial relationships show a further particularity: in addition to the distinct interests of those involved, which are to be brought into accord in a subtle way, ethical views of the public have to be taken into account. These constellations of interests cannot be mediated without the presence of authority, and this can only be the authority of law.

---

[19] Teubner (Recht als autopoietisches System, s. supra, note 15, p. 82) puts this very suggestively: "Law regulates society by regulating itself."

[20] Teubner, ibid. p. 90.

Legal regulation is thus necessary, even indispensable. And any allusion to an autonomy, to a self-regulation of social life obscures the correct theoretical approach of the role law plays in present-day society. Law should not be viewed as an external, alien force, which intervenes and "colonizes", and even destroys the "inner" logic of the subject matter under consideration. Law is, as has been pointed out, an expression of the political authority of a complex, differentiated society, solely capable of mediating between differing interests. Its specificity lies in its capacity to establish generally binding regulations in a society disposed to conflict.

It is another problem as to how legal regulations are to be shaped in the future. Modern legislation, which already avails of multiple mechanisms of regulation,[21] will have to become more flexible still. It should try to interpret the impulses deriving from political and ethical discourse, which in an open society is conducted on different levels. It has to be improved as far as technique and method of regulation are concerned, and also has to be open to unconventional regulation patterns and to fundamental reforms.

The European integration process raises anew the issue of the role of law. This particularly concerns the nature, function and validity of law. The nature of law will certainly remain the same, because society in an integrated Europe will continue to have plurality and democracy as its aim. Law will express the prevailing political and ethical convictions and the will of major social groups at a certain time. The function of law will not change either. It will also in the future consist of the regulation of the essential structures of society according to the above mentioned political will. It is to be expected that the legislature is going to change its configuration. Beside the different national parliaments and a unified Pan-European parliament, legislative power is going to be conferred on regional and specialised bodies. All this will not lead to a denaturation of validity, to a restriction of the binding force of law. The law may perhaps alter its mode of governing social relationships, e.g. by diminishing the use of sanctional provisions, but legal norms will not be of a lesser binding character.

Thus, we may well state that the cardinal problems of our time will continue to be solved with the assistance of law. It is not likely that spontaneous social arrangements will sweep aside law's domain. In any case, the way that lies ahead will not lead away from law. We still need law, a law whose socio-axiological foundations are constantly subjected to philosophical reflexion. This will be the flexible, democratic and social law of the 21st century.

---

[21] Cf. I. Maus, Perspektiven "flexiblen Rechts" im Kontext gegenseitiger Deregulierungstendenzen, in: Kritische Justiz 1986, pp. 391 - 400; H. Rottleuthner, Legal Evolution and the Limits of Law, in: A. Aarnio / K. Tuori (eds.), Law, Morality and Discursive Rationality, Helsinki 1988, pp. 217 seq.

Formalism or Anti-Formalism

Reconsidering an Important Dispute in Jurisprudence

By Ota Weinberger, Graz

I. Preface

The dispute between formalism and anti-formalism in jurisprudence and legal practice is one of the main fields of interest of Professor Robert S. Summers. His contributions to this field of research are remarkable, yet – as he underlines himself – the problems in this area are not explained and settled definitively. Therefore, as a homage on his jubilee, I shall try to contribute to the clarification of these theoretically and practically essential problems by applying logical analysis to the main issues of this field of juristic work.

The main contributions of Professor Summers to this field – as I see it – are:

(i) an explanation of lawyer's instrumentalism and the clarification of its limits,

(ii) the justification of the view that formality is a general feature of law, and

(iii) the recognition that the notion of formality in law, state organization and jurisprudence is a kind of family notion (in the sense of Wittgenstein) which has its varieties of cases in different fields. Professor Summers' enumeration of the main areas in which formality is applied in law as well as his characterization of these different problems is important.

(iv) Summers analyzes different legal systems with respect to their tendencies to be formalistic or anti-formalistic. He detects important differences between the American and the English legal system in this regard.

(v) Professor Summers distinguishes first-level and second-level rationales which can be used to underpin legal opinions and decisions. First-level arguments are based mainly on the recognition of social aims which are intended by the law, and which, therefore, justify the content of legal rules or decisions. Second-level rationales take the structure and effects of legal processes into consideration and aim to secure formal justice and the rule of law in social reality. Second-level reasons often modify the content of the law even at the expense of choosing a solution which is sub-optimal from the point of view of first-level considerations.

The main topics of law in which formality can apply in different degrees are the following:

a) the features of rules and other legal precepts,

b) the determination of legal validity,

c) the use of the principle of stare decisis,

d) the limited power of judges to modify law,

e) the methods of interpreting statutes and other legal norms, and

f) the formality of legal processes and the adherence of governmental activities to the rule of law.

The structure of legal and political systems may reveal differences in being more or less formalistic.[1]

Summers' underlining of the essential role of formality in law and in the body of the state and the political system is in fact not in conflict with his accepting some basic ideas of pragmatic instrumentalism in jurisprudence as it is reasonable both to regard law as an instrument for realizing social and political aims and to understand the essential role of formal or even formalistic elements in the legal system and in legal procedures.

II. Programme of My Approach

Starting from some remarks about the difficulties of using family notions in science and philosophy I shall first argue that different elements of formality in law and politics should be treated separately, and that the argumentation for more or less formality is distinct in different fields even though we are accustomed to characterize them all commonly as 'formal' or 'non-formal'. Next I shall give a short account of the structure theoretical approach to jurisprudence and explain the connection of this approach with the conception of lawyer's argumentation. The purpose of this part of my paper is to show the relevance of structure theory of law and of the general theory of lawyer's argumentation with regard to the dispute of formalism and anti-formalism in jurisprudence. On this theoretical basis I shall explain my views about the dispute between the partisans of formalism and the partisans of anti-formalism. Besides structural theoretical arguments I shall adduce other arguments following from communication theory and from my conception of neo-

[1] Cf. R. S. Summers, The Formal Character of Law, *Cambridge Law Journal,* 51 (2), July 1992, pp. 242 - 262; the same, On Analyzing and Characterizing the General Style of a Legal System as Formal or as Substantive, RECHTSTHEORIE, 23 (1990), pp. 27 - 34; the same, Instrumentalismus und amerikanische Rechtstheorie, Darstellung und Kritik, Freiburg/München 1983.

institutionalism.[2] Finally, I shall deal with the relation between Summers' approach and the consequences of neo-institutionalism for the methodology of jurisprudence.

III. Family Notions

Notions constituted by family resemblance have specific logical and methodological features. A family notion (the class of objects to which this notion refers) is not defined by a common quality of all designata of the notion, but the field of reference of the notion is determined by similarity which holds between pairs of elements of the extension of the family notion.

Family notions are useful tools of ordinary language, but they lead to great difficulties when applied in scientific or philosophical analysis; there are no nomic theses which would be valid for all designata of the notion. Therefore, it is necessary to split the field of the family notion into subclasses (subnotions) which exhibit the same feature in such a way that it becomes possible to state nomic assertions about the elements of the subclass.

Concerning the fields of the attribution of greater or smaller formality of legal phenomena we have to distinguish different fields in which we evaluate formality, and in which we can argue for or against formalistic conceptions. It can be shown that in these different areas non-formality means rather different things.

An important consequence of the distinction of different fields in which we consider formalism or anti-formalism is the fact that we can often reasonably argue for formality in one field and against formality in the other.

IV. A Sketch of Structure Theory of Law

The structural theoretical approach to jurisprudence has a great tradition which ressembles closely the general aims of analytical philosophy. This study is directed towards the understanding of the general features of our linguistic tools to express the law; it leads to the analysis of logical relations and argumentative operations in the legal system.

The analytical approach is based on the distinction of form and content in such a way that the logical and linguistic form in which legal content can be

[2] Concerning my conception of neo-institutionalism (or normative institutionalism) see: D. N. MacCormick/O. Weinberger, *An Institutional Theory of Law. New Approaches to Legal Positivism,* Dordrecht et al. 1986; O. Weinberger, *Law, Institution and Legal Politics. Fundamental Problems of Legal Theory and Social Philosophy,* Dordrecht et al. 1991.

expressed is not in conflict with the analysis of the content, but on the contrary, formal structures are only receptacles used to present a content.[3]

The analytical tradition encompasses Bentham, Austin, Kelsen, Merkl, Weyr, Hart etc. A kind of logical structuring of jurisprudence was always implied by the analytical endeavour. Only seldom philosophers of this attitude confined their considerations to formal (this means here: to logical) aspects, but they generally were convinced that any juristic consideration has its logical-linguistic aspect, but that it is at the same time bound to present also analyses of content.[4]

The structure theoretical approach in jurisprudence is formal in the following sense: it uses formulae in order to characterize formal generality of the expressions by which the content of legal norms of any legal system can be expressed. But this formal characterization based on the abstraction from possible content means nothing else than the fact that the variables of the formulae may take different values out of their range of variability.

The fundamental result of the analytical approach is the recognition of the semantic specificity of normative sentences. Therefore, jurisprudence as well as the whole of practical philosophy is built on the basis of dichotomic semantics which strictly distinguishes descriptive sentences and normative sentences (or more appropriately: practical sentences) as distinct semantic categories.

The structure theoretical approach led with necessity to two results:

(i) It directed attention to the development of logical systems of practical reasoning, namely to the logic of normative sentences (deontic logic), to the logic of preferences, to formal teleology and to formal axiology.

(ii) From the methodological point of view lawyer's reasoning distinguishes clearly the argumentative views of considerations *de lega lata, de lege ferenda* and *de lege applicanda.*

The logical structuring of jurisprudence which is necessarily implied by the structure theoretical approach had two important consequences for legal methodology and the explanation of legal processes:

(1) Legal reasoning is characterized by the interrelation of general rules and individual cases. The determination of decisions of individual cases is justified by general rules, but also the evaluation of individual facts and the justification

---

[3] The controversy of formalism and anti-formalism in legal methodology does not arise from this distinction in logic. Logical analysis deals with formal relations and operations and uses the distinction of form and content. Yet in logic there is no place for the dispute of formalism and anti-formalism which characterizes contemporary jurisprudence.

[4] In logical analysis it is clear from the very beginning that form and content is to be distinguished, but also that formal schemes have to be interpreted in order to give actual information.

of general legal conceptions, i.e. rules, is based on the principle of comparing individual cases and on the principle of generalization. All weighing under the ideals of justice is characterized by a general perspective based on the relation of general rules and individual cases.

[A person who denies the validity of normological deduction, especially the validity of a kind of normlogical rule *de omni et nullo* – as e.g. Hans Kelsen in the latest stage of his teaching[5] – destroys the very nature of all juristic considerations including the analyses of justice.]

(2) The body of the legal system and the complex system of the state linked with this normative nucleus of the state as a social institution form a unity. Even though this unity is formed only as a rational reconstruction of social reality (which may be defective in reality in some respects) it is bound together by logical relations and dynamic processes based on logical relations.

The theory and the reality of law and the state is concieved of as a dynamic process based on legally relevant acts and logical relations. It is clear that these dynamic processes and their logical bases justifying their validity can be characterized as a formal bound – insofar as an evaluation of the respective content of valid law is not necessary, i.e. is not part of the justificatory reasoning, in this process.

The new stage of analytical jurisprudence introduces specific differences of possible structures of legal content. By these steps it comes into conflict with the primary intention of this approach which emphasized initially the unique and universal form of the whole content of law, but it became also much more precise and, therefore, had greater explicative force.[6]

V. Reconsidering the Case of Instrumentalism

In some respects the view of instrumentalism is well founded: Law and the whole legal organization is institutionalized in order to realize certain social and political purposes. It is a piece of human reality which serves certain needs of society. Law is an element of human action and, therefore, instrumental. In principle, it is also a sound view that work in the field of law is something like a piece of social engineering – or that it should have this role.

---

[5] See H. Kelsen, *Allgemeine Theorie der Normen,* ed. by K. Ringhofer/R. Walter, Vienna 1979; O. Weinberger, *Normentheorie als Grundlage der Jurisprudenz und Ethik. Eine Auseinandersetzung mit Hans Kelsens Theorie der Normen,* Berlin 1981.

[6] I refer mainly to the distinction between legal rules and legal principles (implying also different structures of logical argumentation as Dworkin has shown) and to the distinction between rules of behaviour and power-conferring rules. This type of rules is formally irreducible to rules of behaviour. It plays an important role in the dynamic theory of law, in the theory of legal validity and in the explanation of the structure of institutions and their organization.

But the claim for the application of the instrumentalist conception is also intended as a kind of criticism of the formalistic bounds in the construction and application of the law. And in this respect the conception is not free of problems. It is often the case that formality brings about useful social effects in general – e. g. unambiguousness of the content and a strict determination of the stated ought – although it may be the case that in concrete situations it leads to conflict with the presupposed social purposes. Then the existence of a formal regulation may be on the whole more useful than a more adequate solution determinded by teleological considerations in the special case. Nevertheless, I believe that in applying the law officials should have in mind the fact, that their decisions have to serve the role of building up sound social relations. This is extremely important in all cases of judicial discretion, but this consideration should not destroy the clear formal bounds of normative regulations.

Another critical remark restricting the possibilities of instrumentalism seems to me important. It follows from the view of non-cognitivism. We have, of course, some vague idea of the notion of social aims and purposes, but the class of valid social purposes is not the same in all states and collectivities. The idea of social aims is different in different political systems.

Even if a class of certain social purposes is accepted the relative weight of the different aims is not the same for all persons who accept the same class of social purposes. From this consideration it follows that the postulate of instrumentalism is not a clear guide, because it is an indubitable fact, that engineering depends on the presupposed aims, and that these are not given a priori. I admit that here may be a broad consensus about valid social aims, but there is also an important divergence in detail and in the weight of preferences within a single system of instrumental valuation.

Therefore, the case of instrumentalism is not so strong as it seems at first sight. It should not be conceived of as an argument against normative bounds and in favour of anti-legalism.

VI. Formal or Teleological Interpretation

The partisans of formality in law adduce strong arguments in favour of strictly linguistically based legal hermeneutics. The two main reasons for formally restricted interpretation in jurisprudence are the following: (a) Only an interpretation restricted by linguistically valid arguments can guarantee a faithful recognition of the legal sources since any teleological consideration is liable to the danger of distortion and of replacing the views of the empowered legislator by the ideas of the interpreter, and (b) the so-called creative interpretation when executed only on the doctrinal level means taking influence from outside on the system of orders given by legally empowered instances: namely from persons without legislative power.[7]

There is, I believe, a strong argument – resulting from general hermeneutics – in favour of the view that the interpretation of precepts (as well as of individual legal acts, contracts, etc.) is by its very nature not only formally determined by linguistic elements, but realized also under teleological aspects. The process of understanding communications in interpersonal processes of communication is always realized in light of the presupposition that the message has been communicated with a certain intention and as an act directed towards certain aims (which, of course, in general are not part of the communication, but are its implicit presupposition). The same holds, of course, also in the field of legal communication: It would be in some way impossible to realize the process of understanding normative communications if we would strictly abstract them from their intention. The open question is then only how to clarify by convincing arguments the real intention of the law (which is by no means always clear or explicitly expressed).

In legal practice it is more or less a question of degree whether we (or the tradition of a legal system) put greater weight on linguistic, historical, or instrumental considerations as arguments for interpretative justification.

There is a tendency to name interpretative argumentation guided primarily by linguistic arguments formal and the use of teleological and instrumental arguments non-formal. I would prefer to avoid this terminology.

Legal production of norms has the character of heteronomous ordering. Therefore, interpersonal communication is always essential in this field. It is much easier to communicate normative rules of behaviour particularly if the ordered behaviour is determined by a single description than to communicate teleological determination. Purposes are sometimes characterized only vaguely, and in most cases the teleological determination is established by a class of purposes not by one single objective. This situation leads to the effect that teleological determination is not unambiguous. The application of different objectives as criteria of teleological determination depends also on the weighing of the importance of the single purposes of the teleological deliberation. The choice or the justification on the basis of purposes is not sufficiently characterized by the class of aims, but depends also on the preferences attached to the different objectives.

To establish normative rules consists both in producing rules of behaviour or power-conferring rules and on the determination of social objectives of the law. But normative rules of behaviour and power-conferring rules, teleological determinants – even if stated explicitly – are not unambiguous determinants.

---

[7] This does not concern official interpretation which is an indispensable element of applying the law, and which is therefore realized on the basis of an empowered legal process. Doctrinal interpretation must take into consideration the results of official interpretation.

Therefore, teleological or instrumental considerations have only a supplementary function.

VII. Formal Determination of Legal Validity

Legal validity concerns either the whole legal system, namely a system of norms to which validity is attributed, or the functional relation between this corpus of norms and the institution of the state, or a certain norm under consideration which is conceived as valid within an established system of law. In both cases neo-institutionalism justifies the recognition of validity based on the actual relation between norms and social reality of institutional character. Following the fundamental conception of neo-institutionalism the finding that an institution in fact works on the basis of the normative system under consideration is the necessary and sufficient reason for the view that this system of norms is valid, i.e. is part of the respective social reality.

A question concerning the validity of the normative system as a whole can be answered only on the basis of an empirical examination of institutional facts, namely the functioning of the institution on the basis of the respective system of norms. Also, the validity of a specific norm as an element of a valid normative order is an institutional fact. It must be analyzed as an actual social fact which should be in empirical accordance with life in the institution. The structure of modern legal systems establishes explicit rules by which we can get an immediate insight into the question of validity of specific norms of the system. The essential way of proving *ad oculos* the validity of a norm is to examine the process by which the norm has been created. This means that the construction of a legal system is conceived of as a dynamic process realized by rule-abiding creation acts of norms. [Cf. the dynamic conception of law in the mind of the pure theory of law or in the conception of neo-institutionalism.[8]] In a similar way Hart introduces secondary rules, namely rules of recognition and rules of change, which are used to justify the recognition of validity.

Modern law systems clarify by help of special institutions, namely formal promulgation, the recognition of the validity of norms, and they generally give also clear answers about the relative force of different kinds of precepts. We can regard these institutions as tools by which the law is formalized. The usefulness of formalization in these matters is evident. But in a certain respect univocity of legal precepts is not granted even by this formalization: the actual content of the law depends on the interpretation of formally established sources. In fact, valid law is more the result of interpretation than the wording of the rules in statutes or other kinds of precepts.

---

[8] Cf. O. Weinberger, Nuove considerazioni sulla teoria della nomodinamica, in: L. Gianformaggio (ed.), *Sistemi normativi statici e dinamici. Analisi di una tipologia Kelseniana,* Torino 1991, pp. 36 - 66.

VIII. The Determining Function of the Content of Rules

In principle all normative rules serve to determine what is ordered (or what is allowed), but this determination can be more or less strictly dependent on the structure and the content of the rule.

Rules of behaviour can express the condition under which the normative consequences apply in different ways, namely so that subsumption can be determined simply by observable features, or value decisions of different kinds are necessary in order to decide whether the subsumption of a certain case is justified. Principles are normative rules of a special kind: they express a more abstract legal content which does not justify subsumption, but which determine only criteria of valuation or objectives which should be realized. We may say that rules determining subsumption are more formal than principles which state only a relevant view of the legal consideration, but do not by themselves provide a strict determination of legal decisions.

The formulation of the legal content can restrict or open fields for discretion or give very strict guidance on how cases are to be decided. Whether the rules may give strict guidance or be open to discretion concerning the decision is – in my view – not so much a matter of preference for or against formalistic procedures, but more a question of appropriateness in relation to the kind of cases under consideration.

IX. Conclusion

Formality and formalistic views mean very different things in different fields of law and politics. Therefore, it would be misleading to be globally for or against formality. In some fields of legal life formalistic methods are able to bring considerable improvement. The thesis that in principle law is an institution with instrumental character and having therefore its teleological determination is by no means in conflict with formal legal structures and processes. Teleological arguments are of essential importance in the field of legislation, juridical discretion and in a specific way in legal hermeneutics. If we wish to understand legal norms, we must be aware of the fact that establishing legal rules and communicating them is always realized with a certain social intention. This fact does not mean that interpretation of law should not be based primarily on valid texts of legal sources. In cases of doubt it seems reasonable in my opinion to argue also by social aims and to adduce also considerations about the effect of different possible interpretations. The fact that there is a certain interplay and also a certain tension between juristic formality and teleological interpretation in the mind of political and social ideas seems to be useful. The understanding of the law should not be confined to teleological analysis and not be restricted to the weighing under teleological aspects, but we should realize also a functional analysis of legal institutions. We have learned that the working of norms and legal institutions change in dependence of the different context of institutional reality. Functional analysis in the sense of neo-institutionalism transgresses the view of instrumentalism, but is not anti-formalistic in principle.

Robert Samuel Summers

A Bibliography of his Publications 1960 - 1994

(Through March 1994)

A. Books and Monographs

1. *Law: Its Nature, Functions, and Limits* (Prentice Hall, Inc., Englewood Cliffs, N.J. 1965) (with Charles G. Howard) 1st ed. 466 pp.
2. *Commercial Transactions* (West Pub. Co., St. Paul 1969) (with Richard E. Speidel and James J. White) 1st ed. 1144 pp.
3. *Law: Its Nature, Functions, and Limits* (Prentice Hall, Inc. Englewood Cliffs, N.J. 1972) (with Charles G. Howard) 2nd ed. 798 pp.
4. *The Uniform Commercial Code* (West Pub. Co., St. Paul 1972) (with James J. White) 1st ed. 1054 pp.
5. *The American Legal System* (Ginn and Co., Boston 1973) (with A. B. Campbell and G. Hubbard) 317 pp.
6. *Justice and Order Through Law* (Ginn and Co., Boston 1973) (with A. B. Campbell and G. Hubbard) 237 pp.
7. *Commercial and Consumer Law* (West Pub. Co., St. Paul 1974) (with Richard E. Speidel and James J. White) 2nd ed. 1475 pp.
8. *Collective Bargaining and Public Benefit Conferral – A Jurisprudential Critique* (Cornell Univ. ILR Monograph, Ithaca 1976) 65 pp.
9. *Het pragmatisch instrumentalisme* (Standaard Wetenschappelijke Uitgeverij, Amsterdam 1980) 261 pp.
10. *The Uniform Commercial Code* (West Pub. Co., St. Paul 1980) (with James J. White) 2nd ed. 1250 pp.
11. *Commercial and Consumer Law* (West Pub. Co., St. Paul 1981) (with Richard E. Speidel and James J. White) 3rd ed. 1490 pp.
12. *Instrumentalism and American Legal Theory* (Cornell U. Press, Ithaca 1982) 295 pp.
13. *Pragmatischer Instrumentalismus und amerikanische Rechtstheorie* (Karl Alber, Freiburg 1983) 208 pp.

14. *Lon L. Fuller* (Stanford U. Press, Stanford 1984) 174 pp.; paperback edition: Arnold Press, London.

15. *Law: Its Nature, Functions, and Limits* (West Pub. Co., St. Paul 1986) (with Kevin Clermont, et al.) 3rd ed. 801 pp.

16. *Commercial Law – Teaching Materials* (West Pub. Co., St. Paul 1987) (with Richard E. Speidel and James J. White) 4th ed. 1448 pp.

17. *Contract and Related Obligation: Theory, Doctrine and Practice* (West Pub. Co., St. Paul 1987) (with Robert A. Hillman) 1st ed. 1074 pp.

18. *Form and Substance in Anglo-American Law* (Oxford U. Press, Oxford 1987) (with Patrick S. Atiyah) 437 pp.

19. *The Uniform Commercial Code* (for students) (West Pub. Co., St. Paul 1988) (with James J. White) 3rd ed. 1386 pp.

20. *The Uniform Commercial Code* (for scholars, judges and practitioners) (West Pub. Co., St. Paul 1988) (with James J. White) 3rd ed. 2 vols., 1787 pp.

21. *Article 2A of the Uniform Commercial Code – Leases of Goods* (West Pub. Co., St. Paul 1991) (with James J. White) 419 pp.

22. *Interpreting Statutes – A Comparative Study* (Dartmouth Pub. Co., Aldershot 1991) (with D. Neil MacCormick) (co-editor, and contributor to four chapters) 560 pp.

23. *Form and Substance In Anglo-American Law* (Oxford U. Press, Oxford 1991) (with Patrick S. Atiyah) paperback edition with minor revisions, 437 pp.

24. *Essays on the Nature of Law and Legal Reasoning* (Duncker and Humblot, Berlin 1992) (previously published essays with revisions), 217 pp.

25. *Contract and Related Obligation: Theory, Doctrine and Practice* (West Pub. Co., St. Paul 1992) (with Robert A. Hillman) 2nd ed., 1037 pp.

26. *Commercial Law – Teaching Materials* (West Pub. Co., St. Paul 1993) (with Richard E. Speidel and James J. White) 5th ed., 1738 pp.

27. *The Uniform Commercial Code – Negotiable Instruments and Funds Transfers: Revised Articles 3 and 4, and Article 4A* (West Pub. Co., St. Paul 1993) (with James J. White) 401 pp.

B. Books edited

28. *Essays in Legal Philosophy* (U. of Calif. Press, Berkeley 1968) (general editor, and contributor) 307 pp.

29. *More Essays in Legal Philosophy* (U. of Calif. Press, Berkeley 1971) (general editor, and contributor) 161 pp.

30. *American Legal Theory* (New York Univ. Press, N.Y. 1992) (A collection of readings with a general introduction and biographical sketches; editor and contributor) 605 pp.

C. Articles, Review-Articles, and Commentaries

31. "A Critique of the Business Purpose Doctrine," vol. 41 *Oregon L. Rev.*, pp. 38 - 48 (1961).

32. "A Note on Symbolic Logic and the Law, vol. 13 *J. Legal Ed.*, pp. 486 - 492 (1961).

33. "Should Oregon Adopt the Uniform Commercial Code Concept of Floating Lien?", vol. 41 *Oregon L. Rev.*, pp. 182 - 188 (1961).

34. "H. L. A. Hart on Justice," vol. 59 *J. of Philosophy*, pp. 497 - 499 (1962).

35. "Symbolic Logic and the Law," vol. 15 *J. Legal Ed.*, pp. 60 - 63 (1962).

36. "Secured Transactions Under the Uniform Commercial Code," vol. 42 *Oregon L. Rev.*, pp. 1 - 24 (1962).

37. "Justiciability," vol. 26 *Modern L. Rev.*, pp. 530 - 538 (1963).

38. "Logic in the Law," vol. 72 *MIND*, pp. 254 - 259 (1963).

39. "Is and Ought in Legal Philosophy," vol. 13 *The Philosophical Quarterly*, pp. 147 - 159 (1963).

40. "Professor H. L. A. Hart's Concept of Law," vol. 1963 *Duke L. J.*, pp. 629 - 670 (1963).

41. "Security Interests in a Retail Merchant's Inventory: California Amends the Code," vol. 16 *Stanford L. Rev.*, pp. 149 - 159 (1963).

42. "A Rejoinder to Professor Mullock," vol. 1965 *Duke L. J.*, pp. 76 - 81 (1965).

43. "Professor Fuller on Morality and Law," vol. 18 *J. Legal Ed.*, pp. 1 - 27 (1965).

44. "The New Analytical Jurists," vol. 41 *New York Univ. L. Rev.*, pp. 861 - 896 (1966).

45. "Good Faith in General Contract Law and the Sales Provisions of the Uniform Commercial Code," vol. 54 *Virginia L. Rev.*, pp. 195 - 267 (1968).

46. "Law, Adjudicative Processes and Civil Justice," in *Law, Reason and Justice*, pp. 169 - 185 (1969) (New York Univ. Press, G. Hughes, ed.).

47. "A Critique of Professor Fried's Anatomy of Values," vol. 56 *Cornell L. Rev.*, pp. 598 - 625 (1971).

48. "The Technique Element in Law," vol. 59 *Calif. L. Rev.*, pp. 733 - 751 (1971).

49. "Evaluating and Improving Legal Processes – A Plea for Process Values," vol. 60 *Cornell L. Rev.*, pp. 1 - 52 (1974).

50. "The Present State of Legal Theory in the United States," vol. 6 *Rechtstheorie,* pp. 65 - 82 (1975).

51. "Naive Instrumentalism and the Law," in *Law, Morality and Society – Essays in Honor of H. L. A. Hart,* pp. 119 - 131 (1977) (Oxford U. Press, P. Hacker and J. Raz, eds.).

52. "Two Types of Substantive Reasons in the Common Law," X *Beiheft,* (Neue Folge) *Archiv für Rechts- und Sozialphilosophie,* pp. 217 - 230 (1978).

53. "Two Types of Substantive Reasons – The Core of a Theory of Common Law Justification", vol. 63 *Cornell L. Rev.*, pp. 707 - 788 (1978).

54. "Comment on the Adversary System and Justice," in *Philosophical Law,* pp. 122 - 126 (1978) (Greenwood Press, R. Bronaugh, ed.).

55. "Professor Fuller's Jurisprudence and America's Dominant Philosophy of Law," vol. 92 *Harvard L. Rev.*, pp. 433 - 449 (1978).

56. "General Equitable Principles Under Section 1 - 103 of the Uniform Commercial Code," vol. 72 *Northwestern L. Rev.*, pp. 906 - 946 (1978).

57. "Pragmatic Instrumentalism – The Most Influential Philosophy of Law in the United States During the Twentieth Century," *Archiv für Rechts- und Sozialphilosophie* Supplementa Vol. 1, pt. 2, pp. 511 - 524 (1979).

58. "Public Employee Collective Bargaining Substantially Diminishes Democracy," vol. 1 *Government Union Rev.*, pp. 5 - 22 (1980).

59. "Pragmatic Instrumentalism in Twentieth Century American Legal Thought – A Synthesis and Critique of Our Dominant Theory About Law and Its Use, vol. 66 *Cornell L. Rev.*, pp. 861 - 948 (1981), translated, in part, into Italian: "Lo Instrumento Pragmatico e la teoria America del Diritto," vol. 37 *Rivista Trimestrale di Diritto Procedura Civile,* pp. 1083 - 1093 (1983).

60. "Economists' Reasons for Common Law Decisions – A Preliminary Inquiry," vol. 1 *Oxford J. Legal Studies,* pp. 213 - 255 (1981), with Leigh B. Kelly.

61. "What Factors Explain Our Failure to Progress Toward Efficiency?", vol. 4 *Research in Law and Economics,* pp. 65 - 74 (1981) (JAI Press, Inc., R. Zerbe ed.).

62. "Working Conceptions of the Law," vol. 1 *Law and Philosophy,* pp. 263 - 289 (1982) (also appears in *Law, Morality and Rights,* pp. 3 - 30 (1983) (Reidel Pub. Co., M. Stewart ed.).

63. "Reply to Mr. Mackie," vol. 1 *Law and Philosophy,* pp. 303 - 314 (1982).

64. "The General Duty of Good Faith – Its Recognition and Conceptualization in the New Restatement of Contracts," vol. 67 *Cornell L. Rev.,* pp. 810 - 840 (1982).

65. "Concluding Comments" (the Summers-Mackie exchange) in *Law, Morality and Rights,* pp. 51 - 63 (1983) (Reidel Pub. Co., M. Stewart ed.).

66. "Comments on the Foundations of Legal Reasoning," Metatheorie juristischer Argumentation, *Schriften zur Rechtstheorie, Heft* 108, pp. 145 - 157.

67. "Professor MacCormick on H. L. A. Hart's Legal Theory," vol. 31 American J. Comp. Law, pp. 481 - 488.

68. "Pragmatic Instrumentalism and American Legal Theory," vol. 13 *Rechtstheorie,* pp. 257 - 268 (1982).

69. "Comments on Alan R. White's Facts in the Law," *Beiheft,* (Neue Folge) *Archiv für Rechts- und Sozialphilosophie,* pp. 120 - 126 (1983).

70. "The Future of Economics in Legal Education," vol. 33 *J. Legal Ed.,* pp. 337 - 358 (1983).

71. "Goal Reasons in Common Law Cases – Are They Predictive?", in *Theory of Legal Science,* pp. 345 - 355 (1984) (A. Peczenik ed.).

72. "On Identifying and Reconstructing a General Legal Theory: Some Thoughts Prompted by Professor Moore's Critique," vol. 69 *Cornell L. Rev.,* pp. 1014 - 1046 (1984), translated, in part, into Japanese: in *Kansai Gakuin U. L. J.* 47 (1987).

73. "Fuller on Legal Education," vol. 34 *J. Legal Ed.,* pp. 8 - 21 (1984).

74. "Comment on the Foundations of Constitutional Economics" in *Constitutional Economics,* pp. 157 - 160 (1984) (Lexington Books, R. McKenzie ed.).

75. "Toward a Better General Theory of Legal Validity," vol. 16 *Rechtstheorie,* pp. 65 - 83 (1985).

76. "Some Considerations Which May Lead Lawmakers to Modify a Policy When Adopting It As Law," vol. 141 *Zeitschrift für die gesamte Staatswissenschaft,* pp. 41 - 57 (1985).

77. "The Virtues and Vices of Conceiving of Law As If It Were a Machine Technology," vol. 17 *Rechtstheorie,* pp. 1 - 12 (1986).

78. "Summers' Primer on Fuller's Jurisprudence – A Wholly Disinterested Assessment of the Reviews of Professors Wueste and Le Bel," vol. 71 *Cornell L. Rev.*, pp. 1231 - 1251 (1986).

79. "Form and Substance in Legal Reasoning," in *Essays in Honor of Torstein Eckhoff,* pp. 700 - 715 (Tano Press, S. Evju ed.) (also included in *Rotterdam Lectures in Jurisprudence* (Gouda Press, J. Van Dunné, ed. 1989)), translated into Italian: "Form e Sostanza Ragionaimento Guiridico, vol. 110 *Studi Senesi,* pp. 143 - 167 (1986).

80. "Economics and the Autonomy of Law, Legal Analysis and Legal Theory," *Rechtstheorie* Beiheft 10, pp. 395 - 408 (1986).

81. "Why Common Law Courts Seldom Need to Assess Closely the Comparative Force of Conflicting Substantive Reasons," in vol. 1 *Reason in Law,* pp. 207 - 223 (1987) (Giuffré, Milan, E. Pattaro, ed.).

82. "Positivism, Natural Law, and the Theory of Legal Validity," *Archiv für Rechts- und Sozialphilosophie,* Supplementa III, pp. 62 - 67 (1988).

83. "The Ideal Socio-Legal Order – Its Rule of Law Dimension," vol. 1 *Ratio Juris* 154 - 161 (1988).

84. "The Emergence of the Doctrine of Good Faith in 20th Century American Contract Law," in *Rechtsdogmatik und Praktische Vernunft,* pp. 127 - 142 (1989) (Vandenhoeck and Ruprecht, R. Dreier und O. Behrends, eds.).

85. "The Dominant Legal Theory in the U. S. A. in the Twentieth Century," vol. 7 *Journal of Soviet State and Law* 109 - 116 (1989) (translated into Russian by Viktor Mozolin).

86. "Theory, Formality and Practical Legal Criticism," vol. 106 *Law Quarterly Rev.*, pp. 407 - 430 (1990).

87. "Strict Liability in Tort for Personal Injuries Caused by Dangerously Defective Products – Aspects of the American Experience," in *Lectures on Products Liability – U. of Helsinki Jubilee Seminar,* pp. 23 - 48 (L. Kallioma, ed.) (1990).

88. "Peirce and America's Dominant Philosophy of Law" in *Peirce and Law,* pp. 153 - 162 (Peter Lang Pub. Co., R. Kevelson, ed.) (1991).

89. "Judge Richard Posner's Jurisprudence," vol. 89 *Michigan L. Rev.*, pp. 1302 - 1333 (1991).

90. "Statutes and Contracts as Founts of Formal Reasoning," in *Essays for Patrick Atiyah,* pp. 71 - 85 (P. Cane and J. Stapelton eds., Oxford U. Press) (1991).

91. "On Analyzing and Characterizing The General Style of a Legal System as Formal or as Substantive," vol. 23 *Rechtstheorie,* pp. 27 - 34 (1992).

92. "The Formal Character of Law," vol. 51 *Cambridge L. J.,* pp. 242 - 262 (1992).

93. "The Argument from Ordinary Meaning in Statutory Interpretation", vol. 43 *Northern Ireland Law Q.,* pp. 213 - 236 (1992) (with G. Marshall).

94. "Interpreting Statutes – A Comparative Study; *Archiv für Rechts- und Sozialphilosophie* Beiheft 51, pp. 255 - 263 (1993).

95. "The Limited Efficacy of Law", *Rechtsnorm und Rechtswirklichkeit – Festschrift für Werner Krawietz,* pp. 417 - 425 (1993) (Duncker & Humblot, Aulis Aarnio et al. eds.)

96. "A Formal Theory of the Rule of Law", vol. 6 *Ratio Juris* 127 - 142 (1993).

97. "Der formale Charakter des Rechts II", vol. 80 *Archiv für Rechts- und Sozialphilosophie,* pp. 66 - 84 (1994).

98. "The Formal Character of Law III", forthcoming in vol. 25 *Rechtstheorie* (1994).

99. "Rudolf von Jhering's Influence on American Legal Theory – A Selective Account", forthcoming in *Jhering Todestag Symposion.*

D. Book Reviews

100. Wasserstrom, *The Judicial Decision,* vol. 37 *New York Univ. L. Rev.,* pp. 962 - 968 (1962).

101. Hart, *Law, Liberty, and Morality,* vol. 38 *New York Univ. L. Rev.,* pp. 1201 - 1213 (1963).

102. Stone, *Legal System and Lawyer's Reasonings,* vol. 53 *Calif. L. Rev.,* pp. 386 - 395 (1965).

103. Shuman, *Legal Positivism, Its Scope and Limitations,* vol. 16 *Philosophical Q.,* pp. 88 - 91 (1966).

104. MacGuigan, *Jurisprudence: Readings and Cases,* vol. 2 *Ottawa L. Rev.,* pp. 249 - 252 (1967).

105. Hart, *Punishment and Responsibility,* vol. 19 *U. of Toronto L. J.,* pp. 642 - 653 (1968).

106. Bentham, *Of Laws in General,* vol. 21 *Univ. of Toronto L. J.,* pp. 445 - 448 (1971).

107. Christie, *Jurisprudence,* vol. 74 *Michigan L. Rev.,* pp. 178 - 184 (1975).

E. Brief Essays, Notes, and Tributes

108. "Annual Survey of Oregon Law – Commercial Law and Contracts", vol. 40 *Oregon L. Rev.*, pp. 197 - 211 (1961).

109. "Annual Survey of Oregon Law – Commercial Law and Contracts", vol. 41 *Oregon L. Rev.*, pp. 200 - 210 (1962).

110. "General Introduction to the Code", *California Commercial Law I* (U. of California), pp. 1 - 19 (1966).

111. "Legal Philosophy at Oxford", VIII *Foreign Exchange Bulletin*, pp. 9 (1966).

112. "On Writing & Editing a Law Book: An Interview with Professor Robert S. Summers," vol. 21 *Cornell Law Forum* 1969 No. 2, pp. 8 - 9 (1969).

113. *Bankruptcy – Problem, Process, Reform* (Brookings, D. T. Stanley and Marjorie Girth eds. and coauthors) (served as one of the six principal field researchers for this empirical study of the workings of the bankruptcy system) (1971).

114. "The Nature, Functions and Limits of Law," vol. 24 *Cornell Law Forum*, pp. 2 - 5 (1972).

115. "Free Press, Closed Shops, And the Value of a Bill of Rights, vol. 3 *Cornell Law Forum* No. 1, pp. 12 - 15 (1976).

116. "Pragmatic Instrumentalism: America's Leading Theory of Law," vol. 5 *Cornell Law Forum* No. 1, pp. 15 - 20 (1978).

117. "What is the Area of Greatest Deficiency in Legal Education?," vol. 6 *Cornell Law Forum* No. 3, pp. 17 - 21 (1980).

118. "Dean Cramton and Cornell Law School," vol. 65 *Cornell L. Rev.*, pp. 733 - 736 (1980).

119. "Pragmatic Instrumentalism – The Most Influential Philosophy of Law in the United States During the Twentieth Century," *Archiv für Rechts- und Sozialphilosophie* Supplementa Vol. 1, Part 2, pp. 511 - 524 (1983).

120. "Lawyers, Professors, and A Leading Law School," vol. 10 *Cornell Law Forum* No. 3, pp. 2 - 5 (1983).

121. "Lon L. Fuller's Jurisprudence and the Possibility It Was Much Influenced by G. W. F. Hegel," vol. 10 *Cornell Law Forum* No. 1, pp. 9 - 13 (1983).

122. "Roscoe Pound" in *Biographical Dictionary of the Common Law* pp. 427 - 431 (1984) (Butterworths, B. Simpson ed.).

123. "Hans A. Linde as Seen by a Junior Colleague – A Personal Tribute," 1984 New York Univ. *Survey Am. Law*, pp. 11 - 13 (1984).

124. "Vienna – Spring Semester 1985," vol. 12 *Cornell Law Forum* No. 3, pp. 2 - 5 (1986).

125. "Form and Substance in Anglo-American Law," vol. 14 *Cornell Law Forum* No. 1, pp. 2 - 6 (1987).

126. "Frank Robinson Lacy. Jr. – A Personal Tribute," vol. 67 *Oregon L. Rev.*, pp. 473 - 475 (1987).

127. "The First Hour of the Course in Commercial Law, Spring Semester 1990," vol. 17 *Cornell Law Forum* No. 1, pp. 12 - 15 (1990).

128. "The Comparative Statutory Interpretation Project," vol. 17 *Cornell Law Forum* No. 2, pp. 7 - 10 (1990).

129. "Chapin D. Clark – A Personal Tribute," vol. 71 *Oregon L. Rev.*, pp. 245 - 247 (1992).

130. "A Year At Cambridge", vol. 19 *Cornell Law Forum* No. 3 pp. 8 - 12 (1993).

Addresses of the Authors

Aarnio, Aulis, LL. D., Prof. Dr., University of Tampere, Research Institute for Social Sciences, P.O. Box 607, SF-33101 Tampere

Alexy, Robert, Prof. Dr., Christian-Albrechts-Universität Kiel, Juristisches Seminar, Olshausenstraße 40, D-24118 Kiel

Barceló, John J. III, A. R. Noll Professor of Law, Director, Berger International Legal Studies Program, Cornell Law School, 318 Myron Taylor Hall, Ithaca, New York 14853, USA

Behrends, Okko, Prof. Dr., Georg-August-Universität Göttingen, Institut für Römisches und Gemeines Recht, Prinzenstraße 27, D-37073 Göttingen

Bell, John S., Prof., The University of Leeds, Faculty of Law, GB-Leeds LS2 9JT

Campbell, Tom D., Professor of Law, The Australian National University, Faculty of Law, GPO Box 4, Canberra ACT 2601, Australia

Coenen, Dan T., Prof., The University of Georgia, School of Law, Athens, Georgia 30602, USA

Cramton, Roger C., Stevens Professor of Law, Cornell Law School, 216 Myron Taylor Hall, Ithaca, New York 14853, USA

Dreier, Ralf, Prof. Dr., Universität Göttingen, Juristisches Seminar, Lehrstuhl für Allgemeine Rechtstheorie, Platz der Göttinger Sieben 6, D-37073 Göttingen

Eckhoff, Torstein, Prof. Dr., Universitetet i Oslo, Institutt for Offentlig Rett, Department of Public and International Law, Karl Johansgate 47, N-0162 Oslo

Evans, Jim, Prof., University of Auckland, Faculty of Law, Private Bag 92019, Auckland, New Zealand

Fentiman, Richard G., M. A., B. C. L., Director of Studies in Law, Queens' College, GB-Cambridge CB3 9ET

Garzón Valdés, Ernesto, Prof. Dr., Universität Mainz, Institut für Politikwissenschaft, Colonel-Kleinmann-Weg 17, D-55128 Mainz

Greenawalt, Kent, Prof., Columbia University in the City of New York, School of Law, 435 West 116th Street, New York, New York 10027, USA

Harwood, Sterling, J. D., Ph. D., Professor and Pre-Law Advisor, San José State University, Department of Philosophy, One Washington Square, San José, California 95192, USA

Hausmaninger, Herbert, o. Univ.-Prof. Dr., Universität Wien, Rechtswissenschaftliche Fakultät, Institut für Römisches Recht und Antike Rechtsgeschichte, Schottenbastei 10 - 16, A-1010 Wien

Hellner, Jan, Prof. Dr., Stockholms Universitet, Faculty of Law, S-10691 Stockholm

Helmholz, R. H., Ruth Wyatt Rosenson Professor of Law, The University of Chicago, The Law School, 1111 East 60th Street, Chicago, Illinois 60637, USA

Hillman, Robert A., Associate Dean for Academic Affairs and Professor of Law, Cornell Law School, 220 Myron Taylor Hall, Ithaca, New York 14853, USA

Hruschka, Joachim, Prof. Dr., Universität Erlangen-Nürnberg, Lehrstuhl für Strafrecht, Strafprozeßrecht und Rechtsphilosophie, Kochstraße 2, D-91054 Erlangen

Jensen, Erik M., Professor of Law, Case Western Reserve University, School of Law, 11075 East Boulevard, Cleveland, Ohio 44106, USA

Kaufmann, Arthur, Prof. Dr. Dr. h.c. mult, Longinusstraße 3, D-81247 München

Kirkpatrick, Laird, Professor of Law, University of Oregon, School of Law, 1101 Kincaid Street, Eugene, Oregon 97403, USA

Krawietz, Werner, Prof. Dr. Dr. Dr. h. c., Westfälische Wilhelms-Universität Münster, Lehrstuhl für Rechtssoziologie, Rechts- und Sozialphilosophie, Bispinghof 24/25, D-48143 Münster

La Torre, Massimo, Prof. Dr., Lecturer, Europäisches Hochschulinstitut, Badia Fiesolana, Via dei Roccettini, 9, I-50016 San Domenico di Fiesole (Florence)

Lucas, J. R., F.B.A., Merton College, GB-Oxford OX1 4JD

MacCormick, Neil, Prof. Dr., The University of Edinburgh, Centre for Criminology and the Social and Philosophical Study of Law, Old College, South Bridge, GB-Edinburgh EH8 9YL

Marshall, Geoffrey, Provost, The Queen's College, GB-Oxford

Müller-Graff, Peter-Christian, Prof. Dr., Universität Trier, Fachbereich Rechtswissenschaft, Postfach 38 25, D-54228 Trier

Osgood, Russell K., Dean and Professor of Law, Cornell Law School, 265 Myron Taylor Hall, Ithaca, New York 14853, USA

Pattaro, Enrico, Prof. Dr., Centro Interdipartimentale di Ricerca in Filosofia del Diritto e Informatica Giuridica "H. Kelsen" dell'Università degli Studi di Bologna (CIRFID), Via Zamboni, 27/29, I-40126 Bologna

Paulson, Stanley L., Prof., Washington University in St. Louis, School of Law, Campus Box 11 20, One Brookings Drive, St. Louis, Missouri 63130, USA

Peczenik, Aleksander, Prof. Dr., Lunds Universitet, Juridiska institutionen, Box 2 07, S-221 00 Lund

Petev, Valentin, Prof. Dr., Westfälische Wilhelms-Universität Münster, Institut für Internationales Wirtschaftsrecht, Universitätsstraße 14 - 16, D-48143 Münster

Prebble, John, Barrister & Professor of Law, P.O. Box 6 00, Wellington, New Zealand

Rottleuthner, Hubert, Prof. Dr., Freie Universität Berlin, Fachbereich Rechtswissenschaft, Institut für Rechtssoziologie und Rechtstatsachenforschung, Boltzmannstraße 3, D-14195 Berlin

Samu, Mihály, Prof. Dr., ELTE Állam-és Jogtudományi Kar, Egyetem tér 1 - 3, H-1053 Budapest V.

Taruffo, Michele, Prof. Dr., Università di Pavia, Istituto di Diritto Privato e Processuale, Strada Nuova, 65, I-27100 Pavia

Troper, Michel, Prof. Dr., Université Paris X - Nanterre, U.F.R. de Sciences Juridiques Administratives et Politiques, 200, Avenue de la République, F-92001 Nanterre (Cedex)

Varga, Csaba, Prof. Dr., Senior Fellow, Scientific Adviser, Institute for Legal Science, Hungarian Academy, P.O. Box 25, H-1121 Budapest

Weinberger, Ota, Prof. DDr. Dr. h.c., Karl-Franzens-Universität Graz, Institut für Rechtsphilosophie, Merangasse 70, A-8010 Graz

White, James J., Prof., University of Michigan Law School, 625 S. State Street, 300 Hutchins Hall, Ann Arbor, Michigan 48109, USA

Wieacker, Franz, Prof. Dr. Dres. h.c., Otfried-Müller-Weg 10, D-37075 Göttingen

Wright, Georg Henrik, Prof. Dr. Dr. h.c. mult., Skepparegatan 4, SF-00150 Helsingfors

Wyduckel, Dieter, Prof. Dr., Juristische Fakultät der TU Dresden, Lehrstuhl für öffentliches Recht insbes. Verfassungsgeschichte, Allgemeine Rechts- und Staatslehre, Staatskirchenrecht, Mommsenstraße 13, D-01062 Dresden

FSC
www.fsc.org
MIX
Papier | Fördert
gute Waldnutzung
FSC® C083411

Kolibri 360 GmbH
Ferdinand-Jühlke-Straße 7
99095 Erfurt, Deutschland
produktsicherheit@kolibri360.de

Druck:
CPI Druckdienstleistungen GmbH
im Auftrag der
Kolibri 360 GmbH
Ferdinand-Jühlke-Str. 7
99095 Erfurt